T0207311

Lecture Notes in Computer Science

Lecture Notes in Artificial Intelligence   14272

Founding Editor

Jörg Siekmann

Series Editors

Randy Goebel, *University of Alberta, Edmonton, Canada*
Wolfgang Wahlster, *DFKI, Berlin, Germany*
Zhi-Hua Zhou, *Nanjing University, Nanjing, China*

The series Lecture Notes in Artificial Intelligence (LNAI) was established in 1988 as a topical subseries of LNCS devoted to artificial intelligence.

The series publishes state-of-the-art research results at a high level. As with the LNCS mother series, the mission of the series is to serve the international R & D community by providing an invaluable service, mainly focused on the publication of conference and workshop proceedings and postproceedings.

Huayong Yang · Honghai Liu · Jun Zou ·
Zhouping Yin · Lianqing Liu · Geng Yang ·
Xiaoping Ouyang · Zhiyong Wang
Editors

Intelligent Robotics and Applications

16th International Conference, ICIRA 2023
Hangzhou, China, July 5–7, 2023
Proceedings, Part VI

Springer

Editors

Huayong Yang
Zhejiang University
Hangzhou, China

Jun Zou ⓘ
Zhejiang University
Hangzhou, China

Lianqing Liu ⓘ
Shenyang Institute of Automation
Shenyang, Liaoning, China

Xiaoping Ouyang ⓘ
Zhejiang University
Hangzhou, China

Honghai Liu ⓘ
Harbin Institute of Technology
Shenzhen, China

Zhouping Yin
Huazhong University of Science
and Technology
Wuhan, China

Geng Yang ⓘ
Zhejiang University
Hangzhou, China

Zhiyong Wang
Harbin Institute of Technology
Shenzhen, China

ISSN 0302-9743   ISSN 1611-3349 (electronic)
Lecture Notes in Artificial Intelligence
ISBN 978-981-99-6479-6   ISBN 978-981-99-6480-2 (eBook)
https://doi.org/10.1007/978-981-99-6480-2

LNCS Sublibrary: SL7 – Artificial Intelligence

This Springer imprint is published by the registered company Springer Nature Singapore Pte Ltd.
The registered company address is: 152 Beach Road, #21-01/04 Gateway East, Singapore 189721, Singapore

Paper in this product is recyclable.

Preface

With the theme "Smart Robotics for Sustainable Society", the 16th International Conference on Intelligent Robotics and Applications (ICIRA 2023) was held in Hangzhou, China, July 5–7, 2023, and designed to encourage advancement in the field of robotics, automation, mechatronics, and applications. It aimed to promote top-level research and globalize quality research in general, making discussions and presentations more internationally competitive and focusing on the latest outstanding achievements, future trends, and demands.

ICIRA 2023 was organized and hosted by Zhejiang University, co-hosted by Harbin Institute of Technology, Huazhong University of Science and Technology, Chinese Academy of Sciences, and Shanghai Jiao Tong University, co-organized by State Key Laboratory of Fluid Power and Mechatronic Systems, State Key Laboratory of Robotics and System, State Key Laboratory of Digital Manufacturing Equipment and Technology, State Key Laboratory of Mechanical System and Vibration, State Key Laboratory of Robotics, and School of Mechanical Engineering of Zhejiang University. Also, ICIRA 2023 was technically co-sponsored by Springer. On this occasion, ICIRA 2023 was a successful event after the COVID-19 pandemic. It attracted more than 630 submissions, and the Program Committee undertook a rigorous review process for selecting the most deserving research for publication. The Advisory Committee gave advice for the conference program. Also, they help to organize special sections for ICIRA 2023. Finally, a total of 431 papers were selected for publication in 9 volumes of Springer's Lecture Note in Artificial Intelligence. For the review process, single-blind peer review was used. Each review took around 2–3 weeks, and each submission received at least 2 reviews and 1 meta-review.

In ICIRA 2023, 12 distinguished plenary speakers delivered their outstanding research works in various fields of robotics. Participants gave a total of 214 oral presentations and 197 poster presentations, enjoying this excellent opportunity to share their latest research findings. Here, we would like to express our sincere appreciation to all the authors, participants, and distinguished plenary and keynote speakers. Special thanks are also extended to all members of the Organizing Committee, all reviewers for peer-review, all staffs of the conference affairs group, and all volunteers for their diligent work.

July 2023

Huayong Yang
Honghai Liu
Jun Zou
Zhouping Yin
Lianqing Liu
Geng Yang
Xiaoping Ouyang
Zhiyong Wang

Organization

Conference Chair

Huayong Yang   Zhejiang University, China

Honorary Chairs

Youlun Xiong   Huazhong University of Science and Technology, China

Han Ding   Huazhong University of Science and Technology, China

General Chairs

Honghai Liu   Harbin Institute of Technology, China
Jun Zou   Zhejiang University, China
Zhouping Yin   Huazhong University of Science and Technology, China
Lianqing Liu   Chinese Academy of Sciences, China

Program Chairs

Geng Yang   Zhejiang University, China
Li Jiang   Harbin Institute of Technology, China
Guoying Gu   Shanghai Jiao Tong University, China
Xinyu Wu   Chinese Academy of Sciences, China

Award Committee Chair

Yong Lei   Zhejiang University, China

Publication Chairs

Xiaoping Ouyang   Zhejiang University, China
Zhiyong Wang   Harbin Institute of Technology, China

Regional Chairs

Zhiyong Chen   University of Newcastle, Australia
Naoyuki Kubota   Tokyo Metropolitan University, Japan
Zhaojie Ju   University of Portsmouth, UK
Eric Perreault   Northeastern University, USA
Peter Xu   University of Auckland, New Zealand
Simon Yang   University of Guelph, Canada
Houxiang Zhang   Norwegian University of Science and Technology,
                                  Norway
Duanling Li   Beijing University of Posts and
                                  Telecommunications, China

Advisory Committee

Jorge Angeles   McGill University, Canada
Tamio Arai   University of Tokyo, Japan
Hegao Cai   Harbin Institute of Technology, China
Tianyou Chai   Northeastern University, China
Jiansheng Dai   King's College London, UK
Zongquan Deng   Harbin Institute of Technology, China
Han Ding   Huazhong University of Science and Technology,
                                  China
Xilun Ding   Beihang University, China
Baoyan Duan   Xidian University, China
Xisheng Feng   Shenyang Institute of Automation, Chinese
                                  Academy of Sciences, China
Toshio Fukuda   Nagoya University, Japan
Jianda Han   Nankai University, China
Qiang Huang   Beijing Institute of Technology, China
Oussama Khatib   Stanford University, USA
Yinan Lai   National Natural Science Foundation of China,
                                  China
Jangmyung Lee   Pusan National University, Korea
Zhongqin Lin   Shanghai Jiao Tong University, China

Hong Bao	Hefei Institute of Technology, China
Hongli Liu	University of Portsmouth, UK
Jianwei Ma	Ritsumeikan University, Japan
Hai Kai Chen	Beijing Robot and Automation Co., Ltd., China
Ming Tao	Institute of Automation, Chinese Academy of Sciences, China
Kevin Warwick	Coventry University, UK
Guowei Wang	National Robot Science and Technology Center, China
Laurence Wang	Beihang University, China
Tao Wan Wang	Shenyang Institute of Automation, China
Shaobo Wang	Shenyang Institute of Automation, Chinese Academy of Sciences, China
Benjamin Whiteside	Auburn University, USA
Ming Xie	Nanyang Technological University, Singapore
Hengxing Se	Chinese University of Hong Kong, China
Huaibin Yang	Zhejian University, China
Jie Zhao	Harbin Institute of Technology, China
Xiuqing Zheng	Harbin Institute of Technology, China
Xingyun Zhao	Shanghai Jiao Tong University, China

Contents – Part VI

Clinically Oriented Design in Robotic Surgery and Rehabilitation

Visual and Visual-Tactile Perception for Robotics

Design and Control of Legged Robots

Leg Mass Influences the Jumping Performance of Compliant One-legged Robots

Guifu Luo[1], Ruilong Du[2], Anhuan Xie[2(✉)], Hua Zhou[1(✉)], and Jason Gu[3]

[1] State Key Laboratory of Fluid Power and Mechatronic Systems, Zhejiang University, Hangzhou, China
hzhou@zju.edu.cn
[2] Intelligent Robot Research Center, Zhejiang Lab, Hangzhou, China
xieanhuan@163.com
[3] Department of Electrical Engineering, Dalhousie University, Halifax, NS, Canada

Abstract. Compliant leg behavior and the spring-loaded inverted pendulum (SLIP) model help understand the dynamics of legged locomotion while few works could be found discussing the effects of leg mass, which is an intriguing and worthwhile question for designers of compliant legged robots. This work is focused on the influence of leg mass on jumping performance using a compliant one-legged robot designed by the authors. An extended SLIP model with the center of mass of the torso offset from the hip and with the leg mass considered is presented for the designed robot, and the bio-inspired virtual pendulum posture control (VPPC) and the velocity-based leg adjustment method (VBLA) are used to achieve stable jumping of the robot. Afterward, the maximum forward pushed velocity at which the robot can recover its stability is investigated for different leg masses, and this velocity is used as a criterion to analyze the effect of leg mass. Results show that the maximum allowed pushed velocity decreases as the leg mass increases, suggesting that leg mass leads to a reduction in the stability of the robot. Results also show that stability decreases sharply when the ratio of leg mass to the total mass of the robot is higher than 0.35, which is close to the ratio of leg mass to the total mass in humans, according to human anatomical data. It suggests that the leg mass ratio should be kept below 0.35 in the practical design of legged robots so that the leg mass would have less effect on the locomotion performance of the robot.

Keywords: Leg mass · Compliant one-legged robot · Jumping · Bio-inspired control

1 Introduction

Compliant leg behavior helps understand the dynamics of walking and running of legged systems from a biological perspective, and the spring-loaded inverted pendulum (SLIP) model serves as one of the most used template models for designing and controlling the legged robots [1, 2]. By putting the whole-body mass concentrated in one point and the leg being taken as a massless spring, the SLIP model can describe the legged locomotion

© The Author(s), under exclusive license to Springer Nature Singapore Pte Ltd. 2023
H. Yang et al. (Eds.): ICIRA 2023, LNAI 14272, pp. 3–16, 2023.
https://doi.org/10.1007/978-981-99-6480-2_1

conceptually and abstractly [3]. However, in a practical legged robot design, legs without mass are not available.

Utilizing the concept of the SLIP model, researchers have constructed several compliant leg robots with different morphologies. These leg robots usually have three common features to take advantage of the SLIP model-based control, the first is a spring-like leg via introducing elastic elements in the legs, such as springs or leaf springs, the second is a very short torso that crosses the hip to coincide the center of mass (CoM) of the torso with the hip as much as possible, and the third is that the legs are desired to be as light as possible. The Raibert's Hopper developed in 1984 represents a fairly typical design of compliant leg robots that utilize the exact morphology of the SLIP model. In the design of the Hopper, a mechanical guided spring was placed at the distal end of the leg, and the torso was deliberately designed so that its CoM coincided with the hip, and its leg mass to torso ratio was 1/18 [4]. A three-part decomposition control strategy was proposed that demonstrated the successful application of the SLIP-like robot from the perspective of academic research [5]. However, Raibert's Pogo stick-like Hopper cannot stretch as articulated legs, limiting its practical applications in general human-built environments. In 2015, Hurst et al. designed a biped robot Atrias to approximate the SLIP model by placing the heavy motors above and leaf springs in series with the motors in the lower leg. Though the ratio of the leg mass to the torso mass was not reported, it could be seen that the majority of the mass was concentrated close to the hip and the leg was deliberately designed to be light by using carbon fiber material [6]. Based on Atrias, Hurst et al. further developed the biped robot Cassie, whose ratio of leg mass to the torso is higher than Atrias because Cassie has some motors placed in his legs. Nevertheless, Cassie exhibits similar SLIP model features to Atrias because it has a short torso with a large mass whose CoM is close to the hip [7, 8]. From Hopper to Cassie, it is a very intriguing and worthwhile question for the legged robot designers to investigate what the maximum ratio of leg mass to torso mass would cause the SLIP model to no longer be satisfied, and how that ratio affects the locomotion behavior of the robot. However, most of the publications concerning these robots mainly focus on the gait planning and control strategy, et al. [9–11], and few publications could be found addressing the details of the robot design.

In addition, it is worth mentioning that the CoM of the torso is usually offset from the hip, and thus the leg mass would exert an inertia effect on the torso, which would directly affect the dynamics and stability of the torso. Noticing the typical SLIP model that characterizes the torso as a point mass on the hip fails to address this issue, an extended SLIP model was proposed which replaced the point mass with an extended torso [12, 13]. Seyfarth et al. compared the extended SLIP model with and without leg mass and investigated the influence of the leg mass based on the virtual pendulum posture control (VPPC) method [14], in which a virtual pivot point (VPP) above the center of mass that was experimentally observed in walking humans and in running chickens [15]. In the study of Seyfarth et al., the parameters for the extended SLIP model were parameters measured from humans, and to investigate the influence of the leg mass, the total mass and CoM were kept constant by adjusting the mass and CoM of the torso. Following the control concept of the VPP, researchers continued to study the extended SLIP model using parameters measured from humans, many of which focused on template models while rarely discussing the effects of the leg mass [16–18]. Poulakakis applied the extended SLIP model to the compliant legged robot Thumper and Mabel, however, he mainly worked on the compliant hybrid zero dynamics controllers, and the leg was taken as a massless spring [19]. After a thorough review of other compliant-legged robots, such as Durus, the Cornell biped, et al. [20–22], there were still few publications that could be found to discuss the influence of the leg mass on the locomotion behavior of the robot.

In this work, we applied the extended SLIP model to represent the compliant one-legged robot designed by ourselves as shown in Fig. 1. The bio-inspired VPPC and the velocity-based leg adjustment method (VBLA) were utilized to stabilize the jumping. After that, by examining the maximum forward pushing velocity that the robot could withstand, the effect of the leg mass in a compliant-legged robot was investigated, which could guide the design of compliant-legged robots.

The rest of this work is organized as follows. Section 2 briefly describes the compliant one-legged robot designed by ourselves. Section 3 depicts the dynamic modeling and bio-inspired control of the robot's jumping motion considering the leg mass. Section 3.4 introduces the design of the controller that enables the robot to jump stably and recover its stability in case of a sudden forward push. Afterward, Section 4 brings the simulation results and discusses the effect of the leg mass. Lastly, Section 5 concludes this work and presents future work including some preliminary experiments we have conducted on the robot.

Fig. 1. Compliant one-legged robot designed by ourselves [23]

2   Brief Description of the Compliant One-legged Robot

Figure 2 illustrates the CAD model of the compliant one-legged robot developed by ourselves. The dimensions of the robot's leg were derived from human leg proportions. The robot is primarily composed of two major components: a 12 kg torso with its center of mass (CoM) offset from the hip and a 6.5 kg leg. The leg comprises two actuated motors connected in series, a thigh equipped with a compliant linkage mechanism utilizing two leaf springs, and a shank with a point-foot configuration.

The swing angle and length adjustment of the leg's rest length are controlled by motors M and N, respectively. In this study, the leg length is maintained at 700 mm, although it is capable of reaching approximately 900 mm when fully extended and 300 mm when fully contracted. The introduction of a compliant six-bar linkage mechanism, incorporating two leaf springs in the thigh, allows the leg length to change in response to forces applied along the leg, resembling the behavior of a spring. This design feature enables the application of the extended SLIP model. Details regarding the robot's design parameters are presented in Table 1. For further information on the robot design, please refer to our previously published work [23, 24].

3　Modeling and Bio-inspired Control of the Robot's Jumping Motion Considering the Leg Mass

Figure 3 presents the extended SLIP model, which is utilized to represent the planar jumping behavior of the compliant one-legged robot. Notably, this model accounts for the non-trivial masses of both the torso and the leg. As previously mentioned, motor N is responsible for adjusting the leg length. On the other hand, motor M actively rotates to generate a hip torque τ, facilitating the swing angles of both the leg and the torso.

The world coordinate system for the robot's jumping motion was defined with the x-direction representing the forward movement and the z-direction representing the hopping direction of the robot. The jumping motion can be divided into three consecutive processes: the flight phase in the air, the stance phase on the ground, and the transition process between these two phases. In the following subsections, we would provide a detailed description of the dynamic modeling of these processes using the extended SLIP model, taking into account the leg mass.

Table 1. Design parameters of the one-legged robot

Term	Symbol	Value [units]
Torso mass	m_T	12 [kg]
Torso moment of inertia	I_T	1.0 [kg·m^2]
Distance from hip to torso CoM	r_T	0.2 [m]
Leg mass	m_L	6.5 [kg]
Leg moment of inertia	I_L	0.188 [kg·m^2]
Distance from hip to leg CoM	r_L	0.25 [m]
Rest length of Leg	L_0	0.45 [m]
Leg stiffness	k	6000 [N/m]

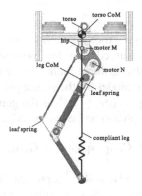

Fig. 2. CAD model of our compliant one-legged robot with the extended SLIP model [23]

3.1 Flight Phase

During the flight phase, the robot's foot remains off the ground, and the leg length is maintained at a constant value of L_0. As a result, the extended SLIP model for this phase incorporates four degrees of freedom (DoFs). We selected $\mathbf{q}_f = (x_T, z_T, \theta_T, \gamma)^T$ as the generalized variables, where x_T, z_T, and θ_T represent the translational displacement in the x-direction, translational displacement in the z-direction, and the rotation angle of the torso with respect to the z-direction, respectively. Thus, the dynamic modeling of the flight phase can be expressed as follows:

$$\mathbf{M}_f(\mathbf{q}_f) \cdot \ddot{\mathbf{q}}_f + \mathbf{C}_f(\mathbf{q}_f, \dot{\mathbf{q}}_f) \cdot \dot{\mathbf{q}}_f + \mathbf{G}_f(\mathbf{q}_f) = \mathbf{B}_f \cdot \mathbf{u}_f \qquad (1)$$

where $\mathbf{M}_f \in \mathbf{R}^{4 \times 4}$, $\mathbf{C}_f \in \mathbf{R}^{4 \times 4}$ and $\mathbf{G}_f \in \mathbf{R}^{4 \times 4}$ denote the inertia matrix, Coriolis and centrifugal matrix, and gravity vector respectively, $\mathbf{B}_f \in \mathbf{R}^{4 \times 4}$ denotes the coefficient matrix of generalized forces, and $\mathbf{u}_f = (0, 0, 0, \tau)^T$ denotes the vector of generalized forces.

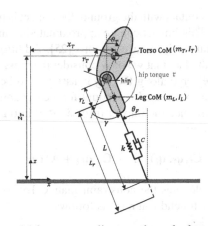

Fig. 3. Extended SLIP model for our compliant one-legged robot considering leg mass [23]

3.2 Stance Phase

During the stance phase, the robot's foot maintains contact with the ground, acting as a pivot joint with no slipping assumed. The leg, possessing spring-like compliance, undergoes a change in length L due to the influence of the ground reaction force (GRF). Consequently, the extended SLIP model for the stance phase incorporates three degrees of freedom (DoFs). We select $q_s = (\theta_T, \gamma, L)^T$ as the generalized variables. Thus, the dynamic modeling of the stance phase can be expressed as

$$M_s(q_s) \cdot \ddot{q}_s + C_s(q_s, \dot{q}_s) \cdot \dot{q}_s + G_s(q_s) = B_s \cdot u_s \tag{2}$$

where $M_s \in R^{3 \times 3}$, $C_s \in R^{3 \times 3}$, and $G_s \in R^{3 \times 3}$ represent the inertia matrix, Coriolis and centrifugal matrix, and gravity vector in the stance phase, respectively. $B_s \in R^{3 \times 3}$ denotes the coefficient matrix of generalized input torques, and $u_s = (0, \tau, F_s)^T$ $u_s = (0, \tau, F_s)^T$ represents the vector of generalized input torques. F_s denotes the passive spring force produced by the change of the leg real length $F_s = -k \cdot (L - L_0)$.

3.3 Transit Maps

From Eqs. (1) and (2), it is evident that there are variations in the DoFs and generalized variables between the flight phase and the stance phase. Consequently, transit maps are required to establish the relationships between the generalized variables across different phases. The transit maps consist of two components: the touchdown map and the lift-off map.

Touchdown Map: The touchdown map is a transformation that converts variables from the flight phase to the stance phase. This map comes into play when the robot's foot makes contact with the ground, indicated by the foot's displacement in the z-direction reducing to zero. There are two key aspects to consider: the transient change of variables resulting from the impact with the ground and the conversion of variables between the flight and stance phases.

When the robot makes contact with the ground, the impact is treated as instantaneous and completely inelastic. This impact can be approximated as an impulse, causing the foot's velocity to instantaneously reduce to zero [25]. Additionally, considering our compliant leg design and the fact that we only consider the mass above the leg's spring-like structure, the impulse force along the leg is assumed to be zero, acting solely in the direction perpendicular to the leg. To account for the dynamic characteristics at the moment of impact, we introduce the impact force $\delta_\lambda \in R$ into Eq. (1), resulting in the following modified Equation:

$$M_f(q_f) \cdot \ddot{q}_f + C_f(q_f, \dot{q}_f) \cdot \dot{q}_f + G_f(q_f) + A^T(q_f) \cdot \delta_\lambda = B_f \cdot u_f \tag{3}$$

where $A \in R^{1 \times 1}$ $A \in R$ denotes the constraint matrix. By integrating both sides of Eq. (3), we can express the touchdown map as follows:

$$M_f \cdot (\dot{q}_f^+ - \dot{q}_f^-) + A^T \cdot \lambda = 0 \tag{4}$$

where $\lambda \in R^1$ $\lambda \in R$ denotes the intensity of the impulse, $\dot{\mathbf{q}}_f^-$ and $\dot{\mathbf{q}}_f^+$ $\dot{\mathbf{q}}_f^-$, $\dot{\mathbf{q}}_f^+$ denote the generalized velocity of the robot before and after the impact. The orientation of the leg is parallel to the straight line connecting the hip joint and the contact point. As a result, the leg is subject to a holonomic constraint, which can be expressed as Eq. (5).

$$h = \tan(\theta_F(\mathbf{q}_f)) - \frac{z_{hip}(\mathbf{q}_f) - z_{con}}{x_{hip}(\mathbf{q}_f) - x_{con}} = 0 \tag{5}$$

where (x_{hip}, z_{hip}) and (x_{con}, z_{con}) represent the coordinates of the hip joint and the contact point of the robot, respectively. The derived velocity constraint function can be expressed as

$$\dot{h}(\mathbf{q}_f) = \frac{\partial h}{\partial \mathbf{q}_f} \cdot \dot{\mathbf{q}}_f = \mathbf{A}(\mathbf{q}_f) \cdot \dot{\mathbf{q}}_f = 0 \tag{6}$$

By combining Eqs. (4) and (6), the impulse intensity and the velocity after impact can be obtained as

$$\lambda = \left(\mathbf{A} \cdot \mathbf{M}_f^{-1} \cdot \mathbf{A}^T\right) \cdot \mathbf{A} \cdot \dot{\mathbf{q}}_f^- \tag{7}$$

$$\dot{\mathbf{q}}_f^+ = \dot{\mathbf{q}}_f^- - \mathbf{M}_f^{-1} \cdot \mathbf{A}^T \cdot \lambda = \Delta_{imp} \cdot \dot{\mathbf{q}}_f^- \tag{8}$$

To account for the transformation of variables between the flight phase and the stance phase, the following expression can be utilized:

$$\mathbf{x}_{s0} = \Delta_{f \to s}\left(\mathbf{x}_f^+\right) \tag{9}$$

where $\mathbf{x}_{s0} = \left(\mathbf{q}_{s0}^T, \dot{\mathbf{q}}_{s0}^T\right)^T \in R^6$ denotes the states of the stance phase after impact $\mathbf{x}_f^+ = \left(\mathbf{q}_f^{+T}, \dot{\mathbf{q}}_f^{+T}\right)^T \in R^8$ denotes the flight states after impact, $\Delta_{f \to s}$ denotes the reset map from flight to stance.

Lift-off map: The lift-off map refers to the transformation of variables from the stance phase to the flight phase. The lift-off event occurs when the leg length L returns to its rest length L_0. As the ground cannot exert a pulling force on the robot, there is no impact involved, and hence we only need to address the states reset map from the stance phase to the flight phase:

$$\mathbf{x}_{f0} = \Delta_{s \to f}\left(\mathbf{x}_s^-\right) \tag{10}$$

where $\mathbf{x}_{f0} = \left(\mathbf{q}_{f0}^T, \dot{\mathbf{q}}_{f0}^T\right)^T \in R^8$ denotes the states in the flight phase after the lift-off event, $\mathbf{x}_s^- = \left(\mathbf{q}_s^{-T}, \dot{\mathbf{q}}_s^{-T}\right)^T \in R^6$ denotes the states in the stance phase before the lift-off event, $\Delta_{s \to f}$ denotes the reset map from the flight phase to the stance phase.

3.4 Bio-inspired Jumping Control

A jumping controller for our compliant one-legged robot would be designed first to enable the robot to jump stably. The jumping controller needs to address the two phases described above: the stance phase and the flight phase.

Stance Phase Control: As shown in Fig. 4, the bio-inspired virtual pendulum posture control was implemented for achieving stable jumping in compliant-legged robots. This control strategy draws inspiration from experimental findings in biological-legged locomotion systems, including walking humans and running chickens [15].

The ground reaction force (GRF) F_c is the combined force of two orthogonal directions, along the leg and perpendicular to the leg. The force along F_s the leg is the spring force produced by the deformation of the leg spring defined as $F_s = -k\cdot(L-L_0)F_s = -k(L - L_0)$, while the force perpendicular to the leg F_τ is produced by the hip torque τ from motor M. Via regulating the hip torque τ, it is expected that the GRF F_c is directed to a virtual pivot point (VPP) which is located above the total CoM of the robot. In this work, to simplify the control strategy, we leave the VPP located on the torso at a distance of r_v from the torso CoM. The value of r_v needs to be chosen carefully, and the hip torque τ yields

$$\tau = -F_s \cdot (r_L + L) \cdot \frac{(r_L + r_v) \cdot \sin(\gamma)}{r_L + L + (r_L + r_v) \cdot \cos(\gamma)} \tag{11}$$

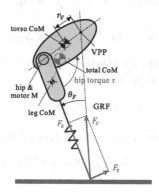

Fig. 4. Schematic of the VPP control strategy for our compliant one-legged robot [23]

Flight Phase Control: The angle of attack θ_F θ_F, at the moment the robot touchdown on the ground, plays a crucial role in achieving stable jumping behavior. In this work, the VBLA method [26] was used for the flight phase control. The method was shown the best one in mimicking human leg adjustment. Let the angle of attack be composed of the velocity vector of the torso CoM of the robot $V_{TCoM} = (\dot{x}_T, \dot{y}_T)$ $\mathbf{v}_{TCoM} = (\dot{x}_T, \dot{y}_T)^T$ and the vector of the gravitational acceleration $G = (0, -g)^T$ $\mathbf{G} = (0, -g)^T$, the angle of attack θ_F θ_F can be expressed as

$$\mathbf{v} = (v_x, v_y)^T = \mu \cdot \mathbf{v}_{TCoM} + (1 - \mu) \cdot \mathbf{G} \tag{12}$$

where $\mu \in (0, 1)$ $\mu \in (0,1)$ denotes the weight of the component $\mathbf{v}_{TCoM}$, which needs to be carefully chosen. Hence, the desired angle of attack θ_F when the leg touches the ground yields

$$\theta_{Fdes} = \arctan\left(\frac{v_y}{v_x}\right) \tag{13}$$

Since the angle of attack cannot be controlled directly, the desired angle of attack is transformed to desired swing leg angle $\gamma_{des} = \theta_T + \theta_{Fdes}$, where θ_T is estimated using the IMU located on the torso. A PD control strategy is adopted to track the desired swing leg angle $\tau = k_p \cdot (\gamma - \gamma_{des}) + k_d \cdot \dot{\gamma}$, where k_d and k_p are control parameters that need to be chosen carefully.

4 Results and Discussion

The jumping motion of our compliant one-legged robot was simulated using MATLAB 2019b and the related dynamics functions were solved using the ODE45 solver. The robot was initially lifted to a height of 0.1m above the ground and imposed an initial forward velocity $\dot{x}_{T0}$ to the torso CoM. The design parameters for our compliant leg are displayed in Table 1, Section 2. A criterion was set for choosing the optimally matched controller parameters of the robot (r_v, μ, k_p, k_d), i. e., the minimum time to recover its stable jump under the initial forward velocity $\dot{x}_{T0} = 0.2 m/s$ $\dot{x}_{T0} = 0.2$ m/s under the constraint of the maximum torque and speed of the motor M.

Figure 5 depicts the convergence process regarding the case of the initial forward velocity $\dot{x}_{T0} = 0.5$ m/s. Figure 5 (a) displays the snapshots of the locomotion of the robot from its initial state with a forward velocity to its stable jumps with the forward velocity converging to zero. The blue lines denote the compliant leg and the red lines denote the torso of the robot. As modeled, one can see that the leg is first compressed and then extended, rotating around the foot, in the stance phase; in the flight phase, the same leg length is maintained, rotating around the hip to regulate the angle of attack. The torso can be seen to swing back and forth around the hip and remain above the hip, similar to the posture of humans performing jumps.

Figure 5 (b) depicts the GRF of the robot in 0–1 s, where the blue curve denotes the GRF in the x-direction and the red curve denotes the GRF in the z-direction evaluated as

$$\text{GRF} = (m_T + m_L) \cdot (\ddot{x}_{CoM}(\mathbf{q}_s, \dot{\mathbf{q}}_s, \ddot{\mathbf{q}}_s), \ddot{z}_{CoM}(\mathbf{q}_s, \dot{\mathbf{q}}_s, \ddot{\mathbf{q}}_s))^T \qquad (14)$$

where $\ddot{\mathbf{q}}_s$ denotes the acceleration of generalized variables in the stance phase.

As observed, the GRF in Fig. 5 (b) exhibits a pattern similar to the GRF measured during human running [2], justifying the modeling and the designed controller. It deserves noting that before the forward velocity converges to zero, the GRF is not strictly symmetrical within a stance phase because the robot was doing a deceleration jumping.

Figure 5 (c) depicts the convergence of the torso orientation with its angular velocity dropping to zero, indicating that the torso eventually stabilized in the vertical direction. Figure 5 (d) depicts the convergence of the displacement of the robot in the x-direction with its forward velocity dropping to zero. The convergence of these variables also justifies the modelling and the designed controller.

Figure 6 depicts the jumping performance with regard to different initial forward velocities and leg masses. It should be noted that when changing the mass of the leg, the

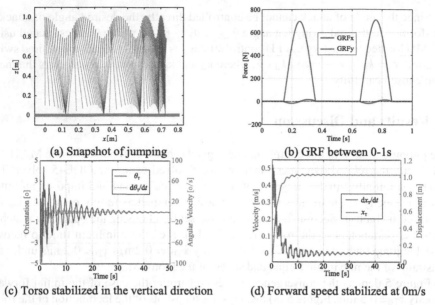

Fig. 5. Convergence process of the jumping regarding $\dot{x}_{T0}$=0.5 m/s $\dot{x}_{T0}$ = 0.5m/s

inertia of the leg would also change

$$I_L^{(b)} = I_L^{(a)} \cdot \left(\frac{m_L^{(b)}}{m_L^{(a)}}\right)^2 \tag{15}$$

where the superscripts (a) and (b) denote different cases with regard to different leg masses.

To ensure the fairness of the comparison, the controller parameters of the robot (r_v, μ, k_p, k_d) were optimally matched based on the criterion described above. As observed in Fig. 6 (a), with regard to the leg mass of 6.5 kg, a stable jumping motion can still be achieved at an initial forward velocity of 2.1 m/s, however, the robot cannot resume a stable jumping motion while the initial forward velocity increases to 2.3 m/s. It suggests that the maximum initial forward velocity that the robot could withstand could be taken as a criterion to evaluate the stability of the jumping system of a one-legged robot.

A similar phenomenon can be observed in Fig. 6 (b) corresponding to the case of the leg mass of 10 kg. Moreover, it can be seen that the robot cannot resume stability when the initial forward velocity increases to 1.7 m/s, justifying the effects of the leg mass on the jumping performance of the one-legged robot.

To further explore the effects of the leg mass on the jumping performance, we have conducted more simulations with regard to different leg masses. Defining a leg mass ratio α as the ratio of the leg mass to the total mass of the robot $\alpha = m_L / (m_L + m_T)\alpha = m_L/(m_L + m_T)$, the relationship between the leg mass ratio and the maximum initial forward velocity that the robot could withstand could be obtained as shown in Fig. 7.

It can be seen that as the leg mass ratio increases, the maximum initial forward velocity decreases, suggesting poorer stability of the robot. This is believed to be because

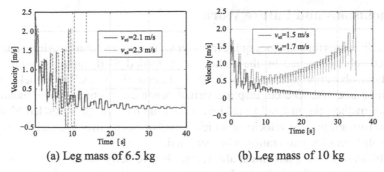

(a) Leg mass of 6.5 kg   (b) Leg mass of 10 kg

Fig. 6. Jumping performance with regard to different initial forward velocities and leg masses

as the leg mass increases, greater hip torque is required to swing the leg during the flight phase, which results in greater counteracting torque on the torso and therefore greater perturbation in the torso orientation. In addition to that, greater leg mass adds to the difficulty of tracking the desired angle of attack, which results in errors in the touchdown state of the leg, and consequently decreases stability.

Two evident sharp decreases in velocity can be observed in Fig. 7, one of which occurs at the leg mass ratio above 0.1 and the other at the ratio above 0.35. It suggests that when the leg mass ratio is below 0.1, the effect on jumping performance is rather small. However, frankly speaking, with regard to the practical design of legged robots, it is fairly difficult for robot designers to keep the leg mass ratio below 0.1 unless the robot is intended for academic research, such as Raibert's Hopper, because motors are needed to be placed in the legs to drive the knee and ankle joints.

When the leg mass ratio falls within the range of 0.1–0.35, the decrease in velocity is not significant, proving that the effect of mass is relatively insignificant; while when it is above 0.35, the velocity decreases sharply again and the effect becomes significant again. This is a rather interesting finding because the leg mass ratio of humans is approximately 0.35 according to the anatomical data of humans [27]. It suggests that the leg mass ratio should be kept below 0.35 in the practical design of legged robots so that the leg mass has less effect on the locomotion performance of the robot.

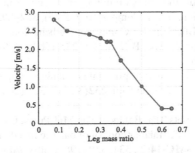

Fig. 7. The maximum initial forward velocities with regard to different leg mass ratios

5 Conclusions and Future Work

This work discusses the influence of leg mass on jumping performance using a compliant one-legged robot designed by the author. An extended SLIP model is employed to represent the robot approximately, which incorporates the leg mass. The model equations are provided in detail. The bio-inspired virtual pendulum posture control method and the VBLA method are utilized to achieve stable jumping of the extended SLIP. The maximum forward pushed velocity at which the robot can recover to a stable jump with respect to different leg mass ratios is investigated.

Results show that the maximum allowed pushed velocity decreases as the leg mass increases, suggesting that leg mass leads to a reduction in the stability of the robot. Results also show two sharp decreases in the stability of the jumping, one of which occurs at the leg mass ratio above 0.1 and the other at the ratio above 0.35.

With regard to the practical design of legged robots, it is fairly difficult for robot designers to keep the leg mass ratio below 0.1, while 0.35 is close to the ratio of leg mass to the total mass in humans, according to human anatomical data. Since the stable jumping controller employed in this study was inspired by biological mechanisms, the obtained results provide valuable insights into the locomotion capabilities of the robot in relation to its structural parameters. It suggests that the leg mass ratio should be kept below 0.35 in the practical design of legged robots so that the leg mass would have less effect on the locomotion performance of the robot.

In the next step, experiments will be conducted on our compliant one-legged robot to validate the results and analysis above, the influence of the mass/inertia distribution on the robot jumping performance will be further explored. We have conducted some preliminary experiments on the jumping motion of the robot. However, the robot has not achieved stable jumps without external support due to some issues that still need to be addressed, such as data filtering and fusion. In the long term, we will optimize the design of the compliant leg based on the analysis of this work and further build a biped robot capable of compliant walking and running.

References

1. Daley, M.A.: Understanding the agility of running birds: sensorimotor and mechanical factors in avian bipedal locomotion. Integr. Compar. Biol. **58**(5), 884–893 (2018)
2. Geyer, H., Seyfarth, A., Blickhan, R.: Compliant leg behaviour explains basic dynamics of walking and running. Proc. R. Soc. B Biol. Sci. **273**(1603), 2861–2867 (2006). https://doi.org/10.1098/rspb.2006.3637
3. Geyer, H., Seyfarth, A., Blickhan, R.: Spring-mass running: simple approximate solution and application to gait stability. J. Theoret Biol. **232**(3), 315–328 (2005). https://doi.org/10.1016/j.jtbi.2004.08.015
4. Raibert, M.H.: Legged Robots That Balance. The MIT Press, Cambridge (1986)
5. Raibert, M.H., Wimberly, F.C.: Tabular control of balance in a dynamic legged system. IEEE Trans. Syst. Man Cybern. **SMC-14**(2), 334–339 (1984). https://doi.org/10.1109/TSMC.1984.6313221
6. Grimes, J.A., Hurst, J.W.: The design of ATRIAS 1.0 a unique monopod, hopping robot. In: Adaptive Mobile Robotics, pp. 548–554 (2012)

7. Abate, A.M.: Mechanical design for robot locomotion. Ph.D. thesis, School of Mechanical, Industrial, and Manufacturing Engineering, Oregon State University, Oregon, USA (2018)
8. Cassie - Next Generation Robot. https://www.youtube.com/watch?v=Is4JZqhAy-M. Accessed 24 May 2023
9. Xiong, X., Ames, A.D.: Bipedal hopping: reduced-order model embedding via optimization-based control. In: Proceedings of IEEE/RSJ International Conference on Intelligent Robots and Systems, IEEE, Madrid, pp. 3821–3828 (2018)
10. X. Xiong, A. D. Ames.: Coupling reduced order models via feedback control for 3d underactuated bipedal robotic walking. In: Proceedings of IEEE-RAS 18th International Conference on Humanoid Robots (Humanoids), pp. 67–74 IEEE, Beijing (2018)
11. Gong, Y. Grizzle, J.: One-step ahead prediction of angular momentum about the contact point for control of bipedal locomotion: validation in a lip-inspired controller. In: IEEE International Conference on Robotics and Automation (ICRA), pp. 2832–2838 IEEE, Xi'an (2021)
12. Poulakakis, I., Grizzle, J.: Formal embedding of the spring loaded inverted pendulum in an asymmetric hopper. In: Proceedings of European Control Conference, Kos, pp. 3159–3166 (2007)
13. Maus, H.M., Rummel, J., Seyfarth, A.: Stable upright walking and running using a simple pendulum based control scheme. In: 11th International Conference on Climbing and Walking Robots and the Support Technologies for Mobile Machines (CLAWAR), pp. 623–629 (2008)
14. Sharbafi, M.A., Maufroy, C., Ahmadabadi, M.N., et al.: Robust hopping based on virtual pendulum posture control. Bioinspir. Biomim. 8(3), 036002 (2013)
15. Maus, H.-M., Lipfert, S.W., Gross, M., Rummel, J., Seyfarth, A.: Upright human gait did not provide a major mechanical challenge for our ancestors. Nat. Commun. 1(1), 1–6 (2010). https://doi.org/10.1038/ncomms1073
16. Sharbafi, M.A., Seyfarth, A.: FMCH: a new model for human-like postural control in walking. In: Proceedings of IEEE/RSJ International Conference on Intelligent Robots and Systems (IROS), Hamburg, pp. 5742–5747 (2015)
17. Ossadnik, D., Jensen, E., Haddadin, S.: ULT-model: towards a one-legged unified locomotion template model for forward hopping with an upright trunk. In: IEEE International Conference on Robotics and Automation (ICRA), pp. 3040–3046. IEEE, Xi'an (2021)
18. Ossadnik, D., Jensen, E., Haddadin, S.: Nonlinear stiffness allows passive dynamic hopping for one-legged robots with an upright trunk. In: IEEE International Conference on Robotics and Automation (ICRA), pp. 3047–3053 IEEE, Xi'an (2021)
19. Poulakakis, I.: Stabilizing monopedal robot running: reduction-by-feedback and compliant hybrid zero dynamics. Ph.D. thesis, Electrical Engineering: Systems, University of Michigan, Michigan, USA (2009)
20. Ma, W.L., et al.: Bipedal robotic running with DURUS-2D: bridging the gap between theory and experiment. In: 20th International Conference on Hybrid Systems: Computation and Control (HSCC), Pittsburgh, pp. 265–274 (2017)
21. Collins, S., Shishir, K., Ambrose, E.R., et al.: Efficient bipedal robots based on passive-dynamic walkers. Science 307(5712), 1082–1085 (2005)
22. Iida, F., Minekawa, Y., Rummel, J., et al.: Toward a human-like biped robot with compliant legs. Robot. Autonom. Syst. 57(2), 139–144 (2009)
23. Luo, G., Du, R., Song, S., et al.: Stable and fast planar jumping control design for a compliant one-legged robot. Micromachines 13(8), 1261 (2022)
24. Du, R., Song, S., Zhu, S., et al.: Design and analysis of the leg configuration for biped robots' spring-like walking. In: 2021 IEEE International Conference on Robotics and Biomimetics (ROBIO). IEEE (2021)
25. Westervelt, E.R., Grizzle, J.W., Chevallereau, C., Choi, J.H., Morris, B.: Feedback control of dynamic bipedal robot locomotion. CRC Press (2018). https://doi.org/10.1201/9781420005 3739

26. Sharbafi, M.A., Seyfarth, A.: VBLA, a swing leg control approach for humans and robots. In 2016 IEEE-RAS 16th International Conference on Humanoid Robots (Humanoids). IEEE, 952–957 (2016)
27. Stanley Plagenhoef, F., Evans, G., Abdelnour, T.: Anatomical data for analyzing human motion. Res Q Exerc. Sport **54**(2), 169–178 (1983). https://doi.org/10.1080/02701367.1983. 10605290

The Topologies Characteristics and Behaviors Design of the Curling Hexapod Robot

Yuguang Xiao⬤, Feng Gao⁽⊠⁾ ⬤, Ke Yin, and Zhijun Chen

Shanghai Jiao Tong University, Shanghai 200240, China
gaofengsjtu@gmail.com

Abstract. This paper introduces a new curling robot, the curling hexapod robot. It is the first robot to imitate human curling stone throwing behavior in the world. Under the special design, the curling hexapod robot can switch among different topologies characteristics such as hexapod topology, quadruped topology and biped topology. Aiming at the humanoid curling stone delivering behavior, the task chain and behavior chains of the curling hexapod robot curling stone throwing are designed by using task decomposition method and behavior decomposition method. The experimental result show that the curling hexapod robot has the ability of topologies switching and humanoid curling stone throwing function. The success of the curling hexapod robot expands the application field of legged robot and promotes the further development of legged robot application.

Keywords: Hexapod robot · Curling stone · Topology characteristics · Behaviors design

1 Introduction

Curling originated in Scotland in the 14th century and is a throwing competition on ice. Curling not only pays attention to throwing skills, but also pays more attention to throwing strategy, so it is also known as ice Chess.

How to make robots participate in human-led curling is a research problem in academic circles. In 2015, Kawamura T [1] et al. developed a curling throwing robot, which main unit can be roughly classified as the delivering board, the linear guide, the frame, the delivery direction change mechanism, the pushing-out mechanism, and the rotation applying mechanism. With the cooperation of the operating simulator, this curling throwing robot can deliver the curling stone to the desired position. In 2017, Chinese scholar designed a curling robot based on Sysmac control platform [2], which adopts the design scheme of parallel manipulator. This curling robot utilizes the terminal platform controlled by serve motors to delivery curling stones. What attracted the most attention was the curling robot Curly [3–6] developed by South Korea after the 2018 Pyeongchang Winter Olympics, which consists of two cameras, a robotic arm, two driving front wheels, a rear wheel and a gripper, and can be used as both a throwing robot and an observation robot. Curly grips and rotates the curling stone through the gripper and drives the robot

© The Author(s), under exclusive license to Springer Nature Singapore Pte Ltd. 2023
H. Yang et al. (Eds.): ICIRA 2023, LNAI 14272, pp. 17–30, 2023.
https://doi.org/10.1007/978-981-99-6480-2_2

to release the curling stone at the desired speed and angle by controlling the two front wheels.

Although all the above robots can throw curling stones, and some of them have achieved good results in curling competitions with people, the behaviors of these robots delivering curling stones are quite different from that of people. How to make the robot have the humanoid curling stone throwing behaviors, so as to make it better participate in the human-led curling, is the research content of this paper.

The curling hexapod robot introduced in this paper is the first curling robot in the world that imitates human pedaling hack, gliding, rotating curling stone and so on. The second section of this paper will introduce the design of the curling hexapod robot, the third section will introduce the topology characteristics of the curling hexapod robot, and the fourth section will introduce the task chain and behavior chains of the robot delivering curling stone. The fifth section is the related experiments and analyses of the robot. Finally, the research of this paper is summarized.

2 Design of the Curling Hexapod Robot

Fig. 1. Curling Hexapod robot: 1. HIKROBOT MV-CH0120-10UC camera, 2. HESAI Pandar64 64-Channel Mechanical Lidar, 3. Driving Wheel controlled by servo motor, 4. Driven wheel, 5. Single degree of freedom mechanical arm, 6. 16000mAH lithium battery, 7. Supports for gliding.

The curling hexapod robot is an intelligent robot designed to simulate human curling behavior. Its overall size is about 1.50 m long, 0.86 m wide, 0.65 m high and weighs about 63kg, as shown in Fig. 1. There are two driving wheels controlled by servo motor at the knee joint of the front legs, and two driven wheels near the tip of the front legs. They are used to rotate the curling stone. And there are four supports for gliding at the hip joint of the front legs and the knee joint of the middle legs. In addition, the curling hexapod robot uses Advantech MIO-5373 embedded single-board computer as the motion controller, and TWOWIN TECHNOLOGY T505 computer as the vision processor. At the same time, the robot is equipped with HESAI Pandar64 Lidar and HIKROBOT MV-CH0120-10UC camera, which are used to detect the environment of the curling venue and the movement of the curling stone in real time. The camera is installed on the single degree of freedom mechanical arm on the robot, and the view field of camera is expanded by extending the arm. And the robot is equipped with two 16000 mAh lithium batteries, which can provide the robot with continuous operation for nearly 2 h.

The curling hexapod robot is different from the general hexapod robots. It has a variety of different topologies characteristics: hexapod walking and standing topology, quadruped posture adjustment topology and biped curling stone delivering topology, as shown in Fig. 2. The hexapod walking and standing topology is used for robot walking on ice task, the quadruped posture adjustment topology is used for robot finding hack and adjusting direction tasks, the biped curling stone delivering topology is used for robot pedaling hack and delivering curling stone tasks. When in the biped curling stone delivering topology, the front legs of the robot are transformed into the gripper to realize the action of holding and rotating the curling stone. The knees of the middle legs and the hips of the front legs are combined into four points to contact with the ice, thus realizing the function of supporting the robot glide, as shown in the yellow dotted line in Fig. 2.c. The rear legs pedal the hack to accelerate the robot to glide. In addition, the front legs will complete the task of throwing the curling stone during the glide process of the robot. After finish the curling stone delivering task, the curling hexapod robot will change from the biped curling stone delivering topology to the hexapod walking and standing topology.

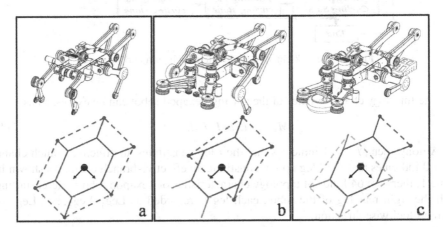

Fig. 2. Different topology characteristics of curling hexapod robot: a. hexapod walking and standing topology, b. quadruped posture adjustment topology, c. biped curling stone delivering topology

3 Topology Characteristics of the Curling Hexapod Robot

As shown in Fig. 3, the task chain of an athlete to deliver a curling stone is to step into the hack, confirm the target, pedal the hack to glide and release the curling stone. Among them, the behaviors that athletes need to complete are: stepping into the hack with one foot, supporting the body with other foot, confirming the target angle, holding the curling stone, pedaling the hack, gliding assisted by broom, rotating the curling stone and releasing the curling stone.

In order to imitate the behavior of human throwing the stone, the curling hexapod robot has different topologies characteristics (see Fig. 2) to complete different actions. The topologies variations of the curling hexapod are introduced below.

The topology characteristics of the legged robot is defined as a parallel mechanism composed of "ground- mechanical leg- robot body". In the process of mechanism motion, its mechanism topology is divided according the whether the mechanical leg forms an effective branch chain or not. Each mechanical topology is the topology characteristics of the robot.

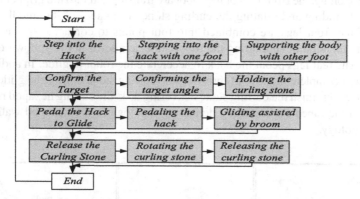

Fig. 3. The task chain of an athlete to deliver a curling stone.

The topology characteristics of the curling hexapod robot can be expressed as

$$M_T = (L_1 L_2 L_3 L_4 L_5 L_6) \tag{1}$$

Among them, $L_i = 1$ indicates that the i leg constitutes an effective branch chain, $L_i = 0$ indicates that the i leg do not constitute an effective branch chain. As shown in Table 1, there are 64 kinds of topology characteristics of hexapod robots. Here, starting with the right rear leg of the robot, each leg is recorded as $\text{Leg}_1, \text{Leg}_2, \ldots, \text{Leg}_6$ in counterclockwise direction.

As shown in Fig. 2.a, the curling hexapod robot is in the hexapod walking and standing topology, its topology characteristic can be expressed as $M_T^{0-6}=(1\ 1\ 1\ 1\ 1\ 1)$. At this time, it is equivalent to a 6-SRRR parallel mechanism, and the point at which the tip of leg touches the ground is equivalent to the spherical joint in each branch chain. In this topology, when the robot needs to walk, it can switch from M_T^{0-6} to $M_T^{3-3}=(1\ 0\ 1\ 0\ 1\ 0)=(0\ 1\ 0\ 1\ 0\ 1)$. That is, the robot uses 3–3 gait to walk on the ice.

As shown in Fig. 2.b, the curling hexapod robot is in the quadruped posture adjustment topology, its topology characteristic can be expressed as $M_T^{2-4}=(1\ 1\ 0\ 0\ 1\ 1)$. The front legs of robot ($\text{Leg}_3,\text{Leg}_4$) is folded and rotated inward to form a curling stone gripper, and they are no longer the effective branch chains of the robot. In this time, the curling hexapod robot is equivalent to a 4-SRRR parallel mechanism. In this topology, the robot can adjust the position and angle of the body.

Table 1. Expression of 64 kinds of topology characteristics

Type	Expression
0–6	$^{(1)}M_T^{0-6} = (111111)$
1–5	$^{(1)}M_T^{1-5} = (011111)$ $^{(3)}M_T^{1-5} = (110111)$ $^{(5)}M_T^{1-5} = (111101)$
	$^{(2)}M_T^{1-5} = (101111)$ $^{(4)}M_T^{1-5} = (111011)$ $^{(6)}M_T^{1-5} = (111110)$
2–4	$^{(1)}M_T^{2-4} = (001111)$ $^{(6)}M_T^{2-4} = (100111)$ $^{(11)}M_T^{2-4} = (110101)$
	$^{(2)}M_T^{2-4} = (010111)$ $^{(7)}M_T^{2-4} = (101011)$ $^{(12)}M_T^{2-4} = (110110)$
	$^{(3)}M_T^{2-4} = (011011)$ $^{(8)}M_T^{2-4} = (101101)$ $^{(13)}M_T^{2-4} = (111001)$
	$^{(4)}M_T^{2-4} = (011101)$ $^{(9)}M_T^{2-4} = (101110)$ $^{(14)}M_T^{2-4} = (111010)$
	$^{(5)}M_T^{2-4} = (011110)$ $^{(10)}M_T^{2-4} = (110011)$ $^{(15)}M_T^{2-4} = (111100)$
3–3	$^{(1)}M_T^{3-3} = (000111)$ $^{(8)}M_T^{3-3} = (011001)$ $^{(15)}M_T^{3-3} = (101010)$
	$^{(2)}M_T^{3-3} = (001011)$ $^{(9)}M_T^{3-3} = (011010)$ $^{(16)}M_T^{3-3} = (101100)$
	$^{(3)}M_T^{3-3} = (001101)$ $^{(10)}M_T^{3-3} = (011100)$ $^{(17)}M_T^{3-3} = (110001)$
	$^{(4)}M_T^{3-3} = (001110)$ $^{(11)}M_T^{3-3} = (100011)$ $^{(18)}M_T^{3-3} = (110010)$
	$^{(5)}M_T^{3-3} = (010011)$ $^{(12)}M_T^{3-3} = (100101)$ $^{(19)}M_T^{3-3} = (110100)$
	$^{(6)}M_T^{3-3} = (010101)$ $^{(13)}M_T^{3-3} = (100110)$ $^{(20)}M_T^{3-3} = (111000)$
	$^{(7)}M_T^{3-3} = (010110)$ $^{(14)}M_T^{3-3} = (101001)$
4–2	$^{(1)}M_T^{4-2} = (110000)$ $^{(6)}M_T^{4-2} = (011000)$ $^{(11)}M_T^{4-2} = (001010)$
	$^{(2)}M_T^{4-2} = (101000)$ $^{(7)}M_T^{4-2} = (010100)$ $^{(12)}M_T^{4-2} = (001001)$
	$^{(3)}M_T^{4-2} = (100100)$ $^{(8)}M_T^{4-2} = (010010)$ $^{(13)}M_T^{4-2} = (000110)$
	$^{(4)}M_T^{4-2} = (100010)$ $^{(9)}M_T^{4-2} = (010001)$ $^{(14)}M_T^{4-2} = (000101)$
	$^{(5)}M_T^{4-2} = (100001)$ $^{(10)}M_T^{4-2} = (001100)$ $^{(15)}M_T^{4-2} = (000011)$
5–1	$^{(1)}M_T^{5-1} = (100000)$ $^{(3)}M_T^{5-1} = (001000)$ $^{(5)}M_T^{5-1} = (000010)$
	$^{(2)}M_T^{5-1} = (010000)$ $^{(4)}M_T^{5-1} = (000100)$ $^{(6)}M_T^{5-1} = (000001)$
6–0	$^{(1)}M_T^{6-0} = (000000)$

As shown in Fig. 2.c, the curling hexapod robot is in the biped curling stone delivering topology, its topology characteristic can be expressed as $M_T^{4-2}=(1\ 0\ 0\ 0\ 0\ 1)$. The middle legs touch the ground with the discs at the knee joint and the front legs touch the ground with the support at the hip joint to form a four-point support. And these legs are no longer effective branch chains of the robot. In this case, the curling hexapod robot is equivalent to a 2-URRR parallel mechanism and has 3 degrees of freedom in ice plane, which is one translation and two rotations. So, the robot realizes the glide function on the ice through the rear legs (Leg_1,Leg_6) pedal hack.

Through the switching of the above different topologies, the curling hexapod robot has the conditions to realize the humanoid delivering curling stones behaviors. In order to realize the delivering curling stone function, further behaviors design is need for the robot.

4   Behaviors Design of the Curling Hexapod Robot

When facing the practical application task, the robot needs to decompose the complex task into several subtasks to form a task chain. Subtask is a logical concept used for task decomposition, which divides complex tasks into more detailed and simple tasks. According to the sequence of subtasks execution, the subtasks can be summarized into two categories: serial structure and parallel structure. Serial structure means that all subtasks are executed according to time series, while parallel structure means that all subtasks are executed at the same time. The task is represented by A_M, the serial structure is represented by vector that has order character, and the parallel structure is represented by set that has disorder character, then the mathematical model of decomposing task into subtask chain can be expressed as

$$A_M = \left(\left\{ \begin{matrix} A_{M1} \\ A_{M1} \\ A_{M1} \end{matrix} \right\}, \cdots, \left\{ \begin{matrix} A_{M(n+1)} \\ A_{M(n+2)} \end{matrix} \right\} \right) \tag{2}$$

After the task is decomposed into subtask chain, its behavior chain needs be further constructed. The behavior chain consists of a series of basic behaviors, and defines all the behaviors required by the task and the logical relationship between them. The continuous derivable trajectory with the same motion mode and trajectory production mode is defined as the basic behavior of the robot, which is represented by B_R, then the basic behavior can be clearly described by an independent continuous trajectory equation. Based on this, the mapping relationship between the subtask and the behavior chain can be established, which is

$$A_{Mi} \rightarrow (B_{Ri1}, B_{Ri2}, \cdots, B_{Rin}) \tag{3}$$

In this way, the task decomposition pattern and expression of "task-subtask chains-behavior chains" for complex tasks are formed.

The basic behavior includes topology characteristic, motion characteristic and trajectory characteristic. The motion characteristic is used to describe which output dimension move at the end. A hexapod robot has two types of ends: a body with six complete output dimensions and a toe with three output dimensions. They can be expressed in G_F Sets [7] as

$$G_{Fb} = G_F^I = (T_a, T_B, T_C, R_a, R_\beta, R_\gamma), G_{Ff} = G_F^{II} = (R_a, R_\beta, T_a, 0, 0, 0) \tag{4}$$

where T_a, T_b, T_c are three non-coplanar moving direction vectors, and R_α, R_β, R_γ are three non-coplanar rotation line vectors. G_{Fb} is used to describe the motion characteristics of the robot body, there are 25 types, as shown in Table 2. G_{Ff} is used to describe the motion characteristics of the leg tip, there are 8 types, as shown in Table 3.

Table 2. The motion characteristic of the robot body

Dimension	The first kind of G_F set	The second kind of G_F set	The third kind of G_F set
1	$^{(1)}G_{Fb}^{I}=(T_a,0,0,0,0,0)$	$^{(1)}G_{Fb}^{II}=(R_\alpha,0,0,0,0,0)$	/
2	$^{(2)}G_{Fb}^{I}=(T_a,T_b,0,0,0,0)$	$^{(2)}G_{Fb}^{II}=(R_\alpha,R_\beta,0,0,0,0)$ $^{(3)}G_{Fb}^{II}=(R_\alpha,T_a,0,0,0,0)$ $^{(4)}G_{Fb}^{II}=(T_a,R_\alpha,0,0,0,0)$	/
3	$^{(3)}G_{Fb}^{I}=(T_a,T_b,T_c,0,0,0)$ $^{(4)}G_{Fb}^{I}=(T_a,T_b,R_\alpha,0,0,0)$	$^{(5)}G_{Fb}^{II}=(R_\alpha,R_\beta,R_\gamma,0,0,0)$ $^{(6)}G_{Fb}^{II}=(T_a,R_\alpha,R_\beta,0,0,0)$ $^{(7)}G_{Fb}^{II}=(R_\alpha,R_\beta,T_a,0,0,0)$ $^{(8)}G_{Fb}^{II}=(T_a,T_b,R_\alpha,0,0,0)$ $^{(9)}G_{Fb}^{II}=(R_\alpha,T_a,T_b,0,0,0)$ $^{(10)}G_{Fb}^{II}=(T_a,R_\alpha,T_b,0,0,0)$	/
4	$^{(5)}G_{Fb}^{I}=(T_a,T_b,T_c,R_\alpha,0,0)$	$^{(11)}G_{Fb}^{II}=(R_\alpha,R_\beta,R_\gamma,T_a,0,0)$ $^{(12)}G_{Fb}^{II}=(T_a,R_\alpha,R_\beta,R_\gamma,0,0)$ $^{(13)}G_{Fb}^{II}=(R_\alpha,R_\beta,T_a,T_b,0,0)$ $^{(14)}G_{Fb}^{II}=(T_a,T_b,R_\alpha,R_\beta,0,0)$	$^{(1)}G_{Fb}^{III}=(T_a,T_b,R_\alpha,R_\beta,0,0)$ $^{(2)}G_{Fb}^{III}=(R_\alpha,T_a,T_b,R_\beta,0,0)$
5	$^{(6)}G_{Fb}^{I}=(T_a,T_b,T_c,R_\alpha,R_\beta,0)$	/	$^{(3)}G_{Fb}^{III}=(T_a,T_b,R_\alpha,R_\beta,R_\gamma,0)$ $^{(4)}G_{Fb}^{III}=(R_\alpha,R_\beta,T_a,T_b,R_\gamma,0)$
6	$^{(7)}G_{Fb}^{I}=(T_a,T_b,T_c,R_\alpha,R_\beta,R_\gamma)$	/	/

Table 3. The motion characteristic of the leg tip

Dimension	The first kind of G_F set	The second kind of G_F set	The third kind of G_F set
1	$^{(1)}G_{Ff}^{I}=(T_a,0,0,0,0,0)$	$^{(1)}G_{Ff}^{II}=(R_\alpha,0,0,0,0,0)$	/
2	$^{(2)}G_{Ff}^{I}=(T_a,T_b,0,0,0,0)$	$^{(2)}G_{Ff}^{II}=(R_\alpha,R_\beta,0,0,0,0)$ $^{(3)}G_{Ff}^{II}=(R_\alpha,T_a,0,0,0,0)$	/
3	$^{(3)}G_{Ff}^{I}=(T_a,T_b,T_c,0,0,0)$	$^{(4)}G_{Ff}^{II}=(R_\alpha,R_\beta,T_a,0,0,0)$ $^{(5)}G_{Ff}^{II}=(R_\alpha,T_a,T_b,0,0,0)$	/

Trajectory characteristic describe what kind of trajectory is used in each motion output. The trajectory characteristics can be divided into three planning methods: one is to plan with a given target position, the second is to plan with a given target force, and the third is to plan with a given joint motor position or speed.

B_{Ri} denotes the i basic behavior, M_{Ti} represents the topology characteristic, G_{Fi} represents the motion characteristics and T_{Ei} represents the trajectory characteristics, then:

$$B_{Ri} = \{M_{Ti}, G_{Fi}, T_{Ei}\} \tag{5}$$

When the body and legs are moving at the same time, the motion characteristics include body motion and toe motion characteristics, and the corresponding trajectory characteristics also include these two items. Therefore,

$$B_{Ri} = \left\{M_{Ti}, \left\{G_{Fbi}, G_{Ffi}\right\}, \left\{T_{Ebi}, T_{Efi}\right\}\right\} \tag{6}$$

It is a complex task for the curling hexapod robot to deliver the curling stone. Using the task decomposition method and behavior decomposition method, this paper develops the robot throwing the curling stone method, as shown in Fig. 4. The curling stone throwing task can be decomposed into 6 subtasks: A_{M1} quadruped topology, A_{M2} seeking hack, A_{M3} angle adjustment, A_{M4} holding and rotating the curling stone, A_{M5} delivering the curling stone and A_{M6} hexapod topology. These 6 subtasks are executed sequentially in chronological order, so the task chain can be expressed as

$$A_M = (A_{M1}, A_{M2}, A_{M3}, A_{M4}, A_{M5}, A_{M6}) \tag{7}$$

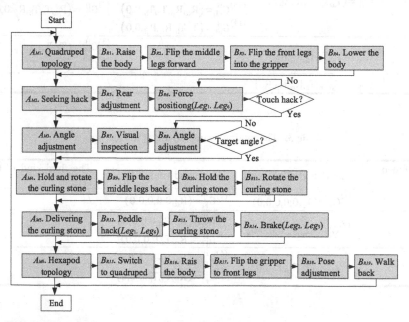

Fig. 4. The task chain and behavior chains of the robot delivering the curling stone

These 6 subtasks can be further decomposed to 19 basic behaviors to form behavior chains. The mapping relationship between the task chain and the behavior chains can be expressed as

$$
\begin{aligned}
A_{M1} &\to (B_{R1}, B_{R2}, B_{R3}, B_{R4}) \\
A_{M2} &\to (B_{R5}, B_{R6}) \\
A_{M3} &\to (B_{R7}, B_{R8}) \\
A_{M4} &\to (B_{R9}, B_{R10}, B_{R11}) \\
A_{M5} &\to (B_{R12}, B_{R13}, B_{R14}, B_{R15}) \\
A_{M6} &\to (B_{R16}, B_{R17}, B_{R18}, B_{R19})
\end{aligned}
\tag{8}
$$

In the subtask of A_{M1} quadruped topology, the curling hexapod robot first raises the height of the body, then flips the middle legs forward to achieve stable quadruped support, then folds the front legs and flips them inward to form the curling stone gripper, and finally lowers the body to the ice. The basic behaviors in this process are

$$
\begin{aligned}
B_{R1} &= \left\{ {}^{(1)}M_T^{0-6}, {}^{(1)}G_{Fb}^{I}, T_{Eb1} \right\} \\
B_{R2} &= \left\{ {}^{(8)}M_T^{2-4}, {}^{(2)}G_{Ff}^{I}, T_{Ef2} \right\} \\
B_{R3} &= \left\{ {}^{(10)}M_T^{2-4}, {}^{(3)}G_{Ff}^{I}, T_{Ef3} \right\} \\
B_{R4} &= \left\{ {}^{(10)}M_T^{2-4}, {}^{(1)}G_{Fb}^{I}, T_{Eb4} \right\}
\end{aligned}
\tag{9}
$$

where

$$
\begin{aligned}
&T_{Eb1}: z = (1 - s_b)H_{Init} + s_b H_{Tar} \\
&T_{Ef2}: \begin{cases} q_t = (1 - s_f)\theta_{tInit} + s_f \theta_{tTar} \\ q_s = (1 - s_f)\theta_{sInit} + s_f \theta_{sTar} \end{cases} \\
&T_{Ef2}: \begin{cases} q_a = (1 - s_f)\theta_{aInit} + s_f \theta_{aTar} \\ q_t = (1 - s_f)\theta_{tInit} + s_f \theta_{tTar} \\ q_s = (1 - s_f)\theta_{sInit} + s_f \theta_{sTar} \end{cases} \quad, \quad s_b = s_f = \begin{cases} 2\left(\frac{t}{T}\right)^2, \ 0 = \frac{t}{T} = \frac{1}{2} \\ -2\left(\frac{t}{T}\right)^2 + 4\left(\frac{t}{T}\right) - 1, \frac{1}{2} < \frac{t}{T} = 1 \end{cases} \\
&T_{Eb4}: z = (1 - s_b)H_{Init} + s_b H_{Tar}
\end{aligned}
\tag{10}
$$

In the subtask of A_{M2} seeking hack, the curling hexapod robot moves the body back through the quadruped topology, and then determines whether the rear legs in on the hack through the force perception. The basic behaviors in this process are

$$
\begin{aligned}
B_{R5} &= \left\{ {}^{(10)}M_T^{2-4}, {}^{(3)}G_{Fb}^{I}, T_{Eb5} \right\} \\
B_{R6} &= \left\{ {}^{(10)}M_T^{2-4}, {}^{(1)}G_{Ff}^{I}, T_{Ef6} \right\}
\end{aligned}
\tag{11}
$$

Where

$$
T_{Eb5}: \begin{cases} x = (1 - s_b)D_{Init} + s_b D_{Tar} \\ y = (1 - s_b)D_{Init} + s_b D_{Tar} \\ z = (1 - s_b)H_{Init} + s_b H_{Tar} \end{cases}, \quad s_b = s_f = \begin{cases} 2\left(\frac{t}{T}\right)^2, \ 0 = \frac{t}{T} = \frac{1}{2} \\ -2\left(\frac{t}{T}\right)^2 + 4\left(\frac{t}{T}\right) - 1, \frac{1}{2} < \frac{t}{T} = 1 \end{cases}
$$
$$
T_{Ef6}: x = (1 - s_f)D_{Init} + s_f D_{Tar}
\tag{12}
$$

In the subtask of A_{M3} angle adjustment, the curling hexapod raises the manipulator to expand the camera's field, then combine with lidar to detect the curling stone, and finally adjusts the body angle to the desired angle for throwing curling stone. The basic behaviors in this process are

$$
\begin{aligned}
B_{R7} &= \left\{ {}^{(10)}M_T^{2-4}, {}^{(1)}\,G_{Ff}^{II}, T_{Ef7} \right\} \\
B_{R8} &= \left\{ {}^{(10)}M_T^{2-4}, {}^{(3)}\,G_{Fb}^{II}, T_{Eb8} \right\}
\end{aligned}
\tag{13}
$$

Where

$$
T_{Ef7}: q = (1 - s_f)\theta_{Init} + s_f\theta_{Tar}
$$

$$
T_{Eb8}:
\begin{cases}
z = (1 - s_b)H_{Init} + s_bH_{Tar} \\
yaw = (1 - s_b)\theta_{Init} + s_b\theta_{Tar}
\end{cases}
, \quad s_b = s_f =
\begin{cases}
2\left(\frac{t}{T}\right)^2, \ 0 = \frac{t}{T} = \frac{1}{2} \\
-2\left(\frac{t}{T}\right)^2 + 4\left(\frac{t}{T}\right) - 1, \frac{1}{2} < \frac{t}{T} = 1
\end{cases}
\tag{14}
$$

In the subtask of A_{M4} holding and rotating the curling stone, the curling hexapod robot flips the middle legs backward, and constructs a stable supporting quadrilateral through the knee joint supports of the middle legs and the hip joint supports of the front legs. And then the front legs gripper clamps the curling stone to achieve the function of holding the stone and rotates the stone through the driving wheels of the knee joint. The basic behaviors in this process are

$$
\begin{aligned}
B_{R9} &= \left\{ {}^{(10)}M_T^{4-2}, {}^{(2)}\,G_{Ff}^{II}, T_{Ef9} \right\} \\
B_{R10} &= \left\{ {}^{(10)}M_T^{2-4}, {}^{(1)}\,G_{Ff}^{II}, T_{Ef10} \right\} \\
B_{R11} &= \left\{ {}^{(10)}M_T^{2-4}, {}^{(1)}\,G_{Ff}^{II}, T_{Ef11} \right\}
\end{aligned}
\tag{15}
$$

Where

$$
T_{Ef9}:
\begin{cases}
q_t = (1 - s_f)\theta_{tInit} + s_f\theta_{tTar} \\
q_s = (1 - s_f)\theta_{sInit} + s_f\theta_{sTar}
\end{cases}
, \quad s_f =
\begin{cases}
2\left(\frac{t}{T}\right)^2, 0 = \frac{t}{T} = \frac{1}{2} \\
-2\left(\frac{t}{T}\right)^2 + 4\left(\frac{t}{T}\right) - 1, \ \frac{1}{2} < \frac{t}{T} = 1
\end{cases}
$$

$$
T_{Ef10}: q_t = (1 - s_f)\theta_{tInit} + s_f\theta_{tTar}
$$

$$
T_{Ef11}: q_t = (1 - s_f)V_{Init} + s_fV_{Tar}
\tag{16}
$$

In the subtask of A_{M5} delivering the curling stone, the curling hexapod robot pedals the hack to accelerate the glide of robot, then throws the curling stone through the front legs, and finally brakes down the robot glide through the middle legs. The basic behaviors in this process are

$$
\begin{aligned}
B_{R12} &= \left\{ {}^{(10)}M_T^{4-2}, {}^{(1)}\,G_{Ff}^{I}, T_{Ef12} \right\} \\
B_{R13} &= \left\{ {}^{(10)}M_T^{2-4}, {}^{(1)}\,G_{Ff}^{I}, T_{Ef13} \right\} \\
B_{R14} &= \left\{ {}^{(10)}M_T^{2-4}, {}^{(1)}\,G_{Ff}^{II}, T_{Ef14} \right\}
\end{aligned}
\tag{17}
$$

where

$$T_{Ef12}:x = a_0 + a_1t + a_2t^2 + a_3t^3 + a_4t^4 + a_5t^5 + a_6t^6 + a_7t^7$$
$$T_{Ef13}:x = a_0 + a_1t + a_2t^2 + a_3t^3 + a_4t^4 + a_5t^5 + a_6t^6 + a_7t^7 \tag{18}$$
$$T_{Ef14}:q_t = (1 - s_f)\theta_{tInit} + s_f\theta_{tTar}, s_f = \begin{cases} 2\left(\frac{t}{T}\right)^2, 0 = \frac{t}{T} = \frac{1}{2} \\ -2\left(\frac{t}{T}\right)^2 + 4\left(\frac{t}{T}\right) - 1, \frac{1}{2} < \frac{t}{T} = 1 \end{cases}$$

The boundary conditions corresponding to T_{Ef12} and T_{Ef13} are

$$x(0)=0, \dot{x}(0)=0, \ddot{x}(0)=0, x^{(3)}(0)=0,$$
$$x(T)=D_{end}, \dot{x}(T)=V_{Tar}, \ddot{x}(T)=0, x^{(3)}(T) = 0 \tag{19}$$

where D_{end} is the set distance for acceleration, and V_{Tar} is the target speed of acceleration.

In the subtask of A_{M6} hexapod topology, the curling hexapod robot folds the rear legs and flips the middle legs forward into the quadruped topology. Then it raises the body, restores the front legs, and flips the middle legs backward into the hexapod topology. After that, the robot can walk back to hack with the 3–3 gait. The basic behaviors are

$$B_{R15} = \left\{ {}^{(10)}M_T^{2-4}, {}^{(2)}G_{Ff}^{II}, T_{Ef15} \right\}$$
$$B_{R16} = \left\{ {}^{(1)}M_T^{0-6}, {}^{(1)}G_{Fb}^{I}, T_{Eb16} \right\}$$
$$B_{R17} = \left\{ {}^{(10)}M_T^{2-4}, {}^{(3)}G_{Ff}^{I}, T_{Ef17} \right\} \tag{20}$$
$$B_{R18} = \left\{ {}^{(6)}M_T^{3-3}, {}^{(3)}G_{Ff}^{I}, T_{Ef18} \right\}$$
$$B_{R18} = \left\{ {}^{(15)}M_T^{3-3}, \left\{ {}^{(3)}G_{Fb}^{I}, {}^{(3)}G_{Ff}^{I} \right\}, \left\{ T_{Eb19}, T_{Ef19} \right\} \right\}$$

These trajectories characteristics can be referred to subtask A_{M1}.

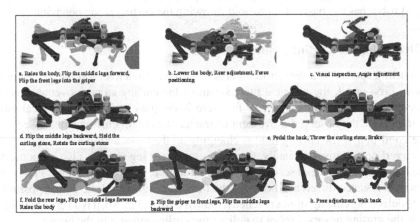

Fig. 5. The humanoid delivering curling stone action of the curling hexapod robot

The humanoid delivering curling stone action of the robot is shown in Fig. 5.

5   Experiments and Analysis

This section presents results from experiments of the curling hexapod robot. These experiments results highlight the functional completeness and accuracy of the curling hexapod robot by topologies change and behavior design.

5.1   Topologies Switching

Fig. 6. Topologies switching: a. from hexapod topology to quadruped topology, b. from biped topology to hexapod topology

The curling hexapod robot has the function of topologies switch. It can switch from the hexapod topology to the quadruped topology (see Fig. 6.a). And it also can switch from the biped topology to the hexapod topology (see Fig. 6.b). That means the curling hexapod robot has the basis of humanoid throwing the curling stone behavior.

5.2   Delivering the Curling Stone

In the curling sport, it is a very difficult task for athletes to deliver a stone to the desired position. First of all, the physical mechanism of the curling stone movement has not yet been fully understood [8–10], so far there is no quantitative mathematical model that can explain the observed movement characteristics of all curling stones. Secondly, the ice condition of the curling field is changing all the time, and these changes cannot be observed quantitatively. Finally, the trajectory of curling stone is also influenced by athletes' throwing skills and scrubbing skills. Therefore, in the 2018 Winter Paralympic Games, the distance difference between the desired position and the actual position of athletes delivering curling stones reached a span of 0.81–1.3 m. So, it is a very challenging task for the curling hexapod robot to deliver the curling stone into the house.

Figure 7 shows the experiments of the curling hexapod robot delivering curling stones into the house. Figure 7.a shows the video screenshots of one cast. It demonstrates that the robot can perform humanoid delivering stone action and can deliver the stone into

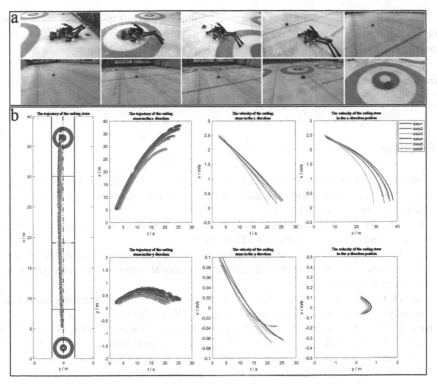

Fig. 7. Delivering the curling stone: a. the video screenshots of one cast, b. the trajectory of the robot throwing curling stone six times in the same control parameters

the house area. And Fig. 7.b shows the trajectory of the robot throwing curling stone six times in the same control parameters. It can be seen from the figure that the initial trajectories of these curling stones have a high degree of coincidence, while in the second half of these trajectories, the trajectories of different casts are more scattered. The high coincidence in the initial stage of these trajectories shows that the curling hexapod robot has high repetition accuracy of throwing stone in the same control parameters. The discretization of the second half of these trajectories is due to the deterioration of the ice condition with the passage of time. And the cumulative effect of ice deterioration on the curling stones movement is highlighted in the second half of these trajectory.

6   Conclusion

The curling hexapod robot introduced in this paper is the first robot to imitate human curling stone throwing behavior in the world. The various topologies characteristics of the curling hexapod robot are the basis for its humanoid curling stone throwing behavior. On this base, according to the task decomposition method and behavior decomposition method, we design the task chain and behavior chain of humanoid curling stone throwing behavior of the curling hexapod robot. And we validate the topology changing ability and curling stone delivering function of the curling robot by experiments.

The development of demonstration application of the hexapod robot is ours next work. By developing the suitable curling stone throwing strategy algorithm for the curling robot, the robot can participate in the human-led curling competition.

Acknowledgements. This work was funded by the National Natural Science Foundation of China (No. 92248303).

References

1. Kawamura, T., Kamimura, R., Suzuki, S., et al.: A study on the curling robot will match with human result of one end game with one human, In: 2015 IEEE Conference on Computational Intelligence and Games (CIG) (2015)
2. Xiang, G.: Design and simulation of curling robot based on Sysmac control platform. Shandong Indus. Technol. **000**(022), 127–129 (2017)
3. Choi, J. H., Song, C., Kim, K., et al.: Development of stone throwing robot and high precision driving control for curling. In:2018 IEEE/RSJ International Conference on Intelligent Robots and Systems (IROS) (2018)
4. Won, D.-O., Kim, B.-D., Kim, H.-J., et al.: Curly: an AI-based curling robot successfully competing in the olympic discipline of curling. In: IJCAI (2018)
5. Kim, K., Song, C., Jin, W.: Design and Implementation of Wheeled Curling Robots (2018)
6. Won, D.-O., Müller, K.-R., Lee, S.-W.: An adaptive deep reinforcement learning framework enables curling robots with human-like performance in real-world conditions. Sci. Robot. **5**(46), abb9764 (2020). https://doi.org/10.1126/scirobotics.abb9764
7. Feng, Gao., Jialun, Yang., Qiaode,Ge.: GF sets theory for synthesis of parallel robots.SCIENCE PRESS,Beijing (2011)
8. Nyberg, H., Alfredson, S., Hogmark, S., et al.: The asymmetrical friction mechanism that puts the curl in the curling stone. Wear **301**(1–2), 583–589 (2013)
9. Nyberg, H., Hogmark, S., Jacobson, S.: Calculated trajectories of curling stones sliding under asymmetrical friction: validation of published models. Tribol. Lett. **50**(3), 379–385 (2013)
10. Lozowski, E.P., Szilder, K., Maw, S., et al.: Towards a first principles model of curling ice friction and curling stone dynamics, In: The Twenty-fifth International Ocean and Polar Engineering Conference (2015)

Hierarchical Trajectory Optimization for Humanoid Robot Jumping Motion

Junbao Sun[1,2], Haopeng Liu[2], Xu Li[2], Haibo Feng[2], Yili Fu[1,2(✉)], and Songyuan Zhang[2]

[1] Intelligent Robot Research Center, Zhejiang Laboratory, Hangzhou 311100, China
meylfu@hit.edu.cn

[2] State Key Laboratory of Robotics and System, Harbin Institute of Technology, Harbin 150001, China
{hitlx,fenghaibo,zhangsy}@hit.edu.cn

Abstract. In order to make the robot have high dynamic motion ability, this paper uses the trajectory optimization method to plan the jumping motion trajectory of the humanoid robot quickly and effectively, and carries out the jumping motion experiment on the HIT-HU humanoid robot platform. In order to improve the solving speed of trajectory optimization problem, simplified centroid dynamics model and single rigid body model are established. Differential dynamic programming (DDP) based on the combination of the centroid dynamic model and the whole body joint kinematic model is used to solve the hopping trajectory optimization problem with high accuracy, and the external penalty function method is used to deal with the relevant constraints. In order to overcome the problem that the solver is sensitive to the initial point selection, a hierarchical trajectory optimization framework is proposed. The framework uses the direct collocation method based on the single rigid body model. The trajectory of the simplified model is used as the initial trajectory guess, and the differential dynamic programming method is introduced to solve the optimal trajectory of the whole joint. The differential dynamic programming algorithm using the direct method of warm start is about twice as fast as the method of manually given initial trajectory. The simulation and experimental verification of the vertical jump trajectories generated by the algorithm on the humanoid robot HIT-HU show that the jump trajectories generated by the algorithm can be effectively transformed into the motion trajectories of humanoid robots, and can be effectively executed on the physical prototype. This further verifies the effectiveness of the algorithm and plays an important role in practical application.

Keywords: Humanoid jumping · Hierarchical trajectory optimization · Differential dynamic programming · Direct collocation method

1 Introduction

The jump motion planning of legged robots is a complex task. It is necessary to find the optimal contact force sequence and joint trajectory sequence under given initial and end positions, attitude and other constraints, so as to achieve stable take-off and landing, and achieve preset targets such as jump heights [1]. In the research of jump planning for legged robots, there are currently some challenges and difficulties. The jump process is a nonlinear mixed dynamic complex system, so it is necessary to use advanced control theory and methods to solve the problems in jump trajectory planning [2]. Boston Dynamics' hydraulic driven humanoid robot Atlas can jump a certain height and perform a variety of tasks, but there are few public literatures on how to achieve stable and complex jump trajectory planning and control method on the humanoid robot [3]. Unlike industrial robots with fixed bases, humanoid robots belong to underactuated floating base systems [4].

There are various methods of jumping motion planning for legged robots [5]: Motion capture-based planning methods use captured human or animal jumping data to guide the robot's jumping planning. Machine learning-based planning methods use machine learning algorithms to learn patterns and features in jumping motion, and plan jumps based on these patterns and features. The optimization-based planning method implements skip planning by finding the optimal solution. Each planning method has its advantages, disadvantages and scope of application, and it is very important to choose a suitable method. Although there are many jump planning schemes for different legged robot hardware platforms, there is no general framework for trajectory planning. Since each hardware platform has its specific limitations and constraints, the performance limitations of the hardware platform need to be considered when designing and constraining the jump planning scheme.

Some researchers use human motion capture to generate complex movements of humanoid robots [6], since the kinematics and dynamics of humanoid robot movements are different from human movements, the captured trajectories must be modified to meet the kinematics and dynamics constraints. Some researchers have tried to combine robot dynamics and motion capture data to generate feasible trajectories [7]. Most studies have discussed motion planning in the case of relatively slow speed. In the case of high-speed dynamic motion, the dynamic stability of humanoid robot motion is a key issue, and the high cost of motion capture equipment is the primary constraint to its development [8]. R Batke et al. proposed a method to generate reference trajectories for biped robots performing highly dynamic actions using reinforcement learning [9]. The method can adapt to the walking and action requirements in different environments, can continuously optimize the behavior of the robot through feedback learning and adaptive learning, and can reduce the dependence on prior knowledge, thereby improving the autonomy and flexibility of the robot. However, machine learning algorithms require a large amount of data for training, so they require a long learning time and a large amount of data storage space. Machine learning algorithms may have problems such as overfitting or under fitting, and feature selection and parameter optimization are required.

The optimization-based trajectory optimization method refers to a class of methods that use mathematical optimization algorithms to optimize the trajectory of the robot [10]. The advantage of this method is that it can better balance the motion efficiency and motion stability of the robot, while satisfying different constraints. Optimization-based trajectory optimization is essentially an optimal control problem. The solution methods include indirect analytical method and direct numerical method [11]. The direct numerical method converts the optimization problem into a nonlinear programming problem, and uses the nonlinear programming algorithm to solve the optimization problem, so as to obtain the optimal control strategy. The collocation method usually requires a large number of numerical calculations, which has high computational complexity and consumes a large amount of computing resources. But the direct advantage is that it can handle high-latitude problems and can handle very complex constraints. Indirect trajectory optimization is a method based on optimal control theory, the main idea is to transform the optimization problem into the conditions satisfied by its optimal solution. The indirect method can obtain the global optimal solution, which has higher accuracy than the direct method. However, the indirect method deals with more complex constraints than the direct method, and the indirect method is more sensitive to the initial trajectory.

Robot modeling is a very important step in optimization-based jump trajectory planning, which greatly affects the effect of trajectory optimization. Raibert first used the spring-loaded inverted pendulum model, and successfully applied it to single-legged, bipedal, and quadrupedal [12] robots to achieve balanced running, jumping and other dynamic gaits. Yu simplified the wheel-legged robot into the double-mass spring inverted pendulum (DM-SLIP) model [13], and MIT's "Cheetah" series robots used the SRBM simplified model to plan the trajectory of the robot [14]. Imperial College London proposed a unified model to plan highly dynamic jumps [15]. An overly complex model may lead to too long calculation time of the trajectory optimization algorithm, thus affecting the real-time and practicality of trajectory optimization. Therefore, in practice there is a trade-off between model accuracy and computational efficiency [16].

The main contribution of this paper is to propose a hierarchical trajectory optimization framework. In order to overcome the sensitivity of the solver to the initial point, this paper adopts the direct method and the indirect method for layered optimization based on models of different complexity, combining the advantages of the direct method and the indirect method. The direct collocation method based on the single rigid body model converts the motion planning problem of the legged robot into a nonlinear optimization problem, solves the initial trajectory, and combines the differential dynamic programming method to solve the optimal whole-body joint trajectory. Numerical simulation results show that this framework can significantly save convergence time.

2 System Modeling

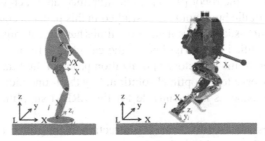

Fig. 1. Coordinate System of Humanoid Robot System on Floating Base.

Humanoid robots usually have many degrees of freedom. To optimize their trajectory, it is necessary to analyze and establish the kinematics and dynamics models of the robot. As shown in Fig. 1, all the vectors describing the robot in this article are under the four coordinate systems, namely the inertial coordinate system $\{L\}$, the base coordinate system $\{B\}$, the center of mass coordinate system $\{G\}$ and the joint coordinate system $\{i\}$. The superscripts in front of all the vectors in this paper, such as i or B, mean that they are $\{i\}$ represented in the local coordinate system and the base coordinate system $\{B\}$ respectively. If not written, all are assumed to be represented in the inertial coordinate system $\{L\}$.

2.1 Model of Dynamics

The first step in building a complete rigid body model of the robot is to describe the state of the robot. The structural configuration of the robot can be described by a complete and independent set of generalized coordinates $q \in R^n$ [17], which correspond to the position of each joint, and n is the total number of degrees of freedom of the robot. The floating base system can be described $q_{fb} \in R^6$ by an enhanced set of generalized coordinates, which $q = [q_{fb}^T, q_j^T] \in R^{n+6}$ describe the position and orientation of the floating base while $q_j \in R^n$ describing the position of each non-virtual joint.

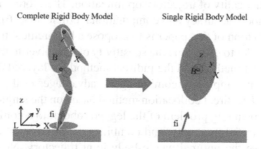

Fig. 2. Simplified Single Rigid Body Model.

In this paper, the robot is simplified to a simpler model based on the center of mass, the Single Rigid Body Model (SRBM), the single rigid body model of a biped robot is a model composed of two massless rods and a rigid body whose mass is concentrated at the center of mass of the robot [9, 17]. This simplified approach is shown in Fig. 2. The torso of the hydraulic humanoid robot studied in this paper accounts for more than 60%. Although the high-speed movement of the limbs has a great impact on the moment of inertia of the simplified single rigid body, the calculation results can be used as an approximate solution to the trajectory optimization problem, and the subsequent optimization results converge to the optimal solution. Lay the foundation, so the humanoid robot studied in this paper is more suitable for this SRBM simplification to a certain extent.

The Euler angles are used to define the direction of the robot, a fixed rigid body coordinate system $\{B\}$ is established at the center of mass of the rigid body, and the coordinate axis is consistent with the inertial axis of the rigid body. The axes are determined by the right-hand rule. Then the complete state of the SRBM can be expressed as.

$$x = \begin{bmatrix} q_{fb} \\ \dot{q}_{fb} \end{bmatrix} = [r_c, \theta, v_c, {}^B\omega]^T \tag{1}$$

where $r_c \in R^3$ is the position of the center of mass, $\theta \in R^3$ is the direction of the rigid body represented by ZYX Euler angles, $v_c \in R^3$ is the velocity of the center of mass, ${}^B\omega \in R^3$ and is the angular velocity of the rigid body expressed in the fixed system $\{B\}$ relative to the inertial system. The resulting rigid body dynamics are much simpler than full multi-rigid body dynamics.

$$\dot{x} = \frac{d}{dt} \begin{bmatrix} r_c \\ \theta \\ v_c \\ {}^B\omega \end{bmatrix} = \begin{bmatrix} v_c \\ B(\theta){}^B\omega \\ \frac{1}{m}f - g \\ {}^BI^{-1}\left(R_{body}^T\tau - {}^B\hat{\omega}{}^BI{}^B\omega\right) \end{bmatrix} \tag{2}$$

wherein $B(\theta) \in R^{3\times3}$ is the conversion matrix from angular velocity to Euler angle change rate, m is the rigid body mass, $f \in R^3$ is the net external force acting on the center of mass, and $g \in R^3$ is the acceleration of gravity, ${}^BI \in R^{3\times3}$ is the center of mass inertia tensor expressed in the fixed system $\{B\}$, and R_{body} is the rotation matrix from the center of mass coordinate system to the inertial coordinate system. $\tau \in R^3$ is the net moment about the center of mass.

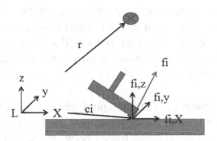

Fig. 3. Foot-to-ground Contact Model.

Since the mass of all the connecting rods of the robot is concentrated into a rigid body, it is assumed that the moment of inertia of the rigid body ${}^BI$ is constant. The reaction forces at each foot contact point determine the net resultant external forces and moments transferred to the rigid body. The net external force and net moment acting on the center of mass is.

$$\begin{bmatrix} f \\ \tau \end{bmatrix} = \sum_{i=1}^{n} \begin{bmatrix} f_i \\ \hat{p}_i f_i \end{bmatrix} \tag{3}$$

where $f_i \in R^3$ is the ground reaction force of the i-th contact point, and p_i is the position vector of the i-th contact point relative to the

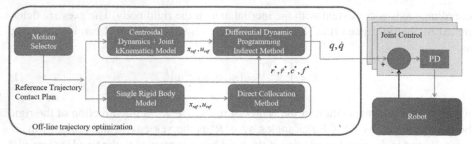

Fig. 4. Jump Motion Trajectory Optimization Framework. Hierarchical programming framework, hot start based on direct collocation method, and differential dynamic programming framework to achieve the dynamic air motion of humanoid robots.

of mass of the rigid body (for all p_i, $y \in R^3$, there is $\hat{p}_i y = p_i \times y$). The centroid momentum of the humanoid robot $h_G \in R^6$ is linearly related to the generalized coordinates of the humanoid robot $\dot{q} \in R^{n+6}$ through the centroidal momentum matrix (CMM) $A_G \in R^{6\times(n+6)}$[18].

$$h_G = \begin{bmatrix} h \\ p \end{bmatrix} = A_G(q)\dot{q} \tag{4}$$

2.2 Contact Model

In order to facilitate the analysis of the force and contact of the soles of the feet, assuming that the ground is flat, there are eight contact points between the feet of the humanoid robot and the ground, which are respectively located at the four corners of the soles of the feet. The position of each contact point in the inertial coordinate system is $c_i \in R^3$, There are contact forces on points $f_i \in R^3$, $i = 1, 2, ..., n_c$, the number of contact points in this paper $n_c = 8$.

During the jumping process of the humanoid robot, it will experience three motion situations: the take-off phase, the flying phase and the landing phase. Under different motion phases, the contact points and forces between the external environment and the robot will also change, thus changing the dynamic constraint characteristics of the robot. During the movement of the robot, when the foot of the robot is in contact with the ground, the collision that occurs is assumed to be a rigid body collision model. The contact model between the foot end and the ground is shown in Fig. 3.

$$\begin{aligned} (c_{i,z} - h_{ground})f_{i,z} = 0, & \quad i = 1, 2, ...n_c \\ f_{i,z} \geq 0, & \quad c_{i,z} - h_{ground} \geq 0 \end{aligned} \tag{5}$$

Complementary constrain a unified dynamic model between different contact phases, simplifying multi-phase trajectory optimization to single-phase trajectory optimization.

3　Planning Framework

Using differential dynamic programming to plan the vertical jump of the humanoid robot, the simplified center-of-mass dynamics model and the whole-body joint kinematics model can effectively avoid dealing with complex whole-body dynamics. In the face of complex dynamic motion, it is difficult to manually guess the initial reference trajectory, and it often takes a long time. Therefore, cold-start optimization, i.e. setting the starting point of all optimization variables to zero, usually results in longer solution times than empirically based warm-start [17].

3.1　Trajectory Optimization Framework

The trajectory optimization framework is shown in Fig. 4. This trajectory optimization framework consists of three steps: The first one is a motion selector, which selects the necessary motions for the robot, such as vertical jumps, etc., based on the evaluation of the terrain and the task at hand. In this work, this step is performed by a human, and it is necessary to manually give the reference motion trajectory and the contact plan of the foot end with the ground.

The focus of this paper is the following two steps: based on different levels of models and methods layered trajectory optimization. Firstly, according to the given reference trajectory and contact plan, the trajectory optimization based on the direct collocation method based on the single rigid body model is performed to obtain the optimal trajectory of the robot approximating a single rigid body. Then, considering the joint horizontal kinematic constraints of the robot, the center of mass momentum matrix is used to establish the link between joint kinematics and centroid angular momentum is established, and then the robot's centroid dynamics and joint kinematics models are established, and the optimal trajectory obtained by the direct collocation method is used as the initial value into the differential dynamic programming method to solve the optimal whole-body joint trajectory.

The framework has certain universality. It adopts the same trajectory optimization formula and the same task hierarchy for all dynamic motions, and is suitable for any robot with legs, regardless of the size or number of legs. Another advantage is that the framework adopts a hierarchical optimization scheme. By using the direct method to obtain the approximate value of the optimal solution, the initial solution is brought into the indirect method to quickly obtain the high-precision solution, so as to effectively overcome the indirect method's sensitivity to the initial trajectory and quickly converge to the high-precision optimal trajectory. At the same time, direct method adopts approximate single rigid body model for trajectory optimization, which reduces the problem of local optimal solution caused by complex system dynamics.

3.2　Direct Collocation Warm Start

Based on the direct collocation method of a single rigid body model, the optimization variables include discrete single rigid body model state variables $x \in R^{12}$, the position of the end effector foot $c \in R^{3n_c}$, and the ground reaction force acting on the end foot $f \in R^{3n_c}$. These trajectories are discretized into n_t time steps, and the time interval for dt.

These variables are compressed into a single optimization variable $X_{SRBM} \in R^{(12+6n_c)n_t}$, while $X_{SRBM} = [X_{SRBM,1}, X_{SRBM,2}, ..., X_{SRBM,n_t}]$, where

$$X_{SRBM,k} = \begin{bmatrix} x_k \\ c_k \\ f_k \end{bmatrix}, \quad k = 1, 2, ..., n_t$$

$$x = [r, \theta, v, {}^B\omega]^T \tag{6}$$

$$c = [c_1, ..., c_{n_c}]^T$$

$$f = [f_1, ..., f_{n_c}]^T$$

The direct method trajectory optimization adopts the quadratic cost function form as follows, where, $Q_x \in R^{12}$ is $Q_f \in R^{3n_c \times 3n_c}$ the weight matrix, and the reference trajectory $x_k^{ref} \in R^{12}$ comes from the manual motion selector. The cost function includes the expected trajectory error and ground reaction force, which can make the trajectory smoother and more efficient and meet the requirements of the target state.

$$\min_{X_{SRBM}} J = \sum_{k=1}^{n_t-1} \left\| x_k^{ref} - x_k \right\|_{Q_x}^2 + \|f\|_{Q_f}^2 \tag{7}$$

For the simplified SRBM model, the dynamic constraints perform Euler integration between adjacent points, where $\dot{x}$ given by the single rigid body dynamics.

$$x_{k+1} = x_k + \dot{x}dt \tag{8}$$

Since joint kinematics is not explicitly considered, there is no joint level constraint, but the approximate constraint uses the maximum distance from the foot end to the hip joint.

$$\|c_{i,k} - c_{i,hip,k}\| \leq l_{max,i}, \quad i = L, R$$

$$c_{L,k} = \frac{1}{4} \sum_{i=1}^{4} c_{i,k}, \quad c_{R,k} = \frac{1}{4} \sum_{i=5}^{8} c_{i,k} \tag{9}$$

Among them, $c_{i,hip}$ is the position of the limb at the attachment point of the body, $l_{max,i}$ and is the maximum feasible movement distance of the limb. For the entire contact plan, the foot position and ground reaction forces need to satisfy complementary constraints.

$$(c_{i,z,k} - h_{ground})f_{i,z,k} = 0, \quad i = 1, 2, ...n_c \tag{10}$$

$$f_{i,z,k} \geq 0, \quad c_{i,z,k} - h_{ground} \geq 0 \tag{11}$$

In order to keep the end foot of the robot from sliding when it touches the ground during jumping, consider the friction constraint in the horizontal direction.

$$-\mu f_{i,z,k} \leq f_{i,x,k} \leq \mu f_{i,z,k}, \quad i = 1, 2, ..., n_c \tag{12}$$

$$-\mu f_{i,z,k} \leq f_{i,y,k} \leq \mu f_{i,z,k}, \quad i = 1, 2, ..., n_c \tag{13}$$

Actuator constraints are reduced to simple boundary constraints, estimated using ground reaction forces.

$$f_{i,\min} \leq f_{i,k} \leq f_{i,\max}, \quad i = 1, 2, \ ..., \ n_c \tag{14}$$

This SRBM optimization is still nonlinear in terms of simplified dynamic constraints and approximate kinematic constraints, but the dimensionality of the problem is greatly reduced, avoiding complex joint kinematic constraints and whole-body dynamic constraints. The output of the trajectory optimization provides a rough approximation of the desired motion of the buoy and the reaction forces and foot-end trajectories required to produce that motion.

3.3 Differential Dynamic Programming

The indirect trajectory optimization method based on Differential Dynamic Programming (DDP) considers the centroid dynamics and joint level general kinematics of humanoid robots, which can effectively avoid dealing with complex general dynamics. At the same time, the consistency constraints of whole-body kinematics and centroid dynamics ensure the feasibility of the trajectory, which can better fit the real motion of the humanoid robot. The state variables and control variables $u \in R^{48}$ of the robot $x \in R^{30}$ are.

$$x = \begin{bmatrix} q & h & r & \dot{r} \end{bmatrix}^T$$
$$u = \begin{bmatrix} c & f \end{bmatrix}^T \tag{15}$$

where $q \in R^{21}$ is the joint position of the humanoid robot, $h \in R^3$ is the angular momentum of the center of mass, and $r \in R^3$, $\dot{r} \in R^3$ is the position and velocity of the center of mass. The dynamic model of the center of mass of the humanoid robot is.

$$\dot{x} = f(x, u) = \frac{d}{dt} \begin{bmatrix} q \\ h \\ r \\ \dot{r} \end{bmatrix} = \begin{bmatrix} A_{CAM}^{-1}(q)h \\ \sum_{i=1}^{n_c} (c_i - r) \times f_i \\ \dot{r} \\ \frac{1}{m} \sum_{i=1}^{n_c} f_i - g \end{bmatrix} \tag{16}$$

Differential dynamic trajectory planning can be understood as an optimal control problem based on a linear quadratic regulator (LQR) [19, 20]. The initial controller is given artificially based on experience as.

$$u[n] = k[n] + Kx[n], \quad n = 0, 1, 2, ..., N \tag{17}$$

The initial trajectory can be generated from the dynamic model of the system $\dot{x} = f(x, u)$ and the initial state $x(0) = x_0$.

$$x_{ref}[n], n = 0, 1, 2, ..., N$$
$$u_{ref}[n], n = 0, 1, 2, ..., N \tag{18}$$

The loop is then constructed. First, the system dynamics equation is linearized along the nominal trajectory, then a local LQR problem is constructed, and the quadratic cost function is defined. After the local LQR problem is solved, the controller is updated.

$$\min_{\overline{u}} \overline{J} = \left(\overline{x}(N) - \overline{x}_N^*\right)^T Q_f \left(\overline{x}(N) - \overline{x}_N^*\right)$$

$$+ \sum_{i=0}^{N-1} \overline{x}^T Q\overline{x} + \overline{u}^T R\overline{u} \tag{19}$$

$$s.t. \ \dot{\overline{x}}(n) = A(n)\overline{x}(n) + B(n)\overline{u}(n),$$
$$\overline{x}(0) = 0$$

$$A[n] = \left.\frac{\partial f}{\partial x}\right|_{x=x_{ref}[n]}, \ B[n] = \left.\frac{\partial f}{\partial u}\right|_{u=u_{ref}[n]} \tag{20}$$

$$\overline{x} = x - x_{ref}$$
$$\overline{u} = u - u_{ref} \tag{21}$$
$$\overline{x}_N^* = x_N^* - x_{ref}[N]$$

$$\overline{u}(n) = \overline{K}(n)\overline{x}(n) + \overline{k}(n) \tag{22}$$

$$u'[n] = \overline{K}(n)\left(x[n] - x_{ref}[n]\right) + \overline{k}(n) + u_{ref}[n] \tag{23}$$

The unconstrained optimization problem is constructed using the penalty function method. The following constraints are given for the jumping motion of the humanoid robot HIT-HU.

The allowed initial state χ_0 is the state of the robot at the time of planning, and the allowed terminal state χ_F depends on the desired motion. At the same time, joint kinematic constraints are given by a set of motion ranges for each joint. χ The initial time is t_0, the end time is t_F, and the state of the robot system is $x(t)$.

$$x(t_0) \in \chi_0$$
$$x(t_F) \in \chi_F \tag{24}$$
$$x(t) \in \chi$$

The dynamic constraints can be established by the Newton Euler method of the floating base system, where the center-of-mass momentum includes angular momentum h and linear momentum p, and r is the position of the robot's center of mass. Although still non-linear due to the external torque term, the equations of motion for these dynamics are much simpler than the full-body dynamics equations.

$$\dot{h} = \sum_{i=1}^{n_c} (c_i - r) \times f_i$$

$$\dot{p} = m\ddot{r} = \sum_{i=1}^{n_c} f_i - mg \tag{25}$$

Kinematic constraints generally include two parts, which consist of forward and inverse kinematics of the robot and consistency of the center of mass. Where $f_{com}(q)$ is the function to calculate the position of the center of mass based on the configuration of the robot joints, and $f_c(q)$ is the function to calculate the position of the i-th contact point based on the state of the robot joints. These constraints ensure the consistency between the center of mass dynamics and the whole-body kinematics.

$$r = f_{com}(q)$$
$$c = f_c(q)$$

(26)

Another constraint that ensures consistency between center-of-mass dynamics and whole-body kinematics is the center-of-mass momentum constraint. The evolution of the center-of-mass momentum of the robot is determined by the external resultant force and moment acting on the robot's center of mass. However, at each moment, the robot's center-of-mass momentum must also be consistent with the moment of mass calculated from the robot's whole-body kinematics. Where $A_{CAM}(q)$ is the center-of-mass momentum matrix given in [18].

$$h = A_{CAM}(q)\dot{q}$$

(27)

There are different contact constraints at different phases during the jumping process of the robot, given by the complementary constraints above. In order to keep the end foot of the robot from sliding when it touches the ground during jumping, the friction constraint in the horizontal direction is considered here. Where is μ the coefficient of static friction between the end foot and the ground.

$$(c_{i,z} - h_{ground})f_{i,z} = 0, \ i = 1, 2, \dots n_c$$
$$f_{i,z} \geq 0, \ c_{i,z} - h_{ground} \geq 0$$
$$-\mu f_{i,z} \leq f_{i,x} \leq \mu f_{i,z}, \ i = 1, 2, \dots, n_c$$
$$-\mu f_{i,z} \leq f_{i,y} \leq \mu f_{i,z}, \ i = 1, 2, \dots, n_c$$

(28)

The drive constraints and sensor range constraints are directly or indirectly given by the feasible region ψ of the control variable u.

$$u(t) \in \psi$$

(29)

4   Experimental Results

Taking vertical jump as an example, numerical experiments on jumping trajectory optimization are carried out. The Drake platform is used for the simulation analysis of the vertical jumping motion of the humanoid robot, the optimal jumping trajectory planned above is tracked, and the feasibility of the trajectory optimization result is verified. At the same time, the vertical jump trajectory no-load tracking experiment and the actual take-off phase tracking experiment were carried out on the humanoid robot HIT-HU physical platform, which preliminary verified the accuracy of the kinematics and dynamics constraints of the jump trajectory optimization algorithm proposed in this paper. At the

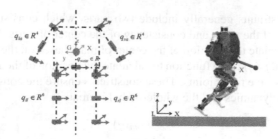

Fig. 5. The HIT-HU Humanoid Robot. Kinematic modeling of the robot HIT-HU, and the robot has a total of 21 degrees of freedom.

same time, the rationality of the trajectory planned by the framework is verified. The new generation of hydraulic humanoid robot HIT-HU is close to the Boston Dynamics robot Atlas at the hardware level, and can theoretically achieve complex and highly dynamic movements such as jumping. Jumping can make the humanoid robot give full play to the advantages of biped [21].

4.1 Robot Platform and Control

The real object of the hydraulic humanoid robot HIT-HU is shown in Fig. 5. The hydraulic humanoid robot HIT-HU stands about 1.5 m tall and weighs about 63 kg. About 64.6% of the mass is contained in the robot's torso and hips, 25.2% in the robot's legs, and the remaining 10.2% in the robot's arms. The robot has a total of 21 degrees of freedom. The setting details of the degrees of freedom are shown in Fig. 5. The joints on both sides are distributed symmetrically. Each leg has 6 degrees of freedom, each arm has 4 degrees of freedom, and the waist has 1 pitching freedom degree.

$$q = (q_{fb}, q_{ll}, q_{rl}, q_{waist}, q_{la}, q_{ra})^T \in R^{6+21} \tag{30}$$

The PID control scheme of the whole-body joints is adopted, and the optimal angle of the planned single joint is realized by using the PID position tracking method, so as to verify the effectiveness of the optimal trajectory of jumping [22].

Table 1. Trajectory solving times.

Methods	Jumping Motions		
	Vertical jump	*Jump forward*	*Jump backward*
Warm Start-DDP	186 ms	235ms	247 ms
DDP	358 ms	476 ms	495 ms

The robot control block diagram is shown in Fig. 6. According to the trajectory optimization results $q \in R^{21}$, solve the corresponding hydraulic cylinder stroke for the hydraulically driven joints $l \in R^{19}$, and then use PID position feedback tracking it. The PID Angle feedback tracking control is carried out directly for the motor driven joint $q \in R^2$.

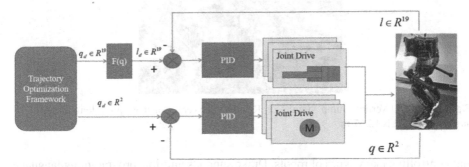

Fig. 6. HIT-HU Feedback Control Framework. According to the trajectory optimization results, the corresponding hydraulic cylinder stroke of the hydraulic drive joint was solved, and then the PID position feedback was used to track its 21 DOF.

4.2 Optimized Jump Trajectory

The trajectory optimization simulation experiment of the first-layer single rigid body model was built in MATLAB using the CasADi optimization algorithm, and the constructed nonlinear optimization problem was directly solved by a solver based on IPOPT. Due to the limited onboard computing capability of the robot, trajectory optimization and simulation experiments are performed offline on a laptop with an i5 processor. The second layer of simulation experiments uses the Crocoddyl library to construct the indirect trajectory optimization algorithm. The constructed nonlinear optimization problem is solved based on a high-performance DDP solver. The Crocoddyl library uses Pinocchio to quickly calculate the robot dynamics and its analytical derivatives. This paper mainly uses the solution library to calculate the partial derivative of the differential dynamic programming algorithm and the nonlinear programming to solve the initial trajectory of the direct method, both of which are very time-consuming, so the calculation is carried out offline.

A better initialization trajectory speeds up the convergence speed of the indirect method trajectory optimization algorithm and can achieve faster solution, as shown in Table 1. It can be seen that for high dynamic jumping motions with different difficulties, the direct method hot start algorithm is faster than the manual method. The trajectory optimization framework can save an average of 49.59% convergence time.

4.3 Simulation and Experiment

Drake is an open source robot control and simulation platform developed by the MIT CSAIL research team. It provides a rich set of tools and algorithms for simulating

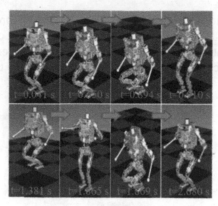

Fig. 7. HIT-HU Vertical Jump Simulation Results. The center of mass jump height of HIT-HU humanoid robot is 1.267 m.

and controlling many types of robots. Drake supports multiple programming languages such as MATLAB, Python and C++ for development and control. It provides efficient mathematical tools, such as solving optimization problems, symbolic calculations and numerical integration, which can help users quickly establish robot control algorithms. At the same time, Drake also provides a graphical simulation environment, which is convenient for users to conduct virtual experiments and visual analysis.

The dynamics simulation results of HIT-HU are shown in Fig. 7 and Fig. 8 shows the position tracking of the hydraulic cylinder based on Drake's dynamic simulation of vertical jump motion. It can be seen that the position tracking of each joint of the simulated hydraulic cylinder is good. In the whole jump phase, the position tracking error of each joint is small, the simulation trajectory and the optimal trajectory have a good correspondence, and the planned limit position of the hydraulic cylinder of each joint can be effectively tracked. The initial value of the robot jumping centroid height is 0.8 m, and the highest height is 1.267 m. Compared with the expected height of 1.280 m in trajectory planning, the error is 1.02%. And the movement time is about 2.68 s, which is roughly similar to the planning time of 2.6 s. It can be seen that although the simple PID control has tracking lag, it basically achieves the expected joint trajectory target.

In order to verify the rationality of the above trajectory optimization framework and compare the differences between the simulation and the real platform, a vertical jump trajectory tracking experiment was carried out on the humanoid robot HIT-HU real platform.

Based on the safety factor and the actual movement ability of the robot, this paper first tests the tracking ability of the robot HIT-HU for the vertical jump trajectory under no-load conditions. The response speed of the STAR200 hydraulic servo valve used in the hydraulic system is 200Hz, so the control signal sending frequency is set to 0.005 ms.

As the initial phase of jumping, the take-off phase of the robot is crucial to the success of the jumping motion. The take-off phase refers to the body state between the start of the movement and the departure of the feet from the ground when the robot is jumping. In order to further verify the effectiveness of the algorithm, verify whether the

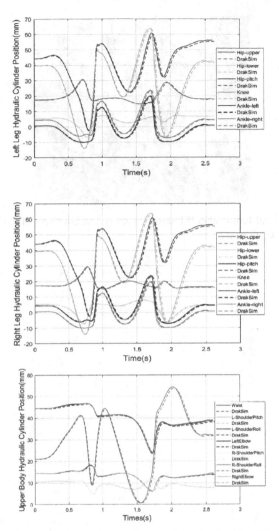

Fig. 8. HIT-HU Vertical Jump Simulation Hydraulic Cylinder Position Tracking. According to the feedback of displacement sensor data, the output positions of 19 hydraulic cylinders in the whole body are obtained and compared with the planned optimal trajectory.

take-off posture of the humanoid robot HIT-HU satisfies the plan. Figure 9 shows the tracking test results of the robot HIT-HU's vertical jump take-off phase trajectory. It can be seen that the robot HIT-HU has achieved a stable squat movement under the control of the planned take-off phase trajectory. The initial center of mass height of the robot is 0.8 m, and the maximum squat depth is 0.327 m. Compared with the trajectory planning of 0.321 m, the error is small, which verifies the validity of the simulation results. The take-off phase posture is naturally stable.

Fig. 9. HIT-HU Vertical Jump Takeoff Phase Trajectory Tracking Test. HIT-HU humanoid robot to achieve a stable takeoff phase.

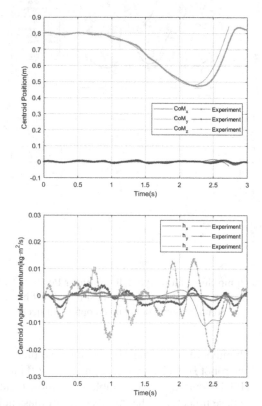

Fig. 10. HIT-HU Takeoff Phase Centroid Tracking. The centroid position r (top) and the centroid angular momentum h (bottom) of HIT-HU.

Constraints such as kinematics and actuator limitations of the trajectory optimization framework are embodied through center-of-mass dynamics. Through the position of the hydraulic cylinder of each joint, the motion angle of each joint can be obtained according to the joint fitting relationship, and then the centroid information of the humanoid robot HIT-HU can be obtained, as shown in Fig. 10. It can be seen from the figure that the position of the center of mass of the robot has been effectively tracked during the take-off and squatting phases, and the angular momentum of the robot is also stably tracking the planned trajectory, fluctuating between $\pm$ 0.02 kg·m^2/s, and the above simulation results are close. In short, the robot did not overturn when tracking the trajectory of the take-off phase to achieve squatting, which shows the reliability of the trajectory optimization framework. The center of mass dynamics and actuator constraints adopted by the framework are in line with the real situation of the robot HIT-HU.

5 Conclusion

This paper proposes a layered trajectory optimization framework, which overcomes the sensitivity of the solver to the initial point, and gets rid of the difficulty of manually setting the reference initial trajectory. Compared with manually setting the initial trajectory, the optimization solution speed is increased by 49.59%. Through the dynamics simulation based on Drake and the trajectory tracking experiment test on the physical prototype of the humanoid robot HIT-HU, a jump height of 1.267 m has been achieved, compared with the expected height of 1.280 m in trajectory planning, the error is 1.02%, which verifies that the jumping trajectory generated by the algorithm can be effectively transformed into the motion of a humanoid robot, and can be effectively executed in practical applications.

The research results of this paper provide an effective optimization method and experimental verification for the motion ability of high degree of freedom humanoid robot systems, and have important practical application value. Although this paper has made some achievements in the research of skip motion trajectory optimization of high degree of freedom humanoid robot systems, the algorithm can only be carried out offline because the partial derivative calculation and nonlinear programming are used in this paper to solve the initial trajectory. In the future, the analytical partial derivative approximation can be directly given to improve the real-time performance, and the initial trajectory library of off-line hopping motion can be established according to the direct collocation method, which has the possibility of realizing online trajectory optimization.

Acknowledgments. This work was supported by Key Research Project of Zhejiang Lab [No. 115002-AC2101], the Natural Science Foundation of Heilongjiang Province of China [YQ2021F011].

References

1. Kuindersma, S., Deits, R., Fallon, M., et al.: Optimization-based locomotion planning, estimation, and control design for the atlas humanoid robot. Auton. Robot. **40**(3), 429–455 (2016)
2. Yu, H.: Research on Gait Control of Foot Robot Based on SLIP Reduction Model. Harbin Institute of Technology (2014)

3. Chignoli, M., Kim, D., Stanger-Jones, E, et al.: The MIT humanoid robot: design, motion planning, and control for acrobatic behaviors. In: 2020 IEEE-RAS 20th International Conference on Humanoid Robots (Humanoids), pp. 1–8. IEEE (2021)

4. Liu, M.: Design and Implementation of Biped Robot Control System. University of Electronic Science and Technology of China (2022)

5. Xin, L., Xiaojun, D.: Research on motion planning and control of ground mobile robots. J. Harbin Inst. Technol. 53(1), 1–15 (2021)

6. Huang, Q., Peng, Z., Zhang, W., et al.: Design of humanoid complicated dynamic motion based on human motion capture. In: 2005 IEEE/RSJ International Conference on Intelligent Robots and Systems, pp. 3536–3541. IEEE (2005)

7. Koenemann, J., Burget, F., Bennewitz, M.: Real-time imitation of human whole-body motions by humanoids. In: 2014 IEEE International Conference on Robotics and Automation (ICRA), pp. 2806–2812. IEEE (2014)

8. Bravo, M.D.A., Rengifo, R.C.F.: Generation of gait trajectories for a humanoid robot from motion capture. Ciencia en Desarrollo 12(2), 31–42 (2021)

9. Batke, R., Yu, F., Dao, J., et al.: Optimizing bipedal maneuvers of single rigid-body models for reinforcement learning. In: 2022 IEEE-RAS 21st International Conference on Humanoid Robots (Humanoids), pp. 714–721. IEEE (2022)

10. He, Z.: Research on motion planning of legged robot based on trajectory optimization. Wuhan University (2021)

11. Dai, H., Valenzuela, A., Tedrake, R.: Whole-body motion planning with centroidal dynamics and full kinematics. In: 2014 IEEE-RAS International Conference on Humanoid Robots, pp. 295–302. IEEE (2014)

12. Raibert, M.H., Brown, H.B., Jr., Chepponis, M.: Experiments in balance with a 3D one-legged hopping machine. Int. J. Robot. Res. 3(2), 75–92 (1984)

13. Yu, H.: Research on jumping control of hydraulic biped wheel-legged robot. Harbin Institute of Technology (2021)

14. Wang, K., Xin, G., Xin, S., et al.: A unified model with inertia shaping for highly dynamic jumps of legged robots. arXiv preprint arXiv:2109.04581 (2021)

15. Kelly, M.: An introduction to trajectory optimization: how to do your own direct collocation. SIAM Rev. 59(4), 849–904 (2017)

16. Chignoli, M.M.T.: Trajectory optimization for dynamic aerial motions of legged robots. Massachusetts Institute of Technology (2021)

17. Wensing, P.M., Orin, D.E.: Improved computation of the humanoid centroidal dynamics and application for whole-body control. Int. J. Humanoid Rob. 13(01), 1550039 (2016)

18. Stewart, D.E.: Rigid-body dynamics with friction and impact. SIAM Rev. 42(1), 3–39 (2000)

19. Wang, Y.S., Matni, N., Doyle, J.C.: Localized LQR optimal control. In: 53rd IEEE Conference on Decision and Control, pp. 1661–1668. IEEE (2014)

20. Xie, Z., Liu, C.K., Hauser, K.: Differential dynamic programming with nonlinear constraints. In: 2017 IEEE International Conference on Robotics and Automation (ICRA), pp. 695–702. IEEE (2017)

21. Kojima, K., Kojio, Y., Ishikawa, T, et al.: A robot design method for weight saving aimed at dynamic motions: Design of humanoid JAXON3-P and realization of jump motions. In: 2019 IEEE-RAS 19th International Conference on Humanoid Robots (Humanoids), pp. 586–593. IEEE (2019)

22. Zhang, C.: Research on compliance control of single-leg joints of hydraulically driven legged robots. Harbin Institute of Technology (2019)

A Navigation and Control Framework of Quadrupedal Robot for Autonomous Exploration in Cave Environments

Yong Hu[1], Lisong Jiang[2], Ke Kang[2], Dandan Cao[2], Zhongda Zhou[2], Junfeng Liu[2], Yong Wang[1], Maodeng Li[1], and Haidong Hu[1,2(✉)]

[1] National Key Laboratory of Science and Technology On Space Intelligent Control, Beijing Institute of Control Engineering, Beijing 100190, China
haidong_2005@163.com

[2] China Academy of Space Technology Hangzhou Institute, Hangzhou 310001, China

Abstract. This article introduces XiaoTian, a quadrupedal robot with high mobility, dynamic motion skills, and autonomous ability. The robot uses backdriveable joint actuators with high force density, and robustness to impacts during trotting. Considering the specific application environment, we design the overall navigation and control framework of the robot, including the motion controlling, mapping, and planning methods. The experiment proved that XiaoTian can perform walking gaits, dynamically trot on the uneven ground and achieve autonomous exploration in the dark cave environments.

Keywords: Legged Robot · Autonomous Exploration · Navigation and Control

1 Introduction

Legged robots offer potential advantages for application in challenging man-made and natural terrains compared to tracked or wheeled vehicles. So far, the technical complexity of manufacturing and controlling such robots has made it impossible to be applied to real-world scenarios, for example, the dark cave environments. With significant advances in recent years, driven by initiative of practical application, we are poised to overcome the last technical hurdles and design a quadrupedal robot XiaoTian available for real-world applications.

At present, the available solutions for quadruped robots dynamic locomotion can be mainly divided into three categories, namely traditional control algorithms based on simplified model and control decoupling, modern popular control algorithms based on rigid body model and numerical optimization, and AI algorithms based on data and learning.

In the traditional control algorithms, the Zero Moment Point [1] is an important theory for analyzing the stability of quadruped robots. The control method based on zero moment point has been widely used in the field of legged robots such as HYQ [2], Little Dog [3], etc. Raibert presented SLIP based heuristic controllers for hopping and bounding [4], which are far-reaching. Inspired by SLIP model, the virtual model control [5] based method has many applications in the motion control of quadruped robots, StarlETH [6] and HyQ [7]achieved excellent motion control effects.

The structure of quadruped robots is becoming more and more complex, and the control dimensions are tightly coupled. Both have great limitations in control dynamics and robustness, and cannot meet the needs of practical applications. Therefore, the motion control algorithm based on model and numerical optimization has become the mainstream control algorithm of legged robots [8]. For motion planning of the quadrupedal robots, the corresponding map needs to be established first. Lidar is widely used to construct map. Many SLAM algorithm base on 3D laser are put forward in different conditions [12–14]. For rough terrain, many traversability estimation approaches are usually used based on stereo camera images [15–19].

This paper presents XiaoTian, a highly mobile quadrupedal robot developed for autonomous exploration in cave environments. XiaoTian is designed to combine the motion capability to cross large obstacles with the autonomous perception and planning. The autonomous robot paves the way for real-world applications. It can be used in the search and rescue for harsh cave environments. In the following, we introduce the robot, illustrate navigation and control framework, autonomous control, mapping and planning design for autonomous exploration, and finally summarize the overall system performance through cave experiment.

2 System Description

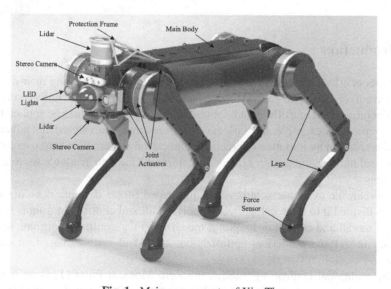

Fig. 1. Main components of XiaoTian

XiaoTian is specifically designed for long autonomous exploration in dark cave environments. Focus is put on high mobility, dynamic motion skills, and autonomous ability. XiaoTian, the quadrupedal robot features four low-inertia legs, three backdriveable joint actuators per leg with a large range of motion. The backdriveable actuator are also known as proprioceptive actuator which can provide the high-bandwidth and critical contact force for response in an unstructured environment [20]. The link length is 360 mm for thigh and shank. The total weight is slightly less than 60 kg. The payload capacity is up to 30 kg and a light robotic arm can be equipped while executing manipulation tasks. The onboard batteries are 5 kg weight and contain more than 1000 Wh energy which can support more than 1 h autonomous operation. A protection frame on the head and rubber pads attaching to the legs protect the robot from damage when colliding with the environment. Several sensors such as lidar, stereo camera, and IMU are provided to detecting the surroundings in front the robot. The robot is equipped with a commercial 60 V, Li-Ion battery. It is easy charging and contains battery management system. Main components of XiaoTian are shown in Fig. 1.

3   Navigation and Control Framework

The overall navigation and control framework of the robot is shown in Fig. 2. Each algorithm block is designed to be modular so that every block can be easily updated and replaced without modifying other blocks of the system. The blue blocks, which are described in Sect. 4, are associated with the stable quadruped motion and only the remote input from an operator is required to make the robot move freely. The red blocks only work in autonomous exploration mode. The cost map and terrain map are needed in this mode. This mode will be described in Sect. 5.

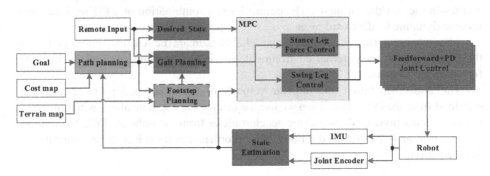

Fig. 2. Navigation and Control Framework Block Diagram

4   Autonomous Control

In Fig. 1, a gait is defined as a sequence of contact states. Contact states are defined at uniformly spaced time steps, typically at intervals of approximately 30 ms. On one hand, the selection of the time step is fine enough to accurately describe the timing of a gait, on the other hand, it is rough enough to make the number of contact states in a plan within a reasonable range.

The contact state of each foot is a flag indicating whether it is in a swing or flight state. Let $c[i] \in \{0, 1\}^4$ denote the contact state of all 4 legs at time step i, where 1 represents contact and 0 represents swing. Most commonly used gaits are periodic, that is, the ground contact sequence is repeated. Ideally, the motion of the robot in these gaits can also be expected to be periodic, with a period equal to the gait period.

Periodic gaits considered here include diagonal gait, diagonal-running gait, and the like. A common feature of these gaits is that the cycle is relatively short, and it takes the robot 200–500 ms to complete a gait cycle. Each gait cycle is divided into 10 time steps. For these gaits, at least one full gait cycle is included in each controller's plan, which guarantees possible periodic constraints on body motion.

With a cyclic phase-based gait scheduler, only two parameters are required to determine the gait type, the phase offset for each foot, and the stance period. Since most gaits are essentially cyclical, properly arranging swing and stance cycles in a cycle can define different gaits. Change the gait frequency by adjusting the cycle length.

Simplify the robot into a single rigid body, concentrate the mass and inertia, and consider the influence of the motor and legs. The approximate single rigid body motion of the robot is analyzed in the global coordinate system, with the legs in contact with the ground modeled as forces acting on the rigid body at the point of contact. The upper-level controller is used to determine the force at the contact point, and the lower-level controller calculates the joint torque to obtain the desired force.

We adopts the model predictive control algorithm of quadruped robot based on the linearized state transition equation, which can realize the real-time calculation frequency of about 30 Hz. Desired ground reaction forces can be acquired by a discrete-time finite-horizon model predictive controller. The trajectory of each swing leg is planned by splines in the world coordinate. The controller is a combination of a PD feedback and inverse dynamic feedforward term.

The state estimator can accurately and reliably estimate the state of a quadruped robot that interacts with the external environment, and is an important auxiliary technology for control problems.

The body orientation and angular velocity of the quadruped robot are directly obtained from the IMU data. Then we use the orientation estimate along with kinematic measurements from the legs and the accelerometer from the onboard IMU to compute the position and velocity of the body. This problem can be solved by a conventional Kalman filter.

5 Mapping and Planning for Autonomous Exploration

In the autonomous exploration tasks, the robot has two autonomous mapping and planning modes. In the first mode, a large range of cost map is established and path planning is carried out to obtain an obstacle avoidance path in real time. The adaptation for uneven terrain relies on the robustness of motion control method introduced in the previous section. A relatively fast speed can be achieved. In the second mode, in addition to establishing a cost map for path planning, it is also necessary to establish a terrain map

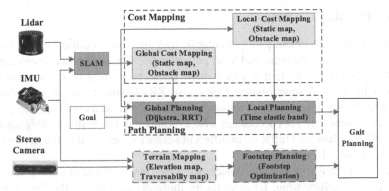

Fig. 3. Block diagram of the mapping and planning

so as to analysis the adaptability for footstep. Footstep planning is carried out to obtain a series of footstep points on the terrain map. In this mode, the amount of calculation is relatively large, and the robot needs to control the landing position for each leg, which is safer and moves slowly. The process of the two modes are shown in Fig. 3.

5.1 SLAM

We use a tightly-coupled laser-inertia odometer approach to obtain the globally consistent pose of the robot by optimizing the LiDAR odometer factor, IMU pre-integration factor and loop factor. The author uses frame-local map matching instead of frame-global map matching in LOAM, which improves the efficiency of frame - map matching. The above method builds a three-dimensional map, which needs to be converted into a two-dimensional map for path planning. Considering the laser information of different heights, the three-dimensional spatial information is mapped to the two-dimensional space to build a map.

5.2 Cost Mapping

The map constructed by SLAM is static, while the obstacle information is variable. When approaching the edge of an obstacle, the robot may collide with the obstacle due to some factors such as the turning of robot with irregular shape. Therefore, static maps cannot be directly applied. Instead, some auxiliary information needs to be added to the maps, such as obstacle data acquired from time to time and expansion area data added based on static maps. The optimized map is called the cost map.

Cost maps include global cost maps for global path planning and local cost maps for local path planning. Both cost maps require the superposition of multiple map layers, including the static map constructed by SLAM, the obstacle map layer used by sensors to perceive obstacle information, and the inflation layer expands on the above two maps to prevent the robot from hitting obstacles.

5.3 Path Planning

Path planning include global path planning to find the shortest effective path from the starting point and the end point and local path planning for local obstacle avoidance.

Global planning is to find a global path from the current robot position to the given goal location. A search-based Dijkstra or RRT-Connect sample algorithm over the updated 2D occupancy map (cost map) is utilized to find a collision free path that contains a sequence of 2D coordinates of waypoints. Global path planning takes into account different levels of inflation in different scenarios, setting it to 0.4 m in a factory environment and 0.15 m in a cave.

Local Planning is to find a local trajectory which is composed of a series of discrete poses with time information. By optimizing these discrete poses, the final trajectory composed of these discrete poses can achieve the shortest time, shortest distance, far away from obstacles and other goals, and at the same time limit the speed and acceleration to satisfy the capacity of the robot.

5.4 Terrain Mapping

The cost map only considers the two-dimensional spatial information and has some limitations. The elevation map preserves the three-dimensional spatial information without making the map calculation too complicated. Traversability map is a method of weighting information such as roughness, slope and curvature of terrain on the basis of elevation map to obtain the score of landing point $s(x, y) \in [0, 1]$ at each grid.

$$s(x, y) = \max\left(1 - \sum_i w_i \frac{v_i(x, y)}{v_{crit}}, 0\right)$$

where w_i represents the weight factor for each quality measure i with value $v_i(x, y)$ and allowed value v_{crit}. As quality measures, we evaluate the slope and curvature (derived from the surface normal) and the roughness (height standard deviation) from the neighboring cells. To further simplify the foothold selection process, we create a binary foothold scores based on a threshold to maps to either 0 or 1, where means not traversable or fully traversable.

5.5 Footstep Planning

By using terrain map, we can directly judge whether the landing point of each leg of the quadruped robot meets the dynamic requirements. By judging the traversability of the map, the special terrain such as stairs and gullies can be planned. We first obtain a series of nominal footstep points by gait planning. Then, the overall adaptability of the position of the points in terrain map is optimized. The results is safer and satisfies a variety of constraints such as kinematics, friction of the robot. The method has more general applications instead of designing an obstacle judgment mode for each terrain.

6   Experiments

To investigate the disturbance rejection of the controller, we perform the experiment in the cave, as Fig. 4 shows. The cave is about thirty meters, and there are uneven places on the ground and a little humid. Gait cycle of XiaoTian is made at period between 0.5 to 0.8 s. MPC was run at about 30 Hz, the result from the optimization is used directly. Joint control and state estimation run at 300 Hz.

It can be seen from Fig. 5 that the robot can walk smoothly in the cave, and keep the tracking error of the position and posture of the position and the posture. The torque is within a reasonable range in Fig. 6. J0, J1, and J2 correspond to the torque of abduction/adduction joint, hip joint, and knee joint, respectively. The cost map and terrain map in the cave experiments are shown in Fig. 7 and Fig. 8, respectively.

Fig. 4. Trotting in the cave

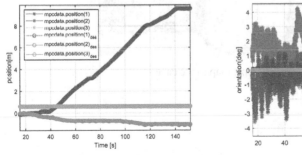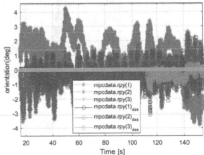

Fig. 5. Position and orientation of the robot

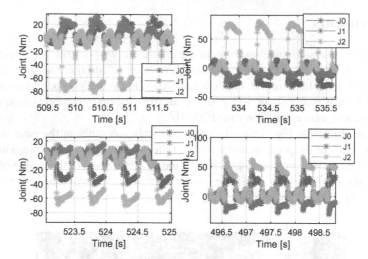

Fig. 6. Joint torque of the robot

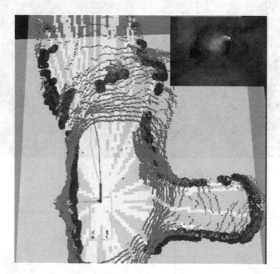

Fig. 7. Cost map in the cave

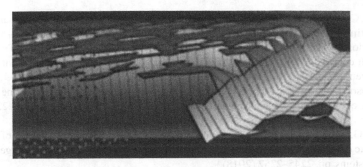

Fig. 8. Terrain map in the cave

7 Conclusion

This paper has introduced XiaoTian, a quadrupedal robot as a new platform designed for the autonomous exploration in the dark cave environments. In order to adapt the specific application environment, we design an appropriate navigation and control framework based on the measurement data of the sensory system. The experiment confirms that XiaoTian can achieve autonomous exploration in the dark cave environments.

Acknowlegment. This work was supported in part by the "Leading Goose" R&D Program of Zhejiang under Grant 2023C01177, in part by the Major Project of Science and Technology Innovation 2030—"New Generation Artificial Intelligence"—under Grant 2018AAA0102700, in part by the Artificial Intelligence Science and Technology Innovative Major Program of Hangzhou under Grant 2022AIZD0155, and in part by the National Natural Science Foundation of China under Grant U20B2054.

References

1. Vukobratović, M., Borovac, B.: Zero-moment point—thirty five years of its life. Int. J. Humanoid Rob. 1(1), 157–173 (2004)
2. Orsolino, R., Focchi, M, Caldwell, D.G, et al.: A combined limit cycle-zero moment point based approach for Omni-directional quadrupedal bounding. In: Human-Centric Robotics: Proceedings of CLAWAR 2017: 20th International Conference on Climbing and Walking Robots and the Support Technologies for Mobile Machines, pp. 407–414 (2018)
3. Kalakrishnan, M., Buchli, J., Pastor, P., et al.: Fast, robust quadruped locomotion over challenging terrain. In: 2010 IEEE International Conference on Robotics and Automation, pp. 2665–2670 (2010)
4. Raibert, M.H.: Legged Robots that Balance. MIT Press, Cambridge (1986)
5. Fukuoka, Y., Kimura, H.: Dynamic locomotion of a biomorphic quadruped 'Tekken' robot using various gaits: walk, trot, free-gait and bound. Appl. Bionics Biomech. 6(1), 63–71 (2009)
6. Hutter, M., Gehring, C., Bloesch, M., et al.: Adaptive Mobile Robotics, pp. 483–490. World Scientific, Baltimore (2012)
7. Winkler, A., Havoutis, I., Bazeille, S., et al.: Path planning with force-based foothold adaptation and virtual model control for torque controlled quadruped robots. In: IEEE International Conference on Robotics and Automation, Hong Kong, China, pp. 6476–6482 (2014)

8. Monje, C.A., Martinez, S., Pierro, P., et al.: Whole-body balance control of a humanoid robot in real time based on ZMP stability regions approach. Cybern. Syst. **49**(7–8), 521–538 (2018)

9. Di Carlo, J., Wensing, P.M., Katz, B., et al.: Dynamic locomotion in the MIT Cheetah 3 through convex model-predictive control. In: 2018 IEEE/RSJ International Conference on Intelligent Robots and Systems, pp. 1–9 (2018)

10. Bellicoso, C.D., Jenelten, F., Gehring, C., et al.: Dynamic locomotion through online nonlinear motion optimization for quadrupedal robots. IEEE Robot. Autom. Lett. **3**(3), 2261–2268 (2018)

11. Bledt, G., Powell, M.J., Katz, B., et al.: MIT Cheetah 3: design and control of a robust, dynamic quadruped robot. In: 2018 IEEE/RSJ International Conference on Intelligent Robots and Systems, pp. 2245–2252 (2018)

12. Zhang, J., Singh, S.: Low-drift and real-time lidar odometry and mapping. Auton. Robot. **41**(2), 401–416 (2017)

13. Shan, T., Englot, B., Meyers, D., Wang, W., Ratti, C., Rus, D.: LIOSAM: tightly-coupled lidar inertial odometry via smoothing and mapping. In: IEEE/RSJ International Conference on Intelligent Robots and Systems, pp. 4758–4765 (2020)

14. Chilian, A., Hirschmuller, H.: Stereo camera based navigation of mobile robots on rough terrain. In: IEEE/RSJ International Conference on Intelligent Robots and Systems, pp. 4571–4576 (2009)

15. Chestnutt, J.: Navigation Planning for Legged Robots. Ph.D., thesis, Carnegie Mellon University, Pittsburgh, PA (2007)

16. Wermelinger, M., Fankhauser, P., Diethelm, R., Krüsi, P., Siegwart, R., Hutter, M.: Navigation planning for legged robots in challenging terrain. In: 2016 IEEE/RSJ International Conference on Intelligent Robots and Systems, pp. 1184–1189 (2016)

17. Gilroy, S., et al.: Autonomous Navigation for Quadrupedal Robots with Optimized Jumping through Constrained Obstacles. Cornell University - arXiv, July 2021

18. Fankhauser, P., Bloesch, M., Hutter, M.: Probabilistic terrain mapping for mobile robots with uncertain localization. IEEE Robot. Autom. Lett. (RA-L). **3**(4), 3019–3026 (2018)

19. Norby, J., Johnson, A.M.: Fast global motion planning for dynamic legged robots. In: 2020 IEEE/RSJ International Conference on Intelligent Robots and Systems, pp. 3829–3836 (2020)

20. Wensing, P.M., Wang, A., Seok, S., Otten, D., Lang, J., Kim, S.: Proprioceptive actuator design in the MIT Cheetah: impact mitigation and high-bandwidth physical interaction for dynamic legged robots. IEEE Trans. Robot. **33**(3), 509–522 (2017). https://doi.org/10.1109/TRO.2016.2640183

Design and Development of the Small Hexapod Walking Robot HexWalker III

Qian Wang and Bo Jin[✉]

State Key Laboratory of Fluid Power and Mechatronic Systems,
Zhejiang University, Hangzhou, China
bjin@zju.edu.cn

Abstract. This paper presents the design and implementation of the HexWalker III, a small electric hexapod robot suitable for various applications. The mechanical structure of the robot is designed with a mammalian leg arrangement, and the hardware components, including servo motors, sensors, and control system, are described in detail. The hierarchical-distributed control system involving the main controller and the embedded controller is designed to meet the control requirements of the robot. The control algorithm, which includes gait planning, motion planning, and inverse kinematics, is also described. The walking experiment results demonstrate that the robot has good controlled performance and walking ability.

Keywords: hexapod robot · mechanical design · control system

1 Introduction

Legged robots have gained significant attention due to their ability to navigate complex and challenging terrains. They find applications in various fields such as search and rescue, exploration, and surveillance. Dozens of legged robots have been developed over the last decades. There existing quadruped robot research platforms, such as BigDog [1], MIT Cheetah 3 [2], ANYmal [3] and HyQ2Max [4], which have focused on fast, dynamic locomotion. On the other hand, the hexapod robots such as RHex [5], LAURON V [6], HITCR-II [7], and the DLR Crawler [8] have focused on rough terrain locomotion, as they are inherently more stable over rough terrain with a wider support polygon, lower centre of gravity, larger locomotion workspace and statically stable, fast gaits. Hexapod robots trade off stability and speed in rough, unstable and slippery terrain for increased hardware complexity and weight compared to the quadruped robots [9].

This paper introduces the HexWalker III, a small electric hexapod robot designed to be used in daily life. The design focuses on the mechanical structure, actuators and sensors, and the control system of the robot. The hardware and software components are described in detail, and the control algorithm, including gait planning and motion planning, is also presented. Compared to the previous version HexWalker II [10], the HexWalker III has a more compact structure,

H. Yang et al. (Eds.): ICIRA 2023, LNAI 14272, pp. 59–68, 2023.
https://doi.org/10.1007/978-981-99-6480-2_5

a higher load-bearing capacity, and a more powerful control system. Besides, the HexWalker III is equipped with a monocular camera, an IMU sensor and a force sensor on each foot for perception and feedback control. The HexWalker III provides a versatile platform for further research and development in legged robotics.

2 Hardware Design

2.1 Mechanical Structure

The HexWalker III is a small electric hexapod robot designed for everyday use in various fields such as education, entertainment, and surveillance, as shown in Fig. 1. The dimensions of the robot are about 410 mm (L) × 220 mm (W) × 260 mm (H) at the standing position. The overall weight of the robot is around 3.8 kg, and it can carry additional payloads of approximately 2 kg. When walking on a flat terrain with tripod gait, it can achieve a maximum speed of 20 cm/s.

Fig. 1. The hexapod walking robot HexWalker III

Unlike other spider-shaped hexapod robots such as PhantomX [11], the leg joints of the HexWalker III are arranged in a mammalian structure, which allows for greater load-bearing capacity and better adaptation to different terrain, as shown in Fig. 2. The axis of the root joint is parallel to the body of the robot and the legs are entirely under the body. Each leg of the robot has three joints: root joint, hip joint and knee joint, which are actuated by servo motors. The length of each link l_1, l_2, l_3 is 50 mm, 100 mm and 100 mm, respectively.

2.2 Actuators and Sensors

The joints of the HexWalker III are actuated by DYNAMIXEL XM430-W350 servo motors. The servo motor has a maximum torque of 4.1 N·m and a maximum speed of 46 rpm, which has a balanced performance between power and speed

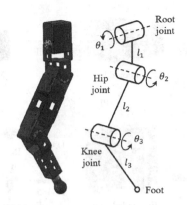

Fig. 2. Leg configuration of HexWalker III

and is suitable for the joints of small legged robots. The servo motor can be controlled via a serial communication interface and the present position, present speed and present load of the servo motor can be read for feedback control.

The HexWalker III is equipped with a monocular camera, an IMU sensor and a force sensor on each foot for perception and feedback control. The camera MV-CB013-A0UC is a global shutter camera with a resolution of 1280×1024 pixels and a max frame rate of 201 fps, which will be used for visual odometry and terrain perception. The IMU sensor is MTi-3, which can measure the angular velocity, linear acceleration and magnetic field of the robot, with an output data rate of 100 Hz, and will be used for attitude estimation and motion planning. The force sensor is a single axis force sensor with a range of 0–100 N and a resolution of 0.01 N, which will be used for ground contact detection.

2.3 Control System

The HexWalker III is equipped with a hierarchical-distributed control system [12], as shown in Fig. 3. The onboard computer Intel NUC i5 is used as the main controller, which is responsible for high-level tasks such as gait planning, motion planning and terrain perception. Users can control the robot with a mobile APP via a WiFi connection, which can send motion commands and receive feedback information from the robot. An embedded board with the STM32H723 microcontroller is used as the embedded controller, which is responsible for low-level tasks such as joint control and data collection. The main controller communicates with the embedded controller via SPI bus, utilizing the USB converter chip CH347, which sends joint commands and receives sensor data from the embedded controller. The embedded controller communicates with the servo motors via 6 RS485 buses, where the 3 servo motors of each leg share one RS485 bus, enabling relatively high communication speed and low latency [13]. And the embedded controller receives data from the IMU sensor and the force sensors via UART bus and RS485 bus, respectively.

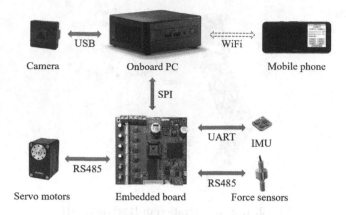

Fig. 3. The control system of HexWalker III

3   Software Design

3.1   Embedded Controller Software Design

The tasks of the embedded controller include joint control, sensor data collection and communication with the main controller, etc. The program of the embedded controller is mainly consists of two interrupts [14]: the SPI receive interrupt and the timer interrupt. The SPI receive interrupt is triggered when the main controller sends a SPI message to the embedded controller, the frequency of which is determined by the control frequency of the main controller. And the timer interrupt is triggered periodically with a frequency of 2 kHz, during which the servo positions are send to the servo motors, the present servo positions, velocities and loads are read from the servo motors, and the attitude data and foot force data are read from the IMU sensor and the force sensors, respectively. Besides, the monocular camera on the robot is triggered by the embedded controller to capture images in a fixed frequency, and the images are directly transferred to the host computer via the USB interface.

The servo motors, the IMU sensor, the force sensors and the camera are all triggered by the embedded controller, and the timestamps of the sensor data recorded, as shown in Fig. 4, so that the timestamps of the sensors are from the same clock source, which is important for sensor fusion and pose estimation [15]. The MCU sends triggering pulses to the camera to start image exposure, and receives the strobe signal which indicates the exposure state of the camera. The exposure timestamp and a increasing sequence number are recorded and sent to the host computer, and the timestamp will be matched with the corresponding image based on the sequence number.

3.2   Main Controller Software Design

The tasks of the main controller include motion planning, communication with the embedded controller and receiving commands from the user, etc. The soft-

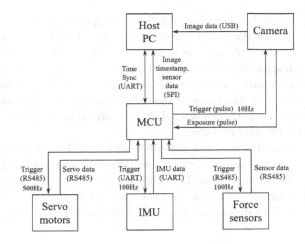

Fig. 4. Triggering method and frequency of the sensors

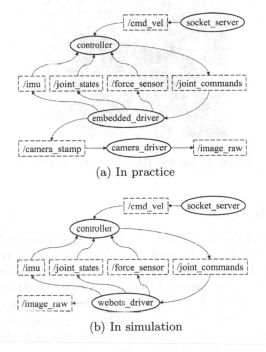

(a) In practice

(b) In simulation

Fig. 5. The ROS nodes and topics

ware framework of the main controller is developed based on the Robot Operating System (ROS) [16]. The software framework is composed of several ROS nodes, as shown in Fig. 5. The node *embedded_driver* is responsible for communication with the embedded controller, which receives the sensor data from the embedded controller and publishes the sensor data to the corresponding ROS topics. The node *controller* is responsible for motion planning and control, which subscribes to the sensor data topics and the command topics, and publishes the joint commands to the embedded controller. The node *socket_server* is responsible for communication with the user, which receives the user commands from the mobile APP and publishes the command topics. The node *camera_driver* is responsible for receiving the images from the camera, which subscribes to the *camera_stamp* topic from the *embedded_driver* node and publishes images with timestamps to the *image_raw* topic.

In the simulation situation, the *embedded_driver* node and the *camera_driver* node are replaced by the *webots_driver* node, which is responsible for communication with the Webots simulator [17]. This makes it easy to switch between the real robot and the simulated robot, and the same control algorithm can be used in both situations. The simulation of the HexWalker III in Webots is shown in Fig. 6.

Fig. 6. Hexwalker III in Webots simulation

3.3   Control Algorithm

The main contents of the robot's control algorithm is shown in Fig. 7. According to the user's command and the configuration of the gait parameters, the gait planner generates the gait sequences and the trajectory planner generates the foot trajectories. Then the inverse kinematics solver calculates the joint angles of the robot based on the foot trajectories. The joint angles are sent to the embedded controller to control the robot. The gait planning and foot trajectory planning can be adjusted online according to the sensor feedback, such as the correction of the yaw angle of the robot [10].

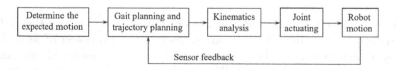

Fig. 7. Main contents of the control algorithm

Some different kinds of gaits and the online transformation of the gaits has been implemented on the robot [10]. The foot trajectory of the leg is mainly composed of four parts: the swing phase, the touchdown phase, the stance phase and the lift-off phase, which are planned using the polynomial fitting curves. The kinematic model of the robot is established based on the product of exponential (POE) model [18]. The errors of kinematic parameters was calibrated using the method proposed in [19] to improve the accuracy of the kinematic results and the inverse kinematics method in a numerical way is used to calculate the joint angles of the robot.

4 Experiment Result

The HexWalker III is tested by walking experiment. In the experiment, the robot walks on the flat ground with the tripod gait. The parameters of the gait are set

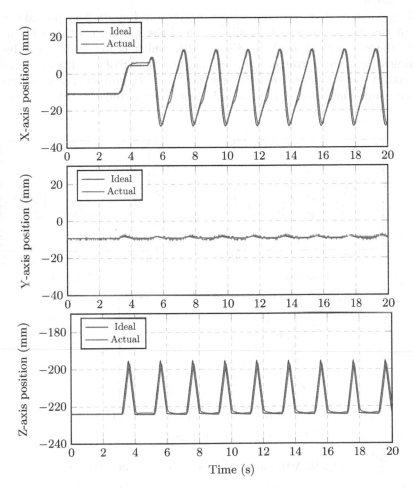

Fig. 8. Comparison between the ideal foot trajectory and the actual computational foot trajectory of leg 1

as follows: body height H =230 mm, step length $S = 30$ mm, max lift height L = 30 mm, and the period of the gait cycle $T = 2$ s.

Based on the actual position of each joint reading from the encoder, the actual foot trajectory of each leg is calculated and compared with the ideal foot trajectory to verify whether the robot can achieve the desired motion. Taking leg 1 as an example, the comparison between the ideal foot trajectory and the actual computational foot trajectory is shown in Fig. 8. It can be seen that the actual foot trajectory is close to the ideal foot trajectory.

The attitude angle data when the robot walks is shown in Fig. 9, where the roll angle and pitch angle indicate the fluctuation of the robot body plane relative to the horizontal plane. According to the experimental data, the fluctuation of the roll angle and pitch angle is within 1°, indicating that the robot's motion is relatively stable. The drift of the yaw angle is relatively large during the motion, which may be caused by mechanical errors, slippage, etc. However, the change in the yaw angle during the motion will not affect the stability of the robot's motion much.

The ground contact force of each leg is shown in Fig. 10. The ground contact force in the swing phase is basically 0N, and the ground contact force in the stance phase differs from about 3N to 20N, which is maybe affected by the mechanical structure error of each leg and the center of gravity of the robot. The ground contact forces are currently only used for ground contact detection, and the compliance control method will be studied in future work.

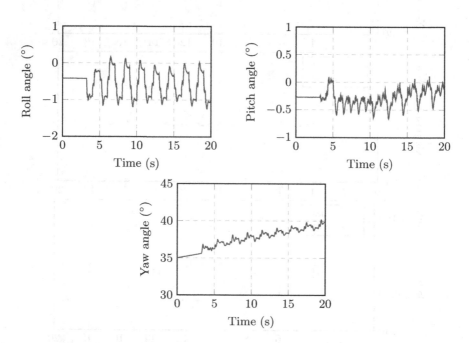

Fig. 9. Attitude angle data when the robot walks

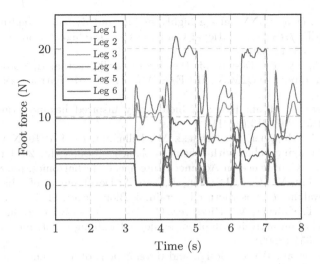

Fig. 10. The ground contact force of each leg when the robot walks

5   Conclusion and Future Work

In this paper, the small electrical hexapod walking robot named HexWalker III is developed. The robot's mammalian leg arrangement provides improved load-bearing capacity and terrain adaptability. The hardware components, such as servo motors and sensors, were carefully selected to ensure optimal performance. The control system, consisting of an embedded controller and a main controller, enables hierarchical-distributed control and communication between the robot and the user. The software design, based on ROS, allows for flexible and efficient development of control algorithms. The experimental results demonstrated the robot's walking performance.

In future work, more control strategies and algorithms will be studied on HexWalker III. We will make use of the existing sensors to develop a state estimation algorithm for the robot, which will be used for the closed-loop control of the robot. We will also study more advanced control algorithms, such as terrain adaptation and obstacle avoidance, to improve the robot's adaptability to the environment.

References

1. Raibert, M., Blankespoor, K., Nelson, G., Playter, R.: BigDog, the rough-terrain quadruped robot. IFAC Proc. Volumes **41**(2), 10822–10825 (2008)
2. Bledt, G., Powell, M.J., Katz, B., Di Carlo, J., Wensing, P.M., Kim, S.: MIT Cheetah 3: design and control of a robust, dynamic quadruped robot. In: 2018 IEEE/RSJ International Conference on Intelligent Robots and Systems (IROS), pp. 2245–2252 (2018)

3. Hutter, M., et al.: ANYmal - a highly mobile and dynamic quadrupedal robot. In: 2016 IEEE/RSJ International Conference on Intelligent Robots and Systems (IROS), pp. 38–44 (2016)
4. Semini, C., et al.: Design of the hydraulically actuated, torque-controlled quadruped robot HyQ2Max. IEEE/ASME Trans. Mechatron. **22**(2), 635–646 (2017)
5. Altendorfer, R., et al.: RHex: a biologically inspired hexapod runner. Auton. Robots **11**(3), 207–213 (2001)
6. Roennau, A., Heppner, G., Nowicki, M., Dillmann, R.: LAURON V: a versatile six-legged walking robot with advanced maneuverability. In: 2014 IEEE/ASME International Conference on Advanced Intelligent Mechatronics, pp. 82–87 (2014)
7. Zhang, H., Liu, Y., Zhao, J., Chen, J., Yan, J.: Development of a bionic hexapod robot for walking on unstructured terrain. J. Bionic Eng. **11**(2), 176–187 (2014)
8. Wimböck, T., Görner, M., Hirzinger, G.: The DLR Crawler: evaluation of gaits and control of an actively compliant six-legged walking robot. Ind. Robot: Int. J. **36**(4), 344–351 (2009)
9. Steindl, R., et al.: Bruce - design and development of a dynamic hexapod robot. In: Australasian Conference on Robotics and Automation, ACRA, vol. 2020-December, pp. 1–7 (2020)
10. Zhang, F., Zhang, S., Wang, Q., Yang, Y., Jin, B.: Straight gait research of a small electric hexapod robot. Appl. Sci. **11**(8), 3714 (2021)
11. Tikam, M., Withey, D., Theron, N.J.: Standing posture control for a low-cost commercially available hexapod robot. In: 2017 IEEE/RSJ International Conference on Intelligent Robots and Systems (IROS), pp. 3379–3385 (2017)
12. Zhai, S., Jin, B., Dong, J., Liu, Z.: Design, development and control of the hydraulic walking robot WLBOT. In: 2021 7th International Conference on Control, Automation and Robotics (ICCAR), pp. 71–75 (2021)
13. Bestmann, M., Güldenstein, J., Zhang, J.: High-frequency multi bus servo and sensor communication using the Dynamixel protocol. In: Chalup, S., Niemueller, T., Suthakorn, J., Williams, M.A. (eds.) RoboCup 2019: Robot World Cup XXIII, pp. 16–29. Lecture Notes in Computer Science, Cham (2019)
14. Liu, Z., Zhang, C., Jin, B., Zhai, S., Dong, J.: Design and development of an embedded controller for a hydraulic walking robot WLBOT. Appl. Sci. **11**(12), 5335 (2021)
15. Tschopp, F., et al.: VersaVIS-an open versatile multi-camera visual-inertial sensor suite. Sensors **20**(5), 1439 (2020)
16. Macenski, S., Foote, T., Gerkey, B., Lalancette, C., Woodall, W.: Robot operating system 2: design, architecture, and uses in the wild. Sci. Robot. **7**(66), eabm6074 (2022)
17. Michel, O.: Cyberbotics Ltd., Webots: professional mobile robot simulation. Int. J. Adv. Robot. Syst. **1**(1), 5 (2004)
18. Chen, I.M., Yang, G., Tan, C.T., Yeo, S.H.: Local POE model for robot kinematic calibration. Mech. Mach. Theory **36**(11), 1215–1239 (2001)
19. Wang, Q., Jin, B., Zhang, C.: Kinematic calibration of a hexapod robot based on monocular vision. Mach. Vis. Appl. **33**(6), 86 (2022)

A Rigid-Flexible Coupling Recursive Formulation for Dynamic Modeling of Biped Robots

Lingling Tang[1,2], Dingkun Liang[1,2(✉)], Xin Wang[1,2], Anhuan Xie[1,2], and Jason Gu[1,2,3]

[1] Research Center for Intelligent Robotics, Research Institute of Interdisciplinary Innovation, Zhejiang Laboratory, Hangzhou 311100, China
liangdk@zhejianglab.com
[2] Zhejiang Engineering Research Center for Intelligent Robotics, Hangzhou 311100, China
[3] Department of Electrical and Computer Engineering, Dalhousie University, Halifax, NS B3H 4R2, Canada

Abstract. Biped robots are complex rigid-flexible coupling multibody systems that achieve the desired stable locomotion through foot-ground interactions. In the recent bio-inspired structure designs for biped robots, flexible parts are usually adopted to absorb the foot-ground impact and store the contact energy. However, most existing modeling formulations can only treat biped robots as rigid multibody systems, and the flexible parts are simply replaced by some linear or torsion springs. Since the deformations of the flexible parts have significant effects on the dynamic responses of the biped robot, the rigid multibody modeling method inevitably leads to a gap between the simulation model and the real prototype, and makes the sim-to-real transfer more difficult. To address this problem, a rigid-flexible coupling recursive modeling formulation is presented in this paper. In addition, the foot-ground interaction is modeled via a smooth normal contact model and a velocity-based Coulomb friction model. Finally, several numerical examples including inverse dynamics, kinematic closed-loop and frictional contact are given to verify the rigid-flexible coupling formulation.

Keywords: Biped robot · Multibody dynamics · Rigid-flexible coupling · Contact dynamics

1 Introduction

The biped robot is a kind of legged robots, which achieves the locomotion ability through foot-ground interactions. Compared with the extensively studied locomotion control methods for biped robots, the dynamic modeling is also a challenging research area but receives less attention. In the reduced-order models

Supported by Key Research Project of Zhejiang Lab (No. G2021NB0AL03), Zhejiang Provincial Natural Science Foundation of China (No. LQ23F030010).

for locomotion control, like the linear inverted pendulum model (LIPM) [6] and the single rigid body model (SRBM) [3], the biped robot is usually simplified as one point mass or one rigid body. In addition, due to the previous biped robots are mainly designed with rigid structures, the deformation effects are also ignored. However, since increasing bio-inspired structures are adopted in the newly designed biped robots, it is necessary to establish a rigid-flexible coupling full dynamic model. One reason is the dynamic responses of the biped robot can be strongly affected by the deformations of the flexible parts. Another reason is with flexible parts included in the biped robot, the foot-ground impact can be absorbed, and the contact energy can be stored for the locomotion control in the next gait, which means high energy efficiency and high agility.

Most existing multibody dynamic models for biped robots are based on the rigid multibody formulations. The generalized coordinates can be defined as joint coordinates (i.e., Lagrangian coordinates) or Cartesian coordinates [5]. Joint coordinates with clear physical meanings are usually independent with each other, and can be directly used as state variables in the locomotion control of biped robots. One disadvantage of the joint coordinates is that the generalized mass matrix and the generalized inertial force vector are accompanied with complex expressions, and the derivations should be implemented in a recursive manner. Cartesian coordinates are redundant coordinates and can't be directly used for control. In addition, the constraint conditions are usually required, which leads to a set of differential-algebraic equations with a larger scale.

Regarding the kinematics description, in the multibody community, the linear velocity of the center of mass (CoM) and the angular velocity of the rigid body are adopted in the Newton-Euler equations. With superimposed small deformations, this kinematics description can be easily extended to the rigid-flexible coupling case [5]. While in the robotics community, the 6-dimensional spatial velocity vector is usually preferred, like Featherstone's method [4]. The motion of the rigid body is described by its angular velocity and the linear velocity of the body-fixed point that coincides with the origin at the current instant. This method is computationally efficient, and the computational complexity is only $O(n)$. However, it is generally used for solving rigid multibody problems, and the flexible part can only be approximated as a linear or torsion spring.

Modeling the biped robot only as a rigid multibody system will inevitably lead to a gap between the simulation model and the real prototype, and makes the sim-to-real transfer more difficult. Several formulations can be used for modeling of flexible bodies. In the floating frame of reference formulation (FFR), a floating frame of reference is established for the flexible body, and the motion of the flexible body is described as the superposition of the large overall motion of the floating frame and the deformation with respect to that frame [5]. This formulation is suitable for flexible bodies undergoing small deformations and large overall motions. If the deformations are expressed in terms of a reduced set of modal coordinates, the computational efficiency can be improved. In addition, when the deformation components are ignored, the floating frame of reference formulation can be degenerated to a rigid multibody formulation. The absolute nodal coordinate formulation (ANCF) is a total Lagrangian finite element formulation, where the nodal coordinates are defined by the global position vector and the gradient vectors [9]. This formulation is proposed for flexible bodies undergoing large deformations and large overall motions, like the soft robots.

Considering that the deformations of the real prototype are small and the locomotion control requirements, a proper dynamic model for the biped robot includes the following features: (1) The joint coordinates are chosen as the generalized coordinates of the rigid body, and the dynamics equations are derived in a recursive manner. (2) The linear velocity of the center of mass and the angular velocity of the rigid body are adopted to describe the kinematics. (3) The flexible body is modeled by the floating frame of reference formulation.

The objective of this paper is to present a rigid-flexible coupling recursive modeling formulation for biped robots. The rest of this paper is organized as follows. In Sect. 2, the rigid-flexible coupling recursive modeling formulation is presented. A smooth normal contact model and a velocity-based Coulomb friction model are briefly reviewed in Sect. 3, which are employed to model the foot-ground interactions. Several numerical examples, including inverse dynamics, kinematic closed-loop and frictional contact, are demonstrated in Sect. 4 to verify the formulation. Summary and conclusions are presented in Sect. 5.

2   Rigid-Flexible Coupling Recursive Formulation

Based on the statement in the penultimate paragraph of the introduction, the rigid-flexible dynamic model is established via the single direction recursive assembly method [5, 12], which is a forward recursive formulation and takes joint coordinates and modal coordinates as the generalized coordinates.

2.1   Dynamics of Single Flexible Body

As shown in Fig. 1, the floating frame of reference of the flexible body B_i is defined at the point C_i, which is the center of mass before deformation.

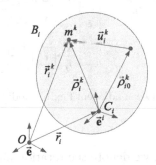

Fig. 1. Dynamics of single flexible body

The flexible body is discretized using the lumped mass finite element method, and the deformation is described via a reduced set of modal coordinates $\mathbf{a}_i =$

$[a_{i1} \cdots a_{is}]^{\mathrm{T}}$. For an arbitrary node k, the modal vector is $\mathbf{\Phi}_i^k = \left[\phi_{i1}^k \cdots \phi_{is}^k\right]^{\mathrm{T}}$, and the absolute velocity vector of this node can be expressed as

$$\dot{\mathbf{r}}_i^k = \mathcal{B}_i^k \mathbf{v}_i, \quad \mathcal{B}_i^k = \left[\mathbf{I}_3 \ -\tilde{\rho}_i^k \ \mathbf{\Phi}_i^k\right], \quad \mathbf{v}_i = \left[\dot{\mathbf{r}}_i^{\mathrm{T}} \ \omega_i^{\mathrm{T}} \ \dot{\mathbf{a}}_i^{\mathrm{T}}\right]^{\mathrm{T}} \tag{1}$$

where ρ_i^k is the absolute position vector of the node k with respect to the origin C_i, the notation $\sim$ over a vector represents a skew-symmetric matrix, $\dot{\mathbf{r}}_i$ is the absolute linear velocity vector of the origin C_i, and ω_i is the absolute angular velocity vector of the floating frame of reference.

Based on the principle of virtual power, the variational form of the equations of motion for the flexible body B_i is written as

$$\delta \mathbf{v}_i^{\mathrm{T}} \left(-\mathbf{M}_i \dot{\mathbf{v}}_i - \mathbf{w}_i + \mathbf{f}_i^o - \mathbf{f}_i^u\right) = 0 \tag{2}$$

where $\mathbf{M}_i$ is the generalized mass matrix, $\mathbf{w}_i$ is the generalized inertial force vector, $\mathbf{f}_i^o$ is the generalized external force vector, and $\mathbf{f}_i^u$ is the generalized elastic force vector.

2.2   Recursive Kinematics Between Adjacent Flexible Bodies

The kinematic relation between adjacent flexible bodies B_i and B_j is illustrated by Fig. 2, where B_j is the inside connecting body of B_i, and the labeling of all bodies is assumed to be regular [11].

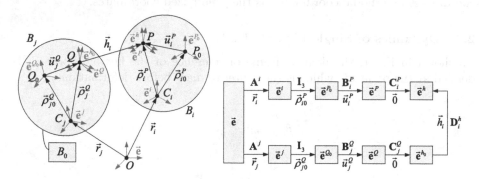

Fig. 2. Kinematic relations between adjacent flexible bodies (**Left**) and between frames of reference (**Right**)

For the flexible body B_i, we denote the rotation matrix of the floating frame of reference with respect to the global reference frame as $\mathbf{A}^i$. Then, the recursive relation between rotation matrices can be expressed as

$$\mathbf{A}^i = \mathbf{A}^j \mathbf{A}^{ji}, \quad \mathbf{A}^{ji} = \mathbf{B}_j^Q \mathbf{C}_j^Q \mathbf{D}_i^h \mathbf{C}_i^{P\mathrm{T}} \mathbf{B}_i^{P\mathrm{T}} \tag{3}$$

where $\mathbf{B}_j^Q$ and $\mathbf{B}_i^P$ are rotation matrices due to deformations, $\mathbf{C}_j^Q$ and $\mathbf{C}_i^P$ are constant matrices representing the joint orientations on B_j and B_i, and $\mathbf{D}_i^h$ is the rotation matrix of the joint, which is discussed in Sect. 2.3.

Similarly, the recursive relations between absolute angular velocity vectors $\boldsymbol{\omega}_i$ and $\boldsymbol{\omega}_j$ and between absolute linear velocity vectors $\dot{\mathbf{r}}_i$ and $\dot{\mathbf{r}}_j$ can be obtained. With the definition of $\mathbf{v}_i$ in Eq. (1), these relations are assembled as follows:

$$\mathbf{v}_i = \mathbf{T}_{ij}\mathbf{v}_j + \mathbf{U}_i\dot{\mathbf{y}}_i \tag{4}$$

where $\mathbf{y}_i = \begin{bmatrix} \mathbf{q}_i^\mathrm{T} & \mathbf{a}_i^\mathrm{T} \end{bmatrix}^\mathrm{T}$ is the vector of generalized coordinates of body B_i, and $\mathbf{q}_i$ is a set of joint coordinates. The absolute acceleration vector can be derived in a similar way

$$\dot{\mathbf{v}}_i = \mathbf{T}_{ij}\dot{\mathbf{v}}_j + \mathbf{U}_i\ddot{\mathbf{y}}_i + \boldsymbol{\beta}_i \tag{5}$$

where $\mathbf{T}_{ij}$, $\mathbf{U}_i$ and $\boldsymbol{\beta}_i$ are auxiliary matrices and vector.

2.3 Relative Kinematics of Joints

Fig. 3 shows the relative kinematics of joints. From top left to bottom right, they are the revolute joint ($\mathbb{R}$), the universal joint ($\mathbb{U}$), the prismatic joint ($\mathbb{P}$), the cylindrical joint ($\mathbb{C}$), the spherical joint ($\mathbb{S}$) and the free joint ($\mathbb{F}$), respectively.

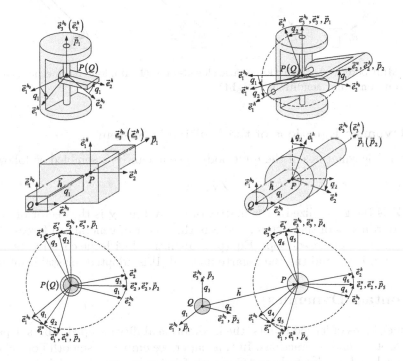

Fig. 3. Relative kinematics of joints

Table 1. Relative degrees of freedom and rotation matrices of joints

Joint type	Revolute ($\mathbb{R}$)	Universal ($\mathbb{U}$)	Prismatic ($\mathbb{P}$)	Cylindrical ($\mathbb{C}$)	Joint type	Spherical ($\mathbb{S}$)	Free ($\mathbb{F}$)
DOFs	1	2	1	2	DOFs	3	6
Translation/rotation	Rz	RzRy	Pz	Pz-Rz	Translation/rotation	RzRyRx	PxPyPz-RzRyRx
Rotation matrix $\mathbf{D}_i^h$	$\begin{bmatrix} c_1 & -s_1 & 0 \\ s_1 & c_1 & 0 \\ 0 & 0 & 1 \end{bmatrix}$	$\begin{bmatrix} c_1c_2 & -s_1 & c_1s_2 \\ s_1c_2 & c_1 & s_1s_2 \\ -s_2 & 0 & c_2 \end{bmatrix}$	$\begin{bmatrix} 1 & 0 & 0 \\ 0 & 1 & 0 \\ 0 & 0 & 1 \end{bmatrix}$	$\begin{bmatrix} c_2 & -s_2 & 0 \\ s_2 & c_2 & 0 \\ 0 & 0 & 1 \end{bmatrix}$	Rotation matrix $\mathbf{D}_i^h$	$\begin{bmatrix} c_1c_2 & -s_1c_3 + c_1s_2s_3 & s_1s_3 + c_1s_2c_3 \\ s_1c_2 & c_1c_3 + s_1s_2s_3 & -c_1s_3 + s_1s_2c_3 \\ -s_2 & c_2s_3 & c_2c_3 \end{bmatrix}$	

The relative degrees of freedom (DOFs), the translation/rotation sequences and the rotation matrices of these six joints are given in Tab. 1, where $c_i = \cos q_i$ and $s_i = \sin q_i$.

2.4   Kinematic Closed-Loop

For multibody systems with closed-loops as shown in Fig. 4, some specific joints in the loops need to be cut off, and the cut-off joint constraint conditions are introduced [5]. It should be noted that some constraint conditions may be redundant and need to be removed, like that in the four-bar mechanism.

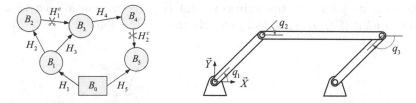

Fig. 4. Multibody system with kinematic closed-loops (**Left**), four-bar mechanism with redundant constraint conditions (**Right**)

2.5   Dynamic Equations of the Multibody System

The dynamic equations of the multibody system can be assembled as follows

$$\mathbf{Z}\ddot{\mathbf{y}} = \mathbf{z} \tag{6}$$

where $\mathbf{Z}$ is the generalized mass matrix of the system, $\mathbf{y}$ is the vector of generalized coordinates of the system, and $\mathbf{z}$ is the vector of generalized forces of the system. In cases of closed-loops, Eq. (6) is augmented with the constraints at the acceleration level, and the Baumgarte method [1] is adopted for stabilization.

3   Contact Dynamics

Like other kinds of legged robots, the locomotion ability of biped robots depends on the foot-ground interactions. In this paper, we employ a smooth normal contact model and a velocity-based Coulomb friction model to model the interactions as follows.

3.1   Normal Contact Model

The normal non-penetration condition is formulated via the penalty method, where the normal contact force is modeled as a spring-damper force [8].

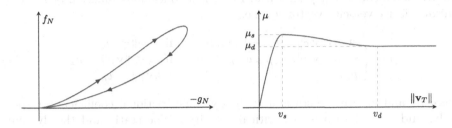

Fig. 5. Normal contact force model (**Left**) and frictional coefficient model (**Right**)

The measure of normal interaction is based on the normal penetration g_N and the normal relative velocity v_N. When the smooth spring-damper force model is adopted, the normal contact force can be defined in terms of g_N and v_N as follows:

$$f_N = \begin{cases} \max\left(0, -kg_N - cv_N\right), & \text{if } g_N \leq 0 \\ 0, & \text{otherwise} \end{cases} \tag{7}$$

Here, the operator max ensures the normal force is zero at the end of the contact decompression or restitution phase. The overall force-penetration relation consisting of the compression and decompression phases is depicted in Fig. 5.

The stiffness and damping coefficients are defined as functions of the normal penetration g_N, which lead to a smooth transition of the normal force between the separation state and the contact state.

$$k = \text{step}\left(-g_N, 0, 0, w, k_{\max}\right), \quad c = \text{step}\left(-g_N, 0, 0, w, c_{\max}\right) \tag{8}$$

where w is the penetration transition depth, $k_{\max}$ and $c_{\max}$ are the maximum stiffness and damping coefficients, respectively. In the modeling of the foot-ground interaction, the maximum damping coefficient $c_{\max}$ should be sufficient enough to simulate the inelastic contact behavior.

The step(x, x_0, y_0, x_1, y_1) function is a piecewise cubic polynomial as follows:

$$\text{step} = \begin{cases} y_0, & \text{if } x \leq x_0 \\ y_0 + (y_1 - y_0)\left(\dfrac{x - x_0}{x_1 - x_0}\right)^2 \left(3 - 2\dfrac{x - x_0}{x_1 - x_0}\right), & \text{if } x_0 < x < x_1 \\ y_1, & \text{if } x \geq x_1 \end{cases} \tag{9}$$

3.2   Friction Model

The tangential interaction is formulated via the velocity-based Coulomb friction model [8], which unifies both the static and the dynamic friction cases.

According to this model, the frictional force can be expressed as

$$\mathbf{f}_T = -\mu |f_N| \frac{\mathbf{v}_T}{\|\mathbf{v}_T\|} \tag{10}$$

The frictional coefficient μ shown in Fig. 5 is a continuous function of the tangential relative velocity vector $\mathbf{v}_T$, i.e.,

$$\mu = \begin{cases} \text{step} \left(\|\mathbf{v}_T\|, -v_s, -\mu_s, v_s, \mu_s\right), & \text{if } \|\mathbf{v}_T\| \leq v_s \\ \text{step} \left(\|\mathbf{v}_T\|, v_s, \mu_s, v_d, \mu_d\right), & \text{if } v_s < \|\mathbf{v}_T\| < v_d \\ \mu_d, & \text{if } \|\mathbf{v}_T\| \geq v_d \end{cases} \tag{11}$$

where μ_s and μ_d are the static and the dynamic frictional coefficients, respectively, and v_s and v_d are two critical velocities. The static and the dynamic frictional cases are located within the ranges of $[0, v_s]$ and $[v_d, \infty)$, respectively, and the range (v_s, v_d) represents the Stribeck effect transition zone.

4   Numerical Examples

In this section, three numerical examples are presented to verify the rigid-flexible coupling formulation. These examples focus on rigid multibody problems with inverse dynamics, kinematic closed-loop and frictional contact, while cases that consider deformation effects are currently in progress.

4.1   Inverse Dynamics of a Rigid Manipulator

Figure 6 depicts the reference configuration of a rigid manipulator, which consists of four bodies interconnected by revolute joints [5,7].

Since all revolute joints are subject to the prescribed motions defined in Eq. 12, this is an inverse dynamic problem. Here, the critical instant T_s is 15 s, the effect of gravity is ignored, and all model parameters can be found in Ref. [7].

$$\theta_1 = \begin{cases} \dfrac{3\pi}{2} + \dfrac{\pi}{2T_s} \left(t - \dfrac{T_s}{2\pi} \sin\left(\dfrac{2\pi t}{T_s}\right)\right), & \text{if } 0 \leq t < T_s \\ 2\pi, & \text{if } t \geq T_s \end{cases}$$

$$\theta_2 = \begin{cases} \dfrac{\pi}{2} - \dfrac{\pi}{4T_s} \left(t - \dfrac{T_s}{2\pi} \sin\left(\dfrac{2\pi t}{T_s}\right)\right), & \text{if } 0 \leq t < T_s \\ \dfrac{\pi}{4}, & \text{if } t \geq T_s \end{cases} \tag{12}$$

$$\theta_3 = \dfrac{\pi}{2} - \theta_2, \quad \theta_4 = \theta_1 - \dfrac{3\pi}{2}$$

The configurations of the rigid manipulator at different instants are illustrated by Fig. 6, and the actuator torques at the revolute joints presented in Fig. 7 are consistent with that in Ref. [5].

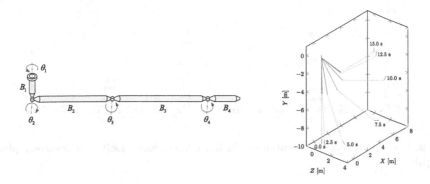

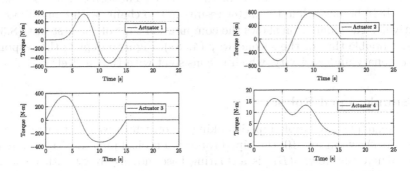

Fig. 6. Reference configuration without rotation (**Left**) and configurations at different instants (**Right**) of a rigid manipulator

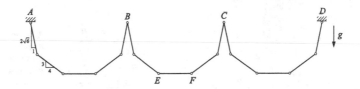

Fig. 7. Actuator torques at the revolute joints

4.2 Catenary with Closed-Loop

The second example is a catenary with closed-loop shown in Fig. 8. It consists of 15 identical links interconnected by revolute joints, and each link has a length of 0.3048 m m and a mass of 1 kg [5,10]. Both ends of the catenary are connected to the fixed base by revolute joints, and thus there is a kinematic closed-loop.

Fig. 8. Catenary with closed-loop falls under gravity

As mentioned in Sect. 2.4, one revolute joint should be cut off here and replaced by the cut-off joint constraint, which restricts the relative translations

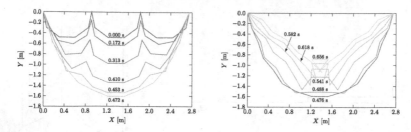

Fig. 9. Configurations of the catenary during falling phase (**Left**) and recovery phase (**Right**)

along two directions. There are two ways to break this closed-loop, that is to cut off the revolute joint at the point D or the point F. The former leads to a single chain with 15 bodies, while the latter results in two chains with 8 and 7 bodies, respectively. The simulation shows the computation time of the first way (8.32 s) is almost double that of the second way (4.38 s). Figure 9 depicts the responses of the catenary under gravity, which is consistent with that in Ref. [5].

4.3   Simple Biped Robot

The last example is a simple biped walking robot, which was first introduced in Ref. [2]. As shown in Fig. 10, the biped robot is a typical underactuated dynamic system, where the pelvis (B_1) is a floating base moving freely with respect to the ground (B_0). The left thigh (B_5) is connected to the pelvis by a spherical joint, and the rotation sequence RzRyRx represent the hip yaw, roll and pitch motions. A revolute joint representing the knee pitch motion is defined between the left shank (B_6) and the left thigh. In addition, the left foot (B_7) and the left shank are interconnected by a universal joint, where the rotation sequence RzRy indicates the ankle pitch and roll degrees of freedom. The right leg has similar definitions of joints, and the kinematic topology is also illustrated by Fig. 10.

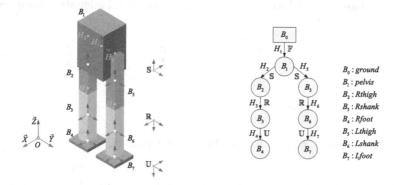

Fig. 10. Simple biped walking robot (**Left**) and its kinematic topology (**Right**)

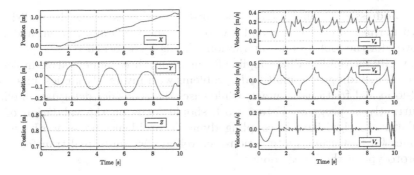

Fig. 11. Position and velocity components of the center of mass of the pelvis

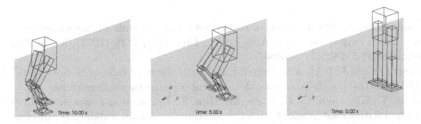

Fig. 12. Configurations of the biped robot at different instants

The joints on both legs are actuated by prescribed motions, which are generated in advance via a trajectory planning procedure. For each leg, these motions satisfy the following rules: the hip yaw motion is disabled, the sum of hip roll and ankle roll motions is always zero, and the sum of three pitch motions is also kept at zero. This means that each foot is designed with a global flat orientation.

The time plots of the position and velocity components of the pelvis is given by Fig. 11, where the forward walking of the biped robot is stable, and the height of the pelvis remains almost unchanged after 1 s. Figure 12 shows the initial, middle and final configurations of the biped robot, which is consistent with the results in Ref. [2].

5   Conclusions

In order to model the biped robots with flexible parts, a rigid-flexible coupling formulation is presented in this paper, which is based on the single direction recursive assembly method. The deformation of the flexible body is described by a reduced set of modal coordinates, which together with the joint coordinates are selected as the generalized coordinates. For the adjacent flexible bodies, the recursive relations between rotation matrices, absolute velocity vectors and absolute acceleration vectors are derived, and the relative kinematics of six different joints are presented. Based on these derivations, the dynamic equations of the multibody system can be assembled, and the cases with kinematic closed-loops can be addressed by introducing the cut-off joint constraints. In addition, a smooth normal contact model and a velocity-based Coulomb friction model are employed for the foot-ground interactions during locomotion.

To verify the rigid-flexible coupling formulation, three numerical examples are presented, including rigid multibody problems with inverse dynamics, kinematic closed-loop and frictional contact, while cases that consider deformation effects are currently in progress. Future work should focus on the validation of the formulation in rigid-flexible coupling dynamic problems, non-smooth contact dynamics for foot-ground interactions, as well as the sim-to-real transfer to the real prototype of the biped robot.

References

1. Baumgarte, J.: Stabilization of constraints and integrals of motion in dynamical systems. Comput. Methods Appl. Mech. Eng. **1**(1), 1–16 (1972). https://doi.org/10.1016/0045-7825(72)90018-7
2. Castro, S.: MATLAB and Simulink Robotics Arena: Walking Robot. MathWorks (2019). https://github.com/mathworks-robotics/msra-walking-robot
3. Ding, Y., Khazoom, C., Chignoli, M., Kim, S.: Orientation-aware model predictive control with footstep adaptation for dynamic humanoid walking. In: International Conference on Humanoid Robots, pp. 299–305 (2022). https://doi.org/10.1109/Humanoids53995.2022.10000244
4. Featherstone, R., Orin, D.E.: Dynamics. In: Siciliano, B., Khatib, O. (eds.) Springer Handbook of Robotics, pp. 37–66. Springer, Cham (2016). https://doi.org/10.1007/978-3-319-32552-1_3
5. Hong, J.Z.: Computational Dynamics of Multibody Systems. Higher Education Press, Beijing (1999)
6. Kajita, S., Tani, K.: Study of dynamic biped locomotion on rugged terrain, derivation and application of the linear inverted pendulum mode. In: International Conference on Robotics and Automation (ICRA), pp. 1405–1411 (1991). https://doi.org/10.1109/ROBOT.1991.131811
7. Kim, S.S., Haug, E.J.: A recursive formulation for flexible multibody dynamics, part i: open-loop systems. Comput. Methods Appl. Mech. Eng. **71**(3), 293–314 (1988). https://doi.org/10.1016/0045-7825(88)90037-0
8. MSC.Adams: Adams/View help. MSC.Software (2012). https://simcompanion.hexagon.com/customers/s/article/adams-view-help---adams-2012-1-2-doc10021
9. Shabana, A.A.: Computational Continuum Mechanics, 2nd edn. Cambridge University Press, New York (2012)
10. Wang, J.T., Huston, R.L.: Kane's equations with undetermined multipliers-application to constrained multibody systems. J. Appl. Mech. **54**(2), 424–429 (1987). https://doi.org/10.1115/1.3173031
11. Wittenburg, J.: Dynamics of Multibody Systems. Springer, Berlin (2008). https://doi.org/10.1007/978-3-642-86464-3
12. Yu, Q., Chen, I.M.: A general approach to the dynamics of nonholonomic mobile manipulator systems. J. Dyn. Syst. Meas. Contr. **124**(4), 512–521 (2002). https://doi.org/10.1115/1.1513178

Robots in Tunnelling and Underground Space

Path Planning for Muck Removal Robot of Tunnel Boring Machine

Lijie Jiang[1,2] , Yanming Sun[1](✉) , Yixin Wang[1], Xiaowei Yuan[1], and Hao Qian[1]

[1] China Railway Engineering, Equipment Group Co., Ltd., Zhengzhou 450016, China
symcrec@126.com
[2] School of Mechanical Engineering, Zhejiang University, Hangzhou 310027, China

Abstract. The muck removal operation in tunnel boring machine (TBM) construction seriously restricts the safety and efficiency of tunnel engineering. To meet the requirements of muck removal at the bottom of the tunnel, a mechanism design and path planning algorithm were proposed to address the complex structure and frequent interference of the robot operating environment. Firstly, a robot cleaning plan and the robot body structure were proposed, the kinematic model of the robot was designed. Secondly, an improved RRT algorithm suitable for TBM and robot working environment was proposed to meet the requirements, which conclude obstacle avoidance, short time-consuming, and path smoothness. A collision detection strategy based on distance judgment, a random point generation strategy under goal-oriented constraints, a redundant path point deletion strategy, and a path smoothing processing strategy based on cubic B-splines were proposed to optimize the final path. Finally, the simulation platform has been built for traditional RRT and improved RRT algorithm were used for simulation. The results showed that the improved algorithm reduces the path cost by 27.13%, which verifies the effectiveness of the method.

Keywords: Tunnel Engineering · Muck Removal Robot · Path Planning · Improved Rapid-exploration Random Tree; Collision Detection; Path Optimization

1 Introduction

The tunneling boring machine (TBM) has been widely promoted and applied to excavate underground tunnels [1, 2]. During the construction process, slag and stones will be accumulated at the bottom of the tunnel from rock bursts, top collapses, and falling blocks. Therefore, the removal of muck has become an essential part of TBM construction.

To achieve mechanization of muck removal operations, research on muck removal systems has been conducted both domestically and internationally [3]. However, currently, the muck removal system is controlled by the worker inside the tunnel. As TBM tunnel construction moves towards complex geological conditions, the working environment is becoming increasingly harsh. For example, the minimum temperature of the Sichuan Tibet project reaches -30 °C, with oxygen deficiency and the presence of harmful gases, which can easily lead to casualties. Therefore, to improve the automation and intelligence of the tunnel bottom muck removal will be a powerful measure to speed up the construction progress and improve the work safety. However, due to the special environment in the tunnel, the robot movement path should avoid the anchor bolt drill, steel arch assembly device, and other moving equipment on both sides of the main beam. The application of kinematics theory and path planning algorithm is the core content to achieve the automatic operation of the muck removal robot.

At present, mostly used path planning algorithms include traditional path planning algorithms such as "artificial potential field (APF)", "A* algorithm", "rapid exploration random tree", and intelligent path planning algorithms such as "genetic algorithm", "ant colony optimization", "particle swarm optimization". However, many studies have reduced robots to particles for planning. Or due to the simple working environment of robots, without considering the obstacle avoidance requirements of the robot body. However, the complex working environment, large working range, and flexibility require-ments of the muck removal robot result in more degrees of freedom for the robot. Not only do we need to ensure the obstacle avoidance of the end effector in 3-D space, but we also need to consider the obstacle avoidance of each link and the surrounding environment. Therefore, using the above method for path planning of the muck removal robot in the configuration space will result in a significant increase in time cost [4], so that cannot be directly used for the muck removal robot.

The RRT algorithm based on random sampling is suitable for high-dimensional space search. In response to the problems of slow convergence speed and unstable directionality of traditional RRT algorithms, Hsien L et al. [5] proposed the bi-RRT algorithm, which accelerates the convergence speed of the algorithm by expanding the random tree at both the initial and target positions; Gammell J D et al. [6] proposed the Informed-RRT* algorithm, which limits the sampling range of nodes by generating elliptical sampling sets, improves path convergence speed, and reduces time costs; Li Wei et al. [7] proposed an RRT algorithm that adds gravitational weight coefficients. By biasing the extension direction with the gravitational weight coefficients, it can quickly grow toward the goal direction. However, in complex obstacle environments, random trees may fall into local optima. In addition, when conducting path planning in complex spaces, the convergence speed of the algorithm is slow and there are a large number of unnecessary nodes, resulting in uneven paths.

In response to the above issues, this paper proposes an improved RRT algorithm suitable for the path planning of muck removal robots. Firstly, a mathematical description of the cleaning robot with its working environment is demonstrated. Then, the current posture of the robot is obtained based on sensor. And a preliminary path is planned under the constraint of not colliding with the surrounding environment. Through redundant point deletion strategy and path smoothing strategy, the optimized path is made more suitable for the cleaning robot's operation, which providing a reference for the safe and efficient operation of the cleaning robot.

2 Scheme Design

2.1 Structure Design

Based on the environment inside the tunnel and the characteristics of robot operation, a muck removal robot operation plan is designed as shown in Fig. 1. The robot is installed at the bottom of the main beam, and during the muck removal operation, it avoids equipment such as anchor rod drilling machines and steel arch assembly machines that move on both sides of the main beam, and grasps and transports the rock slag at the bottom of the tunnel.

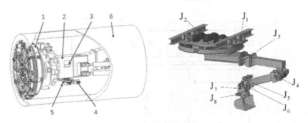

1-Cutter head; 2-main beam; 3-slag chute; 4-muck removal robot; 5-version system; 6-ground

Fig. 1. Muck removal robot operation plan and the structure of the robot.

The structure of the robot is shown in Fig. 1, mainly consisting of 8 joints. J1 is driven by an electric motor, which enables the robot to move along the direction of the main beam and meet the cleaning requirements of rock debris along the tunnel axis direction; J2 is driven by an electric motor, which rotates the robot in a vertical direction to meet the cleaning requirements of the tunnel section stone slag and avoid the occurrence of cleaning blind spots; The coordination of J3, J4, and J5 joints meets the requirements of the end effector for grasping the large operating range of rock debris at the bottom of the tunnel. J6, J7, and J8 achieve the adjustment of the robot's end posture.

2.2 Robot Modeling

The standard D-H parameter method is used to establish the robot link coordinate system, as shown in Fig. 2, and its D-H parameters are obtained to establish its kinematics model, to realize the robot's pose description in space [8].

3 Principles of Improved RRT Algorithm

To achieve obstacle avoidance of the muck removal robot body in a narrow and unstructured working environment under the TBM main beam, and to complete the muck removal task faster and more automatically, a path planning algorithm suitable for the muck removal robot is proposed. The process is shown in Fig. 3, which is mainly divided into modules such as initialization, obstacle avoidance RRT, and path optimization.

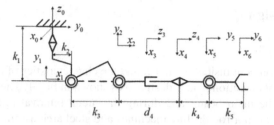

Fig. 2. Robot link coordinate system.

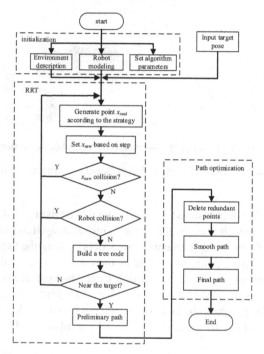

Fig. 3. Flow chart of path planning algorithm for muck removal robot.

3.1 Robot Link Collision Detection Method

According to the muck removal robot operation plan, the robot operation process needs to avoid collisions between each connecting rod and the surrounding environment, but the obstacles inside the warehouse are difficult to express using accurate mathematical formulas. This article uses bounding box technology to simplify the obstacles into bounding balls [3], and uses the cylindrical envelope method [9] to simplify the robot connecting rod into a cylinder, as shown in Fig. 4.

According to the simplified collision detection model established in Fig. 4, each segment of the robotic link i, it can be represented as an equivalent line segment $\overrightarrow{p_{i-1}p_i}$, with its two end points p_i and p_{i-1} with the origin of the coordinate system $\{i\}$ and $\{i-1\}$ respectively. So, the pose matrix of the endpoint in the base coordinate system $\{0\}$ is

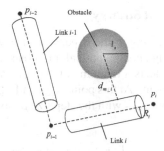

Fig. 4. Collision detection model.

obtained from the equation bellow:

$$^0_i\mathbf{T} = {}^0_1\mathbf{T}^1_2\mathbf{T} \cdots {}^{i-1}_i\mathbf{T} \tag{1}$$

$$p_i = [{}^0_i\mathbf{T}(1,4), {}^0_i\mathbf{T}(2,4), {}^0_i\mathbf{T}(3,4)] \tag{2}$$

$$p_{i-1} = [{}^0_{i-1}\mathbf{T}(1,4), {}^0_{i-1}\mathbf{T}(2,4), {}^0_{i-1}\mathbf{T}(3,4)] \tag{3}$$

$$\vec{l}_i = \overrightarrow{p_{i-1}p_i} = \begin{bmatrix} {}^0_i\mathbf{T}(1,4) - {}^0_{i-1}\mathbf{T}(1,4) \\ {}^0_i\mathbf{T}(2,4) - {}^0_{i-1}\mathbf{T}(2,4) \\ {}^0_i\mathbf{T}(3,4) - {}^0_{i-1}\mathbf{T}(3,4) \end{bmatrix}^{\mathrm{T}} \tag{4}$$

According to the established simplified collision detection model, the sphere envelope box model for recording obstacles is $S_m (P_m, R_m)$, where P_m represents the coordinates of the sphere center, R_m represents the radius of the sphere envelope box, and R_i represents the envelope radius of the connecting rod i. The spatial sphere can be represented as:

$$(x - x_0)^2 + (y - y_0)^2 + (z - z_0)^2 = R_m^2 \tag{5}$$

So, the distance d_{m_i} from the center P_m of the spherical envelope box to the equivalent line segment $p_{i-1}p_i$ is recorded, and the collision problem is simplified as a comparison between d_{m_i} and R_m.

$$\begin{cases} \text{free} & d_{m\_i} > R_m + R_i \\ \text{collision} & d_{m\_i} \le R_m + R_i \end{cases} \tag{6}$$

By calculating the distance between each connecting rod and the center of the spherical envelope box, it is possible to determine whether the muck removal robot collides with obstacles in any posture. If there is a collision, sample point x_{rand} and new node x_{new} are regenerated.

3.2　Goal-Oriented Constraint Strategy

In response to the lack of targeting in the expansion of new nodes in traditional RRT algorithms, which results in high computational time costs, this paper sets a probability threshold p_{tr} and randomly selects a random value p_{rand}; When $p_{tr} < p_{rand}$, the target point is used as the sampling point. At this point, x_{near} and x_{goal} are directly connected, a new node x_{new} is extended from x_{near} with the step size ρ, so that the random tree grows towards the target point.

$$x_{rand} = \begin{cases} x_{goal} & (p_{tr} < p_{rand}) \\ x_{sample} & (p_{rand} \leq p_{tr}) \end{cases} \tag{7}$$

3.3　Redundant Point Deletion Strategy

The above goal-oriented constraint strategy enables the improved algorithm to select the target point as the sampling point with a certain probability, which can make the random tree grow towards the target point, reduce the randomness of path generation, and reduce the length of the path. However, as shown in Fig. 5, there may still be a large number of unnecessary path points in the generated path, and there may be a large angle phenomenon at the node connection. To address this issue, a redundant point deletion strategy is proposed for redundant path point deletion.

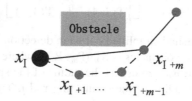

Fig. 5. Schematic diagram of redundant point deletion strategy

Assume the starting point of the initial path be $x_I(x_I, y_I, z_I)$, the m-th node behind this point $x_I(x_I, y_I, z_I)$ is $x_{I+m}(x_{I+m}, y_{I+m}, z_{I+m})$; then determine whether the line segment formed by x_I and x_{I+m} is in the obstacle area, if not, set x_{I+m} as x_{II}, Delete other path point between x_I and x_{II} in the initial path, so that the robot moves directly from x_I to x_{II}; otherwise judge whether the line segment formed by x_I and x_{I+m-2}, $x_{I+m-3}\cdots x_{I+m-t}$ ($t = 1, 2, \cdots, m - 1$), repeat the above steps and eventually generate a preliminarily optimized path consisting of $x_I, x_{II}, x_{III}\cdots$.

3.4　Path Smoothing Strategy

A method based on B-spline curve smoothing is proposed to address the problem of unsmooth path planning in the RRT algorithm [10, 11]. Due to the large order of the spline curve, the generated path differs greatly from the initial path, resulting in the motion path encountering obstacles. Therefore, this article proposes a method for path smoothing based on cubic B-spline curves.

$$N_{0,3}(u) = \frac{1}{6}\left(-u^3 + 3u^2 - 3u + 1\right) \tag{8}$$

$$N_{1,3}(u) = \frac{1}{6}\left(3u^3 - 6u^2 + 4\right) \tag{9}$$

$$N_{2,3}(u) = \frac{1}{6}\left(-3u^3 + 3u^2 + 3u + 1\right) \tag{10}$$

$$N_{3,3}(u) = \frac{1}{6}u^3 \tag{11}$$

Then the cubic B-spline curve segment is as follows:

$$P_{0,3}(u) = P_0 \times N_{0,3}(u) + P_1 \times N_{1,3}(u) + P_2 \times N_{2,3}(u) + P_3 \times N_{3,3}(u) \tag{12}$$

In the equation, P_0, P_1, P_2, P_3 is the curve control point, then using the above equation, an optimized motion path of the muck removal robot can be calculated.

4 Simulation Calculation

To verify the effectiveness of the proposed method, a simulation platform was built using MATLAB to simulate the path planning of the muck removal robot.

The description of obstacles and the movement of the muck removal robot in space is based on the foundation coordinate system of the robot. The simulation environment built using MATLAB is shown in Fig. 6, where the obstacle is simplified as a sphere with center coordinates of $[-1, -1.1, -1.6]$ and a radius of 0.25; Set the starting point coordinates of the muck removal robot $[-1.5, -1, -1.7]$ and the target point coordinates $[-0.5, -1.5, -1.5]$.

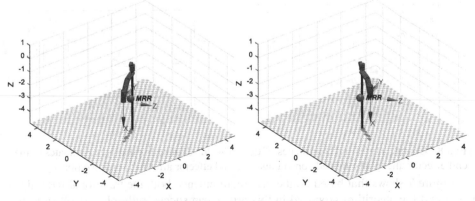

Fig. 6. Initial and target configurations of robots

Set the path planning parameters for the muck removal robot as shown in Table 1 Based on the proposed algorithm, calculate the initial motion path and the optimized path as shown in Fig. 7.

Table 1. Parameters of path planning

Number	Type	value
1	Step ρ/m	0.08
2	probability threshold p_{tr}	0.6
3	The upper limit of iterations N	5000
4	Distance Threshold r	0.05
5	path optimization m	5

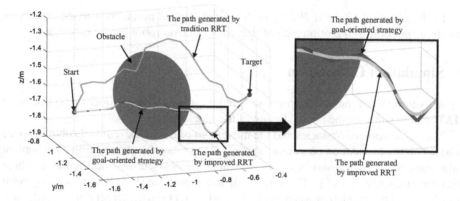

Fig. 7. Comparison of paths planned under different algorithms

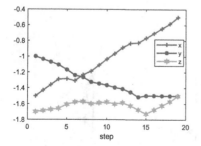

Fig. 8. Change in position coordinates of the end effector after goal-oriented constraints

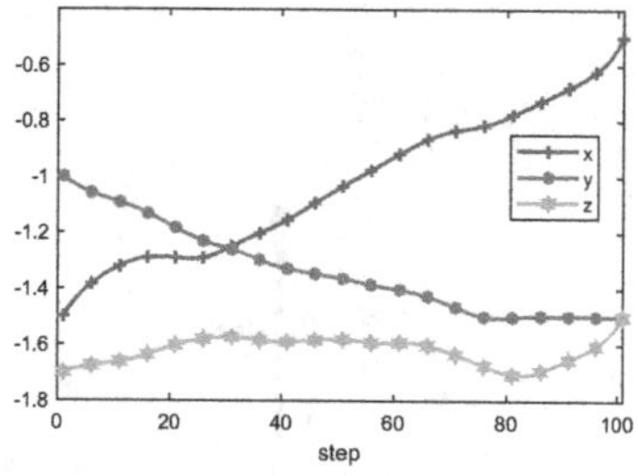

Fig. 9. Change in position coordinates of the end effector after final optimization

Figure 7 shows that based on the task requirements, both the traditional RRT algorithm and the algorithm proposed in this article can successfully plan a collision-free motion path suitable for the muck removal robot to operate in an obstacle environment. The traditional RRT algorithm results in longer path lengths and more turning points in the path. However, with the goal-oriented constraint strategy, the algorithm can make the path grow toward the target point, resulting in significant improvements in path length and smoothness. Meanwhile, Fig. 8 and Fig. 9 show that with the redundant point deletion strategy and the smooth track strategy, the number of turning points in the path can be further reduced, improving the smoothness of the robot's end motion. Through 10 repeated experiments in this scenario, using goal-oriented constraints, redundant point deletion strategies, and path smoothing strategies, the length of the path can be reduced by 27.13%.

5 Conclusion

This paper presents a path planning algorithm for muck removal robots based on improved RRT has been proposed to address the demand for intelligent path planning during muck removal operations.

(1) In response to the slow convergence speed of traditional RRT algorithms, a method is proposed that takes the target point as a random point with a certain probability to make the random tree grow toward the goal point.
(2) A redundant path point deletion strategy is proposed, in order to optimize the initial path for the first time for the case that there are still redundant nodes in the path point.
(3) In response to the problem of unsmooth paths after optimization, the optimized paths were optimized again based on B-spline curves.

Finally, the performance of the improved algorithm was verified through simulation. Compared to traditional algorithms, the improved algorithm proposed in this paper can reduce the length of the planned path by 27.13%.

References

1. Hong Kairong, D., Yanliang, C.K., et al.: Full-face tunnel boring machine (shields/TBMs) in China: history, achievements, and prospects. Tunnel Constr. **42**(05), 739–756 (2022)
2. Jianbin, L.: Current status, problems and prospects of research, design, and manufacturing of boring machine in China. Tunnel Constr. **41**(06), 877–896 (2021)
3. Fei, H., Xingjian, Z., Yanming, S., et al.: Design and experiment of muck removal robot for tunneling boring machine. Advanced Engineering Sciences **54**(04), 12–19 (2022)
4. Chen, Q., Zheng, Y., Jiang, H., et al.: Improved particle swarm optimization algorithm based on neural network for dynamic path planning. J. Huazhong Univ. Sci. Technol. (Nat. Sci. Edn.) **49**(02), 51–55 (2021)
5. Ma, J., Wang, Y., He, Y., et al.: Motion planning of citrus harvesting manipulator based on informed guidance point of configuration space. Trans. Chin. Soc. Agric. Eng. (Trans. CSAE) **35**(08), 100–108 (2019)
6. Lin, H.I., Yang, C.S.: 2D-span resampling of bi-RRT in dynamic path planning. Int. J. Autom. Smart Technol. **5**(1), 39–48 (2015)
7. Gammell, J.D., Barfoot, T.D., Srinivasa, S.S.: Informed sampling for asymptotically optimal path planning. IEEE Trans. Rob. **34**(4), 966–984 (2018)

8. Wei, L., Shijun, J.: Optimal path convergence method based on artificial potential field method and informed sampling. J. Comput. Appl. **41**(10), 2912–2918 (2021)

9. Bo, C., Bi, S., Zheng, J., et al.: Obstacle avoidance algorithm for redundant manipulator of improved artificial potential field method. J. Harbin Inst. Technol. **51**(07), 184–191 (2019)

10. Xu, J., Liu, Z., Yang, C., et al.: A pseudo-distance algorithm for collision detection of manipulators using convex-plane-polygons-based representation. Robot. Comput. Integr. Manuf. **66**, 101993 (2020)

11. Liu, J., Fan, P.: Path planning of manipulator based on improved RRT*-connect Algorithm. Comput. Eng. Appl. **57**(06), 274–278 (2021)

12. Du, M., Mei, T., Chen, J., et al.: RRT-based motion planning algorithm for intelligent vehicle in complex environments. Robot **37**(04), 443–450 (2015)

Research on Snake-Like Robot for Cutter Inspection in Tunnel Boring Machine

Xiantong Xu, Haibo Xie[✉], Cheng Wang, and Huayong Yang

State Key Lab of Fluid Power and Mechatronic Systems, Zhejiang University,
Hangzhou 310027, Zhejiang, China
hbxie@zju.edu.cn

Abstract. While the applications of tunnel boring machine (TBM) are growing due to its high performance, the working mode of "robot replacing labor"
is continuously increasing because of TBM's harsh and confined space. Thus,
snake-like robot, which is with superior dexterity and obstacle avoidance ability, are highly suitable for TBM cutter inspection. However, its large number of
degrees of freedom (DOFs) makes the inverse kinematics and control strategy
very complex. Therefore, the paper researches the efficient kinematics algorithm
based on the geometric method, including tip-following and serpentine-scanning
methods. Tip-following method achieves to send the end-effector to the target area,
while serpentine-scanning method promises the scanning inspection on every cutter. Because of the particularity of the geometric method in this paper, the local
coordinate frame and joint space are abandoned, but the "link eigen vector" is
utilized to construct a simpler and more direct kinematic model. Simulation and
experiment results show the proposed methods satisfy the real-time control and
obstacle avoidance. Especially the engineering test shows the snake-like robot can
meet the quick and reliable inspection task of the cutter and cutterhead.

Keywords: Geometric method · Inverse kinematics · snake-like robot · tunnel
boring machine

1 Introduction

In the past decades, exploitation of underground space has been developed unprecedent-
edly. Modern tunnel boring machine (TBM) in particular, which integrates excavating
tunnels, removing excavated debris, assembling tunnel-supporting structures and other
functions [1, 2], has been increasingly widely used. Compared to the traditional drill and
blast methods, TBM has significant advantages in excavation efficiency, quality, safety,
environment protection [3], etc. As a result, the excavation technology utilizing TBM
is becoming the mainstream. Nevertheless, the cutters in TBM are highly susceptible
to wear and damage due to the high work intensity [4]. It is usually for people to enter
the excavation chamber and perform the inspection and maintenance of the cutterhead
and cutters. However, due to the high integration and harsh environment of the TBM, its
interior is a complex, narrow and closed space. Especially in the excavation chamber,

© The Author(s), under exclusive license to Springer Nature Singapore Pte Ltd. 2023
H. Yang et al. (Eds.): ICIRA 2023, LNAI 14272, pp. 93–106, 2023.
https://doi.org/10.1007/978-981-99-6480-2_8

mud and water are mixed in the confined space, and often accompanied by weak light, toxic gas, high temperature, high pressure, high humidity and other environmental factors. These severe conditions not only seriously weaken the labor power and impair the health, but also demand the workers and cutters to travel between the high-pressure and atmospheric-pressure environments. Hence, the time and manpower consume for the inspection of TBM cutterhead and cutters are extremely high. According to engineering statistics, during the excavation of Qinling Tunnel, the time consumed by cutter inspection, replacement and repair accounts for almost one-third of the total time of tunneling [5–8]. And many safety accidents, which caused casualties and even death, may occur during the manual inspection [9].

Therefore, "robot replacing labor" is a significant and imperative TBM technology for the tasks of cutter inspection. And the cable-driven snake-like robot (CSR), which is with superior flexibility and obstacle avoidance ability, has a very broad foreground. However, CSR belongs to hyper-redundant robot [10–14] whose inverse kinematics has always been a challenge. The conventional robotic kinematics can be divided into numerical and analytical methods. The calculation cost of the numerical method with sufficient accuracy is too high, which does not meet the real-time control, so it is not considered in this paper. And the analytical method can be divided into algebraic and geometric methods. Algebraic method is suitable for low DOF robots, but for hyper-redundant robots, it often comes with problems such as high computation complexity, non intuitive configuration space, and multiple solutions. The computation time for algebraic method even grows with fourth power of the number of DOFs [15]. On the other side, geometric method, which is with high efficiency, singularity avoidance ability, and easy to meet the constraints of the task space, is widely applied. Back in the 1990s, Naccarato et al. [16, 17] presented an inverse kinematic solution by forcing the hyper-redundant robot to track reference shape curve. Chirikjian et al. [18, 19] extended the reference shape curve to backbone curve reference set including both of bending description and torsion description. Moreover, the follow-up studies have put more attention on it, such as the methods of segmented geometry [20], follow-the-leader [21], tractrix [22], FABRIK [23], path-following [24].

Also based on the geometric method, the paper studies the tip-following and serpentine-scanning method, which are both used for cutterhead and cutter inspection in TBM. Tip-following motion means all links of CSR move along the serpentine path, that is, each joint of the robot moves along the trajectory of the tip. This motion mode is appropriate for the CSR to cross the obstacles and reach to the observation area of cutters. Serpentine-scanning motion means the body and tail parts of CSR move along the serpentine path for obstacle avoidance, while the head part moves along the scanning path for cutter inspection. And according the specialty of the above two methods, the paper studies the method of how to describe the CSR pose through the link eigen vectors, so as to establish a more intuitive and simpler kinematic model. In the simulation and experiment parts, the paper applies the remote operation based on the digital twin system. Operator can monitor the motion and environmental status according to the graphical interface, thereby adjusting the movement of CSR in real time and achieving the best inspection effect.

Figure 1(a) shows a 3-D drawing of CSR assembled on TBM. The figure demonstrates the relative spatial positions of CSR, excavation chamber, cutterhead, etc. When CSR performs the task of cutter inspection, the pressure inside the robot cabin would increase until it is up to the same as the pressure in excavation chamber. Then the gate is opened and the CSR enters the excavation chamber to conduct the inspection task according to the operator's instructions. After the mission is completed, the CSR automatically retracts along the serpentine path to the robot cabin, which can effectively avoid the collisions. When the CSR is on standby, it stays in the robot cabin. Figure 1(b) shows a photo of CSR assembled on TBM. The figure demonstrates the CSR's operation for cutter inspection. On the end-effector of CSR, there are operation tools for inspection, such as camera, LED, nozzle and laser.

(a) 3-D drawing of CSR assembled on TBM. (b) Photo of CSR assembled on TBM.

Fig. 1. CSR assembled on TBM.

2 Kinematics Modelling

Since the CSR is driven by the cables, the kinematic model studies the relations between configuration space and the shifts of the cables.

2.1 Structure of CSR

The structure of CSR is shown in Fig. 2. The specific structure can be divided into 3 parts, i.e., sliding table, robot arm and base box. The sliding table achieves the translation movement of the whole robot. And the robot arm is driven by the cable, and the cable is driven by the base box. The power device with large mass is located on the base box, which is the mechanical power source of the robot and converts the driving moments of the motors into the driving forces of the cables. The structure puts the bulky power unit rear and effectively reduces the inertia of the robotic arm, making the arm span's movement more flexible.

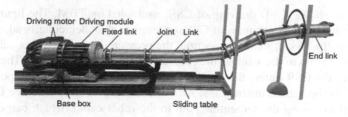

Fig. 2. Mechanical structure of CSR.

2.2 Construction of Kinematic Model

This section will abstract the robot arm into a geometric object. And based on the geometric object, this section defines the link eigen vectors for kinematics modelling.

1) Geometric object of CSR

As is shown in Fig. 3, $Link_0$ is the fixed link and $Link_6$ is the end link. $Joint_0$ located on the start end of $Link_0$ is the fixed joint. The end of the robot arm is defined as $Joint_7$. The rest are all normal links and universal joints. Every normal universal joint is with 2 DOFs and is driven by 3 cables. Each joint, except $Joint_0$ and $Joint_7$, has two discs, which are indexed as $Disc_{1,i}$ and $Disc_{2,i}$ respectively. And $Disc_{1,i}$ is also located on the distal end of $Link_{i-1}$, while $Disc_{2,i}$ is also located on the proximal end of $Link_i$. The center position of $Joint_i$ is indexed as O_{mi}. Correspondingly, O_{ai} is the center position of $Disc_{1,i}$ and O_{bi} is the center position of $Disc_{2,i}$.

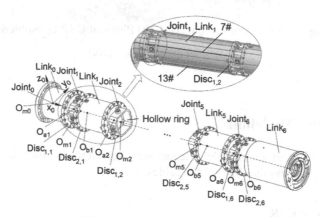

Fig. 3. Geometry object of CSR.

As is shown in Fig. 3, the reference coordinate system is established: Set O_{m0} as the origin, set $\overrightarrow{O_{m0}O_{m1}}$ as x_0-axis, set z_0-axis vertically upward and y_0-axis horizontally to the right. Then, the cable, which is intersected with y_0-axis, is indexed as 1#. The rest cables are indexed counterclockwise as 2#, $\cdots$ 18#. The cables driving $Joint_i$ would pass through the holes on $Disc_{1,1}, Disc_{2,1} \cdots Disc_{2,i}$ and fixed to $Disc_{1,(i+1)}$. As is shown in the partial image of Fig. 3, the cables 1#, 7# and 13# which are fixed to $Disc_{1,2}$ of $Link_1$ are used to drive $Joint_1$ (1# is covered by the robot arm). And the other cables would

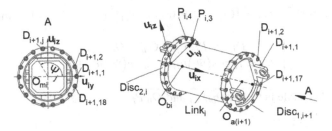

Fig. 4. Illustration of $Link_i$.

pass through $Link_1$. As is shown in Fig. 4, for $Link_i$, the hole on $Disc_{2,i}$ for cable $j\#$ passing through is indexed as $P_{i,j}$ and the hole on $Disc_{1,i+1}$ for cable $j\#$ passing through is indexed as $D_{i+1,j}$. All holes are evenly distributed circumferentially on the disc.

2) Definition of the link eigen vectors

Definition: $Link_i$'s independent link eigen vector is a unit vector pointing from proximal end to distal end of $Link_i$. It is,

$$u_{ix} = \overrightarrow{O_{mi}O_{m(i+1)}}/|\overrightarrow{O_{mi}O_{m(i+1)}}| \tag{1}$$

There are two another derived link eigen vectors, u_{iy}, u_{iz}, which is shown in Fig. 4.
Let $u_{dirz} = u_{ix} \times u_{(i-1)y}$, then u_{dirz} is collinear with u_{iz}.
Let $u_{diry} = u_{dirz} \times u_{ix}$, then u_{diry} is collinear with u_{iy}.
Therefore,

$$\begin{cases} u_{iz} = u_{dirz}/|u_{dirz}| \\ u_{iy} = u_{diry}/|u_{diry}| \end{cases} \tag{2}$$

According to the structure of CSR, the rotation axis between $Link_i$ and $Joint_{i+1}$ coincides with u_{iy}, and the rotation axis between $Link_i$ and $Joint_i$ coincides with u_{iz}.

2.3 Mapping from Link Eigen Vectors to Cables' Lengths

The cable $j\#$ within the scope of arm span can be divided into the part between $P_{i-1,j}$ and $D_{i,j}$, and the part between $D_{i,j}$ and $P_{i,j}$. The cable's length of $j\#$ between the two discs in $Joint_i$, is approximately equal to the distance between $D_{i,j}$ and $P_{i,j}$. Thus, the driving of the universal joint is achieved by changing the cables' lengths, which also refers to the driving shifts of the cables. The following will only consider the length between $D_{i,j}$ and $P_{i,j}$. The symbols are predefined as follows:

d : Distance from O_{mi} to adjacent disc's center, $d = |O_{mi} - O_{ai}| = |O_{mi} - O_{bi}|$.

r_d : Radius of the distribution circle of the hole on the disc.

$s_{i,j}$: Distance between $D_{i,j}$ and $P_{i,j}$.

C_{sj}: Total cable's length of cable $j\#$, which is calculated through $s_{i,j}$.

Then,

$$\begin{cases} O_{ai} = O_{mi} - du_{(i-1)x} \\ O_{bi} = O_{mi} + du_{ix} \end{cases} (i = 1, 2, \cdots 6) \tag{3}$$

Let $O_{b0} = [000]^T, P_{0,j} = \left[0 \, r_d \cos(\Psi_j) \, r_d \sin(\Psi_j)\right]^T (j = 1, 2, \cdots 18)$, then

$$\begin{cases} D_{i,j} = P_{i-1,j} + O_{ai} - O_{b(i-1)} \\ P_{i,j} = r_d \cos(\Psi_j)\boldsymbol{u_{iy}} + r_d \sin(\Psi_j)\boldsymbol{u_{iz}} + O_{bi} \end{cases} \tag{4}$$

Ψ_j : Included angle between $\overrightarrow{O_{bi}P_{i,j}}$ and $\overrightarrow{O_{bi}P_{i,1}}$.
Thus,

$$s_{i,j} = |P_{i,j} - D_{i,j}| \tag{5}$$

Let n_j be the remainder of j divided by 6, then,

$$C_{sj} = \sum_{k=1}^{k=n_{j-1}+1} s_{k,j} \tag{6}$$

If the cable is tensioned, C_{sj} can be taken as the real total cable's length. Thus, the mapping is solved.

3   Strategy of Motion Control

The specific geometric method in this paper, which refers to the CSR's tracking of the reference polyline, is especially suitable for the kinematic model in Sect. 2. The method normally generates the reference polyline that the manipulator can track in the task space firstly, and then force the manipulator to fit the polyline. That means the joint's center O_{mi} would be solved in this way and then the link eigen vectors could also be calculated. And then, the driving cables' lengths can be figured out according to the kinematic model in Sect. 2. Finally, the motors drive the cables to the desired displacement so as to achieve the motion control of the robot arm.

3.1   Tip-Following Method

The reference polyline, which is for CSR's tracking, is also called the serpentine path. The following will illustrate the generation, update strategy and tracking method of the serpentine path.
    1) Generation
    The serpentine path is generated by connecting the key points linearly, i.e., the reference polyline. The turning points in the serpentine path are also the key points, so the setting of the key points will achieve the goal of obstacle avoidance. Hence, according to CSR's initial pose, obstacles' distribution and target position, the number and positions of the key points can be figured out. Besides, sometimes a key point is additionally set for the target wrist position, which is utilized to set the posture of the end-effector.
    Figure 5 shows a typical method of how to generate the serpentine path. Firstly, according to the initial pose of CSR, the key point P_0 is determined. Then according to the obstacles that the CSR needs to pass, i.e., the narrow pipeline in the figure, the turning key points P_1, P_2, P_3 are determined. And P_4 is the target wrist position, P_5 is

the final target position. Therefore, the required key points are $P_0, P_1 \cdots P_5$. Then, the serpentine path can be can be generated by connecting these key points.

Real-time operation requires the real-time update strategy of the serpentine path. The update strategy rules the way of how the serpentine path is generated and rectified, correspondingly, determines the interactive strategy of human-machine. There are 3 basic update ways which meet the requirements of tip-following motion, i.e., 1) extend the serpentine path on the head side; 2) add key points on the head side; 3) truncate the serpentine path on the head side. Using a combination of the basic update ways, any desired serpentine path can be obtained. As is shown in Fig. 6(a), the path $P_0P_1 \cdots P_5$ is needed to be updated to $P_0P_1 \cdots P_{in}P_6$. Then, as is shown in Fig. 6(b), firstly P_4P_5 is truncated as P_4P_{in}. And then, as is shown in Fig. 6(c), the desired serpentine path is generated by connecting $P_{in}P_6$.

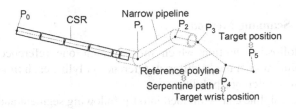

Fig. 5. Generation of serpentine path.

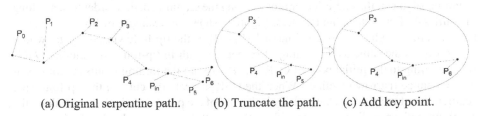

(a) Original serpentine path. (b) Truncate the path. (c) Add key point.

Fig. 6. Example of update strategy of serpentine path.

2) Tracking method

The CSR's tracking of serpentine path is fulfilled by forcing the joint center O_{mi} on the serpentine path. This is a recursive process for solving the position of each O_{mi}. According to the direction of recursion, the tracking method can be divided into inward and outward tracking.

The recursive direction of inward tracking method is from head to tail. That means if the end-effector is the head, O_{mi} is calculated through $O_{m(i+1)}$. And the position of O_{m7} is the initial value, which is given as the target value. As is shown in Fig. 7, O'_{m7} is the original position of $Joint_7$'s center and O_{m7} is obtained by moving O'_{m7} along $\overrightarrow{P_4P_5}$ according to the specified step length. Then, $O_{m6}, O_{m5} \cdots O_{m0}$ can be calculated by inward recursion. One inward tracking of the whole CSR corresponds to one movement step. As the inward tracking runs cyclically, CSR's end can reach the final target position along the serpentine path. It is worth noting that the step length needs not to be constant. Please refer to Sect. 3.3 for the detailed solution of the recursive equations.

The recursive direction of outward tracking method is from tail to head, which can be solved by the analogy of the inward tracking.

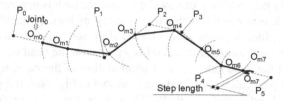

Fig. 7. Inward tracking.

3.2 Serpentine-Scanning Method

Unlike the tip-following motion which moves along one reference polyline, the serpentine-scanning motion tracks different reference polyline each time.

1) Generation of reference polylines

The reference polyline can be divided into tip-following segment and scanning segment. For the tip-following segment, the joint center moves along the same polyline in order to ensure the reliable obstacle avoidance for the proximal part CSR. For the scanning segment, the end-effector moves along the scanning path in order to scan along the surface of cutterhead and cutters. Figure 8 shows an example of how to generate the reference polylines. The polyline of $P_0P_1P_2P_3$ is the tip-following segment, whose generation is the same as the setting of serpentine path in tip-following method. P_0 is set according to the initial pose of CSR. P_1, P_2, P_3 are the turning points set for obstacle avoidance (narrow pipeline). When the CSR inspects the cutters, the tip-following segment would remain unchanged. P_5 is the end of the polyline, which moves along the scanning path according to the specified step length as time goes by. Furthermore, the key point P_4 is added for wrist joint in the scanning segment, in order to ensure the stable posture for the end-effector. Therefore, $\overrightarrow{P_4P_5}$ keeps collinear at different time and its modulus is the same as the length of end-effector. Thereby, the orientation of the end effector remains unchanged, ensuring the stability of the camera's view.

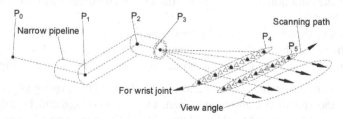

Fig. 8. Generation of reference polylines for serpentine-scanning method.

Unlike tip-following method, whose update strategy is to modify the unique serpentine path, serpentine-scanning motion generates different reference polyline in real time. That means the update strategy is included in the generation of reference polylines.

In addition, sometimes the posture of the end-effector needs to be adjusted for the better view angle of the camera or better cleaning angle of the jet water flow. At this time, the serpentine-scanning motion should be suspended and end-effector adjusting mode could be executed. In this mode, only $Joint_6$ keeps moving. When the end-effector is adjusted to the proper posture, then CSR carries on the serpentine-scanning motion with the adjusted end-effector posture.

2) Tracking method

During the serpentine-scanning motion, the robot end moves along the specified scanning path, which clarifies the position of O_{m7}. Then, O_{m7} is the initial value of the recursive equation. As a result, serpentine-scanning motion is only suitable with inward tracking method. The inward tracking methods of the two geometric methods are basically the same. And the detailed solution of the recursive equations is also shown in Sect. 3.3.

3.3 Recursive Equations

Since the tip-following and serpentine-scanning methods both are the CSR's tracking of the reference polyline, they are with the same recursive equations. Firstly, as the joint centers of CSR are constrained on the polyline, the polyline constraint equations are obtained. Polyline constraint Eqs. (7) are in the form of inward tracking. And by analogy, the polyline constraint equations of outward tracking can be deduced easily. Suppose the polyline, whose key points are $P_0, P_1 \cdots P_k \cdots P_n$, is composed by connecting n straight line segments in series. Thus, Eqs. (7) include n groups of piecewise lines, i.e., $eq_1, eq_2 \cdots eq_n$. Secondly, since the links are continuous and rigid, which means the distal end of $Link_i$ coincides with the proximal end of $Link_{i+1}$ and every link's length keeps unchanged, the continuity equation can be derived as (8).

$$\begin{cases} x_i = x_{P_1} + v_{x_1}t, y_i = y_{P_1} + v_{y_1}t, z_i = z_{P_1} + v_{z_1}t(eq_1) \\ \vdots \\ x_i = x_{P_k} + v_{x_k}t, y_i = y_{P_k} + v_{y_k}t, z_i = z_{P_k} + v_{z_k}t(eq_k) \\ \vdots \\ x_i = x_{P_n} + v_{x_n}t, y_n = y_{P_n} + v_{y_n}t, z_i = z_{P_n} + v_{z_n}t(eq_n) \end{cases} \qquad (7)$$

$$(x_{i+1} - x_i)^2 + (y_{i+1} - y_i)^2 + (z_{i+1} - z_i)^2 = l_i^2 \qquad (8)$$

$[x_{P_k} y_{P_k} z_{P_k}]^T$: Coordinates of P_i ($k = 0, 1, 2 \cdots n$).

$[x_i y_i z_i]^T$: Coordinates of O_{mi}, i.e., coordinates of $Link_i$'s proximal end.

l_i: Length of $Link_i$.

$[v_{xk} v_{yk} v_{zk}]^T$: Direction vector of $\overrightarrow{P_{k-1}P_k}$ ($k = 1, 2 \cdots n$) and its value is,

$$[v_{xk} v_{yk} v_{zk}]^T = (P_k - P_{k-1})/|P_k - P_{k-1}| \qquad (9)$$

Then the first recursive equations are obtained by combining (7) and (8). When the recursive initial value is set, the first recursive equations are with 4 equations and 4 unknown variables (x_i, y_i, z_i, t). Therefore, the equations have the unique solution. Additionally, instead of the ordinary curves or lines, the polyline is utilized in the paper, so sometimes u_{ix} would coincides with the reference polyline. In this case, (7) and (8) can be substituted by the second recursive Eqs. (10) for a simpler solution.

$$\begin{cases} x_i = x_{i+1} - v_{x_k} l_i \\ y_i = y_{i+1} - v_{y_k} l_i \\ z_i = z_{i+1} - v_{z_k} l_i \end{cases} \tag{10}$$

Because (7) includes n groups of straight line, it is necessary to figure out which line O_{mi} lies on. Let

$$l_{Re} = O_{m(i+1)} - P_{k-1} \tag{11}$$

Then, if $l_{Re} \geq l_i$, O_{mi} lies on $P_{k-1}P_k$. Else, O_{mi} lies on P_0P_{k-1} or O_{mi} is out of the reference polyline. Fortunately, if O_{mi+1} and O_{mi} both lie on $P_{k-1}P_k$, the second recursive equations are effective. Figure 9 shows the flowchart of the solution process.

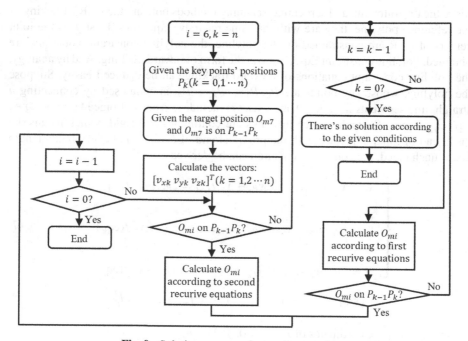

Fig. 9. Solution process of recursive equations.

After all coordinates of O_{mi} are obtained, the driving lengths of the cables can be calculated according to Sect. 2.

4 Simulation and Experiment

In order to verify the effectiveness of the geometric method in this paper, simulation and experiment have been tested. The tests can be divided into laboratory test and engineering test.

4.1 Laboratory Test of Simulation and Experiment

In the laboratory, quantities of simulation and experiment have been conducted on CSR prototype.

1) Setup of the simulation and experiment

The CSR prototype is shown in Fig. 2 and the interactive platform has been developed for CSR's real-time operation and motion analysis. The platform can not only run independently, so as to complete the simulation analysis, but also can control the CSR in real time, so as to achieve the digital twin system as is shown in Fig. 10.

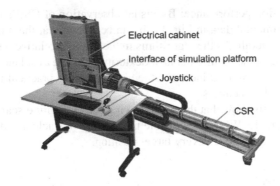

Fig. 10. Digital twin system of CSR.

2) Process of simulation and experiment

Various serpentine and scanning paths have been conducted on CSR prototype to test the performance of the geometric methods. And the motion with typical serpentine and scanning paths is shown in Fig. 11(a). CSR first passes through the narrow pipeline and arrives at the target position. And then the end effector scans along the rectangular, meantime the view angle keeps unchanged. Figure 11(b) shows the relation between the coordinates of $O_{m2}, O_{m3} \cdots O_{m7}$ and the time. And according to the experimental data in Fig. 11, the relation between the link eigen vectors and the time can also be derived.

3) Result of simulation and experiment

Analysis of calculation efficiency: The structures of tip-following and serpentine-scanning algorithms are similar, so their efficiency is basically the same. Measuring the execution time of the two algorithms, the average time is only 1.5 μs per movement step for C++ program. These programs run on the hardware with Intel processor i5-13400 and 16 GB RAM. For instance, the typical motion in Fig. 11, tip-following motion has a total of 6379 steps with 9.1 ms running time, so the average time is 1.4 μs per movement step. Serpentine motion has a total of 3000 steps with 4.6 ms running

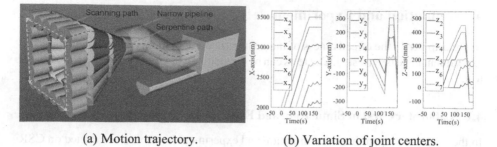

(a) Motion trajectory.   (b) Variation of joint centers.

Fig. 11. Motion trajectory and experiment data.

time, so the average time is 1.5 μs per movement step. Compared to the numerical or algebraic method, the algorithms are with significant efficiency improvement in inverse kinematics. Furthermore, the computation time is almost linear with the number of DOFs.

Analysis of motion performance: By visual observation of CSR's motion and analyzing of the experimental data in Fig. 11, it can be drawn that the movement of CSR is coordinated and smooth. As the algorithms in the paper is relatively simple and intuitive, it is easier to meet the requirements of dexterity, obstacle avoidance and singularity avoidance simultaneously. That indicates the algorithms are practical in the inspection task of the cutterhead and cutters.

The laboratory tests show that the tip-following and serpentine-scanning algorithms are efficient and reliable. While they enable the reliable obstacle avoidance ability, the end-effector can smoothly reach every target position.

4.2 Engineering Test

The CSR was assembled and tested on TBM in order to make further verification of the reliability of the tip-following and serpentine-scanning methods. Figure 12 is the photos of CSR during engineering test. The left photo was taken in the assembly shop, and the right two photos were taken when TBM and CSR were at the tunnel excavation site.

Engineering test result: Engineering test shows that the CSR works stably and reliably in the complex and harsh environment of TBM. The CSR prototype successfully accomplishes the task of cleaning and inspecting the cutterhead and cutters. The significance and feasibility of the working mode, "robot replacing labor", have been verified.

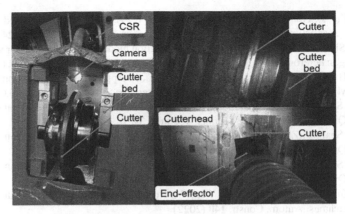

Fig. 12. Photos of CSR during engineering test.

5 Conclusion

The paper studies the application of a hyper-redundant robot, that is, the cable-driven snake-like robot (CSR), on a TBM. Because of the harsh and confined interior space of TBM, the manual operation is costly and unsafe. CSR, therefore, whose motion is extremely flexible due to it super high DOFs, is very suitable for the unstructured environment with limited space. However, its inverse kinematics is really complicated. Thus, aiming to study the real-time and stable kinematics algorithms of the CSR, the tip-following and serpentine-scanning methods, which are applied for cleaning and inspecting the cutterhead and cutters, are proposed. And because of the special properties of the two geometric kinematics methods, the simple and effective kinematic model is also constructed.

Although the two geometric methods run well currently, the more accurate control is difficult to fulfil. That is because of the complex and nonlinear mechanics of the robot arm, which makes its dynamics hard to analyze. In the future, we would study the statics and dynamics of the CSR and try to figure out the close-loop control, so as to realize the more reliable and precise motion.

Acknowledgement. This work was supported by the Fundamental Research Funds for the Central Universities, Award Number: 226-2022-00016, the State Key Laboratory of Fluid Power and Mechatronic Systems Independent Project, Award Number: SKLoFP_ZZ_2106, and the National Key R&D Program of China, Award Number: 2022YFC3802300.

References

1. Zheng, Y., Zhang, Q., Zhao, J.: Challenges and opportunities of using tunnel boring machines in mining. Tunn. Undergr. Space Technol. **57**, 287–299 (2016)
2. Liu, Q., et al.: A wear rule and cutter life prediction model of a 20-in. TBM cutter for granite: a case study of a water conveyance tunnel in China. Rock Mech. Rock. Eng. **50**(5), 1303–1320 (2018)

3. Yu, H., Tao, J., Huang, S., Qin, C., Xiao, D., Liu, C.: A field parameters-based method for real-time wear estimation of disc cutter on TBM cutterhead. Autom. Constr. **124** (2021)

4. Ren, D., Shen, S., Arulrajah, A., Chen, W.: Prediction model of TBM disc cutter wear during tunnelling in heterogeneous ground. Rock Mech. Rock. Eng. **51**(11), 3599–3611 (2018)

5. Liu, Q., Huang, X., Gong, Q., Du, L., Pan, Y., Liu, J.: Application and development of hard rock TBM and its prospect in China. Tunn. Undergr. Space Technol. **57**, 33–46 (2016)

6. Wan, Z., Sha, M., Zhou, Y.: Study on disk cutters for hard rock (1), application of TB880E TBM in Qinling tunnel. Modern Tunnel. Technol. **39**(5), 1–11 (2002)

7. Wan, Z., Sha, M., Zhou, Y.: Study on disk cutters for hard rock (2), application of TB880E TBM in Qinling tunnel. Modern Tunnel. Technol. **39**(6), 1–12 (2002)

8. Wan, Z., Sha, M., Zhou, Y.: Study on disk cutters for hard rock (3), application of TB880E TBM in Qinling tunnel. Modern Tunnel. Technol. **40**(1), 1–6 (2003)

9. Du, L., Yuan, J., Bao, S., Guan, R., Wan, W.: Robotic replacement for disc cutters in tunnel boring machines. Autom. Constr. **140** (2022)

10. Chirikjian, G.S., Burdick, J.W.: An obstacle avoidance algorithm for hyper-redundant manipulators. In: Proc. IEEE Int. Conf. Rob. Autom., pp. 625–631. Cincinnati, OH, USA (1990)

11. Chirikjian, G.S., Burdick, J.W.: Parallel formulation of the inverse kinematics of modular hyper-redundant manipulators. In: Proc. IEEE Int. Conf. Rob. Autom., Sacramento, CA (1991)

12. Hannan, M.W., Walker, I.D.: Novel 'elephant's trunk' robot. In: IEEE ASME Int Conf Adv Intellig Mechatron AIM, Atlanta, pp. 410-415. GA, USA (1999)

13. Hannan, M.W., Walker, I.D.: The 'elephant trunk' manipulator, design and implementation. In: IEEE ASME Int Conf Adv Intellig Mechatron AIM, pp. 14–19. Como, Italy (2001)

14. Hannan, M.W., Walker, I.D.: Kinematics and the implementation of an elephant's trunk manipulator and other continuum style robots. J. Robot. Syst. **20**(2), 45–63 (2003)

15. Xiong, Z., Tao, J., Liu, C.: Inverse kinematics of hyper-redundant snake-arm robots with improved tip following movement. Robot. **40**(1), 37–45 (2018)

16. Naccarato, F., Hughes, P.C.: An inverse kinematics algorithm for a highly redundant variable-geometry-truss manipulator. In: Proc. 3rd Annual Conf. Aerospace Computational Control, pp. 89–45. D.E. Bernard and G.K. Man, Eds. Oxnard (1989)

17. Naccarato, F., Hughes, P.C.: Inverse kinematics of variable-geometry truss manipulators. J. Robotic. Syst. **8**(2), 249–266 (1991)

18. Chirikjian, G.S., Burdick, J.W.: A geometric approach to hyper-redundant manipulator obstacle avoidance. J. Mech. Design **114**(4), 580–585 (1992)

19. Chirikjian, G.S., Burdick, J.W.: A modal approach to hyper-redundant manipulator kinematics. IEEE Trans. Robot. Autom. **11**(3), 343–354 (1994)

20. Mu, Z., Yuan, H., Xu, W., Liu, T., Liang, B.: A segmented geometry method for kinematics and configuration planning of spatial hyper-redundant manipulators. IEEE Trans. Syst., Man, Cybern., Syst. **50**(5), 1746–1756 (2020)

21. Xie, H., Wang, C., Li, S., Hu, L., Yang, H.: A geometric approach for follow-the-leader motion of serpentine manipulator. Int. J. Adv. Robot. Syst. **16**(5) (2019)

22. Sreenivasan, S., Goel, P., Ghosal, A.: A real-time algorithm for simulation of flexible objects and hyper-redundant manipulators. Mech. Mach. Theory **45**(3), 454–466 (2010)

23. Aristidou, A., Lasenby, J.: FABRIK: a fast, iterative solver for the Inverse Kinematics problem. J. Robot. Syst. **73**, 243–260 (2011)

24. Wang, C., Li, S., Xie, H.: Interactive path-following method of snake-like robot. In: Int. Conf. Robot. Autom. Eng., pp. 178–185. Singapore (2022)

Shield Tail Seal Detection Method Based on Twin Simulation Model for Smart Shield

Lintao Wang, Zikang Liu[✉], Ning Hao, Meng Gao, and Zihan Wang

School of Mechanical Engineering, Dalian University of Technology, Dalian 116024, China
liuzikang@mail.dlut.edu.cn

Abstract. The tail sealing system of the shield machine is an important guarantee to ensure the tunneling of the shield machine underground. The safety warning of the shield tail sealing system is an important part of the intelligent shield machine, a prerequisite for the attitude adjustment of the shield machine and an important reference for the segment intelligent assembly robot. However, since the shield tail seal system works underground, it is difficult to construct experiments to verify the sealing performance and working state, so there is no mature Detection method for the shield tail seal. Therefore, this paper proposes a new detection method based on twin simulation-driven shield tail seal working status. First, a part of the working condition data of the existing construction site is selected as the training set of the simulation model to establish a twin simulation model, and then the reliability of the model is verified by using the verification set data. Then, based on this twin system, a large number of sample points are randomly selected for simulation to obtain corresponding data sets, so as to obtain the parameter range and corresponding relationship of various working states of the shield tail. Then according to the corresponding relationship between these data sets and states, a BP neural network detection and classification model is established. Finally, the twin simulation model is set to a new working condition, and the data generated by the simulation under this working condition is placed in the classification model to judge the working state, so as to verify the reliability of the detection model. The results showed that the detection accuracy was as high as 99.2%, which verified the reliability of the detection method. In short, the detection system has good stability and reliability, and meets the expected requirements of the design.

Keywords: Smart Shield System · Siamese simulation model · Sample point · BP neural network · Detection and classification model · Reliability

1 Introduction

When the shield tunneling machine is working, it often produces various risk problems and even accidents because of the complex construction environment and the change of working condition. Shield tail sealing system is one of the important systems for shield tunneling machine to cope with construction risks such as groundwater leakage and grouting leakage and ensure construction safety. The sealing state of the shield tail also directly affects the assembly process of the shield tail segment assembly robot [2]. Figure 1 shows the schematic diagram of the shield tail system.

© The Author(s), under exclusive license to Springer Nature Singapore Pte Ltd. 2023
H. Yang et al. (Eds.): ICIRA 2023, LNAI 14272, pp. 107–118, 2023.
https://doi.org/10.1007/978-981-99-6480-2_9

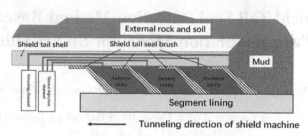

Fig. 1. Shield tail sealing principle

In the field of shield tail simulation, predecessors have done some basic research, which laid the foundation for the establishment of the twin model in this paper. Li Guang and Wang Ning used multiphase flow simulation (VOF) to prove the feasibility of the computational fluid method in the shield tail seal research [2]; Jing Jing et al. studied the pressure distribution and variation characteristics of the shield tail seal oil chamber, and designed the leakage criterion based on pressure monitoring by using the pressure distribution law of the oil chamber under different conditions [3]; Sun Kaixin studied the wear characteristics of the tail brush. The wear of the tail brush is mainly related to the force of the tail brush [4]. In this paper, the twin model of shield tail system is established by numerical calculation method, and a large number of sample points are simulated as data sets.

Neural networks have already had practical applications in mechanical fault diagnosis. Neural network is used in the diagnosis of bearing faults [5] and rotating machinery fault diagnosis [6, 7]. In this paper, the pressure distribution in the shield tail cavity, the oil consumption, the stress and strain of the tail brush are used as the criteria to classify the working state of the shield tail system. Corresponding the sample point information with the classification results, a back propagation neural network fault diagnosis classification model is established. The new working condition twin model data is transmitted to the system for experimental verification, proving its reliability and stability.

2 Establish Twin Simulation Model Based on Working Condition Data

2.1 Modeling Theory of Shield Tail Seal

When the grease seal principle of shield tail sealing system works normally, the fluid dynamics equation should satisfy the basic flow equation, including the mass conservation equation, momentum conservation equation and energy conservation equation:

$$\frac{\partial \rho}{\partial t} + \text{div}(\rho \boldsymbol{u}) = 0 \tag{1}$$

$$\begin{cases} \dfrac{\partial(\rho u)}{\partial t} + div(\rho u\,\boldsymbol{u}) = div(\mu gradu) - \dfrac{\partial p}{\partial y} + S_u \\[2mm] \dfrac{\partial(\rho v)}{\partial t} + div(\rho\upsilon\,\boldsymbol{u}) = div(\mu gradv) - \dfrac{\partial p}{\partial y} + S_v \\[2mm] \dfrac{\partial(\rho w)}{\partial t} + div(\rho w\,\boldsymbol{u}) = div(\mu gradw) - \dfrac{\partial p}{\partial z} + S_w \end{cases} \qquad (2)$$

In formula (1) to formula (2), ρ is the density, t is time, u is the velocity vector, μ is the dynamic viscosity, u, v and w are the components of u in the x, y and z directions., S_u, S_v, S_w is the generalized source term of the momentum conservation equation.

2.2 Numerical Solution Model of Shield Tail Seal

This paper takes the shield tail sealing system of a certain type of earth pressure bal-ance shield machine used in an actual project as the research object. Based on the shield tail sealing principle shown in Fig. 1, parametric modeling is carried out to establish a three-dimensional simulation physical model of the shield tail sealing sys-tem flow field, as shown in Fig. 2. In order to simplify the fluid calculation of the exposed brush filament part of the shield tail brush. Simplify this part to the porous media region so that it can be used in fluid calculations. The tail brush is com-posed of steel wires in the middle of the guard plates on both sides. In this paper, the guard plates are modeled separately, as shown in Fig. 3(a). Corresponding materials are set for the middle steel wire and the guard plate model, making the simulation model closer to the actual situation. Since the tail brush guard plate is composed of many steel plates pressed one by one, there are many gaps between the steel plate guard plates. When the grease is pressurized, a lot of grease in the grease chamber is released from the fender gap overflows, so a simplified fender gap is built in the sim-ulation model. The gap is reflected in the fluid domain of the grease cavity, as shown in Fig. 3(b).

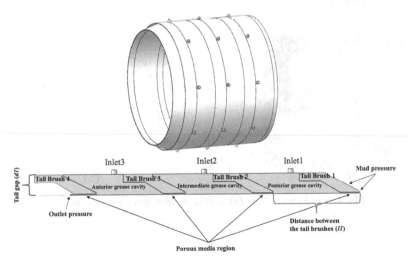

Fig. 2. Overall 3D simulation model of shield tail system

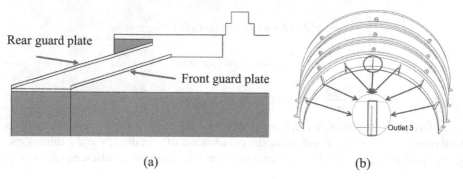

Fig. 3. 3D model cross section (a) & Guard Gap Model (b)

2.3 Meshing

The size of the finite element simulation model is relatively large. Therefore, under the premise of ensuring the simulation quality, the number of grids should be reduced as much as possible. Otherwise, too many grids will affect the calculation speed. Tetrahedral meshes are used in porous media domains. The grid size at the oil inlet should be smaller than that of the surrounding grids, and the grid refinement effect should also be achieved at the gap outlet. The grid of the fluid domain is shown in Fig. 4(a).

The result values are obtained through computational fluid dynamics simulation analysis, such as the pressure value of the circumferential section of the oil chamber, and the change of the pressure value curve is observed to verify the grid independence. As shown in Fig. 4(b), the number of grids in the eighth group in the pressure value change curve basically does not change after it reaches 9×10^6. The grid division size and quantity scheme of group 10 is used to grid the watershed model for subsequent solution and test design optimization, which can meet the requirements of calculation accuracy and grid quality.

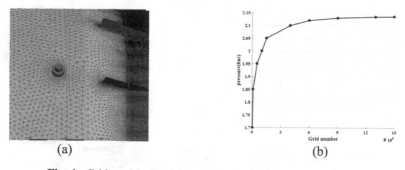

Fig. 4. Grid partitioning (a) & grid independence verification (b)

2.4 Simulation Boundary Condition Settings

Under normal working conditions of the shield machine, the grease inside the shield tail has been leaking and sticking to the segment, and is constantly being worn out. Fluid flows out from outlet 1 and outlet 2 to simulate the process of grease adhering to the segment, and fluid flows out from outlet 3 to simulate the process of grease overflowing from the guard plate gap. When the shield machine is moving forward, the shield tail sealing system adopts the pressure grease injection method to inject grease, continuously fills the grease and maintains the pressure in the grease chamber so that the grease chamber is not penetrated by the external mud.

The pressure and temperature sensors in the grease chamber are evenly distributed in the circumference of the tail of the shield. Figure 5 shows the distribution of sensors.

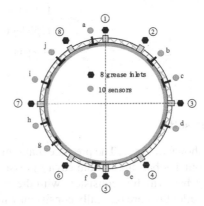

Fig. 5. Distribution map of pressure and temperature sensors

As shown in Fig. 6, knowing the pumping pressure and the pressure values of the rear, middle and front chambers, under normal circumstances the pressure of the rear chamber (1.4 bar–2 bar) > the pressure of the middle chamber (1.1 bar–1.3 bar) > the pressure of the front chamber (0.8 bar–1.2 bar), the boundary conditions of the simulation model are set based on this pressure value.

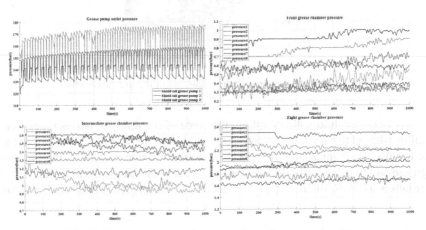

Fig. 6. Pump pressure and pressure in each grease chamber

Set up the model of the fluid domain in the fluent simulation. The boundary conditions are shown in Table 1.

Table 1. Boundary condition settings for the initial model

boundary type	Value
Porous media viscous drag coefficient	$4.12 \times 10^5 \mathrm{m}^{-2}$
Inlet1 pressure (P_1)	1.4–2 bar
Inlet2 pressure (P_2)	1.1–1.3 bar
Inlet3 pressure (P_3)	0.8–1.2 bar
Mud pressure (P_4)	1.5–1.8 bar
Front outlet pressure (P_5)	1–1.5 bar
Grease density (ρ)	1250 kg/m^3
Grease viscosity	800 pa·s

2.5 Simulation Partial Results

The simulation results are shown in Fig. 7. The pressure diagram shows that the pressure in the oil rear cavity is about 1.8 bar, the middle cavity pressure is about 1.3 bar, and the front cavity is about 1.1 bar, which is consistent with the pressure sensor data. The simulation results of each outlet flow are basically consistent with the actual monitoring values, and the error does not exceed 1.5% (as shown in Table 2), which proves the reliability of the simulation.

Fig. 7. The pressure distribution diagram of the grease chamber

Using one-way fluid-solid coupling, the force of the fluid domain is transmitted to the tail brush, and the stress and strain of the tail brush are obtained, as shown in Fig. 8. Since the non-Newtonian fluid has good force transmission capability, the pressure in the grease cavity is basically the same as the pressure in the grease injection port. The deformation and stress of the first tail brush (the gap is in contact with the mud) and the last

Table 2. Each export flow

export name	Simulation value of egress traffic (kg/s)	Monitoring value (kg/s)	error value
outlet1	0.00628	0.00619	1.43%
outlet2	0.00762	0.00761	0.13%
outlet3	0.01073	0.01075	0.19%

tail brush (the gap is in contact with the atmosphere) are the largest. The deformation and stress of the tail brush in the middle grease chamber depends on the pressure difference in the grease chamber, and there is a pressure difference that minimizes the stress and deformation of the tail brush.

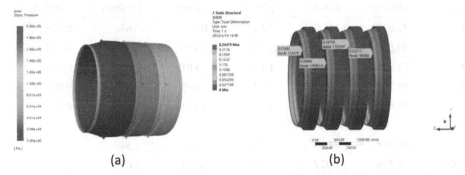

Fig. 8. One-way fluid-solid coupling simulation - fluid domain pressure (a) and tail brush deformation (b)

3   Parametric Simulation to Create Data Sets

The complete input information of the sample point is shown in Fig. 9, the input information of the sample point includes two categories of working condition parameters and design parameters (Code name). In this paper, the shield machine with a diameter (D) of 6.9 m is taken as the research object (The distance between the tail brushes $(l1)$ is 500 mm, and the shield tail gap $(d1)$ is 100 mm), and other input parameters are adjusted within a reasonable range, and the output parameters are obtained through the established simulation model.

The design parameters and working condition parameters are limited within a reasonable range, and 1000 groups of model input parameters are generated in Table 3. Then these input parameters are fed into the debug twin model for calculation, and some calculation results and Corresponding fault type (It has been explained in Sect. 4.2) are shown in Table 4.

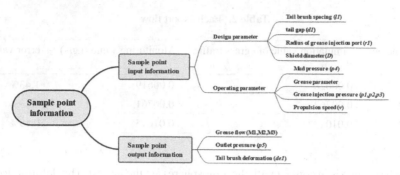

Fig. 9. Sample point information

Table 3. Input parameters data

S/N	$r1$(mm)	$p1$(bar)	$p2$(bar)	$p3$(bar)	$p4$ (bar)	v(mm/s)
1	32.895	1.929	1.195	0.841	1.638	0.925
2	30.502	1.988	1.118	1.165	1.791	0.811
3	31.445	1.483	1.148	0.801	1.544	0.675
4	37.294	1.581	1.273	1.095	1.778	0.757
5	34.823	1.755	1.301	1.111	1.676	0.701
......						
999	30.768	2.022	1.291	1.130	1.546	0.620
1000	30.558	2.027	1.008	0.951	1.675	0.592

Table 4. Calculation results and Corresponding fault type

S/N	$p5$(bar)	de_1(mm)	M_1(kg/s)	M_2(kg/s)	M_3(kg/s)	type
1	0.921	0.0248	0.018	0.013	0.056	c
2	1.023	0.0247	0.005	0.003	0.015	b
3	0.756	0.0251	0.021	0.014	0.063	b
4	0.954	0.0248	0.014	0.007	0.032	a
5	1.036	0.0247	0.018	0.013	0.055	c
......						
999	1.083	0.0247	0.015	0.011	0.047	a
1000	0.806	0.0248	0.015	0.011	0.045	a

4 BP Neural Network Fault Classification Model of Shield Tail System

4.1 Introduction to BP Neural Network

The training of BP neural network includes two processes: forward propagation of signal and reverse feedback of error. Among them, the forward propagation is that the signal enters the hidden layer after parallel weighted calculation from the input layer, and then enters the output layer through weighted processing to obtain the output; while the reverse feedback process is carried out in the direction from output to input, and the weight is adjusted according to the actual error. Adjust the value and threshold. After repeated forward calculation and reverse feedback, the final output results meet the requirements. The fault diagnosis model based on BP neural network is shown in Fig. 10. In the figure: $(x_1, x_2,..., x_j,..., x_m)$ is the input quantity, the subscript is the number of inputs, corresponding to the input layer nodes; $(y_1, y_2,..., y_k,..., y_l)$ is the output quantity, The subscript is the number of outputs, corresponding to the output layer nodes; $(\theta_1, \theta_2,..., \theta_i,..., \theta_q)$ is the threshold introduced by the hidden layer, and the subscript is the number of hidden nodes. There may be multiple hidden layers in a neural network; $(a_1, a_2,..., a_l,..., a_k)$ is the threshold introduced by the output layer, the subscript is the number of output nodes, a neural network has only one output layer; ε is the error value [8].

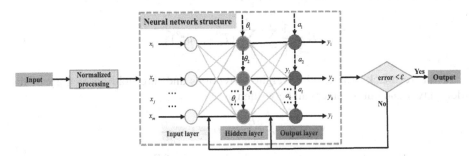

Fig. 10. Schematic diagram of neural network structure

During forward propagation, the input n_i of the ith node of the hidden layer, and output o_i are calculated as follows:

$$n_i = \sum_{j=1}^{m} w_{ij} x_j + \theta_i \tag{3}$$

$$o_i = \phi(net_i) = \phi \sum_{j=1}^{m} (w_{ij} x_j + \theta_i) w_{ij} \tag{4}$$

In the process of forward propagation, the calculation formula of the input net_k and output out_k of the kth node of the output layer is as follows:

$$net_k = \sum_{i=1}^{q} w_{ki} o_i + a_k = \sum_{i=1}^{q} w_{ki} \phi \left(\sum_{j=1}^{m} w_{ij} x_j + \theta_i \right) + a_k \tag{5}$$

$$out_k = \psi(net_k) = \psi \left(\sum_{i=1}^{q} w_{ki} \phi \left(\sum_{j=1}^{m} w_{ij} x_j + \theta_i \right) + a_k \right) \tag{6}$$

In the above formula: w_{ij} is the weight of the jth input variable in the ith node of the hidden layer; ϕ is the activation function of the hidden layer; ψ is the activation function of the output layer; In order to enhance the ability of large-scale nonlinear fitting, according to practical experience, the activation function of the hidden layer chooses the bipolar S-type *tansig* function, and the activation function of the output layer chooses the linear *purelin* function. The error function E_p of the pth sample is shown in formula (5), where T_k is the expected output value of the kth node.

$$E_p = \frac{1}{2} \sum_{k=1}^{l} (T_k - out_k)^2 \tag{7}$$

The total error E of P training samples is:

$$E = \frac{1}{2} \sum_{p=1}^{P} \sum_{k=1}^{l} (T_k^p - out_k^p)^2 \tag{8}$$

In the feedback process, the weight corrections and threshold corrections of the hidden layer and output layer can be written as:

$$\Delta w_{ij} = -\eta \frac{\partial E}{\partial w_{ij}}, \ \Delta \theta i = -\eta \frac{\partial E}{\partial \theta_i}$$
$$\Delta w_{ki} = -\eta \frac{\partial E}{\partial w_{ki}}, \ \Delta a_k = -\eta \frac{\partial E}{\partial a_k} \tag{9}$$

In the formula, η is a coefficient that determines the adjustment rate.

4.2   Build a Neural Network Diagnosis Model

The working state of the shield tail seal can be divided into three categories:

(a) Work normally
(b) Risk of mud penetration
(c) Excessive oil leakage

These three types of faults should be determined by comprehensively considering the outlet flow of the twin simulation, the pressure value of the grease chamber and the deformation of the tail brush.

Schematic diagram of the shield tail seal fault neural network diagnosis model. The twin model generated data (sample point data) is first normalized, and then randomly divided into training (70%) and test (30%) data sets to train the model. During model training, the training data is split 9:1 for model training and validation. The reliability of the model is tested by using newly generated 1000 sets of sample points. The diagnostic accuracy results are shown in Table 5. There is no misjudgment of the sample points in the normal state, only 0.05% of the misjudgment is caused by the risk of mud penetration, and only 0.03% of the misjudgment is made in the state of large oil leakage. The 992 groups of sample points are consistent with the actual state type. Consistent, with an accuracy rate of 99.2%, the detection system has good reliability. It is proved that inputting the design parameters (such as grease injection radius, tail brush spacing, etc.) and working condition parameters (inlet pressure) into the fault diagnosis model will obtain credible shield tail working states (a, b, c). If the pressure data monitored by the sensors is input into the model, the status of the tail seal will be monitored in real time.

Table 5. Comparison of 1000 sets of diagnostic results with actual faults

Fault type	Diagnostic result	Actual fault	Error rate of each type of fault
a	560	560	0
b	256	253	0.03%
c	184	179	0.05%

5 Conclusions

In this paper, aiming at the difficulty of detecting and diagnosing the faults of the shield tail scaling system, the actual shield tail system is replaced by the method of establishing a twin model through simulation. Using this simplified model for parametric simulation, a large number of sample points are obtained. Then use these sample points to train the corresponding BP neural network model. Then, the reliability of the model was tested by using the newly generated sample point information, and the diagnostic accuracy reached 99.2%, which reached the expected ideal result. Future work will focus on improving the twin model in more detail, and training a more accurate neural network model, so that the diagnostic model has a wider and more detailed state classification. For example, each of the three broad categories of working status is finely divided into 3–4 categories. The fault diagnosis of the shield tail seal will provide an important reference for the intelligent assembly of segments, and is an important part of the intelligent shield.

Acknowledgements. This article was supported by the National Key R&D Program Project: Research on Monitoring and Early Warning Technology for Safety Critical Systems of Large Tunnel Boring Machine Construction, 2020YFB2007203.

References

1. Jianbin, L., Liujie, J., Chen, Y., Fulong, L., Na, Z., Pengyu, L.: Discussion on the technical characteristics and realization path of intelligent shield. Tunnel Construct. (Chinese and English) **43**(03), 355–368 (2023)
2. Guang, L., Ning, W.: Research on sealability of shield tail sealing system based on multiphase flow numerical simulation. Tunnel Construct. (Chinese and English) **41**(S1), 490–496 (2021)
3. Jing, J.: Research on pressure distribution characteristics of shield tail sealing system of shield machine. Dalian University of Technology (2021). https://doi.org/10.26991/d.cnki.gdllu.2021.000864
4. Sun, K., et al.: Simulation analysis of tail brush wear characteristics of shield tail sealing system. Mod. Machin. **5**, 6–10 (2022). https://doi.org/10.13667/j.cnki.52-1046/th.2022.05.004
5. Xu, X., et al.: Application of neural network algorithm in fault diagnosis of mechanical intelligence. Mech. Syst. Signal Process. **141**, 106625 (2020)
6. Lin, C.J., Lin, C.H., Lin, F.: Bearing fault diagnosis using a vector-based convolutional fuzzy neural network. Appl. Sci. **13**(5), 3337 (2023)
7. Liu, R., et al.: Artificial intelligence for fault diagnosis of rotating machinery: a review. Mech. Syst. Signal Process. **108**, 33–47 (2018)
8. Peng, X., et al.: Fault diagnosis of ship power system based on optimized BP neural network. Chin. Ship Res. **16**(Suppl), 1–8 (2021)

Support Boot Mechanisms of Shaft Boring Machine for Underground Vertical Tunnel Construction

Qizhi Meng[1,2(✉)], Lianhui Jia[3], Lijie Jiang[3], Yongliang Wen[3], Ruijie Tang[1], Xin Yuan[1], and Xin-Jun Liu[1,2(✉)]

[1] The State Key Laboratory of Tribology in Advanced Equipment, Department of Mechanical Engineering (DME), Tsinghua University, Beijing 100084, China
qizhi.meng@foxmail.com, xinjunliu@mail.tsinghua.edu.cn
[2] Beijing Key Lab of Precision/Ultra-Precision Manufacturing Equipment and Control, Tsinghua University, Beijing 100084, China
[3] China Railway Engineering Equipment Group Co., Ltd., Zhengzhou 450016, Henan, China

Abstract. Shaft boring machines are significant to the mechanized construction of underground vertical tunnels in water conservancy projects, underground mining, transport infrastructure, etc. As one of the main components, the support boot mechanism should apply large pressure on the sidewall to provide enough friction for balancing the gravity and boring torque of the shaft boring machine. In this paper, novel support boot mechanisms are presented to output desired pressure along the radial direction of the cylindrical tunnel, as well as to provide steady support during the vertical tunnel construction. The proposed support boot mechanisms are based on deployable modules with one degree of freedom by converting axial translation into radial one. With this characteristic, synchronous unfolding movements of multiple support boots can be realized. To avoid the failure of the support due to the damage to the tunnel surface, the adjusting modules are adopted at the ends of support boots for changing their radial position. In addition, an adjustment device is presented based on the 3-RPS parallel mechanism to control the direction of the boring head and realize the advancement of the whole shaft boring machine. Combined with the support boot mechanism, the adjustment device, as well as the advancement mechanism, the concept designs of shaft boring machines are presented. This work provides a reference for the structural design and candidates of deployable-module-based support boot mechanisms in shaft boring machines for underground vertical tunnel construction.

Keywords: Design and Analysis · Support Boot Mechanism · Shaft Boring Machine · Deployable Module · Vertical Tunnel Construction

1 Introduction

A vertical shaft typically refers to a well-like, upright-walled passage that serves as a vital pathway for transporting personnel, materials, equipment, and providing ventilation to the underground space. By installing cables and pipes in the shaft, it enables the supply and transmission of electricity, water, gas, communication, and other essential functions. Vertical shaft engineering has become an integral part of various underground projects such as water conservancy construction, underground mining, and measures for large tunnels, highways, and railway tunnels.

With the increasing demand for vertical shafts, the construction techniques for vertical shafts are constantly evolving. Currently, the drill-and-blast method is widely used in vertical shaft construction due to its mature equipment and high economic efficiency. However, there are problems with construction workers working in harsh environments, such as dampness, high-intensity noise, and dust pollution. Moreover, they may also face hazards such as harmful gas leakage, local collapse, and falling objects at height, which may compromise their safety. In recent years, equipment manufacturing technology has rapidly developed. Particularly with the widespread application of tunnel boring machine construction technology, traditional manual drill-and-blast methods for breaking rock in underground mines have gradually been replaced by mechanical rock drilling or construction methods. The mechanical construction methods for vertical shafts mainly include: (1) the drilling method, in which a vertical drilling machine drills down from the surface to form a well; (2) the inverse drilling method, in which an inverse drilling machine drills forward through a guide hole and backward through an expanded hole to form a vertical shaft; and (3) the full-section excavation method, in which a vertical shaft boring machine (SBM) drills and supports parallel to form a shaft. All three construction methods use a controllable mechanical rock-breaking strategy instead of a drill-and-blast strategy, which is the mainstream direction for the future development of shaft construction.

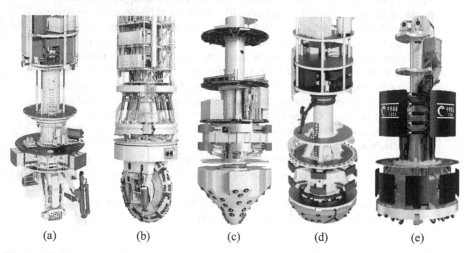

(a)   (b)   (c)   (d)   (e)

Fig. 1. Shaft boring equipment: (a) the shaft boring roadheader, (b) the shaft boring machine, (c) the shaft boring extension machine, (d) the shaft boring cutterhead from Herrenknecht AG [1], (e) the full cross-section hard-rock shaft boring machine from China Railway Engineering Equipment Group Co., Ltd. [2].

As one of the most advanced mechanical excavation equipment at present, the shaft excavation machine has received much attention. Herrenknecht AG [1] from Germany has proposed various feasible solutions for shaft excavation equipment, completed the production of the shaft boring roadheader, as shown in Fig. 1(a), and applied it to the shaft construction of a potassium salt mine. Subsequently, three more designs were presented, called shaft boring machine, shaft boring extension machine, and shaft boring cutterhead, as shown in Fig. 1(b), Fig. 1(c), and Fig. 1(d), all of which were equipped with disc cutters, as opposed to the pencil bits on the SBR. China Railway Engineering Equipment Group Co., Ltd. [2] has constructed a full cross-section hard-rock shaft boring machine, as shown in Fig. 1(e), which was adopted for the construction of a hydropower station in Zhejiang Province of China.

As one of the main components, the support boot mechanism in shaft excavation machines should apply large pressure on the sidewall to provide enough friction for balancing the gravity and boring torque of the shaft boring machine. In this paper, novel support boot mechanisms are presented to output desired pressure along the radial direction of the cylindrical tunnel, as well as to provide steady support during the vertical tunnel construction. To avoid the failure of the support due to the damage to the tunnel surface, the adjusting modules are adopted at the ends of support boots for changing their radial position before development. By being equipped with the presented support boot mechanism and adjusting module, concept designs of two shaft boring machines are provided. This work provides a reference for the structural design and candidates of deployable-module-based support boot mechanisms in shaft boring machines for underground vertical tunnel construction.

2 Structure Design of Support Boot Mechanisms

2.1 Support Boot Mechanisms Based on Deployable Modules

The support boot mechanism is a vital component of a shaft boring machine, which supports and stabilizes underground excavation operations. According to the operational requirements of shaft excavation, the support boot mechanism generally fulfills the following functions: (1) Strong support capacity: It applies substantial pressure on the side wall, generating adequate friction to counterbalance the weight and torque of the excavation machine; (2) Radial adjustment capability: With radial adjustment capability, it enables folding and expansion, providing support for the excavation machine and facilitating their passage through tunnels; (3) Multi-point support feature: By utilizing a design that uniformly distributes support force, it improves the stress state of the wall and prevents collapse.

In recent years, deployable mechanisms [3] have attracted much attention due to their excellent support stiffness and good deformation ability. Given this, the idea of adopting deployable mechanisms is presented to design support boot mechanisms. As two examples, two deployable modules that can be folded and unfolded radially, are shown in Fig. 2 and Fig. 3, respectively. The deployable module in Fig. 2 is based on the scissor mechanisms, while that in Fig. 3 is based on the parallelogram mechanisms. Compared to the deployable module based on scissor mechanisms, that based on the parallelogram mechanisms is more concise, and the rods are not subjected to shear force, resulting in better stress conditions. In addition, it is worth emphasizing that the deployable module based on parallelogram mechanisms can have a large space in the middle, which is beneficial for the slag discharge, material, and personnel transportation of the shaft boring machine. For this purpose, the deployable module based on parallelogram mechanisms is adopted to carry out the design of the support boot mechanism in the shaft boring machine.

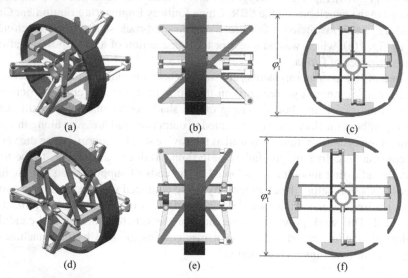

(a)   (b)   (c)

(d)   (e)   (f)

Fig. 2. Deployable module based on scissor mechanisms: (a), (b), (c) folded configurations with the tunnel diameter of φ_1^1, (d), (e), (f) expanded configurations with that of φ_1^2.

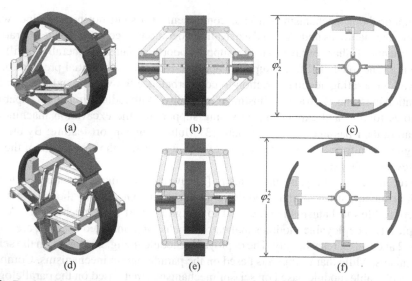

(a)   (b)   (c)

(d)   (e)   (f)

Fig. 3. Deployable module based on parallelogram mechanisms: (a), (b), (c) folded configurations with the tunnel diameter of φ_2^1, (d), (e), (f) expanded configurations with that of φ_2^2.

To avoid the failure of the support due to the damage to the tunnel surface, the adjusting modules are adopted at the ends of support boots for changing their radial position. The concept design of a support boot mechanism with four branches and four adjusting modules is presented in Fig. 4.

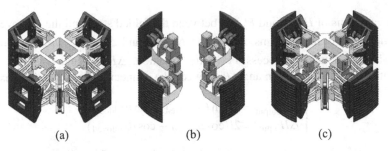

(a)   (b)   (c)

Fig. 4. The support boot mechanism: (a) the deployable module with four branches, (b) four adjusting modules, (c) the support boot unit composed of deployable and adjusting modules.

2.2 Kinematics and Statics of Support Boot Mechanism

The kinematics should be conducted to achieve the relationship between the output motion of the support boots and the input of the actuation, and thus realize the motion control of the support boot mechanisms. The mechanism schematic of the support boot mechanisms is presented in Fig. 5. A coordinate system is established with the y-axis being along with the symmetric axis of the support boot mechanisms, and the x-axis passes the upper end of the actuation of the deployable module E_1. Suppose that the inputs of the actuation of the deployable module and the adjusting module are H_{input} and D_{input}, respectively; the output motion of the support boot mechanisms is R_{output}. Suppose that the distance between the y-axis and revolute joint A_1 or A_4 is r; the distance between revolute joint A_3 and its symmetrical revolute joint A_2 along the y-axis is h_1; the distance between revolute joint A_4 and point E_1 along the y-axis is h_2.

According to the geometric constraints of the deployable module, the output motion of the deployable module is marked as R and should satisfy

$$R = 0.5\sqrt{4l^2 - \left(H_{input} - h_1 - 2h_2\right)^2} + r \tag{1}$$

Therefore, the relationship between the input motion of the actuation and the output motion of the support boot mechanisms R_{output} should satisfy

$$R^i_{output} = D^i_{input} + R = D^i_{input} + 0.5\sqrt{4l^2 - \left(H_{input} - h_1 - 2h_2\right)^2} + r \tag{2}$$

The first-order differentiation of H_{input}, D_{input}, and R_{output} can be written as

$$\dot{R}^i_{output} = \dot{D}^i_{input} - \frac{H_{input} - h_1 - 2h_2}{2\sqrt{4l^2 - \left(H_{input} - h_1 - 2h_2\right)^2}}\dot{H}_{input} \tag{3}$$

The second-order differentiation of H_{input}, D^i_{input}, and R^i_{output} can be written as

$$\ddot{R}^i_{output} = \ddot{D}^i_{input} - \frac{H_{input} - h_1 - 2h_2}{2\sqrt{4l^2 - (H_{input} - h_1 - 2h_2)^2}}\ddot{H}_{input} - \frac{4l^2}{2\left[4l^2 - (H_{input} - h_1 - 2h_2)^2\right]^{1.5}}\dot{H}^2_{input}$$

(4)

The variations of H_{input} and R^i_{output} between the folded state and the deployed state of the support boot mechanisms, marked as ΔH_{input} and ΔR^i_{output}, are the main concern during the actuation process. For better intuition, ΔH_{input} and ΔR^i_{output} can be represented by the intersection angle θ between the connection rods and the y-axis as

$$\begin{cases} \Delta R^i_{output} = l\left(\sin\theta_{deployed} - \sin\theta_{folded}\right) \\ \Delta H_{input} = 2l\left(\cos\theta_{folded} - \cos\theta_{deployed}\right) \end{cases}$$

(5)

where $\theta_{deployed}$ and θ_{folded} represent θ at the folded state and the deployed state of the support boot mechanisms, respectively. Given that $\Delta R^i_{output} = 0.1$ m, the calculation results of ΔH_{input} when $\theta_{deployed}$ and l are different are presented in Fig. 6. According to the calculation results, the required variation of the actuation input ΔH_{input} can be reduced by selecting smaller $\theta_{deployed}$ and shorter lengths of connecting rods, i.e., shorter l.

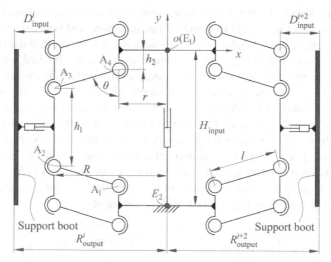

Fig. 5. The mechanism schematic and geometric parameters of the support boot mechanisms.

The statics should be conducted to achieve the relationship between the output force of the support boots and the input of the actuation, so that the required force from the actuation system can be determined to provide steady support during the construction. Meanwhile, the static analysis can serve as the basis of the structural design. As shown in Fig. 7(a), the adjusting modules are locked during the construction process. The output force of the support boots is provided by the actuation of the deployable module. Suppose that the input of the actuation system is F_{input}; the required output force of the support boots is F_{output}; the produced friction from the support boots is f_{output}; the force born by the connecting rods is F_1, F_2, F_3, and F_4, from bottom to top.

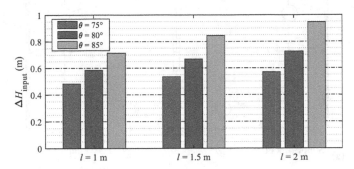

Fig. 6. The calculation results of ΔH_{input} when $\theta_{deployed}$ and l are different.

The intersection angle θ between the connection rods and the y-axis is one of the key parameters during the static analysis. According to the force balance of the support boot mechanisms, the concerned force including F_{input}, $(F_1 + F_2)$, and $(F_3 + F_4)$ should satisfy

$$\begin{cases} F_{output} = (F_1 + F_2 + F_3 + F_4)\sin\theta \\ f_{output} = (-F_1 - F_2 + F_3 + F_4)\cos\theta \\ F_{input} = (F_3 + F_4)k\cos\theta \end{cases} \tag{6}$$

Suppose that F_{output} and f_{output} are determined. Then, F_{input}, $(F_1 + F_2)$, and $(F_3 + F_4)$ can be written as

$$\begin{cases} F_{input} = \frac{k}{2\tan\theta}F_{output} + \frac{k}{2}f_{output} \\ (F_1 + F_2) = \frac{1}{2\sin\theta}F_{output} - \frac{1}{2\cos\theta}f_{output} \\ (F_3 + F_4) = \frac{1}{2\sin\theta}F_{output} + \frac{1}{2\cos\theta}f_{output} \end{cases} \tag{7}$$

where k represents the number of the support boots of the mechanisms.

Given that $k = 4$, $F_{output} = 10000$ kN, and $f_{output} = 2500$ kN, F_{input}, $(F_1 + F_2)$, and $(F_3 + F_4)$ when θ is different are presented in Fig. 7(b). With the rise of θ, F_{input} decreases and thus the input force of the actuation system can be smaller. Besides, the larger value between $(F_1 + F_2)$ and $(F_3 + F_4)$ dramatically increases when θ approaches 90°. Therefore, the connecting rods should be sturdier to bear the external loads. An appropriate θ should be selected as the working angle of the support boot mechanisms to balance the actuation selection and structural design. According to Fig. 7(b), the working angle is approximately taken as an integer of 80°.

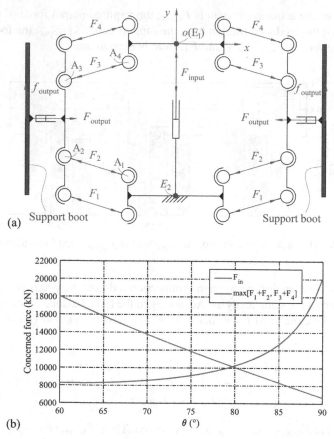

Fig. 7. The static analysis of the support boot mechanisms: (a) the mechanism schematic and concerned force; (b) the calculation results of the concerned force.

3 Integrated Shaft Boring Machine

3.1 Adjustment Device Based on the 3-RPS Parallel Mechanism

In the 3-RPS parallel mechanism, all three kinematic chains are driven by prismatic joints, enabling the mechanism to achieve two-dimensional rotation within the plane of the moving platform and one-dimensional translation along the z-axis. The schematic diagram of the 3-RPS parallel mechanism is shown in Fig. 8(a), where points O and O' represent the centers of the base and the moving platform, respectively. The radii of the base and the moving platform are denoted as R_b and R_p, respectively, and the initial distance between the base and the moving platform is Z. Global coordinate system $\{O\text{-}xyz\}$ and moving coordinate system $\{O'\text{-}x'y'z'\}$ are established at points O and O', respectively. In addition, the x-axis and x'-axis are along with B_3O and P_3O', respectively.

Due to the structural constraints at the revolute joints, the kinematic chain B_iP_i will always remain perpendicular to its respective revolute axis. As a result, the moving platform generates the parasitic motion along the x-axis and y-axis. Let the coordinates of the center point O' of the moving platform in the global coordinate system $\{O\text{-}xyz\}$ be (x, y, z). The parasitic motion of the 3-RPS parallel mechanism can be expressed as:

$$x = \frac{R_p}{2}\cos 2\alpha(1 - \cos\beta), \text{ and } y = -\frac{R_p}{2}\sin 2\alpha(1 - \cos\beta) \tag{8}$$

where α and β represent tilt and torsion angles of the moving platform respectively by using the description of T&T angles. To evaluate the local motion/force transmission and constraint performance of the mechanism comprehensively, the minimum values among ITI, OTI, ICI, and OCI are defined as the local transmission and constraint index (LTCI) [4]. Furthermore, the set of poses that satisfy LTCI ≥ 0.7 is defined as the good transmission and constraint workspace (GTCW). Within the GTCW, there is a maximum inscribed circular region ς ($0 \leq \alpha \leq 2\pi$ and $0 \leq \beta \leq \beta_{\max}$), where $\beta_{\max}$ is defined as the maximum orientation capacity (MOC). To evaluate the global transmission and constraint performance of the mechanism within the maximum inscribed circular region ζ, the average value of LTCI within this region is defined as the global transmission and constraint index (GTCI), which is expressed as follows:

$$\text{GTCI} = \iint_\zeta \text{LTCI}\, d\alpha d\beta \bigg/ \iint_\zeta d\alpha d\beta \tag{9}$$

Based on MOC and GTCI, dimensional optimization of the 3-RPS parallel mechanism can be carried out. The parameters to be optimized include R_p, R_b, and Z, which is the distance between point O' and plane O along the z-axis. If R_p is selected as the normalization factor, under the design requirements, the range of these parameters is given as $R_b/R_p \in [0.5, 2]$, $Z/R_p \in [0.5, 2]$.

The distributions of MOC and GTCI of the 3-RPS parallel mechanism are presented in Fig. 8(b) and Fig. 8(c), respectively. The region with MOC $\geq 30°$ and GTCI ≥ 0.9 is selected as the optimal region, as shown in Fig. 8(d). In this optimal region, a set of parameters is derived as $R_b/R_p = 0.8$, $Z/R_p = 1.1$. The values of performance indices are MOC $= 34°$, GTCI $= 0.9264$. Considering the size of the tool disk connected to the moving platform, R_p is set to 3600 mm. Consequently, the optimal parameters for the mechanism are determined as $R_p = 3600$ mm, $R_b = 2880$ mm, and $Z = 3960$ mm. Under the optimal parameters, the distributions of the GTCW and MOC of the 3-RPS parallel mechanism are illustrated in Fig. 9. It can be observed that the mechanism exhibits the best orientation capability at $\alpha = 0°$, $\alpha = 120°$, and $\alpha = 240°$. In this case, the MOC approximately reaches $35.5°$, which means the 3-RPS parallel mechanism obtains the orientation capacity of $35.5°$ in any direction with a minimum index value 0.7 of the motion/force transmission and constraint performance.

3.2 Concept Designs of Shaft Boring Machines

By equipped with the presented support boot mechanism and adjusting device, two concept designs of shaft boring machines are presented in Fig. 10 and Fig. 11. Their difference is the number of the support boot mechanism. The shaft boring machine in Fig. 11 adopts two support boot mechanisms and an adjustment device based on the

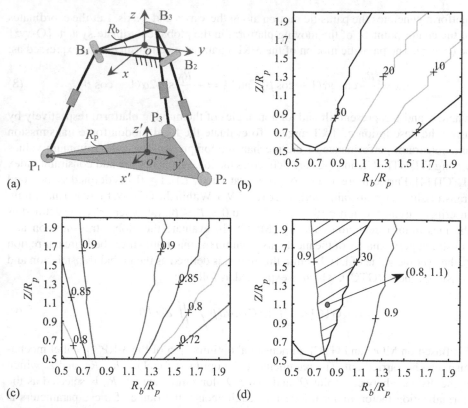

Fig. 8. Dimensional optimization of the 3-RPS parallel mechanism: (a) the schematic diagram, (b) the MOC atlas, (c) the GTCI atlas, (d) the optimal design region.

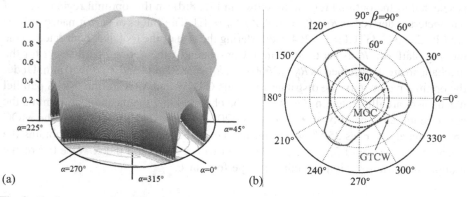

Fig. 9. Performance atlas of the 3-RPS parallel mechanism: (a) the distribution of the LTCI, and (b) the distributions of the GTCW and MOC.

3-RPS parallel mechanism. The upper support boot mechanism is connected with the central column through the advancement mechanism. The lower support boot mechanism is solidly connected to the central column. Meanwhile, the lower support boot mechanism is connected to the boring head through the adjustment device.

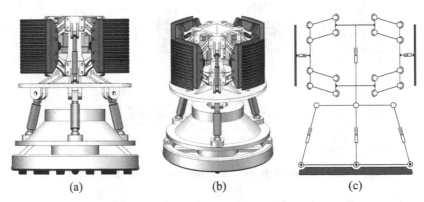

Fig. 10. The concept design of the shaft boring machine with one support boot mechanism: (a) the front view, (b) a view between the front and top views, and (c) the schematic diagram.

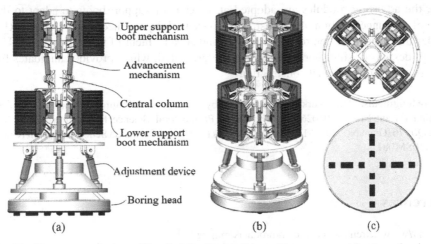

Fig. 11. The concept design of the shaft boring machine with one support boot mechanism: (a) the front view, (b) a view between the front and top views, and (c) two top views.

During the advancement process, the two support boot mechanisms can provide steady support to resist the gravity of this proposed shaft boring machine and the reaction torque from the boring head. The adjustment device can realize the forward movement and pose adjustment of the boring head during the boring process. Meanwhile, the adjustment device can coordinate with the advancement mechanism to conduct the advancement of the whole shaft boring machine. The diagram of this advancement process of the whole shaft boring machine is presented in Fig. 12.

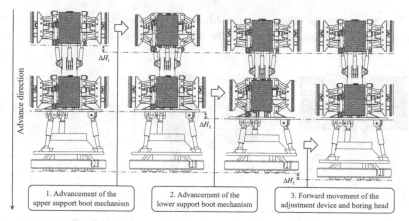

Fig. 12. The process diagram of the advancement of the whole shaft boring machine.

4 Conclusion

In this paper, novel support boot mechanisms are presented based on deployable modules. Then, the adjusting modules are adopted at the ends of support boots to adapt to the shape of the tunnel section. An adjustment device is also presented based on the 3-RPS parallel mechanism to control the direction and advancement of the boring head. The concept designs of shaft boring machines are presented, which provide candidates for underground vertical tunnel construction.

Acknowledgments. This work was supported by the National Natural Science Foundation of China (Grant No. 52105026) and the China Postdoctoral Science Foundation (Grant No. 2021TQ0176, Grant No. 2021M701885), as well as the Shuimu Tsinghua Scholar Program (Grant No. 2020SM081).

References

1. https://www.herrenknecht.com/en/products/mining
2. https://www.crectbm.com/product-detail/7588/334.html
3. Meng, Q., Liu, X.-J., Xie, F.: Structure design and kinematic analysis of a class of ring truss deployable mechanisms for satellite antennas based on novel basic units. Mech. Mach. Theory **174**, 104881 (2022)
4. Chong, Z., et al.: Design of the parallel mechanism for a hybrid mobile robot in wind turbine blades polishing. Robot. Cim.-Int. Manuf. **61**, 101857 (2020)

Development and Application of Rectangular Tunneling Boring Machine for Trenchless Urban Rail Transit Station Construction

Chengjie Zhang[✉]

Shanghai Urban Construction Tunnel Equipment Co., Ltd., Shanghai, China
zhangchengjie@stecmc.com

Abstract. Urban rail transit stations usually use the open excavation method for construction, which requires the installation of supporting structures, pipeline relocation, and other processes. The construction involves a large amount of work, site requirements, difficulty, and long construction period. This article relies on the construction project of Jing'an Temple Station on shanghai rail transit line 14, and innovatively develops rectangular excavation equipment that is applied to the construction of station platform layer and station hall layer underground excavation in response to the significant environmental impact and complex geological conditions of the project located in the core urban area. And elaborate on its many key adaptive technologies and provides reference methods for the construction of stations using excavation equipment underground excavation method in complex strata.

Keyword: Subway Station · Trenchless · Innovation · Key Technologies · Rectangular Tunneling Machine

1 Backgroud

1.1 Project Introduction

Jing'an Temple Station is the core part of the Civil Engineering Section 9 of shanghai rail transit line 14, located below Huashan Road at the intersection of Huashan Road and Yan'an Middle Road. It is an underground three story island platform station, forming a three line transfer hub with the completed and open Jing'an Temple Station of Line 2 and Line 7. As shown in Fig. 1, Channel B connects the main structures A and C, with a tunnel depth of 4.6 m in the station hall layer and 15.2 m in the platform layer. The vertical distance between the platform layer and the station hall layer is 5.4 m, and the distance between the two platform layers is 2 m. The distance between the east line tunnel and the elevated pile foundation is 5.6 m, and the distance between the west line tunnel and the elevated pile foundation is 6.3 m.

H. Yang et al. (Eds.): ICIRA 2023, LNAI 14272, pp. 131–141, 2023.
https://doi.org/10.1007/978-981-99-6480-2_11

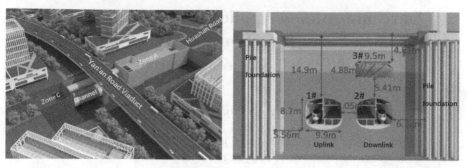

Fig. 1. Schematic diagram of Jing'an Temple Station project on Shanghai Line 14

1.2 Surrounding Environment

The Jing'an Temple Station of Line 14 is located in the gathering area of living and business areas, adjacent to building facilities. Surrounding buildings are arranged along both sides of Huashan Road. From south to north, it is Shanghai International Guidu Hotel, Yan'an Road Elevated Building, and Huide Feng Building. To the east is Lane 229 of Huashan Road, Huashan Greenland, Yan'an Road Elevated Building, Jing'an Park, the main substation of Jing'an Temple Station of Line 2, and Yimei Square.

As shown in Fig. 2, the station crosses the elevated Yan'an Road. Due to its close proximity to the elevated bridge pier, construction may cause disturbance to the pier. The construction of the station mainly involves Huashan Road, which runs in a north-south direction with a width of about 22.8 m and is equipped with 7 lanes in both directions, resulting in heavy daily traffic.

There are various specifications of water supply and drainage, communication, power, gas and other pipelines buried within a range of 1 m to 3 m below the ground level along the station, with a complex distribution.

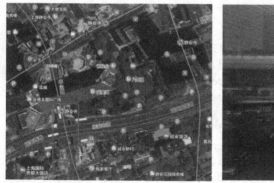

Fig. 2. Surrounding environment of Jing'an Temple Station on Line 14

1.3 Geological and Hydrological Conditions

According to geological survey data, the soil for crossing the station hall layer is mainly composed of ③ gray silty clay and ④ gray muddy clay. The soil for crossing the platform layer is mainly composed of ④ gray muddy clay, ⑤$_{1-1}$ Gy clay, and ⑤$_{1-2}$ Gy silty clay.

Groundwater mainly consists of phreatic water stored in shallow soil layers, micro confined water in the ⑤$_2$ layer, confined water in the ⑦$_{2-1}$ and ⑦$_{2-2}$ layers, and confined water in the ⑨ layer. Below the bottom plate of the engineering structure, there is a confined aquifer of sandy silt, with abundant water supply [1] and the buried depth of the water head is 6.85 m.

If the open excavation method is used for the construction of the station in this project, both Yan'an Road and Huashan Road will need to reduce several lanes, which will bring more severe challenges to the already congested traffic. The pipeline will need to be relocated 5 times in total, causing significant disturbance to the surrounding environment and buildings, making it difficult to control. The total open excavation period is expected to be 70 months, which increases the difficulty of the project and cannot meet the requirements of the project nodes.

After comparing and studying the schemes, it was decided to design a rectangular tunneling machine to excavate the station hall and platform layers using the concealed excavation process [2].

2 Research on Rectangular Pipe Jacking Machine for Platform and Hall Layers

2.1 9.93 m × 8.73 m Rectangular Tunneling Machine Used for Platform Floor Construction

See Fig. 3.

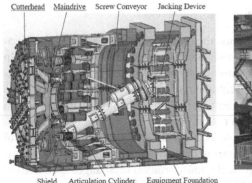

Fig. 3. 9.93 m × 8.73 m earth pressure balanced rectangular tunneling machine

2.2 9.54 m × 4.91 m Rectangular Tunneling Machine Used for Hall Floor Construction

See Fig. 4.

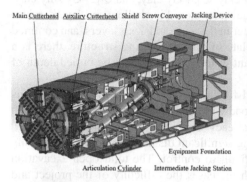

Fig. 4. 9.54 m × 4.91 m earth pressure balanced rectangular tunneling machine

9.93 m × 8.73 and 9.54 m × 4.91 m earth pressure balanced rectangular tunneling machineis are respectively developed for the adaptability of the section size of the platform floor and the hall floor of Jing'an Temple Station [3], and its structure is mainly composed of the combined cutter head, main drive, hinge, screw machine, jacking device (top ring, U-shaped iron, oil cylinder support, steel backrest) and rear supporting power control system. In addition to differences in cross-sectional dimensions, there are also differences in the form of the cutterhead, shell structure, hinge correction device, and rear supporting system between the two devices, but their working principles are basically similar.

3 Key Adaptability and Innovative Technologies

3.1 Multiform Combined Cutterhead

For the section of the platform and hall floors, the traditional tunnel excavation equipment with a single circular cutter head can no longer meet the cutting requirements. In this project, multiple forms of combined cutter heads are used. 9.93 m × 8.73 m rectangular tunnel boring machine adopts the central circular main cutter head + eccentric multi axis auxiliary cutterhead combined cutterhead [4]. The combination of the two can achieve 100% full section cutting, which can not only ensure the construction efficiency, but also give consideration to the construction accuracy and left and right corner control sensitivity. At the same time, due to the diameter of the cutterhead reaches 9.93 m, it cannot meet the width requirements for large-scale transportation in Shanghai. Therefore, the central cutterhead adopts a block combination design. 9.54 m × 4.91 m rectangular tunnel boring machine adopts a combined cutter head of circular main cutter head + circular auxiliary cutter head. The circular cutter head has the advantages of wide adaptability to geological conditions, strong support stability for the excavation face, good settlement control, high cutting efficiency, reliable performance, etc. [5] (Fig. 5).

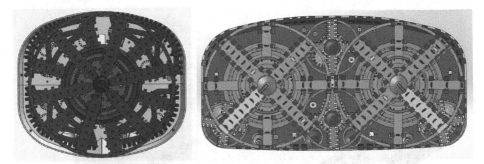

Fig. 5. Combined cutterhead of rectangular tunneling machine

3.2 Modular Shell with Large Aspect Ratio

The design length and width of the rectangular tunnel boring machine used for hall floor construction is 9.54 m × 4.91 m due to the segment ring section, the load on the front shell is mainly divided into two parts [6]. The first part is the external soil and water pressure, and the second part is the self gravity and soil pressure of the installed components inside the shell. According to the actual construction conditions of the project, the downward water and soil pressure borne by the top of the shell is 102.8 kN/m^2, the lateral water and soil pressure at the top is 71.96 kN/m^2, the upward water and soil pressure at the bottom is 233.49 kN/m^2, and the lateral water and soil pressure at the bottom is 133.83 kN/m^2. By using finite element simulation software to model and simulate the shell, a stress-strain cloud diagram can be obtained as shown in Fig. 7. From the simulation results, it can be seen that the maximum stress of the shell structure (material Q345) is located at the position of the reinforcement plate on the driving installation side, which is 285 MPa, and the maximum strain is 5.2 mm, meets the design and construction requirements (Fig. 6).

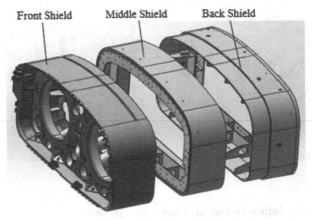

Front Shield   Middle Shield   Back Shield

Fig. 6. Large aspect ratio shell of rectangular tunneling machine

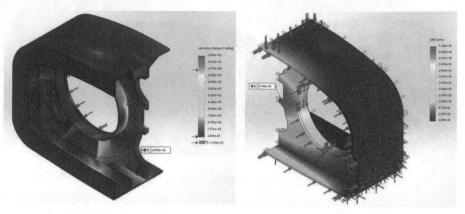

Fig. 7. Finite Element Simulation Model of Large Aspect Ratio Shell

3.3 Intensive Jacking Device

As shown in Fig. 8, the jacking device mainly consists of a base, top ring, U-shaped ring, jacking oil cylinder, and fixed frame, with a compact structure. The cylinder body of the jacking oil cylinder is installed on a fixed frame, and the end of the piston rod is connected to a U-shaped ring. Through the U-shaped ring, 16 cylinders with a maximum jacking force of 40000 kN are transmitted to the top ring, pipe joint, and the front host to complete tunnel excavation construction. When design the various components of the jacking device, while fully consider the processing and installation process of the components, its size and detachable structure meet the requirements of equipment lifting and transportation.

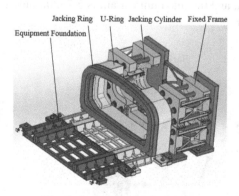

Fig. 8. Intensive jacking device

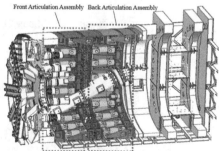

Fig. 9. Double Articulation deviation correction device

3.4 Double Articulation Deviation Correction Device

In response to the difficulties of shallow soil cover and close spacing between the upper and lower tunnels of the platform and hall floors in this project, in order to improve the deviation correction control ability of the tunneling machine, an articulated relay room with active hinge function is added at the rear of the rear shell [7], forming a double hinge (deviation correction) function with the front host hinge device, as shown in Fig. 9, which increases the deviation correction ability and flexibility. Compared with a single articulated tunneling machine, the use of a double articulated device can achieve a smaller deviation correction angle, and the sealing pressure of the articulated device is also smaller, adapting to variable working conditions and improving safety [8].

3.5 Multiform Combined Articulation Seal

Due to its unique structural shape design, rectangular tunneling machines have a higher risk of leakage in their articulated positions compared to circular tunneling machines. Therefore, in the design of the rectangular tunneling machine in this project, the main seal adopts three reinforced toothed sealing rings. In addition to the traditional main seal, a slurry baffle is added to the rear side for protection. Through engineering practice, this slurry baffle can effectively block mud, sand, and slurry, providing good protection for the joint seal. In addition, an emergency sealing device is also equipped. When an emergency situation occurs and the hinge seal leaks, the emergency sealing airbag is quickly inflated through the inflation nozzle. The inflated airbag can establish a temporary seal, improving the reliability of the hinge seal in this project with high groundwater level and pressurized water conditions, the design structure is shown in Fig. 10.

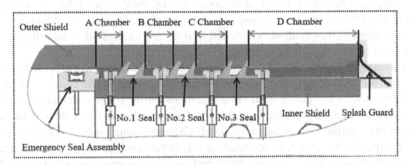

Fig. 10. Multiform combined articulation seal

3.6 High Precision Automatic Fill Friction Reduction System

Design a high-precision automatic fill friction reducing system, as shown in Fig. 11. There are holes for adding friction reducing slurry around the shell. During the excavation of the tunneling machine, the friction reducing slurry is automatically discharged from the filling port (based on flow and pressure feedback) by the system, forming a uniform slurry sleeve around the shell, avoiding direct contact between the shell and the soil, reducing friction and disturbance to the soil, and avoiding the occurrence of the shell's "back soil" phenomenon, it has achieved good results in settlement control.

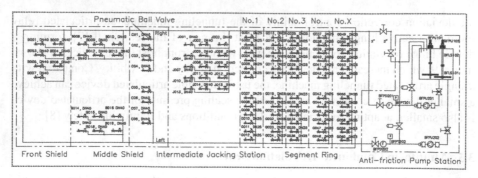

Fig. 11. Schematic diagram of automatic fill friction reduction system

3.7 Status Monitoring and Health Assessment System

3.7.1 Health Assessment of Shield Tunneling Machine Cutterhead Based on T-SNE Data-Driven Model

As the core component of shield tunneling equipment, the health status of the cutter-head directly affects the safety and progress of engineering construction. Aiming at the traditional evaluation method based on cutter head failure mechanism, which to some extent depends on the complex structural problems of the actual working conditions and shield equipment, this paper proposes a health evaluation method for the cutter head of shield equipment based on T-SNE data driven model, establishes a data driven model for cutter head health evaluation, and uses actual engineering data validation to verify the effectiveness of this method, which can analyze and evaluate the cutter head health status in real time in actual engineering.

Considering that in the actual driving process, when the tool is worn, the reduction of cutting performance of the cutter head will cause the change of the cutter head driving parameters such as the cutter head speed, penetration degree and driving speed, and the related performance parameters of the drive motor will also fluctuate to balance the change of the external load of the cutter head. Therefore, nine kinds of parameters such as driving speed, total thrust, cutter head torque, cutter head speed, penetration degree, motor speed, motor torque, specific thrust and specific torque are selected for analysis in each ring driving process of shield machine. The deviation degree between high-dimensional sample data and baseline data is characterized by Mahalanobis distance MD [9]. The larger the MD, the more serious the deviation from the normal state of the equipment. Otherwise, the equipment is in good working state, so the MD reflects the working state performance of the equipment. Figure 12 shows that the distance fluctuations in the Markov space of samples under normal and fault repair conditions are relatively small, while the distance fluctuations in the decay domain samples are relatively large. The trend is consistent with the actual situation, indicating that the performance changes of the cutterhead are well measured in the Markov space.

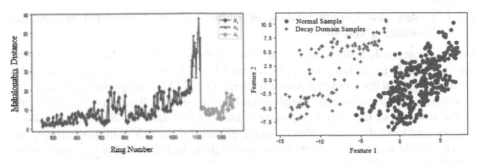

Fig. 12. Markov space metrics and T-SNE low dimensional feature distribution maps

3.7.2 Real Time Prediction of Shield Tunneling Machine Cutterhead Torque Based on Long-term and Short-term Memory Network

The torque of the cutterhead is an important guarantee for shield tunneling construction, and timely and accurate prediction of torque helps to provide warnings before faults occur and avoid major accidents. LSTM is a special case of Recurrent Neural Network (RNN), mainly to solve the problem of "gradient disappearance" in the training process, and is the most widely used RNN architecture. A real-time prediction model for shield tunneling machine cutter head torque based on LSTM network was proposed and constructed [10], parameters such as cutterhead torque and current were used for variable detection, the objective function was used for training and testing the LSTM model, the mean square error (MSE) was used to evaluate the final prediction results, and the average absolute error (MAE) was used for performance evaluation indicators. Through correlation analysis, the key state parameters of predicted torque include the pressure of the propulsion cylinder, the given propulsion speed of the propulsion cylinder, the actual speed of the cutter head and the given speed, and the front earth pressure. Batch processing was carried out every 100 moments during the construction of tunnel boring machine, and perform 50 times, as shown in Fig. 13, the prediction model based on LSTM network always maintains a small average absolute error in the entire training set, with an average absolute error of 0.0367, which can well fit the nonlinear relationship between the key state parameters and the cutter head torque [11], accurately predict the torque of the cutterhead shield machine, with high prediction accuracy.

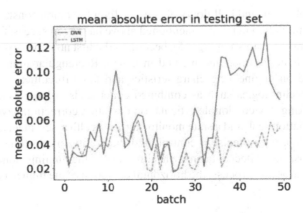

Fig. 13. MAE every 100 moments on the LSTM and BP network test set

3.7.3 Design and Implementation of Industrial Cloud Platform and Status Monitoring System

Design a reasonable architecture for the project to build a shield machine status monitoring cloud platform, as shown in Fig. 14, use the MELSEC protocol as the communication protocol between the industrial personal computer and PLC, design the hardware composition, software architecture, database architecture and the functions of each module of the software of the monitoring system, and compile the software that can collect, display, and store the torque, thrust, speed, propulsion speed Monitoring software for various shield tunneling machine status information, including screw machine torque, and finally monitoring the entire system in actual construction environments.

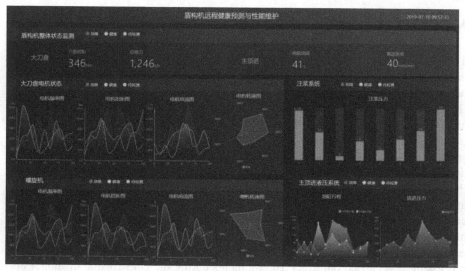

Fig. 14. Tunnel boring machine remote monitoring and health status perception interface diagram

4 Conclusion

At present, the platform and hall floors of Jing'an Temple Station constructed using the two rectangular tunneling machines mentioned above have been successfully completed and put into operation (shown in Fig. 15), becoming the first non open excavation station built using the tunneling machine method in China. Rectangular tunneling machines developed based on engineering characteristics and key difficulties, with a series of innovative key technologies such as combined cutterheads, a large aspect ratio shell, an intensive jacking device, double articulation deviation correction device, multiform combined articulation seal, and a state monitoring and health assessment cloud platform, has high reliability, high-precision control, and the ability to real-time warn, control, correct deviations, and collect data on the health status of the running tunneling machine. In the actual construction process, the horizontal deviation of the tunnel axis is −8 mm ~

+9 mm, and the elevation deviation is −12 mm ~ +10 mm, effectively controlled ground settlement and ensured the normal transportation of the traffic artery (Yan'an Elevated Line), avoided many foreseeable and unforeseeable problems and hidden dangers in open-cut construction and solved the three major problems of underground engineering in the central urban area that cannot be placed, dismantled, or touched, providing a new construction method for the trenchless construction of urban rail transit stations, while also improving the competitive level of independent research and development of tunnel excavation equipment in China.

Fig. 15. Construction drawings for platform and hall floors of Jing'an Temple Station on Line 14

References

1. Zhang, R.: Key techniques for construction of super large cross section rectangular pipe jacking in soft and rich water strata. Construct. Techniq. **47**(S1), 723–727 (2018)
2. Xiong, C.: Application of large section rectangular top pipe in urban underground pedestrian passages. Life Disast. **S1**, 76–79 (2009)
3. Zhao, J.: Construction technology of shallow buried and concealed excavation method for urban street crossing. Shanghai Tunnel **1**, 16–20 (2015)
4. Lu, J., Shi, Y., Lou, R.: Design and application of eccentric multi axis pipe jacking machine for large section rectangular tunnel in Shanghai tunnel. Shanghai Construct. Sci. Technol. **2**, 16–18 (2004)
5. Wu, L., Li, X.: Research on the evaluation method for the excavation performance of shield tunneling cutterhead system. Mod. Tunnel. Technol. **5**, 108–114 (2017)
6. Zhang, C.: Anti-deformation control of shield tail of large section quasi-rectangular shield machine. Shanghai Tunnel **1**, 115–122 (2018)
7. Li, Q., Yu, X.: Application of active articulation system in shield tunneling attitude adjustment. Traffic Eng. Technol. Natl. Defence **9**, 68–72 (2011)
8. Sun, Y., Liu, C.: Deviation and torsion correction technology for long distance and large diameter pipe jacking construction. Railway Standard Technol. **3**, 24–27 (2003)
9. Zhao, S., Huang, Y., Wang, H.: Laplacian eigenmaps and mahalanobis distance based health assessment methodology for ball screw. J. Mech. Eng. **53**(15), 125–130 (2017)
10. Ling, J., Sun, W., Yang, X.: Analysis of stress intensity factors for a TBM cutterhead crack incomplex stress states. J. Harbin Eng.Univ. **38**(4), 633–639 (2017).
11. Xia, Y., Bian, Z., Hu, C.: Performance comprehensive evaluation of composite earth pressure balanced shield machine cutterhead. J. Mech. Eng. **50**(21), 1–9 (2014)

The Gordian-Innovation Technology and Recent Construction Application of Special-Shaped Tunnel Boring Machine

Yuanqi Shi[✉]

Shanghai Urban Construction Tunnel Equipment Co., Ltd., Shanghai, China
zhangchengjie@stecmc.com

Abstract. Underground space resources in urban construction are increasingly scarce, but at present, tunnels are mostly circular sections that occupy more underground space. Compared with traditional circular sections, special-shaped sections adapted to various functions can save tunnel space and realize shallow soil covering construction. Using tunnel boring machine to construct special-shaped section tunnels is an important means to solve such problems. How to solve the two key technologies of special-shaped full-section cutting and special-shaped segment assembly, and the development and practical engineering application of special-shaped tunnel-boring machines with high precision control and the characteristics of special-shaped boring machine and pipe Jacking inter-conversion, etc., are increasingly urgent. Based on the author's more than ten years of research and experience, this paper expounds the advanced technology of the special-shaped section tunnel boring machine applied not only to the construction of pedestrian, rail traffic and vehicle tunnels, but also to the construction of subway stations and crossing sections.

Keywords: Special-shaped Tunnel Boring Machine · Inter-conversion of Special-shaped Tunnel Shield Machine and Pipe Jacking · Full Section Cutting · Special-shaped Segment Assembly

1 Background

With the gradual development of urban underground space, the available underground space has become less and less, especially the shallow underground space in the core area of megacities is seriously saturated, so it is urgent to find effective means of underground engineering development to save urban underground space.

The double track subway tunnel uses two single round tunnels to form a maximum width of at least 18 m (Fig. 1). When the road surface width is less than 18 m, houses will be demolished. If the single round large diameter shield is used, the section is wasteful (Fig. 2), the burial depth is deep, and the section utilization rate is low, however, the rectangular section tunnel, due to its good section space utilization rate and its outstanding environmental protection advantages under the limited space (such as the core old urban area of the city, etc.), it has become an inevitable choice to solve the

© The Author(s), under exclusive license to Springer Nature Singapore Pte Ltd. 2023
H. Yang et al. (Eds.): ICIRA 2023, LNAI 14272, pp. 142–151, 2023.
https://doi.org/10.1007/978-981-99-6480-2_12

problem of severely saturated underground space environment utilization. Therefore, research on excavation equipment and related technologies for rectangular or quasi rectangular sections has emerged [1].

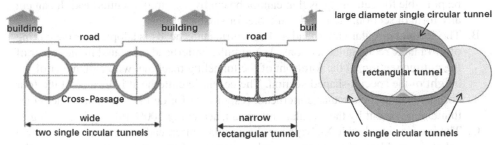

Fig. 1. Comparison of single circular double track and special-shaped double track tunnel

Fig. 2. Comparison of space utilization between single circular tunnel and special-shaped tunnel

For over a century, due to the ease of achieving mechanized full face excavation and lining assembly, and the economic manufacturing of the structure, the vast majority of tunneling machines have a circular cross-section. Compared with the traditional round tunnel boring machine, the development of rectangular tunnel boring machine needs to solve three key technologies: 100% cutting of special-shaped full section, assembly of special-shaped segments, and sealing of special-shaped articulation. According to engineering requirements, special-shaped tunnel boring machines are also divided into two categories: rectangular tunnel boring machine and rectangular pipe jacking machine [2].

2 Special-Shaped Full Section Cutting Technology

The development of special-shaped full section cutting is not achieved overnight. Traditional circular cutterheads have the characteristics of high cutting efficiency and reliability. Eccentric multi axis drive cutterheads use the motion principle of parallel double crank mechanism, and are driven by several sets of eccentric crankshafts simultaneously. Each tool moves in a planar circular motion, the cutting radius is the Radius of gyration of the crankshaft, and the shape of the cutterhead can be designed according to the required cross-sectional shape of the tunnel. The outer contour is designed to imitate the outer contour of a rectangular tunneling machine, So when the eccentric cutterhead rotates, the edge can be well cut along the outer edge of the tunneling machine, combined with the axial propulsion stroke to complete 100% cutting and excavation of the entire section. After more than 20 years of research, combined with the respective advantages of the circular cutterhead and eccentric cutterhead, the only combination of various types of cutterheads in the world has been achieved, which has strong adaptability to geological conditions and has achieved super large section 100% full section cutting.

Currently, there are three commonly used methods for 100% full section cutting of special-shaped sections:

A. The form of circular cutterhead and double eccentric cutterhead is that the circular cutterhead is located in the center of the cutting section, at the forefront of the tunneling machine, with a diameter of the height of the special-shaped section. The eccentric cutterhead is located on both sides behind the circular cutterhead and is responsible for cutting areas that cannot be cut by the circular cutterhead. It can cut any form of section, but is only suitable for small sections.

B. The form of circular cutterhead + 4 eccentric cutterheads is adopted for the cutting of ultra large rectangular sections. The circular cutterhead is located in the center of the cutting section, at the forefront of the tunneling machine, with a diameter of the height of the special-shaped section. The eccentric cutterhead is located at the four corners behind the circular cutterhead, responsible for cutting the four corner areas that cannot be cut by the circular cutterhead, achieving 100% full section cutting.

C. The intersecting double X-shaped spoke circular cutterhead and eccentric cutterhead solve the problem of avoiding mutual interference between two cutterheads on the same plane during operation. It is the first in the world to have synchronous control and correction functions under normal cutting conditions for intersecting double circular cutterheads on the same working surface. For ultra large rectangular sections, the combination of the same plane double X-shaped spoke circular cutterhead and eccentric cutterhead is adopted, The double circular cutterhead and eccentric cutterhead are arranged in staggered layers before and after, and the spoke type cutterhead cuts the maximum area in the rectangular section. The eccentric cutterhead compensates for the part that the circular cutterhead cannot cut, and the quasi rectangular section is cut 100% full section (Figs. 3, 4, 5, 6, and 7).

Fig. 3. Center circle cutterhead + double eccentric cutterheads

Fig. 4. Center circle cutterhead + 4 eccentric cutterheads

Fig. 5. Double X-shaped spoke type circular cutterhead + eccentric cutterhead

3   Multi Degree of Freedom Special-Shaped Boring Machine Segment Assembly Technology with Central Pillar Assembly Function

The traditional circular tunnel segment erector arranges two hydraulically driven lifting arms parallel and symmetrically along a certain radius direction in the rotation plane. It relies on the rotation of the erector around the excavation axis and the expansion and contraction of the lifting arm to achieve the positioning of the segments within the tunnel section. For rectangular tunnels, due to its one tunnel double track design, the segment ring is equipped with a central column to separate the upper and lower lines,

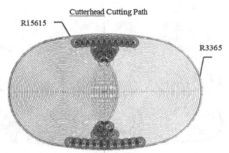

Fig. 6. Physical image of double X-shaped spoke type circular cutterhead and eccentric cutterhead

Fig. 7. Full section cutting trajectory map

and the unequal and significant distance between different segments and the rotation center of the erector, the traditional erector cannot complete the assembly of segments in limited space. The single robotic arm segment erector uses a mechanism similar to the excavator bucket driving arm to achieve the positioning of segments within the tunnel section, which has the characteristics of compact structure and long segment transfer distance. Therefore, it is more suitable for segment assembly in rectangular tunnels and other non circular tunnels.

The assembly of rectangular tunnel segments adopts two hollow axis rotary single arm segment erectors (Fig. 8), which are composed of a rotary system, a translation system, a manipulator system (a swinging mechanical arm system, a robotic arm system, and a segment clamping device). It is the world's first to create a dual machine ring arm segment assembly technology with 6 degrees of freedom, including 1 horizontal section, 5 rotations, and a segment clamping device. The two erectors can operate independently or work together simultaneously. The translation mechanism allows the entire erector to move forward and backward along the supporting cantilever beam through rollers, allowing the erector to move to the segment storage area and insert the sealing block. It is driven by two parallel oil cylinders. The lifting of the pipe segment is controlled by a swinging robotic arm system and a rotating mechanism through a computer program. It also has left and right swinging and front and back swinging mechanisms (the pipe segment swings longitudinally back and forth along the tunnel), and a horizontal swinging mechanism (the pipe segment rotates horizontally) can achieve 90° rotation of the middle column, thereby achieving the assembly of the middle column.

4   Latest Application of Special-Shaped Tunnel Boring Machine

4.1   The World's First Example of Using a Rectangular Tunnel Boring Machine and Pipe Jacking Inter-conversion Equipment Constructs a Subway Turnaround Line Tunnel

The total length of the turnaround line project at Sijiqing Station on Hangzhou Metro Line 9 is 231.1 m, including a 67.2 m long crossover area (shown on the left below Fig. 9). The original plan for the project was to use one 11.83 m × 7.27 m type rectangular shield

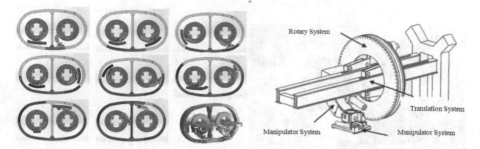

Fig. 8. Erector of special-shaped tunnel boring machine

tunneling machine is used for excavation construction. The crossing section adopts steel pipe segments without columns and is filled with concrete, while other positions use reinforced concrete segments with columns. The crossing section is covered with deep soil (about 11 m deep), and rectangular steel pipe sheets without columns are still being studied. There are no successful applications under deep soil conditions, and the project schedule is also tight. Due to the same inner dimensions of the crossover section and the main section, the main section separates the uplink and downlink, the segment ring is equipped with columns. The uplink and downlink lines of the crossover section have the function of crossing, so the segment lining does not have columns, the crossover section has been changed to tube. Taking advantage of the characteristics of pipe jacking, the inner size remains unchanged, while the outer size is enlarged in parallel (not greater than the outer size of the original rectangular shield body), the thickness of the tube is increased, and the columns are removed (shown on the right below Fig. 9). Therefore, the cross crossover section is constructed using the rectangular pipe jacking method, The remaining parts are constructed using the rectangular shield tunneling method.

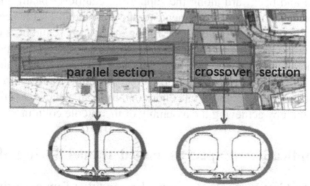

Fig. 9. Construction section of parallel and crossover at Sijiqing Station

According to the needs of the project, through the research on the combination of quasi rectangular shield and rectangular pipe jacking equipment, the key technical problem of inter-conversion between shield and pipe jacking on the same equipment of non-circular special-shaped TBM was solved. This technology can switch between pipe jacking and shield mode according to the needs of the project, effectively improving the engineering adaptability of non-circular special-shaped TBM, while reducing the cost of equipment repeated manufacturing, opening up a new idea for the development of tunnel boring machine.

The project adopts a height of 11.83 m × 7.27 m type rectangular shield machine is remanufactured, and according to the different component structures and propulsion methods of the shield and top pipe, the shield tail is connected to the rear shell in the shield mode, and the adapter ring is connected to the rear shell in the top pipe mode (Fig. 10). In shield tunneling mode, the propulsion cylinder is the propulsion system, while in top pipe mode, the propulsion cylinder is the force transmission support system. During shield tunneling and pipe jacking modes, each has its own independent control room. Therefore, during mode switching, some control systems need to transfer connections from one control room to another. At the same time, individual systems (such as jacking systems and erector systems) are only used in a single mode and connected to the corresponding control room. Complete the 67.2 m top pipe section, install the erector and shield tail, convert it into a shield machine, and resume the shield driving.

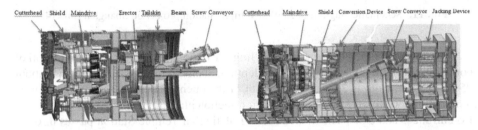

Fig. 10. Rectangular shield and pipe jacking inter-conversion tunneling machine

4.2 The World's First Subway Station Built with a Rectangular Tunnel Boring Machine

The Jing'an Temple Station of Shanghai Metro Line 14 is an underground three story island platform station arranged in a north-south direction along Huashan Road. It is a hub station replaced by Line 2 and Line 7, and the station is elevated across Yan'an Road (Fig. 11). The Yan'an Road Elevated Road is a major thoroughfare in Shanghai, with heavy traffic that cannot be interrupted and numerous underground pipelines. The headroom under the Yan'an Road Elevated Road is only 10 m, which poses challenges in low headroom construction such as underground walls and excavation of foundation pits. Therefore, the construction process of underground excavation needs to be adopted in the elevated area of Jing'an Temple Station on Line 14 to reduce pipeline relocation and avoid road traffic interruption. Therefore, applying the above achievements, in order to adapt to the high environmental requirements of Jing'an Temple located in the center of Shanghai and crossing the elevated Yan'an Road, it is necessary to innovate and develop more advanced platform floor 9.93 m × 8.73 m, station hall floor 9.53 m × 4.91 m rectangular tunnel boring machine with high reliability, high-precision control, full section 100% cutting, and real-time warning and control functions for the health status, under the condition of ensuring the smoothness of the ground roads, three rectangular tunnels in the shape of "品" were constructed by the rectangular underground tunnel boring machine (Fig. 11), and the subway station (including the platform floor and ticket sales floor) was built at one time. This is the first time in the world that the trenchless rectangular pipe jacking method was used to build a subway station.

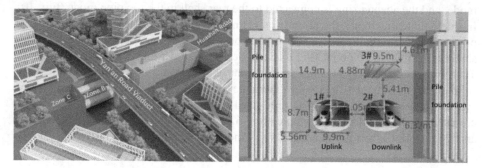

Fig. 11. Schematic diagram of Jing'an Temple Station project on Shanghai Line 14

The top plate of the platform center at Jing'an Temple Station is covered with soil of about 3 m, the bottom plate is buried at a depth of about 24 m, the station length is about 225 m, the net width is 20.54 m, the width of the open excavation section platform is 13 m, and the width of the hidden excavation section platform is 2 × 4.6 m, with a total of 6 entrances and exits. The main structure of Jing'an Temple Station passes through the Yan'an section (zone B in Fig. 11) and is constructed using top pipe concealed excavation. The platform layer adopts two 82 m long sections with a cross-sectional size of 8700 × 9900 mm top pipe tunnel connects the platforms on the north and south sides of Yan'an Road (areas A and C in Fig. 11), and a 82 m long sections with a cross-sectional size of 4880 × 9500 mm is used for the station hall floor pipe jacking tunnel connects the station halls on the north and south sides of Yan'an Road. The buried depth of the top pipe tunnel on the platform floor is 15.17–15.37 m, and four connecting channels are set up. The buried depth of the top pipe tunnel on the station hall floor is 4.84–5.01 m. The single line length of the top pipe section channel is 82 m, the horizontal distance between the two top pipes on the platform layer is 2.0 m, the vertical distance between the platform layer and the station hall layer is 5.4 m, the soil cover on the top pipe on the station hall layer is 4.6 m, and the soil cover on the top pipe on the platform layer is 15.2 m.

To achieve this project, three major difficulties must be addressed:

Difficulty 1: high requirements for settlement control and the need to solve the problem of special-shaped full section cutting;
Difficulty 2: Narrow site, high-precision small block design, manufacturing, lifting, and installation of super large and special-shaped section tunneling machines;

Difficulty 3: Research on the excavation technology inside the soil chamber of a 9.53 m × 4.91 m large aspect ratio rectangular section tunneling machine.

In view of difficulty 1, combined with the engineering geological conditions and engineering conditions of Jing'an Temple Station, from the comprehensive comparison of the full cutting rectangular section, the support of the excavation face, the stratum adaptability, the control performance of left and right corners, the total power equipped, and the price, it is decided to select a rectangular tunnel boring machine with a round cutterhead + 4 eccentric multi axis cutterheads (Fig. 12). The main cutterhead is located in the center of the cutting section, the front end of the tunnel boring machine, and the eccentric cutterhead is located at the rear side of the large cutterhead, the four corners on the front of the rectangular tunneling machine are responsible for cutting areas that cannot be cut by the large cutterhead. The contour of the eccentric cutterhead is designed to imitate the outer edge contour of the rectangular tunneling machine, so when the eccentric cutterhead rotates, the edge can be cut well along the outer edge of the tunneling machine, achieving 100% full section cutting (Fig. 13).

Fig. 12. Central cutterhead + 4 eccentric multi axis combined cutterhead

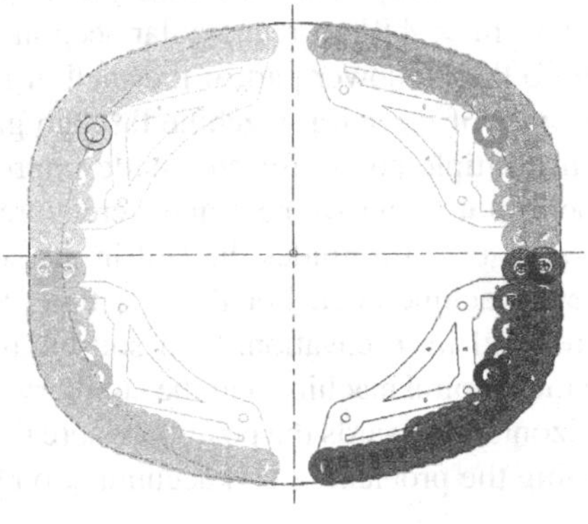

Fig. 13. Full section cutting trajectory map

In response to difficulty 2, we have solved the high-precision small block design, manufacturing, lifting, and installation of super large cross-section pipe jacking, with a height of 9.93 m × 8.73 m rectangular tunneling machine shell can be divided into a front shell and a rear shell. The front and rear shells are connected by an articulated system, and the front shell can be further divided into two parts: the front shell 1 and the front shell 2, which are connected by bolts. For ease of transportation, the front housing 1, front housing 2, and rear housing can be split into upper and lower halves to reduce the size and weight of a single piece for transportation. The shell can be split into upper and lower parts at the flange. During final assembly, the flange is aligned and connected with high-strength bolts, equipped with positioning pins and shear pins to locate and transmit shear force. At the same time, the outer connecting gaps are welded tightly with water tight welding to prevent water leakage at the gaps (as shown on Fig. 14). The circular cutterhead is also divided into a central disc body and three outer blocks, which are assembled on site (as shown on Fig. 15).

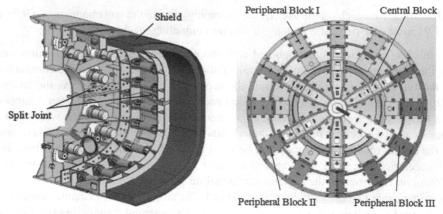

Fig. 14. Structure diagram of detachable shell   **Fig. 15.** Structure diagram of detachable main cutterhead

For difficulty 3, it is extremely difficult for the soil to flow inside the soil chamber of 9.53 m × 4.91 m rectangular section tunneling machine with a large aspect ratio. Due to the flat lower part of the shell, it is difficult for the soil to flow naturally to the soil inlet of the spiral machine through gravity. The technology of using a single area with multiple points for automatic improvement, divided into 5 areas (Fig. 16), and synchronous improvement in different areas not only allows the filling port to improve the soil, but also guides the soil in the soil warehouse to flow in the direction of the screw machine inlet. For the first time, two main and two auxiliary spiral machines were used for excavation. Four soil improvement filling ports were arranged between the main spiral machine and the auxiliary spiral machine. The filling ports were sprayed horizontally towards the position where the screw machine inlet was located, effectively solving the problem of soil accumulation between the screw machine purge ports.

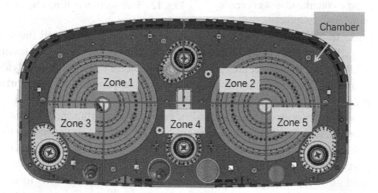

Fig. 16. Layout of improved filling ports in large aspect ratio soil chamber

In view of the solution of difficult problems and more than 20 years of experience in the design, manufacture and construction of special-shaped tunnel boring machine, the project achieved the expected results in land subsidence within 10 mm during construction.

5 Conclusion

By solving the two key technologies of full section cutting and assembling of special-shaped segments [4], and at the same time, the development of special-shaped tunnel boring machine with characteristics of high-precision control and mutual rotation of special-shaped shield tunneling, the special-shaped tunnel boring machine can not only be reliably applied to the construction of pedestrian, rail transit and vehicle tunnels, but also be innovatively and flexibly applied to the construction of subway stations, crossover sections and other key and difficult construction projects, so as to effectively and intensively reduce underground space, this makes the special-shaped tunnel boring machine a better construction choice under special working conditions. More than 40 special-shaped tunnels have been constructed in multiple cities in China, achieving significant economic and social benefits, and promoting technological progress in the manufacturing industry of special-shaped tunnel excavation equipment in China.

References

1. Japan Civil Engineering Society. Tunnel Standard Specification [Shield] and Interpretation. Zhu, W. (Trans.). China Architecture and Building Press, Beijing (2011)
2. Zhang, F., Zhu, H., Fu, D.: Shield Tunnel. China Communications Press, Beijing (2004)
3. Chengming, S., Yanming, L., Sheng, H.: Adaptive coordinated control for collision prevention in extreme working conditions of double cutterheads of special-shaped shield tunnels. Mod. Tunnel. Technol. 1, 23–26 (2016)
4. Zhu, Y., Zhu, Y., Huang, D., Yang, Z., Yang, L., Liu, S.: Research and application of key technologies for rectangular shield tunneling. Tunnel Construct. 9, 55–60 (2017)

Research on Visual Localization of Cutter Changing Robot in Unstructured Environments

Qiankun Wu[1] ⓘ, Hang Yang[1] ⓘ, Zhengdao Li[1], Feihu Peng[1], and Lijie Jiang[1,2(✉)]

[1] China Railway Engineering Equipment Group Co., Ltd., Zhengzhou 450016, China
376632068@qq.com, jianglijie001@126.com
[2] School of Mechanical Engineering, Zhejiang University, Hangzhou 310027, China

Abstract. Due to the non-closed-loop control of the cutter head and the uncertain environments of the excavation chamber, it is impossible to obtain the precise positioning of the cutter. Therefore, a robot cutter changing method based on visual navigation was proposed. Analyzed the working environment, disc cutter features, and installation accuracy of the cutter changing robot, and designed a visual positioning method based on scaled sub pixel features. To solve the problem that changes in visual distance will affect the positioning robustness and accuracy, a variable scale precise approximation target point control strategy was designed, and an adaptive adjustment robot motion step algorithm based on bolt circle center distance error was proposed. The feasibility of the algorithm was verified through a disc cutter change test bench. The results show that the proposed visual positioning method has a comprehensive positioning accuracy less than 1 mm under non-structured environmental conditions such as different disc cutter positions, lighting, and visual distances, which meets the requirements of dynamically adjusting the position and posture of the end effector of the cutter changing robot for precise cutter changing.

Keywords: Cutter Changing Robot · Visual Positioning · Sub-pixel · Unstructured environments

1 Introduction

The full face rock tunnel boring machine is widely used in rail transit, water conservancy, national defense and other tunnel engineering construction due to its fast excavation construction speed and high safety [1, 2]. Whether the shield can be bored smoothly, the condition of the cutterhead plays a crucial role. The disc cutter on the cutter head cuts the formation, the wear and fall off of the cutter is inevitable, and the cutter needs to be checked and replaced in time [3, 4]. At present, cutter inspection and change mainly rely on manual work, and hidden safety hazard in the construction environment such as large burial depth and high water pressure, and major safety hazards such as casualties are prone to occur, which can not meet the requirements of safe and rapid boring of tunnel boring machines. With the increasingly prominent issue of cutter changing, the efficient and safe "machine-to-human" operation mode for cutter inspection and changing is imperative due to the strong environmental adaptability and high level of automation of robots [5, 6].

H. Yang et al. (Eds.): ICIRA 2023, LNAI 14272, pp. 152–163, 2023.
https://doi.org/10.1007/978-981-99-6480-2_13

Currently, many scholars and institutions have conducted research on robot cutter changing technology. Visual navigation is the most core technical bottleneck in the development process of robot cutter changing, and has become a research hotspot in the industry. SCHWOB et al. [7] used KUKA robots for cutter changing operations, but only for manual guidance control and did not achieve high-precision automatic cutter changing by robots. Junke Guo et al. [8] proposed a visual positioning method for robot cutter changing, but the visual system is only suitable for known environments, without considering situations such as feature occlusion and changes in sight distance. The end-effector positioning system for TBM Cutter-Changing Robot based on binocular vision proposed by Dongjian Yang [9] from Dalian University of Technology. Its visual positioning accuracy is 2.5 mm, which does not meet the precision requirements for robot cutter changing navigation. The disc cutter system visual positioning based on PnP proposed by Dandan Peng et al. [10] which is greatly influenced by the number and quality of feature points on the cutter holder. In summary, the development of visual navigation systems for cutter changing robot was only under the known environment. However, the visual high-precision positioning under the influence of unstructured factors such as the delay of the cutter head braking, the variation of excavation chamber illumination, the occlusion of feature points, and the change of the relative position between the cutter head and the robot system has not been studied.

In view of this, this paper proposes a robot visual navigation method suitable for uncertain environment. Verify the feasibility of the proposed scheme by establishing mathematical models and carrying out visual positioning experiments under various uncertain factors.

2 Analysis of Disc Cutter System

2.1 Analysis of Disc Cutter System Working Environment

The internal environment of the shield tunneling machine is harsh, filled with mud, water, sand, and stones. The disc cutter system works in the excavation chamber for a long time, which can cause wear and corrosion of the disc cutter system (see Fig. 1). Therefore, pasting labels on the cutter holder or recognizing the color characteristics of the cutter system is not suitable for the working environment of shield tunneling machines.

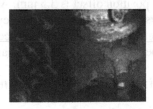

Fig. 1. Cutter system working environment.

2.2 Analysis of Cutter System Feature Points

Figure 2 illustrates the structure of the cutter system, it is found that the fastening bolts may be damaged after multiple disassembly and assembly of the robot, and the fixed flange block is affected by disassembly and assembly, which affects the repeatability positioning accuracy. Moreover, considering the installation position of the visual system on the end effector of the robot, the features on the fastening bolts and fixed flange blocks are not suitable as visual positioning feature points. Considering that the C-type block tensioning device is basically not disassembled and includes fixed bolts and installation slots, its features are more abundant and the feature points can more adequately face the center of the visual system. Therefore, it meets the requirements of visual image feature positioning of the cutter system.

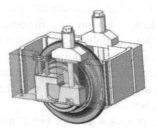

Fig. 2. Cutter system.

2.3 Analysis of Disc Cutter Installation Accuracy

Taking the 19-inch disc cutter and cutter box of a certain project as the research object, through the analysis of the cutter box structure, the accuracy of visual positioning is affected by the interference between the cutter shaft and the cutter box, the interference between the cutter hub and the cutter box side, and the deviation between the robot bolt disassembly and assembly mechanism and the bolt. Among them, the deviation of the robot bolt disassembly and assembly mechanism and the bolt (position and angle deviation) is solved by the flexible alignment of the end effector of the robot.

Through analysis, it can be seen that the cutter is installed in the cutter box under the ideal situation, the maximum deviation of the cutter axis rotation angle is 1.7°, and the maximum deviation of the position offset is 3.5 mm. At the same time, considering the comprehensive error analysis of robot control accuracy, cutter axis pose deviation, and processing error, etc. Therefore, the position control accuracy and visual positioning accuracy of the robot should be less than 1 mm during changing disc cutter.

3 Study on Feature Point Localization of Cutter System

After analyzing the feature points of the cutter system, it is mainly focused on straight line features and circular features. The circular feature target feature is obvious and the center of the circle will not change with rotation, which is easy to detect and identify. Therefore, a visual positioning method for cutter systems based on scaled sub pixel features was designed.

3.1 Sub-pixel Feature Extraction

Using Canny edge detection to extract subpixel edges and using double threshold to further judge edges to extract target subpixel features [11–13].

To eliminate the influence of noise, use the following Gaussian function to filter the collected image.

$$\begin{cases} h(x,y) = \frac{1}{2\pi\sigma^2}e^{\left(-\frac{x^2+y^2}{2\sigma^2}\right)} \\ g(x,y) = f(x,y) * h(x,y) \end{cases} \tag{1}$$

where $h(x,y)$ is the Gaussian function, $f(x,y)$ is the original image, and $g(x,y)$ is the filtered image.

The location where the grayscale intensity changes the most is the gradient direction, and the horizontal gradient G_x and vertical gradient G_y are calculated to detect horizontal, vertical, and diagonal edges in the image, that is, to determine the gradient amplitude and direction of the pixels.

Horizontal gradient:

$$G_x = \frac{f[i,j+1] - f[i,j] + f[i+1,j+1] - f[i+1,j]}{2} \tag{2}$$

Vertical gradient:

$$G_y = \frac{f[i,j] - f[i+1,j] + f[i,j+1] - f[i+1,j+1]}{2} \tag{3}$$

The amplitude and direction of the gradient are expressed as:

$$\begin{cases} M = \sqrt{G_x^2 + G_y^2} \\ \theta = \arctan\left(G_y/G_x\right) \end{cases} \tag{4}$$

The edge points are processed by double threshold, and the subpixel edge contours of the image are extracted by length, circularity and other conditions. Use formula (5) to filter the edge features of the obtained edge image.

$$\begin{cases} 0.9 < circularity < 1 \\ L - 20 < contlenth < L \end{cases} \tag{5}$$

where L is taken as 600.

Figure 3 shows the process of extracting sub pixel edge features.

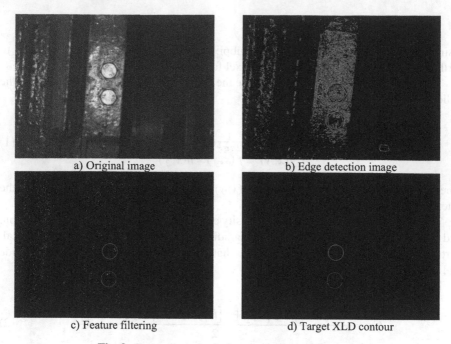

a) Original image   b) Edge detection image

c) Feature filtering   d) Target XLD contour

Fig. 3. Extracting sub pixel process of target features.

3.2 Sub-pixel Scaled Template Matching

Create a scalable template based on the subpixel contour to adapt to different viewing distances, types, and sensor models of the tested target. At the same time, in order to quickly search for the target, the pyramid model is combined to improve the matching speed [14, 15].

Figure 4, Fig. 5, and Fig. 6 show the positioning results of the cutter system using XLD templates with scaling for different viewing distances, different detection target models, and different visual sensors.

Fig. 4. Different types of tested bolts.

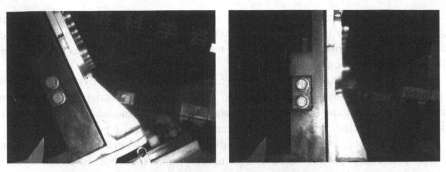

Fig. 5. Different types of visual sensors.

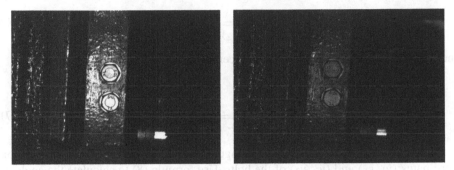

Fig. 6. Different types of visual sensors and object distances.

It can be seen from Fig. 4, Fig. 5, and Fig. 6 that the sub pixel template matching with scaling satisfies accurate positioning under uncertain factors such as changes in viewing distance and different detection target models.

3.3 Adaptive Adjustment of Robot Motion Step

According to the pinhole imaging model of the camera, as shown in Fig. 7, the point P_1 at visual distance Z_1 corresponds to point $p_1(u_1, v_1)$ in the image, and the point $P_1{}'$ at visual distance Z_2 corresponds to point $p_1{}'(u_1{}', v_2{}')$ in the image. Therefore, under different viewing distances, the center distance of the two circle features in the cutter system is represented by h and $h{}'$ respectively.

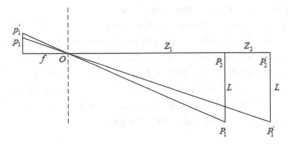

Fig. 7. Schematic diagram of imaging at different viewing distances.

The main drive telescope drives the cutterhead to move forward and backward, the robot cannot move in place along the axis direction, and the position of the cutter head system and the robot system changes, resulting in scaling problems in the images collected by the monocular vision system.

To ensure the accuracy of visual navigation, the robot needs to dynamically adjust its position to accurately approach the target. The article uses a variable scale subpixel circular template to match the collected image information, and adaptively adjusts the robot's motion step based on the center distance error for precise positioning.

In the image coordinate system, the coordinates of the bolts in the cutter tools system are (u_1, v_1) and (u_2, v_2). Combined with formula (6) adjust the robot movement strategy. If $\triangle \varepsilon > \varepsilon$, the robot needs to move forward; otherwise, the robot needs to move backward.

$$\Delta\varepsilon = \frac{L}{\sqrt{(u_1 - u_2)^2 + (v_1 - v_2)^2}} \tag{6}$$

where, ε is the ideal distance, L is the bolt center distance.

Robot motion step distance:

$$\Delta z = \left| \frac{Lf}{h} - \frac{Lf}{\sqrt{(u_1 - u_2)^2 + (v_1 - v_2)^2}} \right| \tag{7}$$

Screen out the same features in the image coordinate system to obtain the position coordinates (u_1, v_1) and (u_2, v_2) of the bolts. Use formula (8) to calculate the angle of the cutter tools box relative to the end effector of the robot.

$$\begin{cases} \theta = \frac{v_2 - v_1}{u_2 - u_1} & u_2 > u_1 \\ \theta = \frac{v_1 - v_2}{u_1 - u_2} & u_1 > u_2 \end{cases} \tag{8}$$

4 Robot Cutter Changing Visual Localization Test

4.1 Laser Tracker Positioning Accuracy Test

Use a three coordinate laser tracker to measure the accuracy of the designed cutter changing robot vision system, as shown in Fig. 8. Due to the inconsistency of the coordinate system between the cutter changing robot and the three coordinate laser tracker, the X and Y axis deviations are gradually measured, and the corresponding three coordinate changes are $\Delta l = \sqrt{\Delta x^2 + \Delta y^2 + \Delta z^2}$, in which Δx, Δy, and Δz is the changes in the three directions of the laser tracker coordinate system.

The visual detection system carried by the robot performs different position offsets and records the offsets. The visual system is used to detect position deviations at each position, and the laser tracker is used for synchronous detection to measure accuracy in the X and Y directions, as shown in Fig. 9, Fig. 10, Fig. 11, and Fig. 12.

According to Fig. 9, Fig. 10, Fig. 11, and Fig. 12, it can be concluded that the positioning accuracy of the visual system is less than 1 mm, which meets the requirements of robot visual navigation in uncertain environments.

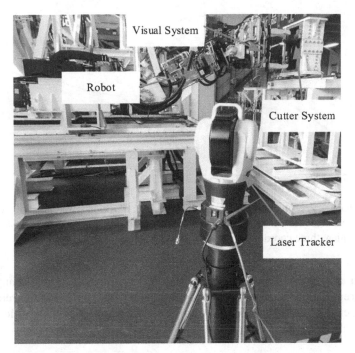

Fig. 8. Visual positioning accuracy detection of laser tracker.

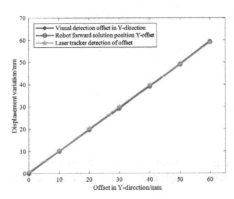
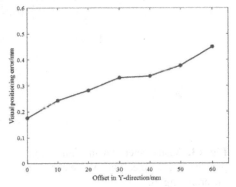

Fig. 9. Change curve in Y-direction, which includes visual detection offset, robot forward solution position, three coordinate position.

Fig. 10. Position error curve in Y-direction of visual detection and robot forward solution.

The visual guide angle error is measured through the inclinometer sensor on the cutterhead simulation platform. The cutterhead simulation platform drives the cutter system to rotate a certain relative angle and records it. Then the visual system detects the relative rotation angle at this pose and records it. Then detect the rotation relative angle of the tool seat system at this posture through the visual system. Calculating the difference between the two angles to obtain the positional accuracy of the visual navigation in

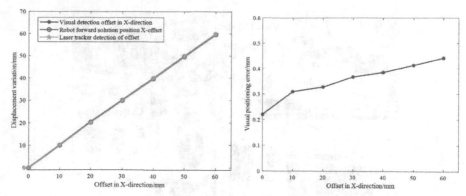

Fig. 11. Change curve in X-direction, which includes visual detection offset, robot forward solution position, three coordinate position.

Fig. 12. Position error curve in X-direction of visual detection and robot forward solution.

the rotation around the Z-axis. Figure 13 and Fig. 14 shows the angle change curves under different angle changes under visual positioning, with a maximum average angle positioning error of less than 0.5°, meeting the requirements of visual positioning.

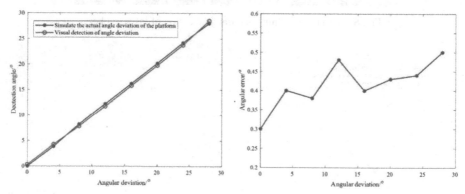

Fig. 13. Visual detection and simulation platform angle detection change curve under different angles.

Fig. 14. Visual detection and simulation platform angle error curves at different angles

4.2 Visual Localization Test Under Different Poses

Simulate different cutter positions on the cutter head simulation platform by driving the disc cutter holder to perform movements such as translation and rotation. At the same time, construct scenarios such as darkness, different pressures, and humidity to simulate the uncertain environment of the shield machine excavation or slurry chamber. As shown in Fig. 15, the automatic cutter changing experiment based on visual navigation is carried out under unknown rolling tool pose. As shown in Fig. 17, the automatic cutter changing experiment based on visual navigation is carried out under dark conditions. Figure 16 shows the visual positioning results under unknown pose; Fig. 18. Shows the visual localization results under partial occlusion of feature points.

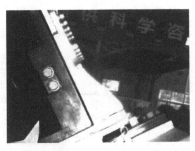

Fig. 15. Visual positioning experiment under different postures.

Fig. 16. Visual positioning experiment under unknown pose.

Fig. 17. Visual positioning experiment under dark conditions.

Fig. 18. Visual positioning experiment under feature occlusion.

Figure 15, Fig. 16, Fig. 17, and Fig. 18 show that under unknown pose and feature occlusion conditions, the method proposed in this paper can accurately locate feature points.

The uncertainty factors in robot cutter changing include unstable positions of the cutter pallet and robot system, unknown orientation of the cutter system, unknown lighting conditions in the excavation chamber, and unknown blockage rate of bolt feature points. To address this, the visual system was tested for cutter changing under uncertain conditions. The robot drives the visual system to move within the visible range of the disc cutter holder system. By collecting and analyzing the image of the disc cutter holder at this position, the relative pose of the disc cutter holder system and the robot end system at this position is obtained, and guide the robot to perform the cutter changing operation. Figure 19 shows the simulated curve of the visual navigation system in uncertain environments. It can be seen that the designed visual navigation method has an accuracy of less than 1 mm even with uncertainty factors such as changes in visual distance by 20 mm, 15% blockage of feature points, and changing lighting conditions. Meet the visual navigation requirements of cutter changing robots in uncertain environments.

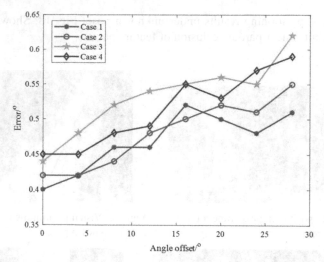

Fig. 19. Visual navigation accuracy curve under uncertain factors: Case 1 standard visual range + 20 mm, feature point occlusion 15%; Case 2 standard visual range-20 mm, feature point occlusion 15%; Case 3 dark environment, standard visual range + 20 mm, feature point occlusion 15%; Case 4 dark environment, standard visual range-20 mm, feature point occlusion 15%.

5   Conclusion

This paper propose a monocular vision method based on circular features to estimate the pose of the cutter holder.

Utilizing sub-pixel features with scale reduction for initial localization of the captured cutter image, which addresses the problem of measuring feature scaling caused by changes in visual distance. The designed variable-scale precision target point approximation control strategy first filters located circle center coordinates and calculates circle center distance errors in the cutter image, guiding the robot to adaptively adjust its motion steps to achieve accurate approximation of the measured target location and enable precise cutter positioning.

Experimental validation shows that the proposed method has good high-precision visual navigation capabilities in uncertain environments with varying work environments, bolt features partially covered by mud, different types of bolts, and changes in the relative position between the cutter changing robot and the cutter head.

References

1. Li, J.: Research status, problems and prospects of excavating machines in China. Tunnel Construct. **41**(6), 877–896 (2021)
2. Aydan, Ö, Hasanpour, R.: Estimation of ground pressures on a shielded TBM in tunneling through squeezing ground and its possibility of jamming. Bullet. Eng. Geol. Environ. **78**(7), 5237 (2019)
3. Yang, Y., et al.: Analysis of influencing factors on scraper wearing of full-surface rock tunneling machine. Tunnel Construct. **36**(11), 1394–1400 (2016)

4. Han, B., et al.: Analysis and prediction of cutter wear in composite strata shield tunneling. J. Civ. Eng. **53**(S1), 137–142 (2020)
5. Huang, Z., et al.: Design and key technology analysis of tunnel maintenance robot system. J. Railway Sci. Eng. **18**(3), 767–776 (2021)
6. Jiang, L., Wang, Y., Sun, Y., et al.: Design and analysis of a shield machine cutter changer robot suitable for narrow spaces. J. Railway Sci. Eng. (2022)
7. Schwob, A., et al.: Tuen Mun-Chek Lap Kok Link: an outstanding subsea tunnel project in Hong Kong. Proc. Inst. Civil Eng. Civil Eng. **173**(5), 33 (2020)
8. Guo, J., Wang, D.: Research on shield robot cutter change technology based on visual navigation positioning. Tunnel Construct. **41**(2), 300–307 (2021)
9. Yang, D.: Research on End Pose Determination of TBM Cutter Changing Robot Based on Binocular Vision. Dalian University of Technology (2021)
10. Peng, D., et al.: Pose determination of the disc cutter holder of shield machine based on monocular vision. Sensors (2022)
11. Li, M., Bai, M., Lü, Y.: Adaptive threshold image edge detection method. Pattern Recogn. Artif. Intell. **29**(2), 177–184 (2016)
12. Du, X., Chen, D., Ma, Z., Liu, F.: An improved image edge detection algorithm based on canny operator. Comput. Digit. Eng. **50**(2), 410–413 (2022)
13. Chao, Y., et al.: Measurement method of shaft parts based on improved Zernike moment. Electron. Measur. Technol. **45**(3), 169 (2022)
14. Liu, Y., et al.: Extraction method of deep information on steel plate surface based on image pyramid. Acta Metrolog. Sin. **36**(04), 356–359 (2015)
15. Xinyi, Y., et al.: An improved ORB feature extraction algorithm based on quadtree. Comput. Sci. **45**(S2), 222–225 (2018)

Design of Hybrid Shield Cutter-Changing Robot and Its Motion Control Method

Zhen Wu[✉], Hao Chen, Shangqi Chen, and Junzhou Huo

School of Mechanical Engineering, Dalian University of Technology, Dalian 116024, China
wuzhen0808@mail.dlut.edu.cn

Abstract. The shield machine is facing the problem of difficult cutter change at the beginning of its application. Its current dangerous and inefficient manual cutter change method did not match the requirements of safe, efficient and intelligent tunnel construction. Especially in the high pressure, high humidity and harsh operating environment of mud and water shield, the life safety of the cutter changer is at great risk, so the safe operation mode of "machine cutter changing" has become an inevitable trend. Based on the special working environment of slurry shield tunneling, this paper first designs a hydraulic-driven seven-degree-of-freedom cutter-changing robot that can adapt to a 12.6 m diameter shield tunneling. Then, combined with the combination of high-order polynomial and trapezoidal velocity curves, an optimal trajectory planning method based on time and strike combination is proposed and applied to the operation process of the cutter-changing robot. Finally, a PD control rate based on dynamic compensation was designed based on the structure of the cutter-changing robot. The simulation results show that the end movement has neither flexible nor rigid strikes, and the running time of a single stroke is maintained within 30 s to 70 s, which greatly shortens the cutter change time and ensures that the end positioning accuracy is less than 1 mm, while the cutter-changing robot has full coverage of the cutter-changing range.

Keywords: Shield cutter-changing robot · Trajectory planning · Motion control

1 Introduction

During the excavation process of tunnel boring machine, it mainly relies on the extrusion cutting of the hob and rock to break the rock. Under a series of harsh service environments [1] such as heavy load, strong strike and mud immersion, the hob consumption is huge, so the hob needs to be replaced frequently. Now the project mainly adopts the manual method to replace the hob. When faced with high pressure, high humidity, corrosion and other extreme operating environments, "difficult detection and cutter replacement risk" has become an internationally recognized industry challenge.

In terms of robot cutter change, foreign research institutions and relevant scholars took the lead in exploring. In 2007, the French company Bouygues was the first to propose TELEMACH, a cutter-changing robot [2] for the replacement of hobs in tunnel boring machines, and to conduct certain studies on control and trajectory planning, the project is mainly in conceptual design. In 2015, Bouygues and NFM [3], a subsidiary of Werder in Germany released a robot cutter change solution using a KUKA industrial robot as the body, equipped with a self-designed end effector [4] and corresponding new cutter holder system. In 2017, Bouygues successfully applied the TELEMACH project demonstration to a full-section Herrenknecht tunnel boring machine with a diameter of 17.6 m, which can significantly reduce the cutter-changing time and protect the health and safety of cutter-changing workers, but the cutter-changing range is only about 30%, which cannot realize the industrialization of cutter-changing robot operation. In 2019, Huo Junzhou's team at Dalian University of Technology proposed a TBM-applicable cutter-changing robot, which has an end load of 300 kg, uses radial operation, and is designed with a shear lift, which can make the cutter-changing range cover most of the positive hobs of the blade, but cannot replace the side hobs. In summary, the research on shield cutter-changing robots at home and abroad is still immature, and most of them are in the structural design stage, and there are certain problems in the cutter-changing range and robot control accuracy.

In response to the problems of small cutter-changing range and poor control accuracy of the robot in the design and research of shield cutter-changing robots, this paper designs a hybrid-type seven-degree-of-freedom hydraulically driven cutter-changing robot that can adapt to large-load operation in narrow and long spaces of shield machines. This robot design method can greatly reduce the cutter change time while ensuring the positioning accuracy of the end-effector. The rest of this paper is as follows: In Sect. 2, the design method of metamorphic mechanism is used to design the cutter-changing robot body scheme applied to the narrow and long working space. In Sect. 3, a trajectory planning method based on the optimal combination of time and strike is proposed. In Sect. 4, the PD control rate based on dynamics compensation is designed based on the structure of the cutter-changing robot. In Sect. 5, simulation experiments are performed.

2   Design of Task-Oriented Shield Cutter-Changing Robot Solution

2.1   Robot Task Analysis

The cutter changing robot operation area can be divided into the positive hob operation area and side hob operation area, and the positive hob operation area can be divided into three different areas for the robot cabin: upper, middle and lower. The robot poses variations of the cutter-changing robot under different operational tasks in a narrow operating space as shown in Fig. 1.

In the process of cutter changing, it is necessary to move the joint to send the robot out of the robot cabin, move the telescopic joint so that the end-effector can cross multiple hobs, turn the joint so that the telescopic joint is parallel to the cutter plate surface, and turn the joint so that the end-effector is perpendicular to the cutter plate surface. A comprehensive analysis [5, 6] of the robot configuration for the four task areas requires two moving and two turning motion subsets. The actual cutter change process has a certain angular deviation θ between the cutter stop position and the robot's installation axis, and the hob position changes as shown in Fig. 2.

A new rotating and moving joint are needed to solve the problem of inaccurate cutter docking, and the following seven-degree-of-freedom robot body design scheme is finally formed according to the distribution of human arm joints [7], as shown in Fig. 4.

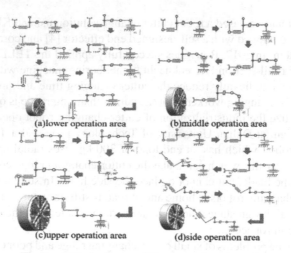

Fig. 1. Attitude change of the cutter-changing robot

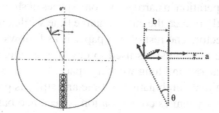

Fig. 2. Deflection diagram of cutter disc

2.2 Structure Design of Hybrid-Type Cutter-Changing Robot

Taking a 12.6 m diameter slurry shield tunnel as an engineering case, the body design of the cutter-changing robot is based on the metamorphic mechanism. Due to the large robot load, all driving sources are hydraulically driven, while the helical hydraulic oscillating motor can realize the role of driving joints and save space as a frame. Combined with the designed end-effector and the adapted new cutter holder, it forms a complete hybrid seven-degree-of-freedom hydraulically driven cutter-changing robot structure design that can adapt to the long and narrow space of the shield machine with a large load, as shown in Fig. 3.

From the figure, it can be seen that the cutter-changing robot consists of ten parts, including the base, horizontal push joint (first joint), pitch joint (second joint), left and right fine-tuning joint (third joint), two-axis rotating joints (fourth and fifth joints), telescopic joint (sixth joint), end rotating joint (seventh joint), end-effector, and new cutter system. The spiral hydraulic swing motor of joint four is both the driving source and the frame, and the cutter-changing robot has full coverage of the cutter-changing range.

Fig. 3. Cutter-changing robot structure scheme

3 Design of Trajectory Planning Method

The high-order polynomial interpolation method [8] replaces the trapezoidal velocity interpolation method with the linear segment of acceleration and deceleration, to solve the problem of the acceleration discontinuity of trapezoidal velocity trajectory planning [9]. Meanwhile, the continuous and stable characteristics of the high-order polynomial [10] are introduced into it. Thus, a new combined trajectory planning method with excellent performance of both curves is formed [11, 12]. The equations of displacement, velocity, acceleration and sharpness are shown in Eqs. (1) to (4).

$$
S(t) = \begin{cases}
\displaystyle\sum_{i=0}^{6} a_i t^i & 0 \le t < t_1 \\[2ex]
\displaystyle\sum_{i=0}^{6} a_i t_1^i + v_{\max}(t - t_1) & t_1 \le t < t_2 \\[2ex]
\displaystyle\sum_{i=0}^{6} a_i t_1^i + \sum_{i=1}^{6} b_i (t - t_2)^i + v_{\max}(t_2 - t_1) & t_2 \le t \le T
\end{cases}
\tag{1}
$$

$$
V(t) = \begin{cases}
\displaystyle\sum_{i=1}^{6} i a_i t^{i-1} & 0 \le t < t_1 \\[2ex]
v_{\max} & t_1 \le t < t_2 \\[2ex]
\displaystyle\sum_{i=1}^{6} i b_i (t - t_2)^{i-1} & t_2 \le t \le T
\end{cases}
\tag{2}
$$

$$
A(t) = \begin{cases}
\displaystyle\sum_{i=2}^{6} i(i - 1) a_i t^{i-2} & 0 \le t < t_1 \\[2ex]
0 & t_1 \le t < t_2 \\[2ex]
\displaystyle\sum_{i=2}^{6} i(i - 1) b_i (t - t_2)^{i-2} & t_2 \le t \le T
\end{cases}
\tag{3}
$$

$$
J(t) = \begin{cases} \sum_{i=3}^{6} i(i-1)(i-2)a_i t^{i-3} & 0 \le t < t_1 \\ 0 & t_1 \le t < t_2 \\ \sum_{i=3}^{6} i(i-1)(i-2)b_i (t-t_2)^{i-3} & t_2 \le t \le T \end{cases} \tag{4}
$$

where a_i and b_i are the coefficients of the velocity function during the acceleration and deceleration stages, respectively; t_1, t_1-t_2, and t_2-T are the time of joint motion during the acceleration, uniform, and deceleration stages, respectively.

The maximum velocity of the joint is 0.25 mm/s, the maximum acceleration is 0.25 mm/s^2, the starting displacement s0 is 0, and the ending displacement sf is 0.6535 m. A new trajectory planning method based on the combination of seventh-order polynomial and trapezoidal velocity trajectory planning-an optimal trajectory planning method based on the combination of time and strike. The displacement, velocity, acceleration and sharpness curves of the joint motion are shown in Fig. 4.

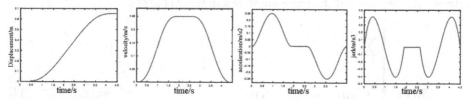

Fig. 4. The optimal trajectory planning curve based on the combination of time and strike

Analysis of the trajectory planning method based on the optimal combination of time and shock takes 4.494 s to complete the same displacement, which is 27.3% shorter than the interpolation method with seven polynomials; The velocity and acceleration curves are continuous and without sudden changes, and there is no flexible or rigid shock in the joint motion, which meets the requirements of trajectory planning; The jerk is continuous without sudden change, and there is no residual vibration at the beginning and end positions, but the maximum value of jerk is increased. In general, the new trajectory planning method effectively shortens the motion time and reduces the shock at the start-stop time of joint motion.

4   Design of Motion Control Methods

4.1   Dynamics Model

The general motion of a rigid body generally includes two forms of traverse and rotation. The velocity of each point on the rigid body varies, and Newton's equation for a general rigid body is:

$$
F = \sum_i m_i \frac{d^2}{dt^2} r_i = \frac{d^2}{dt^2} \sum_i m_i r_i = \frac{d^2}{dt^2} mr_C = m\ddot{r}_C \tag{5}
$$

The relative moment of momentum of a rigid body towards its centroid is:

$$L_C^r = \sum_i m_i[r_{c_i} \times (\omega \times r_{c_i})] = \sum_i m_i\left[\left(r_{C_i}^T r_{c_i}\right)\omega - \left(r_{c_i}^T\omega\right)r_{c_i}\right] \tag{6}$$

Suppose that the expression r_{C_i} in the coordinate system solidly connected to the rigid body is $\bar{r}_{C_1} = [\bar{x} \ \bar{y} \ \bar{z}]^T$, brought into Eq. (6) to obtain:

$$\tilde{L}_c^r = \begin{bmatrix} \sum_i m_i(\bar{y}_i^T + \bar{z}_i^2) & -\sum_i m_i\bar{x}_i\bar{y}_i & -\sum_i m_i\bar{x}_i\bar{z}_i \\ -\sum_i m_i\bar{x}_i\bar{y}_i & \sum_i m_i(\bar{x}_i^2 + \bar{z}_i^2) & -\sum_i m_i\bar{y}_i\bar{z}_i \\ -\sum_i m_i\bar{x}_i\bar{z}_i & -\sum_i m_i\bar{y}_i\bar{z}_i & \sum_i m_i(\bar{x}_i^2 + \bar{y}_i^2) \end{bmatrix} \triangleq \tilde{I}_C\tilde{\omega} \tag{7}$$

where $\tilde{I}_C$ the rotational inertia at the centroid.

Combining (7), the Euler equation for a general rigid body can be found as:

$$\frac{d}{dt}(\tilde{I}_C\tilde{\omega}) + \omega \times (\tilde{I}_C\tilde{\omega}) = \left(\frac{d}{dt}\tilde{I}_C\right)\tilde{\omega} + \tilde{I}_C\frac{d}{dt}\tilde{\omega} + \tilde{\omega} \times (\tilde{I}_C\tilde{\omega}) = \tilde{I}_C\dot{\omega} + \tilde{\omega} \times \tilde{I}_C\tilde{\omega} = \tilde{M}_C \tag{8}$$

Using the outward iterative method to calculate the velocity and acceleration, assuming that the coordinate system $\{C_i\}$ is fixed at the centroid of i, the equation for the transfer of velocity between the connecting rods is as follows:

$$^{i+1}\omega_{i+1} = \begin{cases} ^{i+1}_i R^i\omega_i + \dot{\theta}_{i+1}^{i+1}Z_{i+1} \\ ^{i+1}_i R^i\omega_i \end{cases} \tag{9}$$

where ω_{i+1} is the angular velocity of joint $i + 1$ in coordinate system $\{i + 1\}$, $^i\omega_i$ is the angular velocity of joint i in coordinate system $\{i\}$, $\dot{\theta}_{i+1}$ is the angular velocity of joint $i + 1$ itself, $^{i+1}Z_{i+1} = [0 \ 0 \ 1]^T$.

The corresponding angular acceleration transfer equations when the two connecting rods are the rotating and moving joints are:

$$^{i+1}\dot{\omega}_{i+1} = \begin{cases} ^{i+1}_i R^i\dot{\omega}_i + ^{i+1}_i R^i\omega_i \times \dot{\theta}_{i+1}^{i+1}Z_{i+1} + \ddot{\theta}_{i+1}^{i+1}Z_{i+1} \\ ^{i+1}_i R^i\dot{\omega}_i \end{cases} \tag{10}$$

The linear acceleration transfer equations corresponding to the origin of the linkage coordinate system when the two linkages are rotating and moving joints are:

$$^{i+1}\dot{v}_{i+1} = \begin{cases} ^{i+1}_i R[^i\omega_i \times {}^iP_{i+1} + {}^i\omega_i \times ({}^i\omega_i \times {}^iP_{i+1}) + {}^i\dot{v}_i] \\ ^{i+1}_i R[^i\omega_i \times {}^iP_{i+1} + {}^i\omega_i \times ({}^i\omega_i \times {}^iP_{i+1}) + {}^i\dot{v}_i] \\ +2^{i+1}\omega_{i+1} \times \dot{d}_{i+1}{}^{i+1}Z_{i+1} + \ddot{d}_{i+1}{}^{i+1}Z_{i+1} \end{cases} \tag{11}$$

Linear acceleration at the centroid of each linkage:

$$^i\dot{v}_{C_i} = {}^i\dot{\omega}_i \times {}^iP_{C_i} + {}^i\omega_i \times ({}^i\omega_i \times {}^iP_{C_i}) + {}^i\dot{v}_i \tag{12}$$

Combining (5), (8) Newton-Euler formula [13] and (9) to (12) yields the linkage centroid inertia force and moment as:

$$\begin{cases} F_i = m\dot{v}_{Ci} \\ N_i = {}^{C_i}\mathbf{I}\dot{\omega}_i + \omega_i \times {}^{C_i}\mathbf{I}\omega_i \end{cases} \tag{13}$$

After obtaining the inertial force and torque of the connecting rod centroid, the driving torque of each joint need to be calculated. The equations of force balance and torque balance of the connecting rod in the gravity-free state are:

$$\begin{cases} {}^i f_i = {}^i_{i+1}R^{i+1}f_{i+1} + {}^i F_i \\ {}^i n_i = {}^i N_i + {}^i_{i+1}R^{i+1}n_{i+1} + {}^i P_{C_i} \times {}^i F_i + {}^i P_{i+1} \times {}^i_{i+1}R^{i+1}f_{i+1} \end{cases} \tag{14}$$

the inward iteration method of force and torque can be used to obtain the driving torque of the rotating joint and the linear driving force of the moving joint:

$$\begin{cases} \tau_i = {}^i n_i^T {}^i Z_i \\ \tau_i = {}^i f_i^T {}^i Z_i \end{cases} \tag{15}$$

extrapolation of the outward iterative method for velocity and acceleration:$0 \to 9$

$$\begin{cases} {}^{i+1}\omega_{i+1} = \begin{cases} {}^{i+1}_i R^i \omega_i + \dot{\theta}^{i+1}_{i+1} Z_{i+1} \\ {}^{i+1}_i R^i \omega_i \end{cases} \\ {}^{i+1}\dot{\omega}_{i+1} = \begin{cases} {}^{i+1}_i R^i \dot{\omega}_i + {}^{i+1}_i R^i \omega_i \times \dot{\theta}^{i+1}_{i+1} Z_{i+1} + \ddot{\theta}^{i+1}_{i+1} Z_{i+1} \\ {}^{i+1}_i R^i \dot{\omega}_i \end{cases} \\ {}^{i+1}\dot{v}_{i+1} = \begin{cases} {}^{i+1}_i R[^i \omega_i \times {}^i P_{i+1} + {}^i \omega_i \times ({}^i \omega_i \times {}^i P_{i+1}) + {}^i \dot{v}_i] \\ {}^{i+1}_i R[^i \omega_i \times {}^i P_{i+1} + {}^i \omega_i \times ({}^i \omega_i \times {}^i P_{i+1}) + {}^i \dot{v}_i] + 2^{i+1}\omega_{i+1} \times \dot{d}_{i+1}{}^{i+1}Z_{i+1} + \ddot{d}_{i+1}{}^{i+1}Z_{i+1} \end{cases} \\ {}^{i+1}\dot{v}_{C_{i+1}} = {}^{i+1}\dot{\omega}_i \times {}^{i+1}\mathbf{P}_{C_{i+1}} + {}^{i+1}\omega_{i+1} \times ({}^{i+1}\omega_i \times {}^{i+1}\mathbf{P}_{C_{i+1}}) + {}^{i+1}\dot{v}_{i+1} \\ {}^{i+1}F_{i+1} = m_{i+1}{}^{i+1}\dot{v}_{C_{i+1}} \\ {}^{i+1}N_{i+1} = {}^{C_{i+1}}\mathbf{I}_{i+1}{}^{i+1}\dot{\omega}_{i+1} + {}^{i+1}\omega_{i+1} \times {}^{C_{i+1}}\mathbf{I}_{i+1}{}^{i+1}\omega_{i+1} \end{cases} \tag{16}$$

the inward iteration method for force and torque extrapolation:$9 \to 0$.

$$\begin{cases} {}^i f_i = {}^i_{i+1}R^{i+1}f_{i+1} + {}^i F_i \\ {}^i n_i = {}^i N_i + {}^i_{i+1}R^{i+1}n_{i+1} + {}^i P_{C_i} \times {}^i F_i + {}^i P_{i+1} \times {}^i_{i+1}R^{i+1}f_{i+1} \\ \tau_i = {}^i n_i^T {}^i Z_i \\ \tau_i = {}^i f_i^T {}^i Z_i \end{cases} \tag{17}$$

This completes the mathematical model of the dynamics of the cutter-changing robot based on the Newton-Euler method.

4.2 PD Control Rate Design Based on Dynamics Compensation

For a robot with n degrees of freedom, there exists a generic robot dynamics model:

$$M(q)\ddot{q} + C(q, \dot{q})\dot{q} + G(q) = \tau \tag{18}$$

where $q \in R^n$ is the angle vector or displacement vector of each joint of the robot, $M(q) \in R^{n \times n}$ is the mass matrix, $C(q, \dot{q}) \in R^n$ represents the centrifugal force and Coriolis force matrix, $G(q) \in R^n$ is the gravity matrix, $\tau \in R^n$ is the driving force or torque.

For the robot dynamics system shown in (18), the PD control rate based on dynamic compensation [14] is designed as follows:

$$\tau = -K_p e - K_v \dot{e} + M(q)\ddot{q} + C(q, \dot{q})\dot{q} + G(q)M(q)\ddot{e} + C(q, \dot{q})\dot{e} + K_p e + K_v \dot{e} = 0 \tag{19}$$

From (18) and (19), the error equation for the existence of the control system can be deduced as:

$$M(q)\ddot{e} + C(q, \dot{q})\dot{e} + K_p e + K_v \dot{e} = 0 \tag{20}$$

to prove that the control rate satisfies Lyapunov stability [15] fundamental theorem, define the following Lyapunov function:

$$V(e, \dot{e}) = 1/2 e^T K_p e + 1/2 \dot{e}^T M \dot{e} + \alpha \dot{e}^T M f(e) \tag{21}$$

and define the following functions:

$$\gamma_7 = 2\alpha\beta\lambda_{max}(M) + \alpha\gamma_4 \tag{22}$$

$$\gamma_8 = \lambda_{max}(K_v) + \gamma_3 \tag{23}$$

combining (20) to (23), it can be obtained that:

$$\dot{V}(e, \dot{e}) \leq -(\lambda_{min}(K_v) - \gamma_7 - \frac{1}{2}\alpha\beta\gamma_8)\|\dot{e}\|^2 - \alpha\beta(\lambda_{min}(K_p) - \frac{1}{2}\gamma_8)\|e\|^2 = -\xi_3\|\dot{e}\|^2 - \xi_4\|e\|^2 \tag{24}$$

So it is possible to choose sufficiently large K_p and K_v, then can make $\xi_3 > 0$, $\xi_4 > 0$, such that e and $\dot{e}$ converge exponentially to 0, proving that the system can maintain its stability of the system by adjusting K_p and K_v based on the PD control of dynamics compensation.

5 Simulations

5.1 Effectiveness Analysis of Trajectory Planning

The kinematic model of the cutter-changing robot is built in Adams's virtual space to simulate the replacement of the sixth hob on the cutter head, and the motion performance of each joint in replacing this hob is shown in Table 1.

Table 1. Parameters of each joint when replacing the sixth cutter

Order of motion	Joint	Acceleration time(t_1)	Acceleration displacement/angle	Uniform time(t_1-t_2)	Uniform displacement /angle	Joint movement time	Angle/total displacement
1	Joint 1	1.88 s	0.235 m	0.734 s	0.1835 m	4.494 s	0.6535 m
2	Joint 5	1.88 s	9.40°	16.12 s	161.2°	19.88 s	180°
3	Joint 9	1.88 s	9.40°	16.12 s	161.2°	19.88 s	180°
4	Joint 6	1.88 s	9.40°	7.12 s	71.2°	10.88 s	90°
5	Joint 7	1.50 s	0.10125 m	0.00 s	0.00 m	3.00 s	0.2025 m
6	Joint 8	1.50 s	0.10125 m	0.00 s	0.00 m	3.00 s	0.2025 m
7	Joint 1	1.88 s	0.235 m	0.6588 s	0.1597 m	4.3988 s	0.6297 m

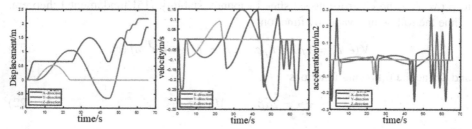

Fig. 5. Comparison of performance parameters of cutter-changing robot ends in three directions

From the above table, it can be seen that the time of single-stroke operation when the cutter-changing robot to replaces the sixth hob is 65.5328 s. Observe the motion of each joint and output the curve of displacement, velocity and acceleration of the end in X, Y and Z directions, as shown in Fig. 5.

Combined with Fig. 6, it can be seen that the end can complete the cutter-changing task without rigid and flexible strike. The same calculation to replace the first, third and seventh hob the single stroke cutter change time of is 40.96 s, 34.6 s and 39.39 s. Considering the replacement and installation of hob, bolt assembly and disassembly, and transport of hob in the hold, the robot cutter change time can be shortened to within 10 min, which greatly reduces the operation time compared with the manual three hours cutter change time.

5.2   Effectiveness Analysis of the Control Method

The virtual prototype of the robot is built using Adams and embedded as a standalone module in Simulink. The algorithms are formulated as functions in the form of S-Functions. And the data is transferred in the form of input to the control algorithm, which outputs the driving force of the joints at this moment based on the designed control rate, and the real motion of each joint under the force is obtained through the solver of Adams, and the flow is shown in Fig. 6:

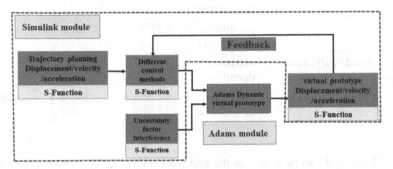

Fig. 6. General flow chart of control joint simulation

With the cutter changing robot replacing the last hob in the radius direction of the cutter head, namely the sixth hob, as an example, the block diagram of dynamic compensation based on is constructed. The comparison of end-effector position errors under different control methods is shown in Fig. 7.

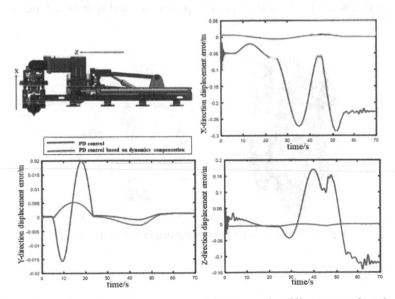

Fig. 7. Comparison of position errors of end-effector under different control methods

By comparing the above curves and extracting the maximum deviation and termination deviation of the end relative to the coordinate system during the motion process under two control methods, the results are shown in Table 2.

Table 2. Statistics of maximum deviation and termination deviation of end-effector

Control method	Deviation	X	Y	Z
PD control	maximum deviation/m	0.2870	0.0180	0.1556
	termination deviation/m	0.2276	0.0012	0.1338
PD control based on dynamics compensation	maximum deviation/m	0.0066	0.0044	0.0037
	termination deviation/m	4.1914e-5	3.5546e-4	0.0013

From Table 2, it can be seen that the end error under PD control is very large and completely fails to meet the requirements of robot cutter replacement. The positioning accuracy of the X, Y and Z directions of the end of the cutter-changing robot based on the PD control with dynamics compensation is 0.042 mm, 0.356 mm and 1.3 mm respectively. The accuracy of the X and Y directions directly affects the docking of the end effector interface and the bolt, as shown in Fig. 8. Combining this positioning accuracy with the guiding positioning interface on the end effector can effectively complete the cutter change task. Therefore, it is proved that the PD control method based on dynamics compensation can ensure the accuracy of end positioning and is suitable for robot cutter changing.

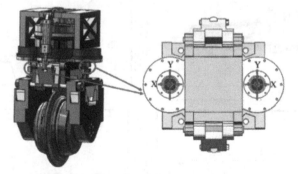

Fig. 8. Grasping cutter positioning diagram of end-effector

6 Conclusion

This paper designs a hybrid seven-degree-of-freedom hydraulically driven cutter-changing robot that can adapt to the long and narrow spaces of shield machines with large loads, in response to the problems of time-consuming and dangerous manual cutter-changing. The cutter-changing range of the robot can reach 100%. To shorten cutter-changing time and avoid shocks, a trajectory planning method based on the optimal combination of time and shocks is proposed, so that the end movement has neither flexible nor rigid strike; Meanwhile, the PD control rate based on dynamic compensation is designed based on the structure of the cutter-changing robot to improve the end positioning accuracy.

Finally, the cutter-changing robot dynamics model is established and the cutter-changing robot control system is built by a joint simulation method of Adams and Simulink. The simulation results show that the end motion has neither flexible nor rigid strike, and the single-stroke cutter change time is between 30 s and 70 s, while ensuring the end positioning accuracy <1 mm.

References

1. Huo, J., Hou, N., Sun, W., Wang, L., Dong, J.: Analyses of dynamic characteristics and structure optimization of tunnel boring machine cutter system with multi-joint surface. Nonlin. Dyn. **87**, 237–254 (2017). https://doi.org/10.1007/s11071-016-3038-0
2. Yang, M., Xia, Y., Jia, L., Wang, D., Ji, Z.: A modular design method based on TRIZ and AD and its application to cutter changing robot. Adv. Mech. Eng. **13**, 168781402110343 (2021). https://doi.org/10.1177/16878140211034369
3. Mansard, N., Khatib, O., Kheddar, A.: A unified approach to integrate unilateral constraints in the stack of tasks. IEEE Trans. Robot. **25**, 670–685 (2009). https://doi.org/10.1109/TRO.2009.2020345
4. Chen, H., Li, H., Huo, J., Yang, B., Yang, F.: Assembly deviation analysis of new integrated TBM disc cutter and design of the supporting cutter-changing robot end-effector. Appl. Sci. **12**, 9549 (2022). https://doi.org/10.3390/app12199549
5. Wang, R., Liao, Y., Dai, J.S., Chen, H., Cai, G.: The isomorphic design and analysis of a novel plane-space polyhedral metamorphic mechanism. Mech. Mach. Theory. **131**, 152–171 (2019). https://doi.org/10.1016/j.mechmachtheory.2018.09.017
6. Tian, H., Ma, H., Ma, K.: Method for configuration synthesis of metamorphic mechanisms based on functional analyses. Mech. Mach. Theory. **123**, 27–39 (2018). https://doi.org/10.1016/j.mechmachtheory.2018.01.009
7. Liu, L., Shi, Y.-Y., Xie, L.: A novel multi-DOF exoskeleton robot for upper limb rehabilitation. J. Mech. Med. Biol. **16**, 1640023 (2016). https://doi.org/10.1142/S0219519416400236
8. Yang, J., Gao, Y., Guo, R., Gao, Q., Zhao, J.: Research on excavator trajectory control based on hybrid interpolation. Sustainability. **15**, 6761 (2023). https://doi.org/10.3390/su15086761
9. Wang, H., Wang, H., Huang, J., Zhao, B., Quan, L.: Smooth point-to-point trajectory planning for industrial robots with kinematical constraints based on high-order polynomial curve. Mech. Mach. Theory. **139**, 284–293 (2019). https://doi.org/10.1016/j.mechmachtheory.2019.05.002
10. Kim, J., Croft, E.A.: Online near time-optimal trajectory planning for industrial robots. Robot. Comput.-Integr. Manuf. **58**, 158–171 (2019). https://doi.org/10.1016/j.rcim.2019.02.009

11. Zanotto, V., Gasparetto, A., Lanzutti, A., Boscariol, P., Vidoni, R.: Experimental validation of minimum time-jerk algorithms for industrial robots. J. Intell. Robot. Syst. **64**, 197–219 (2011). https://doi.org/10.1007/s10846-010-9533-5

12. Yang, Y., Xu, H., Li, S., Zhang, L., Yao, X.: Time-optimal trajectory optimization of serial robotic manipulator with kinematic and dynamic limits based on improved particle swarm optimization. Int. J. Adv. Manuf. Technol. **120**, 1253–1264 (2022). https://doi.org/10.1007/s00170-022-08796-y

13. Jia, Z., Yu, J., Mei, Y., Chen, Y., Shen, Y., Ai, X.: Integral backstepping sliding mode control for quadrotor helicopter under external uncertain disturbances. Aerosp. Sci. Technol. **68**, 299–307 (2017). https://doi.org/10.1016/j.ast.2017.05.022

14. Saramago, S.F.P., Steffen, V.: Optimization of the trajectory planning of robot manipulators taking into account the dynamics of the system. Mech. Mach. Theory. **33**, 883–894 (1998). https://doi.org/10.1016/S0094-114X(97)00110-9

15. Tang, W., Daoutidis, P.: A bilevel programming approach to the convergence analysis of control-lyapunov functions. IEEE Trans. Autom. Control. **64**, 4174–4179 (2019). https://doi.org/10.1109/TAC.2019.2892386

TBM Tunnel Surrounding Rock Debris Detection Based on Improved YOLO v8

Lianhui Jia[1,2(✉)], Heng Wang[2], Yongliang Wen[2], and Lijie Jiang[2,3]

[1] School of Mechanical Science and Engineering, Huazhong University of Science and Technology, Wuhan 430074, Hubei, China
19801355105@163.com
[2] Railway Engineering Equipment Group Co., Ltd., No. 99, 6th Avenue National Economic & Technical Development Zone, Henan 450016 Zhengzhou, China
[3] Zhejiang University, Hangzhou 310058, Zhejiang, China

Abstract. Real time detection of debris particle size is an important means to ensure the safe and efficient construction of TBM. In response to the problems of similar background, random and diverse contours, dense distribution, and overlapping accumulation of TBM debris, an improved YOLO v8 model for TBM tunnel surrounding rock debris detection is proposed. Using the preprocessing methods of ACE algorithm and CLAHE algorithm to improve image illumination intensity and contrast; Introducing deformable convolution to adapt to the irregular shape of debris; Add attention mechanism to the feature channel and selectively emphasize fragment features using global information to solve the problem of similar backgrounds; In the Prediction section, a dynamic non monotonic focusing mechanism is used to improve the quality of the anchor frame and further enhance the detection accuracy of debris recognition. Engineering validation was carried out based on the Dianzhong Water Diversion TBM project, and the results showed that the recognition rate of this method reached 95.7%, and the detection speed reached 43 FPS.

Keywords: TBM · Identification of debris fragments · YOLOv8 · Attention mechanism · Object detection

1 Introduction

Rock debris is various forms of debris produced by the rock layer during TBM excavation under the rolling action of cutting tools, such as block and sheet shapes. Its shape, size, and other physical properties are directly related to the current TBM mechanical state and construction geological conditions [1, 2]. At present, in practical engineering, the main reliance is on manual observation, which poses problems such as poor working environment, high subjectivity, and susceptibility to safety accidents. The use of machine vision technology can achieve low-cost and long-term online real-time monitoring. The particle size distribution of rock debris obtained through visual detection statistics can provide scientific basis for evaluating the characteristics of surrounding rock in the face and guiding excavation parameters [3].

H. Yang et al. (Eds.): ICIRA 2023, LNAI 14272, pp. 177–188, 2023.
https://doi.org/10.1007/978-981-99-6480-2_15

Amankwah and Aldrich used Voronoi map transformation to segment rock images and watershed algorithm to detect rock edges [4], but it is not suitable for situations where rock debris is tightly adhered. Dong and Jiang [5] designed a series of filtering, morphological operations, and watershed transformation processes to ultimately determine the size of ore particles, but in actual engineering, the surrounding rock fragments do not meet the conditions for their target area to be closed and independent. Bai et al. [6] used convex shell algorithm for preliminary segmentation and then separated adhesive particles. Gan Zhangze et al. improved the watershed segmentation algorithm [7] by using the minimum rectangle fitting method to measure the long and short sleeve sizes of rock debris slices. These two methods have certain effects on rock image segmentation, but in cases where there is stacking and overlapping of rocks, they cannot extract a relatively complete contour, and there are certain errors in the contour.

Deep learning has been gradually promoted in the field of tunnel construction due to its end-to-end structure and good robustness. Huang and Zhang et al. summarized the application of deep learning in tunnel construction [8, 9], including rock image segmentation. Reference [10] established LeNet-5 and AlexNet neural network models to detect coal gangue patterns, but did not consider the uneven sample size, making it difficult to ensure the detection accuracy of small-sized debris; Wei et al. [11] formed a fragment instance segmentation model through two sub networks: object detection and semantic segmentation. Although it can achieve object detection, it has not been tested under background interference and overlapping stacking conditions, and there is still a certain gap in performance and speed compared to single stage algorithms represented by the YOLO series.

Aiming at the problem that surrounding rock debris is difficult to detect due to background interference, uneven size, overlapping accumulation and other characteristics, this paper proposes a TBM tunnel surrounding rock debris detection model based on improved YOLO v8. The main contributions are as follows: (1) Design an image preprocessing module based on automatic color balance and limited contrast adaptive histogram equalization algorithm to reduce the impact of dim background; (2) Based on the YOLOv8 object detection network, by establishing a C2f-DCN module and adding an attention module, the recognition accuracy under overlapping debris accumulation is improved; (3) Replace WIoU loss function to improve the quality of anchor frame and realize high-precision identification of uneven size debris pieces. The effectiveness of this method has been verified through the Dianzhong Water Diversion Project. Based on the size distribution results of visual inspection, it is helpful to further evaluate the excavation control parameters.

2 Image Preprocessing

2.1 Automatic Color Enhancement

During TBM excavation, the interior of the tunnel is dark and dusty, and the quality of the image of the debris cannot be effectively guaranteed, and there is interference caused by the similarity of the color and background of the debris. To improve the detection effect of the model on debris, the Automatic Color Equalization (ACE) method is first used to increase brightness and enhance the image effect by changing the contrast of local and nonlinear features in the image. The main process is as follows:

1) Color correction. The region adaptive filter is used to process the initial image I, simulate the lateral inhibition and region adaptability of the human visual system, and adjust the color space to obtain the intermediate result image R.

$$R_c(p) = \sum_{j \in subset, j \neq p} \frac{r(I_c(p) - I_c(j))}{d(p,j)} \tag{1}$$

$R_c(p)$ is the brightness of the processed pixels p; $I_c(p)$ is the brightness of pixels j; $I_c(j)$ is the brightness of pixels j; $d(p,j)$ is the Euclidean distance function between pixels p, j; $r()$ is the brightness representation function as follows.

$$r(x) = \begin{cases} 1, & x > T \\ x/T, & -T < x < T \\ -1, & x < T \end{cases} \tag{2}$$

2) Image dynamic expansion. Stretch and map the resulting image R obtained from Form.1 to the range of 0–255, correct the color difference of the image, reconstruct the image, and obtain the final image L. The calculation formula is as follows:

$$L_c(p) = \frac{R_c(p) - \min R}{\max R - \min R} \tag{3}$$

$\min R$ and $\max R$ are the minimum and maximum values of the defined domain.

2.2 Limited Contrast Adaptive Histogram Equalization

After ACE algorithm is used, there may still be problems such as uneven gray distribution and unclear image details. The restricted contrast adaptive histogram equalization (CLAHE) is used to further enhance the image [12]. Base on limiting the height of the histogram, the CLAHE algorithm also proposes an interpolation method to solve the defect of block discontinuity. The final improved image histogram is:

$$H_{ist}(i) = \{ \begin{matrix} H_{ist}(i) + L, H_{ist}(i) < T \\ H_{\max}, H_{ist} \geq T \end{matrix}, H_{\max} = S_{\max} \times \frac{255}{M \times M} \tag{4}$$

$S_{\max}$ is the maximum slope limited by the $M \times M$ sliding window processing, $H_{\max}$ is the maximum height of the histogram, T is the threshold for partitioning the histogram, and L is the overall height of the histogram.

2.3 Image Effect After Preprocessing

After two image processing steps, the feature of the debris is significantly enhanced, which is conducive to improving the detection effect of the model, as shown in Fig. 1.

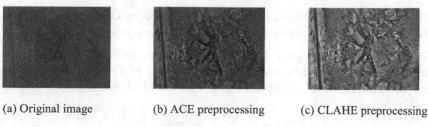

(a) Original image   (b) ACE preprocessing   (c) CLAHE preprocessing

Fig. 1. Image preprocessing effect

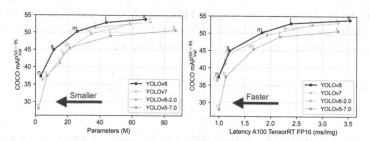

Fig. 2. YOLOv8 Performance Comparison Chart

3 YOLOv8 Basic Model Selection

YOLO is currently the most popular real-time object detector with the following advantages: a) lightweight network structure; b) Effective feature fusion; c) More accurate test results. YOLOv8 builds on the success of previous YOLO versions.

YOLOv8 provides models of different sizes based on scaling coefficients to meet the needs of different scenarios, as shown in Fig. 2. The backbone network uses C2f structure with richer gradient flow. The Head section has been replaced with the current mainstream decoupling head structure, and Loss adopts a Task Aligned Assigner positive sample allocation strategy, which selects positive samples based on the weighted scores of classification and regression, further improving performance and flexibility. This article aims to carry out real-time detection and recognition of debris on TBM, taking into account recognition accuracy and speed, and selecting YOLOv8m as the basic detection model for debris recognition.

4 Proposed AT-YOLOv8 Model

YOLOv8 is comprehensive in all aspects, but it still cannot be directly applied to debris detection tasks due to the following reasons: a) When extracting debris features, small targets are misled by large targets, and the deep extracted features lack a large amount of small target information, reducing accuracy; b) The uneven distribution of debris size is dense, overlapping and stacking with each other, and a large number of features are occluded, which increases the difficulty of model differentiation and localization.

In order to solve the above problems, this article proposes an improved detection algorithm that can ensure the detection effect of normal debris size in complex environments, and improve the detection effect of small and stacked targets. The specific improvements are as follows.

4.1 Introducing Deformable Convolutional Networks

Ballast itself has strong inherent properties, but the shape of the fragments generated by tool compression and crushing is irregular. Fixed block convolution can make the geometric transformation ability inefficient in the feature extraction process, thereby reducing recognition rate. The deformable convolution is introduced here to change the Receptive field from a rectangle or a square to an irregular shape [13], which can preserve the characteristics of the target to be detected to the greatest extent and meet the requirements of slag detection. As shown in Fig. 3

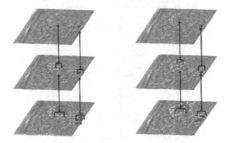

Fig. 3. Ordinary convolutional feature extraction (left) and deformable convolutional feature extraction (right)

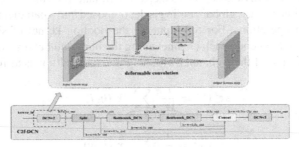

Fig. 4. C2f-DCN module improved based on DCN

For target recognition of debris detection, the DCN concept is introduced to establish a C2f-DCN module to replace the C2f module, as shown in Fig. 4. After using the C2f-DCN module in the backbone network to replace the C2f module in the network, the number of network layers remains unchanged, with parameters increasing by 56430 and gradients increasing by 56430, accounting for 1.87% of the total parameters of the YOLOv8m model. The C2f-DCN module further optimizes the feature information learned by the network model without changing the existing model parameters, greatly improving the detection accuracy of debris.

4.2 Introducing CA Attention Module

Due to the large sampling interval, the original YOLOv8 model is prone to losing small fragment features during convolution operations. The attention mechanism can enable the model to ignore irrelevant information and focus on key information, improving detection efficiency and accuracy. The CA attention mechanism can encode both horizontal and vertical position information into channel attention, model position information and long-range dependencies, without incurring excessive computational complexity. Therefore, this article introduces the CA attention mechanism (Fig. 5).

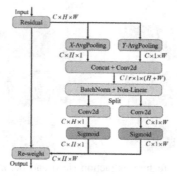

Fig. 5. CA attention mechanism principle

The CA module is divided into two steps: coordinate information embedding and attention generation. Firstly, global pooling is decomposed into a pair of one-dimensional feature encoding operations. For the input X, the pooling kernel of size $(H, 1)$ and $(1, W)$ is first used to encode each channel along the horizontal and vertical coordinate directions. The output of the c channel with height h and width w is as follows:

$$z_c^h(h) = \frac{1}{W} \sum_{0 \le i \le W} x_c(h, i) \tag{5}$$

$$z_c^w(w) = \frac{1}{H} \sum_{0 \le j \le H} x_c(j, w) \tag{6}$$

Secondly, the width and height feature maps with the global receptive field are spliced together, where the dimension is C/r. After batch normalization, input the characteristic graph F_1 into the activation function *Sigmoid* to get the graph f.

$$f = \delta(F_1([z^h, z^w])) \tag{7}$$

$f \in R^{C/r \times (w+h)}$ is the horizontal and vertical intermediate characteristic map of spatial information, r is the down sampling rate. Next, along the spatial dimension, f is divided into two separate tensor sums $f^h \in R^{C/r \times (w+h)}$, $f^w \in R^{C/r \times (w+h)}$, and then its feature map is transformed into the same number of channels as the input X using two 1×1 convolutions to obtain weights in the height h and width w directions.

$$g^h = \sigma(F_h(f^h)), \ g^w = \sigma(F_w(f^w)) \tag{8}$$

By weighting the original feature maps as weights, the final output can be obtained.

$$y_c(i,j) = x_c(i,j) \times g_c^h(i) \times g_c^w(j) \tag{9}$$

After multiple experiments, it has been proven that adding CA attention module in front of YOLOv8's SPPF layer has the best effect, which can strengthen the fused local and global features, and enrich the expression ability of feature maps.

4.3 Introducing Wise IoU Loss Function

The YOLOv8 model uses the CIoU regression loss function. CIoU adds the loss of the detection frame scale on the basis of DIoU, but it does not take into account the direction of the mismatch between the real box and the prediction box, which will obviously affect the detection effect. Therefore, Wise IoU (WIoU) is introduced here [14].

WIoU adopts a dynamic non monotonic focusing mechanism, using "outliers" instead of IoU to evaluate the quality of anchor frames, and providing a wise gradient gain allocation strategy. While reducing the competitiveness of high-quality anchor frames, it also reduces the harmful gradients generated by low-quality examples, improve the overall performance of debris detection.

4.4 Improved YOLOv8m Model

Based on the above theoretical research and analysis, an AT-YOLOv8 model that introduces attention mechanism can be obtained. And the structure is shown in Fig. 6.

5 Experiment

5.1 Dataset Introduction

In the Dianzhong Water Diversion Project, debris images were collected for dataset production. The image acquisition system is shown in Fig. 7. In addition to the industrial camera (5 million pixels, frequency 10 Hz), lens (8 mm fixed focus), and installation bracket, a protective shell was installed to improve image acquisition stability.

The main lithology in the tunnel is basalt, limestone, and dolomite, with a total of 1500 images collected. The statistical results of the dataset are shown in Fig. 8.

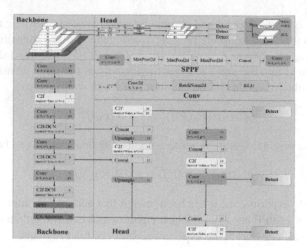

Fig. 6. Improved AT-YOLOv8 network structure

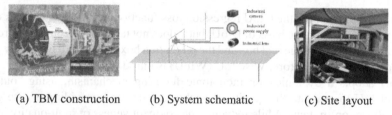

(a) TBM construction   (b) System schematic   (c) Site layout

Fig. 7. Debris data acquisition device equipped in TBM project

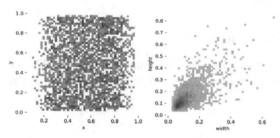

Fig. 8. Statistical results of the center point position (left) and size distribution (right) in dataset

5.2   Experimental Platform and Model Training Configuration

The experimental equipment used is a workstation, with a Quadro RTX 5000 GPU and CUDA10.0. The deep learning framework is Pytorch 1.7.1, and the important parameter settings are shown in Table 1. Evaluate the experimental results using average precision AP (average precision), recall rate (Recall), and inference time per frame.

Table 1. Setting of training parameters for debris recognition

Parameter Name	Parameter value	Parameter Name	Parameter value
Lr0	0.01	Weight_decay	0.0005
Lrf	0.01	Warmup_epochs	3.0
Momentum	0.937	Batch_size	16.0

5.3 Experimental Results and Analysis

Comparative Experiment. In order to objectively analyze the performance of the improved model, a comparative experiment was conducted between the AT-YOLOv8 improved model and mainstream network algorithms shown in the Table 2.

Table 2. Experimental comparison results

Model	Weight/MB	Average accuracy/%	Recall rate/%	Inference time per frame/ms
Faster-RCNN	159.2	56.9	58.3	253
SSD	100.2	42.3	50.1	141
YOLOv4	246.0	51.3	60.7	89
YOLOv5	41.9	60.5	63.6	67
YOLOv8n	14.2	66.8	70.7	21
YOLOv8m	31.6	72.5	75.6	26
AT-YOLOv8m	**33.7**	**95.7**	**96.1**	**23**
AT-YOLOv8x	66.7	96.2	97.1	87

It can be seen that the YOLO series network has the advantage of lightweight and is suitable for application in TBM excavation sites. The improved model AT-YOLOv8m only increases the weight by 1.9 MB compared to YOLOv8m. On the basis of a 2 ms slower inference time per frame compared to YOLOv8n, the average accuracy and recall rate are 23.2 and 20.6% points higher, respectively, confirming that the deformable convolutional module The improvement of attention mechanism and loss function can improve the detection results of YOLO model in debris recognition.

YOLOv8x has advantages in average accuracy and recall compared to YOLOv8m, but its weight is about twice that of YOLOv8m, and its inference speed does not have an advantage; By adding the same modifications to the YOLOv8x model, an improved model AT-YOLOv8x was formed, there is not much difference in average accuracy and recall, with a slight improvement, but there is no advantage in inference speed.

For this experiment, the goal of achieving real-time recognition of debris on embedded devices requires comprehensive consideration of the model's lightness, accuracy, and real-time performance, and AT-YOLOv8m has certain advantages.

Ablation Experiment. The ablation comparison experiment is to verify the optimization effect of each improvement module, and the experimental results are shown in the Table 3. Among them, the improved model 1 indicates that the C2f module is replaced by C2f-DCN module in the backbone network, the improved model 2 adds CA attention mechanism, and the improved model 3 indicates the modification of the loss function.

After replacing the C2f module with C2f DCN, the average accuracy increased by 19.9% points, but the inference time decreased by 3 ms; After adding the attention model, the average accuracy increased by 13.1% points, while the inference time increased by 5 ms; Modifying the loss function can not only improve the recognition accuracy of debris pieces, but also reduce the reasoning speed.

The fully improved model improves the detection accuracy by 23.2% points while ensuring inference speed, which greatly improves the target detection of debris recognition in TBM complex construction sites.

Table 3. Results of ablation experiment

Model	Using DCN Modules	Join CA attention mechanism	Modify loss function	Average accuracy/%	Inference time per frame/ms
YOLOv8m	✗	✗	✗	72.5	26
Improved Model 1	✓	✗	✗	92.4	29
Improved Model 2	✗	✓	✗	85.6	21
Improved Model 3	✗	✗	✓	89.3	22
AT-YOLOv8m	✓	✓	✓	**95.7**	**23**

Analysis of Test Results. Figure 9 shows the detection effect of AT-YOLOv8 on debris in different complex scenes. (a) and (b) demonstrate that the model can still fully extract debris features from the image under dim background conditions; (c) And (d) prove that the model can still have good applicability and accuracy under uneven size, overlapping stacking, and background interference.

In order to better validate the feasibility of the AT-YOLOv8 model, some images were selected in the test set for comparative testing, as shown in Fig. 10. This proves that the AT-YOLOv8 proposed in this paper solves the problems of missed detection, false detection, and insensitivity to uneven size targets in the complex environment of debris detection in the original YOLOv8 model. In complex construction environments, it has better robustness and detection performance.

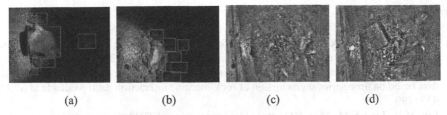

(a)   (b)   (c)   (d)

Fig. 9. The detection effect of AT-YOLOv8 model under dim background, uneven size, and overlapping accumulation of debris

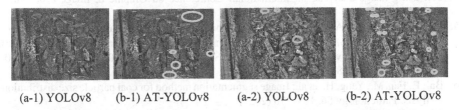

(a-1) YOLOv8   (b-1) AT-YOLOv8   (a-2) YOLOv8   (b-2) AT-YOLOv8

Fig. 10. Comparison of detection effects between YOLOv8 (a) and AT-YOLOv8 (b)

6 Conclusion

1. This paper proposes an improved algorithm AT-YOLOv8 model to address the issues of missed detection and low detection accuracy in current detection algorithms due to background interference, uneven size, and overlapping stacking of surrounding rock fragments. The detection capability of the model for surrounding rock debris in complex environments is improved by adding automatic color balance and limited contrast adaptive histogram equalization pre-processing modules before input to the detection network, establishing C2f DCN structure in YOLOv8m trunk extraction network, adding attention mechanism, improving loss function, etc.
2. The experimental results show that the AT-YOLOv8 model outperforms the YOLOv8 model in detecting small and dense targets of surrounding rock debris generated during TBM excavation, and can achieve good detection accuracy and speed, meeting the accuracy and timeliness requirements for detecting surrounding rock debris generated during TBM complex construction scenarios.
3. This model has good generalization ability and can also be adapted to other types of target detection tasks.
4. The next research focus is to further optimize the model while ensuring speed accuracy. Combined with segmentation algorithms, the volume recognition and detection algorithm for debris is studied, and the recognition results are combined with the current TBM excavation geological conditions to apply to intelligent adjustment of excavation parameters.

Acknowledgments. This work was supported in part by the National Key Research and Development Program of China under Grant 2020YFB2007200.

References

1. Gong, Q.M., Zhou, X.X., Yin, L.J., et al.: Study of rock breaking efficiency of TBM disc cutter based on chips analysis of linear cutting test. Tunnel Constr. **37**(3), 363–368 (2017)
2. Xue, Y., Luo, W., Chen, L., et al.: An intelligent method for TBM surrounding rock classification based on time series segmentation of rock-machine interaction data. Available at SSRN 4331299
3. Liu, M.B., Liao, S.M., Men, Y.Q., et al.: Field monitoring of TBM vibration during excavating changing stratum: patterns and ground Identification. Rock Mech. Rock Eng., 1–18 (2021)
4. Amankwah, A., Aldrich, C.: Automatic estimation of rock particulate size on conveyer belt using image analysis. In: International Conference on Graphic & Image Processing. International Society for Optics and Photonics (2011)
5. Dong, K., Jiang, D.: Automated estimation of ore size distributions based on machine vision. In: Xing, S., Chen, S., Wei, Z., Xia, J. (eds.) Unifying Electrical Engineering and Electronics Engineering. LNEE, vol. 238, pp. 1125–1131. Springer, New York (2014). https://doi.org/10.1007/978-1-4614-4981-2_122
6. Bai, F., Fan, M., Yang, H., et al.: Image segmentation method for coal particle size distribution analysis. Particuology **56**, 163–170 (2021)
7. Gan, Z.Z., Xie, J.H., Xia, Y.M., et al.: Application of improved watershed algorithm in TBM rock debris identification and measurement. Transducer Microsyst. Technol. **39**(11), 155–157 (2020)
8. Huang, M., Ninic, J., Zhang, Q.: BIM, machine learning and computer vision techniques in underground construction: current status and future perspectives. Tunn. Undergr. Space Technol. **108**, 103677 (2021)
9. Zhang, W., Li, H., Li, Y., et al.: Application of deep learning algorithms in geotechnical engineering: a short critical review. Artif. Intell. Rev. **54**(8), 5633–5673 (2021)
10. Su, L., Cao, X., Ma, H., et al.: Research on coal gangue identification by using convolutional neural network. In: IEEE Advanced Information Management, Communicates, Electronic and Automation Control Conference, Xi'an, pp. 810–814 (2018)
11. Qiao, W., Zhao, Y., Xu, Y., et al.: Deep learning-based pixel-level rock fragment recognition during tunnel excavation using instance segmentation model. Tunn. Undergr. Space Technol. **115**, 104072 (2021)
12. Alwakid, G., Gouda, W., Humayun, M.: Deep Learning-based prediction of Diabetic Retinopathy using CLAHE and ESRGAN for Enhancement. Healthcare MDPI **11**(6), 863 (2023)
13. Gao, K., Su, J., Jiang, Z., et al.: Dual-branch combination network (DCN): towards accurate diagnosis and lesion segmentation of COVID-19 using CT images. Med. Image Anal. **67**, 101836 (2021)
14. Tong, Z., Chen, Y., Xu, Z., et al.: Wise-IoU: bounding box regression loss with dynamic focusing mechanism. arXiv preprint arXiv:2301.10051 (2023)

Development and Application of Large Curved-Shaped Pipe Roofing Method with Rectangular Jacking Machine Under the Yangtze River

Yixin Zhai[1]([✉]) and Chi Zhang[2]

[1] Shanghai Shield Research Centre Co., Ltd., Shanghai 200137, People's Republic of China
26851102@qq.com
[2] Shanghai Urban Construction Tunnel Equipment Co., Ltd., Shanghai 200137, People's Republic of China

Abstract. In order to achieve a no-touch and micro-damage salvage under the Yangtze River, a novel underwater wreck salvage method using the large curved shape pipe-roof with rectangular jacking machine (called the CPRJ method in the next study) was proposed. In this study, the feasibility, critical construction parameters and practical application of the novel method were discussed from the equipment, experiment, and on-site construction based on the ancient wreck salvage project named the 'Yangtze River Estuary II'. The reduced-scale model test (1:10) effectively confirmed the feasibility of the CPRJ method, and the clearance between the locks was controlled to around 2 mm. In the full-scale model test (1:1), an embedded rectangular jacking machine ahead of the pipe section and a combination of the oil motor, gear, and rack in the propulsion system were used. Notably, the propulsion time of a single pipe section can be controlled to about 4 h and the thrust force to less than 1500 kN. In the on-site salvage construction, 22 pipe sections were propelled at a thrust force less than 1000 kN and a locking clearance within 10 mm. The CPRJ method was well validated in the ancient wreck salvage project.

Keywords: Yangtze River Estuary II · Ancient wreck salvage · Large curved-shaped pipe roofing method with rectangular jacking machine · Reduced-scale model test · Full-scale model test · Thrust force

1 Introduction

The pipe roofing method originated from pipe jacking technology forms a large overrun support structure by pipe jacking at the head of the excavation area. Specifically, the pipe roofing structure is constructed by using steel pipes and applying prestress along the ring direction, then the individual steel pipes can be stressed collaboratively and loaded bidirectionally to reduce the size of the components and improve the overall stiffness and load-bearing capacity of the pipe roofing structure. The impact of construction on the surface environment can be effectively controlled by this method and it has been widely used in the underground engineering [1]. As early as the 1970s, Antwerp Central Station in Belgium [2] was first constructed using pipe roofing technique, and on the basis of this method, Lunardi [3] proposed the "pipe arch" concept, which improved the overall stiffness of the pipe roofing structure. In the 1990s, Korea completed the structure of station 923 on Line 9 of the Seoul Metro based on the pipe arch concept [4]. The pipe roofing method in China was first applied in Hong Kong in 1984, and later used in Taipei Song Shan Airport underpass and underpass between Hong Xu Road and Bei Hong Road in Shanghai Central Line [5]. In recent years, the pipe roofing method has been used in China for the excavation of the Wuding Road Station of Line 14 in Shanghai [6] and the Ping'anli Station of Line 19 in Beijing [7]. However, most construction cases of pipe roofing method use small diameter and straight pipe sections with short distance, and only a few cases of projects have used curved pipe sections, such as the concealed excavation project of Brandenburg Gate Station of the Berlin underground in Germany and Gongbei Tunnel in Zhuhai, China, to control the deformation of the ground [8].

In the construction of pipe roofing method, the thrust force is the key factor. Scholars at home and abroad have conducted a lot of research on the calculation method of the thrust force for horizontal linear pipe jacking based on empirical formulae, numerical simulation, elasticity theory, etc. [9–11]. Based on the curved shape pipe-roof with jacking machine in the Gongbei tunnel, Zhang et al. [12] studied the contact pressure distribution of curved steel pipe section under burial depth conditions, and consequently established the calculation formula of thrust force. Ding et al. [13] derived a method for calculating the active ultimate support pressure of rectangular pipe sections by improving the classical wedge calculation model. In addition, some scholars have carried out systematic studies on soil deformation and the interaction between pipe sections caused by pipe jacking and pipe roofing construction, and the effects of soil loss, frontal additional thrust, lateral frictional resistance between pipe sections and the ground, and grouting pressure were also studied [14–16].

At present, the traditional methods of salvaging wrecks mainly include sealed chamber pumping salvage, float salvage, ship lift salvage, foam salvage, cofferdam salvage and inflatable drainage salvage, etc. [17]. Notably, these methods mostly require the replacement or modification of the wreck's interior and can cause considerable damage to the wreck itself. In China, the ancient wreck of "Nanhai No.I" was salvaged using the "steel caisson + bottom joist" touch-free method [18, 19]. The South Korean ferry "Seoketsu" was salvaged using the integral method of "steel beam bottoming, full netting, integral floating and lifting to shore" [20]. However, these two salvage methods have a limited application, a long construction period, are heavily influenced by the weather, and the bottom joist jacking will produce a significant crowding effect, which may cause variable damage to the wreck and its cargo. Moreover, offshore operations are restricted by currents, wind and waves, and underwater work usually needs to be done by divers due to the low visibility and limited means of location detection. In this study, techniques from the pipe roofing method will be innovatively applied to the salvage of wreck under the Yangtze River.

2   Engineering Background and Construction Equipment

2.1   Engineering Background

The 'Yangtze River Estuary II' ancient wreck, discovered in September 2015 near Heng Sha Island in the Yangtze River Estuary (Fig. 1), is the largest and best-preserved wooden wreck with a large number of artefacts on board that has ever been discovered by underwater archaeology in China. In this project, the pipe roofing method was innovatively applied to the field of wreck salvage, moreover, the CPRJ method was proposed for the overall salvage and relocation of the 'Yangtze River Estuary II' ancient wreck.

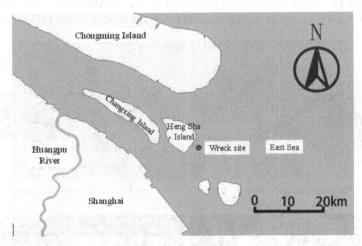

Fig. 1. Location of ancient wreck

2.2   Principle and Equipment

The CPRJ method is a way of forming a monolithic framework by passing curved jacking pipes through the stratum in sequence and then lifting them as a whole, integrating the technical core of curved pipe jacking and pipe roofing method. The main steps of the CPRJ method are as follows:

Step1: Four corner point locating stakes are installed outside the calculated minimum affected area to fix the salvage frame (Fig. 2a). The stakes are to be located a certain distance above the mud surface to facilitate the positioning of the top beam.

Step2: The top beam with four corner pre-drilled holes is placed through the locating stakes until it is sunk to the mud surface (Fig. 2b). The top beam consists of the top ring beam and the end plates on both sides. The top beam is the support for the start and reception of the curved beam and is also the stressing point for the overall lift. Slots are provided in the end plates to act as traction for the first and last curved beams and to seal off the entry of soil and water on both sides. The top beam has pin holes reserved for fixing, which are used as lifting points for the overall lifting after the curved beam has been installed. Pins are left on both sides of the top beam for fixing the curved beam and are inserted after the curved beam has been installed.

Step3: The seat head, curved beam and guide bearing are assembled and lifted into their intended position on the construction vessel, pins are inserted and the hydraulic oil, water lines and electrical system are connected to start the installation of the curved beam. As shown in Fig. 2c, the curved guide frame is installed with a rack that engages with the gears of the propulsion box and provides the propulsion reaction force. A hydraulic motor is fixed to the propulsion box and drives the pinion, which enables the propulsion box to be pushed against the curved beam along a defined curvature (Fig. 2d). Notably, the guide frame has balls on the top, bottom and sides to minimise frictional losses in the thrust force.

Step4: The curved beams are installed in a symmetrical sequence from the outside inwards until the whole bottom tray is formed (Fig. 2e). Moreover, a lug structure is installed on the top beam for the subsequent integral lifting operation (Fig. 2f).

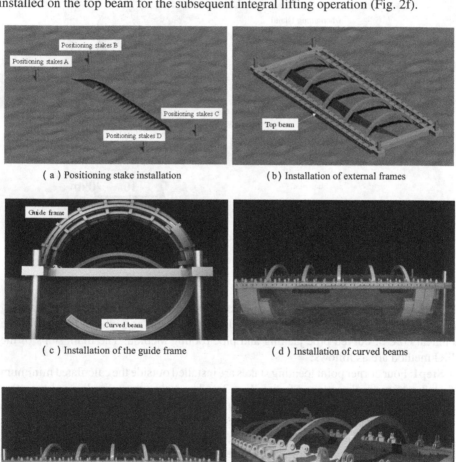

(a) Positioning stake installation   (b) Installation of external frames

(c) Installation of the guide frame   (d) Installation of curved beams

(e) Roof formation   (f) Installation of the lug structure

Fig. 2. Main steps of the CPRJ method

In contrast to the traditional pipe roofing method, a curved pipe section with a matching curved guide frame (Fig. 3) as a guide traction was used in this project. The pipe section was initially placed inside the guide frame. For the characteristics of underwater construction, the propulsion system abandoned the traditional segmental and cylinder jacking method, adopted hydraulic motor and rack for the whole propulsion (Fig. 4), the front of the pipe section is equipped with a rectangular jacking machine (Fig. 5).

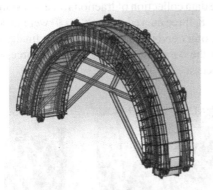

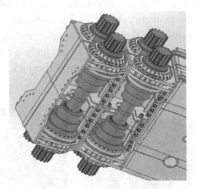

Fig. 3. Guide frame   **Fig. 4.** Propulsion system

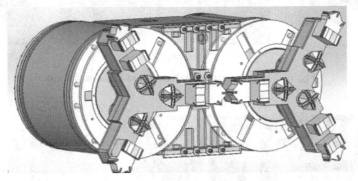

Fig. 5. Rectangular jacking machine

3 Laboratory Tests

3.1 Reduced-Scale Model Test

To verify the feasibility of the CPRJ method and provide experience in terms of equipment and construction, a reduced scale model test was carried out. The test was carried out in a 1.5 m × 2.0 m × 1.8 m soil box filled with iron sheet sand sampled from the wreck site. The sand was buried to a depth of 1.45 m and water was added to submerge the soil. The water surface was kept slightly above the soil surface during the test to simulate the on-site salvage environment. The curved beam of the model has an inner diameter of 0.75 m, an outer diameter of 0.85 m, a cross-sectional width of 0.2 m and a height of 0.1 m. The pipe section and launcher are reduced in size to one tenth of the original design dimension. Due to the restrictions of the test site and size of the soil box, the rectangular jacking machine of the curved pipe section is a gridded extrusion with a pre-drilled inlet and outlet mud hole at the end (Fig. 6). The propulsion method uses a drawbar and a hinge. Specifically, the drawbar is welded to the vertical end surface at the end of the pipe section, the hinge is connected through the pulley. A tension sensor connected to the microcomputer for real-time data collection of traction force is installed on the pulling cable (Fig. 7). As shown in Fig. 8, three curved beams (①–③) were jacked in sequence, then the curved beam (④) at the other end plate was jacked, and finally the closed curved beam (⑤) was jacked to form the complete pallet. The thrust force was measured in real time during the jacking process.

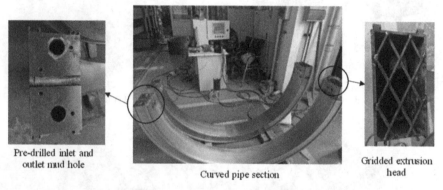

Pre-drilled inlet and outlet mud hole

Curved pipe section

Gridded extrusion head

Fig. 6. The pipe section in the reduced-scale model test

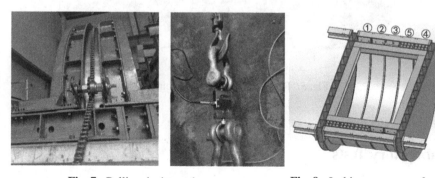

Fig. 7. Pulling device and sensor

Fig. 8. Jacking sequence of curved beams

The variation of thrust force with angle obtained from the test is shown in Fig. 9, and the friction loss is neglected in view of the smoothness of this pipe section. Apart from the pipe sections near the two end plates, the trend and magnitude of thrust force for the middle three pipe sections and single pipe section are relatively similar, with the maximum thrust force being less than 2000 N and the maximum thrust force occurring between approximately 120°–180°. Notably, the initial slope of thrust force for the pipe section near the end plate is greater than that of other pipe sections due to the frictional losses, and it remains stable between 2000 N and 3000 N after about 60° of jacking.

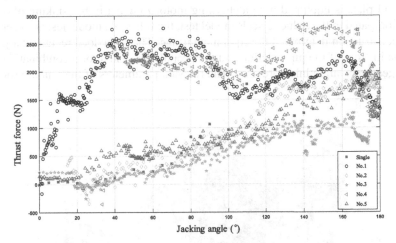

Fig. 9. Variation of thrust force in the reduced-scale model test

The pipe sections are well connected at the latches, with smooth connections and flat end faces. A partial enlargement of the locking area (Fig. 10) shows that the locking clearance is relatively close to 2 mm. This shows the feasibility of the CPRJ method and the excellent attitude control of the pipe section.

Fig. 10. Detail of latch connection

3.2 Full-Scale Model Test

The site of the full-scale model test was located approximately 2 km from the wreck site and was designed to simulate the realistic environment of the wreck site. The mud layer on the river bottom is mainly a layer of iron sheet sand with the thickness of about 3.2 m and a layer of greenish grey mud with the thickness greater than 4.3 m. The dimensions of the testing equipment correspond to the size of the actual salvage equipment, which mainly include the pipe section, end plate and propulsion system (Fig. 11). The bottom of the end plate is equipped with a churning motor to assist in the sinking of the end plate. Compared to the reduced-scale model test, the full-scale model test is closer to the actual construction in terms of the equipment usage. The embedded rectangular jacking machine in front of the pipe section and the propulsion system of a combination of oil motor, gear, rack and pinion are used. The relevant parameters of the unit are shown in Table 1.

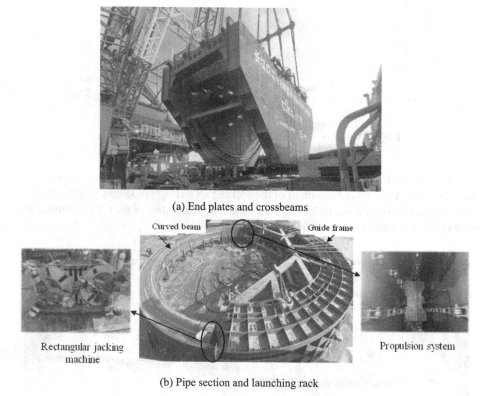

(a) End plates and crossbeams

(b) Pipe section and launching rack

Fig. 11. Equipment used in the full-scale model test

The main initial step of the full-scale model test was to sink the end plate, which was eventually lowered into the mud to a depth of 7.2 m by diving and probing. However, the greenish grey mud was poorly self-supporting, and collapsed in a slippery slope with a maximum height of 2.7 m around the end plate. Three pipe sections were then jacked in the order of the two sides first and then the middle, and the kay parameters for jacking can be seen in Table 2.

Table 1. Key parameters of the equipment

Equipment	Parameter item	Parameter value	unit
End plate	Dimension	19000 × 8500 × 1050	mm
Launching rack	Dimension	Outer arc: R8960 Inner arc: R7030	mm
Pipe section	Dimension	Outer arc: R8505 Inner arc: R7495	mm
Rectangular jacking machine	Dimension	Planetary double cutter 2 × 1	m
Cutter drive	Power	29.7	kw
Cutter drive	Rated torque	91.2	kN·m
Cutter drive	Rotational speed	0–3.11	r/min
Propulsion system	Work pressure	30	MPa
Propulsion system	Thrust force	4000	kN
Propulsion system	Advancing speed	0–50	mm/min

Table 2. The key parameters of jacking

Pipe section	Maximum thrust force/kN	Maximum torque/kN·m	Maximum advancing speed/mm·s^{-1}
Left pipe section	2200	28	500
Right pipe section	1600	25	350
Middle pipe section	1300	18	250

During the jacking of the 1st pipe section, a high advancing speed was used due to lack of construction experience, resulting in high thrust force and torque. The toque of the subsequent two pipe sections were successfully reduced by controlling the advancing speed based on reinforcement of the limit plate. In the end, it was possible to control the advancing time of a single pipe section to around 5 h and the thrust force to below 1500 kN. There was no jamming of the rectangular jacking machine during the whole process.

4 Case Study

Based on the reduced-scale and full-scale model tests, the equipment used for the actual salvage construction was consistent with the full-scale test. The number of pipe sections was increased to 22 and the jacking sequence was shown in Fig. 12. In contrast to the previous tests, the initial positioning work was added to the actual construction by driving positioning stakes around the wreck (Fig. 13). The end plates were sunk into the mud surface on the basis of positioning stakes, followed by the jacking of pipe sections.

Fig. 12. Jacking sequence of pipe sections

Fig. 13. Positioning stakes and end plates

As the data collection system was affected by construction conditions, the typical thrust force data was selected for description (Fig. 14). Specifically, the peak thrust force for most of the pipe sections was kept below 1000 kN. Some of the pipe sections, such as No. 9 and No. 10, had a peak thrust force of over 1200 kN due to the shell layer in which they were located. The whole jacking process of the 22 pipe sections was relatively smooth and the envelope of the wreck was achieved with the small clearance within 10 mm between the locks. Based on previous experimental experience, the fluctuation of each pipe thrust force has been reduced. The propulsion efficiency of each individual pipe section has been improved to 4 h per unit.

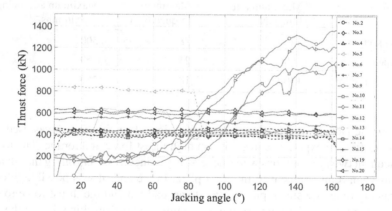

Fig. 14. Variation of thrust force

After the whole lifting of the wreck, the CPRJ method and equipment were evaluated to achieve high precision and mechanization of the salvage, effectively shortened the construction time and greatly reduced the damage rate of cultural relics. The method achieves the requirements of touch-free and micro-damage cultural preservation.

5   Conclusions

In this study, the CPRJ method was proposed for the salvage of the ancient wreck. The principle and equipment of the CPRJ method were specifically elaborated. Moreover, the reduced-scale and full-scale model tests were carried out to confirm the feasibility of this method. The main conclusions were as follows:

(1) The reduced-scale model test (1:10) effectively confirmed the feasibility of the CPRJ method by using the propulsion system of a drawbar and a hinge. The clearance between the locks was controlled to around 2 mm, and the maximum thrust occurred between approximately 120° and 180°.
(2) The full-scale model test (1:1) used an embedded rectangular jacking machine and a propulsion system controlled the propulsion time of a single pipe section to about 4 h and the thrust force to less than 1500 kN.
(3) In the salvage construction on site 22 pipe sections were jacked and the thrust force was basically controlled below 1000 kN and the clearance between the locks was controlled within 10 mm.
(4) The CPRJ method can be further applied in various fields such as ramp excavation, tunnel widening and underwater relocation etc.

Acknowledgment. This research is supported by the Shanghai Science and Technology Innovation Action Plan for 2021 (21XD1431100); Shanghai Science and Technology Commission Social Development Major Project (21DZ1201103).

Author Contributions.   YXZ and CZ conceptualized the study. YXZ conducted the data acquisition, preparation, and analysis. All authors contributed to the interpretation of results and manuscript preparation.

Data Availability Statement.   All data used in this study are true and reliable, it can be freely available through open data portals online.

Compliance with Ethical Standards.

Competing Interest.   The authors declare that they have no known competing financial interests or personal relationships that could have appeared to influence the work reported in this paper.

References

1. Zhang, P.: Research on Key Construction Techniques and Theory of Super Large Curved Pipe Jacking Roof in Gongbei Tunnel. Chinese University of Geoscience, Wuhan (2018)
2. Musso, G.: Jacked pipe provides roof for underground construction in busy urban area. Civil Eng. (ASCE) **11**(49) (1979)
3. Lunardi, P.: Cellular arch technique for large-span station cavern. Tunn. Tunnell., 23–26 (1991)
4. Jeong-Yoon, K., Inn-Joon, P., Kyong-Gon, K.: A study on the applicability of underground structure using steel tubular in Korean geotechnical condition. Tunn. Technol. (Korean) **5**(4), 401–409 (2003)

5. Li, X.Y.: Study on the Mechanical Effects of Pipe Curtain and Excavation Face Stability in the Construction Method of Large Section Pipe Curtain Box Culvert. Tongji University, Shanghai (2006)
6. Zhou, X.S., Li, Z., Chen, J.Q., et al.: Comparative analysis of the influence of underground pile-anchor-pipe curtain excavation on surface settlement in soft soil areas. Tunn. Undergr. Works **3**, 25–28 (2022)
7. Dong, L.P., Yang, S.N., Liu, Z.W.: Research and application of pipe-roof support technology for mined metro stations with ultra-shallow-buried pipe-roof cover method: a case study of Ping'anli Station of Beijing Metro Line 19. Tunn. Constr. **43**(2), 305 (2023)
8. Shi, P.X., Yu, C.C., Pan, J.L., et al.: Analysis on the jacking load of the curved pipe roof supporting the large diameter Gongbei tunnel. Chin. J. Rock Mech. Eng. **36**(9), 2251–2259 (2017)
9. He, S.N., Dou, X.T., Zhao, L.Y., et al.: Analysis of thrust force of adjacent construction of shallow-buried rectangular pipe jacking tunnel group. Tunn. Constr. **39**(03), 383–390 (2019)
10. Lin, Y.X., Peng, L.M., Wu, G.H., et al.: Discussion of a theoretical formula for the friction resistance of a pipe wall in quasi-rectangular pipe jacking. Mod. Tunn. Technol. **54**(04), 180–185 (2017)
11. Jiao, C.L., Zhao, X., Niu, F.J.: Pipe-soil contact state and jacking force prediction of rectangular pipe jacking. J. Northeastern Univ. (Nat. Sci.) **41**(10), 1459–1464 (2020)
12. Zhang, P., Ma, B.S., Zeng, C., et al.: Site monitoring analysis of contact pressure during steel curved pipe jacking with larger buried depth. J. Huazhong Univ. Sci. Technol. (Nat. Sci. Ed.) **44**(05), 93–97 (2016)
13. Ding, W.T., Wang, Z.G., Guo, X.W., et al.: Calculation method of limit support pressure for large diameter rectangular pipe jacking tunnel face. Sci. Technol. Eng. **21**(22), 9563–9569 (2021)
14. Ma, X.F., Chen, F., Wu, B., et al.: Effect of pipe jacking cable tunnel construction on adjacent buildings and underground pipelines. Sci. Technol. Eng. **21**(21), 9074–9080 (2021)
15. Li, Z.H., Li, J.: A study of the interaction between the pipes of a curved pipe-roof. Modern Tunn. Technol. **52**(03), 63–68+102 (2015)
16. Zhang, P., Li, Z.H., Zeng, C., et al.: Prediction of ground deformation induced by curved pipe jacking. Tunnel Construction **37**(09), 1120–1125 (2017)
17. Nie, L.B.: The Plan Optimization and Execution Control of Nanhai I Salvage's Engineering Project. South China University of Technology, Guangzhou (2010)
18. Wu, J.C., Zhang, Y.Q.: The integral salvage of ancient sunken vessel Nanhai I. navigation of China **31**(4), 383–387+399 (2008)
19. Kong, W.D., Hu, M.: Design of the integral floating plan and salvage technology for the Nanhai I Ancient Wreck. Ship Ocean Eng. **38**(4), 148–150 (2009)
20. Chen, S.H., Wang, W.P., Jiang, Y.: Design and implementation of the WEWOL salvage project. World Shipp. **40**(10), 6–23 (2017)

A Shield Machine Segment Position Recognition Algorithm Based on Improved Voxel and Seed Filling

Pei Zhang[1] ⓘ, Lijie Jiang[1,2](✉) ⓘ, Yongliang Wen[1], Heng Wang[1], Mingze Li[1], Ruoyu Wang[1], and Honglei Zhang[1]

[1] China Railway Engineering Equipment Group Co., Ltd., Zhengzhou 450016, China
jianglijie001@126.com
[2] School of Mechanical Engineering, Zhejiang University, Hangzhou 310027, China

Abstract. In response to the problems of low execution efficiency and poor real-time performance of traditional point cloud clustering algorithms when there is a large amount of point cloud data, which cannot meet the requirements of automatic and efficient segment grabbing, this paper proposes a shield machine segment position recognition algorithm based on improved voxel and seed filling. A multi-objective optimization model for point cloud voxel size, nail height, and nail area was established to achieve point cloud voxel space division by constraining the deviation range of segment hanging space. By setting the voxel point cloud threshold and introducing the seed filling method, point cloud clustering was realized, achieving the goal of quickly identifying the spatial coordinates of segment hanging nails. Engineering verification was carried out based on the construction project of China Railway 1084 shield tunneling, and the results showed that under approximate accuracy, the efficiency of this algorithm is 3.2 times that of European Clustering.

Keywords: TBM · Segment · Point Cloud Clustering · Voxel · Seed Filling

1 Introduction

Shield machine is a large-scale underground engineering operation equipment that integrates optical, mechanical, electrical, hydraulic, sensing, and information technology. It has the functions of excavating and cutting soil, transporting soil slag, assembling tunnel lining, measuring and guiding deviation correction, and has been widely used in tunnel engineering such as subways, railways, highways, municipal, and hydropower [1–3]. The shield tunnel segment is the main assembly component during the shield construction process, carrying the function of resisting soil pressure, groundwater pressure, and some special loads, and is the innermost barrier of the tunnel. When the shield tunneling machine advances forward, permanent support for the tunnel needs to be provided through gap assembly. Usually, prefabricated reinforced concrete segments on the ground are transported to the tail of the shield tunneling machine, and then assembled block by block using the shield tunneling segment assembly mechanism [4, 5] (Fig. 1).

© The Author(s), under exclusive license to Springer Nature Singapore Pte Ltd. 2023
H. Yang et al. (Eds.): ICIRA 2023, LNAI 14272, pp. 201–215, 2023.
https://doi.org/10.1007/978-981-99-6480-2_17

a) China Railway 1084 Shield Machine
(Excavation Diameter 2.845m)

b) Tunnel Segment Inner
Diameter 2.1m

Fig. 1. China Railway 1084 Shield and Its Excavated Tunnel

There is a bolt hole in the center of the segment, which allows for the installation of segment lifting bolts, as shown in Fig. 2-a. The segment assembly machine is a mechanical device installed at the tail end of the shield machine, with a clamping mechanism at the end that can cooperate with the segment lifting bolts to complete the grabbing, moving, and assembly actions of the segment, and ultimately achieve tunnel lining, as shown in Fig. 2-b, the segment is picked up by the assembly machine. In the entire segment assembly process, segment recognition and grasping are the foundation and key to achieving the entire step [6, 7].

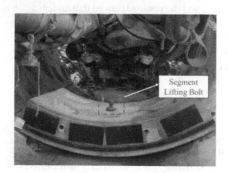

a) Segment Lifting Bolts

b) Segment Lifting

Fig. 2. Assembly Machine Grabbing Segments

During the current construction process, the grabbing of segments is manually operated by a remote control and controlled by assembly machinery [8]. For micro shield tunneling (tunnel inner diameter less than 3 m), the internal space of the tunnel is narrow, making it extremely inconvenient for workers to walk and even difficult to enter. When operating the assembly machine, man-machine interaction is required in the narrow space, which poses extremely high risks. Moreover, when manually operating the assembly machine to grab the segments, it is necessary to repeatedly observe the relative position of the segments and the assembly machine to align the clamping mechanism of the assembly machine with the lifting bolts of the segments, which is a time-consuming process [9, 10]. Therefore, developing autonomous recognition technology for segments and achieving machine assisted or automatic grasping of segments is an effective way to solve the problem of assembling micro shield tunnel segments (Fig. 3).

a) The Space Inside the Tunnel Is Narrow   b) Man-Machine Interaction in the Narrow Space

Fig. 3. Current Situation of Micro Shield Machine Segment Identification and Grasping

Therefore, the automatic grabbing of segments has become a current research hotspot, and the autonomous recognition of segment lifting bolts in complex environments is a prerequisite for achieving automatic grabbing and also one of the core bottlenecks that restrict the implementation of automatic grabbing, which has attracted widespread attention from domestic and foreign experts.

Wang Lintao et al. [11] added an attention mechanism to the Faster RCNN deep learning network, screened out the bolts of the segment to be grabbed, and combined the information from the depth camera to obtain complete three-dimensional coordinates. He Chunhui et al. [12] proposed an automated segment detection method based on close range photogrammetry, which sets marker points on shield tunnel segments, obtains the spatial coordinates of the marker points through close range photogrammetry, and detects the quality of segment assembly and segment posture. Wu Zhiyang et al. [13] used a specially designed two-stage convolutional neural network to recognize the contour features of the surface of the segment, and used a laser ranging system to obtain the depth and pose information of the segment. Xu Younan et al. [14] and others proposed a method of segment position and attitude measurement based on the linear structured light binocular measurement system to solve the problems such as position and attitude error and intelligent position and attitude detection in the segment assembly machine's working process, so as to realize the three-dimensional coordinate transformation and calculation under the segment edge point world coordinate and the manipulator coordinate system of the assembly machine. Gao Xiang et al. [15] used three line laser sensors to scan the edge of the segment, calculated the coordinates of the feature points on the segment based on the relative position coordinates of the edge points, and derived the expressions for the grasping and installation positions of the segment to be installed based on this. This scheme does not require the addition of additional marking points on the segment. Chen Xuyang et al. [16] utilized real-time monocular vision and distance measurement sensors for segment positioning and developed an improved discrete wavelet transform and adaptive multiscale Retinex algorithm based on HSV channel to improve image brightness and color contrast. The recognition accuracy exceeded 90% and the recognition time was about 0.7 s Zhiyang Wu et al. [17] proposed a segment assembly method based on laser displacement sensors (LDS) and intelligent cameras. LDS is used to measure the distance between the assembly machine and the segment, and the intelligent camera senses the gap between the segment to be assembled and the already assembled segment. Kaixian Dong et al. [18] used multiple cameras to obtain image information of the segment, and determined the three-dimensional spatial pose of the segment through image processing methods such as feature extraction and size measurement.

The existing segment recognition technology focuses more on the recognition of segment posture, neglecting the position recognition of segment bolts. However, the existing segment bolt recognition methods have the problem of low execution efficiency. In response to this, this article proposes a shield tunnel segment position recognition algorithm based on improved voxel and seed filling. Firstly, the segment point cloud data obtained from the 3D camera is preprocessed to obtain effective data. Secondly, the point cloud is divided into voxels and stored. Then, point cloud clustering is carried out using the idea of image seed filling method to achieve the segmentation of segment point cloud and lifting bolt point cloud. Finally, Determine the point cloud data of the lifting bolt based on its external dimension characteristics, and calculate its spatial position coordinates. The algorithm has optimized the storage method and clustering method of point cloud voxels, ensuring recognition effectiveness and improving algorithm efficiency (Fig. 4).

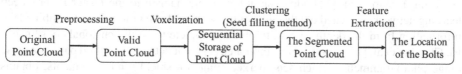

Fig. 4. Algorithm Flowchart of this Article

2 Basic Principles of Voxel and Seed Filling Methods

The core of segment position recognition is the position recognition of segment lifting bolts. After the 3D camera collects point cloud data containing both segments and lifting bolts, a point cloud clustering algorithm needs to be used to segment them. Then, based on the point cloud features, the information of the lifting bolts is identified, and the spatial position coordinates of the lifting bolts are calculated. The clustering of spatial point clouds using the idea of image seed filling can effectively improve clustering efficiency. However, point clouds, unlike images, have disordered features and cannot be directly clustered. Therefore, voxelization of point clouds is an effective means. Point cloud voxelization is the process of dividing point cloud space into grids of a certain size, and classifying, processing, and simplifying storage of point clouds according to their location.

2.1 Point Cloud Voxelization

Before voxelization of point cloud data, a voxel coordinate system is first established, with the direction of the coordinate axis where the point cloud is located as the coordinate axis direction of the voxel coordinate system. The point formed by the minimum values of the three coordinates in the original point cloud data is used as the origin of the voxel coordinate system $(X_{min}, Y_{min}, Z_{min})$. In this way, the coordinates of each voxel are integers not less than 0, and the coordinates represent the position of the voxel in the coordinate system.

The specific process of point cloud voxelization is as follows:

1) Traverse all point clouds and find the boundary of the point cloud in 3D space X_{max}, $X_{min}, Y_{max}, Y_{min}, Z_{max}, Z_{min}$;
2) Set the size A of the point cloud grid and divide the point cloud space into spatial grids based on the cube with side length A;
3) Divide all point clouds into their respective grids according to their coordinate positions: if a point cloud's coordinates are (x, y, z) and its grid number is marked as (i, j, k), then

$$\begin{cases} i = int(\frac{x - X_{min}}{a}) \\ j = int(\frac{y - Y_{min}}{a}) \\ k = int(\frac{z - Z_{min}}{a}) \end{cases} \tag{1}$$

Where $int()$ represents rounding down.

After voxelization of traditional point clouds, if there are multiple point clouds within a voxel, in order to reduce storage space and computational complexity, the average coordinates of these point clouds are calculated as the coordinates of the point cloud within that voxel. However, this approach ignores the spatial distribution of point clouds within voxels and is not very practical in situations where high accuracy is required for segment bolt recognition. As shown in the Fig. 5, point P_{avg} is the coordinates of the points averaged by all point clouds within the voxel:

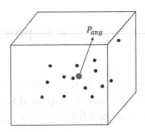

Fig. 5. Point Cloud Voxel Representation

2.2 Seed-Filling

Seed filling method is originally a method of connected area analysis in image processing. Generally, it is aimed at binary image, and adjacent pixels with the same pixel value are marked to achieve the goal of target classification. There are generally two methods for defining the adjacency of pixels: 4-neighborhood and 8-neighborhood, as shown in the Fig. 6:

a) 4 Neighborhood   b) 8 Neighborhood

Fig. 6. Connected Area Definition

Seed filling method is a search in an image that starts from a seed and searches around its neighborhood. It discovers that points with equal pixel features are labeled with the same label, and then continues to search in the neighborhood until there are no pixels with the same pixel value around them, forming a connected region. Then select other seeds and continue searching for the next connected region. Until the entire image search is completed. If the pixel value in the binary image is divided into 0 and 1, the specific process of the seed filling method is as follows:

Traverse the image, if the pixel value is 1, then perform the following actions:

a) Seed the current pixel value and assign it to a label, then add the positions of all neighboring pixels of interest (pixel value 1) to the queue;
b) Delete the pixels at the end of the queue, assign the same label, and add the positions of all neighboring pixels of interest to the queue;
c) Repeat operation b until the queue is empty, at which point a connected region is found and marked with the same label;
d) Add 1 to the label value, continue searching down, and repeat the process a)–c) until all pixels are traversed (Fig. 7).

3 Point Cloud Clustering Based on Improved Voxel and Seed Filling Method

By storing point clouds spatially according to voxels, the spatial ordering of point clouds is achieved, and the voxel storage method is improved to improve the accuracy of point cloud clustering; Apply the idea of seed filling method in images to voxels to achieve rapid clustering of point clouds.

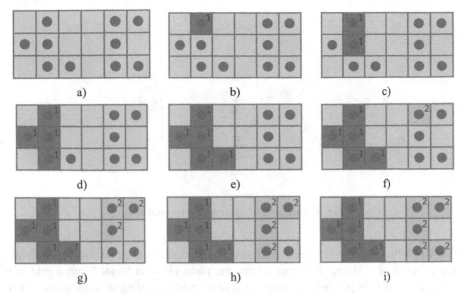

Fig. 7. Principle of Seed Filling Method

3.1 Point Cloud Preprocessing

The captured segments will be placed in a temporary storage area inside the tunnel. When using a 3D camera to obtain the point cloud data of the captured segments, the point cloud of the tunnel wall and the surface point cloud of other mechanisms such as the shield machine pipeline will be simultaneously collected. In addition to the effective data of the captured segments, the presence of other data will increase the workload of subsequent point cloud processing and reduce algorithm efficiency. Therefore, a cross-sectional model of the tunnel can be established, Filter out useless point clouds through mathematical methods.

As shown in the cross-sectional view of the tunnel, O_1 is the center of the tunnel circle, O is the origin of the camera coordinate. If the deviation Δx and Δz between the installation position of the camera and the center of the tunnel are known, then based on the camera coordinate system, the coordinates of the tunnel center can be expressed as $P_0(\Delta x, \Delta z)$。 The effective point cloud is: At the center of the tunnel circle O_1 ∧ point cloud with a center of 0 and a radius of r_1 to r_2. If the distance from the point cloud to the center of the tunnel circle O_1 is expressed as d and the point cloud coordinates are $P(x, y, z)$, then the effective point cloud meets the following conditions (Fig. 8):

$$r_{min} < d = \sqrt{[x + \Delta x]^2 + [z + \Delta z]^2} < r_{max} \tag{2}$$

3.2 Determination of Voxel Size

Due to the disorderly nature of spatial point clouds, the efficiency of point cloud processing is low. If point clouds can be sorted in order and point cloud indexes can be set, the

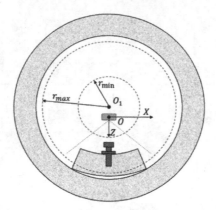

Fig. 8. Location of Segments to be Grabbed

processing efficiency can be improved during calculation. Point cloud voxel partitioning is the process of dividing the space where the point cloud is located into a grid of a certain size, and then placing the point cloud in the grid according to its location, so that each grid has its own position.

The diagram shows the point cloud hitting the segment and bolt, and the purpose of clustering is to separate the point cloud on the segment and bolt. When setting the voxel grid size, it is necessary to consider the relationship between the voxel grid size A and the size h of the segment bolt. If the grid size is too large, the grid resolution will decrease. The same grid may contain both the point cloud of the bolt and the point cloud of the segment, so it cannot achieve the goal of point cloud segmentation; The grid size is too small, resulting in higher grid resolution and reduced algorithm processing efficiency. The following Fig. 9 shows the segment bolt, and it is more appropriate to set the voxel side length as $A = 0.8 * h$.

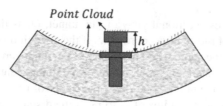

Fig. 9. Point Cloud Distribution on Segments and Bolts

3.3 Optimization of Voxel Storage Methods

In response to the problem of neglecting the spatial distribution of point clouds during voxelization of the original point cloud (as shown in Fig. 10-a), which leads to a decrease in accuracy, this paper proposes an improved voxel information storage method, as shown in Fig. 10-b. After dividing the point cloud into voxels, the minimum and maximum values of all point clouds along the three coordinate axes within the voxel are calculated to obtain two points P_{min} and P_{max}, these two points form the smallest bounding box containing the voxel interior point cloud, which can reflect the spatial distribution range of all point clouds within the voxel.

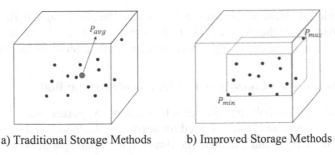

a) Traditional Storage Methods   b) Improved Storage Methods

Fig. 10. Optimization of Voxel Storage Methods

3.4 Point Cloud Clustering Based on Improved Voxel and Seed Filling Method

Apply the idea of seed filling method to point cloud clustering, treat point cloud voxels as pixels in the image, and extend the two-dimensional space in the image to the three-dimensional space of the point cloud. Firstly, define the voxel neighborhood in 3D space as: centered around the voxel, surrounded by 3 × three × The 26 voxels in space 3 are neighborhoods. If the number of point clouds in the neighborhood is not empty, the linear distance dist between the minimum bounding box of the point cloud between the current voxel and adjacent voxels is determined. If dist is less than the set threshold T_d. It is considered that the point clouds in the two voxels are adjacent and meet the clustering criteria (Fig. 11).

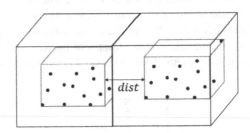

Fig. 11. Rules for Point Cloud Clustering

Based on the above clustering criteria, cluster the entire segment voxel space using the seed filling method, and the process is as follows:

a) Traverse the entire voxel grid. If there is a point cloud inside the voxel, use the current voxel as the seed, assign a new Label, and add all neighboring voxel position indexes that meet the clustering criteria to the queue;

b) Delete the last position index in the queue, assign the same Label, and add the voxel position indexes of all its neighbors that meet the clustering criteria to the queue;

c) Repeat operation b until the queue is empty, at which point a category clustering is completed and marked as the same Label;

d) Repeat operations a–c until the entire voxel mesh traversal is completed.

At this point, adjacent connected voxels that meet the clustering criteria are assigned the same Label, while the point cloud on the segment bolt and the point cloud on the segment do not meet the clustering criteria and are divided into different categories.

3.5   Identification and Coordinate Calculation of Segment Bolts

Segments and segment bolts are divided into different categories. Next, it is necessary to determine which point clouds are used for segment bolts based on the characteristics of point cloud clusters, and calculate the three-dimensional spatial coordinates of the bolts.

a) Set the threshold for the number of point clouds. Based on the surface area S of the bolt on the segment and the point cloud resolution captured by the 3D camera at that location σ, Can calculate the number of point clouds for segment bolts;

$$n = S/\sigma \tag{3}$$

Set the threshold for the number of point cloud: $N_{min} = 0.8 * n$, $N_{max} = 1.25 * n$;

b) Set the point cloud aspect ratio threshold. Find the minimum bounding rectangle of the point cloud cluster along the Z view direction, and set the threshold value of the rectangle length width ratio. The length and width of the rectangle are L and W respectively, and the threshold condition is

$$0.8 < \frac{L}{W} < 1.25 \tag{4}$$

c) Calculation of spatial coordinates for segment bolts. The point cloud that meets the threshold conditions for the number of point clouds and the aspect ratio is regarded as the point cloud of the segment bolt, and the coordinates of a single point cloud are denoted as $P(x_i, y_i, z_i)$, and the spatial coordinates of the segment bolt are denoted as $P_c(x_c, y_c, z_c)$. The calculation method for the spatial coordinates of the segment bolts is as follows

$$\begin{cases} x_c = \sum_{i=0}^{n} x_i \\ y_c = \sum_{i=0}^{n} y_i \\ z_c = \sum_{i=0}^{n} z_i \end{cases} \tag{5}$$

4   Algorithm Verification

To verify the feasibility of the algorithm proposed in this article, the author conducted segment identification verification based on the China Railway 1084 shield tunneling project. The tunnel segment has an outer diameter of 2.6 m, an inner diameter of 2.1 m, and a width of 0.8 m. The processor configuration is as follows: the main frequency is 1.6 GHz Intel i5 8th generation processor, with 16 GB of memory, operating system Windows 10, using Visual Studio 2017 integrated environment, and C++ programming language.

The 3D camera of Tuyang Technology FS820 model is used to collect the point cloud of the pipeline segment. The camera is installed above the storage area of the pipeline segment to be assembled, as shown in Fig. 12-a. The actual pipeline segment data during the construction process is collected, as shown in Fig. 12-b. It can be seen that the original point cloud data of the pipeline segment collected by the camera includes the pipeline segment bolt, the pipeline segment to be grasped, the tunnel wall, and the equipment pipeline, among which the pipeline segment bolt is the target of identification and detection.

 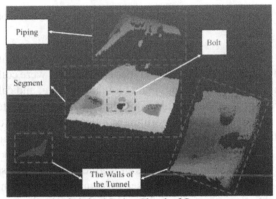

a) Camera Position   b) Original Point Cloud of Segment

Fig. 12. Point Cloud Data of Segment

Point cloud preprocessing: According to the installation position of the camera, in Eq. (2) $\Delta X = -0.15$, $\Delta Z = 0.35$, set $r_{min} = 0.5m$, $r_{max} = 0.95$, according to the boundary conditions of Eq. (2), filter the original point cloud of the segment, delete the invalid point cloud of the tunnel wall and equipment pipeline, and obtain the point cloud data that only includes the segment bolts and the segment to be grasped, as shown in Fig. 13-a;

Point cloud clustering: Based on the specification size of the pipe bolt, set the voxel size to 0.01 m, divide the point cloud into voxels, and use the improved seed filling method for clustering. The segmented point cloud is shown in Fig. 13-b, and it can be seen that the point cloud is divided into three parts, namely the pipe body, pipe bolt, and other point clouds;

Bolt coordinate calculation: screen the three clusters of point clouds according to the number of point clouds and the size of the minimum bounding rectangle of the point cloud, determine the point cloud cluster of the segment bolt, and calculate the bolt spatial coordinates, as shown in Fig. 13-c. The bolt point cloud is represented in red, and other point clouds are represented in blue, and draw the spatial coordinate points of the final segment bolt, which are represented in white. It can be seen that through the method presented in this article, the position of the segment bolts can be effectively detected, laying the foundation for further grasping work of the assembly machine.

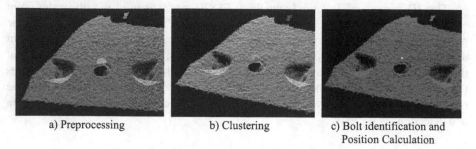

a) Preprocessing   b) Clustering   c) Bolt identification and
                                                            Position Calculation

Fig. 13. The Process of Point Cloud Processing

To further validate the adaptability of the algorithm, six sets of point cloud data with randomly placed different types of segments were collected, and point cloud preprocessing, voxel partitioning, point cloud clustering, and calculation of segment bolt positions were performed. The algorithm time was also calculated, as shown in the Table 1 below. It can be seen that the algorithm proposed in this paper can accurately identify the position of segment bolts for different types of segments in random positions.

To verify the effectiveness of the algorithm proposed in this paper compared to traditional algorithms, six sets of segment data were used. After removing invalid points, Euclidean clustering was used to segment the segment point cloud. The clustering effect and time consumption of this algorithm were observed and compared with the effectiveness of the algorithm proposed in this paper. According to Table 2, it can be seen that Euclidean clustering can effectively segment segments and bolts in 1–5 sets of data. However, in the 6th set of data, due to point cloud adhesion between bolts and segments, the Euclidean clustering algorithm cannot effectively segment bolts and segments; In terms of algorithm efficiency, the algorithm efficiency in this article is 3.326s/1.044s = 3.2 times that of the Euclidean clustering algorithm.

Table 1. The Segment Recognition Effect of the Algorithm in this Article

No	Original Point Cloud	Valid Point Cloud	The Segmented Point Cloud	Bolt Identification and Position Calculation	Time Consumed (s)
1					1.656
2					1.422
3					0.875
4					0.860
5					0.859
6					0.594

Table 2. Comparison of Segment Recognition Effects

No	Number of point clouds	Time Used: European Clustering (s)	Time Used: The Algorithm in this Article (s)	Results of Euclidean Clustering
1	148257	4.891	1.656	
2	127429	4.485	1.422	
3	90836	2.781	0.875	
4	89436	2.875	0.860	
5	86343	2.860	0.859	
6	55190	2.063	0.594	
Average	99582	3.326	1.044	/

5   Conclusion

(1) This article proposes a shield tunnel segment position recognition algorithm based on improved voxel and seed filling, which can effectively preprocess segment point clouds, cluster point clouds, extract features, and ultimately complete the calculation of segment bolt positions;

(2) Compared with traditional European clustering algorithms, the segment recognition performance of this paper is better, and the algorithm efficiency is 3.2 times that of the European clustering algorithms;

(3) Segment recognition can be seen as an application scenario of the algorithm and theory in this paper. In addition, the theory in this paper can also be applied to other point cloud clustering scenarios and effectively improve the efficiency of point cloud processing.

References

1. Li, F., et al.: Overview of key component remanufacturing and repair technology for shield tunneling machines. China Mech. Eng. **32**(07), 820–831 (2021)
2. Miao, W., Yan, S., Li, J., Ding, W., Li, Y.: The development status and trend of China's full face tunnel boring machine. Internal Combustion Engine Accessories **02**, 203–205 (2021). https://doi.org/10.19475/j.cnki.issn1674-957x.2021.02.096
3. Manzoo, S., Jasmin, S.P.: Research on mechanized tunneling technology of tunnel boring machine. J. Progress Civil Eng. **3**(11) (2021)
4. Liu, X., Wang, Z., Shao, C., Wang, Y., Cong, Q.: Overview of research progress on mechanical fault diagnosis of shield machines. Control Eng. **29**(02), 238–245 (2022). https://doi.org/10.14107/j.cnki.kzgc.20200902
5. Bi, X., Liu, X., Li, W., Cao, W., Wang, X., Chen, C.: Research on the application of new connector technology for shield driven subway tunnel segments. Urban Rail Transit Res. **23**(07), 1–11 (2020). https://doi.org/10.16037/j.1007-869x.2020.07.001
6. Li, P., et al.: A study of the segment assembly error and quality control standard of special-shaped shield tunnels. Energies **15**(7) (2022)
7. Yin, Y., et al.: Mechanical behaviour of splicing joints in shield tunnel lining subjected to fire. Tunn. Undergr. Space Technol. Incorp. Trenchless Technol. Res. **123**, 104404 (2022)
8. Li, J.: Current situation, problems, and prospects of development of tunnel boring machines in China. Tunn. Constr. (Chinese and English) **41**(06), 877–896 (2021)
9. Lu, F., et al.: Risk analysis and countermeasures of TBM tunnelling over the operational tunnel. Front. Earth Sci. **11** (2023)
10. Zhang, Z., Wang, B., Wang, X., He, Y., Wang, H., Zhao, S.: Safety-risk assessment for TBM construction of hydraulic tunnel based on fuzzy evidence reasoning. Processes **10**(12), 2597 (2022)
11. Wang, L., Mao, Q.: A method for measuring the grab position of segments based on RGB and deep information fusion. J. Zhejiang Univ. (Eng. Edn.) **57**(01), 47–54 (2023)
12. He, C., Xiao, D., Dai, X.: Multi model shield tunnel segment detection method based on close range photogrammetry. J. Undergr. Space Eng. **17**(03), 840–847 (2021)
13. Wu, Z., Wang, S., Liu, T., Jin, D.: Automatic assembly and positioning method for shield tunnel segments based on deep learning vision and laser assistance. Infrared Laser Eng. **51**(04), 252–260 (2022)
14. Xu, Y., Zhe, H., He, L., Shi, Z.: Orthogonal solution of segment pose based on linear structured light binocular measurement system. Manuf. Autom. **45**(03), 173–178 (2023)
15. X, G., Tao, J., Wang, M., Liu, C., Yang, Z., Zhuang, Q.: A shield tunnel segment pose detection method based on line laser sensors. J. Central South Univ. (Nat. Sci. Edn.) **51**(01), 41–48 (2020)
16. Chen, X., Wang, L., Cai, J., Liu, F., Yang, H., Zhu, Y.: Autonomous recognition and positioning of shield segments based on red, green, blue and depth information. Autom. Constr., 2023146
17. Wu, Z., et al.: Automatic segment assembly method of shield tunneling machine based on multiple optoelectronic sensors. In: International Conference on Optical Instruments and Technology (2020)
18. Dong, K., et al.: Automatic segment assembly in shield method using multiple imaging sensors. In: International Conference on Optical Instruments and Technology (2020)

Kinematics and Workspace Analysis of a Disc Cutter Replacement Manipulator for TBM in a Constrained Motion Space

Tao Zhu, Haibo Xie[✉], and Huayong Yang

State Key Laboratory of Fluid Power Components and Mechatronic Systems, Zhejiang University, Hangzhou, Zhejiang 310027, People's Republic of China
hbxie@zju.edu.cn

Abstract. This paper presents a 6-DOF hydraulic manipulator for replacing the disc cutters in the confined space of a TBM. Firstly, the mechanism design of the manipulator is briefly introduced, and the kinematics coordinate system is built based on the D-H kinematics modeling method. On the basis of the D-H parameters, a kinematics model of the manipulator is established, and forward kinematics analyses are conducted to obtain the relationship between the actuator's position and the manipulator's posture. Lastly, the workspace of the manipulator in restricted space is verified by numerical simulation software. Simulations indicate that the designed manipulator has sufficient motion range to meet the requirements of the disc cutter replacement. Furthermore, the established kinematics model provides a solid foundation for subsequent research on obstacle avoidance trajectory planning of the manipulator.

Keywords: Manipulator · Kinematics · Confined space · Workspace · Disc cutter replacement · TBM

1 Introduction

Tunnel boring machines (TBMs) are widely used in tunnel construction, where the disc cutters experience significant wear and require frequent replacement. The traditional manual cutter replacement methods pose high risks and are time-consuming, significantly impacting construction efficiency and safety. Therefore, developing a robotic arm suitable for cutter replacement in shield tunneling operations is of great significance. In recent years, many researchers both domestically and internationally have conducted extensive studies and designed various solutions, including electrically driven robotic arms and hydraulically driven manipulators [1–3]. One major challenge in the design of the cutter replacement manipulator is to create a compact robot system suitable to the limited space and enable agile operations within the confined workspace. The front-end space of the TBM's cutterhead is already filled with various mechanical equipment, leaving very limited space for the installation of the robotic arm. The installation space for the robotic arm is a rectangular volume measuring $1\,\mathrm{m} \times 1\,\mathrm{m} \times 3\,\mathrm{m}$, with a front

H. Yang et al. (Eds.): ICIRA 2023, LNAI 14272, pp. 216–229, 2023.
https://doi.org/10.1007/978-981-99-6480-2_18

gate near the cutterhead. During operation, the manipulator extends through open of the gate and reaches the position between the submerged wall and the cutterhead to perform cutter replacement for all the disc cutters on the 8.8 m diameter cutterhead. The shape of the gate opening depends on the type of gate design, and in this paper, the gate opening is square-shaped with side lengths of 0.65 m and a length of 0.46 m [4].

To achieve a wide range of cutter replacement operations within a confined space, this paper proposes a 6-DOF hydraulic manipulator, employing a PRRPRR chain. This paper focuses on the kinematic modeling and workspace analysis of the designed manipulator, while the overall design of the robotic system will be presented in Sect. 2. More detailed design specifications will be showcased in our future work (Fig. 1).

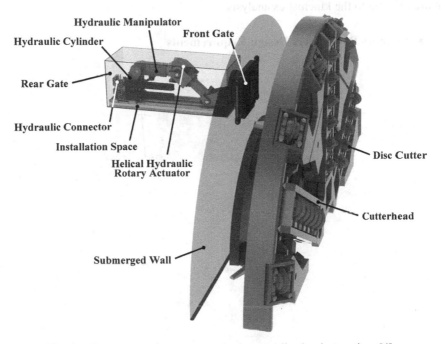

Fig. 1. Disc cutter replacement manipulator application instructions [4].

In order to control the end effector of the manipulator to reach the desired target position, it is necessary to establish the kinematics model of the manipulator to determine the correspondence between the position and orientation of the end effector and each actuator's position. The kinematics analysis in this paper is based on the Denavit-Hartenberg (D-H) method. Additionally, this paper conducts simulation analysis on the entire workspace that the end effector of the robotic arm can reach within the confined space and generates a point cloud diagram of the workspace. The results demonstrate that the motion range of the manipulator can fully cover all the disc cutters on the 8.8 m diameter cutterhead, indicating that the designed kinematic parameters of the robotic arm are reasonable.

The overall structure of this paper is as follows. Section 2 provides a brief introduction of the disc cutter replacement manipulator. Section 3 derives the forward kinematics models of the robotic arm. In Sect. 4, the motion range of the robotic arm is calculated through simulation analysis, and a point cloud diagram of the reachable workspace of the end effector is generated. Finally, Sect. 5 concludes the paper.

2   Manipulator Design

The detailed design of the robotic system involves structural design, actuator design, electrical system design, and motion control software, among others. This paper provides a brief introduction to the structural solution of the robotic arm and its main parameters that are relevant to the kinematics analysis.

2.1   Kinematics Parameters Design Requirements

Fig. 2. Simplified 3D view of the installation space.

Figure 2 illustrates a simplified 3D model relevant to the design parameters. The installation space of the manipulator is a hollow rectangular volume with internal dimensions of 1 m × 1 m × 3 m. The gate opening of the front gate is a square space with side lengths of 0.65 m and a length of 0.46 m. A coordinate system is established with the origin located on the axis of the submerged wall, near the front face of the wall. The z-axis aligns with the central axis of the submerged wall, the y-axis points upwards vertically, and the x-axis direction is determined using the right-hand rule. During the cutter replacement operation, the cutterhead rotates first, adjusting its orientation to align the disc cutters with the working surface of the manipulator. Using this coordinate system as a reference, the target position coordinates that the cutter replacement manipulator needs to reach for each disc cutter can be determined, as shown in Table 1.

Table 1. Target coordinates for each disc cutter (z,y).

The target coordinates of the disc cutters (mm)			
(1150, 1372)	(1150, 1850)	(1150, 2318)	(1150, 2831)
(1150, 3254)	(1150, 3722)	(1150, 1694)	(1150, 2162)
(1150, 2630)	(1150, 3098)	(1150, 3566)	(1150, 1538)
(1150, 2006)	(1150, 2474)	(1150, 2942)	(1150, 3410)
(1150, 3878)	(1150, 1281)	(1150, 1772)	(1150, 2240)
(1150, 2708)	(1150, 3176)	(1150, 3644)	(1150, 1616)
(1150, 2084)	(1150, 2552)	(1150, 3020)	(1150, 3488)
(1150, 3956)	(1150, 1457)	(1150, 1928)	(1150, 2396)
(1150, 2864)	(1150, 3332)	(1150, 3800)	(1230.8, 3802.2)
(1204.0, 3823.3)	(1273.2, 3781.0)	(1153.0, 3918.8)	(1244.3, 3794.2)
(1179.1, 3853.5)	(1218.1, 3811.4)	(1159.3, 3894.4)	(1273.2, 3781.7)
(1191.2, 3837.0)	(1258.5, 3787.3)	(1164.2, 3881.8)	/

2.2 Overall Design

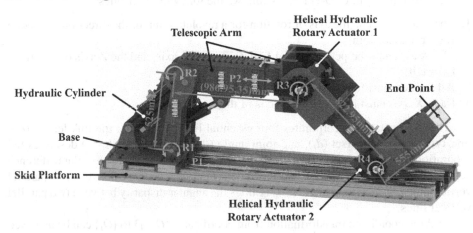

Fig. 3. The overall structure of the robotic system for disc cutter replacement.

The overall structure of the 6-DOF robotic arm, which adopts a PRRPRR chain, is shown in Fig. 3. To differentiate between the joints of the same type, they are labeled as P1, R1, R2, P2, R3, and R4, respectively. The base of the manipulator is mounted on a skid platform, where a servo motor in the skid platform converts rotational motion into translational motion to drive the overall movement of the arm. The first two revolute joints are driven by hydraulic cylinders, enabling the swinging motions of the arms. The third joint is a telescopic arm, driven by an integrated hydraulic cylinder, allowing the retraction and extension of the inner arm. The last two revolute joints are driven by helical hydraulic rotary actuators. The initial positions of each joint are shown in Fig. 3. The distance between the axes of R1 and R2 is 525 mm, denoted by L_{R1R2}. Similarly, the distance between the R2 and R3 is (986.95, 35) mm, representing a horizontal distance of 986.95 mm and a vertical distance of 35 mm. L_{R3R4} is equal to 855.95 mm. The distance between R4 and the end effector, denoted by ED, is $L_{R4ED} = 555$ mm. In the initial state, L_{R1R2} is in a vertical position, perpendicular to the horizontal plane. The P2 joint is horizontal, and L_{R3R4} forms a 45° angle downward with the horizontal plane. L_{R4ED} forms a 40° angle upward with the horizontal plane.

3 Kinematics Analysis

3.1 Denavit-Hartenberg Frames

The kinematic analysis of robotic manipulators commonly employs the Denavit–Hartenberg (D-H) method [5]. This method establishes a coordinate system to describe the geometric parameters and coordinate directions between adjacent links in an articulated kinematic chain.

In this method, a set of coordinate systems is established for the joints of the links. The relative positions and angles between these coordinate systems are determined through homogeneous coordinate transformations.

The establishment of D-H frames follows the following four rules:

1. The Z axis must be the axis of rotation for a revolute joint, or the direction of motion for a prismatic joint;
2. The X axis must be perpendicular both to its own Z axis, and the Z axis of the frame before it;
3. All frames must follow the right-hand rule;
4. Each X axis must intersect the Z axis of the frame before it.

The D-H notation incorporates four essential link parameters: the link length (a_i), link twist (α_i), link offset (d_i), and joint angle (θ_i). The link length (a_i) describes the separation between two joint axes, the link twist (α_i) characterizes the angular difference between two joint axes, the link offset (d_i) determines the distance between two parallel vertical lines, and the joint angle (θ_i) signifies the angular disparity between two parallel vertical lines.

And the coordinate transformation from coordinates $\{O_{i-1}\}$ to $\{O_i\}$ can be achieved using the following procedure:

1. Rotate θ_i around the z_{i-1} axis to align the x_{i-1} and x_i axes.
2. Translate d_i along the z_{i-1} axis to align the x_{i-1} and x_i axes.
3. Translate a_i along the x_i axis to coincide the origins of coordinates $\{O_{i-1}\}$ and $\{O_i\}$.
4. Rotate α_i around the x_i axis to align the z_{i-1} and z_i axes.

By performing these operations, the homogeneous coordinate transformation matrix can be expressed as:

$$A_i = \text{Rot}(z, \theta_i)\text{Trans}(0, 0, d_i)\text{Trans}(a_i, 0, 0)\text{Rot}(x, \alpha_i) \qquad (1)$$

And for the translational transformation, the homogeneous coordinate transformation matrix is

$$A = \text{Trans}(x, y, z) = \begin{bmatrix} 1 & 0 & 0 & x \\ 0 & 1 & 0 & y \\ 0 & 0 & 1 & z \\ 0 & 0 & 0 & 1 \end{bmatrix} \tag{2}$$

The homogeneous coordinate transformation matrices for rotations around the x, y, and z axes are as follows:

$$Rot(x, \theta) = \begin{bmatrix} 1 & 0 & 0 & 0 \\ 0 & c_\theta & -s_\theta & 0 \\ 0 & s_\theta & c_\theta & 0 \\ 0 & 0 & 0 & 1 \end{bmatrix} \tag{3}$$

$$Rot(y, \theta) = \begin{bmatrix} c_\theta & 0 & s_\theta & 0 \\ 0 & 1 & 0 & 0 \\ -s_\theta & 0 & c_\theta & 0 \\ 0 & 0 & 0 & 1 \end{bmatrix} \tag{4}$$

$$Rot(z, \theta) = \begin{bmatrix} c_\theta & -s_\theta & 0 & 0 \\ s_\theta & c_\theta & 0 & 0 \\ 0 & 0 & 1 & 0 \\ 0 & 0 & 0 & 1 \end{bmatrix} \tag{5}$$

3.2 Forward Kinematics

The manipulator has a PRRPRR configuration, and the coordinate systems of the robotic arm links can be obtained using the standard D-H method, as shown in Fig. 4. And the D-H parameters are shown in Table 2.

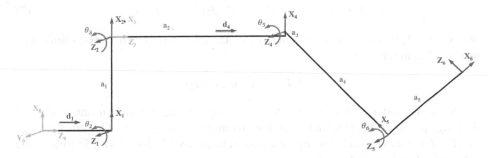

Fig. 4. The D-H frames of the disc cutter replacement manipulator.

Hence, the transformation of the end-effector is given by

$$A_m = A_1 A_2 \cdots A_m = \begin{bmatrix} n_x & s_x & a_x & d_x \\ n_y & s_y & a_y & d_y \\ n_z & s_z & a_z & d_z \\ 0 & 0 & 0 & 1 \end{bmatrix} = \begin{bmatrix} n & s & a & d \\ 0 & 0 & 0 & 1 \end{bmatrix} \quad (6)$$

where $n = [n_x, n_y, n_z]^T$, $s = [s_x, s_y, s_z]^T$, $a = [a_x, a_y, a_z]^T$ represents the vector of the x_m, y_m, z_m in coordinate system $o_0 x_0 y_0 z_0$, respectively. Vector $d = [d_x, d_y, d_z]^T$ represents the vector from the origin o_0 to the origin o_m in coordinate system $o_0 x_0 y_0 z_0$.

Table 2. The D-H parameter table of the disc cutter replacement manipulator.

LinkNumber	θ_i	d_i	a_i	α_i
Link1	0	d_1	0	$-90°$
Link2	θ_2	0	a_1	0
Link3	θ_3	0	0	$90°$
Link4	0	$a_2 + d_4$	a_3	$-90°$
Link5	$45° + \theta_5$	0	$-a_4$	0
Link6	$-95° + \theta_6$	0	a_5	$-90°$

However, the first two rotational joints of the manipulator are driven by hydraulic cylinders, and it is necessary to derive the relationship between the hydraulic cylinders and the joint angles through conversion.

In Fig. 5, $C_{11}C_{12}$ represents the length of hydraulic cylinder 1 (which pushes the boom to rotate around J_2) between its two hinge points. Among them, C_{11} is mounted on the base, and the length of $C_{11}J_2$ is fixed at 370.47 mm, and the length of $C_{12}J_2$ is also fixed at 549.18 mm. When the length of $C_{11}C_{12}$ changes, the angle $\angle C_{11}J_2C_{12}$ changes, thereby driving J_2J_3 to rotate around J_2. The angle $\angle J_1J_2J_3$ is determined by

$$\angle J_1J_2J_3 = \angle C_{11}J_2J_1 + \angle C_{11}J_2C_{12} - \angle J_3J_2C_{12} \quad (7)$$

where $\angle C_{11}J_2J_1$ is a fixed value equal to $21°$ and $\angle J_3J_2C_{12}$ is also a fixed value equal to $10°$. This means that

$$\angle J_1J_2J_3 = 11° + \angle C_{11}J_2C_{12} \quad (8)$$

At the initial state, $\angle J_1J_2J_3$ is $90°$. Since the range of variation in the distance between the hinge points of the cylinder, i.e., the length range of $C_{11}C_{12}$ is 590–855 mm, the range of $\angle C_{11}J_2C_{12}$ can be solved using the cosine function as 72.17–129.41°. Therefore, the range of $\angle J_1J_2J_3$ is 83.17–140.41°.

Similarly, $C_{21}C_{22}$ represents the length of hydraulic cylinder 2 (which pushes the boom to rotate around J_3) between its two hinge points. C_{21} is mounted on the first swing arm, and C_{22} is mounted on the first section of the telescopic arm. The lengths of $C_{21}J_3$

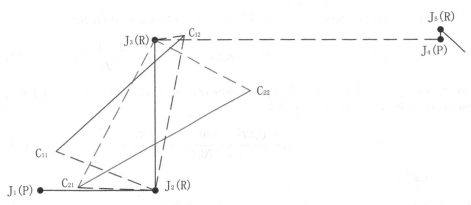

Fig. 5. The relationship between the rotation angle of the rotatory joints (joint 2 and joint 3) and their corresponding hydraulic cylinder displacements.

and $C_{22}J_3$ are fixed at 581.49 mm and 375.42 mm, respectively. When hydraulic cylinder 2 extends or retracts, the angle $\angle C_{21}J_3C_{22}$ changes, thereby driving the telescopic arm to rotate around J_3. The angle $\angle J_2J_3J_4$ is determined by

$$\angle J_2J_3J_4 = \angle C_{21}J_3C_{22} - \angle C_{21}J_3J_2 + \angle C_{22}J_3J_4 \tag{9}$$

where both $\angle C_{21}J_3J_2$ and $\angle C_{22}J_3J_4$ are fixed values of 28°. Therefore,

$$\angle J_2J_3J_4 = \angle C_{21}J_3C_{22} \tag{10}$$

At the initial condition, $\angle J_2J_3J_4$ is 90°. Since the range of variation in the distance between the hinge points of the cylinder, i.e., the length range of $C_{21}C_{22}$ is 630–925 mm, the range of $\angle C_{21}J_3C_{22}$ can be solved using the cosine function as 79.15–149.59°. Therefore, the range of $\angle J_2J_3J_4$ is 79.15–149.59°.

Based on the above, we can obtain the corresponding relationship between the displacement of hydraulic cylinder 1 and the rotation angle of joint 2, as well as the corresponding relationship between hydraulic cylinder 2 and joint 3. $C_{11}C_{12} = 590 + x_1$ (where x_1 is the extension length of the piston rod of hydraulic cylinder 1). Since the initial state is $\angle J_1J_2J_3 = 90°$, the initial value of x_1 should be 72.455 mm. The stroke of hydraulic cylinder 1 is 265 mm. Therefore, it can be concluded that the range of $\angle J_1J_2J_3$ is 83.17–140.41°.

$C_{21}C_{22} = 630 + x_2$ (where x_2 is the extension length of the piston rod of hydraulic cylinder 2). Since the initial state is $\angle J_2J_3J_4 = 90°$, the initial value of x_2 should be 62.149 mm. The stroke of hydraulic cylinder 2 is 295 mm. Therefore, it can be concluded that the range of $\angle J_2J_3J_4$ is 79.15–149.59°.

$J_3J_4 = 986.95 + x_3$ (where x_3 is the extension length of the piston rod of hydraulic cylinder 3 which drives the inner telescopic arm to extend or retract). In the initial pose, $x_3 = 0$, and the stroke of hydraulic cylinder 3 is 330 mm.

The calculation of the correspondence between the rotational joint angle and the hydraulic cylinder stroke is as follows:

$$\angle J_1J_2J_3 = 11° + \angle C_{11}J_2C_{12} = 90° - \theta_2 \tag{11}$$

And the Eq. (11) transforms to Eq. (12) according to the cosine function:

$$\theta_2 = 79° - \angle C_{11}J_2C_{12} = 79° - \arccos(\frac{C_{11}J_2^2 + J_2C_{12}^2 - C_{11}C_{12}^2}{2 \times C_{11}J_2 \times J_2C_{12}}) \quad (12)$$

where $C_{11}J_2 = 370.47\,\text{mm}$, $J_2C_{12} = 549.18\,\text{mm}$, $C_{11}C_{12} = (590 + x_1)\,\text{mm}$, substituting the above equation yields:

$$\theta_2 = 79° - \arccos(\frac{370.47^2 + 549.18^2 - (590 + x_1)^2}{2 \times 370.47 \times 549.18}) \quad (13)$$

Similarly,

$$\angle J_2J_3J_4 = \angle C_{21}J_3C_{22} = 90° + \theta_3 \quad (14)$$

$$\theta_3 = \angle C_{21}J_3C_{22} - 90° = \arccos(\frac{C_{21}J_3^2 + J_3C_{22}^2 - C_{21}C_{22}^2}{2 \times C_{21}J_3 \times J_3C_{22}}) - 90° \quad (15)$$

where $C_{21}J_3 = 581.49\,\text{mm}$, $J_3C_{22} = 375.42\,\text{mm}$, $C_{21}C_{22} = (630 + x_2)\,\text{mm}$, substituting the above equation yields:

$$\theta_3 = \arccos(\frac{581.49^2 + 375.42^2 - (630 + x_2)^2}{2 \times 581.49 \times 375.42}) - 90° \quad (16)$$

The range of motion for each joint is summarized in Table 3.

Thus, the transformation matrix of the end effector of the robotic arm can be expressed in terms of the positions of each actuator according to Eq. (1)–(6), Eq. (13), Eq. (16) and Table 2.

Table 3. The range for each joint of the manipulator.

d_1	θ_2	θ_3	d_4	θ_5	θ_6
0–1900 mm	−50.41–6.83°	−59.59–10.85°	0–330 mm	−30–150°	−171–9°

4   Workspace Analysis

4.1   Analysis Method

Monte Carlo method is commonly used to analyze the motion range of robotic arms. The Monte Carlo method is a numerical computation technique that calculates the position of the robotic manipulator's end effector through numerical simulations, thereby determining the reachable workspace [6–8]. The steps involved in this method are as follows:

1. Determine the range of joint angles for the robotic manipulator.

2. Generate a large number of random joint angle combinations.
3. For each joint angle combination, compute the position of the robotic manipulator's end effector.
4. Analyze and aggregate all computed end effector positions to obtain the reachable workspace of the robotic manipulator.

The Monte Carlo method is a random sampling technique, and the accuracy of the results depends on the number and distribution of samples chosen. Typically, a larger number of samples leads to more accurate results.

However, there is limited literature on the analysis of the reachable workspace of actual robotic manipulators in confined spaces.

In this study, MATLAB SimScape Multibody is utilized to analyze the reachable workspace of the robotic manipulator in a confined space.

The main steps involved in this process are as follows. First, enumerate all possible combinations of joint positions. Second, modify the corresponding pose of the manipulator in SimScape Multibody for each combination. Finally, measure the distance between the manipulator and obstacles. If the distances are all greater than zero (it means that the manipulator is collision-free in that pose), and the coordinates of the end effector are recorded. Otherwise, it indicates that the manipulator collides with the surrounding obstacles in that posture.

4.2 Obstacle Distance Detection

In SimScape Multibody, the detection between models is performed using the 'Spatial Contact Force' module, which can be used to measure the distance between two imported components. However, when processing in MATLAB, the models are represented by convex hulls. The convex hull of a model can be understood as an elastic ball that envelops the component, and the resulting envelope surface represents the convex hull of the component [9, 10]. This means that the convex hulls used by MATLAB to compute distances cannot accurately represent the shape of the components, resulting in deviations in the calculated distances. For example, as shown in Fig. 6, for a T-shaped component (Fig. 6(a)), its convex hull is illustrated in the upper right corner (Fig. 6(b)). In order to achieve more accurate distance detection between the manipulator and obstacles, preprocessing of the manipulator model and obstacles in the 3D modeling software is necessary. For instance, the aforementioned T-shaped component can be split into two separate components, T1(Fig. 6(c)) and T2(Fig. 6(d)). The distance measurement between another object and this T-shaped component can then be transformed into the minimum distance between the components and T1 and T2. This operation improves the accuracy of the measurements but requires twice the usage of the 'Spatial Contact Force' module and increases the computational workload.

The obstacle and manipulator models were appropriately processed before importing them into SimScape Multibody. To reduce the configuration workload in MATLAB, simplification was applied to the 3D models of the manipulator and obstacles. The manipulator model was simplified to retain only the parts that may potentially interfere with the obstacles, while components such as bolts, internal parts, connectors, and hydraulic cylinders were removed before importing.

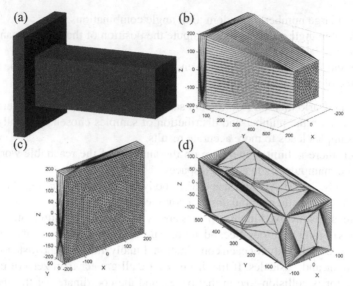

Fig. 6. Convex hull representation of a part.

It has been verified in the 3D software that if the remaining parts of the manipulator do not collide with the surroundings, the hydraulic cylinders will also not collide with obstacles. Therefore, during the analysis, the hydraulic cylinders in the system can be removed.

4.3 Model Setup and Simulation Results

After importing the models, the constraint relationships and coordinate systems between the individual components were configured. The overall model diagram is shown in Fig. 7. The leftmost block of the 'Distance Detection' module is used to calculate the distances between the components of the manipulator and the annular support leg, providing corresponding output. If any component collides with an obstacle, the calculated distance will be less than or equal to zero. Similarly, the other blocks of the 'Distance Detection' module are used to calculate the shortest distances between the manipulator components and the hollow cuboid installation space, front gate, and submerged wall, respectively.

The model for detecting the distances between the components of the robotic manipulator and a specific obstacle is constructed as shown in Fig. 8. And it shows the detailed view of the leftmost submodel in the 'Distance Detection' module. This model connects various parts of the robotic arm and the annular support leg and is used to calculate the distance between the robotic arm and the annular support leg. The annular support leg is divided into four separate parts before import. Figure 9 shows the detailed model that measures the distance between one component of the manipulator and various components of the annular support leg.

The submodel 'Robot System' represents the manipulator model, which defines the connectivity between various components of the manipulator. This subsystem also

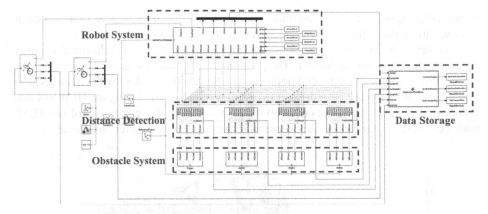

Fig. 7. The overall model in simscape multibody simulation.

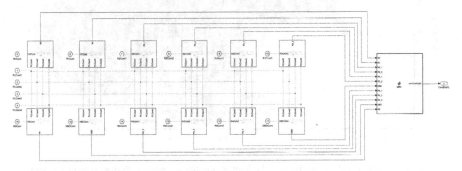

Fig. 8. Details of the leftmost 'Distance Detection' submodel.

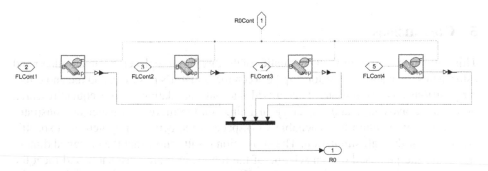

Fig. 9. The details of the upper left corner block in Fig. 8.

defines different connection ports and input/output ports. The connection ports are used to establish connections with 'Distance Detection' module for obstacle distance detection. The input ports receive the desired joint positions of the manipulator, while the output ports provide feedback on the actual joint positions and end effector coordinates. The computations and processing are performed using the Matlab function. If there is no collision between the manipulator components and the obstacle in a particular configuration, the corresponding end effector coordinates are saved.

The target position coordinates that the end point needs to reach during disc cutter replacement are shown in Table 1. The point cloud diagram in Fig. 10 illustrates all the target positions(blue) that the end point can reach without colliding with obstacles. The demanded target points are indicated by a series of crosses(red). Figure 10 shows that the designed manipulator can cover all the disc cutters on the cutterhead of the TBM, and there is sufficient redundancy retained in the specific disc cutter change tasks.

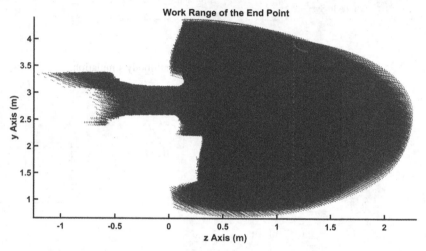

Fig. 10. Point cloud diagram of end effector positions under collision-free condition.

5   Conclusions

This paper derives the forward kinematics of the disc cutter replacement manipulator and establishes the mapping relationship between the actuator's positions and the end effector positions and orientations. This provides a solid foundation for subsequent research on obstacle avoidance and trajectory planning. Furthermore, this paper demonstrates in detail how to obtain the reachable workspace of the actual equipment in a specific environment through simulation. The simulation results show that the designed dimensions and the proposed design scheme of the robotic arm are reasonable and meet the requirements for disc cutter replacement. This case can serve as a design reference for researchers and engineers involved in the development of similar equipment, enabling them to easily validate the rationality of their design solutions.

Acknowledgements. This work was funded by Fundamental Research Funds for the Central Universities [Number: 226-2022-00016]; State Key Laboratory of Fluid Power and Mechatronic Systems Independent Project [Number: SKLoFP_ZZ_2106]; National Key R&D Program of China [Number: 2022YFC3802300].

References

1. Du, L., Yuan, J., Bao, S., Guan, R., Wan, W.: Robotic replacement for disc cutters in tunnel boring machines. Autom. Constr. **140**, 104369 (2022)
2. Yuan, J., Guan, R., Du, J.: Design and implementation of disc cutter changing robot for tunnel boring machine (TBM). In: IEEE International Conference on Robotics and Biomimetics (ROBIO) 2019, pp. 2402–2407. IEEE, Dali (2019)
3. Camus, T., Moubarak, S.: Maintenance robotics in TBM tunnelling. In: International Symposium on Automation and Robotics in Construction 2015, vol. 32, pp. 665-672. IAARC Publications, Oulu (2015)
4. Zhu, T., Xie, H., Yang, H.: Design and tracking control of an electro-hydrostatic actuator for a disc cutter replacement manipulator. Autom. Constr. **142**, 104480 (2022)
5. Denavit, J., Hartenberg, R.S.: A kinematic notation for lower-pair mechanisms based on matrices. J. Appl. Mech. **77**(2), 215–221 (1955)
6. Metropolis, N., Rosenbluth, A.W., Rosenbluth, M.N., Teller, A.H., Teller, E.: Equation of state calculations by fast computing machines. J. Chem. Phys. **21**(6), 1087–1092 (1953)
7. Peidró, A., Reinoso, Ó., Gil, A., Marín, J.M., Payá, L.: An improved Monte Carlo method based on Gaussian growth to calculate the workspace of robots. Eng. Appl. Artif. Intell. **64**, 197–207 (2017)
8. Janson, L., Schmerling, E., Pavone, M.: Monte Carlo motion planning for robot trajectory optimization under uncertainty. In: Bicchi, A., Burgard, W. (eds.) Robotics Research. Springer Proceedings in Advanced Robotics, vol. 3, pp. 343–361. Springer, Cham (2017)
9. Bentley, J.L., Preparata, F.P., Faust, M.G.: Approximation algorithms for convex hulls. Commun. ACM **25**(1), 64–68 (1982)
10. Brönnimann, H., Iacono, J., Katajainen, J., Morin, P., Morrison, J., Toussaint, G.: Space-efficient planar convex hull algorithms. Theoret. Comput. Sci. **321**(1), 25–40 (2004)

Mechanism Surrogate Based Model Predictive Control of Hydraulic Segment Assembly Robot with Sliding Friction

Qi Wei[1,2], Jianfeng Tao[1,2(✉)], Hao Sun[1,2], and Chengliang Liu[1,2]

[1] School of Mechanical Enginnering, Shanghai Jiao Tong University, Shanghai, China
{msv,jftao}@sjtu.edu.cn
[2] State Key Laboratory of Mechanical System and Vibration, Shanghai, China

Abstract. In this paper, we introduce a mechanism surrogate based model predictive controller (MS-MPC) for the motion control of a hydraulically actuated heavy-duty segment assembly robot. Heavy-duty mechanisms in construction machinery frequently employ sliding joint articulations, which exhibit complex mathematical properties that hinder the performance of real-time feedforward control with an accurate model. The mechanism surrogate used in the MPC is developed using a data-driven methodology, which can speed up the dynamics solution with 99.89% of average time savings and low error. The simulation results indicate that the proposed control method can accomplish high-precision motion control for the segment assembly robot's lifting axis, as well as robustness across a variety of loads and friction forces. During frequent reversals, the proposed method is 80.67% more accurate than the feedforward PID controller with no load and 70.68% more accurate with a 700kg load.

Keywords: Segement assembly robot · Surrogate model · Model predictive control · Joint friction

1 Introduction

In shield tunnelling, the segment assembly robot is used for grasping, moving, and assembling various varieties of concrete segments. In recent years, the operation of segment assembly has shifted from manual remote control to semi-automated assistance to fully automated segment assembly [4,18]. During the assembly process, a 0.5mm spacing is required between the segments, placing high demands on the electro-hydraulic servo systems in terms of both time efficiency and precision.

Supported by the National Natural Science Foundation of China (Grant No. 52075320), and the State Key Laboratory of Mechanical System and Vibration (Grant no. MSVZD202006).

Existing research primarily focuses on feedback control [13, 15], impact force or vibration suppression [16, 17], and synchronization control [11]. Most hydraulic construction machinery is operated by humans, and high-precision trajectory tracking control research is lacking. System modelling, especially dynamic modelling of mechanisms with high friction, is the key to high-precision control for heavy-duty construction machines.

There are two types of friction models in mechanisms: reaction-force-independent friction and reaction-force-dependent friction. The reaction-force-independent joint friction is commonly used in scenarios with low loads and joints supported by rolling bearings [7, 9, 10], as its forward dynamical equations can be simplified to a set of ordinary differential equations with relatively easy solvability. However, reaction-force-independent joint friction is not universally applicable [6, 8]. Mechanisms with sliding joints generally require the use of reaction-force-dependent friction for dynamic modeling [5]. This is particularly common in parallel mechanisms with spherical joints and heavy-duty mechanisms utilizing sliding joints.

Model-based feedforward control of hydraulic-actuated heavy-duty mechanisms is problematic due to dynamics modelling problems and hydraulic system nonlinearity. This paper examines the dynamics of heavy-duty sliding friction mechanisms, explains why they are slow to calculate, and proposes a novel approach for real-time solution used in motion controller of forward multi-body dynamics, resulting in precise motion control of the segment assembly robot.

2   Dynamic Models and Problem Formulation

In the single-lift-arm segment assembly robot, the lifting axis is composed of a parallelogram mechanism and consists of seven components, with non-negligible friction torque in each joint. Two valve-controlled hydraulic cylinders drive the mechanism, and are symmetrically arranged on both sides of the mechanism.

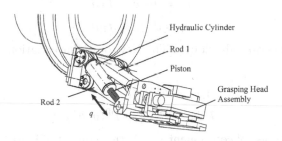

Fig. 1. The structure of lifting axis of the segment assembly robot

2.1   Dynamical Equations of Mechanism

The lifting axis can be simplified into a planar mechanism as shown in 2. The mechanism consists of a frame (component 0) and 5 moving components, where component 5 serves as the driving component, and components 1, 2, 3, 4 are the driven components. The mechanism has degree of freedom $f = 1$.

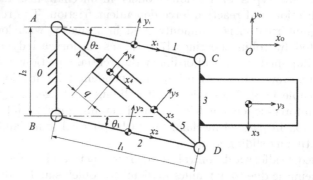

Fig. 2. The simplified planar mechanism of the lifting axis.

The Jacobian matrix of each component obtained by kinematic analysis can be expressed as

$$\begin{bmatrix} \dot{r}_i \\ \omega_i \end{bmatrix} = \begin{bmatrix} J_{Ti} \\ J_{Ri} \end{bmatrix} v$$

Here, $\dot{r}$ and ω_i denote the translational and angular velocity of component i, respectively. Jacobian matrices J_{Ti} and J_{Ri} characterize the virtual translational and rotational displacement of the system [12]. Taking the derivative of the forward kinematic equation with respect to time, we have

$$\ddot{r}_i = J_{Ti}\dot{v} + \dot{J}_{Ti}v$$
$$\dot{\omega}_i = J_{Ri}\dot{v} + \dot{J}_{Ri}v$$

(1)

where v is the generalized velocity. The Newton-Eular equation for each component is

$$m_i\ddot{r}_i = F_i^r + G_i + F_i^a$$
$$I_i\dot{\omega}_i = P_i^r F_i^r + T_i^f(v, F_i^r)$$

(2)

Where m_i is the mass of component i, I_i is the moment of inertia of component i about its center of mass, F_i^r is the reaction force, and the matrix P_i^r converts the reaction force into a moment about the center of mass, T_i^f is the friction torque, G_i is the gravitational force, and F_i^a represents the actuating force (only the hydraulic piston has non-zero values).

The friction torque in sliding joint is a function of the normal force $N_i = \|F_i^r\| + N_0$, where constant N_0 represents initial normal force. Consequently, friction torque is a function of the reaction force F_i^r. By using the Stribeck friction model, we have

$$T_i^f(v, F_i^r) = N_i \operatorname{sgn}(\dot{\theta}) \left[f_c + (f_s - f_c) \exp\left(-\left| \frac{\dot{\theta}}{\omega_s} \right|^2 \right) \right] + B\dot{\theta} \tag{3}$$

According to D'Alembert's principle, the inertial force term can be obtained in terms of generalized coordinates and generalized velocities,

$$-\begin{bmatrix} m_i \ddot{r}_i \\ I_i \dot{\omega}_i \end{bmatrix} = M J_i \dot{v} + k(q, v) \tag{4}$$

Where $M = \operatorname{diag}\{m_1 E_3 \ m_2 E_3 \ \cdots m_5 E_3 \ \cdots I_1 \cdots I_5\}$ represents the inertia matrix, E_3 is a 3×3 identity matrix, and k the Coriolis force contains terms involving both generalized velocities and coordinates.

By combining Eqs. (2) and (4), the generalized coordinate form of the Newton-Euler equations can be obtained as follows

$$M J\dot{v} + k(q, v) + P^r F^r + F^f(v, F^r) + G + F^a = 0 \tag{5}$$

According to the principle of virtual work, the work done by joint reaction forces on virtual displacement is zero, i.e. $J^\top P^r \equiv 0$. Therefore, multiplying both sides of Eq. (5) by $J^\top$ can eliminate the constraint force term, and multiplying both sides of Eq. (5) by $P^r M^{-1}$ can eliminate the generalized accelertion, resulting in

$$J^\top M J\dot{v} = -J^\top \left[k(q, v) + F^f(v, F^r) + G + F^a \right] \tag{6}$$

$$0 = P^r M^{-1} \left[k(q, v) + P^r F^r + F^f(v, F^r) + G + F^a \right] \tag{7}$$

The abstract form of the dynamical equations is

$$\begin{aligned} \bar{M}\dot{v} &= f(q, v, F^a, F^r) \\ 0 &= g(q, v, F^a, F^r) \end{aligned} \tag{8}$$

Where $v = \dot{q}$ due to its holonomic nature. The equations of this mechanism cannot be decoupled using the principle of virtual work because sliding friction is a function of constraint forces. The number of algebraic unknowns (F^r) to be determined is significantly higher than the number of dependent variables in the differential equations (in this case, 14:1). The solution of the semi-explicit DAE (8) is very time-consuming, and real-time solutions are almost impossible in tasks like motion control.

2.2 Dynamical Equations of Hydraulic System

The proportional servo valve used is zero-lap, symmetrical, and matched. The hydraulic system (showed in Fig. 3) is described by the flow equations and continuity equation, and the flow equation are

$$\begin{aligned} Q_1 &= k_q x_v R_1(u, p_1, p_s, p_t) \\ Q_2 &= k_q x_v R_2(u, p_2, p_s, p_t) \end{aligned} \tag{9}$$

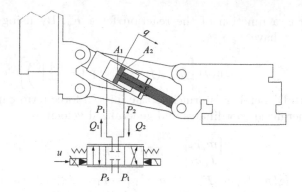

Fig. 3. The diagram of hydraulic circuit.

where

$$s(u) = \begin{cases} 1, & u > 0 \\ 0, & u \leq 0 \end{cases}$$

$$R_1(u, p_1, p_s, p_t) = s(u)\sqrt{p_s - p_1} + s(-u)\sqrt{p_1 - p_t}$$

$$R_2(u, p_2, p_s, p_t) = s(u)\sqrt{p_2 - p_t} + s(-u)\sqrt{p_s - p_2}$$

k_q is the flow gain with respect to the valve spool displacement x_v, p_1 and Q_1, p_2 and Q_2 are the pressure and flow rates of the rodless and rod chambers of the hydraulic cylinder, and p_s and p_t are the supply pressure and tank pressure, respectively. Let the system input be $u = k_q x_v / k_v$, assuming that the dynamic response of the spool can be simplified as a proportional relationship. The hydraulic oil characteristics are considered constant during operation, and the pressure in each chamber of the hydraulic cylinder is equal. Two dynamic equations for pressure in the two chambers can be described as

$$\begin{aligned} Q_1 &= C_i(p_1 - p_2) + \frac{V_1}{\beta}\dot{p}_1 + A_1 v \\ Q_2 &= C_i(p_1 - p_2) - \frac{V_2}{\beta}\dot{p}_2 + A_2 v \end{aligned} \tag{10}$$

where $V_1 = V_{10} + A_1 q$ and $V_2 = V_{20} - A_2 q$, V_{10} and V_{20} are the initial volumes of two chambers at $t = 0$, β is the bulk modulus of the hydraulic oil. Combining the Eq. (9) with the Eq. (10) eliminates the flow term and creates a physical model of the hydraulic system expressed in terms of the pressure in the two chambers (Table 1)

$$\begin{aligned} \dot{p}_1 &= \frac{\beta}{V_1}\left[k_v R_1 u - C_i p_1 + C_i p_2 - A_1 v\right] \\ \dot{p}_2 &= \frac{\beta}{V_2}\left[-k_v R_2 u + C_i p_1 - C_i p_2 + A_2 v\right] \end{aligned} \tag{11}$$

System parameters are provided below:

Table 1. Parameters of segment assembly robot lifting axis

parameters	values	parameters	values
k	2.1324×10^{-3}	A_1	0.0079 m^2
C_i	0	A_2	0.0059 m^2
P_s	14 MPa	V_{10}	$5 \times 10^{-6} \text{ m}^3$
P_t	0	V_{20}	$9.232 \times 10^{-4} \text{ m}^3$
β	680 MPa	f_s	0.005
ω_s	0.2 rad/s	f_c	0.003
B	$3.0 \ N \cdot m \cdot s/rad$		

3   Methodology

As described in Sect. 2 dynamical equations of mechanisms with sliding friction incurs significant time costs. This paper proposes an MPC control method based on a mechanism surrogate that couples the forward dynamics using a model of a mechanism surrogate with the physical model of a hydraulic system. This section describes the proposed control method in detail.

3.1   Mechanism Surrogate

Formalization. The primary challenge in solving Eq. 8 is the determination of constraint Eqs. (6). The proposed approach utilizes a data-driven method to sample and fit dynamical equations of the mechanism, establishing an cheap-to-evaluate approximate ODE form through a surrogate model h:

$$\dot{v} = h(q, v, F^a; \boldsymbol{\omega}) + R \tag{12}$$

$h : \mathbb{R}^3 \to \mathbb{R}$ represents the surrogate model, $\boldsymbol{\omega}$ represents the unknown parameters, and R represents the residual. In theory, any surrogate model that adequately represents nonlinearity can be selected. This paper employs a straightforward and flexible surrogate model structure, which is a linear combination of nonlinear mappings:

$$h(\boldsymbol{x}) = \sum_{i=1}^{m} \mu_i \psi_i(\boldsymbol{a}_i \boldsymbol{x} + b_i) + \beta \tag{13}$$

where m is the number of nonlinear mappings. μ, $\boldsymbol{a}_i$, b_i and β are unknown parameters (in this case, $m = 70$). Several commonly employed nonlinear surrogate models share a similar form to the above [2]. In this paper, chosen nonlinear mapping is the Gaussian radial basis function $\psi_i(x) = \exp(-\|x\|^2/2\sigma_i^2)$; consequently, the RBF surrogate is employed.

Surrogate Fitting Details. Let $\boldsymbol{x} = (q, v, F^{\mathrm{a}})$ be the inputs of the system, and $y = \dot{v}$ be the corresponding output. A large number of accurate value pairs $(\boldsymbol{x}_i, y_i), i = 1, 2, \cdots n$ are sampled from Eq. (8), where n denotes the number of samples. The goal is to fit the surrogate model to represent the majority of the mechanism's dynamic characteristics, i.e., to minimize the residual R (Table 2).

Table 2. Parameter set $\mathcal{X}$

parameters	lower bound	upper bound
q	0	0.148 m
v	−0.085 m/s	0.114 m/s
F^{a}	−5.4 × 10^4 N	−7.1 × 10^4 N

The above parameter set, $\boldsymbol{x} \in \mathcal{X}$, is determined by the hydraulic system. In this paper, the upper and lower bounds of each parameter are chosen independently; coupling relationships between the bounds of each parameter are not taken into account. The Latin Hypercube Sampling (LHS) method is used to sample the multibody dynamics in $\mathcal{X}$ uniformly.

The validation of the surrogate model is determined by the mean squared error(MSE). The values of each unknown parameter are determined by solving the following unconstrained optimization problem:

$$\underset{\mu_j, \boldsymbol{a}_j, b_j, \beta}{\mathrm{argmin}} \sum_{i=1}^{n} \left[\sum_{j=1}^{m} \mu_j \psi_j (\boldsymbol{a}_j \boldsymbol{x}_i + b_j) + \beta - y_i \right]^2 \tag{14}$$

This optimization problem has a loss function with second-order derivatives for each unknown parameter$(\mu_j, \boldsymbol{a}_j, b_j, \beta)$. Therefore, the Broyden-Fletcher-Goldfarb-Shanno (BFGS) method [1] is used for solving it. The optimization process is ended when the loss function value no longer declines after numerous consecutive iterations. At that time, the values of the unknown parameters are considered determined (Table 3).

Table 3. Optimization and prediction performance of mechanism surrogate

Validation MSE	9.40 × 10^{-3} m/s^2
Total Optimization Iterations	10250
Total Optimization Time	1545 sec
Single Step Computation Time(DAE)	85.6 ms
Single Step Computation Time(surrogate)	0.0891 ms

As shown in the Table 3, The mechanism surrogate speeds up mechanism dynamics calculation, allowing real-time online dynamic optimization (MPC).

Compared to the original DAE model, it achieves an average time savings of 99.89%.

3.2   Controller Design

System Prediction Model. Coupling the mechanism surrogate (12) with the hydraulic system (11), we have:

$$
\begin{aligned}
\dot{q} &= v \\
\dot{v} &= h(q, v, F^{\mathrm{a}}) \\
\dot{p}_1 &= \tfrac{\beta}{V_1}\left[k_v R_1 u - C_{\mathrm{i}} p_1 + C_{\mathrm{i}} p_2 - A_1 v\right] \\
\dot{p}_2 &= \tfrac{\beta}{V_2}\left[-k_v R_2 u + C_{\mathrm{i}} p_1 - C_{\mathrm{i}} p_2 + A_2 v\right]
\end{aligned}
\tag{15}
$$

This system will be further simplified. By conducting a coordinate transformation on Eq. (11) using a constant full rank matrix $P = \mathrm{diag}\{1, 1, A_1 - A_2, 1\}$. Considering hydraulic actuating force $F^{\mathrm{a}} = p_1 A_1 - p_2 A_2$, we have the equivalent system:

$$
\begin{aligned}
\dot{q} &= v \\
\dot{v} &= h(q, v, F^{\mathrm{a}}) \\
\dot{F}^{\mathrm{a}} &= -\left[\left(\tfrac{A_1^2}{V_1} + \tfrac{A_2^2}{V_2}\right)\beta v + \left(\tfrac{A_1}{V_1} + \tfrac{A_2}{V_2}\right)(p_1 - p_2)\beta C_{\mathrm{i}}\right] \\
&\quad + \left(\tfrac{A_1}{V_1} R_1 + \tfrac{A_2}{V_2} R_2\right)\beta k_v u \\
\dot{p}_2 &= \tfrac{\beta}{V_2}\left(C_{\mathrm{i}} p_1 - C_{\mathrm{i}} p_2 + A_2 v\right) - \tfrac{\beta k_v R_2}{V_2} u
\end{aligned}
\tag{16}
$$

A new input can be designed as $u^* = \left(\tfrac{A_1}{V_1} R_1 + \tfrac{A_2}{V_2} R_2\right)\beta k_v u$. By neglecting the internal leakage C_i, the system can be described independently using the first three states:

$$
\begin{aligned}
\dot{q} &= v \\
\dot{v} &= h(q, v, F^{\mathrm{a}}) \\
\dot{F}^{\mathrm{a}} &= -\left(\tfrac{A_1^2}{V_1} + \tfrac{A_2^2}{V_2}\right)\beta v + u^*
\end{aligned}
\tag{17}
$$

Velocity Observer. The position q and the hydraulic actuating force F^{a} can be measured through an encoder and pressure transducers. To ensure state feedback, an extended Kalman filter(EKF) [3,14] is used for velocity observer, with the simplified system (17) be the predict model. Since the system is not "noisy", the design parameters(e.g. covariances) are set to constants. A detailed explanation will not be introduced because the EKF design is standardized.

Controller Scheme. Let $x = [q, v, F^{\mathrm{a}}]^{\top}$ denote the system states. By applying the forward Euler method to Eq. (17) for time discretization, we can obtain the discrete state transition equation $x_{k+1} = f_{\mathrm{d}}(x_k, u_k^*)$. The system output is $y_k = q_k$; therefore only the reference trajectory of displacement r_k needs to be planned offline. We have the detailed formulation of MPC:

$$\min_{\boldsymbol{x}_k, u_k} \sum_{k=0}^{T-1} \|W^y (q_k - r_k)\|_2^2 + \|W^u u_k^*\|_2^2$$

$$s.t. \quad \boldsymbol{x}_{k+1} = f_\mathrm{d}(\boldsymbol{x}_k, u_k^*)$$

$$\boldsymbol{x}_0 = \boldsymbol{x}(t) \tag{18}$$

$$q_{T-1} = r_{T-1}$$

$$\boldsymbol{x}_k \in \mathcal{X}$$

$$u_{\min}^* \leq u_k^* \leq u_{\max}^*$$

where $\boldsymbol{x}_0 = \boldsymbol{x}(t)$ denotes the state feedback, while $q_{T-1} = r_{T-1}$ signifies the terminal constraint. The prediction horizon T is set to 20, while the control horizon is 3. The sampling period t_s is 2 ms. This online optimization task is solved using sequential quadratic programming (SQP) method.

4   Simulation Experiment Results

4.1   Simulation Experiment Setup

The complete system model of the lifting axis in the segment assembly robot is established in Simulink. Simscape is used to model the mechanism, whereas s-functions are used to model the hydraulic system. Random noise of 0.1% was added to the feedback voltage of the pressure transducer, and a quantization error of 5μm was introduced to the encoder.

In order to demonstrate the impact of friction on the system, The designed trajectory contains frequent reversals (sine functions with angular velocity of 2π and amplitude of 0.01 m) and introduces a sudden change in velocity at 5 s. The generated trajectory is required to have the same initial value as the system position and is feasible for the constrained system.

4.2   Comparative Experimental Results

The proposed method cannot be compared to a pure feedback-based strategy because the implicit feedforward of MS-MPC eliminates theoretical lag when tracking the offline planned trajectory. System input u is proportional to steady-state flow rate under constant load pressure, thus a segmented velocity feedforward PID controller (FF-PID) is used for comparison. The parameters of PID is carefully tuned.

Two simulation experiments were performed to simulate the actual working conditions of a segment assembly robot: 1. operation without any load. 2. operation with a 700kg concrete segment load attached to the end effecter.

As illustrated in the Fig. 4, the magnitude of friction forces (characterized by pressure spikes) is dependent on the reaction force, directly related to the load. Thus, comparing under different load situations can show friction disturbance robustness without changing model parameters.

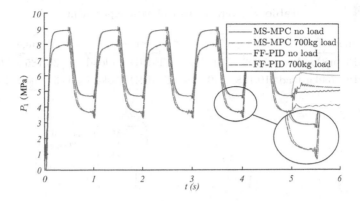

Fig. 4. Pressure in one of the chambers

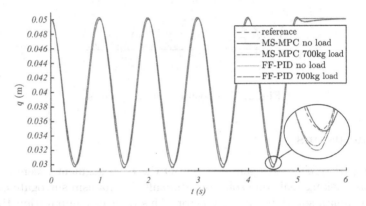

Fig. 5. The position tracking results

The Fig. 5 and Fig. 6 illustrates the position tracking results corresponding to the four experiments. The FF-PID controller exhibits relatively poor tracking performance during piston reversals, and the tracking error shows a clear positive correlation with the load weight. This is primarily due to the model-free nature and fixed gains of the FF-PID controller.

The proposed control method, on the other hand, demonstrates friction compensation capability and robustness, particularly during frequent reversals. Additionally, the proposed method shows a clear advantage in tracking trajectories with abrupt changes in velocity (at 5 s).

Table 4 and Fig. 6 present the trajectory tracking errors for the four experiments. The proposed method improves accuracy during frequent reversals by an average of 80.67% compared to the FF-PID controller in the absence of load and by 70.68% with a 700kg load. This indicates a significant advantage over traditional control methods that lack a model and rely on fixed gains.

Table 4. Average error of each experiment

Experiment	Average Error	Experiment	Average Error
MS-MPC no load	6.993×10^{-5}m	FF-PID no load	36.185×10^{-5}m
MS-MPC 700kg load	10.118×10^{-5}m	FF-PID 700kg load	34.504×10^{-5}m

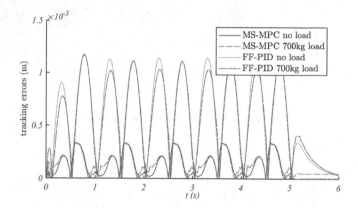

Fig. 6. The position tracking errors

5   Conclusions

(1) Sliding friction creates semi-explicit DAEs on a segment assembly robot's lifting axis, making real-time solutions difficult. Mechanism surrogate can speed up the dynamics solution with low error. This reduces computation time from 85.6ms each time step to 0.0891ms, enabling real-time optimal control and precise segment assembly robot lifting axis control.

(2) The proposed MS-MPC control method combines the mechanism surrogate with the feedback linearized hydraulic equations as the prediction model. Full-state feedback from an Extended Kalman Filter (EKF) velocity observer and sensors allows real-time tracking of the offline intended position trajectory. It achieves high-precision position control.

(3) The suggested control method outperforms standard control methods without a model and fixed gains in monitoring trajectories with frequent reversals and discontinuous velocity. It is resilient to diverse loads and adaptable to mechanism friction forces. These results suggest that the proposed control mechanism can be tested on actural segment assembly robots.

References

1. Numerical Optimization, chap. 6, pp. 135–163. Springer, New York (2006). https://doi.org/10.1007/978-0-387-40065-5_6
2. Bhosekar, A., Ierapetritou, M.: Advances in surrogate based modeling, feasibility analysis, and optimization: a review. Comput. Chem. Eng. **108**, 250–267 (2018)

3. Boutayeb, M., Rafaralahy, H., Darouach, M.: Convergence analysis of the extended Kalman filter used as an observer for nonlinear deterministic discrete-time systems. IEEE Trans. Autom. Control **42**(4), 581–586 (1997)

4. Dong, K., et al.: Automatic segment assembly in shield method using multiple imaging sensors. In: 2019 International Conference on Optical Instruments and Technology: Optoelectronic Measurement Technology and Systems. SPIE (2020)

5. Fraczek, J., Wojtyra, M.: On the unique solvability of a direct dynamics problem for mechanisms with redundant constraints and coulomb friction in joints. Mechanism and Machine Theory **46**(3), 312–334 (2011)

6. Guo, F., Cheng, G., Pang, Y.: Explicit dynamic modeling with joint friction and coupling analysis of a 5-DOF hybrid polishing robot. Mech. Mach. Theory **167**, 104509 (2022)

7. He, Y., et al.: A joint friction model of robotic manipulator for low-speed motion. In: 2021 IEEE International Conference on Robotics and Biomimetics (ROBIO). IEEE (2021)

8. Javanfar, A., Bamdad, M.: Effect of novel continuous friction model on nonlinear dynamics of the mechanisms with clearance joint. Proc. Instit. Mech. Eng., Part C: J. Mech. Eng. Sci. **236**(11), 6040–6052 (2021)

9. Liu, D., et al.: Research on flexible joint friction identification of space lab manipulator. In: 2018 IEEE International Conference on Mechatronics and Automation (ICMA). IEEE (2018)

10. Liu, G., Li, Q., Fang, L., Han, B., Zhang, H.: A new joint friction model for parameter identification and sensor-less hand guiding in industrial robots. Ind. Robot: Int. J. Robot. Res. Appl. **47**(6), 847–857 (2020)

11. Lyu, L., Liang, X., Guo, J.: Synchronization control of a dual-cylinder lifting gantry of segment erector in shield tunneling machine under unbalance loads. Machines **9**(8), 152 (2021)

12. Schiehlen, W.: Multibody system dynamics: roots and perspectives (1997)

13. Shi, H., Gong, G., Yang, H., Wang, L.: Positioning speed and precision control of a segment erector for a shield tunneling machine. In: 2010 IEEE/ASME International Conference on Advanced Intelligent Mechatronics. IEEE (2010)

14. Song, Y.H., Grizzle, J.: The extended Kalman filter as a local asymptotic observer for nonlinear discrete-time systems. American Control Conference (1992)

15. Wang, L., Gong, G., Shi, H., Hou, D.: Positioning precision and impact force control of segment erector for shield tunneling machine. In: 2012 Third International Conference on Digital Manufacturing & Automation. IEEE (2012)

16. Wang, L., Gong, G., Yang, H., Yang, X., Hou, D.: The development of a high-speed segment erecting system for shield tunneling machine. IEEE/ASME Trans. Mechatron. **18**(6), 1713–1723 (2013)

17. Wang, L., Sun, W., Gong, G., Yang, H.: Electro-hydraulic control of high-speed segment erection processes. Autom. Construct. **73**, 67–77 (2017)

18. Wu, Z., et al.: Automatic segment assembly method of shield tunneling machine based on multiple optoelectronic sensors. In: 2019 International Conference on Optical Instruments and Technology: Optical Sensors and Applications. SPIE (2020)

An Investigation into Fatigue Damage and Clearance Evolution of TBM Main Bearings

Zhiwei Liu, Hongliang Zhang, and Chuanyong Qu[✉]

School of Mechanical Engineering, Tianjin University, Tianjin, China
qu_chuanyong@tju.edu.cn

Abstract. This research focuses on investigating the fatigue damage and clearance evolution of TBM main bearings, vital components responsible for load carrying and transfer. The study employs Abaqus to simulate the fatigue damage behavior of TBM main bearings under low speed and heavy load conditions. Analysis of damage evolution patterns is conducted in both the time and space domains, followed by the prediction of clearance evolution in the main bearing using a fatigue damage model. The results indicate that the raceway carries a higher risk of damage compared to the roller, particularly the main pushing raceway. Additionally, as damage progresses, the main bearing experiences a rapid increase in clearance.

Keywords: TBM Main Bearing · Damage Mechanics · Contact Fatigue · Bearing Clearance

1 Introduction

A Tunnel-Boring Machine (TBM) holds increasing significance in various fields, including rail transit and railway tunnel, due to its environmental friendly nature, high efficiency, and enhanced safety features [1–3]. The main bearing, as a critical core component of TBM, assumes the crucial role of carrying and transferring loads. Given the complexities involved in replacing the main bearing, the industry commonly equates its lifespan with that of the entire TBM. Therefore, studying the fatigue damage of the main bearing and its impact on the system response becomes paramount. This research endeavors to promptly detect early faults and predict performance degradation, thereby ensuring the seamless operation of TBM.

Clearance, a critical parameter in bearing quality, plays a vital role in determining rotational accuracy, load distribution, vibration response, and fatigue life [4, 5]. Scholars have conducted extensive research in this domain. Oswald et al. [6] investigated the influence of clearance on load distribution and fatigue life, resulting in the derivation of a life factor-clearance curve. Xu and Ma [7] established a relationship between radial clearance and fatigue life in cylindrical roller bearings through theoretical derivation. Harsha et al. [8] proposed a dynamic model for bearings under high-speed rotation, emphasizing the significant influence of clearance on system vibration response. Bercea et al. [9, 10] proposed a quasi-static model for bearings, analyzing the effects of overturning moment and clearance on fatigue life. Other studies [11, 12] demonstrated the considerable influence of clearance on lubrication, with an optimal clearance reducing contact stress between the roller and the ring, and improving bearing fatigue life. Yang et al. [13] utilized Fe-safe to predict the fatigue life of ball bearings, observing a 24.8% reduction in fatigue life when radial clearance increased from 4μm to 16 μm. Kan [14] established a relationship between fatigue life and clearance of shearer bearings through theoretical analysis. Bi and Zhang [15] recommended a working clearance of no more than 5 μm for ball bearings and 10 μm for cylindrical roller bearings. As fatigue damage progresses, bearing performance gradually deteriorates, accompanied by a gradual increase in clearance that may exceed the threshold values. Abnormal clearance significantly affect the load distribution, leading to stress concentration and accelerated performance decline. Therefore, close monitoring of the clearance allows for real-time assessment of the main bearing's health status, as well as evaluation and prediction of fatigue damage and performance degradation.

The recent advancements in computer technology have facilitated the utilization of the finite element method as a valuable tool in investigating bearing fatigue damage. Scholars have made notable contributions to this field. Li et al. [16] employed octahedral shear stress as the driving force for bearing contact fatigue and used an explicit dynamic method to simulate the evolution of bearing damage. Göncza et al. [17] conducted a finite element simulation of fatigue spalling behavior in bearings using the fracture mechanics approach. Xu et al. [18] predicted the damage life of ball bearings by employing an improved Paris law. He et al. [19] utilized Fe-safe to calculate the fatigue life of a yaw bearing. Zeng et al. [20] investigated the location of wheel fatigue cracks through finite element simulation and contact fatigue testing. He et al. [21] simulated the contact fatigue of gears, considering the coupling effect of elastic damage and plastic damage. Antonio and Guillermo [22] proposed a novel method for calculating rolling contact fatigue life based on raceway survival probability.

The above studies have predominantly focused on investigating the fatigue mechanism and life prediction of bearings, leaving a research gap regarding the evolution of bearing clearance. As fatigue damage progresses, the mechanical properties of materials gradually decline, resulting in a reduction in the contact stiffness between the roller and the raceway, thereby leading to an increase in the clearance of the main bearing. However, limited attention has been given to this particular aspect of bearing behavior in previous research.

In light of this research gap, the objective of this study is to address the aforementioned issue. By employing Abaqus software, the study conduct simulations to analyze the fatigue damage behavior of TBM main bearings under conditions of low speed and heavy load. The study encompasses an investigation of the damage evolution patterns of the main bearing in both the time and space domain, followed by the prediction of clearance evolution behavior, this research aims to enhance the understanding of the performance and behavior of TBM main bearings, contributing to a more comprehensive knowledge in this field.

2 Analysis of Main Bearing Fatigue Damage

2.1 Fatigue Damage Model of Main Bearing

This study focuses on TBM main bearing, which has a diameter of 3.3 m. The bearing structure comprises an outer ring, an inner ring, and three rows of cylindrical rollers, as shown in Fig. 1. An 8m diameter cutterhead is attached to the front of the bearing [23].

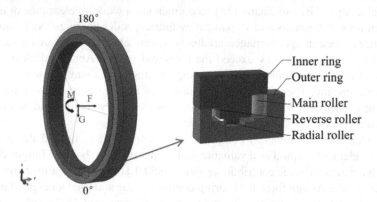

Fig. 1. Structure diagram of TBM main bearing.

Compared to conventional bearing structure, this configuration exhibits enhanced capabilities in withstanding higher levels of thrust, overturning moment, and a certain degree of radial force. The radial force G primarily arises from the cutterhead gravity, which remains relatively stable throughout the tunneling process. However, the dynamic behavior of the thrust force F and overturning moment M is complicated and can significantly contribute to fatigue damage in the rollers and rings. Figure 2 illustrates the dynamic tunneling load and distribution characteristics of an 8 m cutterhead in marble geology [24].

Extensive studies have shown that cyclic shear stress is the primary driving force behind bearing fatigue damage, with the average shear stress having minimal influence. The roller of TBM main bearing are typically manufactured using GCr15 steel, and their torsional S-N equation is described as follows [25]:

$$\tau_{max} = \frac{\Delta\tau}{2} = 2.636N^{-0.102} \tag{1}$$

Generally, the damage evolution equation for high-cycle fatigue can be expressed as follows [26]:

$$\frac{dD}{dN} = \left[\frac{\Delta\sigma}{\sigma_r(1-D)}\right]^m \tag{2}$$

Where D donates the damage variable, N donates the number of cycles, $\Delta\sigma$ denotes the difference between maximum and minimum stresses, σ_r donates the material parameter related to the average stress, and m denotes a material parameter related to the temperature.

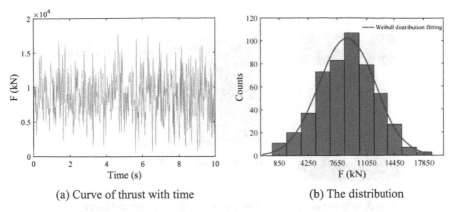

(a) Curve of thrust with time   (b) The distribution

Fig. 2. Thrust and distribution characteristics of the cutterhead

Regarding the contact fatigue of the main bearing, since its main driving force is shear stress, $\Delta\sigma$ is replaced by $\Delta\tau$ in Eq. (2), resulting in the following transformation:

$$\int_0^N dN = \int_0^1 \left[\frac{\sigma_r(1-D)}{\Delta\tau}\right]^m dD \rightarrow \Delta\tau = \frac{\sigma_r}{[(m+1)N]^{\frac{1}{m}}} \tag{3}$$

By comparing Eq. (3) with Eq. (1), the following values can be derived: $m = 9.7874$, $\sigma_r = 6722$ MPa. Therefore, the damage evolution equation for GCr15 steel is shown as follows:

$$\frac{dD}{dN} = \left[\frac{\Delta\tau}{6722(1-D)}\right]^{9.7874} \tag{4}$$

The main bearing ring is typically fabricated from 42CrMo steel. In this study, a similar steel, 18CrNiMo7-6, is used as a replacement. The damage evolution equation for18CrNiMo7-6 steel can be expressed as follows [21]:

$$\frac{dD}{dN} = \left[\frac{\Delta\tau}{3521.2(1-D)}\right]^{10.3} \tag{5}$$

The main bearing of TBM employed cylindrical rollers in all three rows. To simplify the computational complexity, the contact problem between rollers and rings was simplified as a plane strain problem. Figure 3 illustrates the finite element model, where the raceway of the ring is shown in blue and roller is depicted in gray. The material properties of the raceway and roller are provided in Table 1. As the model exhibits symmetry, only one-quarter of the model was considered for the calculation. The contact area between the roller and raceway was meshed with elements having a side length of 0.05 mm. In Abaqus software, the finite element model was assigned CPE4R elements, resulting in a total of 16,000 elements. The contact behavior was defined as "hard contact" for normal contact, and a tangential friction coefficient of 0.05 was applied [16].

Subsequently, two steps were defined in Abaqus to accurately simulate the behavior of the main bearing. In the first step, a small pressure was applied to the upper part of

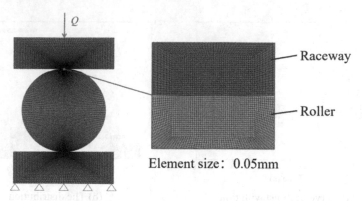

Fig. 3. Finite element model of contact between roller and raceway.

Table 1. Material properties of bearing steel.

	Density	Yong's Modulus	Poisson's Ratio	Yield Strength	Tensile Strength
Raceway	7850 kg·m^{-3}	210 GPa	0.3	1047 MPa	1134 MPa
Roller	7850 kg·m^{-3}	209 GPa	0.28	1617 MPa	2310 MPa

the raceway, allowing the model to establish a stable contact relationship. In the second step, a cyclic load Q was applied to the upper part of the raceway. The variation of this cyclic load over time is shown in Fig. 4. To establish a correlation between time and the number of cycles, an assumption is made regarding the speed of the main bearing, which is set at 6r/min. Based on this assumption and the geometric relationship, the correlation between time and the number of cycles can be derived. This relationship is summarized in Table 2.

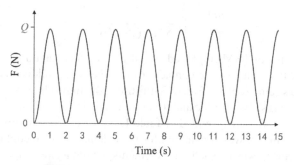

Fig. 4. Curve of cyclic load Q with time.

In the final stage of the analysis, the Property module in Abaqus was utilized to activate a field that established a linear correlation between the elastic modulus E and

Table 2. The relation between the number of load cycles of roller raceway and the working time.

t (h)	Main Roller	Main Raceway	Reserve Roller	Reserve Raceway	Radial Roller	Radial Raceway
1000	2.68×10^7	3.38×10^7	5.46×10^7	2.56×10^7	5.6×10^7	5.76×10^7

a field parameter D. Specifically, when considering a roller, the maximum value of E was set to 209000 MPa, corresponding to $D = 0$, while the minimum value was set to 0, corresponding to $D = 1$. By establishing this relationship, E became linearly dependent on D. Equation (4) and Eq. (5) were then incorporated into USDFLD subroutine and interfaced with Abaqus. This enabled the updating of the roller and raceway damage and stiffness at each occurrence of the shear stress reaching its peak value. For plane problems, the maximum shear stress can be expressed as follows:

$$\Delta \tau = \sqrt{\left(\frac{\sigma_x - \sigma_y}{2}\right)^2 + \tau_{xy}^2} \tag{6}$$

2.2 Fatigue Damage Simulation of Main bearing

Using a tunnelling project as an example, Uniaxial Compressive Strength (UCS) of the rock is measured to be 150 MPa, while the penetration of cutters is observed to be 0.011 m. The thrust force F that the main bearing bears can be determined through the following equation [24]:

$$F = 0.147CP^{0.73}R^{1.27} \tag{7}$$

where C (MPa) denotes UCS of the rock, P (m) denotes the penetration of the cutters, and R (m) denotes the diameter of cutterhead.

Under uniform geological conditions, the thrust force F is distributed among all the main rollers. The load Q on each roller can be determined by the following equation:

$$Q = \frac{f_d F}{n} \tag{8}$$

where f_d denotes the impact load coefficient, which is set to 1.5 in this study [27], and n denotes the number of the main rollers.

The gravity G of the cutterhead is determined to be 800kN, primarily supported by the radial rollers. Among these radial roller, the one positioned at the bottom bears the highest load of 20.2 kN. In the context of uniform geological conditions, the overturning moment M of the cutterhead is assumed to be relatively small. As a result, the load on the reverse roller is considered negligible, hence the analysis does not account for the damage to the reverse roller and the reverse raceway. To conduct the fatigue damage simulation for the main bearing, this study followed the method outlined in the previous

Table 3. The damage D of each part of the main bearing at different times.

t (h)	Main Raceway	Radial Raceway	Main Roller	Radial Roller
3000	0.11	3.0×10^{-5}	6.0×10^{-4}	2.1×10^{-6}
6000	0.99	7.2×10^{-4}	1.1×10^{-3}	4.8×10^{-5}

section. Various working hours were considered, and the resulting damage D of each part of the main bearing is shown in Table 3.

As observed from Table 3, the raceway exhibits a greater susceptibility to damage compared to the roller in the main bearing. Among all rows of the raceway, the main raceway of the outer ring presents the highest risk of damage. Specifically, for the main row, the raceway reaches the failure state after 6000 h of main bearing operation, while the damage to the roller remains significantly smaller in comparison. Figure 5 illustrates the damage nephrogram of the main roller and raceway. For the radial row, the damage to both the rollers and raceways is relatively small after 6000 h of main bearing operation.

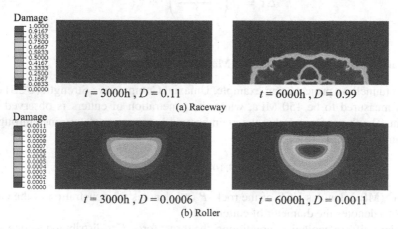

Fig. 5. Damage nephogram of the main roller and raceway.

By utilizing the simulation results of the main raceway, the temporal evolution of damage is shown in Fig. 6. From a spatial perspective, the damage in the raceway originates at a subsurface position 0.6 mm beneath the raceway surface. It then gradually propagates towards the surface, following a horizontal angle of 45°. This gradual fatigue spalling process aligns with the results documented in existing literature [16], as depicted in Fig. 7. In the time domain analysis, it is evident that the damage progression of the main raceway is relatively slow when the working time is below 4500 h. However, beyond 4500 h of operation, the damaged area expands rapidly, and the maximum damage increases from 0.39 to 0.99 within a mere 500-h interval. Based on these observations, it is advisable to establish a critical damage threshold of 0.3.

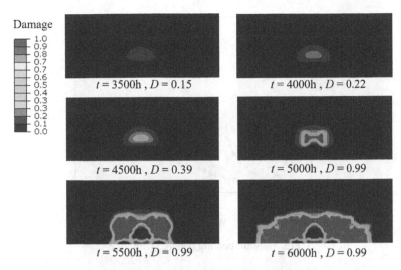

Fig. 6. Damage evolution of main raceway of main bearing outer ring.

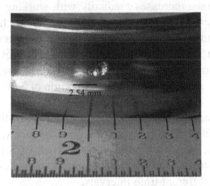

Fig. 7. Typical fatigue spall of bearing raceway

3 Clearance Evolution Prediction of Main Bearing

As damage progresses, the contact stiffness between the roller raceways gradually diminishes, resulting in an increasing in the clearance of the main bearing. It is crucial to note that excessive clearance can have detrimental effects on the load distribution of the main bearing, leading to a reduced service life. Furthermore, it intensifies the vibration response of TBM main drive system, potentially causing impacts and fractures in the cutterhead.

To gain insights into the damage behavior of the main bearing under various geological conditions, this study employed the proposed fatigue damage model. This model facilitates the simulation of the main bearing's damage behavior across three distinct geological conditions. The temporal evolution of the output damage resulting from these simulations is presented in Fig. 8.

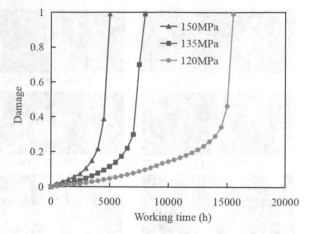

Fig. 8. Main bearing damage with time

Figure 8 provides clear evidence of the main bearing's damage progression over time. When $D < 0.3$, the damage increases gradually with working time. However, once $D > 0.3$, the damage accelerates rapidly. Additionally, the study highlights the sensitivity of the main bearing's damage to geological parameters. For a rock UCS of 120 MPa, it takes approximately 15000 h for the damage to reach a level of 0.99. In contrast, under geological conditions with a rock UCS of 150 MPa, it takes only the same level of damage occurs within a significantly shorter duration of 5,000 h, resulting in a 66.7% reduction in time.

The occurrence of damage affects the elastic modulus of the material, resulting in a decline in contact stiffness between the roller and the raceway. This phenomenon is particularly notable in the working condition with a rock UCS of 150 MPa, as depicted in Fig. 9. The figure illustrates the variation in contact stiffness between the main roller and the main raceway at different time intervals.

The decreasing trend in contact stiffness between the roller and the raceway becomes more pronounced as the working time increases. This decline in contact stiffness is further exacerbated by the presence of damage, leading to nonlinear characteristics in the behavior of contact stiffness.

The decrease in contact stiffness subsequently leads to an increase the clearance of the main bearing. Figure 10 provides a comprehensive visualization of the clearance evolution over time, considering three different geological conditions.

From the observations depicted in Fig. 10, when $D < 0.3$, the clearance of the main bearing is exhibits gradual growth, eventually reaching a relatively stable value of approximately 0.1 mm over an extended period. When $D > 0.3$, the clearance of the main bearing rapidly expands to around 0.2 mm. At this stage, the load distribution becomes distorted, leading to pronounced vibrations in TBM main drive system. These vibrations pose a significant risk of failure and should be a cause for concern.

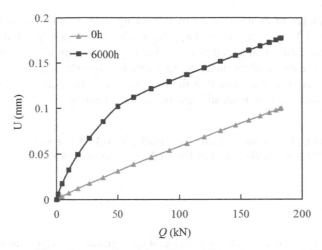

Fig. 9. Contact stiffness between the main roller and the main raceway at different times

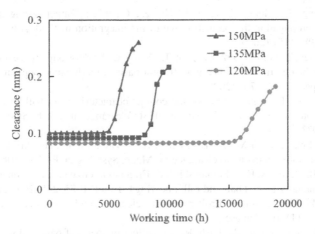

Fig. 10. Clearance of main bearing with time

4 Conclusion

(1) This study employs finite element simulation to investigate the fatigue damage behavior of TBM main bearing. The findings highlight the greater susceptibility of the raceway to damage compared to the roller, with the main raceway posing the highest risk. This emphasizes the need for careful consideration of the main raceway the construction process to ensure its integrity and optimize overall bearing performance.

(2) The damage in the raceway starts from the subsurface position located approximately 0.6 mm away from the raceway surface. Over time, it gradually expands towards the surface, following a horizontal angle of 45° and forming fatigue spalling.

(3) The occurrence of damage in the main bearing leads to an increase in clearance. When $D < 0.3$, the clearance of the main bearing experiences gradual growth, with the axial clearance maintained at approximately 0.1 mm for a long period. When $D > 0.3$, the clearance of the main bearing rapidly expands, reaching approximately 0.2 mm. It is crucial to note that the presence of damage also induces nonlinear characteristics in the contact stiffness of the main bearing.

Acknowledgment. The authors would like to acknowledge the support provided by grant 2020YFB2007202 from the National Key Research and Development Program of China.

References

1. Admiraal, H., Cornaro, A.: Why underground space should be included in urban planning policy-and how this will enhance an urban underground future. Tunn. Undergr. Space Technol. **55**, 214–220 (2016)
2. Li, J., Zhang, Z., Meng, Z., Huo, J., Xu, Z., Chen, J.: Tunnel boring machine cutter-head crack propagation life prediction with time integration method. Adv. Mech. Eng. **11**, 1687814019853451 (2019)
3. Chen, Y., Chen, Z., Guo, D., Zhao, Z., Lin, T., Zhang, C.: Underground space use of urban built-up areas in the central city of Nanjing: Insight based on a dynamic population distribution. Undergr. Space **7**, 748–766 (2022)
4. Xu., H.Y., et al.: Dynamic behaviors and contact characteristics of ball bearings in a multi-supported rotor system under the effects of 3D clearance fit. Mech. Syst. Signal Pr. **196**, 110334 (2023)
5. Cao, H.R., Shi, F., Li, Y.M., Li, B.J., Chen, X.F.: Vibration and stability analysis of rotor-bearing-pedestal system due to clearance fit. Mech. Syst. Signal Pr. **133**, 106275 (2019)
6. Oswald, F.B., Zaretsky, E.V., Poplawski, J.V.: Effect of internal clearance on load distribution and life of radially loaded ball and roller bearings. Tribol. T. **55**, 245–265 (2012)
7. Xu, S.P., Ma, J.M.: Cylindrical roller bearings clearance and bearing service life. J. SYLU. **30**, 43–47 (2011). (in Chinese)
8. Harsha, S.P., Sandeep, K., Prakash, R.: The effect of speed of balanced rotor on nonlinear vibrations associated with ball bearings. Int. J. Mech. Sci. **45**, 725–740 (2003)
9. Nelias, D., Bercea, I., Mitu, N.: Analysis of double-row tapered roller bearings, part I - model. J. Tribol. T. **46**, 228–239 (2003)
10. Nelias, D., Bercea, I., Mitu, N.: Analysis of double-row tapered roller bearings, part II - results: Prediction of fatigue life and heat dissipation. J. Tribol. T. **46**, 240–247 (2003)
11. Yu, H., Ma, W.: Study on two different calculation methods for thrust aerostatic bearings with single supply hole at large gas film clearance. In: International Conference on Mechatronics and Automation, pp. 53–58. IEEE (2010)
12. Upadhyay, S.H., Jain, S.C., Harsha, S.P.: Non-linear vibration signature analysis of a high-speed rotating shaft due to ball size variations and varying number of balls. P I Mech. Eng. K-j Mul, **223**, 83–105 (2009)
13. Yang, Y.L., Li, S.X., Cheng, A.S., Jin, Y.S., Chen, Y.J.: Influences of bearing clearance and residual stress on bearing fatigue life. J. NingboTech. 1–7 (2023)
14. Kan, J.B.: Relation between fatigue life and axial clearance of double row tapered roller bearing in cutting section of shearer. Colliery Mech. Electr. Technol. **40**, 58–61 (2019)

15. Bi, Y.L., Zhang, H.G.: An analysis of fatigue breakdown and the best clearance choice for rolling bearings. J. SMU. **3**, 304–306 (2001)
16. Li, F.K., Hu, W.P., Meng, Q.C., Zhan, Z.X., Shen, F.: A new damage-mechanics-based model for rolling contact fatigue analysis of cylindrical roller bearing. Tribol. Int. **120**, 105–114 (2018)
17. Göncza, P., Potočnik, R., Glodež, S.: Fatigue behaviour of 42CrMo4 steel under contact loading. Procedia Eng. **2**, 1991–1999 (2010)
18. Xu, D., Xu, Y.C., Chen, X., Li, X.L., Yang, Y.M.: Fatigue life prediction of ball bearings by modified Paris law based on critical curved surface. J. Mech. Eng. **47**, 52–57 (2011). (in Chinese)
19. He, P.Y., Hong, R.J., Wang, H., Ji, X., Lu, C.: Calculation analysis of yaw bearings with a hardened raceway. Int. J. Mech. Sci. **6**, 540–552 (2018)
20. Zeng, D.F., Xu, T., Liu, W.D., Lu, L.T.: Investigation on rolling contact fatigue of railway wheel steel with surface defect. Wear **446**, 203207 (2020)
21. He, H.F., Liu, H.J., Zhu, C.Z., Wei, P.T., Sun, Z.D.: Study of rolling contact fatigue behavior of a wind turbine gear based on damage-coupled elastic-plastic model. Int. J. Mech. Sci. **141**, 512–519 (2018)
22. Antonio, G., Guillermo, E.: A model for hybrid bearing life with surface and subsurface survival. Wear **422–423**, 223–234 (2019)
23. Jiang, L.J.: Structure design for main bearing of full face rock tunnel boring machine oriented to reliability and vibration behavior. Master's thesis, Dalian University of Technology, Dalian, China (2013). (in Chinese)
24. Han, M.D.: Study on tunnelling loads and structural performance of cutterhead of full face rock tunnel boring machine. Ph.D. thesis, Tianjin University, Tianjin, China (2017). (in Chinese)
25. Bomidi, J., et al.: Experimental and numerical investigation of torsion fatigue of bearing steel. J. Tribol. **135**, 031103 (2013)
26. Xiao, Y.C., Li, S., Gao, Z.: A continuum damage mechanics model for high cycle fatigue. Int. J. Fatigue **20**, 503–508 (1998)
27. Cheng, D.X.: Mechanical Design Manual. Chemical Industry Press, Beijing (2016). (in Chinese)

Outlier Detection and Correction for Time Series Data of Tunnel Boring Machine

Yitang Wang[1,2], Suhang Wang[1,2], Yong Pang[1,2], and Xueguan Song[1,2(✉)]

[1] School of Mechanical Engineering, Dalian University of Technology, Dalian 116024, People's Republic of China
sxg@dlut.edu.cn
[2] State Key Laboratory of High-Performance Precision Manufacturing, Dalian University of Technology, Dalian 116024, People's Republic of China

Abstract. Time series data mining has attracted ever-growing interest in the past decades thanks to its appealing significance in analyzing the operational statuses of tunnel boring machine (TBM) and extracting valuable information from the collected signals. The quality of raw data is mainly affected by outliers and pre-processing includes the task of detecting and correcting these outliers. In this study, a hierarchical sliding window-based method for handling outliers is proposed. First, the sliding window technique is used to divide the initial time series into several sub-time series. Subsequently, the radius of the confidence interval for the slope of each sub-time series is efficiently calculated to identify any outlier sub-time series. The local outlier factor algorithm is employed to further ascertain the outliers. Finally, for the detected outliers, the k-nearest neighbor algorithm is used to correct the outliers. The experimental results validate the practicality of the proposed method for engineering applications.

Keywords: Outlier Detection and Correction · Time Series Analysis · Tunnel Boring Machine

1 Introduction

In comparison to conventional drill-and-blast technology [1, 2], tunnel boring machines (TBMs) have gained widespread application in large-scale tunnel projects, including urban subways, diversion tunnels, and submarine tunnels, owing to its notable advantages in terms of efficiency, safety, and environmental friendliness [3]. The operational performance and safety of TBMs are significantly influenced by the ground conditions encountered ahead of the tunnel work, particularly when operating in mixed-face ground during construction. Analysis of time-series data, particularly signals from key TBM components, is one of the simplest and most effective methods to assess TBM performance [4–7]. However, the complexity of the construction site environment inevitably creates outliers in the collected data, significantly reducing the utility of the dataset.

There is a considerable literature on various methods for detecting outliers in time series data. In general, algorithmic models for time series-oriented outlier detection are

H. Yang et al. (Eds.): ICIRA 2023, LNAI 14272, pp. 254–261, 2023.
https://doi.org/10.1007/978-981-99-6480-2_21

usually based on predictive, statistical, machine learning and deep learning, window-based methods. The window-based methods involve segmenting the time series by defining the size of a sliding window, extracting features from each sub-time series, and identifying outliers within them. Compared with other methods, this approach has the advantages of ease of understanding, computational simplicity, reductions in time complexity and the ability to handle dynamic data volumes. Therefore, it has gained wide application.

Although existing studies have made great contributions to outlier detection of time series data, there have been only a few studies on the outlier detection method applicable to shield machine data. Motived by this requirement, this paper proposes an outlier detection method based on hierarchical sliding window for TBM data, which named AD-SV-LOF. Meanwhile, we use k-nearest neighbor (KNN) imputation method [8, 9] for correction of outliers in TBM data.

2 Methodology

2.1 Anomalous Sub-time Series Detection

A time series of length n is defined as $X(t) = \{x(t_i)|1 \le i \le n\}$, where $x(t_i)$ is the record of t_i moment, the acquisition time is strictly increasing. A sliding window of length $l(l \ll n)$ is used to segment this time series of equal length in steps m, which is set to 1 here. Sliding $(n - l)/m$ times in succession results in $(n - l)/m + 1$ sub-time series of length l.

Suppose that one of the sub-time series is $X_j(1 \le j \le n - l + 1)$, the slope k between any two adjacent data points in X_j can be calculated by the following equation

$$k(i) = \frac{x(t_i) - x(t_{i-1})}{t_i - t_{i-1}}, (j + 1 \le i \le j + l - 1) \tag{1}$$

The mean $\bar{s}_j$ and mean squared deviation σ_j of the slope of the j-th sub-time series can be calculated as

$$\bar{s}_j = \frac{\sum_{i=j+1}^{j+l-1} k(i)}{l - 1} \tag{2}$$

$$\sigma_j = \sqrt{\frac{\sum_{i=j+1}^{j+l-1} (k(i) - \bar{s}_j)^2}{l - 2}} \tag{3}$$

The radius of the confidence interval for the slope of the j-th sub-time series is expressed as

$$d_j = \frac{|\bar{Z}_j - \underline{Z}_j|}{2} \tag{4}$$

where $\bar{Z}_j$ is the upper confidence limit and $\underline{Z}_j$ is the lower confidence limit, which can be represented as

$$\bar{Z}_j = \bar{s}_j + \frac{\sigma_j}{\sqrt{l}} Y_{\frac{\alpha}{2}} \tag{5}$$

$$Z_j = \bar{s}_j - \frac{\sigma_j}{\sqrt{l}} Y_{\frac{\alpha}{2}} \qquad (6)$$

where Y is a normally distributed random variable satisfying N(0,1), α stands for significance in interval estimation, while 1-α is the confidence level, and α is taken as 0.05.

The characteristics of the sub-time series, i.e., the radius of the confidence interval of the slope, are obtained, and if the radius is greater than the threshold γ, the sub-time series is considered as an abnormal sub-time series, which contains outliers, and the specific outlier information needs further analysis.

2.2 Local Outlier Factor Algorithm

For each detected anomalous sub-time series, the local outlier factor (LOF) algorithm [10, 11] is used to identify outliers by calculating the outlier factor for each data point.

Let the anomalous sub-time series data be $X_t(1 \leq t \leq n-l+1)$. The LOF algorithm first calculates the reachability distance of each data point, calculates the local reachability density of the data point by the reachability distance, and further calculates the local outlier factor of the data point. The more the local outlier factor of a data point is greater than 1, it means that the density of the data point is smaller than the average density of the points in its neighborhood, and the more likely that the data point is an outlier point, and vice versa, it means that the data point is a normal point. In this method, the local outlier factor of each data point in the abnormal sub-data series is calculated, and half of the maximum value of the outlier factor is used as the threshold, if the outlier factor of a data point is greater than the threshold, it is an outlier point, and vice versa, it is a normal point.

The k-th reachability distance from any two points X_p to point X_o is

$$RD_k(X_p, X_o) = max\{k - distance(X_o), dist(X_p, X_o)\} \qquad (7)$$

where $k - distance(X_o)$ is the k-neighborhood distance of point X_o, dist(X_p, X_o) is Euclidean distance from point X_p to point X_o.

The local reachability density at point X_p is defined by

$$LRD_k(X_p) = \frac{1}{\frac{\sum_{o \in N_{k-distance}(X_p)} RD_k(X_p, X_o)}{|N_{k-distance}(X_p)|}} \qquad (8)$$

where $|N_{k-distance}(X_p)|$ is the set of those whose distance from point X_p is less than k-distance(X_p).

The local outlier factor for point X_p is

$$LOF(X_p) = \frac{\sum_{X_o \in N_{k-distance}(X_p)} \frac{LRD_k(X_o)}{LRD_k(X_p)}}{|N_{k-distance}(X_p)|} \qquad (9)$$

Half of the maximum value of the local outlier is selected as the threshold value ρ, and the outlier of each data point is compared with the threshold value, if it is greater than ρ, the data point is an outlier, otherwise it is normal.

2.3   K-Nearest Neighbor Imputation

KNN is one of the most popular imputation methods. In this method, the missing values of each example are imputed with k most similar neighbor values within the training space. For numerical attributes, the mean value of the neighbors is employed, whereas for discrete attributes, the mode value is utilized.

The performance of imputation relies significantly on two key parameters: the number of neighbors and the choice of distance measurement. To address this, we employ the well-established Euclidean distance measure in our study.

The sliding window step in this study is one, so the outlier point exists in multiple sub-time series, and the index of the outlier point in the shield machine actual measurement data is recorded. If there is no such index in the outlier fill data set, the index is created and the value of the predicted outlier point in that sub-time series is recorded; otherwise, the predicted value of the index location point is recorded directly.

3   Experiments

3.1   Evaluation Setup

To evaluate the performance of the proposed method, outlier detection and outlier correction are measured using different metrics. Outlier detection uses recall and accuracy that can be defined as follows

$$Recall = \frac{\text{Number of actual point outliers detected}}{\text{Number of actual point outliers}} \tag{10}$$

$$Accuracy = \frac{\text{Number of actual point outliers detected}}{\text{Number of test results suspected to be point outliers}} \tag{11}$$

The larger the values of Recall and Accuracy, the better the detection performance.

As for the outlier correction, R-square (R^2) is used to evaluate the performance. R^2 is obtained by

$$R^2 = 1 - \frac{\sum_{i=1}^{N}(x_i - \hat{x}_i)^2}{\sum_{i=1}^{N}(x_i - \overline{x}_i)^2} \tag{12}$$

where N is the number of outliers, $\hat{x}_i$ is the corrected result by KNN, x_i is the true value of the source data corresponding to the corrected result, and $\overline{x}_i$ is its mean value. The closer the value of R^2 is to 1, the better the correction performance.

3.2 Project Review and Experimental Setting

The dataset used for analysis in this study was collected from a tunnel project in China. For tunnel excavation, an earth pressure balance (EPB) shield TBM was employed, comprising essential components such as a cutterhead, chamber, screw conveyor, tail skin, and various auxiliary subsystems. The time series data from the TBM encompasses a total of 53 attributes, encompassing signals originating from the electrical system, hydraulic system, grout system, and other supplementary systems. All signals are sampled at a frequency of 1 Hz.

The time series data from the TBM corresponds to a single integral tunnel engineering ring, comprising a total of 1605 time points. To address the issue of scale, a normalization process was applied to each variable within the time series, ensuring values were transformed to the range of [0, 1]. The torque of the cutterhead is selected as the object of analysis, and 20 outliers are randomly inserted into the source data.

3.3 Results and Analysis

The sliding window length is 7, i.e., the step size is 1. The number of neighbors in LOF and KNN is 5. The radius of the confidence interval of the slope of each sub-time series is calculated as shown in Fig. 1, and the optimal threshold γ is set to 0.04. The sub-time series with confidence interval radius greater than the threshold are set as anomalous sub-time series, as shown in Fig. 2. For each detected anomalous sub-time series, the LOF algorithm is used to identify the outliers, as shown in Fig. 3.

Recall and accuracy are used to measure the detection results of different algorithms, and the results are compared with the proposed method by AD-SV-GG, AD-Variance-LOF, and LOF algorithms. The AD-SV-GG method is the same as this method in the anomalous sub-recognition sequence identification stage, but the Gath-Geva clustering algorithm is used in the outlier identification. The AD-Variance-LOF method selects the traditional confidence interval threshold judgment in the identification of anomalous sub-time series. 10 times of repeated experiments, and the mean values of each index are taken, and the results are shown in Table 1.

Table 1. Comparison of outlier detection results.

Methods	Recall (%)	Accuracy (%)
AD-SV-GG	92.00	70.45
AD-Variance-LOF	85.00	80.96
LOF	75.00	50.00
AD-SV-LOF	95.00	90.48

The proposed method utilizes the radius of the confidence interval for the slope of the sub-time series as a characteristic to identify abnormal sub-time series. This characteristic effectively captures the change patterns exhibited by the sub-time series.

In contrast, the AD-Variance-LOF method employs the mean and variance of the sub-time series to describe changes in its structural characteristics, which fails to adequately capture the sub-time series' intrinsic features. Consequently, the evaluation indices of recall and accuracy for the AD-Variance-LOF method are lower than those achieved by the method proposed in this paper.

Furthermore, the AD-SV-GG method employs the Gath-Geva clustering algorithm during the outlier detection stage. However, the results of the Gath-Geva algorithm are influenced by the randomly generated initial matrix and can only provide a binary assessment of whether a data point is an outlier or not. In comparison, the density-based LOF algorithm assigns an outlier factor to each data point based on its neighborhood density, enabling a more nuanced evaluation of outlier status. As a result, the evaluation index of the method proposed in this work surpasses that of the AD-SV-GG method.

Additionally, this proposed method considers the structural change characteristics of time series data during the detection process. It first identifies abnormal sub-time series before applying the LOF algorithm. Consequently, the accuracy and recall rate of this method outperform those of the traditional LOF algorithm.

Finally, KNN is used to correct the outliers, and the R^2 of the corrected results is 0.99, as expected.

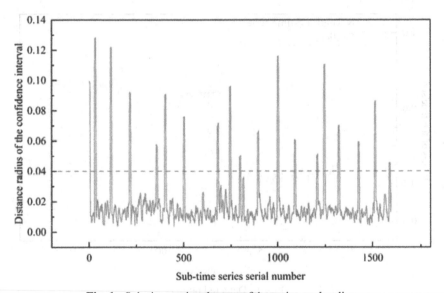

Fig. 1. Sub-time series slope confidence interval radius.

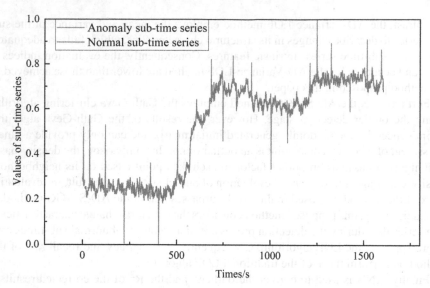

Fig. 2. Detected abnormal sub-time series.

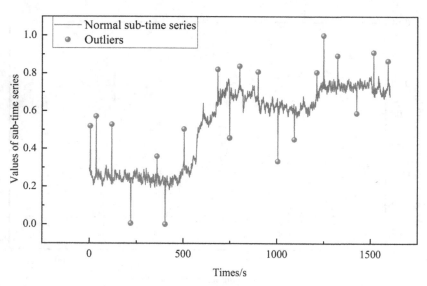

Fig. 3. Detected outliers.

4   Conclusions

In this paper, we propose a sliding window-based method to detect outliers in time series data, specifically to address the issue of point outliers in real measurement data from TBMs. The proposed method consists of identifying anomalous sub-timeseries by calculating the radius of confidence interval of the slope of the sub-timeseries. Subsequently, the LOF algorithm is utilized to detect and classify these abnormal sub-time series as outliers. Experimental results demonstrate that the detection accuracy of this proposed method surpasses that of alternative approaches and the conventional LOF algorithm, which rely on extracting sub-time series features solely from mean and variance information. Moreover, for the identified outlier points, a correction technique based on KNN is employed, yielding satisfactory results as demonstrated by the experimental outcomes. Thus, the point outlier detection and correction method proposed in this paper exhibits promising capabilities for processing engineering data.

References

1. Rehman, H., Ali, W., Naji, A.M., et al.: Review of rock-mass rating and tunneling quality index systems for tunnel design: development, refinement, application and limitation. Appl. Sci. **8**(8), 1250 (2018)
2. Mazaira, A., Konicek, P.: Intense rockburst impacts in deep underground construction and their prevention. Can. Geotech J. **52**(10), 1426–1439 (2015)
3. Shi, M., Zhang, L., Sun, W., et al.: A fuzzy c-means algorithm guided by attribute correlations and its application in the big data analysis of tunnel boring machine. Knowl.-Based Syst. **182**, 104859 (2019)
4. Pang, Y., Shi, M., Zhang, L., et al.: A multivariate time series segmentation algorithm for analyzing the operating statuses of tunnel boring machines. Knowl.-Based Syst. **242**, 108362 (2022)
5. Qin, C., Shi, G., Tao, J., et al.: An adaptive hierarchical decomposition-based method for multi-step cutterhead torque forecast of shield machine. Mech. Syst. Signal Process. **175**, 109148 (2022)
6. Wang, Y., Pang, Y., Sun, W., et al.: Industrial data denoising via low-rank and sparse representations and its application in tunnel boring machine. Energies **15**(10), 3525 (2022)
7. Yu, H., Qin, C., Tao, J., et al.: A multi-channel decoupled deep neural network for tunnel boring machine torque and thrust prediction. Tunnelling Underground Space Technol. **133**, 104949 (2023)
8. Malarvizhi, R., Thanamani, A.S.: K-nearest neighbor in missing data imputation. Int. J. Eng. Res. Dev. **5**(1), 5–7 (2012)
9. Cubillos, M., Wøhlk, S., Wulff, J.N.: A bi-objective k-nearest-neighbors-based imputation method for multilevel data. Expert Syst. Appl. **204**, 117298 (2022)
10. Zhu, J., Wang, Y., Zhou, D., et al.: Batch process modeling and monitoring with local outlier factor. IEEE Trans. Control Syst. Technol. **27**(4), 1552–1565 (2018)
11. Wang, G., Chen, Y.: Robust feature matching using guided local outlier factor. Pattern Recogn. **117**, 107986 (2021)

Robotic Machining of Complex Components

Error Sensitivity Analysis and Tolerance Allocation Simulation of a Five-Axis Parallel Machining Robot

Yuhao He[1], Fugui Xie[1,2(✉)] ⓘ, Xin-Jun Liu[1,2], and Zenghui Xie[1,2]

[1] State Key Laboratory of Tribology in Advanced Equipment, Department of Mechanical Engineering (DME), Tsinghua University, Beijing 100084, China
xiefg@mail.tsinghua.edu.cn

[2] Beijing Key Lab of Precision/Ultra-Precision Manufacturing Equipments and Control, Tsinghua University, Beijing 100084, China

Abstract. With the advantages of flexible attitude adjustments and high stiffness, parallel robots have the potentials to be used in the machining of complex parts. However, the multi-closed-loop structures of parallel robots result in more error terms and make the error transfer relationships complicated. It is costly to keep all the error terms small. To maintain relatively high theoretical accuracy in a cost-effective way, the error model of the five-axis parallel machining robot is established and the sensitivity analysis is carried out at the design stage. The global position sensitivity index and global orientation sensitivity index are presented to evaluate the influence of each error term on the position and orientation error of the end-effector. On this basis, the vital and trivial error terms are identified. Tolerance allocation simulation shows that compared to reducing the value of trivial error terms, reducing the value of vital error terms has a much more significant effect on the reduction of position and orientation error. By implementing strict control over vital error values and appropriately loosening the control over trivial error values, it is possible to achieve relatively high accuracy while minimizing manufacturing costs. The identified results of the vital and trivial error terms are helpful for the prototype design.

Keywords: Kinematic Error Model · Sensitivity Analysis · Tolerance Allocation

The List of Symbols and Nomenclature

$\delta O'$ Position error of the end-effector
δR Orientation error of the end-effector
ε Error vector
J_{CVC} Error mapping matrix
LSI Local sensitivity index
GSI Global sensitivity index
$AGSI$ Average global sensitivity index

© The Author(s), under exclusive license to Springer Nature Singapore Pte Ltd. 2023
H. Yang et al. (Eds.): ICIRA 2023, LNAI 14272, pp. 265–274, 2023.
https://doi.org/10.1007/978-981-99-6480-2_22

1 Introduction

In the last decades, with the rapid development of aerospace industry, shipping, and energy, the demand for the parts with complex surface (such as marine propellers and turbine blades) is becoming more and more urgent. The machining of such parts requires the equipment be capable of five-axis linkage motion, high-efficiency and high-precision machining.

Serial robots [1], which have serial structure [2] and simple kinematics, have been used for machining complex parts [3, 4]. However, the stiffness of serial robots varies largely in the workspace. Moreover, defects and reduction in machining efficiency may occur at the open-and-close angle transitions [5] due to the generally used A/C rotating head and its synthetic attitude adjustment motion. Therefore, their applications in high-efficiency and high-precision machining are limited. In contrast, parallel robots, which characterized with compact structure and relatively high stiffness [6–8], can realize attitude coupling motions. This feature makes them have the potentials to machine complex parts with high efficiency and high precision. The accuracy of machining equipment will directly affect machining quality. The multi-closed-loop structures of parallel robots result in more error terms and make the error transfer relationships complicated. Obviously, it will cost a lot to keep all error terms small [9]. Thus, how to improve theoretical accuracy of parallel robots in a cost-effective way at the design stage is the first problem to be solved.

As a response to the issue, this paper performs error modeling and error sensitivity analysis of a five-axis parallel machining robot. The geometric errors as important factors affecting its accuracy [10] should be considered at the design stage. To select the geometric error terms that have critical impact on the accuracy of end-effector, sensitivity analysis is necessary. Huang et al. [11] defined the sensitivity indexes of a 3T1R parallel robot using the average value of the sum of error vectors in the workspace. Chai et al. [12] proposed local sensitivity indexes of a 2UPR-2RPU parallel robot. The local sensitivity indexes are unit consistent and have physical significance, based on which the link parameters were optimized. Shen et al. [13] defined sensitivity matrices using variational method, and a non-fully symmetric parallel Delta robot was designed, which was less sensitive to variation of geometric parameters compared to the original Delta robot. Inspired by the works above, this paper establishes the error model of the five-axis parallel machining robot and proposes a global sensitive index to evaluate the contribution of each error term to the error of the end-effector. A tolerance allocation simulation is carried out to verify the correctness.

The remainder of this paper is organized as follows: in Sect. 2, a brief introduction to the five-axis parallel machining robot is presented. In Sect. 3, the error model of the five-axis parallel machining robot is established and a global sensitive index is defined. Based on the index, the contribution of each error term to the position and orientation error of end-effector is evaluated. Tolerance allocation simulation is conducted in Sect. 4. The paper is concluded in Sect. 5.

2 Introduction to the Five-Axis Parallel Machining Robot

Complex parts place high demands on machining equipment's motion dexterity. The five-axis parallel machining robot presented in this paper is based on the 5-DoF (degree of freedom) special parallel mechanism [14], which is a 4-UCU&UCR mechanism.

The CAD model and kinematic scheme are shown in Fig. 1. Points B_1–B_5 are on the base and on the same circle, which has point O as its center and r_b as its radius. Points A_1–A_3 are on the end-effector and on the same circle, which has p' as its center and r_p as its radius. Points A_4 and A_5 are on the end-effector and on the same circle, which has s' as its center and r_s as its radius, and $s'p'$ is perpendicular to circle $A_1A_2A_3$. The global coordinate frame O-xyz is fixed with the base, and the origin O is the center of the circle $B_1B_2B_3B_4B_5$. The local coordinate frame O'-$x'y'z'$ is fixed with the spindle, and the origin O' coincides with the tool tip point. For simplicity, B_iA_i will be referred to be as limb i.

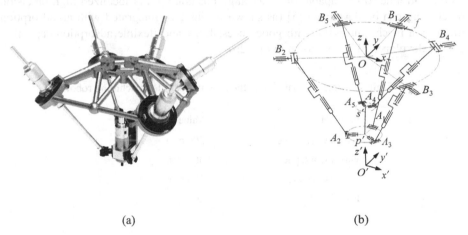

(a)   (b)

Fig. 1. Five-axis parallel machining robot: (a) CAD model, (b) kinematic scheme

Limb 1 is a UCR kinematic chain, which is a five-DoF chain. It provides a one-dimensional force constraint on the end-effector. As shown in Fig. 1(b), the constraint force f passes through the center of Hooke joint (point B_1) on the base and is parallel to the axis of the revolution joint (point A_1) on the end-effector. Limb 2–5 are UCU kinematic chains, which are six-DoF chains and do not provide constraint on the end-effector. Thus, the five-axis parallel machining robot is a 2T3R parallel robot, and can achieve flexible attitude adjustments. The structural parameters are shown in Table 1.

Table 1. Structural parameters of the five-axis parallel machining robot

Parameters	Value	Parameters	Value
r_b	650 mm	$\angle B_1 O B_2 = \angle B_1 O B_3$	120°
r_p	181.2 mm	$\angle B_1 O B_4 = \angle B_1 O B_5$	50°
r_s	90 mm	$\angle A_1 p' A_2 = \angle A_1 p' A_3$	120°
$s'p'$	371.2 mm	$\angle A_4 s' A_5$	45°

As shown in Table 2, the five-axis parallel machining robot has a cube workspace with 300 mm × 300 mm × 200 mm, and can realize at least 20° rotational angle in an arbitrary direction, which allows for good motion dexterity. The five-axis parallel machining robot can be used as a plug-and-play module to develop different kinds of mobile machining equipment. For example, integrated with a robotic arm and an AGV, a mobile robot capable of wide-range positioning and localized high-precision machining can be developed [5] (as shown in Fig. 2a); integrated with an adsorption module, a machining robot with good accessibility and flexible adsorption capability can be developed [15] (as shown in Fig. 2b).

Table 2. Motion capability of the five-axis parallel machining robot

Parameters	Value
x-axis workspace	300 mm
y-axis workspace	300 mm
z-axis workspace	200 mm
Rotational angle	20°

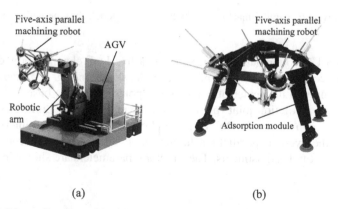

(a)   (b)

Fig. 2. Possible applications of the five-axis parallel machining robot: (a) integrated with a robotic arm and an AGV; (b) integrated with an adsorption module

3   Error Modeling and Sensitivity Analysis

3.1   Error Modeling of the Five-Axis Parallel Machining Robot

The geometric errors are important factors affecting accuracy, and they can be controlled at the design stage. Therefore, it is necessary to investigate how each geometric error affects the position and orientation error of the end-effector. The error model can be obtained through the closed-loop vector chain (CVC) method mentioned in [16], and it can be written as

$$
J^{ee} \begin{bmatrix} \delta O' \\ \delta R \end{bmatrix} = J^{cl} \varepsilon_0 \tag{1}
$$

where J^{ee} and J^{cl} are error mapping matrices. $\delta O'$ is the position error of the end-effector, and δR is the orientation error of the end-effector. ε_0 is a column vector comprising 55 error terms, which can be further categorized into 30 length error terms, 20 angle error terms, and 5 joint zero position error terms. The length error terms consist of position error of point A_i and point B_i. The angle error terms consist of orientation error of the fixed axes of each universal joint and the axis of revolute joint in limb 1.

Except for the 55 error terms, the length error of the tool along the spindle axis needs to be considered. Therefore, the error model of the five-axis parallel machining robot can be further rewritten as

$$
\begin{aligned}
\begin{bmatrix} \delta O' \\ \delta R \end{bmatrix} &= J_{CVC} \varepsilon \\
J_{CVC} &= \begin{bmatrix} [I_3\ 0]J^{ee^{-1}}J^{cl}\ Re_3 \\ [0\ I_3]J^{ee^{-1}}J^{cl}\ 0 \end{bmatrix}, \varepsilon = \begin{bmatrix} \varepsilon_0 \\ \delta t \end{bmatrix}
\end{aligned} \tag{2}
$$

where R is the rotating matrix of the end-effector. I_3 is a third-order unit matrix and e_3 is a unit column vector whose third element is 1 and the rest are 0. δt is the length error of the tool along the spindle axis.

3.2   Sensitivity Analysis of the Five-Axis Parallel Machining Robot

Reducing the value of error terms facilitates the improvement of the accuracy of the end-effector. However, it will cost a lot to keep every error term small. Thus, it is necessary to conduct sensitivity analysis to evaluate the extent that each error term contributes to the position and orientation error of the end-effector. Under a specific configuration of the five-axis parallel machining robot, the contribution of the kth error term ε_k to the position and orientation error of end-effector can be defined as local sensitivity index (LSI) as follows

$$
\begin{aligned}
LSI_{P1}(\varepsilon_k) &= \frac{e_1^{\mathrm{T}} J_{CVC} e_k}{e_1^{\mathrm{T}} \delta O'}, \quad LSI_{P2}(\varepsilon_k) = \frac{e_2^{\mathrm{T}} J_{CVC} e_k}{e_2^{\mathrm{T}} \delta O'}, \quad LSI_{P3}(\varepsilon_k) = \frac{e_3^{\mathrm{T}} J_{CVC} e_k}{e_3^{\mathrm{T}} \delta O'} \\
LSI_{O1}(\varepsilon_k) &= \frac{e_4^{\mathrm{T}} J_{CVC} e_k}{e_1^{\mathrm{T}} \delta R}, \quad LSI_{O2}(\varepsilon_k) = \frac{e_5^{\mathrm{T}} J_{CVC} e_k}{e_2^{\mathrm{T}} \delta R}, \quad LSI_{O3}(\varepsilon_k) = \frac{e_6^{\mathrm{T}} J_{CVC} e_k}{e_3^{\mathrm{T}} \delta R}
\end{aligned} \tag{3}
$$

It is obviously that *LSI* satisfies the following equation.

$$\sum_{k=1}^{56} LSI_{P1}(\varepsilon_k) = \sum_{k=1}^{56} LSI_{P2}(\varepsilon_k) = \sum_{k=1}^{56} LSI_{P3}(\varepsilon_k) = 1$$

$$\sum_{k=1}^{56} LSI_{O1}(\varepsilon_k) = \sum_{k=1}^{56} LSI_{O2}(\varepsilon_k) = \sum_{k=1}^{56} LSI_{O3}(\varepsilon_k) = 1$$
(4)

To synthesize the effect of each error term on the position and orientation error of end-effector, the local position sensitivity index (*LSI_P*) and local orientation sensitivity index (*LSI_O*) are defined as follows

$$LSI_P(\varepsilon_k) = a_1 LSI_{P1}(\varepsilon_k) + a_2 LSI_{P2}(\varepsilon_k) + a_3 LSI_{P3}(\varepsilon_k)$$

$$LSI_O(\varepsilon_k) = b_1 LSI_{O1}(\varepsilon_k) + b_2 LSI_{O2}(\varepsilon_k) + b_3 LSI_{O3}(\varepsilon_k)$$
(5)

where a_1–a_3 and b_1–b_3 are the weighting factors. This paper considers the position error in three directions to be equally important, and the error of rotation angle around the spindle axis is not as important as that around the other two axes. Therefore, the parameters below will be used in the analysis to follow.

$$a_1 = a_2 = a_3 = \frac{1}{3}, b_1 = b_2 = \frac{1}{2}, b_3 = 0$$
(6)

To represent the overall influence of each error term on the position and orientation error of end-effector in the robot workspace (as shown in Table 2), the global position sensitivity index (*GSI_P*) and global orientation sensitivity index (*GSI_O*) are defined as follows

$$GSI_P(\varepsilon_k) = \frac{\int_V LSI_P(\varepsilon_k) dV}{\int_V dV}, \quad GSI_O(\varepsilon_k) = \frac{\int_V LSI_O(\varepsilon_k) dV}{\int_V dV}$$
(7)

The average of *GSI_P* and *GSI_O* (*AGSI_P* and *AGSI_O*) can be defined as

$$AGSI_P = \frac{\sum_{k=1}^{56} GSI_P(\varepsilon_k)}{56}, \quad AGSI_O = \frac{\sum_{k=1}^{56} GSI_O(\varepsilon_k)}{56}$$
(8)

Usually, the trivial error terms are considered to be one order of magnitude smaller than the vital error terms [17]. Thus, the error terms whose *GSI* is larger than *AGSI* are defined as the vital error terms, while the error terms whose *GSI* is smaller than 0.1*AGSI* are defined as the trivial error terms. Histograms of the *GSI* of error terms are shown in Fig. 3. By taking the concurrent set for vital error terms and the intersection set for trivial error terms obtained by *GSI_P* and *GSI_O*, the vital error terms and trivial error terms are identified as shown in Table 3.

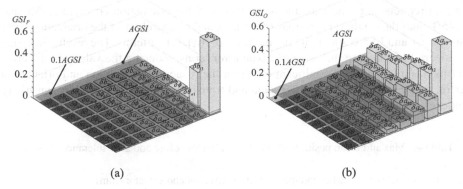

Fig. 3. Histograms of the GSI of error terms: (a) GSI_P, (b) GSI_O

Table 3. Vital error terms and trivial terms

Sensitivity index	Vital error terms	Trivial error terms
GSI_P	$\delta a_{13}, \delta b_{13}, \delta\phi_{a1}, \delta\theta_{a1}$	$\delta a_{11}, \delta b_{11}, \delta\theta_{b1}, \delta\theta_{a2}, \delta\phi_{b2}, \delta\theta_{b2},$ $\delta\theta_{a3}, \delta\theta_{b3}, \delta\phi_{a4}, \delta\theta_{b4}, \delta\phi_{a5}, \delta\theta_{b5}$
GSI_O	$\delta a_{12}, \delta a_{13}, \delta b_{13}, \delta\phi_{a1}, \delta\theta_{a1}, \delta a_{33},$ $\delta b_{33}, \delta a_{41}, \delta a_{42}, \delta b_{41}, \delta b_{42}, \delta a_{51},$ $\delta a_{52}, \delta b_{51}, \delta b_{52}$	$\delta a_{11}, \delta b_{11}, \delta\theta_{b1}, \delta\theta_{a2}, \delta\theta_{b2}, \delta\theta_{a3},$ $\delta\theta_{b3}, \delta b_{42}, \delta\phi_{a4}, \delta\theta_{a4}, \delta\phi_{b4}, \delta\theta_{b4},$ $\delta a_{52}, \delta\phi_{a5}, \delta\theta_{a5}, \delta\phi_{b5}, \delta\theta_{b5}$

4   Tolerance Allocation Simulation

To validate the vital and trivial error terms mentioned in Sec. 3, tolerance allocation simulation needs to be carried out. Assuming that in the initial state, all 31 length error terms have a value of 0.1 mm and all 25 angle error terms have a value of 0.1°. The tolerance allocation process was simulated by reducing the length error term to 0.01 mm and the angle error term to 0.01°.

To quantitatively describe the importance of tolerance allocation, the max and mean errors of position and orientation of the end-effector are shown in Table 4 and Table 5. It can be seen from Fig. 4 that the largest reductions of the max and mean values of the position error are 40.32% and 42.24%, and the smallest reductions of the max and mean values of the position error are 38.60% and 40.23% after reducing the value of vital error terms. The largest reductions of the max and mean values of the orientation error are 49.36% and 50.14%, and the smallest reductions of the max and mean values of the orientation error are 38.62% and 46.31% after reducing the value of vital error terms. In contrast, the largest reductions of the max and mean values of the position error are 1.46% and 0.98%, and the smallest reductions of the max and mean values of the position error are 0.26% and 0.66% after reducing the value of trivial error terms. The largest reductions of the max and mean values of the orientation error are 2.46% and 2.45%, and the smallest reductions of the max and mean values of the orientation error are 0.26% and 1.85% after reducing the value of trivial error terms. The results show that compared to reducing the value of trivial error terms, reducing the value of vital error terms has a much more significant effect on the reduction of position and orientation error, and it verifies the validity of vital and trivial error terms identified by sensitivity indexes proposed in this paper.

Table 4. Max and mean position errors of end-effector before and after tolerance allocation

Pendulum angle of end-effector	Max and mean position errors of end-effector (mm)		
	Keep initial state	Reduce the value of vital error terms	Reduce the value of trivial error terms
$\theta = 5°$	1.602/1.271	0.956/0.760	1.579/1.263
$\theta = 10°$	1.613/1.288	0.967/0.766	1.589/1.280
$\theta = 15°$	2.041/1.451	1.232/0.839	2.019/1.437
$\theta = 20°$	3.093/1.966	1.761/1.135	2.912/1.946

Table 5. Max and mean orientation errors of end-effector before and after tolerance allocation

Pendulum angle of end-effector	Max and mean orientation errors of end-effector (°)		
	Keep initial state	Reduce the value of vital error terms	Reduce the value of trivial error terms
$\theta = 5°$	0.369/0.285	0.186/0.142	0.359/0.278
$\theta = 10°$	0.373/0.288	0.191/0.144	0.364/0.281
$\theta = 15°$	0.503/0.321	0.276/0.162	0.492/0.314
$\theta = 20°$	0.613/0.441	0.352/0.237	0.587/0.433

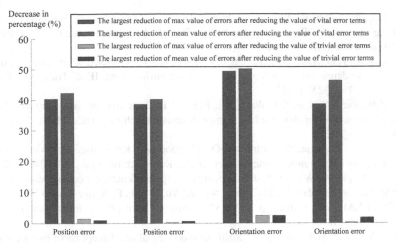

Fig. 4. Comparison of simulation results

5 Conclusion

The geometric errors are important factors affecting accuracy of end-effector. Aiming to improve theoretical accuracy of the five-axis parallel machining robot in a cost-effective way, this paper presents a method to identify the vital and trivial error terms. The five-axis parallel machining robot is designed based on a 4-UCU&UCR mechanism, which is a 2T3R mechanism and can achieve good motion dexterity. The error model of the five-axis parallel machining robot is established and two global sensitivity indexes (GSI_P and GSI_A) are proposed to evaluate the impact of each geometric error term. The vital error terms and trivial error terms are identified base on the indexes. The simulation shows that compared to reducing the value of trivial error terms, reducing the value of vital error terms has a much more significant effect on the reduction of position and orientation error, and it verifies the validity of the vital and trivial error terms identified by sensitivity indexes.

The error model and sensitivity indexes presented in this paper are useful for reasonable tolerance allocation and reducing manufacturing cost at the design stage.

Acknowledgements. This work was supported in part by the National Key R&D Program of China under Grant 2022YFB3404101, and National Natural Science Foundation of China under Grants 92148301 and 91948301.

Referencess

1. Lei, P., Zheng, L.: An automated in-situ alignment approach for finish machining assembly interfaces of large-scale components. Rob. Comput. Integr. Manuf. **46**, 130–143 (2017)
2. Zhao, X.W., Lu, H., Yu, W.F., Tao, B., Ding, H.: Vision-based mobile robotic grinding for large-scale workpiece and its accuracy analysis. IEEE/ASME Trans. Mechatron. **28**(2), 895–906 (2023)

3. DeVlieg, R., Sitton, K., Feikert, E., Inman, J.: ONCE (one-sided cell end effector) robotic drilling system. In: Proceedings of the 2002 SAE Automated Fastening Conference & Exhibition, Chester,UK (2002)
4. Zhao, X.W., Han, S.B., Tao, B., Yin, Z.P., Ding, H.: Model-based actor−critic learning of robotic impedance control in complex interactive environment. IEEE Trans. Ind. Electron. **69**(12), 13225–13235 (2022)
5. Xie, Z.H., Xie, F.G., Liu, X.J., Wang, J.S., Mei, B.: Tracking error prediction informed motion control of a parallel machine tool for high-performance machining. Int. J. Mach. Tools. Manuf. **164**, 103714 (2021)
6. Brahmia, A., Kelaiaia, R., Company, O., Chemori, A.: Kinematic sensitivity analysis of manipulators using a novel dimensionless index. Robot. Auton. Syst. **150**, 104021 (2022)
7. Wen, J., Xie, F., Bi, W., Liu, X.-J.: Conceptual design and kinematic optimization of a gantry hybrid machining robot. In: Liu, X.-J., Nie, Z., Yu, J., Xie, F., Song, R. (eds.) ICIRA 2021. LNCS (LNAI), vol. 13014, pp. 743–753. Springer, Cham (2021). https://doi.org/10.1007/978-3-030-89098-8_70
8. Wang, Y.Y., Liu, H.T., Huang, T.: Stiffness modeling of the Tricept robot using the overall Jacobian matrix. J. Mech. Robot. **1**, 21002 (2009)
9. Li, Z.B., Li, S., Luo, X.: An overview of calibration technology of industrial Tobots. IEEE/CAA J. Autom. Sin. **8**(1), 23–36 (2021)
10. Kim, S.H., et al.: Robotic machining: a review of recent progress. Int. J. Precis. Eng. Manuf. **20**(9), 1629–1642 (2019)
11. Huang, C.H., Xie, F.G., Liu, X.J., Meng, Q.Z.: Error modeling and sensitivity analysis of a parallel robot with R-(SS)2 branches. Int. J. Intelli. Robot. Appl. **4**(4), 416–428 (2020)
12. Chai, X.X., Zhang, N.B., He, L.Y., Li, Q.C., Ye, W.: Kinematic sensitivity analysis and dimensional synthesis of a redundantly actuated parallel robot for friction stir welding. Chin. J. Mech. Eng. **33**(1), 1–10 (2020)
13. Shen, H.P., Meng, Q.M., Li, J., Deng, J.M., Wu, G.L.: Kinematic sensitivity, parameter identification and calibration of a non-fully symmetric parallel Delta robot. Mech. Mach. Theory **161**, 104311 (2021)
14. Liu, X.J., Xie, Z.H., Xie, F.G., Wang, J.S.: Design and development of a portable machining robot with parallel kinematics. In: 16th International Conference on Ubiquitous Robots (UR), pp. 133–136. IEEE, South Korea (2019)
15. Chen, J.K., Xie, F.G., Liu, X.J., Bi, W.Y.: Stiffness evaluation of an adsorption robot for large-scale structural parts processing. J. Mech. Robot. **13**, 40907 (2021)
16. Mei, B., Xie, F.G., Liu, X.J., Yang, C.: Elasto-geometrical error modeling and compensation of a five-axis parallel machining robot. Precis. Eng. **69**, 48–61 (2021)
17. Luo, X., Xie, F.G., Liu, X.J., Li, J.: Error modeling and sensitivity analysis of a novel 5-degree-of-freedom parallel kinematic machine tool. J. Eng. Manuf. **233**(6), 1637–1652 (2019)

High-Precision Point Cloud Data Acquisition for Robot Based on Multiple Constraints

Bingbing Li[1], Teng Zhang[1], Hao Sun[2]([✉]), Runpeng Deng[1], Fangyu Peng[1,3],
Rong Yan[1], and Xiaowei Tang[1]

[1] The National NC System Engineering Research Center, School of Mechanical Science and Engineering, Huazhong University of Science and Technology, Wuhan 430074, China
{zhang_teng,m202270655,yanrong,tangxw}@hust.edu.cn

[2] The Wuhan Digital Design and Manufacturing Innovation Center Co. Ltd., Wuhan 430074, China
sunhao@niiddm.com

[3] The State Key Laboratory of Digital Manufacturing Equipment and Technology, School of Mechanical Science and Engineering, Huazhong University of Science and Technology, Wuhan 430074, China

Abstract. The foundation of high-precision 3D reconstruction is the acquisition of high-precision point clouds. Through multi-view point cloud scanning and alignment, the point cloud of parts can be obtained. The great flexibility of the robot enables it to carry out scanning operations that require multi-view. However, the robots are limited in position error, and the accuracy of the camera varies depending on the range of vision. In addition, the point cloud density is influenced by the curvature of the workpiece, which seriously limits the accuracy of point cloud acquisition and registration. To solve these problems, a method of high-precision point cloud data acquisition for robots based on multiple constraints is proposed. The precision of the measuring system is increased by imposing constraints. So the high-performance field of vision of the camera and the high-performance motion space of the robot are obtained. The effect of workpiece curvature on point cloud scanning is thought to require increased camera viewpoints. After obtaining the camera viewpoints, the moving route planning of the robot is implemented using the ant colony voting method. In this paper, a curved blade experiment was carried out to prove the advantages of our method. It is not necessary for the point cloud overlap rate or the parts with many features. The accuracy of scanned point clouds is 0.249 mm, which is less than the results of using intelligent algorithms and marked points.

Keywords: Point cloud scanning · Multiple constraints · Robot measurement system · High-precision

H. Yang et al. (Eds.): ICIRA 2023, LNAI 14272, pp. 275–287, 2023.
https://doi.org/10.1007/978-981-99-6480-2_23

1   Introduction

The precision of 3D reconstruction, which is dependent on measurement accuracy, has been subject to increasing demands in recent years. Currently, contact measuring devices like the Coordinate Measuring Machine (CMM) are often used in high-precision measurement. The non-contact measurement method is progressively replacing conventional measuring methods due to its simple operation and high measurement speed [1]. It is necessary to figure out how to get high-precision point cloud data since robot motion error, camera measurement performance, and workpiece curvature will all impact measurement accuracy.

Point cloud registration is necessary since it is impossible to get the point cloud of complicated components with a single scan. At this time, there are two sorts of popular registration techniques: free registration and constraint-based registration. The constraint-based alignment method achieves point cloud alignment by applying external constraints to obtain positional relationships. Paoli et al. [2] proposed a measurement system for integrated industrial robot optical scanners, which achieves registration through mechanical positioning. Wang et al. [3] tracked scanning poses and collected the poses from several views using a binocular vision system. Also, prior to measurements, marker points can be pasted in order to achieve point cloud registration based on the relative pose relationship established by the marker points [4]. Additionally, algorithms are mostly used for free alignment. Besl et al. [5] proposed the ICP method for point cloud registration. Yang H. et al. [6] suggested the TEASER++ technique, which runs at the millisecond level and shows remarkable robustness. However, accomplishing effective point cloud registration is a challenge for intelligent registration techniques when the surface of a component lacks geometric characteristics. The use of automatic alignment techniques based on geometric features [7] or picture features [8] has also drawn increased interest in recent studies. This kind of method makes full use of the geometry information on the workpiece surface and improves the stability of alignment.

With the rapid development of industrial robots, robot measuring systems have found widespread application [9]. Wang et al. [10] applied a contour measuring approach of robot to accomplish high-precision three-dimensional measurement of big components. Graumann et al. [11] devised a trajectory planning technique for ultrasound capture to gather regions of interest (ROI) for ultrasound data. The high freedom of robots is advantageous for mobile measurements. However, it is a challenge to ensure the accuracy of the system due to the large motion errors of the robot.

The content of the article can be summarized as follows. In Sect. 2, high-precision point cloud data acquisition for robot based on multiple constraints is presented. In Sect. 3, the methods of scanning viewpoint acquisition and robot motion trajectory planning under various constraints are analyzed. In Sect. 4, the analyses and experiments were carried out. In Sect. 5, the conclusions are made.

2 Multi-constraint Construction of Camera Scanning

2.1 Camera Performance Constraints

Although both RGB-D cameras and structured light cameras can offer a huge working area, these areas frequently exhibit inconsistent measurement accuracy. Being too close or too far away in the field of view can result in inaccurate scanning results. So the high-precision measurement of the camera must be ensured with the proper depth of field distance. Therefore, in order to get high-precision measurement data, it is important to get the appropriate depth of field distance for the camera and the high-precision field of vision area below this distance, which is also known as the region of interest (ROI).

A workpiece is designed in accordance with the advised operating distance of camera, as seen in Fig. 1(a). Test the performance of the camera from various distances:

1) Measure the designed workpieces using CMM: the error value ε_1 between the ideal model point p_i and the corresponding point on the processed workpiece.

$$\varepsilon_1 = \left\| p_i^m - p_i^t \right\|_2 \tag{1}$$

where p_i^t is the theoretical value, p_i^m is the measured value.

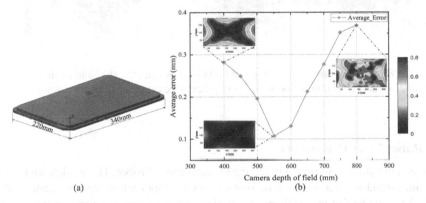

Fig. 1. (a) Standard parts. (b) Camera scanning error at different distances.

2) Divide the working distance $D_0 = 400$ mm–800 mm equidistantly, and sequentially capture point cloud data at different distances. Once the scanned data has been successfully registered with the reference point cloud (the method for obtaining reference point clouds is mentioned in Sect. 4.2). Calculate the exact difference ε_2 between the ideal model and the scanned data.

$$\varepsilon_2 = \left\| p_i^{ca} - p_i^t \right\|_2 \tag{2}$$

where p_i^{ca} is the coordinate value of the point obtained through camera scanning.

3) The measurement error ε_c of camera scanning data can be derived through steps 1) and 2), and it can be expressed as Eq. (3). In Fig. 1(b), it is depicted how to acquire the camera scanning error ε_c at various distances. It can be seen that the error of the camera at 550 mm is the smallest, which is 0.107 mm.

$$\varepsilon_c = \varepsilon_2 - \varepsilon_1 \tag{3}$$

The camera performance test is conducted at a distance of 550 mm since this is where the error is the least. The method for evaluating errors is the same as in the earlier section. Find the low error zone of camera by using the sliding-window. The final size of the performance field of view is set at 100 mm × 200 mm, with a minimal average inaccuracy of 0.1065 mm. As seen in Fig. 2(a), the appropriate camera field of view center point coordinate is $C_P = (10.13$ mm, 8.50 mm$)$, which is the center of the high-performance area.

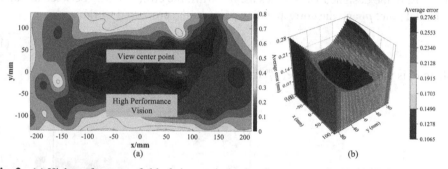

Fig. 2. (a) High-performance field of view optimization for cameras. (b) Field of view error with the sliding window (100 mm × 200 mm, error values at the center of sliding window).

2.2 Robot Error Constraints

There is a matching spherical workspace for each kind of robot. The workpiece that has to be measured is often situated on one side of the robot when measurement work is conducted, and half of the workspace is designated as the measurement space. In order to achieve this constraint, the joint angle range of the robot is limited.

The DH parameter significantly affects the movement accuracy of the robot. In order to increase motion accuracy, it is thought to limit the robot to always being in the low error area. Using the DH parameter values before and after calibration to simulate the motion space of the Staubli TX2-90L robot. The position error of the robot motion space is shown in Fig. 3(a). As a result, the performance space of the robot is the green region, as shown in Fig. 3(b). The motion error of robots is quite low in terms of performance space, which can provide the foundation for highly accurate measurement.

2.3 Workpiece Curvature Constraints

The point cloud will appear as a low-density region during scanning when the surface curvature of the workpiece changes quickly, leading to an obvious deviation in the point

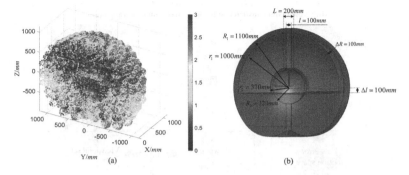

Fig. 3. (a) Position error of robot measurement space. (b) Robot performance space.

cloud data. As a result, while measuring a workpiece, the curvature fluctuation of the component surface should be properly taken into account.

$$\begin{cases} g_i \geq g_h & \text{Add sampling points} \\ g_i < g_h & \text{No need to add sampling points} \end{cases} \tag{4}$$

The viewpoints of the camera must be increased when the surface curvature of the workpiece surpasses threshold g_h. And the setting of threshold is related to target accuracy. The workpiece surface is divided into a grid. To get the camera viewpoint, offset the grid centroid outward by the optimal depth-of-field distance D. The distance has already been explored previously.

3   Scanning Viewpoint Acquisition and Mobile Trajectory Planning Based on Multiple Constraints

The general logic of viewpoint acquisition and path planning is shown in Fig. 4. The constraints of the camera and the workpiece enable the acquisition of viewpoints. The layout of the workpiece is finished using robot constraints, ensuring that the planned camera viewpoint always lies within the low error zone of motion space for the robot. Finally, using the resulting viewpoint set, the TSP problem is solved to produce the ideal scanning path.

3.1   Definition of the Camera Viewpoint Acquisition Issue

The set of scanning viewpoints for the workpiece to be measured must be acquired once the high-precision camera scanning construction with multiple constraints is finished. While keeping a suitable distance between the camera and the surface of the workpiece, the acquisition of camera viewpoints must match the geometric shape of the object being scanned. Extract the surfaces of workpiece to be measured before scanning, and mesh them to get the viewpoint set $\mathbb{C}_{con1}$. The viewpoint set $\mathbb{C}_{con2}$ that grows owing to the pronounced change in curvature is obtained by analyzing the curvature of the workpiece surface.

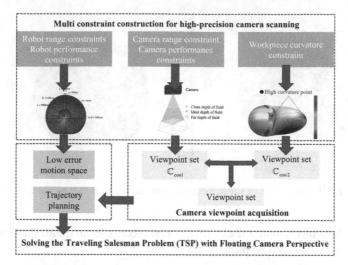

Fig. 4. Logic diagram for planning movement trajectories and acquiring scanning viewpoints.

The objective function for the multi-constraint problem is formed as the sum of the position error of the camera viewpoint in the robot motion space and the double integration of the scan point error in the camera field of view, respectively. In order to realize the planning of the placement of the workpiece to be measured in space, it is assumed that the objective function will be minimized. The resolution $h_{good} \times w_{good}$ of the workpiece surface division and the homogeneous transformation matrix ${}^B_u T$ are then obtained.

$$
\begin{cases}
\min & \begin{aligned}
& F({}^u p(x, y, z)) = \sum_{i=1}^{N} \left\| {}^B p_{ir}(x, y, z) - {}^B p_{it}(x, y, z) \right\| \\
& E(h, w) = \iint_{S} \varepsilon ds \quad (ds = dhdw)
\end{aligned} \\[2em]
s.t. & \begin{aligned}
& N = N_1 + N_2 \\
& N_1 = \sum_{k=1}^{m} \left(\left[\frac{H_{uk}}{h_{good}} \right] \cdot \left[\frac{W_{uk}}{w_{good}} \right] \right) \\
& N_2 = \sum_{j=1}^{n} N_{\Omega j} (when : g_i \geq g_h, default : N_{\Omega j} = 1) \\
& \frac{D}{D_{max}} = \frac{h}{h_{max}} = \frac{w}{w_{max}} \\
& D_{min} \leq D \leq D_{max} \\
& {}^B p(x, y, z) = {}^B_u T \cdot {}^u p(x, y, z) \\
& {}^B p_{ir}(x) \geq 0
\end{aligned}
\end{cases}
\tag{5}
$$

where ${}^u p(x,y,z)$ is the camera viewpoint in the workpiece coordinate system. $F({}^u p(x,y,z))$ is the sum of errors for all camera scanning viewpoints. ${}^B p_{ir}(x,y,z)$ and ${}^B p_{it}(x,y,z)$ are the actual and planned theoretical values of camera viewpoints, respectively. N_1 and N_2 represent the number of camera viewpoints in the viewpoint sets $\mathbb{C}_{con1}$ and $\mathbb{C}_{con2}$.

H_{uk} and W_{uk} represent the distance and width of the k-th surface to be measured. H_{good} and w_{good} are the ideal camera view distance and width, respectively. $_u^B T$ represents the homogeneous transformation matrix between the workpiece coordinate system and the robot base coordinate system. $^B p_{ir}(x)$ is the x coordinates of the camera viewpoint in the robot base coordinate system.

3.2 Calculating the Camera Viewpoint with the Floating Viewpoints

The requirement that incident light be perpendicular to the surface of the workpiece might cause collisions, make it challenging to optimize the movement route, and reduce scanning efficiency [12]. Consider building a cone for each viewpoint and choosing many points on the bottom surface of the cone to create a cluster of camera viewpoints. The deviation threshold of the scanning angle θ_0, which permits the scanning incident direction of the camera to float within a specific range, is the angle between the cone generatrix and the central axis. Will not excessively restrict the scanning direction to correspond with the center point normal to the field of vision, which can fully optimize the moving route of the robot.

3.3 Camera Viewpoint Trajectory Planning

Planning the ideal robot movement path to finish the scanning is required to save time. The goal of this challenge is to resolve the traveling salesman problem (TSP), which uses an ant colony method to establish the viewpoint order of camera movement while ensuring there are no collisions and uses the shortest scanning distance as the optimization target. Using voting algorithms to select a point in the next viewpoint cluster. The final point cloud scan trajectory for the researched workpiece is obtained with the objective of minimizing the spatial motion distance, as shown by the red line in Fig. 5.

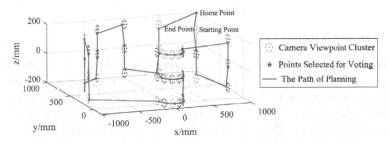

Fig. 5. Mobile path planning of Ant colony-voting algorithm.

4 Experimental Analysis and Discussion

4.1 Experimental Procedure

As seen in Fig. 6, the robot measuring system consists of the ALSONTECH AT-S1000-06C-S structured light camera, the XYR three-axis high-precision motion platform, and the Staubli TX2-90L robot. The camera viewpoint and related normal direction are transformed into the robot base coordinate system following the calibration of the measurement system. The multi-viewpoint trajectory planning of the camera with viewpoint cone is realized using the ant colony-voting technique. Finally, point cloud scanning and registration are conducted based on this path.

Fig. 6. Experimental site of robot measurement system.

4.2 Experimental Result

By comparing this point cloud to the reference point cloud of the object to be measured, the error distribution of the multi-constraint point cloud data is obtained. There are two types of acquisition for the reference point cloud. (1) With a CAD model, the reference point cloud of the object to be measured can be produced by discretizing the CAD model. (2) Without a CAD model, the point cloud data is acquired by scanning with a portable scanner called the HandySCAN. This error formula of the scanner, 0.025 mm + 0.04 mm/m, can satisfy the accuracy of reference point cloud gathering.

Evaluation of the registration error of robot point cloud scanning data is done by comparing the registered point cloud with the reference point cloud. The result is displayed in Fig. 7, and Table 1 displays the error statistics under various constraints.

4.3 Comparative Analysis of Experiments

Results of Experiments Analyzed Under Multiple Constraints. The mean and standard deviation of errors are displayed in Table 1 after statistical analysis of error data under various restrictions using the Gaussian distribution. With an average inaccuracy of 0.249 mm, the registration error of group (a) is much lower than others.

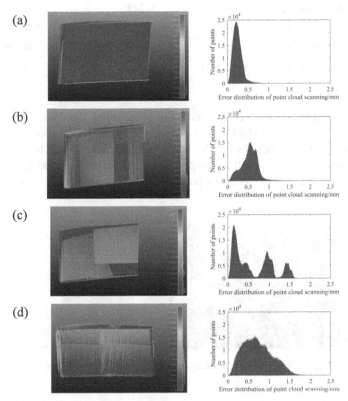

Fig. 7. Experimental error based on multiple constraints. (a) With multiple constraints. (b) Without camera constraints. (c) Without robot constraints. (d) Without workpiece constraints.

It can be seen from Fig. 7 that the wrong choice of the depth-of-field distance for the camera and field-of-view range might raise the bias of the point cloud data overall when the camera constraint is not applied. The camera viewpoint may be in the motion space at a high error location when the robot constraint is not used, producing huge error data. The curvature at the point where the two sides of the workpiece meet varies significantly when the curvature constraint is not applied. Point clouds may contain low-density regions that cause large errors in the point cloud data.

The accuracy of the point cloud data is most affected by whether or not the robot constraint is used, as shown in Table 1. Therefore, it is important to pay attention to the mobility status of the robot when scanning. Avoid placing the camera viewpoints in the high error zone of the motion space.

Comparison with Marked Points Method. The goal of registration based on marker points is to complete data coordinate transformation depending on the location and orientation of the markers in space [4]. Accurate identification of the markers is the

Table 1. Errors with different constraints (The best results are bolded.)

ID	Constraints imposed	Mean value/mm	Variance
(a)	With multiple constraints	**0.249**	**0.135**
(b)	Without camera constraints	0.539	0.225
(c)	Without robot constraints	0.616	0.478
(d)	Without workpiece constraints	0.726	0.364

cornerstone of registration. After denoising the point cloud, the distance matrix of the coordinate values of the marked points is established, and the holes of the markers are fitted with a space circle to get the center coordinates. To get the homogeneous transformation matrix, at least three pairs of marked points must be found. Figure 8 depicts the procedure and outcomes of point cloud registration based on marker points.

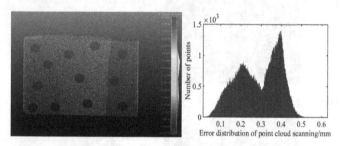

Fig. 8. Point cloud registration results based on marked points.

The quantity of corresponding marker points and the fitting precision of the space circle are the two key factors that influence the registration accuracy of the marker point method. According to the aforementioned studies, high accuracy in registration can be shown. And the average registration error when employing four pairs of marker points is 0.288 mm. The disadvantage of this method is that holes appear in the point cloud data, and hole filling can cause the measured data to be inconsistent with the true surface. The original workpiece surface will be destroyed if the specified locations are pasted, which also limits the application of this method.

Comparison with Intelligent Alignment Algorithm. The intelligent algorithm for point cloud registration has developed rapidly in recent years. The eight approaches that we primarily analyze here are: Global registration Fast [13], Global registration RANSAC [14], ICP (P2P) [5], ICP (P2Plane), Fast + ICP, RANSAC + ICP, CPD [15], and PCA. Table 2 displays the registration results. Point cloud data with a 60% overlap rate was applied during registration. RANSAC outperformed the other three single registration algorithms with an RMSE of 0.489. Since the beginning positions differ significantly from another point cloud, the ICP method becomes stuck in local optimums and incorrect alignment. The combination of two coarse and fine registration methods is significantly better than a single algorithm, with RANSAC + ICP outperforming Fast + ICP with an RMSE of 0.253. Due to their efforts to register point cloud data globally, CPD and PCA, two probability model-based approaches, produce mismatches for point clouds in non-congruent locations. The Fitness is an evaluation indicator during the registration process of two point clouds, which should be equal to the given point cloud overlap rate under optimal registration. When the Fitness is greater than the overlap rate and close to 1, this is an error that occurs in pursuit of global registration.

Table 2. Registration error evaluation based on intelligent registration algorithm. (The best results are bolded.)

Registration Method	Evaluating Indicator	
	Fitness	RMSE
Global registration FAST	0.071	0.377
Global registration RANSAC	**0.643**	**0.489**
ICP(P2P)	1.000	1.834
ICP(P2Plane)	0	0
FAST + ICP(P2Plane)	0.463	0.258
RANSAC + ICP(P2Plane)	**0.624**	**0.253**
CPD	1.000	3.129
PCA	0.915	2.676

It is evident from the experimental study mentioned above. In comparison to the marker point approach, the multi-constraint-based point cloud scanning and alignment has higher precision and avoids holes in the point cloud data. The multi-constraint-based alignment technique also performs better than the eight intelligent alignment techniques mentioned above. High point cloud data overlap rates and various characteristics on the surface of the workpiece are necessary for the intelligent alignment method. Another benefit of our method is that the multi-constraint-based alignment method does not need limits on the overlap rate or the existence of typical characteristics on the workpiece surface.

5   Conclusion and Future Work

In this article, a high-precision point cloud scanning technique based on several constraints is proposed. The high-performance working area of a measurement system is obtained by imposing constraints on both the measuring system and the item to be measured. It can successfully acquire high-precision point cloud data on the surface of complex parts, and the data acquisition accuracy can reach 0.249 mm, which is better than the widely used marker point method and intelligent registration algorithm. In practical applications, it can successfully complete high-precision 3D reconstruction of complex parts using the high-precision point cloud data acquired by this method.

In the future, we will conduct research on other factors that affect the accuracy of point cloud data acquisition and impose more constraints on the point cloud scanning process to achieve higher accuracy in point cloud data acquisition.

Acknowledgement. This research was financially supported by the National Key Research and Development Program of China (Grant No. 2022YFB3404803) and the National Natural Science Foundation of China (Grant No. U20A20294 and No. 52175463).

References

1. Zuo, C., Feng, S., Huang, L., Tao, T., Yin, W., Chen, Q.: Phase shifting algorithms for fringe projection profilometry: a review. Opt. Lasers Eng. **109**, 23–59 (2018). https://doi.org/10.1016/j.optlaseng.2018.04.019
2. Paoli, A., Razionale, A.: Large yacht hull measurement by integrating optical scanning with mechanical tracking-based methodologies. Rob. Comput. Integr. Manuf. **28**, 592–601 (2012). https://doi.org/10.1016/j.rcim.2012.02.010
3. Wang, J., Tao, B., Gong, Z., Yu, S., Yin, Z.: A mobile robotic measurement system for large-scale complex components based on optical scanning and visual tracking. Rob. Comput. Integr. Manuf. **67**, 102010 (2021). https://doi.org/10.1016/j.rcim.2020.102010
4. Franaszek, M., Cheok, G., Witzgall, C.: Fast automatic registration of range images from 3D imaging systems using sphere targets. Autom. Constr. **18**, 265–274 (2009). https://doi.org/10.1016/j.autcon.2008.08.003
5. Besl, P., Mckay, H.: A method for registration of 3-D shapes. IEEE Trans. Pattern Anal. Mach. Intell. **14**, 239–256 (1992)
6. Yang, H., Shi, J., Carlone, L.: TEASER: fast and certifiable point cloud registration. IEEE Trans. Rob. **37**, 314–333 (2021). https://doi.org/10.1109/TRO.2020.3033695
7. Rusu, R., Blodow, N., Marton, Z., Beetz, M.: Aligning point cloud views using persistent feature histograms. In: 2008 IEEE/RSJ International conference on Robots and intelligent Systems, vol.1–3, pp. 3384–3391(2008)
8. Sipiran, I., Bustos, B.: Harris 3D: a robust extension of the Harris operator for interest point detection on 3D meshes. Vis. Comput. **27**, 963–976 (2011). https://doi.org/10.1007/s00371-011-0610-y
9. Du, H., Chen, X., Xi, J., Yu, C., Zhao, B.: Development and verification of a novel robot-integrated fringe projection 3D scanning system for large-scale metrology. Sensors **17**, 2886 (2017). https://doi.org/10.3390/s17122886
10. Wang, J., Tao, B., Gong, Z., Yu, W., Yin, Z.: A mobile robotic 3-D measurement method based on point clouds alignment for large-scale complex surfaces. IEEE Trans. Instrum. Meas. **70**, 7503011 (2021). https://doi.org/10.1109/TIM.2021.3090156
11. Graumann, C., Fuerst, B., Hennersperger, C., Bork, F., Navab, N.: Robotic ultrasound trajectory planning for volume of interest coverage. In: 2016 IEEE International Conference on Robotics and Automation(ICRA), pp. 736–741 (2016)
12. Malhan, R., Gupta, S.: Planning algorithms for acquiring high fidelity pointclouds using a robot for accurate and fast 3D reconstruction. Rob. Comput. Integr. Manuf. **78**, 102372 (2022). https://doi.org/10.1016/j.rcim.2022.102372
13. Zhou, Q.-Y., Park, J., Koltun, V.: Fast global registration. In: Leibe, B., Matas, J., Sebe, N., Welling, M. (eds.) ECCV 2016. LNCS, vol. 9906, pp. 766–782. Springer, Cham (2016). https://doi.org/10.1007/978-3-319-46475-6_47

14. Hruda, L., Dvorak, J., Vasa, L.: On evaluating consensus in RANSAC surface registration. Comput. Graph. Forum **38**, 175–186 (2019). https://doi.org/10.1111/cgf.13798
15. Wang, P., Wang, P., Qu, Z., Gao, Y., Shen, Z.: A refined coherent point drift (CPD) algorithm for point set registration. Sci. China Inf. Sci. **54**, 2639–2646 (2011). https://doi.org/10.1007/s11432-011-4465-7

Flexible Functional Component for Fluidic Soft Robots

Liantong Zhang, Anqi Guo, Mengke Yang, Jiakang Zou, and Guoqing Jin[✉]

Robotics and Microsystem Research Centre, School of Mechanical and Electrical Engineering,
Soochow University, Suzhou, China
gqjin@suda.edu.cn

Abstract. In the past few years, inspired by bionics, soft robots have become an emerging research topic in the field of robotics. Currently, almost all pneumatic soft robots rely on hard valves or electronic controls, traditionally air compressor drives, which greatly limit the soft robot from becoming fully flexible. In order to achieve the fully flexible of the soft robots, three different types of flexible functional devices were designed and fabricated. Soft valves were used to control soft robots, soft pumps work as flexible power devices to provide power source as well as flexible pistons work as flexible output devices which enhance the output of soft robot. Finally, by integrating the above-mentioned flexible functional devices, a time-delay control system was purposed and eliminated the need for hard valves, hard pumps and electronic control to achieve a fully soft and intelligent soft robotic system.

Keywords: Soft Robot · Flexible Functional Component · Soft Functional System

1 Introduction

Inspired by bionics, scientists and engineers defined a new class of machine that we refer to as soft robots [1–4]. These robots had a continuously deformable structure and could perform compliant motions, such as robots climbing motion of soft gecko, wing flapping motion of flies, and crawling motion of earthworms [5–7]. The softness and body compliance of soft robots made it be able to bend and twist with high curvatures and thus it could adapt their shape to the environment [8]. To make it be fully compliant and energy-efficient, soft robot should make as much as soft components.

However, there are still few researches on the flexible functional devices of soft robots. At present, the control and driving of soft robots still relied on solenoid valves, pumps and other electronic components [5, 9]. It caused that the control parts and driving parts of the soft robots were difficult to integrated into the soft robots, which greatly limit the soft robots from becoming fully soft. In order to solve the problems above, soft robots urgently need soft control and driving devices [10–12]. The flexible functional devices for soft robots could adapt their shape to go throw narrow spaces, making the

---

L. Zhang and A. Guo—Contributed equally to this study

© The Author(s), under exclusive license to Springer Nature Singapore Pte Ltd. 2023
H. Yang et al. (Eds.): ICIRA 2023, LNAI 14272, pp. 288–297, 2023.
https://doi.org/10.1007/978-981-99-6480-2_24

control and driving components of soft robots more compatible with soft robots and accurately control and drive the motion of soft robots [13–16]. In 2018, Whitesides et al. introduced a new bistable soft valve that utilized snap-through characteristics [17]. In 2019, Menguc's research group at the University of Oregon developed a soft valve that used electrorheological fluids as the working medium [18]. Wendelin J. Stark et al. designed and manufactured a soft pump that imitated an artificial heart by using the traditional rubber manufacturing process [19]. In 2019, Robert J. Wood et al. used origami structures to design a flexible piston that could be driven by negative pressure [20].

In this paper, in order to achieve the fully flexible of the soft robot, three different types of flexible functional devices were designed and manufactured:1) Soft valves, for flexible control devices, which were designed to replace the traditional hard solenoid valve to control the movement of soft robot; 2) Soft pumps, as flexible power devices, were designed to provide a power source for the soft robot; 3) Flexible pistons were used as flexible output devices. This article mainly carried out the following research contents.

2   The Design of Soft Functional Component

According to the different functional requirements of soft robots, flexible functional devices can be divided into flexible control components - flexible valves, flexible power components - flexible pumps and flexible output components - flexible pistons. Flexible systems could bed formed through the combination of different functional components. In this paper, by integrating the above-mentioned flexible functional devices, a time-delay control system was purposed and eliminated the need for hard valves, hard pumps and electronic control to achieve a fully flexible and intelligent soft robotic system.

2.1   Soft Valves

In order to control the flow of gas, soft valves need to have the following properties.

(i) The valve must hold a certain amount of pressure to fully actuate a soft robot.
(ii) The valve is well sealed and do not leak gas.
(iii) The valve should be made of compliant materials, which allow it deformed with the rest of soft body.

To meet those requirements of soft robot, Ecoflex 00-50 was used to create this valve because of its high bonding strength which could allow the valve work under high pressure. The principle of operation of the soft valve was shown in the Fig. 1(a), and the combination of multiple units could be adapted to the needs of multiple airways. Four-way valves and five-way valves (as shown in Fig. 1(b)) were used to illustrate the structural design of valves, which were composed of four and five modules, respectively, each module had an interconnected flow channel and the control chamber was independent of each other. A module unit was tested and the flow rate through the soft valve was shown in Fig. 1(d) as the pressure increases at different membrane thicknesses.

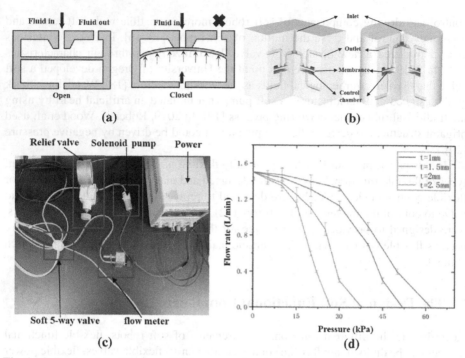

Fig. 1. Soft valves (a) soft valve unit (b) cross-sectional view of directional valve (c) test platform (d) Soft valve closing experiment

2.2 Soft Pumps

The main structure of the soft pump was shown in Fig. 2(a). The left and right were three-dimensional isometric and cross-sectional views respectively. The total pipe length from inlet to outlet was 50 mm. The cross-sectional area of the pipe was a circle of 3 mm. A cone-shaped cavity was in the middle, which served as the sealed cavity of the pump and the state that the magnetic layer deformed downwards and bulges downward was accommodated. The material of the magnetic layer was the mixture of Ecoflex 00-50 and Fe_3O_4 powder, and the main structure below was made of AB silica gel. In order to maximize the displacement of the film, the NdFeB magnets were placed at the midpoint of the cavity perpendicular where is the centre line of the electromagnet. The NdFeB magnets on the upper and lower ends had opposite magnetic properties. When the upper NdFeB magnet was pressed down with the deformation of the film, the repulsive force increased sharply, which made the film spring back to its original shape. This resilience property reduced the use of electromagnetic underneath and simplifies the system structure.

The working process was divided into two steps, one was the suction process, and the other was the discharge process. For the suction process, the output voltage of the power supply was negative at the beginning, the magnetic film bounced up, the volume of the sealed cavity become larger, and the pressure decreased. A pressure difference was formed between the inside and outside of the sealed cavity, the check valve at the inlet was conducted, and which at the outlet was closed, so that the gas is sucked into the sealed cavity. For the discharge process, the output voltage of the power supply was positive, the moving parts moved downwards, the volume of the sealed chamber decreased, the pressure increased, the check valve at the outlet was turned on, and the pressure gas was output. Circulating the suction and discharge process, the soft pump could continuously and stably output pressure gas. The soft valve was tested for performance, and the relationships between the action frequency of the electromagnet and the output pressure and flow rate of the soft pump was shown in the Fig. 2(c).

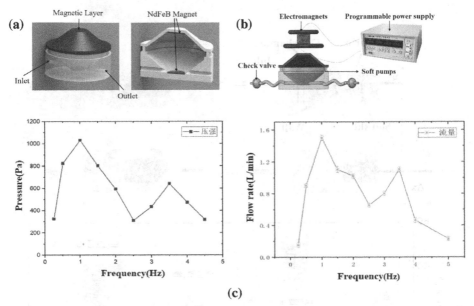

Fig. 2. Soft pumps (a) structure of soft pumps (b) working principle of the soft pumps (c) the relationships between the action frequency and the output pressure and flow rate.

2.3 Soft Piston

The soft piston consisted of three parts: a compressible spring, a soft film that can withstand large deformations and a fluid medium. The spring and the fluid medium were sealed in the soft film and the internal pressure was the same as the external pressure in the initial equilibrium state. When the internal pressure was less than the external pressure, the pressure difference acted on the flexible membrane to drive the deformation of the spring to realize the transformation of the spring structure. The specific working principle was shown in Fig. 3(a).

In this structure, the soft skin wrapped the compressible movable skeleton, fixed the output rod of the piston, and separated the fluid in the piston from the fluid in the movable skeleton, which was made of Ecoflex 00-50. This material was flexible enough to withstand compression and had enough strength to transmit tensile force. The soft outer wall of the inflatable cavity was made of domestic vulcanized rubber AB 950, which was harder than Ecoflex 00-50 and had smaller deformation when subjected to high pressure. The inflatable cavity was fixed with the internal cavity and skeleton to effectively generate tension. The piston frame was a spring with gaps. These gaps allowed the piston frame to be compressed under the pressure difference between the piston and inflation cavity, thereby driving the piston rod to move. This pressure difference could be achieved by inflating the inflation chamber or evacuating the piston chamber. The tensile force that could be generated by pistons with springs of different diameters was shown in the Fig. 3(b).

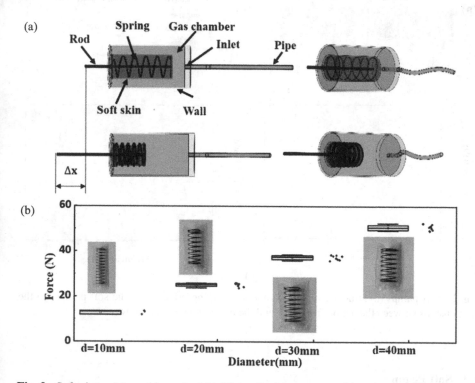

Fig. 3. Soft piston (a) working principle (b) tensile force generated by pistons with springs of different diameters

3   Flexible Time-Delay System

In order to achieve a specific function, existing fluid-driven soft robots often require multiple air paths, and for multiple air sources, if it is necessary to control the opening and closing of multiple flexible valves, multiple control air sources are required. When using tube to connect soft valves together, the control chamber of each valve sequentially reaches a closing pressure due to the presence of fluid viscosity, so that a single input can be used to achieve a response to multiple output delays. Modeling of Delayed Control Systems [21]:

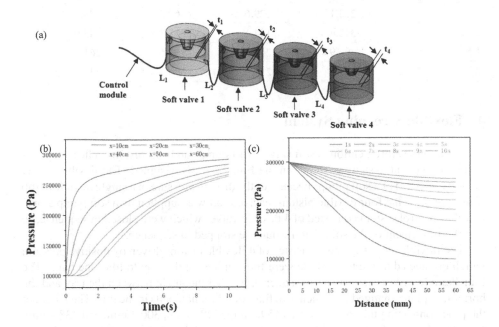

(a)

(b)

(c)

Fig. 4. (a) Schematic diagram of the delay control system (b) The relationship between pressure and time (c) the relationship between pressure and distance

$$\pi r_s^2 \left[\pi \left(1 + \frac{prs}{Ews}\right)^2 + 2pa\left(1 + \frac{prs}{Ews}\right)\frac{rs}{Ews}\right]\frac{\partial p}{\partial t} = \frac{1}{8\pi\mu}\left(\pi r_s^2\right)^2\left[4pa\left(\frac{\partial p}{\partial xx}\right)^2\left(1 + \frac{prs}{Ews}\right) + \left(1 + \frac{prs}{Ews}\right)^4\right] + pa\left(1 + \frac{prs}{Ews}\right)^4\frac{\partial^2 p}{\partial x_x^2}$$

It can be seen from the relationship between pressure and time that when the distance from the entrance was 10 cm, the pressure increased sharply with time. As the distance from the outlet got farther and farther, the pressure increase also slowed down. When the time was constant $t = 1$ s, it could be seen from the relationship between the pressure and the distance that the pressure at a position farther from the entrance was smaller. As time increased, the pressures at various places gradually approached when $t = 10$ s, and they were close to the pressure at the entrance. The pressure was in a controllable range.

As mentioned earlier, for a soft valve with a film which thickness was 1 mm, its closing pressure was 26.5 kPa. Take the control system composed of four soft valves as an example, it was assumed that the pipe which radius is 0.5 mm did not deform under pressure. The pressure at the entrance was 30 kPa and remained unchanged. If the four soft valves were closed in sequence and the intervals were 0.5 s, 1s, 1.5 s and 2 s, the lengths of L_1, L_2, L_3 and L_4 are shown in Table 1.

Table 1. The length of the trachea required at different intervals

Time interval (s)	L_1 (mm)	L_2 (mm)	L_3 (mm)	L_4 (mm)
0.5	222.1	129.6	69.3	48.3
1	312.4	144.1	111.3	43.6
1.5	396.9	201.1	132.6	261.1
2	459.7	228.9	300.4	438.4

4 Flexible Screening System

Combining the aforementioned soft valves, soft pumps and soft pistons, a flexible functional component system as shown in the Fig. 5(a) was designed. The flexible power system consisted of 4 soft pumps because of the driving pressure of a single flexible pump could not drive the four flexible pistons, each circuit was supplied by a soft pump alone. Flexible control system consisted of 4 flexible valves which were closed in sequence, so that the movement of the soft piston would be stopped in sequence.

The flexible output system consisted of 4 flexible pistons driven by positive pressure which connected to the tray. There were four outlets on the tray to filter the balls. The four flexible pistons stop rising in sequence, so that the angle between the tray and the horizontal plane changed in sequence to filter out the small balls in the tray. The length of the pipe connecting the soft valve was 459.7 mm, 228.9 mm, 300.4 mm, and 438.4 mm, respectively, in order to made the valve close sequentially at an interval of 2 s. The air outlet was opened every 10s to restore the piston to its original shape and prepare for the next round of screening.

The process of screening pellets was shown in Fig. 5(b). There were four small holes with a diameter of 5 mm on the screening disc, which were evenly distributed on the circumference, corresponding to the inclination direction of the four flexible pistons. The silver ball was a small steel ball with a diameter of 3 mm, and the yellow ball was a plastic ball with a diameter of 6 mm. The two kinds of balls were screened through the small holes. Under the repeated action of the flexible piston, the inclination angle of the screening disc was cyclically changed. The two kinds of small balls reciprocated continuously on the screening disc. Among them, only the small ball could go through small holes. At the beginning, there were a large number of small balls, colliding with each other, and the screening efficiency was high. As the balls continued to be screened out, the screening efficiency was decreasing. After 466 s, all the small steel balls were screened out (Table 2).

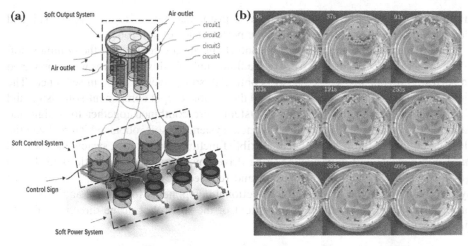

Fig. 5. (a) Design of soft functional device systems (b) The operation of the screening process

Table 2. Result of screening experiments

Time/s	0	37	91	133	191	255	322	385	466
Yellow ball	25	25	25	25	25	25	25	25	25
Steel ball	90	69	51	39	29	20	12	5	0

5 Conclusions

In this paper, in view of the soft control, drive and output requirements of soft robots, flexible control functional devices - soft valves, flexible power functional devices - soft pumps and flexible output functional components - soft pistons were designed and manufactured. Based on this, the soft pump, valve and piston were combined into a flexible functional device system to realize the flexible control and drive of the soft robots. The main conclusions are as follows:

In this paper, soft valve was used as the control part of the pneumatic circuit which could control the movement of the soft robot. The soft valve had light weight, small volume and good compatibility with the soft robot, which reduced the demand of soft robot for hard valve. For the flexible power functional component of soft robot, based on the working principle of positive displacement pump, the soft material and magnetic powder were mixed to produce a soft film with magnetic properties which was used as a moving part to pump fluid under the action of magnetic field. The soft pump was easy to manufacture and could wirelessly drive the soft robot under the action of an external magnetic field, reducing the need for rigid pumps. To eliminate short stroke and uncontrollable output of traditional pneumatic actuator and soft robot, a soft piston based on different structural design was designed by using soft skin and spring which could be divided into positive pressure drive and negative pressure drive. Compared with traditional pneumatic actuators, the flexible piston had longer stroke, larger load, and better controllability, which improved the performance of soft robot.

In order to reduce the number of control signals for controlling the complex soft robot system, based on the viscosity of the fluid, multiple flexible valves were connected in series. Only one air source used to control all soft valves to close in sequence. The flexible power component-soft pump and the flexible output component-soft piston and the above-mentioned flexible control system were combined together to design and manufacture a flexible functional component system for soft robots, which realized the flexible control of the soft robot. The flexible functional component system hardly used hard components and only needed to be driven by an external magnetic field. It had good compatibility with the soft robot and reduced the complexity of the soft robot system. The soft robot used flexible functional components for control and drive was preliminarily realized and the development of the soft robot in the direction of fully flexible soft robotic systems was promoted.

Acknowledgment. Research supported by Postgraduate Research and Innovation Project of Jiangsu Province (SJCX21_1339).

References

1. Cianchetti, M., Ranzani, T., Gerboni, G., et al.: Soft robotics technologies to address short-comings in today's minimally invasive surgery: the STIFF-FLOP approach. Soft Robotics **1**(2), 122–131 (2014)
2. Rus, D., Tolley, M.T.: Design, fabrication and control of soft robots. Nature **521**(7553), 467–475 (2015)
3. Cacucciolo, V., Shintake, J., Kuwajima, Y., et al.: Stretchable pumps for soft machines. Nature **572**(7770), 1–4 (2019)
4. Panagiotis, P., et al.: Soft robotics: review of fluid-driven intrinsically soft devices; manu-facturing, sensing, control, and applications in human-robot interaction. Adv. Eng. Mater. **12**(14), 1136–1152 (2017)
5. Polygerinos, P., et al.: Soft robotics: review of fluid-driven intrinsically soft devices; man-ufacturing, sensing, control, and applications in human-robot interaction. Adv. Eng. Mater. e201700016 (2017)
6. Mosadegh, B., et al.: Pneumatic networks for soft robotics that actuate rapidly. Adv. Funct. Mater. **24**(15), 2163–2170 (2014)
7. Suo, Z.: Theory of dielectric elastomers. Acta Mechanica Solida Sinica **23**(6), 549–578 (2010)
8. Shapiro, Y., Wolf, A., Gabor, K.: Bi-bellows: pneumatic bending actuator. Sens. Actuators A Phys. **167**(2), 484–494 (2011)
9. Resilient, A.: Untethered soft robot. Soft Robot. **1**(3), 213–223 (2014)
10. Wehner, M., Truby, R.L., Fitzgerald, D.J., et al.: An integrated design and fabrication strategy for entirely soft, autonomous robots. Nature **536**(7617), 451–455 (2016)
11. Wang, Z., Volinsky, A.A., Gallant, N.D.: Crosslinking effect on polydimethylsiloxane elastic modulus measured by custom-built compression instrument. J. Appl. Polym. Sci. **131**(22), 547–557 (2015)
12. Elsayed, Y., Vincensi, A., Lekakou, C., et al.: Finite element analysis and design optimization of a pneumatically actuating silicone module for robotic surgery applications. Soft Robot. **1**(4), 255–262 (2014)

13. Liu, H., Huang, W., Gao, J., et al.: Piezoresistive behavior of porous carbon nanotube-thermoplastic polyurethane conductive nanocomposites with ultrahigh compressibility. Appl. Phys. Lett. **108**(1), 918–924 (2016)
14. Elbaz, S.B., Jacob, H., Gat, A.D.: Transient gas flow in elastic microchannels. J. Fluid Mech. **846**, 460–481 (2018)
15. Burkhard, N., et al.: A rolling-diaphragm hydrostatic transmission for remote MR-guided needle insertion. In: 2017 IEEE International Conference on Robotics and Automation (ICRA). IEEE (2017)
16. Acome, E., Mitchell, S.K., Morrissey, T.G., et al.: Hydraulically amplified self-healing electrostatic actuators with muscle-like performance. Science **359**(6371), 61–65 (2018)
17. Rothemund, P., et al.: A soft, bistable valve for autonomous control of soft actuators. Sci. Robot. **3**(16), eaar7986 (2018)
18. Zatopa, A., Walker, S., Menguc, Y.: Fully soft 3d-printed electroactive fluidic valve for soft hydraulic robots. Soft Robot. **5**, 259–271 (2018). https://doi.org/10.1089/soro.2017.0019
19. Kohll, A.X., et al.: Long-term performance of a pneumatically actuated soft pump manufactured by rubber compression molding. Soft Robot. **6**, 206–216 (2018)
20. Li, S., et al.: Tension pistons: amplifying piston force using fluid induced tension in flexible materials. Adv. Funct. Mater. **29**(30), 1901419 (2019)
21. Elbaz, S.B., Gat, A.D.: Axial creeping flow in the gap between a rigid cylinder and a concentric elastic tube. J. Fluid Mech. **806**, 580–602 (2015)

Passive Rotation Compensation for the Cylindrical Joints of the 6-UCU Parallel Manipulators

Lei Fu[1], Zhihua Liu[2(✉)], Meng Tao[1(✉)], Chenguang Cai[2], and Ming Yang[3]

[1] School of Mechanical Engineering, Guizhou University, Guiyang 550025, China
mtao@gzu.edu.cn

[2] Institute of Mechanics and Acoustic Metrology, National Institute of Metrology, Beijing 100029, China
liuzhihua@nim.ac.cn

[3] Electrical Engineering College, Guizhou University, Guiyang 550025, China

Abstract. The 6-UCU parallel manipulator is both ends of the drive chain which are connected to the moving and fixed platform via the Hooke joints. The six drive chains are controlled by six servo-electric cylinders, which should have a prismatic and revolute pair so as to the moving platform producing the 6-DOF motion. However, a relative rotation is inevitably occurred among the Hook joints during the moving of the electric cylinder, which leads to a relative rotation between the electric cylinder rods and their barrel in the direction of the axis, further results in a significant dynamic control error. Therefore, a theoretical derivation of the passive rotation is investigated, which can be used for the 6-UCU parallel manipulator compensation. The simulation analysis indicate that the error is in the millimeter range, which is caused by the passive rotation. The experimental results show a significant improvement in the accuracy of the position after the compensation, where the position error range in the z-direction is reduced from $[-0.762$ mm, 0.855 mm] to $[-0.061$ mm, 0.103 mm].

Keywords: The 6-UCU parallel manipulator · Hooke joints · Passive rotation

1 Introduction

Parallel manipulators are closed-loop mechanisms in which the moving platform is connected to the fixed platform through two or more independent drive chains. The actuators are distributed among different chains and operate in parallel, forming a multi-degree-of-freedom system [1]. Due to its advantages such as high payload-to-weight ratio, high positioning accuracy, and absence of cumulative errors, Parallel manipulators have been widely applied in various fields including motion simulation [2], machine tool [3, 4], and medical devices [5, 6]. However, with the advancement of industrial technology, there are greater challenges in generating precise, complex, and repeatable motion trajectories in three-dimensional space through micro- and nano-level motion control, which pose higher challenges for the parallel manipulators.

H. Yang et al. (Eds.): ICIRA 2023, LNAI 14272, pp. 298–309, 2023.
https://doi.org/10.1007/978-981-99-6480-2_25

Parallel manipulators mainly have the type of 6-SPS and 6-UPS [7, 8]. Here, S represents the spherical joint, P represents the prismatic joint, and U represents the universal joint, which includes two rotational joints, also known as the Hooke or Cardan joints [9]. According to the Kutzbach-Grubler formula [10], each of the six drive chains of parallel manipulators has one redundant degree of freedom, allowing the moving platform to have six degrees of freedom (6-DOF) in space. Therefore, Liu et al. [11, 12] designed a 6-SPS parallel manipulator for the feed support system of the project of Five-hundred-meter Aperture Spherical radio Telescope (FAST), which can realize real-time compensation of the pose error of the terminal. McCann et al. [13] designed a manipulator based on the 6-SPS parallel manipulator, capable of precise motion in all 6-DOF while gripping a target. Qiang et al. [14] studied a 6-UPS parallel manipulator suitable for ship stabilization platforms, with a position accuracy of 0.242 mm and an orientation accuracy of 0.025°. Wu et al. [15] developed a machine tool based on the 6-UPS parallel manipulator, with a position accuracy of 0.082 mm and orientation accuracy of 0.119°.

However, both ends of the drive chain for the 6-UCU parallel manipulators are connected to the moving and fixed platform through Hooke joints, which can further effectively improve the pose accuracy and bearing capacity [16]. C represents the cylindrical joint which have a prismatic and rotational pair. In industrial applications, the drive chains commonly employed the servo electric cylinder control systems, where the rotary motion of the servo motor is converted into linear motion of the cylinder bar through a ball screw mechanism [17, 18]. Therefore, there is an additional passive rotational motion introduced as a dynamic control error in the moving. It is necessary to eliminate this error to enhance the pose accuracy of the moving platform.

In this study, based on the geometric structure of the 6-UCU parallel manipulator, theoretical derivations were made for the passive rotational of the electric cylinder, and the control system of the prototype was compensated to improve the pose accuracy. The remainder of this article is organized as follows. Section 2 provides the kinematic modeling. Section 3 describes the theoretical derivations for the passive rotational. Section 4 presents a simulation of the influence of the passive rotational on the lengths of the drive chains and the pose accuracy. Section 5 presents the verification experiments on the prototype. Finally, Sect. 6 ends with the conclusions.

2   Kinematic Modeling of the 6-UCU Parallel Manipulator

As shown in Fig. 1(a), the 6-UCU parallel manipulator mainly consists of a fixed platform, a moving platform and six electric cylinders, where the upper section of the electric cylinders is connected to the moving platform via the upper Hooke joints and the lower section is connected to the fixed platform via the lower Hooke joints. As shown in Fig. 1(b), a coordinate system $\{O_p\}$ is established with the origin being the center of the moving platform upper surface, and the center coordinates of the upper Hooke joints are $p_i = [p_{xi}, p_{yi}, p_{zi}]^T$ ($i = 1...6$) in $\{O_p\}$. Similarly, a coordinate system $\{O_b\}$ is established with the origin at the center of the fixed platform upper surface, and the lower Hooke joints coordinates are $b_i = [b_{xi}, b_{yi}, b_{zi}]^T$. The structural parameters of the parallel manipulator are shown in Table 1, L_{0i} is the initial offset of the electric cylinder.

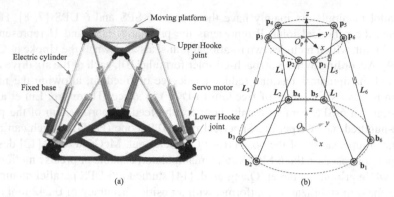

Fig. 1. The 6-UCU parallel manipulator: (a) CAD model; (b) Kinematic scheme.

Table 1. The structural parameters of the 6-UCU parallel manipulator.

i	p_{ix}/mm	p_{iy}/mm	p_{iz}/mm	b_{ix}/mm	b_{iy}/mm	b_{iz}/mm	L_{0i}/mm
1	448.119	−172.017	−127.210	870.056	405.714	108.790	1141.886
2	373.030	−302.074	−127.210	83.670	−956.347	108.790	1141.886
3	−373.030	−302.074	−127.210	−83.670	−956.347	108.790	1141.886
4	−448.119	−172.017	−127.210	−870.056	405.714	108.790	1141.886
5	−75.089	474.090	−127.210	−786.386	550.633	108.790	1141.886
6	75.089	474.090	−127.210	786.386	550.633	108.790	1141.886

According to the Kutzbach-Grubler formula, the degrees of freedom for the 6-UCU parallel manipulator are:

$$M = 6(n - g - 1) + \sum_{i=1}^{g} f_i \tag{1}$$

where M is the degrees of freedom of the mechanism; n is the number of structural members; g is the number of kinematic pairs; f_i is the number of degrees of freedom of the ith kinematic pair.

It is well known that the 6-UCU parallel manipulator has 6-DOF in space. As shown in Fig. 1(a), $n = 14$, $g = 18$, where the Hooke joint has 2-DOF. It shows that the electric cylinder must have 2-DOF to achieve the 6-DOF of motion of the moving platform, namely a prismatic pair and an additional rotation pair, when bringing the above variables into Eq. (3).

The principle of the electric cylinder is to convert the rotation of the servo motor into the linear motion of the cylinder rod through a ball screw. As a result, a passive rotational motion is introduced to the linear motion of the cylinder rod. Generally, a retainer is mounted inside the electric cylinder to eliminate passive rotation and allow only linear motion. However, for the 6-UCU parallel manipulator, the retainer inside the electric cylinder needs to be removed to provide a redundant degree of freedom. Then, when the cylinder rod is running, there is a relative rotation between the upper and lower Hooke joints, which causes a relative rotation between the cylinder rod and barrel along the axis of the electric cylinder. Therefore, there is always an error between the actual and desired length, which needs to be eliminated.

The kinematic model of the 6-UCU parallel manipulator contains the forward and inverse kinematic solutions. The inverse kinematic solution (IKS) is to solve for the length of the six electric cylinders using a known pose, which has an analytic solution, and the operation is simple and fast. The result of IKS is used as the control signal input of the six servo motors to realize the control of parallel manipulators. According to the closed-loop vector method shown in Fig. 1(b), the electric cylinder length L_i can be calculated by p_i and b_i, i.e., IKS is:

$$L_i = R \cdot p_i + t - b_i \quad i = 1 \dots 6 \tag{2}$$

where $R = \begin{bmatrix} c\varphi c\theta & c\varphi s\theta s\psi - s\varphi c\psi & c\varphi s\theta c\psi + s\varphi s\psi \\ s\varphi c\theta & s\varphi s\theta s\psi + c\varphi c\psi & s\varphi s\theta c\psi - c\varphi s\psi \\ -s\theta & c\theta s\psi & c\theta c\psi \end{bmatrix}$ is the rotation matrix, in which $c = \cos$, $s = \sin$, ψ, θ and φ is the rotation angle around the $x-$, $y-$, and z-axis, $t = [x, y, z]^T$ is the translation matrix.

The forward kinematic solution (FKS) is to solve the pose of the moving platform through the known lengths L_i. The operation process is the solution of a non-linear system of equations using numerical methods. Thus, FKS is:

$$F_i(x, y, z, \psi, \theta, \varphi) = \|L_i\|^2 - \left\|L_i^0\right\|^2 = 0 \tag{3}$$

where L_i^0 is the measured telescopic length of the electric cylinder, and L_i is the electric cylinder telescoping length corresponding to the pose $Q(x, y, z, \psi, \theta, \varphi)$. Therefore, FKS can be transformed into a numerical optimization solution problem for the system of multi-objective nonlinear equations F_i, and solved by the *fsolve* function in MATLAB, as shown in Fig. 2, with ε as the threshold value.

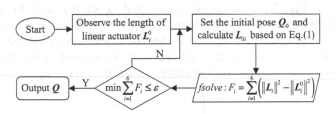

Fig. 2. The operation principle of FKS.

3 Passive Rotation Compensation of the 6-UCU Parallel Manipulator

From the above analysis, the actual length of the electric cylinder during the movement of the 6-UCU parallel manipulator is:

$$L_i = L_{0i} + \Delta L_i \tag{4}$$

in which L_{0i} is the desired telescoping length of the electric cylinder, and ΔL_i is the error caused by the passive rotation.

As shown in Fig. 3(a), k_i, j_i, m_i and n_i represent the unit vectors of the cross axis of the upper and lower Hooke joints, and then the passive rotation between the cylinder rod and barrel can be expressed as the angle between k_i and m_i.

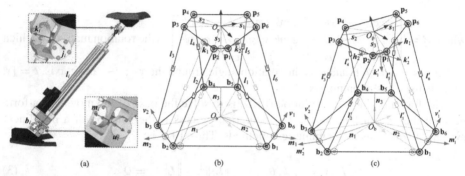

(a)   (b)   (c)

Fig. 3. (a) Vector diagram of Hooke joints at both ends of the electric cylinder, (b) vector diagram of the initial zero position, (c) vector diagram of the motion.

According to the structure of the Hooke joints, there is:

$$k_i \perp j_i, \quad m_i \perp u_i, \quad k_i \perp l_i, \quad m_i \perp l_i \tag{5}$$

As shown in Fig. 3(b), the vectors s_1, s_2, and s_3 are the angle bisectors of the neighboring joints of the moving platform, and the angle between s_1, s_2, and s_3 are 120°. Similarly, the vectors n_1, n_2, and n_3 are the angle bisectors of the neighboring joints of the fixed platform, and the angle between n_1, n_2, and n_3 are 120°. Let $s_1 = (0,1,0)$, $n_1 = (0,-1,0)$, and the rotation matrix around the z-axis be:

$$R_z = \begin{bmatrix} \cos \gamma & -\sin \gamma & 0 \\ \sin \gamma & \cos \gamma & 0 \\ 0 & 0 & 1 \end{bmatrix} \tag{6}$$

then,

$$\begin{cases} s_2 = R_z(\gamma_1)s_1 \quad n_2 = R_z(\gamma_1)n_1 \quad \gamma_1 = 120° \\ s_3 = R_z(\gamma_2)s_1 \quad n_3 = R_z(\gamma_2)n_1 \quad \gamma_2 = 240° \end{cases} \tag{7}$$

The calculation of the passive rotation is divided into two main steps as follows:

Step 1: Calculate the angle between k_i and m_i at the initial zero position of the moving platform. As shown in Fig. 3(a), at the initial zero position, the Hooke joints are located at the center, that is, the vectors m_i, u_i, k_i, and j_i on the cross-axis are simultaneously parallel to its upper and lower bottom planes. According to Eq. (5), there is:

$$s_3 \perp k_1 \ s_2 \perp k_3 \ s_1 \perp k_5$$
$$s_3 \perp k_2 \ s_2 \perp k_4 \ s_1 \perp k_6 \tag{8}$$

Equation (8) illustrates that s_3 is perpendicular to the plane consisting of k_1 and k_2, s_2 is perpendicular to the plane consisting of k_3 and k_4, and s_1 is perpendicular to the plane consisting of k_5 and k_6 when the moving platform is at the initial zero position. Thus, for the upper Hooke joint, there are:

$$k_1 = s_3 \times l_1 \ k_2 = s_3 \times l_2 \ k_3 = s_2 \times l_3$$
$$k_4 = s_2 \times l_4 \ k_5 = s_1 \times l_5 \ k_6 = s_1 \times l_6 \tag{9}$$

in which l_i is the unit vector of the six electric cylinders at the initial zero position, that is, $l_i = L_i/\|L_i\|$. At the same time, for the upper Hooke joints, there are:

$$v_1 = n_2 \times l_1 \ v_2 = n_1 \times l_2 \ v_3 = n_1 \times l_3$$
$$v_4 = n_3 \times l_4 \ v_5 = n_3 \times l_5 \ v_6 = n_2 \times l_6 \tag{10}$$

At the initial zero position, m_i is perpendicular to both v_i and l_i, that is, $m_i = v_i \times l_i$, such that the initial angle between k_i and m_i is:

$$\phi_i = \arccos\left(\frac{k_i}{|k_i|} \times \frac{m_i}{|m_i|}\right) \tag{11}$$

Step 2: Calculate the angle between k'_i and m'_i in the running of the moving platform. The passive rotation is the difference between the angle of k_i and m_i at the initial zero position and the angle of k'_i and m'_i in the running. At this moment, the condition Eq. (9) for the initial zero position does not hold, and then setting the vector h_i, as shown in Fig. 3(c), and satisfying that:

$$h_1 \perp s_3 \qquad h_2 \perp s_3 \qquad h_3 \perp s_2$$
$$h_4 \perp s_2 \qquad h_5 \perp s_1 \qquad h_6 \perp s_1$$
$$h_1 \perp k'_1 \perp l'_1 \ h_2 \perp k'_2 \perp l'_2 \ h_3 \perp k'_3 \perp l'_3$$
$$h_4 \perp k'_4 \perp l'_4 \ h_5 \perp k'_5 \perp l'_5 \ h_6 \perp k'_6 \perp l'_6 \tag{12}$$

in which k'_i and l'_i represent the vectors k_i and l_i in the running. Different from the initial zero position, l'_1, l'_2 and s_3, l'_3, l'_4 and s_2, l'_5, l'_5 s and s_1 are not perpendicular during the operation, and thus there is:

$$h_1 = s_3 \times l'_1 \ h_2 = s_3 \times l'_2 \ h_3 = s_2 \times l'_3$$
$$h_4 = s_2 \times l'_4 \ h_5 = s_1 \times l'_5 \ h_6 = s_1 \times l'_6 \tag{13}$$

then,

$$k'_i = {}^PR_b \frac{h_i \times l'_i}{|h_i \times l'_i|} \tag{14}$$

where ${}^PR_b$ is the rotation matrix of $\{O_p\}$ and $\{O_b\}$. Similarly, as shown in Fig. 3(c), v_i is represented v'_i during the operation, that is:

$$v'_1 = n_2 \times l'_1 \; v'_2 = n_1 \times l'_2 \; v'_3 = n_1 \times l'_3$$
$$v'_4 = n_3 \times l'_4 \; v'_5 = n_3 \times l'_5 \; v'_6 = n_2 \times l'_6 \tag{15}$$

Thus, during the running of the moving platform, m'_i is perpendicular to both v'_i and l'_i, that is, $m'_i = v'_i \times l'_i$. At this moment, the angle between k'_i and m'_i s is:

$$\phi'_i = \arccos\left(\frac{k'_i}{|k'_i|} \times \frac{m'_i}{|m'_i|}\right) \tag{16}$$

Therefore, according to steps 1 and 2, the passive rotation angles are:

$$\Delta\phi_i = \phi'_i - \phi_i \tag{17}$$

Moreover, it should be note that the cylinder rod extends or retracts by 10mm per rotation, so $\Delta L_i = \Delta\phi_i/360 \times 10$, and compensates ΔL_i into Eq. (4) to eliminate the error.

4 Simulation Verification

The structural parameters of the 6-UCU parallel manipulator are shown in Table 1, and its workspace is shown in Table 2. Based on the theoretical calculation of the passive rotation in Sect. 3, a simulation analysis was conducted for the translation and rotation of the moving platform along the x, y, and z-axis.

Table 2. The workspace of the 6-UCU parallel manipulator.

Direction	Range	Direction	Range	Direction	Range
x(mm)	-200–200	z(mm)	-200–200	$\theta(°)$	-25–25
y(mm)	-200–200	$\psi(°)$	-25–25	$\varphi(°)$	-25–25

According to Eq. (19), the results of the passive rotation angle are shown in Fig. 4. It can be seen that the passive rotation angles of the 2nd and 3rd electric cylinders are the largest, at $-0.490°$ and $0.490°$, with corresponding extension and contraction amounts of -0.014 mm and 0.014 mm, during the translation along the x-axis. The passive rotation angles of the 5th and 6th electric cylinders are the largest, at $0.412°$ and $-0.412°$, with corresponding extension and contraction amounts of 0.011 mm and -0.011 mm, during

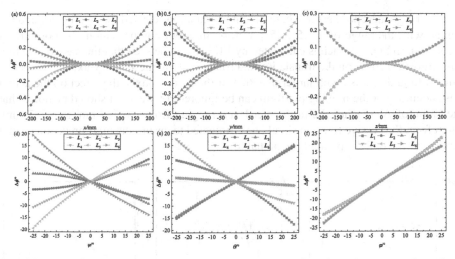

Fig. 4. The passive rotation angle of the translation and rotation along the x-, y-, and z-axis.

the translation along the y-axis. The passive rotation angles of the 1st, 3rd, and 5th are the same, and those of the 2nd, 4th, and 6th are the same, during the translation along the z-axis, and the maximum are $-0.235°$ and $0.235°$, with corresponding extension and contraction amounts of -0.007 mm and 0.007 mm.

Similarly, during the rotation of the moving platform around the x-axis, the passive rotation angles of the 5th and 6th electric cylinders are the largest, at $-19.443°$ and $19.443°$, with corresponding extension and contraction amounts of -0.540 mm and 0.540 mm. During the rotation around the y-axis, the passive rotation angles of the 1st and 4th are the largest, at $-17.599°$ and $17.599°$, with corresponding extension and contraction amounts of -0.489 mm and 0.489 mm. During the rotation around the z-axis, the passive rotation angles of the 1st, 3rd, and 5th are the same, and those of the 2nd, 4th, and 6th are the same, and the maximum is $22.488°$ and $-22.488°$, with corresponding extension and contraction amounts of 0.625 mm and -0.625 mm.

In addition, it can be concluded in Fig. 4 that the passive rotation angles of the six electric cylinders tend to be maximum when the moving platform moves toward the boundary of the workspace. Moreover, the passive rotation angles of the six electric cylinders are symmetrical in pairs which is the symmetrical structure of the 6-UCU parallel manipulator about the y-axis. Relate to the translation, the passive rotation is an order of magnitude larger during the rotation, where the maximum is $22.488°$ introduced by the rotation around the z-axis. In other words, the maximum error is 0.625 mm, which is introduced by the rotation.

As is well known, it is difficult to measure the extension and contraction of the six electric cylinders in the actual experiment. However, the pose of the moving platform can be directly measured. Therefore, it is necessary to conduct a simulation about the influence of the passive rotation on the pose.

As shown in Fig. 4, the rotation around the z-axis generates the largest passive rotation angle, which leads to the largest extension and contraction of the electric cylinder rod, that is, the greatest pose error. Therefore, the simulation selected the rotation around the z-axis, with the range of $[-25°, 25°]$. Before and after compensation, the pose errors are shown in Fig. 5, which is calculated by FKS. It can be seen that the passive rotation has almost no effect on the translation and rotation along the x- and y-axis. At the same time, although $\Delta\varphi$ is much larger than that of the x- and y-axis, the effect on the actual pose accuracy of the moving platform can be ignored. However, it should be noted that the value of Δz reaches the millimeter level, ranging from -0.727 mm to 0.727 mm. Therefore, the passive rotation should be eliminated to ensure the high-precision spatial motion of the 6-UCU parallel manipulator.

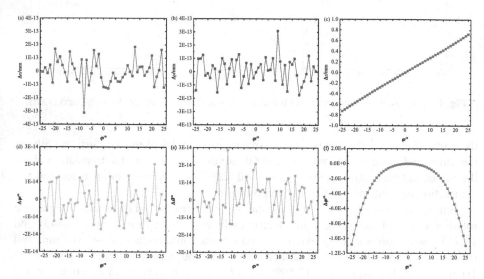

Fig. 5. The pose errors caused by the passive rotation.

5 Experiment and Results

The experiments are conducted using the stereo vision method to measure the actual pose of the moving platform, as shown in Fig. 6, and the structural parameters of the prototype are shown in Table 1, while the workspace is shown in Table 2. The measurement accuracy of the stereo vision measurement system is 20 μm + 20 μm/m [19]. $\{m\}$ represents the measurement coordinate system of the stereo vision system composed of high-speed camera 1 and 2. The origin of coordinate system $\{O_0\}$ is located at the upper surface center of the moving platform. The normal vector of the plane is the z-axis of $\{O_0\}$, and the plane is fitted by the coding targets 2, 3, 4, and 5. Coding target 4 is located on the y-axis, and the x-axis is determined by the right-hand rule.

The experiment mainly consists of the following three steps:

Step 1: According to the standard ASME B89.4.22–2004 [20], the repeatability testing of the prototype is conducted. The principle is to control the moving platform translation along the x-, y-, and z-axis by 150 mm and rotation around the x-, y-, and z-axis by 15°, and using the stereo vision to measure the actual poses. Each pose is measured 10 times, and the ratio of the standard deviation to the mean value of the measurement is calculated as the relative standard deviation. The results presented that the relative standard deviations of the translation and rotation are all below 0.03% in Table 3.

Step 2: According to the simulation results in Sect. 4, an experiment is conducted on the prototype with a rotation around the z-axis. The rotation angle range is $[-25°, 25°]$, with measurements taken at every 5° interval, resulting in a total of 10 pose measurement points, denoted as Q_N.

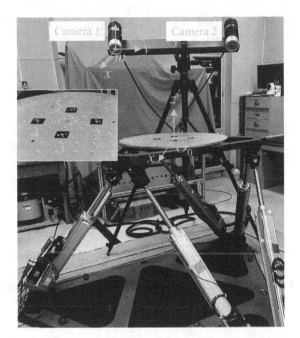

Fig. 6. Experiment of the passive rotation compensation of electric cylinder.

Table 3. The result of the repeatability test.

Axial	x(mm)	y(mm)	z(mm)	ψ(°)	θ(°)	φ(°)
Average	150.095	149.709	150.094	14.989	14.975	15.031
Standard deviation	0.002	0.004	0.005	0.003	0.003	0.003
Relative (%)	0.001	0.003	0.003	0.021	0.022	0.020

Step 3: The moving platform is controlled to the selected 10 measurement poses, and the actual poses Q_0 are measured before the compensation. Similarly, the actual poses Q_1 are measured after the compensation. Then, the pose errors are calculated by $\Delta Q_0 = Q_0 - Q_N$ and $\Delta Q_1 = Q_1 - Q_N$. The results are provided in Fig. 7.

It can be seen that the range of Δx are $[-0.043 \text{ mm}, 0.057 \text{ mm}]$ to $[-0.039 \text{ mm}, 0.053 \text{ mm}]$. The range of Δy are $[-0.029 \text{ mm}, 0.029 \text{ mm}]$ to $[-0.034 \text{ mm}, 0.033 \text{ mm}]$.

The range of $\Delta\psi$ are $[-0.003°, 0.003°]$ to $[-0.004°, 0.002°]$. The range of $\Delta\theta$ are $[-0.003°, 0.004°]$ to $[-0.003°, 0.005°]$. The range of $\Delta\varphi$ are $[-0.018°, 0.024°]$ to $[-0.017°, 0.024°]$. Therefore, it can be concluded that the pose accuracy is limited improvement in the translation along the $x-$, $y-$, and z-axis and the rotation around the $x-$ and y-axis after the compensation. However, there is a one-order-of-magnitude improvement in the translation along the z-axis, that is, the range of Δz are $[-0.762$ mm, 0.855 mm] to $[-0.061$ mm, 0.103 mm]. Therefore, the effectiveness of compensating for the passive rotation angles is validated.

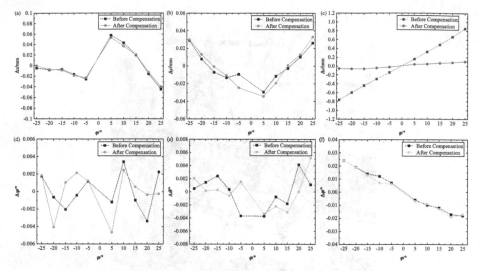

Fig. 7. The pose errors before and after the passive rotation compensation.

6   Conclusions

For the 6-UCU parallel manipulator, there is a relative rotation of the Hooke joints at both ends of the drive link during the running of the moving platform, which introduced a dynamic control error. Therefore, a theoretical derivation of the passive rotation is carried out based on the geometry of the manipulator, and the following conclusions are obtained through simulation and experimentation:

(1) Compared to the translation along the $x-$, $y-$, and z-axis, an order of magnitude larger of the passive rotation angles in the rotation, that is, the maximum pose errors are produced, up to millimeters level.

(2) The experimental results show a significant improvement in the pose accuracy after the compensation, where the position error is reduced from $[-0.762$ mm, 0.855 mm] to $[-0.061$ mm, 0.103 mm] in the z-axis.

Acknowledgement. This research is supported by National Natural Science Foundation of China (No. 52075512, 62203132, and 52265066), Fundamental Research Funds for National Institute of

Metrology of China (AKYZD2302), Youth Science and Technology Talents Development Project of Guizhou Education Department (No. Qianjiaohe KY [2022]138).

References

1. Merlet, J.P.: Parallel Robots, 2nd edn. Kluwer Academic Publishers, Alphen aan den Rijn (2002)
2. Furqan, M., Suhaib, M., Ahmad, N.: Studies on Stewart platform manipulator: a review. J. Mech. Sci. and Technol. 31(9), 4459–4470 (2017)
3. Russo, M., Dong, X.: A calibration procedure for reconfigurable Gough-Stewart manipulators. Mech. Mach. Theory 152, 103920 (2020)
4. Olarra, A., Axinte, D., Kortaberria, G.: Geometrical calibration and uncertainty estimation methodology for a novel self-propelled miniature robotic machine tool. Robot. Cim-Int Manuf. 49, 204–214 (2018)
5. Kuehn, D., Schilling, M., Stark, T., et al.: System design and testing of the hominid robot Charlie. J. Field Robot. 34(4), 666–703 (2017)
6. Zhang, N.B., Huang, P.C.: Modeling, design and experiment of a remote-center-of-motion parallel manipulator for needle insertion. Robot. Cim-Int Manuf. 50, 193–202 (2017)
7. Karmakar, S., Patel, A., Turner, C.J.: Calibration of parallel kinematic machine based on Stewart platform - a literature review. In: Proceedings of the ASME 2021 International Design Engineering Technical Conferences and Computers and Information in Engineering Conference, Virtual, Online, pp. 1–11 (2021)
8. Mekid, S.: A review of machine tool accuracy enhancement through error compensation in serial and parallel kinematic machines. Int. J. Precis. Technol. 1(3), 251–283 (2010)
9. Šalinić, S., Vranić, A., Nešić, N.D.: On the torque transmission by a Cardan-Hooke joint. FME Trans. 45, 117–121 (2017)
10. Qu, H.B., Guo, S., Zhang, Y.: A novel relative degree-of-freedom criterion for a class of parallel manipulators with kinematic redundancy and its applications. J. Mech. Eng. Sci. 231(22), 4227–4240 (2017)
11. Liu, Z.H., Tang, X.Q., Wang, L.P.: Research on the dynamic coupling of the rigid-flexible manipulator. Robot. Cim-Int Manuf. 32, 72–82 (2015)
12. Liu, Z.H., Tang, X.Q., Shao, Z.F., et al.: Dimensional optimization of the Stewart platform based on inertia decoupling characteristic. Robotica 34, 1151–1167 (2016)
13. McCann, C.M., Dollar, A.M.: Design of a stewart platform-inspired dexterous hand for 6-DOF within-hand manipulation. In: 2017 IEEE/RSJ International Conference on Intelligent Robots and Systems (IROS), Vancouver, BC, Canada, pp.1158–1163 (2017)
14. Qiang, H.B., Jin, S.: Model predictive control of a shipborne hydraulic parallel stabilized platform based on ship motion prediction. IEEE Access 8, 181880–181892 (2020)
15. Wu, J.F., Zhang, R.: A systematic optimization approach for the calibration of parallel kinematics machine tools by a laser tracker. Int. J. Mach. Tool Manuf. 86, 1–11 (2014)
16. Kazezkhan, G., Xiang, B.B., Wang, N.: Dynamic modeling of the Stewart platform for the NanShan Radio Telescope. Adv. Mech. Eng. 12(7), 1–10 (2020)
17. Mei, B., Xie, F.G., Liu, X.J.: Elasto-geometrical error modeling and compensation of a five-axis parallel machining robot. Precis. Eng. 69, 48–61 (2021)
18. Li, Y.B., Wang, Z.S.: Dynamic accuracy analysis of a 5PSS/UPU parallel mechanism based on rigid-flexible coupled modeling. Chin. J. Mech. Eng-Eng. 35(33), 1–14 (2022)
19. Fu, L., Yang, M., Liu, Z.H., et al.: Stereo vision-based Kinematic calibration method for the Stewart platforms. Opt. Express 30(26), 47059–47069 (2022)
20. Parry, B., Beutel, D.: Methods for performance evaluation of articulated arm coordinate measuring machines. ASME (2004). B89.4.22–2004

Research on BP Neural Network Prediction of Position Error Considering the Variation of Industrial Robot Center of Mass

Wang Zhiqi, Gao Dong, Lu Yong[✉], Deng Kenan, and Ma Shoudong

Harbin Institute of Technology, Harbin, China
luyong@hit.edu.cn

Abstract. The position error of industrial robots has nonlinear characteristics in the workspace. This paper proposes a back propagation (BP) neural network prediction method for robot position error considering the variation of industrial robot center of mass (CoM). First, the CoM model of the industrial robot is established, which forms a mapping relationship between the joint angle of the robot and the position of the CoM, and the simulation verifies the correctness of the model. Then, the robot position error data set is obtained based on different regional spatial grid sampling methods, and the correlation between the robot end position and CoM about position error is analyzed. Finally, the BP neural network is used to establish position error prediction model that combines the robot end position and the CoM variation. Experimental results show that the constructed model can more effectively predict the robot position error.

Keywords: Industrial Robot · Center of Mass · Position Error Prediction · BP Neural Network

1 Introduction

With the development of industrial robot technology, various performance indicators of robots have also been improved, and robots have gradually shifted from low-precision tasks (such as handling, welding, dispensing, etc.) to high-precision tasks (such as drilling, milling, grinding, etc.) [1, 2]. When industrial robot is used for cutting tasks, it installs actuator for cutting at the end of the robot. However, when the robot performs cutting tasks, due to its poor position accuracy, it is difficult to meet the machining requirements in some high-precision tasks [3, 4]. At this time, it is often necessary to compensate the position error of its end to better adapt to the machining task, so for industrial robots that perform certain high-precision machining tasks, position accuracy compensation is an important prerequisite for ensuring machining accuracy.

The current research on position error compensation of industrial robots is mainly divided into online compensation methods and offline compensation methods. Online compensation methods mainly include joint space compensation and Cartesian space compensation. Devlieg [5] installed optical encoders at the joints to compensate for robot joint rotation error. Li [6] used laser trackers in Cartesian space to realize full closed-loop feedback of robot postures, which greatly improved robot position accuracy. Although the current research method of the online compensation method has achieved good compensation effects, it requires the transformation of the robot body and the introduction of external measuring equipment, and the development cycle is long and the cost is high. The offline compensation method is still the focus of research and application by scholars at home and abroad. The prerequisite for the implementation of the offline compensation method is to obtain the position error of the robot end in advance, so the accurate prediction of the position error is the key. In the prediction research of robot position error, there are methods of robot position error prediction such as fourier series [7], inverse distance weighting [8] and data-driven theory [9]. In the data-driven error prediction method, if the characteristics related to the error can be considered in the prediction model, the prediction accuracy will be improved. Tan [10] used multi-robot characteristics such as robot joint angles, angular velocities and torques to build a temporal convolutional network model to predict robot tracking error and achieved good application effect.

In summary, using a reasonable method to predict robot position error is an important prerequisite for using industrial robots to perform certain high-finishing tasks. This paper focuses on the prediction of robot position error. First, the model of the center of mass of the industrial robot is established with the input of the robot joint angle. Then, the correlation between the center of mass of the robot and the position error is analyzed through the data sets of position error in different regions. Based on this, the center of mass of the industrial robot is used as the input feature to establish the BP neural network position error prediction model. Finally, the application effect of the proposed model is compared and analyzed by using the robot position error data sets in different regions.

2 CoM Model and Correctness Verification of Industrial Robot

2.1 Theoretical Basis of CoM Modeling

Robot kinematics is the basis of robot center of mass (CoM) modeling. This study takes KUKA KR160 industrial robot as the research object, and uses DH parameters to describe the robot kinematics model, DH parameters are shown in Table 1. For a six-freedom industrial robot, its kinematic transfer matrix can be expressed as:

$$T_i^{i-1} = \begin{bmatrix} \cos\theta_i & -\cos\alpha_i \sin\theta_i & \sin\alpha_i \sin\theta_i & l_i \cos\theta_i \\ \sin\theta_i & \cos\alpha_i \cos\theta_i & -\sin\alpha_i \cos\theta_i & l_i \sin\theta_i \\ 0 & \sin\alpha_i & \cos\alpha_i & d_i \\ 0 & 0 & 0 & 1 \end{bmatrix} \tag{1}$$

$$T_6^0 = T_1^0 T_2^1 T_3^2 T_4^3 T_5^4 T_6^5 \tag{2}$$

To model the CoM of the robot, it is necessary to introduce homogeneous coordinates of the mass point [11], the established coordinate system of the robot CoM model in this paper is the robot base coordinate system. The theory is explained below, from the point of view of projective geometry, a point in R^3 can be represented by four homogeneous coordinates:

$$\bar{p} = [x, y, z, w]^T \tag{3}$$

Table 1. KUKA KR160 robot DH parameters.

Link	θ_i (rad)	d_i(mm)	a_i(mm)	α_i(rad)	Range(deg)
1	θ_1	500	250	$\pi/2$	$[-185,185]$
2	$\theta_2 + \pi/2$	0	610	0	$[-130, 20]$
3	$\theta_3 + \pi$	0	70	$-\pi/2$	$[-100,144]$
4	θ_4	710	0	$\pi/2$	$[-350,350]$
5	θ_5	0	0	$-\pi/2$	$[-120,120]$
6	θ_6	215	0	0	$[-s350,350]$

where w is any real number, when $w \neq 0$, it represents a point in the space, and the coordinates of this point is $p = [x/w, y/w, z/w]^T$, this Cartesian coordinate is obtained by projecting the homogeneous coordinate onto a plane of height $1/w$. When $w = 0$, p represents a plane point at infinity. In the homogeneous transformation coordinates, the w value is usually set to 1, corresponding to the coordinates of the position of the point. But in other research related to robotics, it is possible to use the w value to assign relevant quality attributes to points in the alignment transformation for re-coding. In this way, the vector containing the point position and mass properties can be formed, which is the homogeneous coordinates of the mass point, which can be expressed as:

$$\overline{M_i} = [m_i x_i, m_i y_i, m_i z_i, m_i]^T \tag{4}$$

This vector contains mass information and represents the Cartesian coordinates produced by a point in the coordinate plane with height $1/m$. For a multi-CoM system, the sum of the homogeneous coordinates of its subsystem CoM can describe the CoM coordinates of the system. Therefore, the meaning of the sum of this vector is different from the sum of two homogeneous coordinates in Cartesian space. Take the system composed of two CoM as an example, let the coordinates of two mass points be (x_1, y_1, z_1) and (x_2, y_2, z_2), and the masses are m_1 and m_2 respectively, and their sum can be expressed as:

$$\overline{M_1} + \overline{M_2} = [m_1 x_1 + m_2 x_2, m_1 y_1 + m_2 y_2, m_1 z_1 + m_2 z_2, m_1 + m_2]^T \tag{5}$$

In summary, for a multi-body motion system such as industrial robot, the CoM of the overall mechanism is described by the sum of the CoM of each subsystem.

2.2 CoM Model of Industrial Robot

The mass point system composed of a single mechanism, the CoM coincides with the location of the mass point. For industrial robot system composed of multiple mechanisms, the introduction of the quality system of each mechanism causes the translation of the CoM. In addition, the position variation of the CoM of the local mechanism brought about by different robot configurations will also affect the translation of the CoM. The following will focus on how to represent the robot CoM model based on the homogeneous coordinates of the subsystem CoM and the robot motion transfer relationship.

The industrial robot is a multi-body motion system, and its joints are connected by each motion axis. The expression of the CoM model can be obtained more easily by using kinematic equations. To simplify the calculation of the CoM model, the kinematics model of the robot can be introduced to describe the motion state of the robot. Based on describing the motion state of each joint mechanism of the robot, the model can further describe the motion state of the CoM of each joint mechanism. The motion transfer between joints can be described using a homogeneous transformation matrix. In addition, since the position of the CoM of each joint relative to the corresponding coordinate system in the kinematics model remains unchanged during the movement, the position of the CoM of each joint can also be described by means of the coordinate system in the kinematics model.

The CoM of the robot can be calculated by the CoM of each joint mechanism. Industrial robot is composed of a base and six rotating joints, and the position and quality of the CoM corresponding to each part are shown in Fig. 1. The total mass of the robot is the sum of its parts $M = m_0 + m_1 + m_2 + m_3 + m_4 + m_5 + m_6$. The formula for calculating the robot CoM can be deduced from the CoM of each joint of the robot [12]:

$$\overrightarrow{CoM} = \left[\overline{M_0} + T_1^0\overline{M_1} + T_2^0\overline{M_2} + T_3^0\overline{M_3} + T_4^0\overline{M_4} + T_5^0\overline{M_5} + T_6^0\overline{M_6}\right]\Big/ M \qquad (6)$$

where M_i represents the homogeneous coordinates of the mass point, $T0\ i$ represents the homogeneous transformation matrix of the robot first kinematic chain to the i-th kinematic chain, $i = 1,2,\cdots, 6$. This formula uses the robot joint angle as the input to obtain the calculation formula of the CoM of the robot system. The formula uses the robot base coordinate system as the evaluation coordinate system. It should be noted that the first item of the formula represents the homogeneous coordinates of the robot base CoM, and the base does not move during the movement, so this item does not add homogeneous transformation matrix.

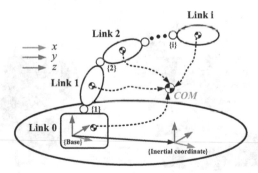

Fig. 1. Schematic diagram of the position and quality of the CoM of each part of the robot

2.3 Verification of Industrial Robot CoM Model

To verify the correctness of the CoM model of the industrial robot established above, it is necessary to clarify the mass of each joint of the robot and the position of the CoM.

In this study, the position and mass of the CoM of each joint of the robot are calculated by using SolidWorks software. The calculation method is: in the coordinate system of the robot kinematics model, respectively calculate the CoM position and mass of each joint of the robot relative to the currently described kinematic coordinate system, and the robot configuration used is [0,0,0,0,0,0], the specific parameters obtained by the calculation are shown in Table 2:

Table 2. Parameter values of each joint of the robot

Joint	Joint mass(kg)	CoM coordinates X, Y, Z (mm)
0	94.689	(−78.12, 0, 91.55)
1	204.196	(−153.16, −99.41, −ss0.12)
2	44.956	(−332.499, 0.537, 334.557)
3	135.638	(−33.582, −55.197, 133.585)
4	6.884	(0.003, −83.397, 0.483)
5	22.346	(0.055, 25.196, 41.080)
6	1.818	(−0.036, 0, −22.794)

The position of the CoM of the industrial robot can be calculated by using the parameters in Table 2 and the joint angles of the robot. In order to verify the correctness of the model, a set of actual CoM coordinates corresponding to the robot configuration is selected for verification (Fig. 2), and compared with the above CoM model The calculated CoM coordinates are compared, and the errors of the two are shown in Table 3. From the error results, the modeling error rate is within 10%, so the proposed method can effectively calculate the CoM of industrial robots.

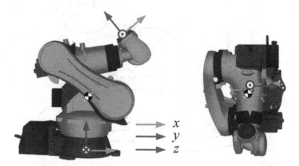

Fig. 2. Robot configuration and corresponding CoM position

For industrial robots for machining task, the end of the robot is equipped with machining device. The calculation of the robot CoM model under this condition needs to integrate the end load into the robot Joint 6, so the reintegrated robot Joint 6 CoM is (−42.064, 0, 72.603) mm and mass is 27.013 kg.

Table 3. Verification of the correctness of robot CoM model

Robot configuration (deg)	Actual CoM (mm)	Calculate CoM (mm)	Error (mm)
[0, −145, 135, 0, −120, 0]	[15.7, −45, 525]	[15.2, −40.8, 499.4]	[−0.5, 4.2, 25.6]

3 Correlation Analysis of Robot CoM and Position Error

3.1 Robot Position Error Acquisition

To verify the correlation between the CoM of the robot and the position error, this study analyzes the data samples of the position error of the robot under different CoM. The position error data sample set is obtained through the spatial grid sampling method. The sampling space size is a spatial grid region of $500 \times 500 \times 300$ mm. There are 216 sampling points in this region (Fig. 3). The position error acquisition experiment was carried out in two different regions (Fig. 4), the sampling spaces of region 1 and region 2 do not overlap, and the programming coordinate systems of these two regions only differ by 500 mm in the y direction of the robot base coordinate system. In the experiment, laser tracker is used to measure the actual robot end position. The difference between the theoretical position and the measured position is the position error. The formula is:

$$\Delta x = x_m - x_a$$
$$\Delta y = y_m - y_a \tag{7}$$
$$\Delta z = z_m - z_a$$

where the measured position coordinate is (x_m, y_m, z_m), and the theoretical position coordinate is (x_a, y_a, z_a).

The above experiment obtained a sample set of robot position error data in different regions, and used these data to analyze the position error of the robot in all directions. The analysis results are shown in Table 4. Figure 5 is a map of robot position error distribution. It can be seen that the position error of region 1 is 0.7722 mm, and region 2 is 0.8234 mm. Compared with region 1, the position error in region 2 is larger. Figure 6 is the robot CoM distribution map. Compared with region 1, it can be found that the CoM variation in region 2 is larger. Figure 7 shows the mean and standard deviation of position error in all direction in different regions, and it can be found that the z-direction error fluctuates greatly.

Table 4. Error distribution in different regions (*mm*)

Category	Δx mean	Δx scope	Δy mean	Δy scope	Δz mean	Δz scope
Region 1	0.619	[0.295,0.960]	0.065	[−0.117,0.316]	0.040	[−0.820,0.729]
Region 2	0.584	[0.378,0.890]	-0.283	[−0.435,0.597]	−0.295	[−1.343,0.597]

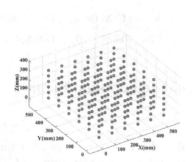

Fig. 3. Collect point grid information

Fig. 4. Different regions error experiment

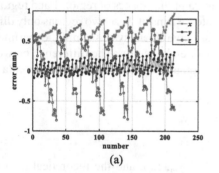

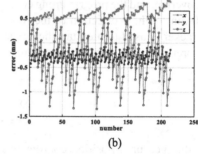

Fig. 5. Robot position error distribution map (a) Region 1. (b) Region 2

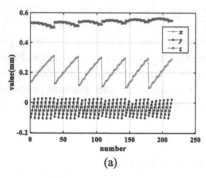

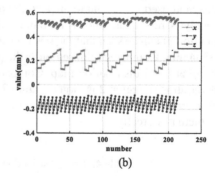

Fig. 6. Robot CoM distribution map (a) Region 1. (b) Region 2

In order to verify the influence of the robot end load on the position error, the position error in the same area was collected under the condition of unloaded and loaded on the robot. The difference between them in each direction of the two experiments is shown in the Fig. 8. It can be seen from Fig. 8 that position error changes greatly, especially

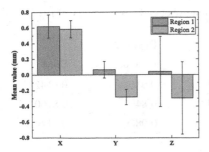

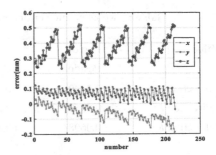

Fig. 7. The mean value and standard deviation of the position error in different regions

Fig. 8. Position error distribution in different regions

the maximum value of the z-direction position error difference can reach 0.524 mm, so it is very important to predict and compensate the robot position error under loaded.

3.2 Correlation Analysis of Robot CoM and Robot Position Error

At present, most of the research on robot position error prediction is carried out using the spatial similarity method. This method believes that the robot position error has a strong correlation with the robot end position, and the position error corresponding to the known point can be used to predict the position error of the relevant region. It can be seen that a strong correlation between the robot end position and position error is a prerequisite for the successful application of this method. Similarly, whether the CoM of the robot can be used to predict the position error of the robot also depends on whether there is a strong correlation between the CoM and the position error. The following analyzes the correlation between the end position and the CoM of the robot about position error.

The statistical product-difference correlation method, Pearson correlation is used to analyze the correlation of data sets, and the calculation formula of correlation coefficient is as follows:

$$R = \frac{\sum\limits_{i=1}^{n} \left(X_i - \overline{X}\right)\left(Y_i - \overline{Y}\right)}{\sqrt{\sum\limits_{i=1}^{n} \left(X_i - \overline{X}\right)^2} \sqrt{\sum\limits_{i=1}^{n} \left(Y_i - \overline{Y}\right)^2}} \tag{8}$$

where R is the correlation coefficient $R \in [-1,1]$, R greater than 0 is positive correlation, R less than 0 is negative correlation, R^2 is the determination coefficient $R^2 < 0.4$ means low linear correlation, $0.4 \leq R^2 < 0.7$ means significant linear correlation, $0.7 \leq R^2 < 1$ means highly linear correlation. The correlation between robot end position and CoM about position error in each direction is shown in Table 5.

It can be seen from Table 5 that the robot end position has a high correlation with the position error in the x and y directions, but the correlation in the z direction is weak. The reason may be related to the gravity of the robot. The CoM of the robot is also highly

Table 5. Robot position error correlation (robot end position and CoM)

Value	Region 1		Region 2	
	Position	CoM	Position	CoM
x direction R^2	0.9440	0.9214	0.9161	0.9142
y direction R^2	0.8859	0.8824	0.8496	0.8760
z direction R^2	0.0698	0.4662	0.0809	0.7144

correlated with the position error in the x and y directions, and its correlation is slightly weaker than that of the robot end position about the position error. However, in the z direction, the correlation degree is much higher than the correlation between the robot end position and the position error, the reason is that the CoM of the robot is the position coordinate related to the quality of each joint mechanism, and the position error is very related to the gravity deformation error of each joint mechanism. After further analysis of the data sets in region 1 and region 2, it can be obtained that the correlation of the CoM in the z direction can be increased by 85.03% in region 1 and 90.76% in region 2 compared with the correlation of the robot end position. The experimental results show that the CoM of the robot has a high correlation with the position error, which can be used to predict the position error of the robot.

4 Position Error Prediction Method Considering the Variation of Robot CoM

Many studies [13, 14] show that the robot position error has nonlinear characteristics in the workspace. In order to adapt to such nonlinear characteristics, the position error prediction can be realized by using data-driven methods, which are often implemented by establishing some nonlinear mapping model. As we all know, BP neural network modelhas strong nonlinear mapping ability [15]. In the application of this black-box nonlinear model, it is proved to be a very effective means to use characteristic parameters related to model output value as model input [10]. Therefore, it is feasible to use BP neural network for robot position error prediction, and its input parameters can use robot characteristic parameters which are strongly related to robot position error.

To sum up, this paper establishes a data-driven BP neural network model for predicting robot position error. The structure of this network is a three-layer BP neural network (Fig. 9). Its input parameters are the coordinates of the robot end position and the coordinates of the robot CoM, and its output is the position error predicted by the model. The input parameters were divided into two cases: One is to input only the robot end position coordinates, and the other is to use the end position and CoM of the end as input parameters. The purpose is to explore the influence of the CoM of the robot on the accuracy of position error prediction.

Using the sample data set obtained above, the position error results predicted by the BP neural network model established with different input features are shown in Fig. 10, and Table 6 shows the prediction and analysis results of the BP neural network model in

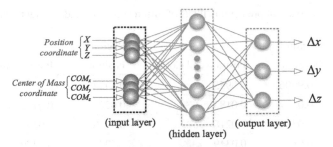

Fig. 9. BP neural network structure

different regions. After analysis and comparison, taking the BP neural network model constructed by the position error data sample set of region 2 as example, adding the CoM of the robot as an input feature to the model, the R^2 of the model is increased by 0.1478, the RMSE (Root Mean Square Error) of the position error prediction in the x, y, and z directions is reduced by 0.1096, 0.01177 and 0.02553 respectively, The MAE (Mean Absolute Error) of the model is reduced by 0.0473, and the MBE (Mean Bias Error) is reduced by 0.05394. It can be seen that adding the CoM of the robot to the position error prediction model can greatly improve the prediction accuracy of the model. It can also be found by comparing the position error prediction effects of region 1 and region 2, the prediction accuracy of the position error prediction algorithm added to the CoM feature in region 2 is significantly improved. The R^2 improvement of region 1 is 0.0049, and the R^2 improvement of region 2 is 0.14778. This may be related to the larger variation range of the CoM of region 2.That is to say, the introduction of this feature has a more positive impact on the accuracy of the model for regions with a large range of CoM.

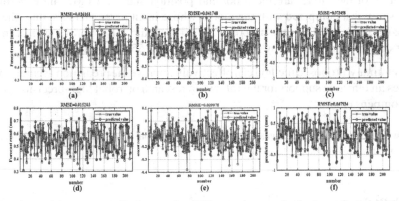

Fig. 10. The position error prediction result of BP neural network, the input feature is the robot end position: (a) x direction (b) y direction (c) z direction. The input feature is the robot end position and CoM: (d) x direction (e) y direction (f) z direction

Table 6. Comparison of prediction effects of different regions and different input features

Value	Region 1		Region 2	
	Position	Position and CoM	Position	Position and CoM
R^2	0.9906	0.9955	0.8444	0.9922
x RMSE	0.0357	0.0183	0.0262	0.0152
y RMSE	0.0332	0.0218	0.0418	0.0299
z RMSE	0.0850	0.0349	0.0735	0.0479
MAE	0.0667	0.0239	0.0801	0.0328
MBE	−0.0107	0.0014	0.0541	0.00016

5 Conclusion

In order to improve the prediction accuracy of nonlinear robot position error, this paper proposes a robot position error BP neural network prediction method considering the variation of industrial robot CoM. Through theoretical and experimental analysis, the following conclusions are drawn:

(1) The CoM model of industrial robot is established, and the correctness of the model is verified by simulation.
(2) Based on the spatial grid sampling method, the robot position error data sample set is obtained, and the analysis shows that the robot CoM has a strong correlation with the position error.
(3) The BP neural network position error prediction model is established, and the input parameters of the model are the robot end position and the CoM. The experimental results show that compared with the model whose input parameters are only the robot end position, the RSME of the proposed model in predicting the position error in the x, y and z directions is reduced by 0.1096, 0.01177, 0.02553 respectively.

In summary, proposed method can effectively improve the prediction accuracy, which provides an effective support for the follow-up research on robot high-precision position error compensation.

Acknowledgement. This work was supported by the National Key R&D Program of China under Grant 2018YFB1306800.

References

1. Verl, A., Valente, A., Melkote, S.: Robots in machining. CIRP Ann. **68**(2), 799–822 (2019)
2. Xie, Z., Xie, F., Liu, X.J., Wang, J., Mei, B.: Tracking error prediction informed motion control of a parallel machine tool for high-performance machining. Int. J. Mach. Tools Manuf. **164**, 103714 (2021)
3. Zhao, X., Tao, B., Han, S., Ding, H.: Accuracy analysis in mobile robot machining of large-scale workpiece. Robot. Comput.-Integr. Manuf. **71**, 102153 (2021)

4. Zhu, W., Li, G., Dong, H., Ke, Y.: Positioning error compensation on two-dimensional manifold for robotic machining. Robot. Comput.-Integr. Manuf. **59**, 394–405 (2019)

5. DeVlieg, R., Szallay, T.: Applied accurate robotic drilling for aircraft fuselage. SAE Int. J. Aerosp. **3**(1), 180–186 (2010)

6. Li, R., Ding, N., Zhao, Y., Liu, H.: Real-time trajectory position error compensation technology of industrial robot. Measurement **208**, 112418 (2023)

7. Alici, G., Shirinzadeh, B.: A systematic technique to estimate positioning errors for robot accuracy improvement using laser interferometry based sensing. Mech. Mach. Theory **40**(8), 879–906 (2005)

8. Tugrul, B., Polat, H.: Privacy-preserving inverse distance weighted interpolation. Arab. J. Sci. Eng. **39**, 2773–2781 (2014)

9. Ma, S., Deng, K., Lu, Y., Xu, X.: Robot error compensation based on incremental extreme learning machines and an improved sparrow search algorithm. Int. J. Adv. Manuf. Technol. **125**(11–12), 5431–5443 (2023)

10. Tan, S., Yang, J., Ding, H.: A prediction and compensation method of robot tracking error considering pose-dependent load decomposition. Robot. Comput.-Integr. Manuf. **80**, 102476 (2023)

11. Xu, K., Chen, H., Mueller, A., Ding, X.: Kinematics of the center of mass for robotic mechanisms based on lie group theory. Mech. Mach. Theory **175**, 104933 (2022)

12. Cotton, S., Murray, A., Fraisse, P.: Statically equivalent serial chains for modeling the center of mass of humanoid robots. In: Humanoids 2008–8th IEEE-RAS International Conference on Humanoid Robots, pp. 138–144. IEEE (2008)

13. Miao, L., Zhang, Y., Song, Z., Guo, Y., Zhu, W., Ke, Y.: A two-step method for kinematic parameters calibration based on complete pose measurement—verification on a heavy-duty robot. Robot. Comput.-Integr. Manuf. **83**, 102550 (2023)

14. Zeng, Y., Tian, W., Liao, W.: Positional error similarity analysis for error compensation of industrial robots. Robot. Comput.-Integr. Manuf. **42**, 113–120 (2016)

15. Ding, S., Su, C., Yu, J.: An optimizing BP neural network algorithm based on genetic algorithm. Artif. Intell. Rev. **36**, 153–162 (2011)

Real-Time Smooth Corner Trajectory Planning for Industrial Robots Under Linear and Angular Kinematic Constraints

Jingfu Peng[1,2,3] (iD), Zhengyang Zhang[1,2,3], and Wenjie Chen[1,2,3](✉)

[1] Blue-Orange Lab, Midea Group, Foshan 528300, China
chenwj42@midea.com
[2] Midea Corporate Research Center, Foshan 528300, China
[3] Midea Corporate Research Center, Shanghai 201702, China

Abstract. Path-invariant corner transition trajectory planning is crucial for industrial robots to achieve error-controllable and smooth motion in many manufacturing applications. It usually consists of a spline-based local smoothing procedure for position and orientation linear segments and a real-time feedrate scheduling process. In traditional parameter-synchronization-based methods, the angular motion is regarded as a slave motion following the linear motion by sharing the same curve parameter, which might result in violation of angular kinematic constraints. To overcome this problem, this paper presents a real-time corner trajectory generation method based on a new time-synchronization algorithm. First, the position and orientation linear segments are G^2-continuously transited by inserting error-controlled cubic B-splines and quaternion B-splines at the corners, and subdivided into numerous pairs of blocks. Then the jerk-limited motion profiles of each block pair are planned separately and synchronized to share the same motion duration. The motion profiles for all block pairs can be efficiently obtained by sequentially applying the proposed method from the first to the end block pair without the bi-directional scanning procedure in the literature. The resulting motion profiles respect tangential linear and angular kinematic limits up to jerk in Cartesian space and guarantee continuous acceleration of joint trajectories simultaneously. Simulation experiments verify the effectiveness of the proposed method.

Keywords: Corner Trajectory · Time Synchronization · Angular Kinematic Constraints · Industrial Robot

1 Introduction

The numerous linear-format segments are widely utilized in robot controller to approximate continuous contour in complex manufacturing tasks. However, the tangential discontinuity of linear segments will cause fluctuation of joint motion profiles, which could deteriorate the motion tracking accuracy [1]. To avoid this problem, the real-time generation of smooth corner trajectory is a necessity for industrial robot controllers.

In the literature, there are a lot of research works focusing on corner transition trajectory planning for industrial robots and five-axis machine tools. These methods can be applied to both robots and machine tools, except that the orientation part should be handled in different ways. Generally, they can be classified into one-step methods [2] and decoupled methods [3]. One-step methods usually separately plan the rest-to-rest motion profiles of linear segments, and directly blends two adjacent motion profiles to form a smooth corner trajectory. The geometry of the corner trajectory is controlled by designing the blending time. For industrial robots, Grassmann et al. [4] planned the rest-to-rest motion profile of position and quaternion segments using a polynomial time law, and then directly blended the two motion profiles of the adjacent segments according to the larger acceleration/deceleration duration to achieve a smooth corner trajectory. However, the geometry of the corner path was not error-controlled. Sun et al. [5] used FIR to design motion profiles of position and orientation segments, and controlled the blending duration by smoothing errors. However, since the corner path is indirectly determined by the blending of motion profiles, its geometry varies with the kinematic conditions, which may not satisfy the requirements in precision manufacturing tasks.

To guarantee the path-invariant property of the corner trajectory, decoupled methods are preferred. It first constructs the smooth transition path by inserting parametric curves at corners, and then plans the feedrate profile for the smooth path. For the construction of the smooth position corner path, different parametric splines such as Bézier [6], B-spline [7, 8], Pythagorean-Hodograph (PH) [9] and Clothoid [10] are well presented in the literature. For the orientation path of industrial robots, the linear segment is usually represented in the parametric space based on the coordinates of the orientation, such as the Euler-angle parameterization [11], exponential-coordinates parameterization [1]. Then the smooth corner path for orientation can be constructed in a similar way as the position path. However, the three-element parameterization of orientation suffers from representation singularity which needs to be carefully addressed. For the real-time feedrate scheduling process, traditional methods take linear motion as the master motion, and the angular motion is regarded as a slave motion. The linear motion is generated under given tangential kinematics limits, and the angular motion is subsequently obtained by sharing the same curve parameter. In this case, kinematic quantities of the angular motion are not strictly satisfied. Besides, to achieve a smooth motion, the orientation path needs to be constructed curve-parameter continuous with respect to the position path, which is usually much difficult compared with constructing the geometrical continuous path.

To overcome the problem of traditional parameter-synchronization process, time-synchronization based methods are proposed recently. Huang et al. [12] proposed a real-time feedrate scheduling method for five-axis machine tools. The linear segment and orientation segment are planned by a jerk-limited motion profile and then synchronized with the analytical time-synchronization profiles. To keep the continuity of velocity profiles, a modified backward and forward scanning process was proposed. However, since the boundary velocity of the new time-synchronization profile might change, the proposed method might still fail as shown in this paper. A reimplementation of the scanning process might solve this problem. Huang et al. [13] presented the time-synchronization method based on the polynomial time law to achieve continuous jerk profile for five-axis machine tools, in which a similar bi-directional scanning process was proposed.

In this paper, the time-synchronization-based feedrate scheduling method is extended for the generation of smooth corner trajectory for industrial robots. The smooth error-controlled corner path is firstly constructed by introducing the G^2-continuous cubic B-splines for position and quaternion B-splines for orientation. Then a new time-synchronization procedure without changing the boundary velocities of the motion profile is proposed. The proposed method is able to plan jerk-limited time-synchronized motion profiles with a high computation efficiency, and generate corner trajectory sequentially without the need of backward and forward scanning process. The tangential linear and angular kinematic limits of corner trajectory in Cartesian space are strictly respected. The effectiveness of the proposed method is validated through simulation experiments.

The remainder of this paper is as follows. Section 2 presents the procedures for the corner (local) smoothing method. Section 3 elaborates the details of the proposed real-time feedrate scheduling process based on the new time-synchronization algorithm. Section 4 validates the correctness and effectiveness of the proposed method through simulation experiments. Conclusions are given in Sect. 5.

2 Local Path Smoothing

In robot controllers, path commands are usually defined by discrete points $\{\mathbf{p}_i, \mathbf{Q}_i\}$, where $\mathbf{p}_i$, $\mathbf{Q}_i$ denote the targeted position and quaternion of the tool, respectively. To generate smooth motion with continuous acceleration, the linear path segments defined by two consecutive discrete points could be locally smoothed to achieve at least G^2-continuous. To this end, the cubic B-spline proposed in [8] for position linear segments is adopted. For the orientation path, to avoid the problem of representation singularity of orientation, the unit quaternion is adopted and the quaternion B-spline is introduced.

2.1 Position Path Smoothing

Without loss of any generality, three consecutive points $\mathbf{p}_i$, $i = 1, 2, 3$ are used to show the construction process of G^2-continuous cubic B-spline for position path. The knot vector of B-spline is $[0,0,0,0,0.5,1,1,1,1]$. The inserted B-spline is represented by

$$C(u) = \Sigma_{i=0}^{4} N_{i,3}(u)\mathbf{B}_i, u \in [0, 1] \tag{1}$$

where $\mathbf{B}_i$ is the control point, $N_{i,3}$ is B-spline basis which can be evaluated by the deBoor-Cox algorithm. As shown in Fig. 1, the control points are constructed as [8]

$$\begin{cases} \mathbf{B}_0 = \mathbf{p}_2 - d_0(1 + c)\mathbf{t}_1, \mathbf{B}_1 = \mathbf{p}_2 - d_0\mathbf{t}_1, \mathbf{B}_2 = \mathbf{p}_2 \\ \mathbf{B}_3 = \mathbf{p}_2 + d_0\mathbf{t}_2, \mathbf{B}_4 = \mathbf{p}_2 + d_0(1+c)\mathbf{t}_2 \end{cases} \tag{2}$$

where d_0 is the character length, $d_1 = cd_0$, c is a positive constant defined by the users, $\mathbf{t}_1$ and $\mathbf{t}_2$ are the unit vectors along the line $\mathbf{p}_1\mathbf{p}_2$ and $\mathbf{p}_2\mathbf{p}_3$. To satisfy the smoothing error limit ε_{pm} and avoid self-intersection of inserted splines, the character length is determined as [7]

$$d_0 = \min\left\{\frac{l_1}{2(1 + c)}, \frac{l_2}{2(1 + c)}, \frac{2\varepsilon_{pm}}{\cos(\beta/2)}\right\} \tag{3}$$

where $l_1 = \|\mathbf{p}_1\mathbf{p}_2\|$, $l_2 = \|\mathbf{p}_2\mathbf{p}_3\|$, β is the angle formed by line $\mathbf{p}_2\mathbf{p}_1$ and $\mathbf{p}_2\mathbf{p}_3$.

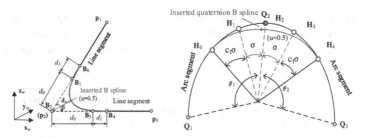

Fig. 1. Schematic of the inserted smooth spline for position and orientation path

2.2 Orientation Path Smoothing Based on Quaternion B-spline

The orientation linear segment is represented by the great arc which connects two consecutive points on the quaternion sphere. The mathematical introduction of quaternion can be found in [14]. As shown in Fig. 1, the great arc from $\mathbf{Q}_1$ to $\mathbf{Q}_2$ is calculated by spherical linear interpolation as

$$\mathbf{q}_{c,0}(u) = \mathbf{Q}_1\left(\mathbf{Q}_1^{-1}\mathbf{Q}_2\right)^u, u \in [0, 1] \tag{4}$$

And the great arc $\mathbf{q}_{c,1}(u)$ from $\mathbf{Q}_2$ to $\mathbf{Q}_3$ is calculated similarly.

To smooth the G^0-continuous arc segments, the cubic quaternion B-spline is inserted at the corner. The algebraic construction of the unit quaternion spline proposed in [15] is used. The knot vector of the B-spline is the same as the position B-spline. The inserted quaternion B-spline is represented as

$$\mathbf{q}_B(u) = \mathbf{H}_0 \prod_{i=1}^{4}\left(\mathbf{H}_{i-1}^{-1}\mathbf{H}_i\right)^{\tilde{N}_i(u)}, u \in [0, 1] \tag{5}$$

where $\mathbf{H}_i$ is the control point and $\tilde{N}_i(u) = \sum_{j=i}^{4} N_{j,3}(u)$ is the cumulative B-spline basis.

To guarantee the G^2 continuity, the control points $\mathbf{H}_0$, $\mathbf{H}_1$ lie on the great arc $\mathbf{q}_{c,0}$, and $\mathbf{H}_3$, $\mathbf{H}_4$ lie on $\mathbf{q}_{c,1}$ and $\mathbf{H}_2$ coincides with $\mathbf{Q}_2$ and the quaternion B-spline is constructed to be symmetrical by

$$\begin{cases} \mathbf{H}_0 = \mathbf{Q}_2\left(\mathbf{Q}_2^{-1}\mathbf{Q}_1\right)^{(1+c_1)\sigma/\theta_1}, \mathbf{H}_1 = \mathbf{Q}_2\left(\mathbf{Q}_2^{-1}\mathbf{Q}_1\right)^{\sigma/\theta_1}, \mathbf{H}_2 = \mathbf{Q}_2 \\ \mathbf{H}_3 = \mathbf{Q}_2\left(\mathbf{Q}_2^{-1}\mathbf{Q}_3\right)^{\sigma/\theta_2}, \mathbf{H}_4 = \mathbf{Q}_2\left(\mathbf{Q}_2^{-1}\mathbf{Q}_3\right)^{(1+c_1)\sigma/\theta_2} \end{cases} \tag{6}$$

where σ is the character parameter, c_1 is a positive constant defined by users, $\theta_1 = \arccos(\mathbf{Q}_1^T\mathbf{Q}_2)$, $\theta_2 = \arccos(\mathbf{Q}_2^T\mathbf{Q}_3)$ are the central angles of $\mathbf{q}_{c,0}$ and $\mathbf{q}_{c,1}$. In this paper, c_1 and c are set 0.25 for simulation.

To limit the orientation smoothing error, the distance ε between the corner point $\mathbf{Q}_2$ and center of the inserted quaternion B-spline is evaluated as

$$\cos\varepsilon = \mathbf{Q}_2^T\mathbf{q}_B(0.5) = \cos^2(\sigma/4) - \sin^2(\sigma/4)\mathbf{n}_1^T\mathbf{n}_2 \tag{7}$$

where $\mathbf{n}_1$ and $\mathbf{n}_2$ are the unit rotation vectors obtained from $\mathbf{Q}_2^{-1}\mathbf{Q}_1$ and $\mathbf{Q}_2^{-1}\mathbf{Q}_3$, respectively. Given orientation smooth error limit ε_{om} in task space, and to avoid self-intersection of the quaternion B-splines, according to Eq. (7), the character parameter is finally given as

$$\sigma = \min\left\{\frac{\theta_1}{2(1+c_1)}, \frac{\theta_2}{2(1+c_1)}, 4\arccos\sqrt{\frac{\left(\cos\left(\frac{\varepsilon_{om}}{2}\right)+\mathbf{n}_1^T\mathbf{n}_2\right)}{1+\mathbf{n}_1^T\mathbf{n}_2}}\right\} \tag{8}$$

3 Time-Synchronization Based Real-Time Feedrate Scheduling

A new real-time feedrate scheduling scheme based on time synchronization is presented in this section. The main steps are: 1) by dividing the smooth path into a sequence of blocks, the jerk-limited S-shape motion profile is used to separately plan the position and orientation trajectory under specified boundary conditions; 2) then the motion durations of the position and orientation profiles for each block are sequentially synchronized using an improved time-synchronization process.

3.1 Jerk-Limited Profile Generation for the Block

As shown in Fig. 2, the smoothed path for position and orientation is divided into a sequence of blocks by the centers of the inserted splines where the curvature extrema occur. These points are denoted as $\mathbf{p}'_i$ for position path and $\mathbf{Q}'_i$ for quaternion path. Each block consists of mixed splines and the remaining linear segment and is then planned by the jerk-limited S-shaped motion profile shown in Fig. 3. The tangential kinematic constraints are set symmetrical, and the null acceleration boundary condition is adopted for simplicity. The details of the jerk-limited motion profile can be found in [12].

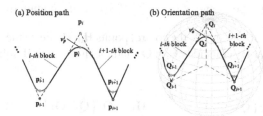

Fig. 2. Schematic of the blocks for the smoothed position and orientation path

To determine the motion profile, the arc length and boundary velocities of each block should be determined first. For the position path, the arc length for the B-spline is calculated by an adaptive numerical integration method [3]. By considering the kinematic limits, the boundary velocity for each position block is given as

$$v_p^i = \min\left\{v_m, \sqrt{a_{p,m}^n\rho_{mi}}, v_{r,p}^i\right\} \tag{9}$$

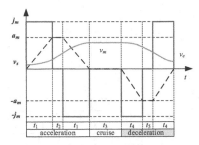

Fig. 3. Jerk-limited piecewise polynomial motion profile [12]

where v_m and $a_{p,m}^n$ are the maximum velocity and normal acceleration for the position path, ρ_{mi} is the curvature radius at $\mathbf{p}'_i$. $v_{r,p}^i$ depends on the path lengths of the consecutive blocks. The derivation of $v_{r,p}^i$ will be described in Sect. 3.2.

For orientation path, the arc length for quaternion curve is calculated similarly by regarding quaternion curve as a curve in R^4. For the quaternion B-spline, its arc length is evaluated by the numerical integration method same as the position B-spline. Considering the normal angular kinematic limit, the boundary velocity for the quaternion block is determined as

$$v_o^i = min\left\{\omega/2, \sqrt{(a_{m,o}^n/2)\Big/\sqrt{\left\|q_{B,ss}^i\right\|^2 - 1}}, v_{r,o}^i\right\} \tag{10}$$

where ω_m is the maximum angular velocity, $a_{m,o}^n$ is the maximum normal angular acceleration, $\mathbf{q}_{B,ss}^i$ is the second order derivative of the quaternion B-spline w.r.t. its arc-length parameter at $\mathbf{Q}'_i$. $v_{r,o}^i$ depends on the path lengths for quaternion blocks.

After obtaining boundary velocities and motion distance for each block and giving the tangential velocity, acceleration and jerk limits, the motion profile for each block can be determined using the well established method in [16].

3.2 Time Synchronization

Since the motion profiles for each block pair are planned separately, the motion profiles must be time synchronized. In [12], a time synchronization algorithm is proposed to extend the jerk-limited S-shaped profile to any longer motion duration. But the boundary velocity of the new motion profile might change, resulting in a modified bi-directional scanning process to achieve the continuity of the feedrate profile. However, the proposed scanning process might fail as shown in the simulation. In this paper, a new time synchronization process without changing the boundary velocities is presented as shown in Fig. 4.

Without loss of generality, assume the original motion profile with $v_s < v_e$, denoted as A_0 in Fig. 4(a). A_0 consists of acceleration (ACC), cruise (CRU), and deceleration (DEC) phase. Let v_s, v_e, v_m, s and T denote the start velocity, end velocity, reachable velocity, motion distance and duration, respectively. Denote the profile for the

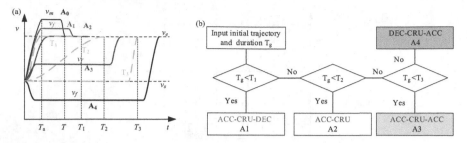

Fig. 4. Schematic of the motion profiles (a) and the flowchart (b) of the proposed time synchronization algorithm

ACC phase as $f(t, v_s, v_m, T_a, s_a)$, where T_a and s_a are the ACC duration and distance. Denote T_d, T_c as the duration for DEC and CRU phases. Then, the profile for DEC phase is $f(T - t, v_e, v_m, T_d, s_d)$. Now A_0 needs to be synchronized to a longer duration $T_g (T_g > T)$ using the profiles A_1–A_4. The cases for A_1 and A_2 are the same as [12] and will be presented for the completeness of the proposed method. The whole procedure is shown in Fig. 4(b) and the details are as follows:

Step 1: Determine the time constant $T_1 = (s + (v_e - v_s)T_a/2)/v_e$ of profile T_1. If $T_g < T_1$, stretch A_0 by an ACC-CRU-DEC profile A_1 which holds the durations of the ACC and DEC phases, and extend the duration for CRU phase to $T_g - T_a - T_d$. The velocity during the CRU phase decreases to $v_f = (T_c + (T_a + T_d)/2)v_m / (T_g - (T_a + T_d)/2)$. Update the ACC and DEC profile analytically [12]; else, go to **Step 2**.

Step 2: Determine duration threshold $T_2 = 2s/(v_s + v_e)$ of profile T_2. If $T_g < T_2$, synchronize A_0 with an ACC-CRU profile A_2. Hold the velocity during the CRU phase and extend the duration of the ACC phase to $T_l = 2(v_e T_g - s)/(v_e - v_s)$. The ACC profile is constructed analytically [12]; else, go to **Step 3**.

Step 3: Determine the profile $f_0(t, v_s, v_e, T_0, s_0)$ for the ACC phase of profile T_3 which transits the velocity from v_s to v_e. Then determine duration threshold $T_3 = T_0 + (s - s_0)/v_s$. If $T_g < T_3$, go to **Step 4**; else, go to **Step 5**.

Step 4: Synchronize A_0 with an ACC-CRU-ACC profile A_3. Calculate v_f and duration T_c for CRU phase, speed profiles $g_s(t), g_e(t)$ for the first ACC phase and the second ACC phase using the bisection method by setting the search range as $v_f \in [v_s, v_e]$.

Step 5: Synchronize A_0 with a DEC-CRU-ACC profile A_4. Then calculate v_f and duration T_c for CRU phase, speed profiles $g_s(t), g_e(t)$ for the DEC phase and the ACC phase using the bisection method. The search range $v_f \in [0, v_s]$.

To guarantee the motion profile of A_4 can be extended to any longer duration, the compatible condition $s - s_s - s_e \geq 0$ should be satisfied, where s_s and s_e are the motion distance for $g_s(t)$ and $g_e(t)$. In this case, if v_f approaches zero, the duration for CRU phase can approach infinite. The motion duration of A_4 profile can be assigned with any value within the interval $[T_3, +\infty)$. Then the bisection method can always find a feasible solution. To satisfy the compatible condition, the upper bound of the boundary velocities of the profile could be determined according to Eq. (11)

$$\tilde{h}(v_r) = \max_{v \in [0, v_r]} h(v, v_r) \leq 0.5s \tag{11}$$

where $h(v, v_r)$ denotes the transition distance when the velocity transits from v to v_r. For the profile in Fig. 3, by direct derivation, $\tilde{h}(v_r)$ can be analytically calculated by

$$\tilde{h}(v_r) = \begin{cases} \sqrt{32v_r^3/27j_m}, & v_r \in [0, 3a_m^2/2j_m) \\ (v_r + a_m^2/(2j_m))^2/2a_m, & v_r \in [3a_m^2/2j_m, +\infty) \end{cases} \quad (12)$$

where a_m and j_m are the tangential acceleration and jerk limits, respectively.

Denote $\tilde{v}_r$ as the upper bound of the velocity satisfying Eq. (11). Denote $L_d = 0.5s$, $L_{cr} = 2a_m^3/j_m^2$. According to Eq. (12), $\tilde{v}_r$ is given by

$$\tilde{v}_r(L_d) = \begin{cases} \sqrt[3]{27L_d^2 j_m/32}, & L_d \in [0, L_{cr}) \\ \sqrt{2a_m L_d} - a_m^2/(2j_m)), & L_d \in [L_{cr}, +\infty) \end{cases} \quad (13)$$

Since the boundary velocity is shared by two adjacent blocks shown in Fig. 2, the velocity $v_{r,p}^i$ in Eq. (9) can be determined as

$$v_{r,p}^i = \min\{\tilde{v}_{r,p}(0.5s_i), \tilde{v}_{r,p}(0.5s_{i+1})\} \quad (14)$$

where $\tilde{v}_{r,p}(s_i)$ is the estimated velocity using Eq. (13) under the length s_i and the tangential kinematic limits for the i-th position block. For the quaternion blocks, the $v_{r,o}^i$ can be determined similarly.

Since the boundary velocities of the profiles hold after the time synchronization, the motion profile for the whole smoothed path can be planned sequentially from the first block to the last block while respecting the continuity of the velocity at block junctions.

Based on the above descriptions, the whole procedure for the proposed method can be given as: 1) construct the smoothing corner paths using the method in Sect. 2; 2) plan the jerk-limited profile for the position and orientation block separately; 3) synchronize the motion profiles in each block pair using the procedure in Fig. 4(b); 4) generate motion commands based on the well-established spline interpolation method.

4 Simulation Validation

In this section, the correctness and effectiveness of the proposed corner trajectory planning method is verified by the comprehensive numerical simulations. All the algorithms are implemented in C + + on a desktop computer with an Intel Xeon E-2236 CPU of 3.4 GHz and 32 G RAM.

As shown in Fig. 5, the four-point path with two corners are adopted. The original paths are smoothed by using the method in Sect. 2. The smoothing error limits are $\varepsilon_{pm} = 0.5$ mm, and $\varepsilon_{om} = 0.01$ deg, respectively. Figure 5(b)-(c) show the smoothed path for the position and orientation. The orientation path is visualized by the trace of the vector $[0,0,1]7$ rotated by the quaternion curve. Figure 5(d) presents the smoothing error at the corners. From Fig. 5 (b)–(d), it can be seen that the position and orientation paths are smoothly transited at corners under the given smoothing error limits.

The smoothed path consists of three blocks subdivided by the centers of the inserted splines. The motion profiles of the position and quaternion blocks are planned simultaneously using the method in Sect. 3. The parameters are as follows: the tangential velocity, acceleration and jerk limits for position block are $v_{mp} = 30$ mm/s, $a_{mp} = 200$ mm/s^2, $j_{mp} = 1000$ mm/s^3; the tangential angular velocity, acceleration and jerk limits are $\omega_m = 15$ deg/s, $a_{mo} = 200$ deg/s^2, $j_{mo} = 1000$ deg/s^3. The half of them gives the tangential kinematic limits for quaternion blocks; the normal acceleration limits are the same as the tangential limits and the sampling period is 1 ms. After determining the boundary conditions for each block pair, the jerk-limited motion profiles for three block pairs are evaluated. The motion durations for the position blocks are 0.543 s, 1.352 s, and 0.441 s, respectively, and for quaternion blocks they are 0.410 s, 0.304 s, and 0.436 s, respectively. Then the motion durations of the three quaternion blocks are synchronized according to durations of the position blocks in this case.

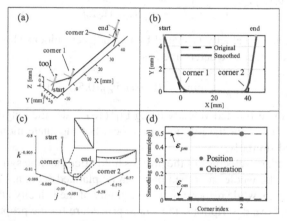

Fig. 5. The smoothing results. (a) The four-point path; (b) Smoothed position path; (c) Smoothed orientation path visualized by the trace of a vector; (d) The smoothing errors at the corners.

The velocity profiles of the proposed method are shown in Fig. 6(a). The blocks in each pair share the same motion duration. The DEC-CRU-ACC motion profile of type A4 is adopted to extend the duration of the second quaternion block. To show the advantage of the proposed method, the SLATP method proposed in [12] is compared with. SLATP establishes the compatibility constraint for the boundary velocity in a different way and uses a bi-directional scanning process with time synchronization to plan the motion profiles. The SLATP is implemented based on the source code provided in [12] and the result is presented in Fig. 6(b). SLATP fails to guarantee the continuity of the linear velocity at the junction between the second and third blocks during the forward scanning process. This is because the SLATP uses a DEC-CRU profile to extend the duration of the second quaternion block, resulting in a smaller start velocity of the third quaternion block. Then the motion duration of the third quaternion block dominates, and the motion profile of the third position block decreases the start velocity to extend the duration. It can be expected that the motion accuracy of robot for the SLATP in this case would decrease. Besides, the total motion duration of SLATP increases to 2.401 s while the proposed method is 2.336 s for this case.

Figure 7 shows the tangential kinematic profiles for the position and orientation. Since the linear and angular profiles are planned separately, the tangential linear/angular

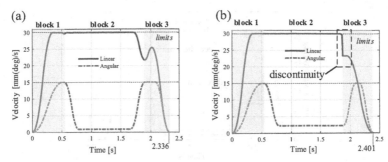

Fig. 6. The linear and angular velocity profiles using (a) the proposed method and (b) the SLATP [12]. The proposed method achieves smooth velocity profiles, while SLATP fails at junction between block 2 and 3.

velocity, acceleration and jerk limits are strictly respected. To show the advantage of the proposed method in aspect of simultaneously satisfying linear and angular kinematic constraints, the traditional parameter-synchronization-based method is performed. The traditional method usually plans the linear motion first, then obtains the angular motion by sharing the same curve parameter. The angular velocity profiles with the proposed method and the traditional method are presented in Fig. 8. One can observe that the angular velocity limit is violated for the traditional method. Besides, the angular velocity profile is not continuous at the junctions between the linear segment and the spline segment. The reason is that the smoothed path is only guaranteed to be geometric continuous in Sect. 2, and a further reparametrization process is needed to guarantee the curve-parameter continuity of the smoothed path as shown in our previous work [1]. This reparametrization process is usually difficult. The proposed method based on time synchronization does not require this treatment.

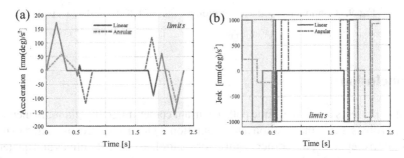

Fig. 7. The tangential linear/angular acceleration and jerk profiles in Cartesian space

To show the real-time scheduling ability of the proposed method, the computation time for the test path with three blocks is summarized. The computation times for the local path smoothing and feedrate scheduling processes are 10 ms, 0.064 ms, respectively. This demonstrates that the proposed feedrate scheduling process is able to be applied in real time for robot controllers. Last, the tested path is executed by a 6-axis Universal Robots UR 10, the interpolated robot commands are used to generate the joint trajectory

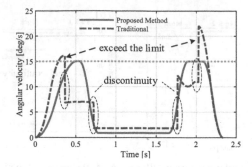

Fig. 8. Compared with the traditional parameter-synchronization method

using inverse kinematics. The joint accelerations of the generated joint trajectory are evaluated and shown in Fig. 9. The accelerations for all the joints are continuous, which further validates the effectiveness of the proposed method.

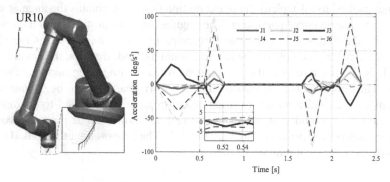

Fig. 9. Continuous joint acceleration profiles of UR10 for the test path

5 Conclusion

This paper presents a new real-time path-invariant corner trajectory planning method for industrial robots. First, the position and orientation segments are reconstructed to be G^2-continuous by replacing the corners with error-controlled cubic B-splines and quaternion B-splines, respectively. The smoothed paths are then subdivided into numerous pairs of blocks. The blocks in each pair are planned separately with the jerk-limited S-shaped motion profile and synchronized with the proposed new time-synchronization procedure. The motion profiles for all the blocks can be generated sequentially by applying the proposed method from the first to the end block pair, with the continuity of velocity profiles always guaranteed. Since the linear and angular trajectories are planned separately, the tangential linear and angular kinematic constraints up to jerk are strictly satisfied in Cartesian space. For the four-point path with three block pairs, the computation time of the feedrate scheduling process is about 64 μs, which demonstrates its potential in real-time implementation. The effectiveness of the proposed method is verified by numerical experiments.

The proposed method could be extended to other applications such as real-time planning corner trajectories for mixed line-arc segments and multi-robot synchronization motion planning. In the present work, the tangential kinematic constraints in Cartesian space are respected. The consideration of other complex constraints such as joint torque and joint kinematic limits is of interest in the future work.

References

1. Peng, J., Huang, P., Ding, Y., Ding, H.: An analytical method for decoupled local smoothing of linear paths in industrial robots. Robot. Comput.-Integr. Manuf. **72**, 102193 (2021). https://doi.org/10.1016/j.rcim.2021.102193

2. Tajima, S., Sencer, B.: Accurate real-time interpolation of 5-axis tool-paths with local corner smoothing. Int. J. Mach. Tools Manuf. **142**, 1–15 (2019). https://doi.org/10.1016/j.ijmachtools.2019.04.005

3. Tulsyan, S., Altintas, Y.: Local toolpath smoothing for five-axis machine tools. Int. J. Mach. Tools Manuf. **96**, 15–26 (2015). https://doi.org/10.1016/j.ijmachtools.2015.04.014

4. Grassmann, R.M., Burgner-Kahrs, J.: Quaternion-based smooth trajectory generator for Via poses in SE(3) considering kinematic limits in Cartesian space. IEEE Robot. Autom. Lett. **4**, 4192–4199 (2019). https://doi.org/10.1109/LRA.2019.2931133

5. Sun, H., Yang, J., Li, D., Ding, H.: An on-line tool path smoothing algorithm for 6R robot manipulator with geometric and dynamic constraints. Sci. China Technol. Sci. **64**, 1907–1919 (2021)

6. Bi, Q., Wang, Y., Zhu, L., Ding, H.: A practical continuous-curvature Bézier transition algorithm for high-speed machining of linear tool path. In: Jeschke, S., Liu, H., Schilberg, D. (eds.) ICIRA 2011. LNCS (LNAI), vol. 7102, pp. 465–476. Springer, Heidelberg (2011). https://doi.org/10.1007/978-3-642-25489-5_45

7. Huang, J., Du, X., Zhu, L.-M.: Real-time local smoothing for five-axis linear toolpath considering smoothing error constraints. Int. J. Mach. Tools Manuf. **124**, 67–79 (2018)

8. Zhao, H., Zhu, L., Ding, H.: A real-time look-ahead interpolation methodology with curvature continuous B-spline transition scheme for CNC machining of short line segments. Int. J. Mach. Tools Manuf. **65**, 88–98 (2013). https://doi.org/10.1016/j.ijmachtools.2012.10.005

9. Hu, Q., Chen, Y., Jin, X., Yang, J.: A real-time C3 continuous local corner smoothing and interpolation algorithm for CNC machine tools. J. Manuf. Sci. Eng. **141**, 041004 (2019)

10. Xiao, Q.-B., Wan, M., Liu, Y., Qin, X.-B., Zhang, W.-H.: Space corner smoothing of CNC machine tools through developing 3D general Clothoid. Robot. Comput.-Integr. Manuf. **64**, 101949 (2020)

11. Yang, J., Li, D., Ye, C., Ding, H.: An analytical C3 continuous tool path corner smoothing algorithm for 6R robot manipulator. Robot. Comput.-Integr. Manuf. **64**, 101947 (2020)

12. Huang, J., Lu, Y., Zhu, L.-M.: Real-time feedrate scheduling for five-axis machining by simultaneously planning linear and angular trajectories. Int. J. Mach. Tools Manuf. **135**, 78–96 (2018). https://doi.org/10.1016/j.ijmachtools.2018.08.006

13. Huang, X., Zhao, F., Tao, T., Mei, X.: A novel local smoothing method for five-axis machining with time-synchronization Feedrate scheduling. IEEE Access **8**, 89185–89204 (2020). https://doi.org/10.1109/ACCESS.2020.2992022

14. Dam, E.B., Koch, M., Lillholm, M.: Quaternions, Interpolation and Animation. Datalogisk Institut, Københavns Universitet, Copenhagen (1998)

334   J. Peng et al.

15. Kim, M.-J., Kim, M.-S., Shin, S.Y.: A general construction scheme for unit quaternion curves with simple high order derivatives. In: Proceedings of the 22nd Annual Conference on Computer Graphics and Interactive Techniques - SIGGRAPH '95, pp. 369–376. ACM Press (1995). https://doi.org/10.1145/218380.218486
16. Lin, M.-T., Tsai, M.-S., Yau, H.-T.: Development of a dynamics-based NURBS interpolator with real-time look-ahead algorithm. Int. J. Mach. Tools Manuf. **47**, 2246–2262 (2007)

Admittance Control for Robot Polishing Force Tracking Based on Reinforcement Learning

Zhouyi Zheng[1], Yu Wang[1], Chen Chen[2(✉)], Zhitao Gao[1], Fangyu Peng[1], and Rong Yan[1]

[1] School of Mechanical Science and Engineering, Huazhong University of Science and Technology, Wuhan, China
[2] Hubei Key Laboratory of Mechanical Transmission and Manufacturing Engineering, Wuhan University of Science and Technology, Wuhan, China
`chenchen_1014@foxmail.com`

Abstract. To achieve a stable interaction between the robot and the environment, stable force control of the robot is required. In this paper, a position-based impedance adaptive controller is proposed. The proposed method tracks the expected contact force based on estimating the parameters of the environment. Within this framework, we analyze environmental parameter estimation, introduce an adaptive algorithm based on reinforcement learning to adjust control parameters, and verify the stability of the system based on the Routh criterion and Lyapunov equation. The collaborative robot for workpieces with different surfaces is used for polishing. The controller is constructed to adjust the reference trajectory and use reinforcement learning training to adaptively adjust the control parameters to reduce the force error. Polishing experiments were carried out on the UR16e robot, and constant force control was carried out on beveled and curved workpieces. The proposed method improved the tracking accuracy of the robot polishing task.

Keywords: Environmental estimation · Steady-state force tracking · Reinforcement learning · Adaptive control · Robot polishing

1 Introduction

Grinding and polishing can reduce the surface roughness of parts, which is very important in the field of machining. Due to its strong adaptability [1] and high safety, robot grinding and polishing have gradually replaced manual grinding. During the grinding process, the grinding-polishing force is an important factor affecting the grinding quality [2], and contact force tracking has received extensive attention due to its value in tasks that require accuracy and safety [3, 4].

Hogan [5] et al. proposed the impedance control algorithm for the first time, introduced the principle of impedance control, and divided it into admittance control and impedance control according to the control force and position. In recent years, with the rapid development of machine learning algorithms, the combination of robot admittance control and machine learning algorithms has been further developed.

© The Author(s), under exclusive license to Springer Nature Singapore Pte Ltd. 2023
H. Yang et al. (Eds.): ICIRA 2023, LNAI 14272, pp. 335–345, 2023.
https://doi.org/10.1007/978-981-99-6480-2_28

Cao et al. analyzed the transient response and steady-state error in classical control methods and proposed a dynamic adaptive hybrid impedance controller to handle dynamic contact force tracking in uncertain environments [6]. Li et al. proposed an adaptive admittance controller based on force error information to compensate admittance parameters in real-time, and introduced a fuzzy loop into the adaptive term to reduce overshoot during force tracking [7]. Luo et al. proposed an adaptive hybrid impedance control algorithm based on subsystem dynamic model design, which solved the problem of inaccurate modeling [8]. There are also some neural network (NN) control schemes [9–11] used to solve constant force tracking.

Impedance control is also gradually combined with reinforcement learning. ROVEDA and others used a combination of reinforcement learning and impedance control to realize human-robot interaction [12]. Zhao et al. proposed a model-based Actor-critic learning algorithm and safe learning strategy to find the optimal impedance control with a safe, fully automatic learning process and unknown system parameters, but for the impedance control of a single joint of the robot [13]. Zhang et al. used a model-based reinforcement learning method to quickly obtain optimal processing parameters for constant force grinding impact and force control in the processing stage [14]. Ding et al. proposed a learning algorithm for robot admittance control parameters based on reinforcement learning to obtain the admittance parameters corresponding to the optimal strategy [15]. However, they predict the contact state through a neural network or a Gaussian model, and then perform off-line reinforcement learning, and there are still deviations between prediction and simulation. At present, there are few studies on the application of reinforcement learning in robot grinding scenarios, mainly focusing on the simulation stage. However, grinding experimental scenarios with high repeatability is conducive to the application of reinforcement learning.

In this paper, by analyzing the steady-state error of the admittance controller, online estimation of environmental parameters is carried out, and the reference trajectory of robot polishing is adjusted to reduce the steady-state error of robot admittance control. An adaptive admittance controller is further proposed, which uses reinforcement learning to adjust the control parameters online.

The paper is organized as follows. Section 2 describes the modeling of the robot admittance control model. Section 3 proposes an adaptive admittance control method and proves its stability and convergence. Section 4 carries out relevant experiments and analyzed the experimental results. Conclusions are drawn in Sect. 5.

2   System Modeling and Control

2.1   Overview of Admittance Control

Most robots generally do not expose the underlying control interface and instead provide a position control mode. Mainly through external force feedback input to change the position of the inner ring while meeting the required admittance characteristics.

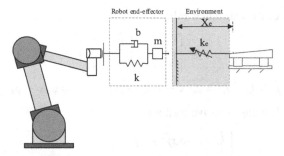

Fig. 1. Robot-environment interaction model.

As shown in Fig. 1, the end of the robot is regarded as a mass-spring-damper system for admittance control [16]. Because the admittance control in each direction is decoupled, the force in a specific axis direction is considered as admittance control, and the equation is transformed into,

$$m(\ddot{x} - \ddot{x}_d) + b(\dot{x} - \dot{x}_d) + k(x - x_d) = f_d - f_e \tag{1}$$

Assume the environment is a stiffness model, and then,

$$f_e = k_e(x - x_e) \tag{2}$$

The details are shown in [17]. The steady-state force tracking error can be expressed as

$$e_{ss} = \frac{k}{k + k_e}[f_d - k_e(x_d - x_e)] \tag{3}$$

To make the force tracking error converge to zero. One option is to set the admittance parameter k = 0. Null stiffness is unreasonable. One reason is that the admittance parameter k is closely related to the natural frequency and damping ratio of the linear second-order system. Since it is a position-controlled robot, it is assumed that the position control is accurate and the following conditions are met:

$$x_d = x_e - \frac{f_d}{k_e} \tag{4}$$

It can ensure that the steady-state force error between the robot with the environment is zero. To reduce the steady-state error of the contact force, it is necessary to know the location and stiffness of the environment. The following section will describe a method for estimating environmental parameters.

2.2 Reference Trajectory Adaptive Adjustment

Estimation in detail using the Lyapunov method,

$$\begin{cases} f_e = k_e(x - x_e) = k_e x - k_e x_e = k_e x - k_x \\ \hat{f}_e = \hat{k}_e(x - \hat{x}_e) = \hat{k}_e x - \hat{k}_e \hat{x}_e = \hat{k}_e x - \hat{k}_x \end{cases} \tag{5}$$

As time $t \to \infty$, the estimated value $\hat{f}_e \to f$,

$$\varphi = \begin{bmatrix} \varphi_e \\ \varphi_x \end{bmatrix} = \begin{bmatrix} \hat{k}_e - k_e \\ \hat{k}_x - k_x \end{bmatrix} \tag{6}$$

$$\tilde{f} = \hat{f}_e - f_e = \hat{k}_e(x - \hat{x}_e) - k_e(x - x_e) = \varphi_e x - \varphi_x \tag{7}$$

Propose the following iterative formula,

$$\begin{cases} \dot{\hat{k}}_e = -\alpha x \tilde{f} + \gamma \tilde{f} \\ \dot{\hat{x}}_e = \frac{\tilde{f}}{\hat{k}_e}(\alpha x \hat{x}_e + \beta - \gamma x - \gamma \hat{x}_e) \end{cases} \tag{8}$$

Among them $\alpha > 0$, $\beta > 0$ and $\alpha\beta < \gamma^2$.

The stability of the method proposed above is proved by selecting a positive definite Lyapunov function,

$$V = \frac{1}{2}(\beta\varphi_e^2 - 2\gamma\varphi_e\varphi_x + \alpha\varphi_x^2) \tag{9}$$

Substituting the updated law of control into the above formula, we can obtain,

$$\begin{aligned} \dot{V} &= \beta\varphi_e\dot{\varphi}_e - 2\gamma\varphi_e\dot{\varphi}_x - 2\gamma\dot{\varphi}_e\varphi_x + \alpha\dot{\varphi}_x\varphi_x \\ &= \alpha\beta\tilde{f}(\varphi_x - \varphi_e x) - \gamma^2(\varphi_x - \varphi_e x) \\ &= -(\alpha\beta - \gamma^2)\tilde{f}^2 \end{aligned} \tag{10}$$

Equation (10) is negative definite. According to Lyapunov's second method, the system can be stable.

Solving by numerical integral formula, $\hat{k}_e$ and $\hat{x}_e$ can be obtained.

$$\begin{cases} \hat{k}_e(t) = k_e(0) - \int_0^t (\alpha x + \gamma)\tilde{f} \, dt \\ \hat{x}_e(t) = x_e(0) + \int_0^t \frac{\tilde{f}}{\hat{k}_e}(\alpha x \hat{x}_e + \beta - \gamma x - \gamma \hat{x}_e) dt \end{cases} \tag{11}$$

Considering that many environments are not flat, add the compensation item of the environment. $\dot{x}_{contour}$ is the offline trajectory normal velocity generated by the CAD model or the point cloud.

$$\begin{cases} \hat{k}_e(t) = k_e(0) - \int_0^t (\alpha x + \gamma)\tilde{f} \, dt \\ \hat{x}_e(t) = x_e(0) + \int_0^t \frac{\tilde{f}}{\hat{k}_e}(\alpha x \hat{x}_e + \beta - \gamma x - \gamma \hat{x}_e + \dot{x}_{contour}) dt \end{cases} \tag{12}$$

It is guaranteed that the reference trajectory can be adjusted adaptively and the actual force converges to the expected force.

3   Control Algorithm

3.1   Control Algorithm and Stability Proof

There is no force closed-loop feedback for the robot admittance control. Consequently, PI control is added to constant admittance control. The following is the stability and convergence of the adaptive admittance control.

$$m\Delta\ddot{x} + b\Delta\dot{x} + k\Delta x = \Delta f + k_p\Delta f + k_i \int \Delta f \tag{13}$$

Suppose that the environment is a stiffness model, then

$$f_e = k_e(x - x_e) = k_e e(t) \tag{14}$$

Because k_e in polishing is so large and has small changes, so consider k_e as time-invariant. Then, we can obtain.

$$e(t) = \frac{f_e}{k_e}, \ \dot{e}(t) = \frac{\dot{f}_e}{k_e}, \ \ddot{e}(t) = \frac{\ddot{f}_e}{k_e} \tag{15}$$

Considering the uncertainty of the environmental location, we use the estimation of the environmental location $\hat{x}_e$ instead of x_e. $\hat{e}$ will replace e in (12) yielding

$$\begin{cases} m\ddot{\hat{e}} + b\dot{\hat{e}} + k\hat{e} = \Delta f + k_p \Delta f + k_i \int \Delta f \\ \delta x_e = \hat{x}_e - x_e \\ \hat{e} = e - \delta x_e \end{cases} \tag{16}$$

The stability and convergence of the adaptive control law are proved as follows. Substituting (1) and (2) into (3), we can obtain

$$\begin{aligned} & m(\ddot{f}_d - \ddot{f}_e) + k(\dot{f}_d - \dot{f}_e) + k(f_d - f_e) + k_e(f_d - f_e) \\ & + k_p k_e(f_d - f_e) + k_i k_e \int (f_d - f_e)dt \\ & = m\ddot{f}_d + b\dot{f}_d + kf_d - mk_e\delta\ddot{x}_e - bk_e\delta\dot{x}_e - kk_e\delta x_e \\ & = m(\ddot{f}_d - \ddot{f}) + b(\dot{f}_d - \dot{f}_e) + k(f_d - f_e) \end{aligned} \tag{17}$$

Let $\varepsilon = f_d - f_e, \xi = f_d - \hat{f}_e$, take Laplace transformation, it will be

$$\begin{aligned} & m\varepsilon(s)s^2 + b\varepsilon(s)s + k\varepsilon(s) + k_e\varepsilon(s) + k_p k_e\varepsilon(s) + k_i k_e\varepsilon(s)/s \\ & = m\xi(s)s^2 + b\xi(s)s + k\xi(s) \end{aligned} \tag{18}$$

$$\frac{\varepsilon(s)}{\xi(s)} = \frac{ms^3 + bs^2 + ks}{ms^3 + bs^2 + ks + k_e s + k_p k_e s + k_i k_e} \tag{19}$$

For stability, using Routh–Hurwitz array, we can obtain,

$$\begin{array}{lll} s^3 & m & k_e + k + k_p k_e \\ s^2 & b & k_i k_e \\ s & k_e + k + k_p k_e - \frac{mk_i k_e}{b} & 0 \\ 1 & k_i k_e & 0 \end{array} \tag{20}$$

$$k_e + k + k_p k_e - \frac{mk_i k_e}{b} > 0 \tag{21}$$

For convergence, according to the final-value theorem, the following equation can be obtained,

$$\varepsilon_s = \lim_{s \to 0} s\varepsilon(s) = \lim_{s \to 0} s\left(\frac{ms^3 + bs^2 + ks}{ms^3 + bs^2 + ks + k_e s + k_p k_e s + k_i k_e}\xi(s)\right) \tag{22}$$

When the input is a step function as $\xi(s) = \frac{1}{s}$, then

$$\varepsilon(s) = \lim_{s \to 0} s \left(\frac{ms^2 + bs + ks}{ms^3 + bs^2 + ks + k_e s + k_p k_e s + k_i k_e} \frac{1}{s} \right) = \lim_{s \to 0} \left(\frac{0}{k_i k_e} \right) = 0 \quad (23)$$

$$\lim_{s \to 0} s\varepsilon(s) = 0 \Rightarrow \lim_{s \to 0} \varepsilon(t) = 0 \quad (24)$$

Thus, as time $t \to \infty$, $f_e \to f_d$. The contact force between the robot and the environment converges with the required force, which shows that the adaptive admittance controller designed in this article is stable.

3.2   Reinforcement Learning Design

The stability of the control will be impacted by the control parameters k_i and k_p. If k_i and k_p are large, oscillations are probably to occur. If k_i, k_p is small, the force tracking error will become large. k_i, k_p need to be dynamically adjusted according to the force tracking error. Based on this, reinforcement learning is used for self-learning of P and I control parameters. The proposed method is called R-AC (reinforcement learning applied in admittance controller) in this article.

Robotic reinforcement learning is a control problem and the goal of reinforcement learning is to maximize a cumulative reward. Said problem is modeled as a Markov Decision Process. We use the state-of-the-art model-free RL method called Proximal Policy Optimization (PPO). The core idea of this method is importance sampling.

In this reinforcement learning model, the state space is $s = [\Delta f, \dot{x}]$. The real-time changing k_p, k_i are related to Δf and $\Delta \dot{f}$. Considering that the actual force measured by the force sensor often has a lot of noise, it is not advisable to directly differentiate the force error. The expected force f_d and environmental parameters in a short time can be regarded as a constant, then there is $\Delta \dot{f} = \dot{f} - \dot{f}_d = -k\dot{x}$. So, the state space can be set as $\Delta f, \dot{x}$.

The action space of reinforcement learning is $a = [k_p, k_i]$. k_p is the real-time changing proportional coefficient, k_i is the real-time changing integral coefficient. We limit the range of parameters k_p, k_i to $[0, 0.2]$, to reduce the training times of reinforcement learning, and only to verify the effectiveness and feasibility of the method.

The goal of robot training is to make error Δf between the actual contact force and the expected contact force as small as possible. Meanwhile, to make the normal speed $\dot{x}$ smaller which is used to reward and punish the amplitude of the end of robot. $\alpha_1, \alpha_2, \alpha_3, \alpha_4$ are positive constants. The reward function is

$$\text{reward} = \frac{1}{\alpha_1 + \alpha_2 \Delta f} + \frac{1}{\alpha_3 + \alpha_4 \dot{x}} \quad (25)$$

The whole adaptive control block diagram Fig. 2 is as follows,

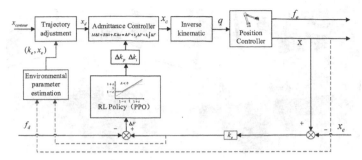

Fig. 2. Admittance control block diagram.

4 Experimental Results

In this section, a series of tests are carried out on the UR16e robot polishing experiment platform to further verify the proposed force control method. OnRobot force sensor and sander are attached at the end of the robot. The communication cycle between the force sensor and controller is 20 ms and is carried out over UDP. The processing workpieces used are beveled workpiece and curved workpiece as shown in Fig. 3.

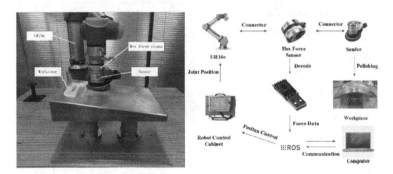

Fig. 3. Polishing experimental platform.

The experiment is conducted on different workpieces which is shown in Fig. 4.

We conducted an experimental training on a beveled workpiece, as shown in Fig. 3(a). The control parameters of the robot are $m = 100$ kg, $b = 4000N/(m/s), k = 5000$ N/m. The parameters for estimating the environmental position are $\alpha = 10, \gamma = 10, \beta = 5$. The speed of the polishing tool is 2000 rpm. The feed speed is 0.035 m/s, and the expected force is set to 20N.

The goal of training needs to satisfy the reward of reinforcement learning to converge to a steady value. As shown in Fig. 5, it is the reward after 100 times of reinforcement learning training. The parameters of PPO are shown in Table 1.

When the PPO reinforcement learning training model converges, the trained model can be directly used for constant force control of polishing. The force tracking performance of the proposed control method is tested in the following experiments.

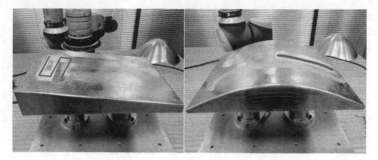

Fig. 4. (a) Beveled workpiece (b) Curved workpiece.

Table 1. The parameters of PPO.

Parameter	Value
Policy Network Learning Rate	0.0003
Value Network Learning Rate	0.0003
Batch Size	64
Max Epochs	600
Discount Factor	0.99
Cropping Rate	0.2

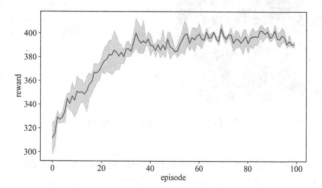

Fig. 5. Total reward value of PPO training.

The constant force in the Fig. 6 shows that there is noise, because a dynamic eccentric polishing tool is used, which inevitably produces vibration during contact, but the force of polishing is stable around the expected force.

In the first two seconds, the robot approached but did not yet contact with the workpiece. As in Fig. 6, the force tracking performance of R-AC and constant admittance control called CAC is shown.

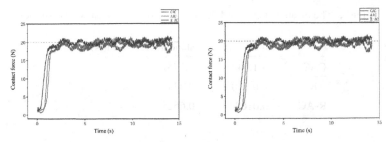

Fig. 6. Comparison of contact force (a) beveled surface; (b) curved surface.

In the case of using the traditional admittance control, the robot contacts the environment in about 2s from the free state to the contact state. The steady-state error of force tracking is large, and the value deviates from the expected contact force by 20 N. In the absence of accurate estimation of environmental parameters, only using admittance control cannot improve the tracking force error.

In the following experiment, the proposed algorithm was compared with the method proposed called AIC in the paper [17] to verify its effectiveness. The results obtained are as follows (Fig. 7).

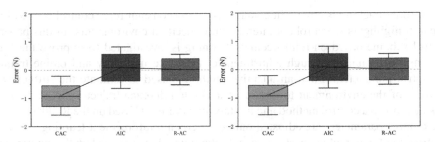

Fig. 7. Comparison of contact force error (a) beveled surface; (b) curved surface.

Table 2. The mean and standard deviation of force error on beveled surface.

	Mean(N)	standard deviation(N)
CAC	−0.6981	0.6899
AIC	0.0865	0.7366
R-AC	0.0254	0.6167

Table 3. The mean and standard deviation of force error on curved surface.

	mean(N)	standard deviation(N)
CAC	−1.0425	0.6751
AIC	−0.2209	0.7342
R-AC	0.01623	0.6625

From the figure above, the proposed method R-AC performs better in terms of standard deviation and mean compared to AIC and CAC. No matter whether on a beveled plane or a curved surface, the mean and standard deviation of the proposed method's performance are minimal (Tables 2 and 3).

In general, the proposed method improves the tracking accuracy of the contact force in the polishing process of the robot. It reduces the steady-state error of the contact force and has better stability and reliability. It can achieve the compliant processing of the robot.

5 Conclusions

Robot force tracking is crucial in contact tasks, and constant force control is one of the research highlights when robots interact with uncertain environments. In this paper, a control scheme based on reinforcement learning is investigated to improve the force tracking performance through adjustment of reference trajectory and online training of control parameters. First, an adaptive method is used to estimate the stiffness and location of the environment to obtain an accurate reference trajectory. And then this paper proposes a control method and its stability is verified based on the Routh criterion. The control parameters are adjusted online based on reinforcement learning to further improve the force tracking performance. In the future, how to speed up the convergence speed of robot reinforcement learning training and realize the strategy transfer of sim2real is an important research direction.

Acknowledgment. The work was supported by the National Natural Science Foundation of China (Grant Nos. 52105515, U20A20294 and 52188102).

References

1. Realyvásquez-Vargas, A., Arredondo-Soto, K.C., García-Alcaraz, J.L., Márquez-Lobato, B.Y., Cruz-García, J.: Introduction and configuration of a collaborative robot in an assembly task as a means to decrease occupational risks and increase efficiency in a manufacturing company. Rob. Comput.-Integr. Manuf. **57**, 315–328 (2019). https://doi.org/10.1016/j.rcim.2018.12.015
2. Brinksmeier, E., et al.: Advances in modeling and simulation of grinding processes. CIRP Ann. **55**, 667–696 (2006). https://doi.org/10.1016/j.cirp.2006.10.003

3. Han, B., Zoppi, M., Molfino, R.: Variable impedance actuation using biphasic media. Mech. Mach. Theor. **62**, 1–12 (2013). https://doi.org/10.1016/j.mechmachtheory.2012.11.001

4. Xu, Z., Li, S., Zhou, X., Cheng, T.: Dynamic neural networks based adaptive admittance control for redundant manipulators with model uncertainties. Neurocomputing **357**, 271–281 (2019). https://doi.org/10.1016/j.neucom.2019.04.069

5. Neville, H.: Impedance control: an approach to manipulation: Part I~ III. Trans. ASME J. Dyn. Syst. Measur. Control **107**, 1 (1985). https://doi.org/10.23919/ACC.1984.4788393

6. Cao, H., Chen, X., He, Y., Zhao, X.: Dynamic adaptive hybrid impedance control for dynamic contact force tracking in uncertain environments. IEEE Access **7**, 83162–83174 (2019). https://doi.org/10.1109/access.2019.2924696

7. Li, Z., Huang, H., Song, X., Xu, W., Li, B.: A fuzzy adaptive admittance controller for force tracking in an uncertain contact environment. IET Control Theor. Appl. **15**, 2158–2170 (2021). https://doi.org/10.1049/cth2.12175

8. Luo, Z., Li, J., Bai, J., Wang, Y., Liu, L.: Adaptive hybrid impedance control algorithm based on subsystem dynamics model for robot polishing. In: Yu, H., Liu, J., Liu, L., Ju, Z., Liu, Y., Zhou, D. (eds.) ICIRA 2019. LNCS (LNAI), vol. 11745, pp. 163–176. Springer, Cham (2019). https://doi.org/10.1007/978-3-030-27529-7_15

9. Hamedani, M.H., Sadeghian, H., Zekri, M., Sheikholeslam, F., Keshmiri, M.: Intelligent impedance control using wavelet neural network for dynamic contact force tracking in unknown varying environments. Control. Eng. Pract. **113**, 104840 (2021). https://doi.org/10.1016/j.conengprac.2021.104840

10. Hamedani, M.H., Zekri, M., Sheikholeslam, F., Selvaggio, M., Ficuciello, F., Siciliano, B.: Recurrent fuzzy wavelet neural network variable impedance control of robotic manipulators with fuzzy gain dynamic surface in an unknown varied environment. Fuzzy Sets Syst. **416**, 1–26 (2021). https://doi.org/10.1016/j.fss.2020.05.001

11. Rahimi, H.N., Howard, I., Cui, L.: Neural impedance adaption for assistive human–robot interaction. Neurocomputing **290**, 50–59 (2018). https://doi.org/10.1016/j.neucom.2018.02.025

12. Roveda, L., et al.: Model-based reinforcement learning variable impedance control for human-robot collaboration. J. Intell. Rob. Syst. **100**, 417–433 (2020). https://doi.org/10.1007/s10846-020-01183-3

13. Zhao, X., Han, S., Tao, B., Yin, Z., Ding, H.: Model-based actor–critic learning of robotic impedance control in complex interactive environment. IEEE Trans. Industr. Electron. **69**, 13225–13235 (2022). https://doi.org/10.1109/TIE.2021.3134082

14. Zhang, T., Xiao, M., Zou, Y., Xiao, J.: Robotic constant-force grinding control with a press-and-release model and model-based reinforcement learning. Int. J. Adv. Manuf. Technol. **106**, 589–602 (2019). https://doi.org/10.1007/s00170-019-04614-0

15. Ding, Y., Zhao, J., Min, X.: Impedance control and parameter optimization of surface polishing robot based on reinforcement learning. Proc. Inst. Mech. Eng. Part B J. Eng. Manuf. (2022). https://doi.org/10.1177/09544054221100004

16. Seraji, H., Colbaugh, R.: Force tracking in impedance control. Int. J. Rob. Res. **16**, 97–117 (1997). https://doi.org/10.1177/027836499701600107

17. Duan, J., Gan, Y., Chen, M., Dai, X.: Adaptive variable impedance control for dynamic contact force tracking in uncertain environment. Robot. Auton. Syst. **102**, 54–65 (2018). https://doi.org/10.1016/j.robot.2018.01.009

Research on the Milling Process Damping and Stability Considering Additional Vibration

Haodong Qu[1], Xiaowei Tang[1(✉)], Tao Ma[2], Fangyu Peng[1,3], Rong Yan[1], and Lei Zhang[2]

[1] School of Mechanical Science and Engineering, Huazhong University of Science and Technology, No. 1037 LuoYu Road, Wuhan, China
{m202170625,pengfy,yanrong}@hust.edu.cn, txwysxf@126.com
[2] State Key Laboratory of Smart Manufacturing for Special Vehicles and Transmission System, Baotou, China
[3] State Key Lab of Digital Manufacturing Equipment and Technology, Huazhong University of Science and Technology, No. 1037 LuoYu Road, Wuhan, China

Abstract. Chatter is a critical factor that impacts both the efficiency and quality of the milling, and the process damping can suppress its occurrence. Process damping is caused by the interference between the machined surface and the flank face of the tool, which is manifested as an effect on the damping term of the system. In this paper, a method of applying additional vibration for workpiece is proposed, and the influence of additional vibration on process damping and milling stability boundary is studied. The calculation and simulation show that the proposed chatter suppression method is reasonable, and applying appropriate additional vibration can make the milling stability boundary higher and improve the machining efficiency.

Keywords: milling · additional vibration · process damping · stability boundary

1 Introduction

Chatter is an important factor in milling process. It will reduce the cutting efficiency and cause the wear of the tool [1]. Process damping is an important condition affecting the stability boundary at low speed. In order to suppress the chatter in milling process, this paper intends to provide greater process damping force for the workpiece caused by additional vibration based on the chatter mechanism, so as to improve the stability of milling chatter.

The research on process damping indicates that the process damping in the milling process can absorb vibration energy, and the research on it mainly focuses on the calibration and its influence on stability. In terms of calibration, E. Budak et al. [2] proposed a method that can directly identify the process damping from the chatter experiment, and established a process damping model based on energy conservation. Altintas et al. [3] calibrated the dynamic ploughing force coefficient by using the sinusoidal excitation provided by the electric vibrator, while Mao et al. [4] calibrated the ploughing force

© The Author(s), under exclusive license to Springer Nature Singapore Pte Ltd. 2023
H. Yang et al. (Eds.): ICIRA 2023, LNAI 14272, pp. 346–357, 2023.
https://doi.org/10.1007/978-981-99-6480-2_29

coefficient by using the transfer function in the dynamic turning process. In the study of the influence of process damping on stability, E. Budak et al. [5] used the indentation coefficient to predict the process damping and critical cutting depth, and verified it by time domain simulation and experiment. Suzuki et al. [6] proposed a tool texture design method, and verified that the structure has sufficient damping effect by frequency domain flutter stability analysis. Yusoff et al. [7] considered the influence of different tool geometries on process damping, and the influence of variable helix/pitch angle was the most significant. The form of process damping force in the dynamic equation is its influence on the damping term of the system, which affects the stability boundary of the system. In addition to considering the process damping of the milling system itself, the external excitation method aiming at improving the stability of the system has also been studied. Muhammad et al. [8] used active damping device to reduce the vibration of milling process based on PI control with high stability and small steady-state error as control objectives. Peng, Z.L et al. [9] used ultrasonic vibration to assist the machining of titanium alloy thin-walled components, that is, the additional vibration of the tool makes the system more stable and reduces the average cutting force.

Based on the method of additional input, this paper proposes a method of inputting additional vibration to the workpiece. The process damping caused by additional vibration provides additional damping force for the system to improve the stability. Finally, this paper verifies that this method can improve the chatter stability of the milling system through theoretical derivation and simulation.

2   Process Damping Modeling with Additional Vibration

2.1   The Relative Vibration of Tool with Additional Vibration

In the milling system shown in Fig. 1, if additional vibration is applied to the tool, it is difficult and may change the dynamic characteristics of the tool. Therefore, this paper intends to select the actuator mechanism to add a simple harmonic vibration in the Y direction to the workpiece such as shaking table, fast tool positioning system or ultrasonic vibration mechanism.

When considering the influence of additional vibration on process damping, its vibration frequency and amplitude can be actively controlled. The change of tool relative radial vibration in the calculation period should be considered when calculating the equivalent process damping coefficient.

The process damping coefficient is modeled by the energy method [2]. This paper intends to use a higher additional vibration frequency. If the additional vibration period T_d is lower than the period of the tool contact angle T_p (the tooth pass period), the period T_p is selected for calculation.

The form of additional vibration can be written as: $y_d = A_d \sin(\omega_d t)$. The additional vibration is equivalent to the relative vibration between the tool and the workpiece. When the additional vibration is applied in the Y direction of the workpiece, the relative radial vibration of the tool is the component of the additional vibration in the radial direction of the tool, which is related to the tool contact angle. Considering the change of tool contact angle, the expression of the relative radial vibration of tool is: $y = A_d \sin(2\pi f_d t) \cos(\varphi_j) = A_d \sin(\omega_d t) \cos(\varphi_j)$.

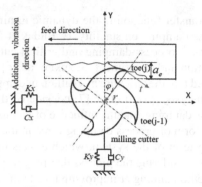

Fig. 1. Milling dynamics model.

Where A_d is the amplitude of the additional vibration, f_d is the frequency of the additional vibration, ω_d is the angular frequency of the additional vibration, and φ_j is the instantaneous radial contact angle of the cutter tooth. When the spindle rotates at an angular velocity ω_n(rad/s), the radial contact angle changes over as this form: $\varphi_j = \omega_n t$. Therefore, the function of tool relative radial vibration changing with time can be written as follows:

$$y = A_d \sin(\omega_d t) \cos(\omega_n t), \, 0 \le t \le T_p \tag{1}$$

2.2 Model of Process Damping Caused by Additional Vibration

According to the analysis of Sect. 2.1 and Fig. 2, the relative radial vibration path of the tool caused by the additional vibration is the path of point A. When the tool has wear W, the flank face AB will press into the workpiece surface (arc ADC) to generate additional damping force, which is the process damping caused by tool wear. In the energy method modeling [2], it is considered that the process damping force F_d in a tooth pass period T_p can be expressed by the equivalent process damping coefficient c_p, which is expressed as the product of c_p and the relative radial vibration velocity $\dot{y}$ of the tool. It is considered that the dissipated energy of equivalent process damping coefficient c_p in a tooth pass period is equal to the energy dissipated by the tool flank pressing into the surface. The equivalent process damping coefficient c_p can be obtained by establishing the above-mentioned equation. Then the equivalent process damping force in the dynamic equation can be expressed by c_p.

Firstly, the energy E_d dissipated by the equivalent process damping coefficient c_p in a tooth pass period can be obtained by integrating the power P_d of the equivalent process damping force in the period T_p. At the same time, the power P_d is the product of the equivalent process damping force F_d and the tool relative radial vibration velocity $\dot{y}$. According to the above, the equivalent process damping force F_d can be expressed as the product of the equivalent process damping coefficient c_p and the tool relative radial vibration velocity $\dot{y}$:

$$
\begin{aligned}
&\dot{y} = A_d \cos(\omega_d t) \cos(\omega_n t) - A_d \sin(\omega_d t) \sin(\omega_n t) \\
&F_d = c_p \cdot \dot{y} \\
&P_d = F_d \cdot \dot{y} \\
&E_d = \int P_d dt = \int F_d \dot{y} dt = \int c_p \dot{y}^2 dt = \int_0^{T_p} c_p (A_d \sin(\omega_d t) \cos(\omega_n t))'^2 dt
\end{aligned}
\tag{2}
$$

The equivalent process damping coefficient can be extracted, and the above expression is expressed as:

$$
E_d = c_p \cdot Q_{cons} \tag{3}
$$

As shown in Fig. 2, there will be a pressing force when the tool flank is pressed into the surface of the workpiece. The pressing force is determined by the volume of the flank pressing into the surface of the workpiece and the pressing coefficient K_d (the pressing force generated by the unit pressing volume), and the pressing volume can be expressed as the product of the cutting depth a_p and the pressing area $U(t)$.

When calculating the total energy dissipated by the flank pressing into the workpiece per unit cutting depth, T_p is discretized into m time intervals for calculation. The calculation process is as follows: The total energy $\overline{E}_d^c$ dissipated by the flank indentation is obtained by summing the dissipated energy of each discrete time period, and the dissipated energy of each discrete time period is obtained by the integration of the indentation force power P_d^c. The indentation force power P_d^c is obtained by the product of the indentation force F_h and the relative radial vibration velocity $\dot{y}$ of the tool, and the indentation force F_h is obtained by the product of the indentation coefficient K_d and the indentation volume. The cutting depth a_p is considered as the unit cutting depth 1, and the indentation volume is numerically equal to the indentation area $U(t)$. The formula can be expressed as follows:

$$
\begin{aligned}
&F_h = a_p K_d U(t) \\
&P_d^c = F_h \cdot \dot{y} \\
&\overline{E}_d^c = \sum_{i=1}^m \int_{dT} P_d^c dt = \sum_{i=1}^m \int_{dT} F_h \dot{y} dt = \sum_{i=1}^m \int_{i \cdot dT}^{(i+1) \cdot dT} K_d U(t) \cdot \dot{y} dt
\end{aligned}
\tag{4}
$$

The indentation area $U(t)$ is calculated as a segmented process. The indentation area is shown in Fig. 2:

The expression of the indentation area $U(t)$ is as follows:

$$
U(t) = \begin{cases} U_1(t) + U_2(t), & \frac{1}{4}T_d \le t \le \frac{3}{4}T_d \\ 0, & other \end{cases}
\tag{5}
$$

$U_1(t)$ is the area surrounded by A, B and D, which can be obtained by integral:

$$
U_1(t) = \int_{v_l \cdot t - W}^{v_l \cdot t} \left[A_d \sin\left(\frac{2\pi}{L_d} s\right) \cos\left(\frac{2\pi}{L_n} s\right) - A_d \sin(\omega_d t) \cos(\omega_n t) \right] ds
\tag{6}
$$

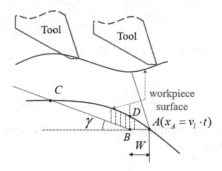

Fig. 2. Schematic diagram of press-in area.

$U_2(t)$ is the area surrounded by B, C and D, which can be obtained by integral:

$$U_2(t) = \int_{xC}^{v_l \cdot t - W} \left\{ \begin{array}{l} A_d \sin\left(\frac{2\pi}{L_d}s\right) \cos\left(\frac{2\pi}{L_n}s\right) \\ -\left[(s - v_l \cdot t - W)\tan\gamma - A_d \sin\left(\frac{2\pi}{L_d} \cdot v_l t\right) \cos\left(\frac{2\pi}{L_n} \cdot v_l t\right)\right] \end{array} \right\} ds \tag{7}$$

$$v_l = \frac{o\pi D}{60}, \ L_d = \frac{v_l}{f_d}, \ L_n = \frac{v_l}{f_n} = \frac{2\pi v_l}{w_n}, \ L_p = \frac{v_l}{f_p} = v_l \cdot T_p$$

where v_l is the tool linear velocity, L_d is the wavelength of additional vibration, L_n is the wavelength of rotation frequency, L_p is the wavelength of tooth frequency, D is the tool diameter, x_C is the intersection of the tool flank and the tool path, and W is the tool wear length.

In summary, the relative radial vibration path of the tool when applied additional vibration is established and the expression of the relative radial vibration velocity of the tool is obtained in Sect. 2.1. The formulas of process damping coefficient in Sect. 2.2 are established on this basis. Finally, the equation of the equivalent process coefficient is: $c_p = \overline{E}_d^c / Q_{cons}$.

3 Stability Model Considering Additional Vibration

3.1 Milling Dynamics Modeling

Without considering the influence of additional vibration on dynamic cutting thickness, the dynamic cutting force can be expressed as:

$$\begin{bmatrix} \Delta f_x(t) \\ \Delta f_y(t) \end{bmatrix} = \begin{bmatrix} a_{xx} & a_{xy} \\ a_{yx} & a_{yy} \end{bmatrix} \begin{bmatrix} x(t) - x(t - T) \\ y(t) - y(t - T) \end{bmatrix} \tag{8}$$

$$a_{xx} = \sum_{j=1}^{N} a_p g(\varphi_j(t)) \sin(\varphi_j(t))[-K_{tc} \cos(\varphi_j(t)) - K_{rc} \sin(\varphi_j(t))]$$

$$a_{xy} = \sum_{j=1}^{N} a_p g(\varphi_j(t)) \cos(\varphi_j(t))[-K_{tc} \cos(\varphi_j(t)) - K_{rc} \sin(\varphi_j(t))]$$

$$a_{yx} = \sum_{j=1}^{N} a_p g(\varphi_j(t)) \sin(\varphi_j(t))[K_{tc} \sin(\varphi_j(t)) - K_{rc} \cos(\varphi_j(t))]$$

$$a_{yy} = \sum_{j=1}^{N} a_p g(\varphi_j(t)) \cos(\varphi_j(t))[K_{tc} \sin(\varphi_j(t)) - K_{rc} \cos(\varphi_j(t))]$$

(9)

For the two-degree-of-freedom milling system shown in Fig. 1, considering the process damping effect, the average tangential and radial process damping force of the J-th cutter tooth can be expressed as:

$$\begin{cases} F_{dr,j} = -c_p \dot{r}_{\varphi j}(t) \\ F_{dt,j} = \mu F_{dr,j} \end{cases}$$

(10)

where μ is the Coulomb friction coefficient, which is usually taken as 0.3 when calculating the process damping. $\dot{r}_{\varphi j}(t)$ is the radial vibration caused by the displacement in X direction and Y direction:

$$\dot{r}_{\varphi j}(t) = \sin(\varphi_j(t)) \cdot \dot{x}(t) + \cos(\varphi_j(t)) \cdot \dot{y}(t)$$

(11)

The average cutting force and radial process damping force are converted to X and Y directions:

$$\begin{cases} F_{dx,j}(t) = -F_{dr,j}(t) \sin(\varphi_j(t)) - F_{dt,j}(t) \cos(\varphi_j(t)) \\ F_{dy,j}(t) = -F_{dr,j}(t) \cos(\varphi_j(t)) + F_{dt,j}(t) \sin(\varphi_j(t)) \end{cases}$$

(12)

Combined with the formula of (10)–(12), the average process damping force in X and Y directions can be written as follows:

$$\begin{bmatrix} f_{dx}(t) \\ f_{dy}(t) \end{bmatrix} = \begin{bmatrix} c_{xx\_d}(t) & c_{xy\_d}(t) \\ c_{yx\_d}(t) & c_{yy\_d}(t) \end{bmatrix} \begin{bmatrix} \dot{x}(t) \\ \dot{y}(t) \end{bmatrix}$$

(13)

$$c_{xx\_d}(t) = \sum_{j=1}^{N} a_p c_p \left(\sin^2(\varphi_j(t)) + \mu \sin(\varphi_j(t)) \cos(\varphi_j(t)) \right) g(\varphi_j(t))$$

$$c_{xy\_d}(t) = \sum_{j=1}^{N} a_p c_p \left(\sin(\varphi_j(t)) \cos(\varphi_j(t)) + \mu \cos^2(\varphi_j(t)) \right) g(\varphi_j(t))$$

$$c_{yx\_d}(t) = \sum_{j=1}^{N} a_p c_p \left(\sin(\varphi_j(t)) \cos(\varphi_j(t)) - \mu \sin^2(\varphi_j(t)) \right) g(\varphi_j(t))$$

$$c_{yy\_d}(t) = \sum_{j=1}^{N} a_p c_p \left(\cos^2(\varphi_j(t)) - \mu \sin(\varphi_j(t)) \cos(\varphi_j(t)) \right) g(\varphi_j(t))$$

(14)

Considering the process damping force caused by additional vibration, the dynamic equation can be expressed as:

$$
\begin{bmatrix} m_x & 0 \\ 0 & m_y \end{bmatrix} \begin{bmatrix} \ddot{x}(t) \\ \ddot{y}(t) \end{bmatrix} + \begin{bmatrix} c_x & 0 \\ 0 & c_y \end{bmatrix} \begin{bmatrix} \dot{x}(t) \\ \dot{y}(t) \end{bmatrix} + \begin{bmatrix} k_x & 0 \\ 0 & k_y \end{bmatrix} \begin{bmatrix} x(t) \\ y(t) \end{bmatrix} = \begin{bmatrix} \Delta f_x(t) \\ \Delta f_y(t) \end{bmatrix} + \begin{bmatrix} f_{dx}(t) \\ f_{dy}(t) \end{bmatrix} \tag{15}
$$

Substituting the formula of (8)–(14) into (15), the stability prediction model can be expressed as:

$$
\begin{bmatrix} m_x & 0 \\ 0 & m_y \end{bmatrix} \begin{bmatrix} \ddot{x}(t) \\ \ddot{y}(t) \end{bmatrix} + \begin{bmatrix} c_x - c_{xx\_d}(t) & -c_{xy\_d}(t) \\ -c_{yx\_d}(t) & c_y - c_{yy\_d}(t) \end{bmatrix} \begin{bmatrix} \dot{x}(t) \\ \dot{y}(t) \end{bmatrix}
$$
$$
+ \begin{bmatrix} k_x & 0 \\ 0 & k_y \end{bmatrix} \begin{bmatrix} x(t) \\ y(t) \end{bmatrix} = \begin{bmatrix} a_{xx} & a_{xy} \\ a_{yx} & a_{yy} \end{bmatrix} \begin{bmatrix} x(t) - x(t - T) \\ y(t) - y(t - T) \end{bmatrix} \tag{16}
$$

It can be seen that the process damping caused by additional vibration is equivalent to adding a new term to the original structural damping of the tool, thus affecting the stability of the system.

3.2 Stability Modeling

According to the f full-discretization method [10], the milling dynamic equation shown in Eq. (16) can be written in state space:

$$
\dot{x}(t) = A_0 x(t) + A(t)x(t) - A(t)x(x - T_p) \tag{17}
$$

where:

$$
A_0 = \begin{bmatrix} -M^{-1}C/2 & M^{-1} \\ CM^{-1}C/4 - K & -CM^{-1}/2 \end{bmatrix} \quad A(t) = \begin{bmatrix} 0 & 0 & 0 & 0 \\ 0 & 0 & 0 & 0 \\ a_{xx} & a_{xy} & 0 & 0 \\ a_{yx} & a_{yy} & 0 & 0 \end{bmatrix}
$$

$$
x(t) = \begin{bmatrix} q(t) & M\dot{q} + Cq/2 \end{bmatrix}^T \quad C = \begin{bmatrix} c_x - c_{xx\_d}(t) & -c_{xy\_d}(t) \\ -c_{yx\_d}(t) & c_y - c_{yy\_d}(t) \end{bmatrix}
$$

By discretizing the dynamic equation, using direct integration and linear approximation, the expression of a is obtained as follows:

$$
x(k + 1) = [I - F_{k+1}]^{-1}(F_0 + F_{0,1})x_k
$$
$$
-[I - F_{k+1}]^{-1}F_{m-1}x_{k+1-m} - [I - F_{k+1}]^{-1}F_m x_{k-m} \tag{18}
$$

According to the above formula, its discrete form can be written as:

$$
y_{k+1} = D_k^{T_p} y_k \tag{19}
$$

where: $y_k = col(x_k x_{k-1} \cdots x_{k-a} \cdots x_{k+1-m} x_{k-m})$

$$D_k^{Tp}$$

$$= \begin{bmatrix} [I-F_{k+1}]^{-1}(F_0+F_{0,1}) & 0 & \cdots & 0\ 0\ 0\ 0 & \cdots & 0 & -[I-F_{k+1}]^{-1}F_{m-1} & -[I-F_{k+1}]^{-1}F_m \\ I & 0 & & 0\ 0\ 0\ 0 & & 0 & 0 & 0 \\ 0 & I & & 0\ 0\ 0\ 0 & & 0 & 0 & 0 \\ \vdots & & & & & & & \\ 0 & 0 & & 0\ 0\ 0\ 0 & & 0 & 0 & 0 \\ 0 & 0 & & I\ 0\ 0\ 0 & & 0 & 0 & 0 \\ 0 & 0 & & 0\ I\ 0\ 0 & & 0 & 0 & 0 \\ \vdots & & & & & & & \\ 0 & 0 & & 0\ 0\ 0\ 0 & & 0 & 0 & 0 \\ 0 & 0 & & 0\ 0\ 0\ 0 & I & 0 & 0 \\ 0 & 0 & & 0\ 0\ 0\ 0 & 0 & I & 0 \end{bmatrix} \quad (20)$$

When the modulus of all eigenvalues of the transfer matrix $\Phi = D_{m-1}D_{m-2}\cdots D_1 D_0$ (m is the discrete number) is lower than 1, the system is stable, otherwise the system is unstable.

4 Stability Prediction and Analysis

After establishing the process damping model of additional vibration, this paper substitutes it into the stability algorithm for simulation to verify whether the stability boundary of the system when applied additional vibration is improved. Because the amplitude and frequency of the additional vibration are actively adjustable factors, the simulation verification of applying the same additional vibration under different cutting widths and applying different additional vibrations under the same cutting width is carried out in this paper to analyze the influence of additional vibration on process damping and stability boundary of the milling system.

4.1 The Influence of the Same Additional Vibration on Different Cutting Widths

The tool modal parameters for stability prediction are shown in the following Table 1.

Table 1. Tool modal parameters

	Frequency (Hz)	Damping (%)	Residue
xx	707	5.63	9.129e-012–3.185e-004j
yy	698	4.66	−7.544e-011–2.758e-004j

This paper plans to use a four-tooth flat-bottom milling cutter with a diameter of 20 mm for simulation. According to the experimental conditions of the laboratory, the tangential cutting force coefficient K_{tc} and the radial cutting force coefficient K_{rc} are set to 3127 MPa and 1769 MPa respectively [11]. Because the cutting force coefficient of the material selected in this paper is large, the maximum radial immersion ratio aD is set to 0.5. Specifically, the radial immersion ratio aD is set to 0.15, 0.25, 0.35, 0.5, and the indentation coefficient K_d is $13.5e^{13}$ N/m^3. The stability prediction results with and without additional vibration $A = 40\,\mu m, f = 1200\,Hz$ are shown in the following figures:

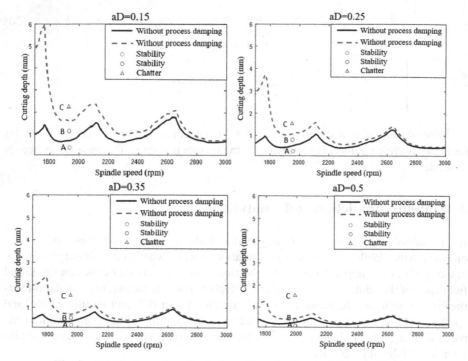

Fig. 3. Stability boundary simulation with and without additional vibration

It can be seen from the Fig. 3 that when the additional vibration of $A = 40\,\mu m, f = 1200\,Hz$ is applied, the resulting process damping will significantly increase the milling stability boundary. The specific analysis is as follows:

The process damping force caused by additional vibration greatly improves the stability boundary. When the radial immersion ratio increases, the stable region increased by the additional vibration decreases. Because the cutting force coefficient selected in this paper is large, when the cutting width increases, the larger dynamic cutting force makes the stability region smaller. At the same time, the energy dissipated by the process damping provided by the additional vibration is only enough to make the stable boundary rise to a smaller area. Although the absolute value of the increase of the stable boundary is not so great when the cut width is large, the improvement level is greater than that without additional vibration.

4.2 The Influence of Different Additional Vibration on the Same Cutting Width

On the basis of 4.1, the influence of several additional vibration data on the stable boundary is added (the additional vibration parameters are marked in the diagram):

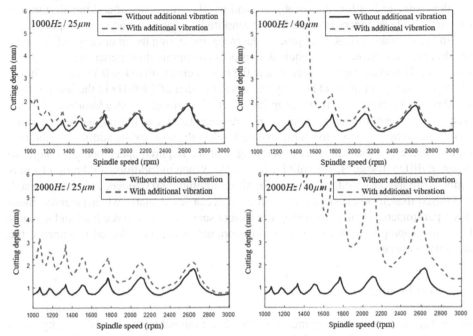

Fig. 4. The influence of different additional vibrations on the stability boundary of the same cutting parameters

From the comparison of Fig. 4, it can be seen that:

Firstly, when the frequency of the additional vibration is constant, the stability boundary of the system will rise sharply when the additional vibration amplitude is increased. In order to avoid the excessive load of the actuator, the appropriate additional vibration amplitude can be selected within the demand range.

Secondly, the process damping effect of additional vibration is different from that caused by forced vibration. In the calculation of the process damping coefficient caused by forced vibration, due to the offset of the analytical formula, c_p is negatively correlated with the tool linear speed v, that is, the degree of improvement of the stable boundary is negatively correlated with the rotational speed. However, in the calculation of the equivalent process damping coefficient c_p caused by additional vibration, the expression of Q_{cons} is as follows:

$$Q_{cons} = \int_0^{\pi/2w_n} (A_d w_d \cos(w_d t) \cos(w_n t) - A_d w_n \sin(w_d t) \sin(w_n t))^2 dt$$
$$= \frac{A_d^2 (w_d^3 \pi - w_n^3 \sin(\frac{w_d \pi}{w_n}) + w_d w_n^2 \pi)}{8 w_d w_n} \tag{21}$$

It can be seen from the calculation in Chapter 3 that the equivalent process damping coefficient c_p represents the equivalent process damping force generated by the additional vibration, which affects the stability boundary at this time. When calculating c_p, the denominator Q_{cons} has no obvious cancellation with the molecule, and its correlation with the rotation speed is complex: the calculation of molecules contains integrals, and the denominator is a function of A_d, w_d and w_n. The influence of additional vibration on the stability boundary is related to the amplitude, frequency and spindle speed.

In the simulation of general process damping, increasing the frequency will increase the damping coefficient of the equivalent process damping, thus increasing the stability boundary. However, it can be seen that in the two figures with $aD = 0.15$ and amplitude of $40\,\mu$m, the effect of 1000 Hz may be better than that of 2000 Hz in the speed before 1600 rpm. This is also due to the coupling effect of rotational speed, additional vibration frequency and amplitude. It can be reasonably speculated that: it is possible to construct a suitable additional vibration form, and then select the appropriate additional vibration and frequency, so that the process damping near the required speed becomes larger to adapt to different speeds, not only for low speed. When the additional vibration form is limited, the spindle speed, additional vibration amplitude and frequency can be traversed, and the equivalent process damping coefficient c_p can be calculated when traversing these three parameters. Then, considering the factors such as cutting force load and actuator load, the appropriate additional vibration parameters can be selected to improve the stability boundary.

5 Conclusions

In this paper, the process damping caused by the additional vibration of the workpiece is analyzed and the model is established. The milling stability prediction model considering the additional vibration is established by bringing it into the full-discretization method. The simulation results show that the process damping caused by additional vibration has a significant effect on the stability boundary. Based on the above research, the following conclusions are generalized:

- The process damping force caused by the additional vibration of the workpiece is equivalent to bring an additional damping term into the milling system, which increases the stability boundary of the tool, and the stability boundary elevation caused by the additional vibration is related to the spindle speed, frequency and amplitude, which provides a possible solution to improve the process damping effect of milling at required speed.
- With the increase of the radial immersion ratio, the improvement of the stability boundary gradually becomes limited, and its influence on the stability needs to be considered when optimizing the parameters to achieve the processing requirements.
- From the existing simulation, the small increase of the additional vibration amplitude can also greatly improve the stable boundary of the low speed. When the additional vibration parameters are selected in low-speed cutting, the frequency can be appropriately reduced and the amplitude can be increased to reduce the load of the actuator to obtain a more stable control effect while meeting the processing requirements.

Acknowledgment. This work was partially supported by the Natural Science Foundation of China (92160301) and National Science and Technology Major Project of China under Grant No. J2019-VII-0001-0141 and the State Key Laboratory of Smart Manufacturing for Special Vehicles and Transmission System (GZ2022KF008).

References

1. Altintas, Y., Budak, E.: Analytical prediction of stability lobes in milling. CIRP Ann.-Manuf. Technol. **44**(1), 357–362 (1995)
2. Budak, E., Tunc, L.T.: A new method for identification and modeling of process damping in machining. J. Manuf. Sci. Eng.-Trans. ASME **131**(5) (2009)
3. Altintas, Y., Eynian, M., Onozuka, H.: Identification of dynamic cutting force coefficients and chatter stability with process damping. CIRP Ann.-Manuf. Technol. **57**, 371–374 (2008)
4. Mao, K.M., Zhu, M., Xiao, W.W., Li, B.: A method of using turning process excitation to determine dynamic cutting coefficients. Int. J. Mach. Tools Manuf. **87**, 49–60 (2014)
5. Budak, E., Tunc, L.T.: Identification and modeling of process damping in turning and milling using a new approach. CIRP Ann.-Manuf. Technol. **59**(1), 403–408 (2010)
6. Suzuki, N., Takahashi, W., Igeta, H., Nakanomiya, T.: Flank face texture design to suppress chatter vibration in cutting. CIRP Ann.-Manuf. Technol. **69**(1), 93–96 (2020)
7. Yusoff, A.R., Turner, S., Taylor, C.M., Sims, N.D.: The role of tool geometry in process damped milling. Int. J. Mach. Tools Manuf. **50**(9–12), 883–895 (2010)
8. Muhammad, B.B., Wan, M., Liu, Y., Yuan, H.: Active damping of milling vibration using operational amplifier circuit. Chin. J. Mech. Eng. **31**(1) (2018)
9. Peng, Z.L., Zhang, D.Y., Zhang, X.Y.: Chatter stability and precision during high-speed ultrasonic vibration cutting of a thin-walled titanium cylinder. Chin. J. Aeronaut. **33**(12), 3535–3549 (2020)
10. Ding, Y., Zhu, L.M., Zhang, X.J., Ding, H.: A full-discretization method for prediction of milling stability. Int. J. Mach. Tools Manuf. **50**(5), 502–509 (2010)
11. Tang, X.W., Peng, F.Y., Yan, R., Zhu, Z.R., Li, Z.P., Xin, S.H.: Nonlinear process damping identification using finite amplitude stability and the influence analysis on five-axis milling stability. Int. J. Mech. Sci. **190**(2021)

Deep Learning-Based CNN-LSTM Model Used for Predicting Pose Error of Stewart Platform

Xin Zhu[1], Ligong Wang[2], Ming Yang[1(✉)], and Lei Fu[3]

[1] Electrical Engineering College, Guizhou University, Guiyang 550025, CO, China
myang23@gzu.edu.cn
[2] Unit 61213 of the People's Liberation Army, Linfen 041000, CO, China
[3] School of Mechanical Engineering, Guizhou University, Guiyang 550025, CO, China

Abstract. The Stewart platform is a typical 6-DOF (six-degree-of-freedom) parallel platform, which has been widely used in aeronautic testing, robot manufacturing, and underwater researching. The accuracy of static pose is considered as one of the critical performance indicators for the Stewart platform. However, the pose accuracy is compromised due to the influences of both geometric and nongeometric errors. Establishing an error model for the Stewart platform is highly complex, especially for modeling and identifying non-geometric error. In this study, a deep learning-based model is proposed to predict the pose error of Stewart platform. This model combines the advantages of Convolutional Neural Network (CNN) in spatial feature extraction and Long Short-Term Memory (LSTM) networks in sequential model, which can better process data with spatial-temporal features. The pose-error pairs dataset of a Stewart platform is established to train and validate the proposed model and the evaluation indicators such as RMSE, MAE, and R^2 are adopted to evaluate the prediction performance of the model. Experimental results indicate that CNN-LSTM model can predict the pose error of Stewart platform with RMSE of 0.02542, MAE of 0.01460, R^2 of 0.99851.

Keywords: Stewart Platform · CNN-LSTM · Deep Learning · 6-DOF · Pose Error Predicting

1 Introduction

Parallel robots are extensively utilized in manufacturing industries to enhance process flexibility and accuracy. By Compared to traditional serial robots, parallel robots have high modularity and rigidity, which has significant advantages in solving the high-quality manufacturing of large and complex components in aeronautic testing. he Stewart platform is a typical six-degree-of-freedom parallel robot [1]. It has been instrumental in numerous applications, such as motion simulation [2, 3], processing and manufacturing [4–6], and space docking [7]. Static pose accuracy is a crucial performance for this manipulator. Since robots are inevitably affected by manufacturing errors, connecting rod deviations, and other error sources in actual manufacturing, the actual pose driven by the nominal actuator length deviates from the desired pose. Therefore, the calibration of the Stewart platform parallel manipulator is extremely important.

The sources of error that contribute to robot inaccuracies include both geometric and nongeometric errors. Currently, there have been numerous research investigations conducted on the identification of geometric error, and among the widely employed techniques, the least squares method stands out as one of the most commonly utilized approaches. J Lin *et al.* [8] established an inverse kinematic model with geometric error and identified geometric parameters through the least squares method. L Fu *et al.* [9] based on the structural traits of the Stewart platform, studied a practical dimensionless error model to improve the effectiveness of the least squares algorithm and the identification accuracy of the platform's geometric parameter errors. However, nongeometric modeling is particularly challenging, as nearly 20% of robot pose error vary with changes in robot configurations. Therefore, establishing a comprehensive error model that considers all error sources is almost impossible [10]. To address this issue, a calibration method without relying on a model has been introduced. This method treats the robot as "black box" and utilizes artificial neural networks to establish the correlation between robot pose error and configurations. Along this track, S Liao [11] proposed a calibration approach for a Tri-Pyramid robot that combines both geometric and non-geometric parameters. The method involves constructing an artificial neural network to estimate the error in non-geometric parameters using actuator length and direction as input. Y Song [12] equivalent the pose error caused by various error sources to the pose error caused by joint motion error related to the pose, and built two artificial neural networks, using nominal joint variables as inputs to predict joint correction quantities. This deep learning approach does not require the construction of explicit models. Instead, it relies on training with relevant historical data to achieve good results. As a result, it has gained increasing attention from many researchers. D Yu [13] proposed a hybrid artificial neural network that composed of BP neural network and RBF neural network and the network was used to predicting the pose error caused by nongeometric parameter error with the actual driven leg length as the input of the hybrid neural network. A time-convolutional prediction model is utilized to predict the tracking error of the joint [14]. Although deep learning methods theoretically have the capability to predict pose error caused by all error sources, their accuracy heavily relies on the measurement data, and a sufficiently large number of samples and configurations are required to achieve good accuracy. One of the challenges in deep learning methods is how to obtain high accuracy with limited data.

In recent years, deep learning has become a powerful tool in data analysis and prediction, and various deep learning models are gradually being applied in the field of robotics. In some complex deep learning models, the CNN layer is often an important component as it can extract deep features from the data. Juan S *et al.* [15] proposed an inverse kinematics model for industrial parallel robots based on three different networks: MLP (Multi-Layer Perceptron), LSTM and GRU (Gated Recurrent Unit) networks. Although LSTM is commonly used for time series prediction, it can also be applied to non-time series prediction tasks. By treating vector sequences or matrix sequences as time series data and reshaping them into a time series with a time step equal to the sequence length.

In this study, a deep learning-based CNN-LSTM model is proposed. It combines two advanced neural networks, CNN and LSTM, which can accurately predict pose error of the Stewart platform. By averaging appropriate pose within the workspace and measuring the actual poses using a stereo vision approach, pose error are obtained by comparing the actual poses with the desired poses. A desired pose is used as input, and the pose error is used as the model output to construct the dataset for training the CNN-LSTM model. Finally, the accuracy of the CNN-LSTM model in predicting pose error is validated on the Stewart platform. The proposed method in this study can accurately predict the pose error of a six-degree-of-freedom parallel platform and has significant implications for improving the accuracy of parallel platforms and establishing digital twin models of parallel robots.

The rest of this study are organized as follows: Section 2 introduces the Stewart platform used in this study and derives the inverse kinematics equations of the Stewart platform. Section 3 presents an elaborate explanation of the proposed deep learning-based CNN-LSTM model. Section 4 describes the experimental setup for predicting pose error using the CNN-LSTM model and provides corresponding experimental results and analysis. Section 5 ends with the conclusion.

2   Inverse Kinematic Analysis

As illustrated in Fig. 1, the Stewart platform is composed by a fixed base, a moving platform, and six symmetrically hydraulic actuators. The ball joint and Hooke joint are respectively connected to the upper and lower ends of the actuator. Since the six legs can move independently in extension and contraction, the moving platform has the ability to translate and rotate along the x, y, and z-axes.

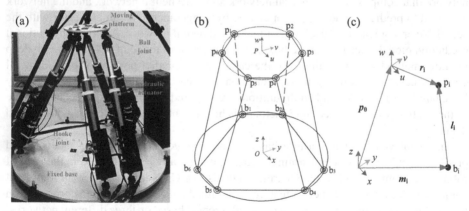

Fig. 1. (a) Stewart platform prototype; (b) Structure of the parallel manipulators; (c) Vector loop of a sub-chain

The relationship between the target pose and the actuator length in the Stewart platform is defined by the inverse kinematics. It enables the determination of the required actuator length for a given pose. Figure 1(c) illustrates a simplified schematic diagram of one sub-chain. The fixed base is associated with the $O\text{-}xyz$ coordinate system, while the moving platform is associated to the $P\text{-}uvw$ coordinate system. Vector l_i starts from the center of Hooke joint b_i to the center of the ball joint p_i. The actuator directly control the length of l_i which is represented by l_i. Vector m_i starts from the origin O to the center of the Hooke joint b_i. The vector p_o represents the position of the moving platform's center relative to the O-xyz coordinate system. Vector r_i starts from the origin P and extends to the center of the ball joint p_i. The orientation of the moving platform relative to the fixed platform can be achieved by sequentially rotating around the x-axis with angle α, followed by rotation around the y-axis with angle β, and finally rotating around the z-axis with angle γ. The rotation matrix of coordinate system P-uvw relative to O-xyz is expressed as:

$$R = R(\psi, \theta, \gamma) = \begin{bmatrix} c\gamma c\theta & c\gamma s\theta s\psi - s\gamma c\psi & c\gamma s\theta c\psi + s\theta c\psi \\ s\gamma c\theta & s\gamma s\theta s\psi - s\gamma c\psi & c\gamma s\theta c\psi + s\theta c\psi \\ -s\theta & c\theta s\psi & c\theta c\psi \end{bmatrix} \tag{1}$$

where s and c denote sine and cosine, $\psi, \theta, \gamma \in [0, \pi]$.

As depicted in Fig. 1(c), the vector loop equation of each sub-chain can be described as:

$$l_i = p_o + r_i - m_i \tag{2}$$

where r_i is calculated by:

$$r_i = Ra_i \tag{3}$$

the actuator length l_i is expressed as:

$$l_i = \|p_0 + Ra_i - m_i\| \tag{4}$$

3 Deep Learning-Based CNN-LSTM Model

3.1 The CNN Principle

Convolutional neural network consists of multiple convolutional kernels and layers, which allow them to automatically extract multi-angle and deep-level features from row signals. A basic structure of CNN is depicted in Fig. 2. The CNN frame has several layers: convolutional layer, pooling layer and fully connected layer. The following is the detailed framework of CNN:

(1) Convolution layer

The convolution layer performs convolution operations to capture spatial features from adjacent points in the input vector. The typical components of a convolutional layer's parameters include the number of kernels, kernel length, and a set of neurons. The operation of convolution layer is to compute the dot product between the input data and the weight matrix of the kernel, this operation is expressed as:

$$x_i^t = \sigma\left(\sum_{j=1}^{n} w_{ij}^t * x_j^{t-1} + b_i^t\right) \tag{5}$$

where x_i^t represents the i-th output of layer t, x_j^{t-1} represents the j-th output of layer t -1, w_{ij}^t represents the weight matrix of convolution kernel, b_i^t represents the convolution kernel biases, $*$ represents the convolution operation, and σ represents the activation function.

(2) Pooling layer

The pooling layer performs down-sampling on the feature maps, reducing the amount of data processing while preserving useful information. Max pooling and average pooling are the most commonly used pooling methods. But the pooling operation will lead a smaller output length. In this study, the pose sequences are relatively short, so the pooling layer is not used.

(3) Fully connected layer

The fully connected layer maps the feature space computed by the convolutional and pooling layers to the sample label space. In simple terms, it integrates the features into a single value.

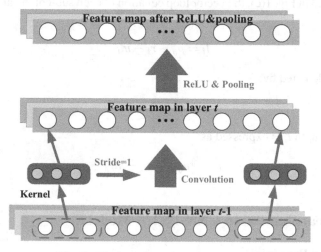

Fig. 2. The basic structure of a CNN layer

3.2 The LSTM Principle

LSTM networks are specialized structural variants of RNN. The internal structure of a LSTM layer is illustrated in Fig. 3. The LSTM is composed by forgetting gate, input gate, and output gate.

The forgetting gate determines what information is discarded. The input of the forgetting gate consists by the current input x_k and the previous output h_{k-1} from the hidden layer. The sigmoid function is applied to transform the output value of the forget gate to the range of [0, 1], which can be expressed as:

$$f_k = \sigma(W_f \cdot [h_{k-1}, x_k] + b_f) \tag{6}$$

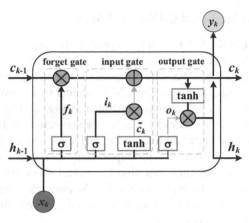

Fig. 3. Internal structure of LSTM

where f_k is the output of the forgetting gate; σ represents the sigmoid activation function; W_f and b_f is the weight matrix bias vector of the forgetting gate.

The input gate determines which information to retain. By utilizing the sigmoid activation function, the output value h_{k-1} of previous time and the new input information x_{k-1} are processed and mapped to the interval [0, 1]. It represents the probability of preserving this part of information. The operation for the input gate can be expressed as follows:

$$i_k = \sigma(W_i \cdot [x_k, h_{k-1}] + b_i) \tag{7}$$

$$\tilde{c}_k = \tanh(W_c \cdot [h_{k-1}, x_k] + b_c) \tag{8}$$

the new state c_k will be generated by adding the $\tilde{c}_k$ and the old state c_{k-1}, which can be expressed as:

$$c_k = f_k \otimes c_{k-1} + i_k \otimes \tilde{c}_k \tag{9}$$

where i_k is the output of the input gate at time k; W_i is the weight matrices of the input gate; b_i is the offset vector of the input gate; tanh is the activation function; W_c is the weight matrices of the calculation unit; b_c is the bias vector of the input gate, $\otimes$ is pointwise multiplication.

The output gate determines which information should be output. The output h_k is generated by multiplying the o_k with the value transformed by the tanh activation function. The o_k and h_k are calculated as following formulas:

$$o_k = \sigma(W_o \cdot [h_{k-1}, x_{k-1}] + b_o) \tag{10}$$

$$h_k = o_k \otimes \tanh(c_k) \tag{11}$$

where W_o is the weight matrices of output gate, b_o is the bias vector of the output gate.

3.3 The Deep Learning-Based CNN-LSTM Model

The structure of the CNN-LSTM model designed in this study is illustrated in Fig. 4, the input vector is the desired pose vector of the Stewart parallel platform, and the output is the error vector. CNN maps one-dimensional pose data into high-dimensional space and learns its spatial features. The CNN contains two convolutional layers, the structure of each convolutional layer is illustrated in Fig. 2. The kernel size of each convolutional layer is set to a vector of 1×3, the step is set to 1, and the ReLU nonlinear activation function is added after each convolutional layer, so that the network captures the nonlinear characteristics between the input data. Subsequently, the multi-channel feature maps undergo a flattening operation to convert them into a one-dimensional sequence, which serves as the input for the LSTM network. The LSTM network is utilized to learn the dependencies and their associated features. Finally, the pose error vector is outputted by the output layer.

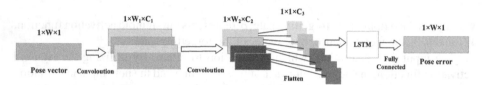

Fig. 4. CNN-LSTM framework

4   Experiment Validation and Results Analysis

4.1   Experiment Setup and Dataset Description

The experiment was conducted on the prototype of the Stewart platform to validate the proposed CNN-LSTM model. Table 1 provides the geometric parameters of the Stewart platform, where R_p and R_b represent the radius of the moving and fixed platforms respectively, θ_p and θ_b are the angles of two adjacent joints on the moving and fixed platforms. The parameters l_{min} and l_{max} is the minimum and maximum length of the actuator respectively, while z_p and z_b represents the distances from the center of the joint to the surfaces of the moving platform and the fixed platform, respectively.

Table 1. Nominal geometric parameters of a Stewart platform

R_p/mm	R_b/mm	θ_p/°	θ_b/°	l_{min}/mm	l_{max}/mm	z_p/mm	z_b/mm
124	454	30	20	696	838	49	39

The 250 poses were selected on average in the workspace which was determined by the method of O Masory *et al.* [16]. The measurement of the position and orientation of Stewart platform (Fig. 5) was carried out using the MoveInspect XR measurement method (20 μm + 20 μm/m accuracy) [9]. The pose error is obtained by calculating the difference between the actual measured pose and the desired pose.

The 250 poses data is divided into 200 sets of training pose and 50 sets of testing pose in a ratio of 0.8:0.2. It is crucial to emphasize that the training poses and the testing pose must be entirely distinct. In order to determine which parameter, desired pose or desired actuator length, is more suitable for predicting pose error, two separate CNN-LSTM models are trained with the desired pose and desired actuator length as inputs while pose error as output. The inverse kinematics equation provided in Sect. 2 is employed to compute the actuator length for the dataset. After training the CNN-LSTM, the testing pose is used to validate the accuracy of this model.

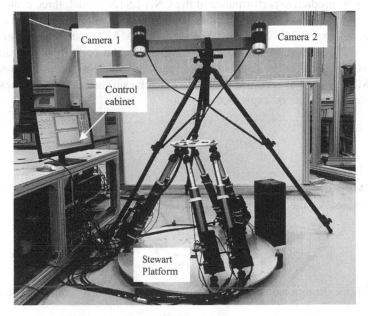

Fig. 5. Stewart platform pose measurement device.

4.2 Hyperparameter Selection

The hyperparameter settings of the CNN-LSTM model are provided in Table 2. The kernel-size represents the size of the convolution kernel used in two convolutional operations; num-kernels is the number of convolution kernels in the two convolutional layers; num-LSTM-layer is the number of LSTM layers; the initial learning rate, decay rate, and decay steps are the detailed settings corresponding to the optimizer; epoch refers to the number of times a model is trained. After the training for the number of decay steps, the learning rate will decay once, and the new learning rate equals the old learning rate multiplied by the decay rate.

Table 2. Hyperparameters of CNN-LSTM model

Hyperparameters	size/number	Hyperparameters	size/number
kernel sizes	$3 \times 1, 3 \times 1$	decay rate	0.1
num-kernels	32, 64	decay step	700
num-LSTM-layer	6	initial learning rate	0.01
optimizer	Adam	epoch	1000

4.3 Evaluation Criteria

To evaluate the predictive performance of the CNN-LSTM model, three evaluation criteria are employed in this study to quantify prediction error and accuracy, including Root Mean Square Error (RMSE), Mean Absolute Error (MAE), and Determination Coefficient (R^2). The smaller MAE and RMSE, the higher the performance of the model, while R^2 is the opposite. The details of the evaluation indicators are as follows:

(1) RMSE is used to measure the deviation between the predicted values and the actual values, which can be expressed as:

$$RMSE = \sqrt{\frac{1}{n} \sum_{j=1}^{n} (\hat{x}_j - \overline{x}_j)^2} \tag{12}$$

(2) MAE represents the represents the average of the absolute errors between the predicted values and the actual values, which can be expressed as:

$$MAE = \frac{1}{n} \sum_{j=1}^{n} |\hat{x}_j - x_j| \tag{13}$$

(3) R^2 is the fitting quality of the data. The calculation of R^2 can be expressed as:

$$R^2 = \frac{SSR}{SST} \tag{14}$$

where

$$SSR = \sum_{j=1}^{n} (\hat{x}_j - \overline{x}_j)^2$$
$$SST = \sum_{j=1}^{n} (x_j - \overline{x}_j)^2 \tag{15}$$

In the above Eqs. (12)–(15), the predicted value is denoted $\hat{x}_j$, the actual value is denoted x_j, and the average of the actual value is denoted $\overline{x}$.

4.4 Experimental Results and Analysis

Figure 6 illustrates the predicting results of the pose error with different input. Figure 7 illustrates the deviation between the actual pose error and the predicted pose error when the desired pose is used as input; Fig. 8 illustrates the deviation when the desired actuator length is used as input. Based on Fig. 7, it is evident that the maximum positional deviation is merely 0.11 mm, and the maximum angular deviation is only 0.038 degrees. These values are considerably superior to the corresponding parameters illustrated in Fig. 8.

The RSME, MAE, and R^2 evaluation indicators are provided in Table 3. With the desired pose as the input of CNN-LSTM, the maximum value of RSME is 0.04994; the maximum MAE among the six parameters is 0.03990; the fitting degree R^2 is greater than 0.99643. This verifies that CNN-LSTM is capable of accurately predicting the pose error of the Stewart platform. The evaluation criteria for predicting pose error with desired actuator length input are all lower than the evaluation criteria with desired pose input. This suggests that predicting pose error is more accurate when using the desired pose rather than the desired actuator length.

Table 3. The performance for CNN-LSTM model

Pose parameter	Desired pose input			Desired actuator length input		
	RMSE	MAE	R^2	RMSE	MAE	R^2
x	0.04994	0.03990	0.99906	0.34583	0.17161	0.95508
y	0.04130	0.03385	0.99881	0.24479	0.13393	0.95810
z	0.03059	0.02302	0.99783	0.12745	0.06446	0.96233
α	0.01207	0.00964	0.99923	0.09594	0.04549	0.95124
β	0.00661	0.00524	0.99643	0.02158	0.01185	0.96197
γ	0.01205	0.00981	0.99967	0.15190	0.07298	0.94717

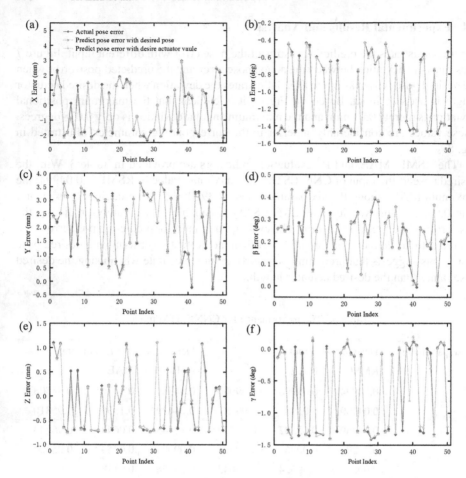

Fig. 6. Predicting results of the pose error with different input.

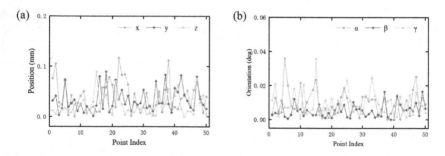

Fig. 7. The deviation between predicted pose error with desired pose input and actual pose error

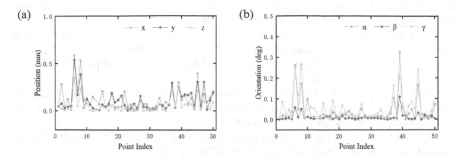

Fig. 8. The deviation between predicted pose error with desired actuator length input and actual pose error

5 Conclusion

This study investigated a deep learning-based CNN-LSTM Model used for predicting pose error of Stewart platform. This model can accurately predict pose error of the Stewart platform by combining the advanced neural networks CNN and LSTM. A pose-error pairs dataset of Stewart platform is established with 250 desired poses and actual poses that measured by the MoveInspect XR measurement method. The CNN-LSTM model was trained using this dataset, and the accuracy of the model in predicting pose error of the Stewart platform was verified. The experimental results confirmed that the proposed CNN-LSTM model achieves the satisfactory prediction accuracy for pose error resulting from both geometric and non-geometric factors. In the future, we will conduct research on online accuracy compensation for universal parallel robots.

Acknowledgement. This work was supported part by National Natural Science Foundation of China (62203132, 52265066, 52075512); National Key R&D Program of China (2017YFF-0205003); Youth Science and Technology Talents Development Project of Guizhou Education Department (No. Qianjiaohe KY [2022] 138); Doctor Foundation Project of Guizhou University (No. GDRJ [2020]30).

References

1. Stewart, D.: A platform with six degrees of freedom. Proc. Inst. Mech. Eng. **180**, 371–86 (1965)
2. Zhang, C., Zhang, L.: Kinematics analysis and workspace investigation of a novel 2-DOF parallel manipulator applied in vehicle driving simulator. Rob. Comput. Integr. Manuf. **29**(4), 113–120 (2013)
3. Zhuang, H., Yan, J., Masory, O.: Calibration of Stewart platforms and other parallel manipulators by minimizing inverse kinematic residuals. J. Rob. Syst. **15**(7), 395–405 (1998)
4. Huang, T., Zhao, D., Yin, F., et al.: Kinematic calibration of a 6-DOF hybrid robot by considering multicollinearity in the identification Jacobian. Mech. Mach. Theory **131**, 371–384 (2019)

5. Peng, H., Wang, J., Wang, L., et al.: Identification of structure errors of 3-PRS-XY mechanism with regularization method. Mech. Mach. Theory **46**, 927–944 (2011)
6. Sun, T., Song, Y., Dong, G., et al.: Optimal design of a parallel mechanism with three rotational degrees of freedom. Rob. Comput.-Integr. Manuf. **28**, 500–508 (2012)
7. Song, Y., Zhang, J., Lian, B., et al.: Kinematic calibration of a 5-DoF parallel kinematic machine. Precis. Eng. **45**, 242–261 (2016)
8. Lin, J., Qi, C., Hu, Y., et al.: Geometrical parameter identification for 6-DOF parallel platform. Intelligent robotics and applications. In: 15th International Conference on Intelligent Robotics and Applications, Proceedings, pp. 70–76 (2022)
9. Fu, L., Yang, M., Liu, Z., et al.: Stereo vision-based Kinematic calibration method for the Stewart platforms. Opt. Express **30**(26), 47059–47069 (2022)
10. Ma, L., Bazzoli, P., Sammons, P.M., et al.: Modeling and calibration of high-order joint-dependent kinematic errors for industrial robots. Rob. Comput.-Integr. Manuf. **50**, 153–167 (2018)
11. Liao, S., Zeng, Q., Ehmann, K.F., et al.: Parameter identification and nonparametric calibration of the tri-pyramid robot. IEEE/ASME Trans. Mechatron. **25**(5), 2309–2317 (2020)
12. Song, Y., Tian, W., Tian, Y., et al.: Calibration of a Stewart platform by designing a robust joint compensator with artificial neural networks. Precis. Eng. **77**, 375–384 (2022)
13. Yu, D.: A new pose accuracy compensation method for parallel manipulators based on hybrid artificial neural network. Neural Comput. Appl. **33**, 909–923 (2021)
14. Tan, S., Yang, J., Ding, H.: A prediction and compensation method of robot tracking error considering pose-dependent load decomposition. Rob. Comput.-Integr. Manuf. **80**, 102476 (2023)
15. Toquica, J.S., Oliveira, P.S., Souza, W.S.R., et al.: An analytical and a deep learning model for solving the inverse kinematic problem of an industrial parallel robot. Comput. Ind. Eng. **151**, 106682 (2021)
16. Masory, O., Wang, J.: Workspace evaluation of Stewart platforms. Adv. Rob. **9**(4), 443–461 (1994)

Research on the Influence of Forced Vibration on Process Damping and Stability Boundary in Milling

Yongqiao Jin[1], Haodong Qu[2], Xiaowei Tang[2(✉)], and Meng Wang[1]

[1] Shanghai Hanghe Intelligent Technology Corporation, No. 3883 Yuanjiang Road, Minhang District, Shanghai, China
wangmengjob@sina.com
[2] School of Mechanical Science and Engineering, Huazhong University of Science and Technology, No. 1037 LuoYu Road, Wuhan, China
{m202170625,tangxw}@hust.edu.cn

Abstract. Due to the constraint of tool wear, the low spindle speeds are usually adopted for the milling of the difficult-to-cut materials, such as AerMet100 and titanium alloy etc. for the stability boundary prediction, the process damping has significant influence in the low spindle speed region. The traditional stability analysis with considering process damping mainly focuses on the effect of waves on the workpiece surface caused by chatter, this paper study the influence of forced vibration on process damping and stability boundary in milling. The formula for calculating the amplitude of forced vibration based on frequency domain is derived, and then the relationship between forced vibration amplitude and spindle speed - cutting depth is analyzed. The process damping model with considering forced vibration is established and introduced to the classical stability prediction model, the simulation of stability boundaries with different cutting parameters are compared and analyzed. The simulation results show that the process damping generated by vibration forced results in a new stability boundary above the chatter region, which provides a new choice for cutting parameter optimization.

Keywords: Process damping · Forced vibration · Chatter region · Stability · Milling

1 Introduction

Chatter is the important factor affecting machining efficiency and quality in milling, and can be avoided by process parameter optimization according the Stable Lobe Diagram (SLD) [1, 2]. Based on the SLD, the optimization of the spindle speed and cutting depth can obtain a higher processing efficiency under the premise of stable processing in the high-speed range. However, only low cutting speed can be adopted for the difficult-to-cut materials, and the low spindle speed will significantly limit the machining efficiency. Fortunately, the process damping is more significant in the low spindle speed region [3] and can significantly improve the stability boundary for achieving the greater cutting

© The Author(s), under exclusive license to Springer Nature Singapore Pte Ltd. 2023
H. Yang et al. (Eds.): ICIRA 2023, LNAI 14272, pp. 371–382, 2023.
https://doi.org/10.1007/978-981-99-6480-2_31

depth to compensate for the loss of efficiency caused by low spindle speed. The process damping comes from process damping force, which is explained due to the contact of the tool flank and undulations left on the workpiece surface, and is in direct proportion to the indentation volume [4, 5]. Thus, the undulations left on the workpiece surface is the key factor affecting the process damping force and stability boundary.

Many scholars have carried out a lot of researches on the milling stability, and the obtained SLDs have well guided the process parameter optimization, such as spindle speed and cutting depth. However the existing researches mainly focused on the SLD at high-speed cutting [6–8], and revealed the mechanism of milling stability, however, when milling at low spindle speed, the actual critical cut depth is greater than the theoretical prediction. Altintas et al. [9] pointed that the contact between the flank face of the tool and undulations left on the surface produces an additional damping effect at low cutting speeds, and studied three dynamic cutting force coefficients related to regenerative chip thickness, velocity and acceleration terms, respectively, and the results shown that the process damping coefficient increases as the tool is worn and increases the chatter stability limit in cutting. Budak et al. [4] calculated the instantaneous indentation volume due to the flank-wave contact and identified the process damping directly from the chatter tests using experimental and analytical stability limits. Rahnama et al. [10] used the equivalent volume interface between the tool and the workpiece to determine the process damping parameter, and given the process damping coefficient related to the waves left on the surface due to the tool movement on the workpiece. Ahmadi et al. [5] investigated the phenomenon of finite amplitude stability with considering the process damping. Tunc et al. [11] investigated the effects of cutting conditions and tool geometry on process stability and pointed that Cutting conditions and tool geometry can enhance chatter stability due to the increased process damping. Feng et al. [12] established the velocity dependent process damping model with considering the relative vibrations of cutter-workpiece system in both feed and normal directions. Tuysuz et al. [13] linearized the process damping force by an equivalent specific viscous damping, and presented an analytical model to predict the process damping forces and chatter stability in low-speed machining. Li et al. [14] established the dynamic milling model including mode coupling and process damping, pointed that process damping plays a vital role in stability improvement mainly at low spindle speeds. Wang et al. [15] established the dynamic milling model for the thin-walled workpiece with considering the material removal and process damping determined by the indentation volume between tool flank face and machined surface. Tang et al. [16] established the nonlinear process damping related to chatter amplitude and proposed a 3D SLD considering the finite amplitude stability.

From the researches on process damping in milling, the waves left on the surface due to the tool movement on the workpiece is the key factor affecting the process damping. In the existing studies, the waves on the surface produced by the chatter are considered as the main factor of process damping. However, forced vibrations excited by intermittently milling force also can produce significant surface waves under certain cutting conditions [17, 18], and result in significant process damping. Thus, this paper establishes process damping model with considering forced vibration, and then calculates the forced vibration amplitude, and analyzes the distribution of cutter-workpiece indentation volume at different spindle speed and cutting depth to investigate the effect of cutting parameters on process damping and stability boundary. The formula of calculating the forced vibration amplitude is derived, and the process damping model with considering forced vibration is established in Sect. 2. The stability prediction model considering the process damping generated by the forced vibration is established, and the influence of process damping on stability boundary is analyzed in Sect. 3. Finally, the conclusions are presented, and the cutting parameters optimization suggestions are given in Sect. 4.

2 Process Damping Generated by Forced Vibration

The ultimate purpose of active control of milling chatter is to suppress the relative vibration of the tool and the workpiece. The workpiece can be actuated by applying a force at the workpiece end to offset the relative motion of the two [16], but it needs to provide greater force and energy in the processing of large parts. Therefore, the use of actuators to control the vibration of the tool is the preferred solution. Smart materials are more widely used in the field of vibration control, among them, piezoelectric actuators have the advantages of small size, large power and fast response, and have gradually become the darling of the field of machining vibration control.

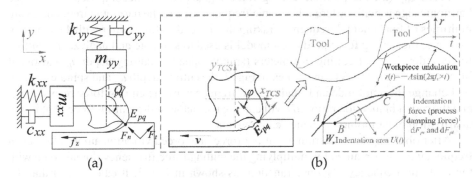

Fig. 1. Dynamics of two DOF system considering process damping.

2.1 Forced Vibration Caused by Intermittently Milling Force

For different tools, such as flat-end milling cutter, ball end milling cutter, bull-nose end milling cutter, etc., there are different cutting force modeling methods [19–21], this paper takes flat-end milling cutter as an example to study. According to Ref. [19] and the coordinate system defined in Fig. 1, the cutting force prediction model is shown as follows:

$$f_x(t) = \sum_{q=1}^{N} \int_0^{a_p} \left(-K_t \cos(\varphi_{pq}) - K_n \sin(\varphi_{pq}) \right) f_z \sin(\varphi_{pq}) g\left(\varphi_{pq}\right) dz$$
$$f_y(t) = \sum_{q=1}^{N} \int_0^{a_p} \left(K_t \sin(\varphi_{pq}) - K_n \cos(\varphi_{pq}) \right) f_z \sin(\varphi_{pq}) g\left(\varphi_{pq}\right) dz$$

(1)

where K_t and K_n are the tangential and radial cutting force coefficients respectively, denotes the instantaneous cutting angle of the p-th differential element of the q-th tooth (Epq), f_z is the feed per tooth, $g(\varphi_{pq})$ is a unit step function determining whether the p-th differential element of the q-th tooth is cutting, N is the number of the cutter teeth, dz represents the cutting depth of differential element and a_p denotes the total depth of cutting.

The frequency domain expression of cutting force with periodic T can be obtained by Fourier transform:

$$F_\gamma(j\omega) = 2\pi \sum_{\kappa=-\infty}^{\infty} \alpha_{\kappa,\gamma}\delta(\omega - \kappa\omega_0), \gamma = x, y \; ; \; \kappa = 1, 2, \ldots$$

$$\alpha_{\kappa,\gamma} = \tfrac{1}{T} \int_T f_\gamma(t)e^{-j\kappa\omega_0 t}dt$$

(2)

where ω_0 is the fundamental frequency and can be expressed as the function of spindle speed n:

$$\omega_0 = \frac{n}{60} \times N$$

(3)

From Eq. (2), the periodic cutting force signals can be decomposed into simple harmonic signals with different harmonic frequencies, and the harmonic frequencies are multiples of fundamental frequency. Taking the flat-end milling cutter with 4 teeth as an example, the cutting force prediction model is used to simulate and analyze the cutting force under different cutting parameters (spindle speed n, cutting depth a_p and radial immersion ratios aD). As can be seen in Fig. 2, the cutting depth a_p and spindle speed n will change the amplitude and fundamental frequency of the cutting force respectively, and the radial immersion ratios aD will change the shape of the cutting force, that is, the distribution of harmonic frequency components.

After obtaining the spectrum of cutting force, the forced vibration amplitude at each frequency can be obtained by multiplying the cutting force frequency domain data with the tool end frequency response function, as shown in Fig. 3. It can be seen that the larger the amplitude of the harmonic component at the mode, the larger the amplitude of the forced vibration, therefore, the amplitude of forced vibration can be changed by changing the cutting parameters. In Fig. 3, the modal frequencies in X and Y direction are 707 Hz and 698 Hz, respectively.

By adding the vibration amplitudes at each harmonic frequency, the total forced vibration amplitude can be obtained, and Fig. 4 shows the amplitude distribution of forced vibration at different speeds and cutting depths. It can be seen that the cut depth will significantly increase the amplitude of forced vibration, and then the vibration amplitude shows rotational speed dependence. For the vibration amplitude caused by cutting force in X direction, vibration amplitude peaks occur at 1760 rpm and 2660 rpm etc. whose harmonic frequency is at the modal frequency ($1760/60 \times 4 \times 6 = 704 \approx 707$, $2660/60 \times 4 \times 4 = 709 \approx 707$), the same for the vibration amplitude in Y direction ($2100/60 \times 4 \times 5 = 700 \approx 698$, $2620/60 \times 4 \times 4 = 699 \approx 698$). In addition, according to cutting forces and FRFs in frequency domain in Fig. 3, the harmonic component value of the cutting force in the X direction is very small around the mode frequency, however the harmonic component in Y direction has a certain value around the mode frequency. Thus,

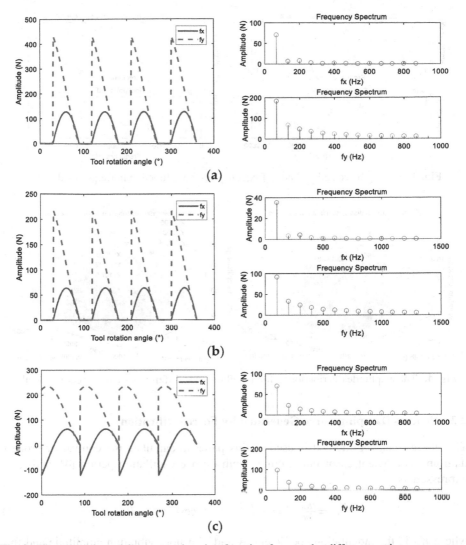

Fig. 2. Time domain and frequency domain of cutting force under different cutting parameters. (a) $n = 1000$ rpm, $a_p = 2$ mm, $aD = 0.25$. (b) $n = 2000$ rpm, $a_p - 1$ mm, $aD = 0.25$. (c) $n = 1000$ rpm, $a_p = 1$ mm, $aD = 0.5$.

the vibration amplitude in Y direction is more sensitive to the spindle speed. According to Fig. 2, the amplitude of forced vibration can be increased by changing the cutting parameters to make the harmonic component present a larger value around the mode frequency of the tool point FRF, so as to increase the process damping.

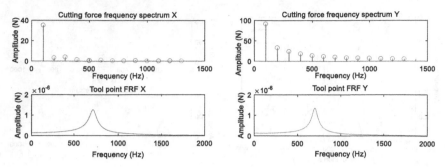

Fig. 3. Cutting force and tool point frequency response function in frequency domain.

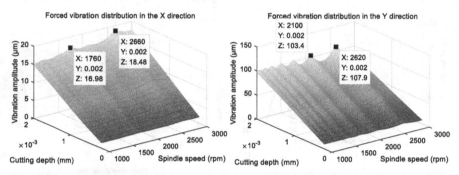

Fig. 4. The amplitude distribution of forced vibration at different speeds and cutting depths.

2.2 Process Damping Force Generated by Forced Vibration

The energy balance method is used in this paper to calculate the equivalent process damping coefficient c_p of unit cutting depth on one oscillation period [4], and c_p is expressed as:

$$c_p = \frac{IK_d}{A\pi}, I = \int_{3/(4f_\kappa)}^{1/(4f_\kappa)} U(t)\cos(2\pi f_\kappa t)dt \tag{4}$$

where K_d is the indentation coefficient, A and f_κ denote vibration amplitude and frequency respectively, and $U(t)$ is the indentation area function with the cutter moving along the workpiece surface wave.

As shown in Fig. 1. Dynamics of two DOF system considering process damping. (b) and Ref. [16], the indentation area $U(t)$ at each vibrational frequency is the function of the simple harmonic vibration workpiece wave $p(t)$ and flank edge with wear land width W and tool flank face.

$$U(t) = \begin{cases} U_1(t) + U_2(t), & t = \left[-1/(4f_\kappa) \ -3/(4f_\kappa) \right] \\ 0, & other \end{cases}$$

$$U_1(t) = \int_{v_l \cdot t}^{v_l \cdot t + W} \left[-A\sin\left(\frac{2\pi}{L}s\right) + A\sin(2\pi f_\kappa \cdot t) \right] ds \tag{5}$$

$$U_2(t) = \int_{v_l \cdot t + W}^{x_C} \left\{ -A\sin\left(\frac{2\pi}{L}s\right) - \left[-A\sin(2\pi f_\kappa \cdot t) + (s - v_l \cdot t - W)\tan\gamma \right] \right\} ds$$

$$v_l = \frac{n\pi D}{60}, L = \frac{v_l}{f_\kappa}$$

where v_l and L are the tool linear velocity and wave length, n and D denotes the spindle speed (rpm) and tool diameter respectively. x_C denotes x-coordinate of the intersection point C and is calculated numerically.

Due to the periodic milling force will excite the forced vibration at different harmonic frequencies, the total I is the sum of the I at each harmonic frequency.

$$I = \sum_{\kappa=1}^{N_\kappa} \int_{3/(4f_\kappa)}^{1/(4f_\kappa)} U_\kappa(t) \cos(2\pi f_\kappa t) dt \tag{6}$$

Combining Eq. (2)–Eq. (6), the equivalent process damping coefficient c_p caused by forced vibration can be obtained.

3 Stability Prediction Model Considers Process Damping

After obtaining the equivalent process damping coefficient c_p, the stability prediction model considering process damping can be established.

3.1 Stability Prediction Model

Considering the dynamic component of the $h(\varphi_{pq})$, the milling force generated by vibration can be expressed as:

$$\begin{bmatrix} \Delta f_x(t) \\ \Delta f_y(t) \end{bmatrix} = \begin{bmatrix} a_{xx} & a_{xy} \\ a_{yx} & a_{yy} \end{bmatrix} \begin{bmatrix} x(t) - x(t-T) \\ y(t) - y(t-T) \end{bmatrix} \tag{7}$$

$$a_{xx} = \sum_{q=1}^{N} \int_0^{a_p} (K_t \sin \varphi_{pq} \cos \varphi_{pq} + K_n \sin^2 \varphi_{pq}) g(\varphi_{pq}) dz$$

$$a_{xy} = \sum_{q=1}^{N} \int_0^{a_p} (K_t \cos^2 \varphi_{pq} + K_n \sin \varphi_{pq} \cos \varphi_{pq}) g(\varphi_{pq}) dz$$

$$a_{yx} = \sum_{q=1}^{N} \int_0^{a_p} -(K_t \sin^2 \varphi_{pq} - K_n \sin \varphi_{pq} \cos \varphi_{pq}) g(\varphi_{pq}) dz$$

$$a_{yy} = \sum_{q=1}^{N} \int_0^{a_p} -(K_t \sin \varphi_{pq} \cos \varphi_{pq} - K_n \cos^2 \varphi_{pq}) g(\varphi_{pq}) dz$$

$$\tag{8}$$

As shown in Fig. 1. Dynamics of two DOF system considering process damping. (b), the tangential and radial process damping forces of the p-th differential element of the q-th tooth can be expressed as:

$$\begin{cases} dF_{dr,pq}(t) = -c_p \dot{r}_{\varphi_{pq}}(t) dz \\ dF_{dt,pq}(t) = \mu dF_{dr,pq}(t) \end{cases} \tag{9}$$

where μ is coulomb friction coefficient, which is usually taken around 0.3 [3, 22]. And radial vibration $\dot{r}_{\varphi_{pq}}(t)$ can be expressed by the vibration of X-direction and Y-direction:

$$\dot{r}_{\varphi_{pq}}(t) = -\sin(\varphi_{pq}(t)) \cdot \dot{x}(t) - \cos(\varphi_{pq}(t)) \cdot \dot{y}(t) \tag{10}$$

The tangential and radial process damping forces are transformed to X-direction and Y-direction.

$$\begin{cases} dF_{dx,pq}(t) = - dF_{pr,ij}(t) \sin(\varphi_{ij}(t)) - dF_{pt,ij}(t) \cos(\varphi_{ij}(t)) \\ dF_{dy,pq}(t) = - dF_{pr,ij}(t) \cos(\varphi_{ij}(t)) + dF_{pt,ij}(t) \sin(\varphi_{ij}(t)) \end{cases} \tag{11}$$

Combining Eq. (9)–Eq. (11), and gathering the process damping forces of every differential element, the total process damping forces are expressed as:

$$\begin{bmatrix} f_{dx}(t) \\ f_{dy}(t) \end{bmatrix} = \begin{bmatrix} c_{xx\_d}(t) & c_{xy\_d}(t) \\ c_{yx\_d}(t) & c_{yy\_d}(t) \end{bmatrix} \begin{bmatrix} \dot{x}(t) \\ \dot{y}(t) \end{bmatrix} \tag{12}$$

$$c_{xx\_d}(t) = \sum_{q=1}^{N} \int_0^{a_p} c_p \left(- \sin^2(\varphi_{pq}(t)) - \mu \sin(\varphi_{pq}(t)) \cos(\varphi_{pq}(t)) \right) g\left(\varphi_{pq}(t)\right) dz$$

$$c_{xy\_d}(t) = \sum_{q=1}^{N} \int_0^{a_p} c_p \left(- \sin(\varphi_{pq}(t)) \cos(\varphi_{pq}(t)) - \mu \cos^2(\varphi_{pq}(t)) \right) g\left(\varphi_{pq}(t)\right) dz$$

$$c_{yx\_d}(t) = \sum_{q=1}^{N} \int_0^{a_p} c_p \left(- \sin(\varphi_{ij}(t)) \cos(\varphi_{ij}(t)) + \mu \sin^2(\varphi_{pq}(t)) \right) g\left(\varphi_{pq}(t)\right) dz \tag{13}$$

$$c_{yy\_d}(t) = \sum_{q=1}^{N} \int_0^{a_p} c_p \left(- \cos^2(\varphi_{pq}(t)) + \mu \sin(\varphi_{pq}(t)) \cos(\varphi_{pq}(t)) \right) g\left(\varphi_{pq}(t)\right) dz$$

According to the dynamics of two DOF system in Fig. 1. Dynamics of two DOF system considering process damping. (a), the dynamical equations can be expressed as:

$$\begin{bmatrix} m_x & 0 \\ 0 & m_y \end{bmatrix} \begin{bmatrix} \ddot{x}(t) \\ \ddot{y}(t) \end{bmatrix} + \begin{bmatrix} c_x & 0 \\ 0 & c_y \end{bmatrix} \begin{bmatrix} \dot{x}(t) \\ \dot{y}(t) \end{bmatrix} + \begin{bmatrix} k_x & 0 \\ 0 & k_y \end{bmatrix} \begin{bmatrix} x(t) \\ y(t) \end{bmatrix} = \begin{bmatrix} \Delta f_x(t) \\ \Delta f_y(t) \end{bmatrix} + \begin{bmatrix} f_{dx}(t) \\ f_{dy}(t) \end{bmatrix} \tag{14}$$

Substitute Eq. (7) and Eq. (12) into Eq. (14), the stability prediction model can be expressed as:

$$\begin{bmatrix} m_x & 0 \\ 0 & m_y \end{bmatrix} \begin{bmatrix} \ddot{x}(t) \\ \ddot{y}(t) \end{bmatrix} + \begin{bmatrix} c_x - c_{xx\_d}(t) & -c_{xy\_d}(t) \\ -c_{yx\_d}(t) & c_y - c_{yy\_d}(t) \end{bmatrix} \begin{bmatrix} \dot{x}(t) \\ \dot{y}(t) \end{bmatrix} + \begin{bmatrix} k_x & 0 \\ 0 & k_y \end{bmatrix} \begin{bmatrix} x(t) \\ y(t) \end{bmatrix}$$
$$= \begin{bmatrix} a_{xx} & a_{xy} \\ a_{yx} & a_{yy} \end{bmatrix} \begin{bmatrix} x(t) - x(t - T) \\ y(t) - y(t - T) \end{bmatrix} \tag{15}$$

It can be seen from Eq. (15) that the damping matrix is changed compared with the traditional stability equation.

3.2 Simulation and Analysis

The FRFs in Fig. 3 is taken as an example for simulation and analysis, the detailed modal parameters are shown in Table 1.

The flat-end milling cutter with 4 teeth and diameter 20 mm is used for simulation, the tangential and radial cutting force coefficients Kt and Kn are set as 3127 MPa and 1769 MPa respectively. The radial immersion ratios aD is set as 0.15, 0.25, 0.37 and 0.5 respectively, the indentation coefficient K_d is set as 13.5e13 N/m^3. The simulation

Table 1. Modal parameters for simulation

	Frequency (Hz)	Damping (%)	Residue
xx	700	5.6	9.1e-012–3.2e-004j
yy	700	4.7	−7.5e-011–2.8e-004j

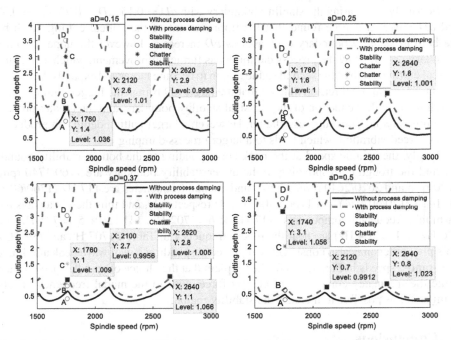

Fig. 5. Simulation results of stability boundary with and without considering process damping.

results of stability boundary with and without considering process damping are shown in Fig. 5.

As can be seen from Fig. 5, the process damping produced by forced vibration has a significant effect on the stability boundary, and detailed performance in the following aspect.

Firstly, process damping leads to two new stability boundaries as shown by the dashed red lines, and the bottom stability boundary improves the original stability boundary, however, with the increase of cutting depth, a new stability boundary appears above the chatter region. In other words, the cutting parameters at point A and point B are stability state and chatter state respectively, but point B also becomes a stable point when considering the damping of the process, and continue as the cut depth increases, the cutting parameters at point C becomes unstable even with considering the process damping. But what is interesting is that as the depth of the cut increases further, a stable region appears, and the cutting parameters at point D becomes a stable cutting point, which is different from the traditional stability prediction with considering process damping. The new stability boundary appears above the chatter region can be explained by that although the increase of cutting depth will lead to the increase of cutting force, further strengthen the conditions for chatter occurrence, however, the increase of cutting force also leads to a larger amplitude of forced vibration, as shown in Fig. 4. When the increased process damping generated by the increased forced vibration amplitude is sufficient to suppress the increased chatter condition, a new stable cutting region appears for the cutting parameters optimization.

Secondly, comparing the stability boundary with $aD = 0.15$, $aD = 0.25$, $aD = 0.37$ and $aD = 0.5$, it can be found that the improvement of the critical cutting depth by the bottom stability boundary decreases as aD increases, however the upper stability boundary produced by the process damping has further improvement, which causes the critical cutting depth of the second stable region to become larger and expands the chatter region. The analytical reason may be that the larger aD brings the bigger cutting force, which leads to the reduction of the classical stability boundary, and the greater process damping is required to suppress chatter. However, a larger cutting depth can produce a larger forced vibration, which leads to a larger process damping.

Lastly, the spindle speed at the peak corresponding to the bottom stability boundary and the trough corresponding to the upper stability boundary are 1760/1740 rpm, 2120 rpm and 2620/2640 rpm, whose fundamental frequencies are 117 Hz (1760/60 × 4), 141 (2120/60 × 4) and 176(2640/60 × 4) respectively, and thus there's always the harmonic frequency components (117 Hz × 6 = 702 Hz, 141 Hz × 5 = 705 Hz and 176 Hz × 4 = 704 Hz) are near the modal frequency in Table 1 (707 Hz and 698 Hz). This phenomenon is also consistent with the corresponding law of wave peak amplitude and spindle speeds in Fig. 4, and further explain that the choice of spindle speed should make the frequency component of cutting force close to the modal frequency of tool point as far as possible to increase the stability region.

4   Conclusions

In this paper, the relationship between forced vibration amplitude and spindle speed - cutting depth is analyzed and then the process damping model with considering forced vibration is established. By introducing the process damping generated by forced vibration, the stability boundary prediction model is established. The simulation results show that the process damping generated by vibration forced has a significant effect on the stability boundary, and the discovery of the secondary stability boundary are the main contribution of this paper. Based on the above research, some conclusions are summarized as follows:

- Above the traditional stability boundary, the process damping generated by vibration forced leads to a new stability boundary. That is, as the cutting depth increases, the cutting state first changes from stable to unstable and then becomes stable again. Therefore, in order to obtain higher cutting efficiency, the secondary stability zone can be explored for milling parameters optimization.
- The stability region influenced by the process damping will decreases as the radial immersion ratios aD increases, thus, aD is also a parameter that can be optimized when considering the process damping generated by vibration forced.

- When the selected spindle speeds have the harmonic frequency components near the modal frequency of tool point, the stability regions are relatively large, and can be used as the preferred spindle speed parameters in milling.

Acknowledgment. This work was partially supported by the Natural Science Foundation of China (92160301, 52005201) and National Science and Technology Major Project of China under Grant No. J2019-VII-0001-0141.

References

1. Altintas, Y., Budak, E.: Analytical prediction of stability lobes in milling. CIRP Ann. Manuf. Technol. **44**(1), 357–362 (1995)
2. Tang, X.W., Peng, F.Y., Yan, R., Gong, Y.H., Li, X.: An effective time domain model for milling stability prediction simultaneously considering multiple modes and cross-frequency response function effect. Int. J. Adv. Manuf. Technol. **86**, 1037–1054 (2016)
3. Tunc, L.T., Budak, E.: Identification and modeling of process damping in milling. ASME J. Manuf. Sci. Eng. **135**(2), 021001 (2013)
4. Budak, E., Tunc, L.T.: A new method for identification and modeling of process damping in machining. ASME J. Manuf. Sci. Eng. **131**(5), 051019 (2009)
5. Ahmadi, K., Ismail, F.: Experimental investigation of process damping nonlinearity in machining chatter. Int. J. Mach. Tools Manuf. **50**(10), 1006–1014 (2010)
6. Merdol, S.D., Altintas, Y.: Multi frequency solution of chatter stability for low immersion milling. ASME J. Manuf. Sci. Eng. **126**, 459–466 (2004)
7. Ding, Y., Zhu, L.M., Zhang, X.J., Ding, H.: A full-discretization method for prediction of milling stability. Int. J. Mach. Tools Manuf. **50**, 502–509 (2010)
8. Tang, X.W., Peng, F.Y., Yan, R., Gong, Y.H., Li, Y.T., Jiang, L.L.: Accurate and efficient prediction of milling stability with updated full-discretization method. Int. J. Adv. Manuf. Technol. **88**, 2357–2368 (2017)
9. Altintas, Y., Weck, M.: Chatter stability in metal cutting and grinding. CIRP Ann. **53**(2), 619–642 (2004)
10. Rahnama, R., Sajjadi, M., Park, S.S.: Chatter suppression in micro end milling with process damping. J. Mater. Process. Technol. **209**, 5766–5776 (2009)
11. Tunc, L.T., Budak, E.: Effect of cutting conditions and tool geometry on process damping in machining. Int. J. Mach. Tools Manuf. **57**, 10–19 (2012)
12. Feng, J., Wan, M., Gao, T.Q., Zhang, W.H.: Mechanism of process damping in milling of thin-walled workpiece. Int. J. Mach. Tools Manuf. **134**, 1–19 (2018)
13. Tuysuz, O., Altintas, Y.: Analytical modeling of process damping in machining. ASME J. Manuf. Sci. Eng. **141**, 061006 (2019)
14. Li, Z.Y., Jiang, S.L., Sun, Y.W.: Chatter stability and surface location error predictions in milling with mode coupling and process damping. Proc. Inst. Mech. Eng. B J. Eng. Manuf. **233**(3), 686–698 (2019)
15. Wang, D.Q., Löser, M., Ihlenfeldt, S., Wang, X.B., Liu, Z.B.: Milling stability analysis with considering process damping and mode shapes of in-process thin-walled workpiece. Int. J. Mech. Sci. **159**, 382–397 (2019)
16. Tang, X.W., Peng, F.Y., Yan, R., Zhu, Z.R., Li, Z.P., Xin, S.H.: Nonlinear process damping identification using finite amplitude stability and the influence analysis on five-axis milling stability. Int. J. Mech. Sci. **190**, 106008 (2021)

17. Shi, Z.Y., Liu, L.N., Liu, Z.Q.: Influence of dynamic effects on surface roughness for face milling process. Int. J. Adv. Manuf. Technol. **80**, 1823–1831 (2015)
18. Xin, S.H., Peng, F.Y., Tang, X.W., Yan, R., Li, Z.P., Wu, J.W.: Research on the influence of robot structural mode on regenerative chatter in milling and analysis of stability boundary improvement domain. Int. J. Mach. Tools Manuf. **179**, 103918 (2022)
19. Liu, Q., Li, Z.: Simulation and optimization of CNC milling process-modeling, algorithms and application, pp. 35–37. Aviation Industry Press, Beijing (2011)
20. Yang, M., Park, H.: The prediction of cutting force in ball end milling. Int. J. Mach. Tools Manuf. **31**(1), 45–54 (1991)
21. Zhu, Z.R., et al.: Parametric chip thickness model based cutting forces estimation considering cutter runout of five-axis general end milling. Int. J. Mach. Tools Manuf. **101**, 35–51 (2016)
22. Shawky, A.M., Elbestawi, M.A.: An enhanced dynamic model in turning including the effect of ploughing forces. ASME J. Manuf. Sci. Eng. **119**(1), 10–20 (1997)

Positioning Error Modelling and Compensation Method for Robot Machining Based on RVM

Jinzhu Wu[1,2], Zhaoyang Liao[2(✉)], Hongmin Wu[2], Li Jiang[1], and Kezheng Sun[2]

[1] Wuyi University, Jiangmen, China
[2] Institute of Intelligent Manufacturing, Guangdong Academy of Sciences,
Guangdong Key Laboratory of Modern Control Technology,
Guangzhou 510070, China
zy.liao@giim.ac.cn

Abstract. The low absolute positioning accuracy of industrial robots leads to low machining accuracy, seriously hindering the development and application of robots in the field of high-precision machining. To solve this problem, this article proposes a robot machining positioning error modeling and compensation method based on RVM. This method takes advantage of RVM's adaptive parameters and high sparsity to identify the strong nonlinear positioning error. Then, based on the error model, the iterative compensation problem is transformed into an optimization problem to reduce the number of inverse kinematic computations of the robot. Finally, through experiments, the effectiveness of positioning error prediction and compensation is demonstrated.

Keywords: Industrial robots · Trajectory accuracy · RVM · Error compensation

1 Introduction

In recent years, robotic manufacturing as a new solution for large complex components has attracted extensive research from domestic and foreign scholars. Compared with traditional CNC machine tools, robots have unique advantages in manufacturing, including low cost, high flexibility, good adaptability, wide working range, and strong parallel co-ordination ability [1]. At the same time, with robots as the center of manufacturing, in combination with external sensing

This work is co-supported by the National Key R&D Program of China [Grant No. 2022YFB4702500], and the National Natural Science Foundation of China [Grant No. U22A20176], the Guangdong HUST Industrial Technology Research Institute, Guangdong Provincial Key Laboratory of Manufacturing Equipment Digitization [Grant NO. 2020B1212060014], the Guangdong Basic and Applied Basic Research Foundation [Grant No. 2021A1515110898], the GDAS' Project of Science and Technology Development [Grant No. 2020GDASYL-20200202001].

H. Yang et al. (Eds.): ICIRA 2023, LNAI 14272, pp. 383–394, 2023.
https://doi.org/10.1007/978-981-99-6480-2_32

and measurement devices such as vision and force sensors, based on optimization algorithms, real-time optimization of process parameters and motion parameters can play a role in active control of the machining process.

In milling machining, machining accuracy is one of the most important evaluation indicators. However, due to the assembly errors at the robot joints and the errors caused by gear backlash and deformation, the absolute positioning accuracy of the robot is low. Positioning errors limit the further application and promotion of robots in high-precision machining and precision operations [2].

Due to the influence of the robot's structure, the positioning accuracy of the robot will vary with the position and posture of the robot throughout the workspace [3]. Usually, before a robot performs a task, the base coordinate system is calibrated and used for the task, thereby reducing some of the absolute positioning errors. However, in large-scale complex tasks such as processing large and complex components using robots, the robot needs to make significant changes in position and posture, causing both the magnitude and direction of its positioning error to change significantly, making it extremely difficult to control machining accuracy. In robot positioning error identification, the method of robot geometric parameter calibration is commonly used, and robot positioning error calibration can be divided into kinematic model [4] and non-kinematic model [5]. Ma L [6] points out that classical model-based robot positioning error calibration methods only consider constant geometric errors and ignore more complex non-geometric errors such as bearing system and gear non-uniformity, which limits the effectiveness of positioning error prediction. Building a mapping relationship between robot configuration and end-point error using intelligent algorithms such as neural networks can accurately identify non-geometric errors and improve compensation accuracy [7]. Xu [8] used the fast backpropagation algorithm to train a feedforward neural network to predict joint errors, and then applied it to the robot's control system to correct positioning errors. Nguyen [9,10] pointed out that due to the difficulties or impossibility of accurately and completely modeling non-geometric error sources such as link deflection errors, joint flexibility errors, gear backlash, etc. Artificial neural networks are used to compensate for these difficult-to-model errors, and the extended Kalman filter algorithm is used to identify the geometrical parameters of each joint of the robot. Combining robot geometric error identification based on the EKF model with compensation technology based on neural networks can effectively solve the correction problem of all robot error sources. Li B [11] proposed a method for predicting robot positioning errors based on genetic particle swarm optimization of neural networks, and used prediction errors to compensate for the end-point position of the robot, thereby improving the machining accuracy of the robot. Zhou W [12] pointed out that there is an inherent relationship between the positioning accuracy of two adjacent points at the end of a robot, and this characteristic is called positioning error similarity. Aiming to leverage the error similarity, Wang W [13] proposed a method for predicting the pose error of industrial robots based on deep belief networks. They established a mapping model between the end-effector pose coordinate and the pose error, and by combining it with offline feedforward compensation methods, they improved the absolute positioning accuracy of the robot. Generally, existing research takes the end-effector position and orientation of the robot as input, establishes a mapping relationship with the positioning error, and predicts the end-effector positioning error. There is a strong correlation between the time and spatial relationships of joint configurations and the end-effector positioning error. If the relative spatiotemporal relationships between the data can be applied to the prediction of robot positioning error, the accuracy of robot positioning error prediction can be improved. Luo [14] proposed a calibration method for robot kinematic parameters that combines Levenberg-Marquardt and differential evolution algorithms. This method not only improves convergence speed but also reduces the impact of high-order nonlinear errors on prediction accuracy. Compensation for robot machining errors can be divided into online feedback compensation and offline preemptive compensation. The offline preemptive compensation method improves positioning accuracy by pre-compensating for errors. The offline preemptive compensation method only needs to pre-correct the tool trajectory based on the predicted joint error to compensate for the error. The online feedback compensation method corrects tracking errors by measuring the robot's absolute position with additional sensing devices [15,16]. Ma [17] predicted the positioning error of robot milling using an incremental extreme learning model and compensated for the error using an offline feedforward compensation method. This method requires minor adjustments to the model with a few measurement points when the robot moves to a new machining position.

Online methods depend on external precision measuring equipment and systems, which are expensive and have time delays during compensation. Therefore, they are difficult to apply in actual machining. On the other hand, offline methods are more efficient due to the ease of obtaining data on positioning errors through measurements and designing algorithms to create prediction models. By using preset prediction models, the offline method can obtain the robot end-effector errors with high efficiency.

2 Modelling of Robot Milling Machining Errors

2.1 Positioning Error Modeling Based on RVM Model

RVM (Relevance Vector Machine) is a machine learning algorithm based on sparse Bayesian inference. Compared with SVM (Support Vector Machine), RVM has the advantages of simpler parameter settings, higher sparsity, probabilistic output, and basis functions that are not restricted by Mercer condition, while maintaining a high accuracy level similar to SVM [18,19]. It can be used for regression and classification problems and has achieved good results in applications such as image classification, fault detection, and various predictions. RVM has the advantage of high accuracy due to its excellent feature selection ability, efficient Bayesian inference algorithm, and the use of sparse vectors.And RVM is able to use fewer support vectors while maintaining high accuracy, as shown in Fig. 1, the mean predicted by RVM is represented by the red curve, and the shaded area represents the position of the standard deviation. In addition, data points are represented by a circle, and points corresponding to the relevant vectors are marked with two circles.

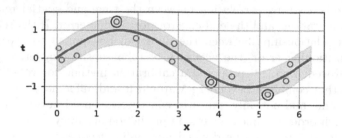

Fig. 1. Diagram of RVM Regression.

The RVM algorithm used in this article adopts the RBF (Radial Basis Function), which is a single hidden layer feedforward neural network that uses RBF as the activation function for the hidden layer neurons, while the output layer is a linear combination of the outputs of the hidden layer neurons. Assuming the training dataset is $\{x_i, t_i\}_{i=1}^n$, where $\{x_i\}_{i=1}^n = [x_1, \cdots, x_n]^T$ is the input vector, $\{t_i\}_{i=1}^n = [t_1, t_2, \cdots, t_n]^T$ is an independent target value vector, $t \in \{1, 2, 3, \cdots, C\}$, and the noise model is:

$$t_i = y(x_i, W) + \varepsilon_i \tag{1}$$

where $W = [w_1, w_2, \cdots, w_n]^T$ is the weight vector, $\mathcal{E}_i$ is Gaussian sample noise with mean 0, variance σ^2, and mutually independent, therefore the Gaussian distribution is:

$$p(t_i|x_i) = N(t_i|y(x_i, W), \sigma^2) \tag{2}$$

The mathematical model of RVM can be represented as:

$$y(x; W) = \sum_{1}^{n} w_i \cdot k(x, x_i) + w_0 \tag{3}$$

where n is the number of samples. Training RVM is to find suitable weights w_i for the kernel function under the sparse Bayesian framework. $k(\cdot, \cdot)$ is the kernel function, and in this paper, the RBF is used as follows:

$$k(x_i, y_i) = \sigma_f^2 \, exp\left(-\frac{(x_i - y_j)^2}{2\sigma_t^2}\right) \tag{4}$$

where is calculated by the squared exponential kernel function. σ_t is the length scale of the kernel, σ_f is the output variance, and $(x_i - x_j)^2$ is the Euclidean distance.

With the introduction of hyperparameter $\beta = \frac{1}{\sigma^2}$, the equation for calculating the likelihood function of the corresponding training dataset is as follows:

$$p(T|W,\beta) = \left(\frac{\beta}{2\pi}\right)^{\frac{-n}{2}} exp\left(-\frac{\beta}{2}||T - \Phi W||^2\right) \tag{5}$$

where $T = (t_1, t_2, \cdots, t_n)^T$, $\Phi = [\Phi(x_1)\ \Phi(x_2)\cdots\Phi(x_n)]^T$, T and $\Phi \in R^{n(n+1)}$ are all pre-designed n*(n+1) matrices, and the RBF vector is denoted as $\Phi(x_i) = [1\ k(x_i, x_1)\cdots k(x_i, x_n)]^T$.

In order to obtain the weight vector and avoid overfitting, ensuring the sparsity of the RVM model, we assume that the weight w_i follows a Gaussian distribution with mean 0 and variance α_i^{-1} within the sparse Bayesian framework. Therefore, the prior probability distribution of the weight vector is given by:

$$p(W|\Lambda) = \prod_{i=0}^{n} N(w_i|0, \alpha_i^{-1}) \tag{6}$$

where Λ is a hyperparameter vector with n+1 dimensions, where $\Lambda = (\alpha_0, \cdots, \alpha_n)^T$ and each independent α_i is only related to its corresponding weight w_i. $N(\cdot)$ represents the normal distribution function.

Hence, the posterior distribution calculation for weight vectors can be formulated based on the Bayesian equation through Eqs. 5 and 6:

$$p(W|T, \Lambda, \beta) = \frac{p(T|W,\beta)\mathbf{p}(W|\Lambda)}{p(T|\Lambda, \beta)} \tag{7}$$

where since both $p(T|W,\beta)$ and $p(W|\Lambda)$ are Gaussian distributions and $p(W|\Lambda)$ does not contain weight vectors, it can be regarded as a normalization coefficient. Therefore, the posterior distribution of weight vectors can be expressed as:

$$p(T|\Lambda, \beta) = N(W|U, \Sigma) \tag{8}$$

where the mean and posterior covariance matrix are respectively:

$$\begin{cases} U = \beta\Sigma\Phi^T T \\ \Sigma = \left(\beta\Phi^T\Phi + A\right)^{-1} \end{cases} \tag{9}$$

where $A = diag(a_0, a_1, \cdots, a_n)$. The posterior distribution of weight vectors is directly influenced by hyperparameters β and Λ. In the process of estimating the convergence of hyperparameters, it is necessary to optimize them to obtain the maximum posterior distribution of weight vectors. When combining with the maximum likelihood method, the hyperparameters Λ_{MP} and noise variance σ_{MP}^2 to be maximized are defined, and:

$$p(t_i|T) = \int p(t_i|W, \Lambda, \sigma^2)p(W, \Lambda, \sigma^2|T)dWd\Lambda d\sigma^2 \tag{10}$$

Taking the partial derivative of Eq. 10 with respect to Λ and setting it to 0, the hyperparameters and noise variance are iterated through the following equation:

$$\begin{cases} \alpha_i^{\text{new}} \equiv \frac{\gamma_i}{\mu_i^2} \\[2mm] \beta^{\text{new}} = \frac{\left(N - \sum_i \gamma_i\right)}{\|T - \Phi U\|^2} \end{cases} \tag{11}$$

Equation 10 can calculate the prediction of the Gaussian distribution. If the input value x_i is given and we have:

$$p(W|T, A, \sigma^2) = (2\pi)^{-\frac{n+1}{2}} |\Sigma|^{-\frac{1}{2}} exp\left\{-\frac{1}{2}(W - \mu)^{\mathsf{T}} \Sigma (W - \mu)\right\} \tag{12}$$

According to Eq. 12, the corresponding output probability distribution is:

$$p\big(t_i|T, \Lambda_{\text{MP}}, \sigma_{\text{MP}}^2)\big) = \int p(t_i|W, \sigma_{\text{MP}}^2) p(W|T, \Lambda_{\text{MP}}, \sigma_{\text{MP}}^2) \mathrm{d}W \tag{13}$$

After simplifying Eq. 13, we have:

$$p\big(t_i|T, \Lambda_{\text{MP}}, \sigma_{\text{MP}}^2\big) = N\big(t_i|y_i, \sigma_i^2\big) \tag{14}$$

where

$$y_i = \mu^{\mathsf{T}} \phi(x_i), \sigma_i^2 = \sigma_{\text{MP}}^2 + \phi(x_i)^{\mathsf{T}} \Sigma \phi(x_i) \tag{15}$$

From Eq. 14, we can see that the prediction results of RVM regression can be intuitively represented as $y(x_i; \mu)$. The noise in the data determines the uncertainty in the prediction process.

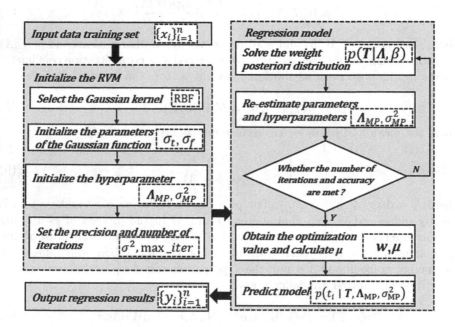

Fig. 2. Construction Process of RVM Prediction Model.

3 Robotic Milling Error Compensation

3.1 Method for Compensating Robot Positioning Error

The general process of error compensation includes predicting the error at the current position, compensating for the position based on the size and direction of the error. Since new errors can be generated after the position compensation, a single compensation often results in new errors (see Fig. 3). To address this issue, multiple iterations are usually required to obtain satisfactory results. However, in the robot pose error model, the input parameters are the robot's joint coordinates. When performing TCP position adjustment, inverse kinematics calculation is required, which leads to long computation time and low efficiency for multiple iterations.

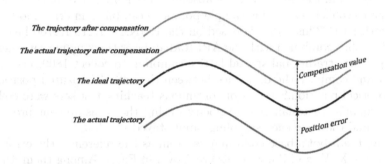

Fig. 3. The situation where error compensation is coupled with error.

In this section, we propose a solution to the compensation problem by transforming it into an optimization problem based on the robot pose error prediction model. This method reduces the number of inverse kinematics calculations and improves computation efficiency. The specific procedure is as follows. First, the ideal robot pose is obtained by inverse kinematics using the desired end-effector pose. Then, an optimization is performed within a specified range to obtain the predicted robot pose based on the robot pose error prediction model. Finally, the current joint coordinates are compared with the desired pose accuracy based on the predicted pose. To accomplish this, an optimization objective function is constructed as follows:

$$
\begin{cases}
\min \Delta_{\text{tran}}(\theta_i) \\
s.t. \theta_{i,e} = f_{ik}^{-1}(p_w^i) \\
\theta_{i,e} - \delta \leq \theta_i \leq \theta_{i,e} + \delta \\
\theta_{\min} \leq \theta_i \leq \theta_{\max}
\end{cases}
\tag{16}
$$

where θ represents the joint angles of the robot, which are coordinate information in the configuration space. p represents the end-effector coordinates in the Cartesian space, while f_{ik} represents the inverse kinematics of the robot, which requires only one calculation to obtain the ideal joint angle information. The joint angles are constrained within a certain range near the ideal values and satisfy the joint limits of the robot. The optimization range is 5 of the ideal joint coordinates based on the error value, and the optimization algorithm uses a genetic algorithm that is directly available through the toolbox in Matlab software. During the optimization iteration process, only forward kinematics computation is required, which avoids efficiency reduction caused by frequent inverse kinematics calculations.

4   Experimental Validation and Analysis

4.1   Validation of Positioning Error Prediction Model Effectiveness

In order to obtain the distribution of absolute positioning error of the robot, it is necessary to collect reasonable sample points to establish an error model of the robot workspace. This paper is based on the KUKA KR210 R2700 heavy-duty industrial robot combined with the API Radian laser tracking measurement system to perform traditional spatial lattice sampling to collect 1800 sets of training data and compare the difference between the actual measured position and the theoretical position.200 sets of continuous teaching test sets were collected, and the robot's Cartesian space velocity during the measurement process was 0.02 m/s, and the time each sampling point stayed was 3 s.

Taking the robot's base coordinate system as the reference, the error distribution of the X, Y, and Z directions are shown in Fig. 4. Among them, the error range of the X direction is [−2.688, 1.8123], the error range of the Y direction is [−2.0267, 2.8543], and the error range of the Z direction is [−2.9617, 2.761]. As a result, the position error of 200 sets of sample points and their corresponding joint coordinates were obtained.

In order to predict the absolute positioning error of any point in any posture of the robot, it is necessary to establish a mapping relationship between the robot's joint space and end-effector error through a set of sample points. Taking the joint coordinates of the six-degree-of-freedom KUKA robot as input and the TCP point position error as output, the RVM was trained to predict the TCP point position error. Figure 2 shows the process of building the RVM prediction model, with the kernel length scale σ_t of 1.5, the output variance σ_f of 1, the hyperparameter Λ_{MP} of 1e5, the noise variance σ^2_{MP} of 1e–5, the number of iterations is 3000, and other parameters use default values.

The positioning accuracy of the robot's TCP point depends on the accuracy of the RVM prediction model. By predicting the errors in X, Y, and Z directions for 200 sets of sample points, the deviation between the actual error values and predicted error values was obtained. As shown in Fig. 5, the deviations in X, Y, and Z directions are ±0.15 mm, ±0.25 mm, and ±0.20 mm, respectively.

Table 1 presents a comparison of fitting accuracy for three kernel functions, RBF, Matern, and RationalQuadratic, which perform well in the RVM. For the same set of 230 sample points, the fitting errors for RBF range from [-0.151,0.236],

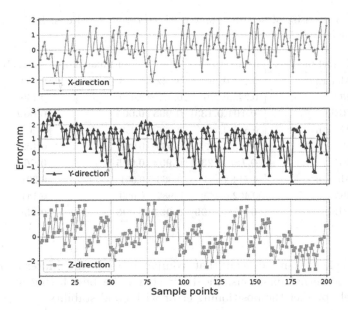

Fig. 4. Position error of the robot in the X, Y, and Z directions.

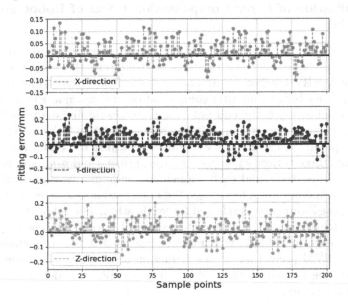

Fig. 5. Deviation between the actual error and estimated value of the sample points in X, Y, and Z directions.

for RationalQuadratic range from [−0.402,0.522], and for Matern range from [−4.714,4.434]. The kernel length scale for all three kernel functions was set to 1.5.

Table 1. Comparison of accuracy among three kernel functions: RBF, Matern, and RationalQuadratic(RQ).

Direction	Kernel function	Fitting error	R^2	Mean square error	Mean absolute error
X	Matern	[−0.151,0.199]	0.942	0.063	0.209
X	RQ	[−0.245,0.370]	0.972	0.030	0.146
X	RBF	**[−0.101,0.133]**	**0.995**	**0.005**	**0.060**
Y	Matern	[−0.586,0.587]	0.935	0.058	0.200
Y	RQ	[−0.363,0.522]	0.969	0.027	0.139
Y	RBF	**[−0.135,0.236]**	**0.993**	**0.005**	**0.063**
Z	Matern	[−4.714,4.434]	0.963	0.061	0.201
Z	RQ	[−0.402,0.389]	0.982	0.029	0.141
Z	RBF	**[−0.151,0.199]**	**0.997**	**0.005**	**0.059**

From Table 1, it can be seen that compared with the Matern and RationalQuadratic kernel functions, the RBF shows the best fitting accuracy, and can precisely predict the positioning error with good stability.

4.2 Verification of Error Compensation Effect of Robot Surface Milling

In order to verify the effectiveness of the proposed localization error compensation method, it is necessary to study and analyze the trajectory accuracy of the KUKA KR210 robot itself. The design of the tested trajectory and the milling trajectory before and after compensation are shown in Fig. 6, where p_0 is the starting point, p_{12} is the end point, and the machining depth is 2 mm. The designed trajectory is programmed in the robot teach pendant, and the positioning error is predicted using the RVM model to adjust the execution trajectory. After milling, three trajectory segments, p_0p_1, $p_1p_2p_6$, and $p_2p_3p_5p_2$, are selected for testing in this study, and each segment is randomly measured with 10 data points using a line laser as a test. Since the main load in this experiment is on the Z direction, the Z direction is selected for verification. The robot trajectory error is obtained by comparing it with the theoretical trajectory. The experimental results are shown in Table 2, which demonstrates that the compensation effect is good after RVM prediction, with a reduction of 0.09591 mm in mean absolute error, confirming the effectiveness of the proposed RVM model in compensating for positioning errors.

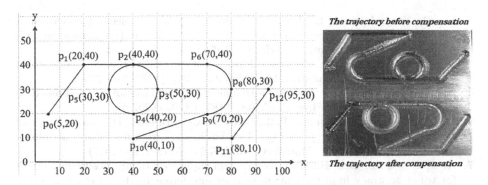

Fig. 6. The schematic of the x-y test trajectory plane and the real milling trajectory before and after compensation are shown.

Table 2. Comparison of the effects before and after compensation of positioning error.

Experiment	Trajectory	Mean absolute error
	p_0p_1	0.11650
Before compensation	$p_1p_2p_6$	0.08800
	$p_2p_3p_5p_2$	0.18099
	p_0p_1	**0.02549**
After compensation	$p_1p_2p_6$	**0.05859**
	$p_2p_3p_5p_2$	**0.03369**

5 Conclusion

(1) In order to improve the positioning accuracy of the robot, this article uses the RVM model to predict the positioning error of the robot end effector and perform offline compensation.

(2) In the process of error compensation, based on the robot pose error prediction model, the compensation problem is transformed into an optimization problem to reduce the number of inverse kinematic computations of the robot.

(3) After validation on the test set, the prediction accuracy of the positioning error model reached 99%. The milling error was reduced by 69.4% after compensation.

(4) The following work will consider comparing RVM with other methods, such as the differences between RVM, neural networks, and Gaussian processes.

References

1. Kai, W., Li, J., Zhao, H., Zhong, Y.: Review of industrial robot stiffness identification and modelling. Appl. Sci. **12**(17), 8719 (2022)
2. Xie, H., Li, W.L., Zhu, D., Yin, Z., Ding, H.: A systematic model of machining error reduction in robotic grinding. IEEE/ASME Trans. Mechatron. **PP**(99), 1 (2020)

3. Ye, C., Yang, J., Zhao, H., Ding, H.: Task-dependent workpiece placement optimization for minimizing contour errors induced by the low posture-dependent stiffness of robotic milling. Int. J. Mech. Sci. **205**, 106601 (2021)
4. Nubiola, A., Bonev, I.A.: Absolute calibration of an ABB IRB 1600 robot using a laser tracker. Robot. Comput. Integr. Manufact. **29**(1), 236–245 (2013)
5. Hu, J., Hua, F., Tian, W.: Robot positioning error compensation method based on deep neural network. J. Phys: Conf. Ser. **1487**, 012045 (2020)
6. Ma, L., Bazzoli, P., Sammons, P.M., Landers, R.G., Bristow, D.A.: Modeling and calibration of high-order joint-dependent kinematic errors for industrial robots. Robot. Comput.-Integrat. Manufact. **50**, S0736584517301965 (2017)
7. Alici, G., Shirinzadeh, B.: A systematic technique to estimate positioning errors for robot accuracy improvement using laser interferometry based sensing. Mech. Machine Theory **40**(8), 879–906 (2005)
8. Xu, W.L., Wurst, K.H., Watanabe, T., Yang, S.Q.: Calibrating a modular robotic joint using neural network approach. In: IEEE World Congress on IEEE International Conference on Neural Networks (1994)
9. Nguyen, A.H.N., Zhou, A.J., Kang, B.H.J.: A calibration method for enhancing robot accuracy through integration of an extended Kalman filter algorithm and an artificial neural network. Neurocomputing **151**, 996–1005 (2015)
10. Nguyen, H.N., Le, P.N., Kang, H.J.: A new calibration method for enhancing robot position accuracy by combining a robot model-based identification approach and an artificial neural network-based error compensation technique. Adv. Mech. Eng. **11**(1), 168781401882293 (2019)
11. Li, B., Tian, W., Zhang, C., Hua, F., Li, Y.: Positioning error compensation of an industrial robot using neural networks and experimental study. Chin. J. Aeronautics **35**(3), 346–360 2021
12. Zhou, W.: Theory and experiment of industrial robot accuracy compensation method based on spatial interpolation. J. Mech. Eng. **49**(3), 7 (2013)
13. Wang, W., Tian, W., Liao, W., Li, B., Hu, J.: Error compensation of industrial robot based on deep belief network and error similarity. Robot. Comput.-Integr. Manufact. **73**(8), 102220 (2022)
14. Luo, G., Zou, L., Wang, Z., Lv, C., Huang, Y.: A novel kinematic parameters calibration method for industrial robot based on Levenberg-Marquardt and differential evolution hybrid algorithm. Robot. Comput.-Integr. Manufact. **71**(1), 102165 (2021)
15. Dongdong, C., Peijiang, Y., Tianmiao, W., Ying, C., Lei, X.: A compensation method for enhancing aviation drilling robot accuracy based on co-kriging. Int. J. Precis. Eng. Manuf. **19**(8), 1133–1142 (2018)
16. Gong, C., Yuan, J., Ni, J.: Nongeometric error identification and compensation for robotic system by inverse calibration. Int. J. Mach. Tools Manufact. **40**(14), 2119–2137 (2000)
17. Ma, S., Deng, K., Lu, Y., et al.: Robot error compensation based on incremental extreme learning machines and an improved sparrow search algorithm. Int. J. Adv. Manuf. Technol. **125**, 5431–5443 (2023)
18. Zhijun, W., Gao, P., Cui, L., Chen, J.: An incremental learning method based on dynamic ensemble RVM for intrusion detection. IEEE Trans. Netw. Serv. Manage. **19**(1), 671–685 (2022)
19. Nao, S., Wang, Y.: Fault detection of gearbox by multivariate extended variational mode decomposition-based time-frequency images and incremental RVM algorithm. Sci. Rep. **13**(1), 7950 (2023)

Design and Implementation of a Novel Agricultural Robot with Multi-Modal Kinematics

Anzheng Zhang[1], Yuzhen Pan[2], Chenyun Zhang[1], Jinhua Wang[3], Guangrong Chen[4], and Huiliang Shang[1(✉)]

[1] School of Information Science, Fudan University, Shanghai 200433, China
shanghl@fudan.edu.cn
[2] Academy for Engineering and Technology, Fudan University, Shanghai 200433, China
[3] Bright Homeport Seed Technology Company, Shanghai 202150, China
[4] Bright Food Group Shanghai Chongming Farm Company, Shanghai 202150, China

Abstract. Robotics applied in agriculture is one of the most prosperous fields in modern technology. In this paper, we design and implement a novel agricultural robot FDU-AgRobot with multi-modal kinematics, making up for the shortage of personnel in a complex and changeable agrarian environment. Considering the low moving efficiency of the existing agricultural machinery, the FDU-AgRobot is an intelligent multi-modal agricultural robot driven by four-wheel independent steering and driving based on the modular design. This novel modular design enables the robot to have multi-modal kinematics characteristics, contributing to higher moving efficiency and less working space. In addition, we present six types of kinematics modalities while analyzing the kinematics characteristics and simplifying the corresponding mode algorithm. In the experiment, We apply the motion model on the robot with motion identification and multiple mode test; the results show that the robot can achieve the desired motion effect. This paper could be an indispensable theoretical and experimental research tool for the intelligent agricultural robot's system design, demonstrating excellent adaptability to complex agricultural scenarios.

Keywords: Agricultural robot · Intelligent farming · Kinematic analysis

1 Introduction

A robot is a complex, intelligent machine that integrates various disciplines, including mechanical engineering, computer technology, electronics, control technology, artificial intelligence, bionics, HIR [1], etc. The application of agricultural robots in agricultural production has promoted the modernization, mechanization, and brightness of agricultural development. Therefore, some researchers call this technology Agriculture 4.0 [2]. The wide application of agricultural robots is changing traditional agricultural labor

This work was supported by the Shanghai Science and Technology Agriculture Promotion Project under Grant 2022-02-08-00-12-F01128.

methods, reducing farmers' labor force, and gradually promoting modern agriculture's development. Agricultural robots are becoming more and more appreciated by countries around the world [3], so agricultural robots are showing a significant trend. Nowadays, agricultural robots are mainly used in fruit picking, weeding, pollination, plant protection [4] and carrying agricultural machinery, which could provide an effective solution for reducing labor and improving agricultural production efficiency. Increasing the research and development of intelligent picking robots is necessary to fill the market demand so that low-cost, high-efficiency and high-precision orchard-picking robots can be applied as soon as possible.

Here we present several typical agricultural robots. Researchers from Norwegian University demonstrate an agricultural robotic system [5] with many types of assembled robots from different modules. Still, the movement of the robot's side may complicate the task of adapting tools. The University of Georgia presents a modular agricultural robotic system for precision farming [6], which is quite inspiring for the robot system's design. However, this paper does not mention its implementation of the navigation algorithm. Indiana University designs an autonomous fertilizing and navigation system for agricultural robots [7] using machine learning algorithms to detect common weeds. However, this has no modular design, and the function is relatively simple. The University of Galati proposes a four-wheel steering vehicle [8] focusing on lateral motion control using a sliding-mode controller (SMC). This outdoor robot has many application scenarios, so it does not have a specific agricultural task.

In this paper, we design and implement a novel agricultural robot FDU-AgRobot with multi-modal kinematics applied to various scenarios. The second section focuses on the design of the FDU-AgRobot. We propose a four-wheel independent steering robot and explain the design scheme of the hardware and software systems. In the third section, we highlight the significance of multi-modal kinematics and present six different types of kinematics modalities (we apply five in our robot). In the next section, we conduct our experiment on the agricultural robot; it can achieve high-precision multi-modal motion control applied to various scenarios.

2   Robot Design

2.1   Mechanical Design

The four-wheel robot FDU-AgRobot in Fig. 1 designed in this paper has better stability for both low and high speed in the kinematics mode. Currently, most four-wheeled mobile robots use differential steering, or Ackermann steering [9]. The differential motion requires the existence of two Omni wheels or two swivel wheels, which is not conducive to the high-precision control of the robot. Meanwhile, the structure of the Omni wheels and swivel wheels may exert a negative impact on the robot due to their dead centers, which require human intervention from time to time, and being prone to less autonomy of the robot. For the Ackermann steering motion, most current cars use the Ackermann steering [10]. Nevertheless, the shortcomings of this Ackermann steering mode are also apparent since parking the vehicle in the parking space and driving backward require the drivers' rich experience. We can see that the flexibility of the Ackermann steering motion is low. In addition, four-wheeled mobile robots are currently popular with Mecanum wheels [11]. But this structure is only suitable for smooth and free of debris (such as clean factories), not for use in the field. We designed this structure because the field operation environment is complex, and the steering ability of the robot is required to be high.

Fig. 1. FDU-AgRobot

For the frame module, the robot's frame consists of steel, which can significantly improve the strength and stability of the structure. The robot is equipped with a rotatable mechanism. Accessory modules such as robotic arms and other agricultural machinery can be installed on it to achieve corresponding functions. As for the power module, we choose four hub motors and four servo steering motors. Each hub motor and steering motor form a module to realize the four wheels' independent drive and steering. The advantage of the in-wheel engine is that the actuator is integrated into the wheel, reducing the drive structure's space and simplifying the mechanical system. Track wheels can also be installed on the hub motor so the robot can also run on the track. Due to the complex working environment, the suspension module is also essential, ensuring that the wheels are fully contacted with the ground and have enough friction to reduce the error of the drive wheel encoder. These modules play a crucial role in subsequent motion control and navigation. The power module is connected to the robot frame module through the suspension module.

2.2 Electrical System Design

The block diagram of the robot electrical system is shown in Fig. 2, which mainly includes the power, high-level, low-level, and motor parts. The power part provides the energy for the whole robot. Lithium battery is the energy source because it has a high energy storage rate and is lightweight; The High-level controller is the robot's brain, which needs to run complicated programs. A computer with Linux is used to do this work. The interaction module and the perception module are directly connected to it; The low-level controller part uses an STM32 single-chip, and it connects with the computer through a serial port to realize data transmission. It receives control commands from the computer to control the motor and sends the robot status information measured by the sensor to the computer; The motor driver communicates with the STM32 through the CAN bus, receives the control command, and drives the motor. The driving motor adopts speed control, and the steering motor adopts position control to realize the robot's various motion modes.

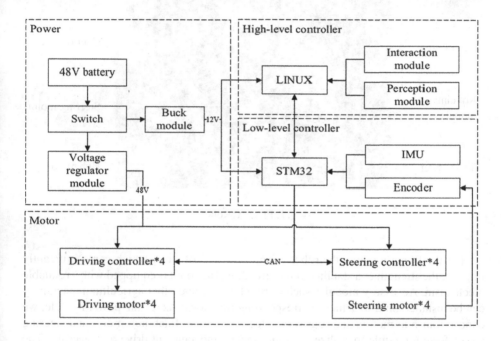

Fig. 2. Electrical System Block Diagram

2.3 Software System Design

The robot's software system is shown in Fig. 3. The computer with Linux runs the ROS2 (Robot Operating System2), encapsulates the code into the ROS2 node, and realizes the message transmission between nodes [12]. It includes an external control node, motion mode transition node, and information fusion node. The STM32 runs the FreeR-TOS(embedded real-time system) and assigns the implemented functions as tasks, each task has a priority, and this way can improve the real-time performance of the system [13]. It includes motor control tasks and information collection tasks.

The working process is as follows: the external input node publishes the control topic, and the mode conversion node calculates the desired state of each motor according to the kinematics model, then sends them to STM32 through the serial port. The motor control task communicates with the motor controller to drive the motor. The information collection task obtains the state of each engine from the encoder, gets the form of the robot from the IMU, then sends these data to the information fusion node. We can estimate the motion state of the robot through the Kalman filter algorithm and visualize it in RVIZ2.

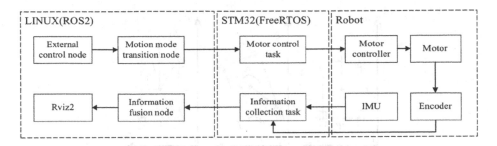

Fig. 3. Software System Block Diagram

3 Multi-Modal Kinematics

3.1 Concept of Multi-Modal

Mobile robots are inclined to be more commonly noticed in daily life and work. As for the agricultural scenarios in this paper, we use wheeled robots when designing the FDU-AgRobot in Sect. 2, which are relatively less complicated to control and could save more energy than legged robots. However, the obstacle-surmounting ability of wheeled robots is inferior to that of legged robots. In future work, we will combine the design of legged robots [14] based on wheeled agricultural robots.

Considering that our four-wheel independent steering and driving mobile robots have higher degrees of freedom, this type of design is significantly more feasible than other mobile robots in terms of steering, motion flexibility, and motion stability control. Some literature calls this type of steering motion four-wheel independent steering (4WIS) [15]. However, few papers mention the multi-modal movement pattern, and even few present its algorithm with mathematical analysis, which will be analyzed in this section. Due to higher degrees of freedom (DOF), this 8-DOF agricultural robot with four steering joints and four driving actuators could demonstrate constructive performance, especially in the intelligent farming scenario. The agricultural robot moves between each line of plants, such as vegetables and fruit trees. The distance between each line may be narrow, so our multi-modal kinematics robot needs to have various movement patterns in different situations. The type of multi-modal kinematics will be judged and decided by the robot regarding the actual situation. Here we present six types of kinematics modalities as shown in Fig. 4 and Fig. 5 to meet different agricultural scenarios:

- (a) Straight driving;
- (b) Pivot steering & spinning;
- (c) Crab steering;
- (d) General active front and rear steering (AFRS) [16];
- (e) Non-eccentric AFRS steering & arc-shape steering;
- (f) Ackermann steering;

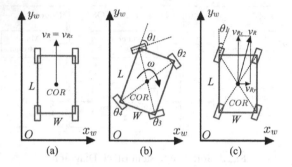

(a)   (b)   (c)

Fig. 4. Multi-modal kinematics of the FDU-AgRobot (a) Straight driving (b) Pivot steering (c) Crab steering

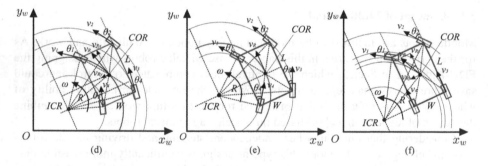

(d)   (e)   (f)

Fig. 5. Multi-modal kinematics of the FDU-AgRobot (d) General active front and rear steering (AFRS) (e) Arc-shape steering (f) Ackermann steering

3.2 Kinematics Analysis of the Robot

This paper introduces six types of kinematics modality, as shown in Fig. 4 and 5. All these kinematics modalities could enhance our robot's ability and effect of movement, making it more flexible for the agricultural robot to engage in production activities. When using ROS (Robot Operation System) to control the robot, it usually requires us input six different parameters: the robot's linear velocity $v = [v_x, v_y, v_z]$, and its angular velocity $\omega = [\omega_x, \omega_y, \omega_z]$ because it is the speed topic message type provided by ROS.

Since this robot only operates close to the ground, $v_z = 0, \omega_x = \omega_y = 0$. At each multi-modal kinematics pattern algorithm, we only need to input three different parameters: $Input = [v_x, v_y, \omega_z]$. The length and width of the robot are expressed as L and W.

In the following calculation, we need to use $\boldsymbol{Input} = [v_x, v_y, \omega_z]$ to express the velocity and angle of each wheel in (1), where k stands for each kinematics pattern and f stands for each algorithm.

$$\begin{bmatrix} \theta_{k1} \; v_{k1} \\ \theta_{k2} \; v_{k2} \\ \theta_{k3} \; v_{k3} \\ \theta_{k4} \; v_{k4} \end{bmatrix} = f_k(v_{kx}, v_{ky}, \omega_{kz}) \tag{1}$$

For straight driving (a) and crab steering (c) in Fig. 4, the robot has no angular velocity. In other words, the instantaneous center of rotation (ICR) is infinite, $\omega_z = 0$. The equation could be written as (2), where i represents each wheel from 1 to 4. Straight driving (a) is a particular case for crab steering (c) when v_{Ry}. Therefore they could be written in the same algorithm. R_i is the distance between the instantaneous center of rotation (ICR) and the center of each wheel.

$$\theta_i = \arctan \frac{v_{Ry}}{v_{Rx}}$$
$$v_i = v_R = \sqrt{v_{Rx}^2 + v_{Ry}^2} \tag{2}$$

3.3   Arc-Shape Steering Algorithm

The following calculation is the symmetric arc-shape kinematics modality, as shown in Fig. 5 (b). When conducting general active front and rear steering (AFRS) (d) in Fig. 5, to increase the life span of each wheel and improve the operating efficiency of the agricultural robot FDU-AgRobot, we need to avoid the phenomenon of slippage between the wheels and the ground as much as possible. So we should make the direction of the wheels the same as the direction of the speed, i.e., $\boldsymbol{\omega} \times \boldsymbol{R}_i = \boldsymbol{v}_i$.

We may see from Fig. 5 that arc-shape steering (non-eccentric AFRS) (e) and Ackermann steering (f) are two exceptional cases for general active front and rear steering (AFRS) (d). Arc-shape steering (e) has a symmetric front and rear steering (non eccentric) since ICR locates at the symmetric point. While the rear wheels of Ackermann steering (f) do not need to turn, i.e., $\theta_3 = \theta_4 = 0$, ICR finds at the line of the rear wheels. It is notable from Fig. 5 that Arc-shape kinematics modality (e) possesses the minimum turning angle for every wheel $\sum \theta_i$ at a designated turning radius R, which is more effective for the robot's kinematics than general AFRS (eccentric) (d). Moreover, this algorithm of the kinematics modality's pattern is less intricate than the general AFRS. As a result, when conducting active front and rear steering, we are inclined to choose Arc-shape steering (e) as the designated algorithm rather than general AFRS (d).

For Arc-shape steering (e), we have (3). R is the distance between the instantaneous center of rotation (ICR) and the center of the robot (COR)... R_1 to R_4 and v_1 to v_4 represent each wheel's instantaneous rotation radius and velocity.

$$R = \frac{v_{Rx}}{\omega} = \frac{v_R}{\omega} \tag{3}$$

In terms of the trigonometric relationship, we can calculate the angle θ_1, θ_2 in (4), while $\theta_3 = -\theta_2$, $\theta_4 = -\theta_1$.

$$
\begin{bmatrix} \theta_1 \\ \theta_2 \end{bmatrix} = \begin{bmatrix} \text{Arctan}\,(\omega L, 2v_R - \omega W) \\ \text{Arctan}\,(\omega L, 2v_R + \omega W) \end{bmatrix}
$$

$$
= \begin{bmatrix} \arctan\,(\omega L/(2v_{R_x} - \omega W)) \\ \arctan\,(\omega L/(2v_{R_x} + \omega W)) \end{bmatrix} (2v_{R_x} - \omega W \neq 0, 2v_{R_x} + \omega W \neq 0) \tag{4}
$$

Afterward, we could calculate the velocity (5). Since $R_1 = R_4, R_2 = R_3$, we have $v_1 = v_4, v_2 = v_3$.

$$
\begin{bmatrix} v_1 \\ v_2 \end{bmatrix} = \frac{\omega L}{2} \begin{bmatrix} \dfrac{1}{\sin \theta_1} \\ \dfrac{1}{\sin \theta_2} \end{bmatrix} \tag{5}
$$

These results is transformed into C++ algorithm in Sect. 4.

3.4   Pivot Steering

As for pivot steering (b), we notice that it could be concluded as non-eccentric AFRS steering or arc-shape steering (e) in Sect. 3.3. We notice that when $v_R = v_{Rx} = v_{Ry} = 0$ for arc-shape steering (e) in (4) and (5), the kinematics modality pattern is converted to pivot steering (b). This is quite surprising and worthwhile so that the number of algorithms could be reduced. As a result, (4) and (5) could be transformed into (6).

$$
\begin{bmatrix} \theta_1 \\ \theta_2 \end{bmatrix} = \begin{bmatrix} \arctan\,(-L/W) \\ \arctan\,(L/W) \end{bmatrix}
$$

$$
\begin{bmatrix} v_1 \\ v_2 \end{bmatrix} = \frac{\omega L}{2} \begin{bmatrix} \dfrac{1}{\sin \theta_1} \\ \dfrac{1}{\sin \theta_2} \end{bmatrix} \tag{6}
$$

3.5   Ackermann Steering Algorithm

Although Ackermann Steering mode (f) possesses a larger turning angle than arc-shape steering (e), it has particular merits. When the robot turns at a slight angle, its rear wheels do not need to turn, i.e., $\theta_3 = \theta_4 = 0$, which highlights the steering accuracy. Furthermore, since ICR is located at the rear wheels' line in Fig. 5, it's easier for sensor systems to locate the robot's position. The distance between ICR and COR is (7).

$$
R = \frac{\sqrt{v_{Rx}^2 + v_{Ry}^2}}{\omega} \tag{7}
$$

The expression of the instantaneous rotation radius of wheel four could be represented as .

$$
R_3 = \sqrt{R^2 - \left(\frac{L}{2}\right)^2} - \frac{W}{2} = \frac{v_{Rx}}{\omega} - \frac{W}{2} \tag{8}
$$

When setting the initial parameter, we should notice that the following equation should be satisfied:

$$v_{R_y} = \frac{L\omega}{2} \tag{9}$$

Here we calculate the angle, while the second equation of (10) must satisfy $\frac{v_{R_x}}{\omega} - \frac{W}{2} > 0$, while $\theta_3 = \theta_4 = 0$.

$$\begin{bmatrix} \theta_1 \\ \theta_2 \end{bmatrix} = \begin{bmatrix} \text{Arctan}\,(L, R_3) \\ \text{Arctan}\,(L, R_3 + a) \end{bmatrix}$$
$$= \begin{bmatrix} \arctan\left(L / \left(\frac{v_{R_x}}{\omega} - \frac{W}{2} \right) \right) \\ \arctan\left(L / \left(\frac{v_{R_x}}{\omega} + \frac{W}{2} \right) \right) \end{bmatrix} \tag{10}$$

Afterward, the velocity vector could be expressed as (11). Based on the advantages of the structure, when the speed is less than 0, the definition of the front and back can be exchanged, and the front wheel of the current direction can be used for steering. Compared with the traditional Ackerman steering mode, the reversing operation can be realized more quickly.

$$\begin{bmatrix} v_1 \\ v_2 \\ v_3 \\ v_4 \end{bmatrix} = \omega \begin{bmatrix} R_1 \\ R_2 \\ R_3 \\ R_4 \end{bmatrix} = \omega \begin{bmatrix} \dfrac{R_3}{\cos \theta_1} \\ \dfrac{R_3 + W}{\cos \theta_2} \\ R_3 \\ R_3 + W \end{bmatrix} \tag{11}$$

We need to point out that although our mathematical derivation in this chapter is based on arc shapes, we can apply these algorithms to most curves. In agricultural application scenarios, we mainly use depth cameras and LIDAR to build maps in many cases so that the robot can navigate SLAM. However, most navigation trajectories of agricultural robots operating in the field are straight lines and non-circular curves. For a non-circular turn, we can imagine it as a combination of many arcs, and each point on the curve has a corresponding curvature. In our practical application, we will divide the turn into a finite number of issues and perform kinematic planning through the radius of curvature of each point. This way, we can use this kinematic segmentation algorithm to perform multi-modal kinematics control in complex agricultural scenes.

4   Experiment and Result

Our tests were designed to verify the basic functionality of the standard agricultural robot chassis prototype with all-terrain wheels and its suspension system. This includes the angular velocity of the three steering models is measured by evaluating the movement performance of the chassis, including speed, ability, and stability in different terrain conditions to ensure that it can travel and operate effectively in various farmland environments. In addition, we will measure the error of the chassis system to understand its accuracy and positioning capability. We take at least five measurements for all tests to minimize random errors. The results shown in Table 1 mainly include speed error, position error, maximum speed, acceleration, and power consumption on the ground. From the experimental results, the robot shows a good movement effect on the environment. But due to the inertia effect, there is a certain degree of motion error, which must be solved by reducing the robot's weight and optimizing the control method.

Table 1. Robot Motion Parameters.

Parameters	Value	Unit
Maximum speed on the ground	0.312	m/s
Lateral movement on the ground	±14.8	mm
Maximum acceleration on the ground	623.6	mm/s^2
Curve motion accuracy	±4	degree
Linear speed error on the ground	±1.2	mm/s
Robot maximum power	700	W
Robot battery life	3.5	h

To verify the correctness of the kinematic model, and because the three motion modes can realize the steering function, we mainly tested the actual angular velocity under different control commands. We obtain real-time angular velocity data from the IMU. The angular velocity of the three steering models is measured by setting various commands(No unit, control the robot to move). The results are shown in Fig. 6. As the control command increases linearly, the angular velocity values in the three modes also increase linearly. So our kinematics model can control the robot to achieve the desired state.

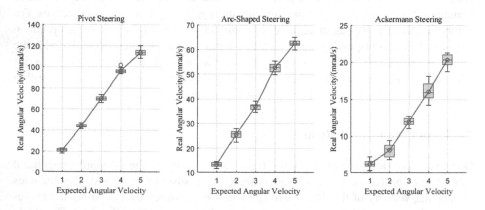

Fig. 6. Angular velocities of three steering models

5   Conclusion

A novel agricultural robot FDU-AgRobot with multi-modal kinematics applied to various scenarios is designed and implemented in this paper. This agricultural robot can realize motion control based on six kinematics modalities. By discovering the existing problems of traditional agrarian machinery and other agricultural robots, we design the mechanical structure of the robot with four-wheel independent steering. Moreover, we highlight the significance of multi-modal kinematics and present and further simplify its algorithm. In the experiment, we applied the kinematics model to the robot. We tested the control accuracy and motion effect, and the results show that the robot can achieve the desired motion effect.

In future work, we will conduct relevant multi-modal kinematics and autonomous navigation test experiments on the FDU-AgRobot in an actual natural field and use multi-sensor perception technologies such as LIDAR and 3D cameras to achieve high-precision visual detection and autonomous navigation. At the same time, we combine a variety of accessory modules, such as robotic arms, agricultural machinery accessories, etc., to improve the agricultural robot's ability further.

References

1. Vasconez, J.P., Kantor, G.A., Cheein, F.A.A.: Human-robot interaction in agriculture: a survey and current challenges. Biosys. Eng. **179**, 35–48 (2019)
2. Zhai, Z., Martínez, J.F., Beltran, V., Martínez, N.L.: Decision support systems for agriculture 4.0: survey and challenges. Comput. Electron. Agricult. **170**, 105256 (2020)
3. Ziwen, C., Chunlong, Z., Nan, L., Zhe, S., Wei, L., Bin, Z.: Study review and analysis of high performance intra-row weeding robot. Trans. Chin. Soc. Agricult. Eng. **31**(5), 1–8 (2015)
4. Jadhav, P.K., Deshmukh, S.S., Khairnar, P.N.: Survey paper on AgRo-Bot autonomous robot. Int. Res. J. Eng. Technol. (IRJET) **6**(12), 434–441 (2019)
5. Grimstad, L., From, P.J.: The Thorvald II agricultural robotic system. Robotics **6**(4), 24 (2017)
6. Xu, R., Li, C.: A modular agricultural robotic system (mars) for precision farming: concept and implementation. J. Field Robot. **39**(4), 387–409 (2022)
7. Khan, N., Medlock, G., Graves, S., Anwar, S.: GPS guided autonomous navigation of a small agricultural robot with automated fertilizing system. Tech. rep, SAE Technical Paper (2018)
8. Solea, R., Filipescu, A., Cernega, D.: Lateral motion control of four-wheels steering vehicle using a sliding-mode controller. In: Proceedings of the 29th Chinese Control Conference, pp. 3699–3703. IEEE (2010)
9. Siegwart, R., Nourbakhsh, I.R., Scaramuzza, D.: Introduction to autonomous mobile robots. MIT press (2011)
10. Mitchell, W.C., Staniforth, A., Scott, I.: Analysis of Ackermann steering geometry. Tech. rep, SAE Technical Paper (2006)
11. Dickerson, S.L., Lapin, B.D.: Control of an omni-directional robotic vehicle with Mecanum wheels. In: NTC1991-National Telesystems Conference Proceedings, pp. 323–328. IEEE (1991)
12. Macenski, S., Foote, T., Gerkey, B., Lalancette, C., Woodall, W.: Robot operating system 2: design, architecture, and uses in the wild. Science Robotics **7**(66), eabm6074 (2022)
13. Guan, F., Peng, L., Perneel, L., Timmerman, M.: Open source FreeRTOS as a case study in real-time operating system evolution. J. Syst. Softw. **118**, 19–35 (2016)

14. Pan, Y., Shang, H.: Design of a hopping robot with its kinetics and dynamics analysis. In: 2021 IEEE International Conference on Robotics and Biomimetics (ROBIO), pp. 411–416. IEEE (2021)
15. Ye, Y., He, L., Zhang, Q.: Steering control strategies for a four-wheel-independent-steering bin managing robot. IFAC-PapersOnLine **49**(16), 39–44 (2016)
16. Ye, Y.: A maneuverability study on a wheeled bin management robot in tree fruit orchard environments. Washington State University (2016)

Research on High Precision Scanning Reconstruction Algorithm for Robot with Line Laser Scanner

Guotao Jiang, Xingwei Zhao[✉], and Bo Tao

School of Mechanical Science and Engineering, Huazhong University of Science and Technology, Wuhan 430074, Hubei, China
zhaoxingwei@hust.edu.cn

Abstract. In order to perform high precision 3D reconstruction it is necessary to acquire high precision point cloud data. Line laser scanners are increasingly used in the field of high-precision point cloud measurement due to their high accuracy and good implementability. However, the traditional method is to fix the line laser scanner above the conveyor belt and scan by the movement of the object. This method has low flexibility in measurement and is more limited. It tends to produce blind areas in the field of view. In addition, it brings new challenges to data fusion because only a single line data can be obtained for each scan. And with the high degree of freedom, the robot has high flexibility. Therefore, we established a high-precision scanning system for robot based on line laser scanner and studied the related high-precision reconstruction algorithm. The hand-eye calibration of the line laser scanner is performed by a simple flat-panel piece. Using the calibration results and the proposed robot scanning strategy, the data fusion problem of a single line point cloud is solved and high precision reconstruction of complex object surfaces is achieved.

Keywords: Surface Reconstruction · Line Laser Scanner · Hand-eye Calibration

1 Introduction

In recent years, in the face of the increasingly fierce competition in the market and the increasingly stringent requirements of consumers for product appearance, companies often adopt the shape design with complex free-form surfaces when designing the product shape. Therefore, inverse modeling technology has been applied in large quantities [1]. Obtaining 3D data on the surface of an object often becomes the first step in the process. And non-contact measurement with its fast measurement speed and high efficiency has gained wide attention and application.

At present, on-site data acquisition mainly relies on manual acquisition and automated equipment acquisition. Manual acquisition [2, 3] is generally carried out by an operator holding a 3D scanner to measure the object to be scanned with high flexibility. However, the measurement efficiency of this approach is low, and the stability and accuracy are insufficient. Commonly used automated devices for scanning are 3D

H. Yang et al. (Eds.): ICIRA 2023, LNAI 14272, pp. 407–416, 2023.
https://doi.org/10.1007/978-981-99-6480-2_34

scanning devices or vision sensors mounted on a tracked moving platform [4]. The 3D measurement is achieved by the on-rail motion of the device or the object to be scanned, which is more efficient. However, this measurement method is less flexible and more limited, often causing inevitable measurement blind spots due to the fixed measurement angle. With the continuous development and maturity of robotics, robots have gradually replaced human labor. With many advantages such as high efficiency, flexibility and intelligence, robots have been widely used in various fields [5]. Using robots as a mobile platform to carry measurement equipment for 3D scanning has become a new method. Compared with traditional handheld scanning or automated scanning with fixed tracks, the robot has good flexibility and controllability. It can adjust the measurement attitude within a certain range to avoid measurement blindness and enhance the system measurement flexibility. Larsson et al. [6] earlier proposed to combine a scanner with an industrial robot for stationary single robot measurement. Theodor Borangiu et al. [7] used an industrial robot and structured light to form a measurement platform. The platform is able to avoid collisions in 3D scanning by setting dynamic constraints. Alexandru Dumitrache et al. [8] used a six-degree-of-freedom robotic arm with a scanner to form a 3D measurement system. The system is capable of quality inspection and 3D scanning of the target object for quality control. Ryo et al.[9] investigated a system based on a mobile robot carrying 3D laser measurement equipment for large-scale constructed 3D measurements. Among many 3D scanning devices, line laser scanners are increasingly used in the field of high-precision point cloud measurement by virtue of their high accuracy and good implementability [10–12].

In order to facilitate high precision scanning and reconstruction of objects, this paper presents a study related to high precision scanning of robots based on a line laser scanner. A high-precision point cloud model of a variety of objects is also acquired and object localization with respect to the robot is achieved. The remainder of this work is organized as follows: Sect. 2 describes the composition of the whole system. Section 3 describes the hand-eye calibration technique of the line laser scanner and robot, and illustrates the strategy and process of scanning reconstruction using the robot. Experiments are given in Sect. 4, and Sect. 5 is a summary.

2 Automatic Scanning System Construction

The automated scanning system consists of a line laser scanner for scanning and a six-axis collaborative robot for motion. The line laser scanner is mounted at the end of the robot and the robot carries the scanner to perform the scanning task. The system equipment composition is shown in Fig. 1(a). The six-axis collaborative robot model is AUBO I5 with a working radius of 886.5 mm, a load of 5 kg, and a repeatable positioning accuracy of ± 0.02 mm. The line laser scanner is a 2430 sensor supplied by Gocator. Its measuring range is 47–85 mm and 75–155 mm in X and Z directions respectively, and the resolution is $X > 0.37$ mm and $Z > 0.8$ μm respectively.

This system is designed to replace 3D manual scanning with a line laser scanner for automatic scanning. It is expected to obtain high-precision point cloud data on the surface of the workpiece and to be able to locate the workpiece position for grinding, placement, picking, etc. with these data. But the data acquired with the scanner are the profile points p_{si} : $[x_{si}, 0, z_{si}]$ located under the scanner coordinate system. In order to obtain the corresponding points p_{bi} : $[x_{bi}, y_{bi}, z_{bi}]$ in the base coordinate system, the hand-eye relationship between the scanner and the robot must be obtained. For convenience, the hand-eye relationship is represented by the rotation matrix R_s with the translation vector t_s, and the robot position is represented by the rotation matrix R_b with the translation vector t_b. The conversion relationship is expressed in Eq. 1.

$$p_{bi} = R_b \left(R_s p_{si} + t_s \right) + t_b \tag{1}$$

p_{si} is the profile read from the scanner and is therefore known. The robot's pose is controllable and can be read from within the robot system, so R_b and t_b are also available. To obtain the actual profile coordinates p_{bi} in the robot's base coordinate system, the hand-eye relationship R_s and t_s must be solved. In addition, since the scanned data are a series of profiles, they need to be combined into a surface point cloud to reconstruct the complete surface. Therefore, it is necessary to solve the problem of hand-eye calibration of robot and scanner and to design the method of scanning reconstruction.

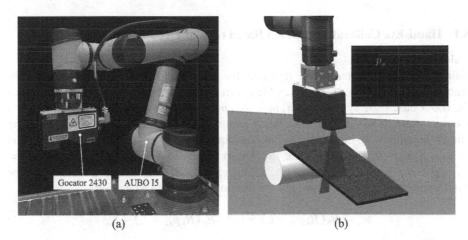

Fig. 1. (a) System equipment composition. (b) Line laser scanner scanning results.

A commonly used calibration method is the one with a fixed standard ball as the calibration object [13, 14]. In this paper we use a flat piece [15] to calibrate the hand-eye matrix. The method scans the straight edges of flat pieces with different robot poses and records the feature points p_s of discontinuous profiles as well as different robot poses R_b and t_b. The used calibrator and the locations of feature point p_s are shown in Fig. 1(b). The recording of the robot pose is done in a kind of grid. The robot pose R_b is recorded in each row of the grid in a consistent manner, but the difference is the robot position t_b. The robot pose R_b and position t_b are recorded differently between rows. The calibration process is performed in two steps. First, the rotation matrix of the hand-eye matrix is calculated, and then the translation component is calculated. The method of collecting data is also relatively simple. Clamp the scanner to the end of the robot and move the robot to a better initial position that allows the line laser scanner to scan one straight edge of the flat piece. After recording the feature points of the robot's pose and profile, we maintain the pose of the robot's end and move the robot's position to a new one. Then we continue to record the feature points of the robot's pose and profile. The steps above are repeated (typically 10 sets of data collected). In this way, one row of the grid data is gathered. When moving the robot, we should avoid only changing the X, Y, or Z data, but instead have all three values changed a certain amount each time.Next, the robot's pose is changed and moved back to the initial position. A new row of grid data is obtained by repeating the above method. Typically, at least 15 different robot poses need to be collected. That means there should be at least 15 rows in the grid.

3 Line Laser Scanner Hand-Eye Calibration and Surface Reconstruction

After setting up the measurement system, the hand-eye calibrated grid data is collected in the way presented. The principles of hand-eye calibration and the method of surface reconstruction are described in this section.

3.1 Hand-Eye Calibration Method Based on Flat Piece

Calculating Rotation
Using the data collected in the first row for discussion, we set the recorded profile feature points as $p_{s1}, p_{s2}, \cdots, p_{sn}$, which corresponds to the profile feature point under the robot base scale system as $p_{b1}, p_{b2}, \cdots, p_{bn}$ In this data set, the variables in Eq. 1 are p_b, p_s and t_b, with the first one being an unknown quantity and the latter two being known quantities. To eliminate the unknown quantity, the subtraction between p_{bi}, that is, $u_{bi} = p_{bi} - p_{b1}, i > 1$. Take Eq. 1 into it we can get Eq. 2. Further set $u_{si} = p_{si} - p_{s1}$, $u_{ti} = t_{bi} - t_{b1}$ can get Eq. 3. This eliminated the translation vector from the hand-eye relationship and kept only the rotation matrix for calculation.

$$u_{bi} = R_b \left(R_s p_{si} + t_s \right) + t_{bi} - R_b \left(R_s p_{s1} + t_s \right) - t_{b1} \tag{2}$$

$$u_{bi} = R_b R_s u_{si} + u_{ti} \tag{3}$$

Next, we consider the two different direction vectors u_{bi} and u_{bj}. Since both are two line segments on a straight edge in physical space, we can deduce that $\| u_{bi} \times u_{bj} \| = 0$, which means the parallelism of u_{bi} and u_{bj}. Bringing Eq. 3 into it leads to Eq. 4, which is further derived to obtain Eq. 5.

$$\| \left(R_b R_s u_{si} + u_{ti} \right) \times \left(R_b R_s u_{sj} + u_{tj} \right) \| = 0 \tag{4}$$

$$\| R_b R_s \left(u_{si} \times u_{sj} \right) + R_b R_s u_{si} \times u_{tj} - R_b R_s u_{sj} \times u_{ti} + u_{ti} \times u_{tj} \| = 0 \tag{5}$$

Using the vectorization of the matrix and the Kronecker product, the rotation matrix R_s of the hand-eye relationship can be derived as follows:

$$R_b R_s \left(u_{si} \times u_{sj} \right) = \left(\left(u_{si} \times u_{sj} \right)^T \otimes R_b \right) r_s = B_1 r_s \tag{6}$$

$$R_b R_s u_{si} = ((u_{si})^T \otimes R_b) r_s = B_2 r_s \tag{7}$$

$$R_b R_s u_{sj} = ((u_{sj})^T \otimes R_b) r_s = B_3 r_s \tag{8}$$

In which, $r_s = Vec(R_s)$. We set $b_r = -u_{ti} \times u_{tj}$, and bring Eqs. 6–8 into Eq. 5 to obtain:

$$\| B_1 r_s + B_2 r_s \times u_{tj} - B_3 r_s \times u_{ti} - b_r \| = 0 \tag{9}$$

The antisymmetric matrix of the vector has the form:

$$
\begin{aligned}
c &= b \times a \\
&= -a \times b \\
&= -\begin{pmatrix} 0 & -a_3 & a_2 \\ a_3 & 0 & -a_1 \\ -a_2 & a_1 & 0 \end{pmatrix} \begin{pmatrix} b_1 \\ b_2 \\ b_3 \end{pmatrix} = \begin{pmatrix} 0 & a_3 & -a_2 \\ -a_3 & 0 & a_1 \\ a_2 & -a_1 & 0 \end{pmatrix} \begin{pmatrix} b_1 \\ b_2 \\ b_3 \end{pmatrix} = a_\times^T b
\end{aligned}
$$

In order to extract r_s, we need to use the above properties, and two terms of Eq. 9 can be rewritten as:

$$B_2 r_s \times u_{tj} = [u_{tj}]_\times^T B_2 r_s \tag{10}$$

$$B_3 r_s \times u_{ti} = [u_{ti}]_\times^T B_3 r_s \tag{11}$$

Substituting $A_1 = B_1, A_2 = [u_{tj}]_\times^T B_2, A_3 = [u_{ti}]_\times^T B_3$ into Eq. 9 yields:

$$\| A_1 r_s + A_2 r_s - A_3 r_s - b_r \| = 0 \tag{12}$$

$$(A_1 + A_2 - A_3) r_s = b_r \tag{13}$$

$$A r_s = b_r \tag{14}$$

In order to Solve r_s, we need to fit the collected data using the least squares method to get the r_s' with minimum error as shown in Eq. 15. By rewriting r_s' as a 3×3 matrix, we will obtain the desired rotation matrix R_s. For this purpose, it is required firstly to construct a super positive definite equation. The same pose-data is stacked into a small block, and then the different small blocks are stacked into a large block to form Eq. 16, where $\tilde{A} \in \mathbb{R}^{3m \times 9}$, $\tilde{b}_r \in \mathbb{R}^{3m \times 1}$ and the value of m is the amount of collected data. Then the least squares formula is used to solve Eq. 16 to gain Eq. 17.

$$r_s' = arg \min \| A r_s - b_r \|^2 \tag{15}$$

$$\tilde{A} r_s = \tilde{b}_r \tag{16}$$

$$r'_s = \left(\tilde{A}^T \tilde{A}\right)^{-1} \tilde{A}^T \tilde{b}_r \qquad (17)$$

However, Eq. 17 will not guarantee that the obtained rotation matrix R_s is positive definite because of the presence of data noise. Thus an additional orthogonalization process is required to project R_s to the nearest rotation matrix. Assuming that the unorthogonalized rotation matrix is $\tilde{R}_s$, the singular value decomposition is used to obtain Eq. 18. The rotation matrix after orthogonalization is shown in Eq. 19.

$$\tilde{R}_s = USV^T \qquad (18)$$

$$R_s = sign\left(\det\left(S\right)\right)UV^T \qquad (19)$$

Calculating Translation

After calculating R_s, many values of u_b can be calculated according to Eq. 3, and its average u_b^* can be found as the direction vector of the straight edge under the robot base scale system. Considering the feature points p_{bi}, p_{bj} scanned at different poses, the direction vectors they form should be parallel to u_b^*, i.e. $\left\|(p_{bj} - p_{bi}) \times u_b^*\right\|$. Equation 20 is obtained by taking Eq. 1 into it. Further separating the known quantity from the unknown quantity gives Eq. 21

$$\left\|\left(R_{bj}\left(R_s p_{sj} + t_s\right) + t_{bj} - R_{bi}\left(R_s p_{si} + t_s\right) - t_{bi}\right) \times u_b^*\right\| = 0 \qquad (20)$$

$$\left\|\left(R_{bj} - R_{bi}\right)t_s \times u_b^* + \left(R_{bj} R_s p_{sj} - R_b R_s^* p_i + t_{bj} - t_{bi}\right) \times u_b^*\right\| = 0 \qquad (21)$$

In order to extract the t_s, the same form of antisymmetric matrix is used to obtain Eq. 22. Moreover, the second half of Eq. 21 is simplified to Eq. 23, and Eqs. 22–23 are brought into Eq. 21 to obtain Eq. 24. Equation 24 is also calculated by a least squares method similar to that in Sect. 3.2. It is solved by simply superimposing the data from two different poses to form the superdeterminant equation.

$$\left(R_{bj} - R_{bi}\right)t_s \times u_b^* = \left[u_b^*\right]_\times^T \left(R_{bj} - R_{bi}\right)t_s = Ct_s \qquad (22)$$

$$\left(R_{bj} R_s p_{sj} - R_{bi} R_s p_{si} + t_{bj} - t_{bi}\right) \times u_b^* = -b_t \qquad (23)$$

$$\left\|Ct_s - b_t\right\| = 0 \qquad (24)$$

3.2 Surface Reconstruction Based on Line Laser Scanner

Once the hand-eye calibration is complete, it is time to use the scanner to scan the workpiece. Due to the limited field of view of the scanner, it is not possible to scan the entire size of the workpiece during a one-movement process. Therefore, it is necessary to split the surface of the workpiece into multiple parts and then move back and forth to scan them in turn. The ROS system enables precise control of the robot and the ability to read and record the robot's current position in real time. Automatically records the robot posture data collected at the same moment together with the profile point cloud data measured by the line laser scanner. The recorded data is saved as a file once a part of the finished part has been scanned. To minimize errors, the speed and acceleration of the robot motion should not be too large. In this way, the effect of vibration on the accuracy of data acquisition can be reduced.

After scanning, we can obtain multiple files with point cloud data in their respective local coordinate systems. In order to rebuild the surface, a further transformation of the point cloud data is required. As shown in Eq. 1, the data is converted to the robot base coordinate system using the robot posture data corresponding to each profile and the hand-eye calibration matrix. In this way each contour is converted to the correct position and interconnected to form a surface. Then each file of data can be converted into a surface point cloud. Each slice of the point cloud data is now in the robot base coordinate system. The superposition of multiple point clouds allows the reconstruction of the workpiece surface. However, due to the existence of errors, there will be deviations in the connection of each point cloud, which requires further fine splicing.

The fine splicing of point clouds mainly relies on the classical iterative closest point (ICP) algorithm, which improves the accuracy of point cloud splicing by iteration. Assuming that the point cloud to be aligned is $P = \{P_1, P_2, P_3, \cdots, P_m\}$ and the target point cloud is $Q = \{q_1, q_2, q_3, \cdots, q_n\}$. The transformation matrix from P to Q is T_Q^P, where R_Q^P and t_Q^P are the rotation and translation relations, respectively.

$$T_Q^P = \begin{bmatrix} R_Q^P & t_Q^P \\ 0 & 1 \end{bmatrix} \tag{25}$$

Find the N_p pairs of corresponding points in the point clouds P and Q whose distances are less than the threshold value and form the set of nearest points $D = \{(p_i, q_j) | 1 \le i \le N_p\}$. Then the objective function as shown in Eq. 26 can be established. The function is the sum of squared Euclidean distances of all corresponding points in the set of nearest points after the point cloud P has undergone one transformation. The core of the ICP algorithm is to calculate the optimal transformation matrix between two point clouds by multiple iterations, which minimizes the objective function. Using the ICP algorithm, all the partial surface point clouds are sequentially aligned to one of the frames. Finally, all the aligned partial point clouds are superimposed to create a complete surface point cloud. Then, the reconstruction of the workpiece surface is completed.

$$f\left(R_Q^P, t_Q^P\right) = \sum_{i=1}^{N_p} \left\| q_i - \left(R_Q^P \cdot p_i + t_Q^P\right) \right\|_2^2 \tag{26}$$

4 Experiment

4.1 Hand-Eye Calibration

The calibrator for this experiment is a straight carbon fiber plate, placed randomly near the robot base. But it needs to be careful to avoid the robot singularity. The robot posture is adjusted according to the measuring range so that the line laser can be clearly imaged when shining on the straight plate. During each translation, change the X, Y and Z position values of the robot. The robot's pose change needs to be larger for each rotation to ensure that the data is sufficiently different from the data. In this experiment, we performed 24 rotations and 10 translations after each rotation, collecting a total of 240 sets of data.

The calibration results are shown in the Fig. 2(a). The points in the figure are the result of converting the collected feature points to the robot base coordinate system. These points should lie on a straight line because of physical constraints of the calibrators. The black line in the figure is the straight line obtained from fitting all feature points. The color of each point represents the distance magnitude from that straight line. To analyze the error, we calculate the Euclidean distance Δd of each feature point from a straight line, which allows to evaluate the goodness of the calibration results. The average distance Δd was found to be 0.78 mm. The source of error is mainly the robot motion accuracy and feature point identification. To further verify the accuracy of the calibration results, we performed multiple scans on a standard ball. The spherical contour point cloud is acquired and converted to the robot base coordinate system using the calibration results. A sphere fit is performed to obtain the parameters of the reconstructed sphere and compare it with the actual values. The nominal diameter of the standard ball is 50 mm, which is measured by the CMM as 50.7968 mm. The fitted ball diameter is 50.7736 mm, with a standard deviation of 0.1876 mm, and the results are shown in the Fig. 2(b). Therefore the calibration results meet the target requirements.

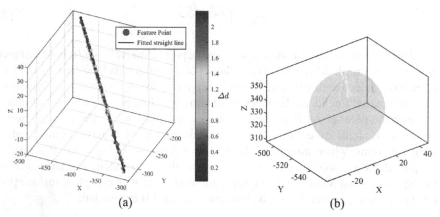

(a)   (b)

Fig. 2. (a) The position of the feature points converted to the robot base coordinate system. (b) Results of fitting multiple contours to a standard ball.

4.2 Surface Reconstruction

Using the calibration results, the robot is operated to scan a variety of workpieces. The scanning results were processed according to the method in Sects. 2 and 3, and the results obtained are shown in Fig. 3. Among them, the board size is large need to be scanned twice. After conversion, we get two point clouds. The complete surface was then reconstructed after fine splicing. The line laser scanner is highly accurate and can recognize the minor changes in the surface. Especially for objects with fine textures like jade pearls, the reconstruction can be achieved successfully as well. It is evident that the system we have built utilizes both the high degree of freedom of the robot and the high accuracy of the line laser scanner, which can be widely applied to the scanning and reconstruction of many kinds of objects. Also, it is able to locate the workpiece with respect to the robot, facilitating the use of the robot for processing, clamping and inspection of the scanned object.

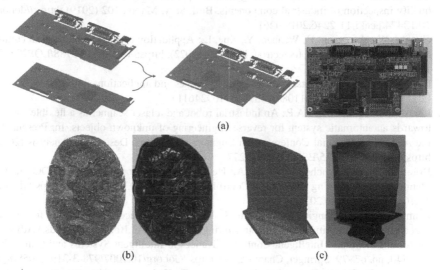

Fig. 3. (a) Circuit board. (b) Jade pendant. (c) Aviation blade.

5 Conclusion

In this paper, a study of algorithms related to high-precision automatic scanning and reconstruction of robots based on line lasers is conducted. An automatic scanning system is built based on a line laser and a collaborative robot. First, a hand-eye calibration method for the coordinate system of a line laser scanner mounted on the end of the robot is introduced. The method is practical and has simple principles because the calibration object is a common straight plate. Then, a strategy for automatic scanning of the system is proposed by combining the characteristics of the line laser scanner and the robot, which introduces the process of reconstructing the surface. Finally, the proposed method is verified. The accuracy of the calibration results of the completed hand-eye calibration experiments meets the practical requirements. And the calibration results are used to scan different objects and successfully reconstruct the surface information of the objects.

Acknowledgement. This work was supported by the National Key Research and Development Program of China under Grant 2022YFB3404102.

References

1. Muslimin, Yoshioka, H., Zhu, J., Tanaka, T.: Automatic segmentation and feature identification of laser scanning point cloud data for reverse engineering. In: 2016 International Symposium on Flexible Automation (ISFA), pp. 278–285 (2016). https://doi.org/10.1109/ISFA.2016.7790175
2. Ameen, W., Al-Ahmari, A.M., Mian, S.H.: Evaluation of handheld scanners for automotive applications. Appl. Sci.-Basel. **8**, 217 (2018). https://doi.org/10.3390/app8020217
3. Yi, L.I., Chao, X.U., Kaixing, L., Hongyao, Z.: Application of handheld 3D laser scanner in quality inspection of industrial components. Bull. Surv. Mapp., 102 (2019). https://doi.org/10.13474/j.cnki.11-2246.2019.0261
4. Chenlu, W., Yuanyuan, F., Wenhao, Y., Xue, L.: Application of laser technology in cultural relics protection. Laser Optoelectron. Prog. **59**, (2022). https://doi.org/10.3788/LOP202259.1700003
5. Bogue, R.: Finishing robots: a review of technologies and applications. Ind. Robot. **36**, 6–12 (2009). https://doi.org/10.1108/01439910910924611
6. Larsson, S., Kjellander, J.A.P.: An industrial robot and a laser scanner as a flexible solution towards an automatic system for reverse engineering of unknown objects. In: Presented at the ASME 7th Biennial Conference on Engineering Systems Design and Analysis (2008). https://doi.org/10.1115/ESDA2004-58277
7. Borangiu, T., Dumitrache, A., Dogar, A.: Heuristic solution for constrained 7-DOF motion planning in 3D scanning application. Control Eng. Pract. **20**, 93–101 (2012). https://doi.org/10.1016/j.conengprac.2011.07.008
8. Dumitrache, A., Borangiu, T., Răileanu, S.: Robotic 3D surface laser scanning for feature-based quality control in Holonic manufacturing. In: Rodić, A., Borangiu, T. (eds.) Advances in Robot Design and Intelligent Control. Advances in Intelligent Systems and Computing, vol. 540, pp. 67–79. Springer, Cham (2017). https://doi.org/10.1007/978-3-319-49058-8_8
9. Kurazume, R., Tobata, Y., Iwashita, Y., Hasegawa, T.: 3D laser measurement system for large scale architectures using multiple mobile robots. In: Sixth International Conference on 3-D Digital Imaging and Modeling (3DIM 2007), pp. 91–98 (2007). https://doi.org/10.1109/3DIM.2007.2
10. Zhang, R., et al.: Local high precision 3D measurement based on line laser measuring instrument. In: Peng, K., Pan, J., Chu, J. (eds.) Young Scientists Forum 2017, p. 107101L. SPIE-Int Soc Optical Engineering, Bellingham (2018). https://doi.org/10.1117/12.2317530
11. Guarato, A.Z., Loja, A.C., Pereira, L.P., Braga, S.L., Trevilato, T.R.B.: Qualification of a 3D structured light sensor for a reverse engineering application. In: Kovacicinova, J. (ed.) Optics and Measurement International Conference 2016, p. 101510C. SPIE-Int Soc Optical Engineering, Bellingham (2016). https://doi.org/10.1117/12.2257601
12. Luo, L., Tang, Y., Lu, Q., Chen, X., Zhang, P., Zou, X.: A vision methodology for harvesting robot to detect cutting points on peduncles of double overlapping grape clusters in a vineyard. Comput. Ind. **99**, 130–139 (2018). https://doi.org/10.1016/j.compind.2018.03.017
13. Yin, S., Guo, Y., Ren, Y., Zhu, J., Yang, S., Ye, S.: A novel TCF calibration method for robotic visual measurement system. Optik **125**, 6920–6925 (2014). https://doi.org/10.1016/j.ijleo.2014.08.049
14. Xie, H., Pang, C., Li, W., Li, Y., Yin, Z.: Hand-eye calibration and its accuracy analysis in robotic grinding. In: 2015 IEEE International Conference on Automation Science and Engineering (CASE), pp. 862–867 (2015). https://doi.org/10.1109/CoASE.2015.7294189
15. Xu, J., Hoo, J.L., Dritsas, S., Fernandez, J.G.: Hand-eye calibration for 2D laser profile scanners using straight edges of common objects. Robot. Comput.-Integr. Manuf. **73**, 102221 (2022). https://doi.org/10.1016/j.rcim.2021.102221

Smooth Joint Motion Planning for Robot Polishing by Redundancy Optimization

Hanqian Wu, Zhoulong Li$^{(\boxtimes)}$, Rui Wang, Zhonghe Luo, and Limin Zhu

School of Mechanical Engineering, Shanghai Jiao Tong University, Shanghai 200240, People's Republic of China
lzl@sjtu.edu.cn

Abstract. With increasing demands on the surface quality of key components in the high-tech fields, ultra-precision polishing technology has received much attention in recent years. Among the numerous ultra-precision polishing technologies, robotic polishing has become the focus of research due to its low cost and high degree of freedom. In robot polishing, ensuring the smooth movement of the robot is an important and challenging issue. This paper presents an algorithm to optimize the smoothness of joint trajectories under variable feedrate conditions. Firstly, the algorithm employs redundant variables to represent the robot's redundant degrees of freedom and selects those which satisfy the established robot motion performance indexes. Subsequently, a one-way graph composed of the selected redundant variables is utilized to derive the graph optimization results. Ultimately, the final results can be obtained using the least squares method. Through simulations and experiments, it is demonstrated that the proposed optimization method can effectively improve the smoothness of robot motion during the polishing process.

Keywords: Robotics · Redundancy · Optimization · Least squares

1 Introduction

In many high-tech fields, the surface quality of critical components is subject to increasingly stringent requirements. To achieve sub-micron-level shape accuracy and nano-level surface roughness, it is essential to investigate the corresponding high-precision polishing processes. Ultra-precision polishing is widely employed and, compared to manual polishing and machine tool polishing, robotic polishing offers unique advantages [1], such as low cost, high freedom and high adaptability. In the robot polishing process, the excellent smoothness of the motion can get a better surface. However, ensuring the smoothness of robot motion is not a simple task. In related studies on robotic polishing, Xiao et al. [2] processed data from the point cloud model of the workpiece, divided the surface into specialized subregions, and planned the direction of the path and the dwell time of the end-effector during the trajectory planning stage. Imran Mohsin's team [3] divided

© The Author(s), under exclusive license to Springer Nature Singapore Pte Ltd. 2023
H. Yang et al. (Eds.): ICIRA 2023, LNAI 14272, pp. 417–429, 2023.
https://doi.org/10.1007/978-981-99-6480-2_35

the surface of the eyeglass holder and polished it according to the predefined path. Wan and his team [4] first performed surface feature extraction, dividing the surface into hexagonal meshes, and finally completing a region-adaptive polishing method through search and fusion, but this method has some limitations when facing complex surfaces.

In robot trajectory planning, ensuring the smoothness of the robot trajectory is a primary research focus. Approaches to achieving this goal include planning the trajectory using a given objective function, interpolating the trajectory during the planning process, or further optimizing it using intelligent optimization algorithms. Sun et al. [5] in 2021 proposed a method to improve the corner motion error by planning the position and attitude of the tool through the FIR filter interpolation method. Wang et al. [6] proposed a real-time motion smoothness method based on cubic polynomial functions while avoiding collisions for a fruit-picking robot task. Nadir and his team [7] proposed multi-quadratic radial basis functions (MQ-RBFs) to construct the joint motion trajectory of the robot and optimize it to obtain the time-optimal smooth motion trajectory. Similarly, Yang built the trajectory curve by 5 times the non-uniform B spline curve (NURBS). Fang [8] used segmented Sigmoid functions to establish time-optimal trajectories that could be found by the analytical method, which greatly reduced the computational cost. In addition, the genetic algorithms [9–11], sparrow search algorithms [12], improved particle swarm algorithms [13,14] and other intelligent algorithms have been applied to the optimization of trajectories.

These aforementioned studies focus more on the polishing process in robot polishing or solely on solving trajectories. In contrast, this paper concentrates on planning smooth joint trajectories for robot polishing through the optimization of redundancy with the ultimate objective of improving polish quality. Based on the robot's joint motion characteristics (velocity, acceleration or jerk, etc.), Dolgui and his team [15] defined an objective function for smoothness, and used graph optimization methods to minimize the cumulative variation and maximum variation in a laser cutting task. Lu's team [16] employed spline curves to fit the joint motion trajectory in segments. Within each segment, a differential evolution algorithm is utilized to perform optimization. Peng [17] used the sequential linear programming (SLP) method to get the smooth trajectory. However, the optimization results of Dolgui's method are suboptimal while Lu's method necessitates segmentation and fitting of the trajectory which is more complicated. In addition, none of these methods adequately address the variable feedrate, which cannot be ignored in the polishing process. Therefore, this paper will take variable feedrate into account and propose an optimization method for robot polishing tasks improved by enhancing the smoothness of joint trajectories.

This paper is structured as follows: Sect. 2 determines the feedrate, and establishes the kinematic model and motion performance indexes using introduced redundant variables. Section 3 outlines the methods employed for robot polishing trajectory optimization. The effectiveness of the proposed strategy is demonstrated through simulations and experiments in Sect. 4. Finally, Sect. 5 summarizes the work presented in this paper and provides an outlook for future research.

2 Background of Robot Polishing Trajectory Optimization

During the polishing process, the tool feedrate is determined by the dwell time and the desired removal. Prior to optimizing the polishing trajectory, the polishing task is modeled using redundant variables and associated motion performance indexes. Redundant variables are introduced to facilitate the description of the effect of redundant degrees of freedom. In order to enhance motion characteristics in the solution space, it is necessary to simultaneously reject certain joint configurations that are incompatible with the robot's motion performance indexes.

2.1 Tool Feedrate

In the workpiece coordinate system $\{WCS\}$, the tool path consists of a set of cutter locations $\{CL_i = (p_i, z_i) \mid i = 1, 2, \ldots, N\}$ which define the position of the tool tip p and the tool-axis direction z. Assuming that the dwell time $\{t_i \mid i = 1, 2, \ldots, N\}$ at each CL in the polishing process has been determined, the feedrate between the tool points is also determined. As shown in Fig. 1, each tool point corresponds to a dwell time, so the robot passes through these two points in half the sum of the dwell times of the two points. Then the feedrate at CLs on the tool path can be obtained by Eq. (1).

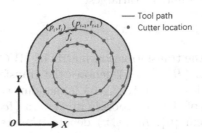

Fig. 1. Calculate the feedrate between the two points based on the dwell time.

$$f_i = \frac{\|\overline{p_i p_{i+1}}\|}{\frac{t_i}{2} + \frac{t_{i+1}}{2}} = \frac{2\|\overline{p_i p_{i+1}}\|}{t_i + t_{i+1}}, i = 1, \ldots, N - 1. \tag{1}$$

where $\|\overline{p_i p_{i+1}}\|$ demotes the Euclidean distance between two points.

2.2 Redundant Variable

Through the implementation of the proper spatial transformations, the robot's polishing poses can be determined from the tool path poses. The transformation matrix of the tool path's initial poses are defined as Eq. (2).

$$^{WCS}T_{i,0} = \begin{bmatrix} x_i^0 & y_i^0 & z_i & p_i \\ 0 & 0 & 0 & 1 \end{bmatrix} \tag{2}$$

where $^{WCS}T_{i,0} \in SE(3)$ indicates the initial tool pose, p_i denotes the tool tip position of i-th point, z_i denotes the tool-axis direction. y_i and x_i are the rotation components of the transformation matrix $^{WCS}T_{i,0}$ and have no special meaning. When $i = 1, 2, ..., N - 1$, $y_i^0 = \frac{z_i \times \overline{p_i p_{i+1}}}{\|z_i \times \overline{p_i p_{i+1}}\|}$, when $i = N$, $y_N^0 = \frac{z_N \times \overline{p_{N-1} p_N}}{\|z_N \times \overline{p_{N-1} p_N}\|}$, $x_i^0 = y_i^0 \times z_i$. In robotic polishing systems, the end-effector is usually installed in such a way that the axis of the tool is at an angle to the central axis of the robot flange. When the robot performs the polishing task, the rotation of the end-effector in the direction of the tool axis has no effect on the geometric position of the tool, thus creating a functionally redundant degree of freedom. Due to the existence of this redundant degree of freedom, there exists an infinite number of feasible tool position descriptions for each tool position point:

$$\psi_i = \{T(\eta_i) \mid T(\eta_i) =^{WCS} T_{i,0} \cdot Rot(z, \eta_i), \quad \eta_i \in [-\pi, \pi]\} \qquad (3)$$

where ψ_i denotes the set of poses for each tool position, $T(\eta_i) \in SE(3)$ denotes redundant poses, $\eta_i \in [-\pi, \pi]$ is the redundant variable and its value indicates the angle of rotation along the initial pose's z axis.

2.3   Robotics Kinematics

The motion of the robot polishing process is modeled using the conventional robot kinematics and redundant variables.

$$^0_{WCS}T \cdot T(\eta_i) \cdot Rot(x, \pi) = ^0_6 T(q_i) \cdot ^6_{tool}T, i = 1, \ldots, N \qquad (4)$$

where $^0_{WCS}T$ denotes the transformation matrix of $\{WCS\}$ with respect to the base coordinate system $\{B\}$. $^0_6 T(q_i)$ denotes the transformation matrix of the robot forward kinematics. $q_i = (\theta_1^i, \ldots, \theta_6^i)$ is the joint vector. $^6_{tool}T$ denotes the transformation matrix of the tool coordinate system $\{tool\}$ with respect to the flange coordinate system $\{6\}$. $Rot(x, \pi)$ denotes the transformation matrix of the rotation angle π around the axis x for aligning the desired tool position with the end tool coordinate system.

At the same time, the corresponding inverse kinematic model is described using Eq. (5).

$$q_i = f^{-1} \left(^0_{WCS}T \cdot T(\eta_i) \cdot Rot(x, \pi) \cdot ^6_{tool} T^{-1}, \mu \right) \qquad (5)$$

where $f^{-1}(\cdot, \cdot)$ denotes the inverse kinematic solution of the robot in a certain robot configuration at a specified pose. For convenience of description and notation, it is noted as $f^{-1}(\eta_i, \mu)$.

2.4   Motion Performance Indexes

Singularity Avoidance. When the robot's end-effector enters or approaches the singularity points, the robot will stop moving or move unexpectedly, creating great instability that may have a large impact on workpiece polishing quality.

One idea to circumvent the singularity phenomenon is to use the monitoring of the robot velocity Jacobi inverse solution results to determine whether the robot movement has reached the singularity point area, and to keep away from such points as far as possible for reasonable trajectory planning. The condition number of the geometric Jacobian matrix of the robot after dimensional normalization [18] is used as an evaluation index, and this index should be less than a preset threshold δ_{thre}.

$$c(\overline{J}) = \left\|\overline{J}\right\|_{Fro} \left\|\overline{J}^{-1}\right\|_{Fro} \leq \delta_{thre} \tag{6}$$

where $\overline{J} \in \mathbb{R}^{6\times 6}$ denotes the dimension-normalized robot geometric Jacobian matrix, Fro means the Frobenius norm, and L denotes the characteristic length which can be obtained by minimizing $c(\overline{J})$.

Joint Velocity and Acceleration. At each tool point $i \in [1, N]$, the joint variable $q_i = (\theta_1^i, \theta_2^i, \theta_3^i, \theta_4^i, \theta_5^i, \theta_6^i)$ can be obtained according to Eq. (5) which contains the redundant variable η. Thus, the motion variables at the corresponding tool point can be approximated by differencing the joint variables at neighboring tool points. Then the velocity and the acceleration can be expressed as:

$$
\begin{cases}
v_{i,j} = \frac{\theta_j^i - \theta_j^{i-1}}{\frac{\|p_{i-1}p_i\|}{f_{i-1}}}, \\
a_{i,j} = \frac{2\theta_j^{i-1}}{\frac{\|p_{i-1}p_i\|}{f_{i-1}}\left(\frac{\|p_{i-1}p_i\|}{f_{i-1}} + \frac{\|p_ip_{i+1}\|}{f_i}\right)} - \frac{2\theta_j^i}{\frac{\|p_{i-1}p_i\|}{f_{i-1}}\frac{\|p_ip_{i+1}\|}{f_i}} \\
\quad + \frac{2\theta_j^{i+1}}{\frac{\|p_ip_{i+1}\|}{f_i}\left(\frac{\|p_{i-1}p_i\|}{f_{i-1}} + \frac{\|p_ip_{i+1}\|}{f_i}\right)}
\end{cases}
\tag{7}
$$

where θ_j^i denotes the j-th joint position at CL_i.

Based on the above formula, the joint velocity $v_i = [v_{i,1}, \cdots, v_{i,6}]^T \in \mathbb{R}^{6\times 1}$ and joint acceleration $a_i = [a_{i,1}, \cdots, a_{i,6}]^T \in \mathbb{R}^{6\times 1}$ can be directly obtained. In order to evaluate the joint velocity and acceleration performance more conveniently, a weighted Euclidean criterion is introduced:

$$\phi_{n,i} = \sum_{j=1}^{6} w_{n,j} n_{i,j}^2 \tag{8}$$

where $n \in \{vel, acc\}$, $w_{n,j}$ is the weight of the corresponding joint. Theoretically, a smaller value of $w_{n,j}$ results in a smoother joint trajectory.

3   Robot Polishing Path Optimization Methodology

3.1   Optimization Model

The sequence of tool points, represented by CLs and defined under $\{WCS\}$, is transformed into the robot base coordinate system $\{B\}$. The poses of tool points are described using the redundant variable η, and the set of robot joints is obtained using Eq. (5). A subset of robot joints that meet the joint motion constraints and singularity avoidance index can then be filtered. Thus, all robot joint paths planned in this subset are solutions that satisfy the above basic motion performance indexes. Then the optimization model can be expressed as Eq. (9).

$$\min_{\eta} \quad \Phi$$
$$\begin{cases} q_i = f^{-1}(\eta_i, \mu) \\ q_{\min} \leq q_i \leq q_{\max} \\ \left\| \overline{J}(q_i) \right\|_{Fro} \left\| \overline{J}^{-1}(q_i) \right\|_{Fro} \leq \delta_{thre} \end{cases} \tag{9}$$

where Φ denotes the optimization objective function, $\eta = (\eta_1, \cdots, \eta_N)^T \in \mathbb{R}^{N \times 1}$ is the redundant variable vector. $q_{\min}$ and $q_{\max}$ denote the joint motion limits.

With the above work, the optimization of the polishing task is transformed into finding a set of most suitable redundant variables. In this paper, the smoothing process for the joint trajectories is as follows: firstly, the graph search method is used to obtain a better solution as the initial solution for the subsequent method, and then the final optimized solution is obtained by the least squares method.

3.2 Graph Optimization

By constructing one-way graphs for discrete search, the result of graph optimization can be obtained. This result serves as an initial solution for further optimization methods.

One-Way Graph Construction. Each redundant variable discrete value corresponds to one node of the joint vector as shown in Fig. 2.

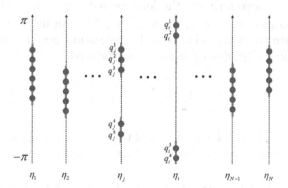

Fig. 2. Discrete redundant variable and corresponding joint vectors. Each dashed axis indicates each redundant variable η_i, the solid green line indicates that the part is a feasible subinterval, and the red circle is the joint position corresponding to the redundant variable there. (Color figure online)

Since the weights of edges can only be defined by adjacent nodes, the weight of an edge is thus the weighted sum of the squared velocities between the two nodes. The edge weight is:

$$ew = \sum_{j=1}^{6} w_{v,j} \left(\frac{\theta_j^i - \theta_j^{i-1}}{\frac{\|\overline{p_{i-1}p_i}\|}{f_{i-1}}} \right)^2 = \sum_{j=1}^{6} w_{v,j} v_i^2 = \phi_{vel,i} \tag{10}$$

where w_j, $j \in [1,6]$ is the impact factor, whose default value is 1. Figure 3 shows the construction of the one-way graph. On this basis, Φ_{graph} is defined as the optimization objective function of the graph search method.

$$\Phi_{graph} = \sum_{i=2}^{N} \sum_{j=1}^{6} w_{v,j} v_i^2 = \sum_{i=2}^{N} \phi_{vel,i} \tag{11}$$

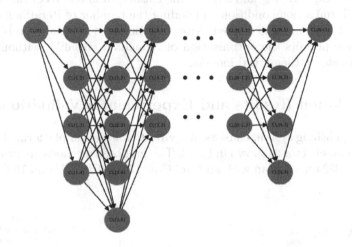

Fig. 3. One-way graph.

Graph Optimization Solution. For one-way weighted graph, there are many methods to search for the shortest path. In this paper, the global optimal solution under the given discrete redundant variables is found by the dynamic search method.

It should be noted that the complexity of this method is sensitive to the number of discrete redundant variables. As mentioned earlier in the process of constructing the one-way graph, η is discretized into M+1 points, when M is large, a relatively smooth joint trajectory can be obtained. However, the computational cost also increases. When M is small, although the calculation speed is accelerated, the desired optimization effect cannot be achieved.

3.3   Least Squares Optimization

To further optimize joint motion performance, the least squares (LS) method is carried out on the basis of graph optimization, with an optimization objective function of Φ_{ls}.

$$\Phi_{ls} = \sum_{i=2}^{N}\sum_{j=1}^{6} w_{a,j} a_{i,j}^2 = \sum_{i=2}^{N} \phi_{acc,i} \tag{12}$$

At this time, the optimization model can be described as Eq. (13).

$$\begin{aligned} \min_{\eta} \quad & \Phi_{ls} \\ & \begin{cases} x_{init} = \eta^0 \\ x_{low} \leq x \leq x_{up} \end{cases} \end{aligned} \tag{13}$$

To solve Eq. (13), Matlab offers an effective function *Lsqnonlin*. The initial values of the variables x_{init} are established as the redundant variables obtained by graph search, and x_{low} and x_{up} are the feasible subintervals of the redundant variables. Termination conditions, including the number of iterations and function value change, are also defined. After iteration, the final solution is achieved. This method permits the optimization of redundant variables without necessitating intricate mathematical models.

4   Simulation Results and Experimental Validations

The robot polishing system consists of a vibration isolation platform, Jaka Zu 18 robot and end-effector as shown in Fig. 4. The proposed methods are programmed in Matlab 2022 on a laptap with an Intel Core I7-9750H CPU and 16 GB RAM.

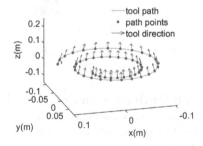

Fig. 4. Experiment system.   **Fig. 5.** Spiral tool path.

4.1   Dwell Time and Feedrate Calculation

A spiral path is utilized to simulate the polishing process of a simple disc-shaped element with a concave interior. As depicted in Fig. 5, the spiral path has a radius of approximately 0.1 m and a depth of about 0.05 m. Wang [19] introduced several

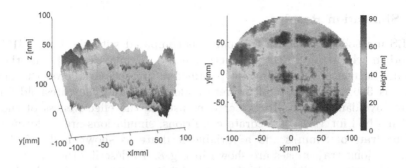

Fig. 6. Rough surface.

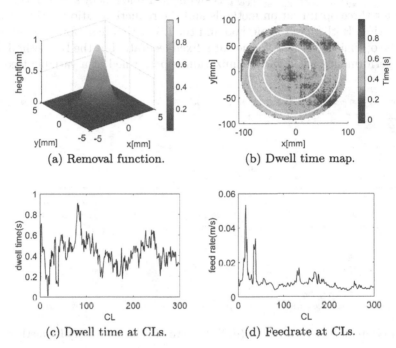

(a) Removal function.

(b) Dwell time map.

(c) Dwell time at CLs.

(d) Feedrate at CLs.

Fig. 7. Dwell time calculation. (a) Gaussian removal function; (b) Calculated dwell time map with the white line on it as the projection of the spiral path; (c) Dwell time at CLs on the spiral path; (d) Variable feedrate.

methods to solve the polishing dwell time, of which the Truncated Singular Value Decomposition (TSVD) method is used in this paper. A simulated rough surface with Gaussian white noise is generated. This rough surface exhibits a peak-to-valley (PV) ratio of 82.0422 nm and a root mean square (RMS) value of 12.8558 nm as shown in Fig. 6.

By employing a Gaussian function as the removal function, the dwell time can be calculated according to the TSVD method. Once the dwell time is obtained, the polishing tool feedrate can be determined as shown in Fig. 7.

4.2   Simulation Results

The LS method proposed in this paper is compared with the Peng's [17] SLP method in which the objective function is $\Phi_{slp} = \max\{\phi_{acc,i}\}$. For the simulation, the relevant experimental parameters are set as follows: the number of CLs is 300, the number of discrete nodes is 80, and the threshold for singularity avoidance is 20. To better demonstrate the effectiveness of the proposed method for variable feedrate conditions, simulations are performed at a fixed feedrate of 8 mm/s and a variable feedrate as shown in Fig. 7(d). The optimized joint trajectories are shown in Fig. 8. To describe the smoothness of trajectories with a uniform criterion, the global optimization objective function $\Phi_{total} = \sum_{i=2}^{N} \phi_{acc,i} + \sum_{i=2}^{N} \phi_{vel,i}$ is defined. Table 1 shows the optimization results for three optimization methods and the reduction ratio relative to graph optimization. Both the SLP method and the LS method can obtain good results when the optimization is performed at a fixed feedrate, but the LS method shows better performance when the optimization is performed at a variable feedrate.

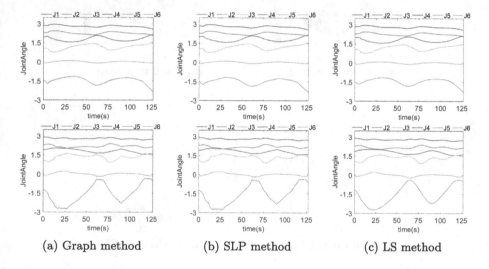

(a) Graph method   (b) SLP method   (c) LS method

Fig. 8. Simulation results, the upper figures are under the condition of fixed feedrate while the lower figures are under the condition of variable feedrate.

4.3   Experimental Results

In the experiments, the robot executes the optimized joint trajectories while sensors collect the acceleration data from the end-effector as shown in Fig. 9. To better demonstrate the optimization effect, Table 2 compares both the proportion of outliers that deviate from the mean by more than three standard deviations and the maximum acceleration. When comparing the maximum acceleration, it is found that the SLP method yields worse results than the LS method.

Table 1. Optimization results.

Method	Feedrate	Φ_{total}	Reduction ratio
Graph	fixed	45.7913	/
SLP	fixed	1.1775	97.4%
LS	fixed	1.0695	97.7%
Graph	variable	24.4413	/
SLP	variable	10.1696	58.4%
LS	variable	3.0542	87.5%

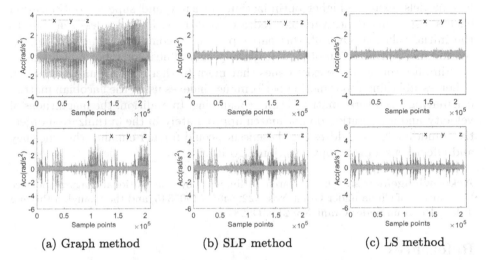

(a) Graph method   (b) SLP method   (c) LS method

Fig. 9. Experimental results, the upper figures are under the condition of fixed feedrate while the lower figures are under the condition of variable feedrate.

Table 2. Acceleration performance.

Method	Feedrate	Ratio of outliers	Max-acceleration
Graph	fixed	0.0780%	4.1313 m/s^2
SLP	fixed	0.0022%	1.0722 m/s^2
LS	fixed	0.0020%	0.7732 m/s^2
Graph	variable	0.0297%	5.6688 m/s^2
SLP	variable	0.0224%	5.2010 m/s^2
LS	variable	0.0095%	3.2008 m/s^2

This appears to be in conflict with the objective functions Φ_{slp} and Φ_{ls}. One possible explanation for this discrepancy is that the SLP method may become trapped within a local optimum, resulting in its suboptimal performance. From the results, it can be seen that the LS method has the best optimization effect, especially when facing the variable feedrate during the robot polishing process.

5   Conclusion

To improve the polishing effect, this paper aims to reduce fluctuations in joint velocity and acceleration to obtain the smoothest joint trajectory. A robot kinematic model is constructed using redundant variables. Kinematic performance indexes for the polishing task are proposed to filter feasible intervals. Thereafter, a sequence of redundant variables on the tool path is obtained using the graph search method. The least sqaures method is used for subsequent optimization to obtain the final joint trajectories. Simulations and experiments demonstrate that the LS method, which eliminates the need for constructing complex mathematical models, exhibits higher optimization efficiency and superior optimization effects, especially under variable feedrate conditions. It is also less sensitive to the initial solution. Overall, this paper presents a complete framework for the redundancy optimization of joint trajectory smoothness for robot polishing.

Simultaneously, there exist issues that merit further research and discussion. When establishing robot motion performance indexes using the Jacobian matrix, calculating the inverse matrix is time-consuming. In addition, the magnitudes of velocity and acceleration do not match appropriately in the optimization objective function Φ_{total}. Addressing these issues could further enhance the efficiency and effectiveness of the optimization algorithm.

Acknowledgements.. This research is financed by the National Natural Science Foundation of China under Grant Nos. 52275451, 51905345, and the Shanghai Pujiang Talent Program under Grant No. 21PJD028.

References

1. Ke, X., et al.: Review on robot-assisted polishing: status and future trends. Robot. Comput.-Integr. Manuf. **80**, 102482 (2023)
2. Xiao, M., Ding, Y., Yang, G.: A model-based trajectory planning method for robotic polishing of complex surfaces. IEEE Trans. Autom. Sci. Eng. **19**(4), 2890–2903 (2022)
3. Mohsin, I., He, K., Li, Z., Ruxu, D.: Path planning under force control in robotic polishing of the complex curved surfaces. Appl. Sci. **9**(24), 5489 (2019)
4. Wan, S., Zhang, X., Min, X., Wang, W., Jiang, X.: Region-adaptive path planning for precision optical polishing with industrial robots. Opt. Express **26**(18), 23782 (2018)
5. Sun, H.W., Yang, J.X., Li, D.W., Ding, H.: An on-line tool path smoothing algorithm for 6r robot manipulator with geometric and dynamic constraints. Sci. China Technol. Sci. **64**(9), 1907–1919 (2021)
6. Wang, H., Zhao, Q., Li, H., Zhao, R.: Polynomial-based smooth trajectory planning for fruit-picking robot manipulator. Inf. Process. Agric. **9**(1), 112–122 (2022)
7. Nadir, B., Mohammed, O., Minh-Tuan, N., Abderrezak, S.: Optimal trajectory generation method to find a smooth robot joint trajectory based on multiquadric radial basis functions. Int. J. Adv. Manuf. Technol. **120**(1), 297–312 (2022)
8. Fang, Y., Hu, J., Liu, W., Shao, Q., Qi, J., Peng, Y.: Smooth and time-optimal s-curve trajectory planning for automated robots and machines. Mech. Mach. Theory **137**, 127–153 (2019)

9. Hong, L., Wenwen, X.: Application in the motion planning of underactuated hexapod robot based on genetic. In: 2011 Third International Conference on Measuring Technology and Mechatronics Automation. vol. 1, pp. 515–518 (2011). https://doi.org/10.1109/ICMTMA.2011.131

10. Cheng, K.P., Mohan, R.E., Khanh Nhan, N.H., Le, A.V.: Multi-objective genetic algorithm-based autonomous path planning for hinged-tetro reconfigurable tiling robot. 8, 121267–121284. https://doi.org/10.1109/ACCESS.2020.3006579

11. Zanchettin, A.M., Messeri, C., Cristantielli, D., Rocco, P.: Trajectory optimisation in collaborative robotics based on simulations and genetic algorithms 6(4), 707–723. https://doi.org/10.1007/s41315-022-00240-4

12. Yu, W., Liu, J., Zhou, J.: A novel sparrow particle swarm algorithm (SPSA) for unmanned aerial vehicle path planning 2021, 5158304. https://doi.org/10.1155/2021/5158304

13. Rigatos, G.G.: Distributed gradient and particle swarm optimization for multi-robot motion planning. Robotica 26(3), 357–370 (2008)

14. Zhenyi, C.: Joint trajectory time optimization of COBOT based on particle swarm optimization 616(1), 012015. https://doi.org/10.1088/1757-899X/616/1/012015

15. Dolgui, A., Pashkevich, A.: Manipulator motion planning for high-speed robotic laser cutting. Int. J. Prod. Res. 47(20), 5691–5715 (2009)

16. Lu, Y.A., Tang, K., Wang, C.Y.: Collision-free and smooth joint motion planning for six-axis industrial robots by redundancy optimization. Robot. Comput.-Integr. Manuf. 68, 102091 (2021)

17. Peng, J., Ding, Y., Zhang, G., Ding, H.: Smoothness-oriented path optimization for robotic milling processes. Sci. China Technol. Sci. 63(9), 1751–1763 (2020)

18. Angeles, J.: Fundamentals of Robotic Mechanical Systems. Mechanical Engineering Series, Springer, Boston (2007). https://doi.org/10.1007/978-0-387-34580-2

19. Wang, T., et al.: Rifta: a robust iterative fourier transform-based dwell time algorithm for ultra-precision ion beam figuring of synchrotron mirrors 10(1), 8135. https://doi.org/10.1038/s41598-020-64923-3, https://www.nature.com/articles/s41598-020-64923-3

Vision-Guided Mobile Robot System for the Assembly of Long Beams on Aircraft Skin

Lei Zheng[1], Huaying Liu[2], Hongsheng Zhu[1], Xingwei Zhao[1(✉)], and Bo Tao[1]

[1] School of Mechanical Science and Engineering, Huazhong University of Science and Technology, Wuhan 430074, Hubei, China
zhaoxingwei@hust.edu.cn
[2] Shanghai Aircraft Manufacturing Co. Ltd., Shanghai, China

Abstract. The current stage of assembly for robotic arms is limited due to the fixed platform, resulting in limited assembly space. To overcome this barrier, this paper proposes a mobile robotic arm assembly system, comprising an AGV, a lifting tool, a robotic arm, an end assembly tool, and a binocular camera. The AGV provides spatial freedom and relocates the entire system to the assembly station, while the lifting tool enhances the assembly height, thereby supplementing the robotic vertical assembly space. The binocular camera provides visual guidance to control the moving tool of the robots, allowing it to approach the target by identifying it. The end tool is the required tool for the actual assembly. Furthermore, the system is established with a communication method that facilitates cooperative control of multiple devices. In the experiment conducted, the end tool successfully reached the assembly position, highlighting the exceptional performance of the assembly system.

Keywords: Robotic Assembly · Visual Guidance · Multi-device Communication

1 Introduction

In the realm of robotic assembly, fixed robotic arms are commonly utilized, however they have limited capabilities and can only perform assembly operations at specific, pre-determined set-up stations [1]. In an industrial environment, if the assembly part is a large, curved plate such as an aircraft wall plate, the confined working space of a single robotic arm is insufficient to fully cover the assembly area. In order to compensate for this, multiple robotic arms could be used. However, using multiple arms increases the assembly cost and introduces potential issues with interference in the robot arm placement. As a solution to these challenges, an assembly robot arm that can achieve freedom of motion and lifting within the workspace is necessary, thereby creating demand for mobile robotic arm assembly systems.

The deployment of robots in industrial modernization has significantly increased, replacing manual labor and becoming prevalent in the areas of handling and assembly due to their flexibility and high load-bearing capacity [2]. In industrial practice, a robotic

H. Yang et al. (Eds.): ICIRA 2023, LNAI 14272, pp. 430–442, 2023.
https://doi.org/10.1007/978-981-99-6480-2_36

arm's operation can be guided by its demonstrator, although this method proves less efficient than offline programming techniques [3]. Offline programming relies mostly on pre-defined trajectories to control robot assembly. However, since the actual assembly position is variable, fixed points can only achieve limited adaptability. Thus, force-controlled assembly and vision-guided assembly have been introduced to accomplish adequate assembly guidance [4]. While force feedback can only be adjusted with contact force feedback, vision is adept at guiding assembly [5–7].

Appropriate calibration of the camera, robotic arm, and end tool is critical in vision-guided robotic arm control, as calibration accuracy directly influences the final assembly precision [8]. Calibration is separated into two parts: camera and tool coordinate system calibration. Tool coordinate system calibration intends to exhibit workpiece information in the robot frame, facilitating the planning of tool motion trajectories. For complete TCP calibration, Yang et al. [9] established a nonlinear constraint equation using inherently constrained target points. Then, the authors utilized a perturbation model to calculate the numerical solution after optimization by the Lie algebra method. Fares et al. [10] proposed the spherical fitting calibration method, which features greater calibration precision by fitting the four collected attitude data. In addition, Krakhmalev [11] formulated a mathematical model for a three-point orientation calibration TCF method for industrial robot tools. Essentially, these calibration techniques collect the robot information under different attitudes of the tool at a fixed point.

Calibrating the camera coordinate system aims to express target information within the robot framework, streamlining robot trajectory planning. Liska et al. [12] collected data with a two-dimensional laser profile scanner, and calibrated the robot and scanner's coordinates. Nissler et al. [13] original approach to calibration involved rotating the robot around an axis and capturing abundant visual features to accurately fit the robot configuration, and establish a precise mathematical model between robot kinematics and the camera reference system. Tsai et al. [14–16] assembled pose information from the camera and robot arm, their approach to calibration varied, as they utilized different computational methods. Overall, these researchers adopted similar strategies to acquire pose information, with varying computational methods applied for the camera coordinate system calibration process.

This paper introduces a mobile robotic arm assembly system that integrates the mobility of a mobile base with the dexterity of a robot, mitigating the constraints associated with traditional fixed assembly systems. The paper is structured as follows: Sect. 2 provides a comprehensive review of the system's configuration. Section 3 details the assembly process's leading technologies. Section 4 features the experimental results, and Sect. 5 concludes the paper.

2   The System and Its Working Scenarios

This section describes the components of this mobile robotic arm assembly system and its working conditions.

2.1   Introduction of Working Conditions

In aircraft assembly processes as shown in Fig. 1, skin splicing requires a locking attachment technique. However, due to the aircraft configuration's large size and the curved nature of its surfaces, manual assembly is problematic, involving excessive operational difficulty and sequential adjustments of the assembly height, while a mobile robotic assembly system can address these issues and provide effective solutions where manual assembly falls short.

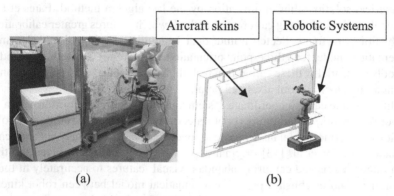

Aircraft skins   Robotic Systems

(a)   (b)

Fig. 1. Experimental scenario (a) and its working condition simulation (b)

2.2   Hardware Composition

The mobile robot assembly system is primarily comprised of four components: the robot arm, mobile base, lifting axis, end tool, and binocular camera, as shown in Fig. 2. Excluding the robot arm, the overall platform measures 800 mm × 560 mm × 960 mm in length, width, and height. The robot base plane is inclined at 90° to the horizontal plane, with a maximum payload of 7 kg, repeat positioning precision of ±0.03 mm, and a working radius of 1125 mm. These attributes effectively support light work needs.

The robotic system comprises several components, including a ROKAE-ER7 PRO robot with seven degrees of freedom. Joints 1, 3, and 5 have a range of motion of ±170°, while joints 2, 4, and 6 have a range of motion of ±120°, and joint 7 has a range of motion of ±360°. The robot's end effector has a 7 kg payload capacity, a working radius of 1125 mm, and a weight of 29 kg. The selected robotic arm provides a high level of precision with its repeatable positioning accuracy of ±0.03 mm and offers an SDK development-supportive inbuilt system, which increases its versatility. Despite its compact size, the robotic arm can accommodate an end effector, camera, and meet basic

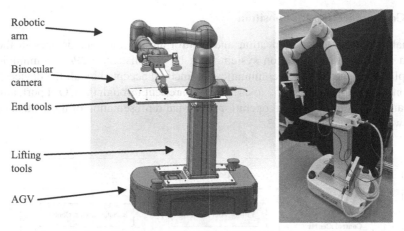

Robotic arm

Binocular camera

End tools

Lifting tools

AGV

Fig. 2. Mobile robotic assembly system. The diagram on the left is the model, and the diagram on the right is the actual diagram.

assembly requirements. The lifting tool utilized in the system is the LIFTKIT-0S by Ewelix, which offers a maximum thrust load of 1500 N and a 900 mm stroke range. At the stroke 0 position, the axis height is 725 mm and can be mechanically locked after reaching the desired height. The positioning accuracy of the lifting tool is 1 mm, and it can be readily controlled using TCP communication. The mobile base chosen for the system is the AMB-150-D by SEER, which relies on laser SLAM for navigation. The motion system of the base has two drive wheels and four omnidirectional wheels, enabling both translational and rotational movements. The base can transport payloads weighing up to 150 kg and offer navigation position accuracy of ± 5 mm and navigation angle accuracy of $\pm 0.5°$. It can be controlled using TCP communication. For imaging, the system employs a high-resolution camera, the acA5742-5 gm by BASLER, matched with a Computer V0826-MPZ lens. The camera boasts a resolution of 5472×3648 pixels with a pixel size of 2.4 μm $\times$ 2.4 μm. The focal length of the lens is 8 mm, with a minimum working distance of 100 mm. Instead of an end effector, the system utilizes a cone-shaped tool.

In conclusion, the entire mobile robotic assembly system is remotely supervised and controlled through a Windows-based platform.

This mobile robot assembly system's key components work in synergy, resulting in its unique functionality and capabilities. The robot offers operational guidance for the assembly of the end tool, while the lifting tool extends the robot arm's vertical height. The camera recognizes image information, providing guidance to the robotic end tool to the position where it is to perform its task. The AGV is instrumental in building a map of the working area and transporting the tools to the assembly station.

2.3 Communication Composition

To enable effective communication and control among the four devices in the system, a suitable communication system must be established. TCP/IP communication is employed as the universal communication method accepted by all the devices. Control commands that are specific to each device are sent through the COM port, allowing for seamless coordination and operation. A visual representation of the system control framework is depicted in Fig. 3.

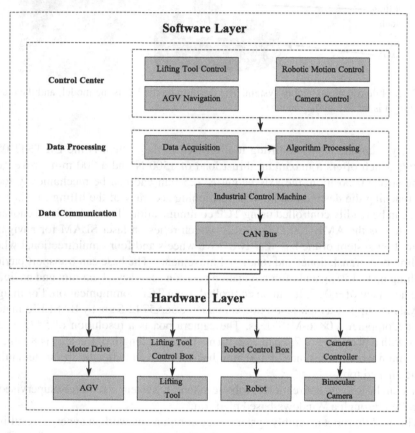

Fig. 3. Control frame of the system.

The system is categorically structured into four layers based on each layer's functionalities: the Control Center layer, Data Processing layer, Data Communication layer, and Hardware layer. The Control Center layer oversees the issuance of directives to the hardware components, while the Data Processing layer involves the AGV gathering information about the operating environment via its laser radar. Additionally, the camera captures data to recognize the required targets. The Data Communication layer facilitates the connectivity of the various devices to the upper computer through a CAN bus. The devices then receive directives from the upper computer and subsequently execute commands via motor drivers, lifting tool control cabinet, robot control cabinet, and camera controller. The Hardware layer makes up the physical components of the system, which includes the AGV, motor drivers, lifting tool control cabinet, robot control cabinet, and camera controller. These four layers collaboratively work towards facilitating effective communication and control within the system.

Received from the Data Communication layer, the information is processed in the Data Processing layer, where it undergoes analysis using relevant algorithms to make informed decisions. The Control Center layer then utilizes this information to perform various tasks like navigating the mobile platform, controlling the robot's motion, overseeing the lifting axis, and managing camera control operations. The information exchange between the Control Center layer, Data Processing layer, and Data Communication layer takes place within the Windows operating system environment.

3   System Control Strategy

This chapter outlines how the mobile robotic arm assembly system performs the assembly work and presents a workflow diagram, as shown in Fig. 4, which illustrates the assembly process in detail.

1. Before starting the assembly task, the mobile base constructs the slam build of the work scene. Following this, several work positions are defined within the generated navigation map to facilitate the mobile base's automatic navigation towards the designated work positions.
2. Once the task begins, the AGV trolley automatically navigates to the assigned working position through the established navigation map.
3. When the system arrives at the designated working position, the lifting tool is operated as needed to raise the required components.
4. Once the lifting axis has elevated the components to the desired height, the mechanical arm starts its operation and moves to the target location within the camera's field of view, at which point it stops moving.
5. As the camera identifies the target, it provides feedback information to the robotic arm, allowing it to operate while simultaneously aligning the end tool's normal vector with the target normal vector.
6. Once the normal vector alignment is complete, spatial position identification of the target is carried out. Once identified, the camera guides the robotic arm to the location to achieve visual guidance.
7. Once the positioning is complete, the assembly process is executed using the end tool.
8. The assembly task is considered complete after the assembly process is executed successfully.

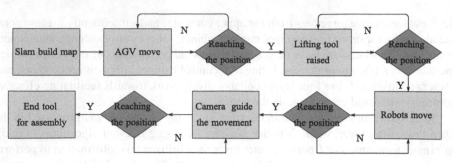

Fig. 4. Visually guided assembly process.

3.1 Visual Guidance Control

This chapter mainly explains how to use the coordinates obtained through visual observation for the motion control of a robot. The coordinate of a space position **P** is obtained through a camera, which is the observation value in the camera coordinate system. Next, we need to control the tool at the end of the robot to reach the observed value. In the control of the robot, we need to transform the coordinates observed by the camera into the coordinate space of the end of the robot, so as to perform motion control. However, if we only transform it into end control, we can only control the end to reach the target position, and cannot control the tool at the end to reach the target position, so it is also necessary to transform the coordinate system of the end of the robot to the tool coordinate system. Therefore, in order to control the robot, two coordinate system transformations need to be carried out first.

Part 1 Hand-Eye Calibration

This subsection focuses on hand-eye calibration, which deals with the transformation of coordinates from the camera to the robot's end-effector. In this context, the representation of the robot's end-effector in the base coordinate system is denoted as $^B_E\mathbf{T}$, while the representation of the calibration board in the camera coordinate system is denoted as $^{CB}_C\mathbf{T}$. Using measurements obtained as $^B_E\mathbf{T}_i$ and $^{CB}_C\mathbf{T}_i, i = 1, 2, ..., N$. The transformation relationship between the two poses is mathematically represented in Eq. (1).

$$
\begin{aligned}
^B_E\mathbf{T}_1{}^C_E\mathbf{T}^{CB}_C\mathbf{T}_1 &= {}^B_E\mathbf{T}_2{}^C_E\mathbf{T}^{CB}_C\mathbf{T}_2 \\
^B_E\mathbf{T}_2^{-1}{}^B_E\mathbf{T}_1{}^C_E\mathbf{T} &= {}^C_E\mathbf{T}^{CB}_C\mathbf{T}_2{}^{CB}_C\mathbf{T}_1^{-1}
\end{aligned}
\tag{1}
$$

where:

$$
\mathbf{T}_a = \begin{bmatrix} R_a & t_a \\ 0 & 1 \end{bmatrix}
\tag{2}
$$

R_a is the rotation matrix and t_a is the translation matrix. Suppose:

$$
\begin{aligned}
\mathbf{T}_a &= {}^B_E\mathbf{T}_2^{-1}{}^B_E\mathbf{T}_1 \\
\mathbf{T}_b &= {}^{CB}_C\mathbf{T}_2{}^{CB}_C\mathbf{T}_1^{-1} \\
\mathbf{T}_x &= {}^C_E\mathbf{T}
\end{aligned}
\tag{3}
$$

By combining Eqs. (2) and (3), we can derive Eq. (4):

$$R_a R_x = R_x R_b$$
$$R_a t_x + t_a = R_x t_b + t_x$$

(4)

To solve Eq. (4), we use an existing hand-eye calibration method [14]. We present only the key solution equation, omitting the solution process:

$$R_x = \left(1 - \frac{|p_x|^2}{2}\right) I + \frac{1}{2}\left(p_x p_x^T + \sqrt{4 - |p_x|^2} \times S(p_x)\right)$$

(5)

Here, $S(\cdot)$ is the antisymmetric matrix and p_x is the rotation vector ($p_x \in \Re^{3\times1}$). p_x is obtained from Eq. (6).

$$p_x = \frac{2p_{x\prime}}{\sqrt{1 + |p_{x\prime}|^2}}$$
$$S(p_a + p_b)p_{x\prime} = p_b - p_a$$

(6)

By combining Eqs. (4–6), we can derive the rotation matrix for the hand-eye calibration.

Part 2 Tool Calibration
Calibrating the tool is the primary topic of this section, which aims to determine the transformation matrix between the tool coordinate system and the robot end-effector coordinate system. The six-point calibration method is used to achieve this objective. Initially, the tool center point is adjusted so that the TCP positions of the first four calibration points coincide to calculate the tool center point. Following this, attitude calibration is utilized to establish a unique orientation relationship between the last three calibration points to measure the tool's coordinate system's attitude concerning the robot end coordinate system. The transformation relation of the robot end coordinate system E concerning the robot base coordinate system B is represented as $_E^B\mathbf{T}$. Furthermore, the transformation relation of the tool coordinate system T with respect to the endpoint coordinate system E is expressed as $_T^E\mathbf{T}$.

The transformation relation of the tool coordinate system T concerning the base coordinate system B is represented by $_E^B\mathbf{T}$, while the transformation relation of the three is denoted by $_E^B\mathbf{T}_T^E\mathbf{T} = _T^B\mathbf{T}$. We can obtain Eq. (7) using the first four data points.

$$_E^B R_1 {_T^E}t + {_E^B}t_1 = {_T^B}t$$
$$_E^B R_2 {_T^E}t + {_E^B}t_2 = {_T^B}t$$
$$_E^B R_3 {_T^E}t + {_E^B}t_3 = {_T^B}t$$
$$_E^B R_4 {_T^E}t + {_E^B}t_4 = {_T^B}t$$

(7)

Equation 8 can be obtained from Eq. 7.

$$_T^E t = \begin{bmatrix} _E^B R_1 - {_E^B}R_2 \\ _E^B R_2 - {_E^B}R_3 \\ _E^B R_3 - {_E^B}R_4 \end{bmatrix} \backslash \begin{bmatrix} _E^B t_2 - {_E^B}t_1 \\ _E^B t_3 - {_E^B}t_2 \\ _E^B t_4 - {_E^B}t_3 \end{bmatrix}$$

(8)

By using the last three points to confirm the posture, we can obtain Eq. (9).

$$\vec{X} = {}_E^B t_5 - {}_E^B t_4$$
$$\vec{Z} = {}_E^B t_6 - {}_E^B t_4 \qquad (9)$$
$$\vec{Y} = \vec{Z}\vec{X}$$

To ensure the orthogonality of coordinate system vectors, vector Z is recalculated.

$$\vec{Z} = \vec{X}\vec{Y} \qquad (10)$$

Combined with Eqs. (8–10), the tool calibration rotation matrix can be derived.

Part 3 Motion Control

Finally, the results of the two calibrations are integrated to enable coordinate transformation and motion control. This integration allows for the conversion of camera observations under the end tool coordinate system.

$${}_T^O P = {}_T^E T {}_E^C T {}_C^O T P \qquad (11)$$

Following this conversion, the robot motion can be controlled in point-to-point mode, i.e., moving from the starting point to the recognized point ${}_T^O P$.

4 Experiment

In this chapter, we perform experimental tests on the system developed in Sect. 2, with the objective of assessing its accuracy and operability in a tightening process. The experimental setup involves a hole point that is to be assembled, and we conduct tests to verify the system's functionality in detecting the hole position and ensuring proper contact.

Specifically, we aim to evaluate whether the system can accurately and reliably detect the hole position, and whether it can execute the tightening process effectively. By testing the system's performance under different conditions and scenarios, we can gain insights into its strengths and limitations, and identify areas for further improvement.

Overall, the experimental tests are a crucial step in validating the functionality and performance of the system, and will inform our decisions moving forward as we continue to develop and refine the technology.

4.1 AGV Navigation Control

As shown in Fig. 4, the initial step in our system involves slam mapping of the workspace using AGV-mounted LIDAR, which enables movement control for the manual construction of a map. During subsequent motion guidance, it is vital to define the working condition position on the previously constructed map. Once the position is defined, the mobile base can be automatically controlled via communication to navigate to the designated target (Fig. 5).

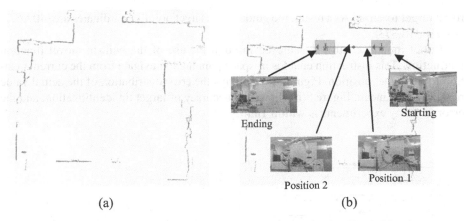

Fig. 5. Slam Map Construction (a) and AGV Navigation Track (b)

4.2 Visually Guided Robotic Movement

Upon reaching the image acquisition position, the system initiates visual guidance to determine the machine's spatial position in the base coordinate system, which is (527.494,9.118,86.413). Figure 6 and 7 display the results of this process.

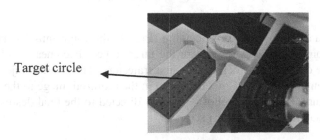

Fig. 6. Visually Guided Starting Posture

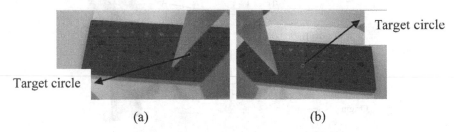

Fig. 7. Visually Guided Starting Posture (a) the left eye, and (b) the right eye

We extract the binocular pixel points of the target's left eye (3866.76, 1352.61) and right eye (1980.01, 1334.96) based on the designated target. These pixel points enable us to determine the target's spatial location, which is subsequently transformed into the robot target location. As a result, the guide space target point's coordinates are (409.672, −8.916, 18.373).

Robot motion control is achieved through the use of the built-in movel function instruction. This instruction enables in-space panning to navigate from the current position to the target position. Figure 8(a) displays the error distribution of the actual value relative to the mean. Figure 8(b) shows the accuracy of target tip identification, and the error of many experiments is within 1mm.

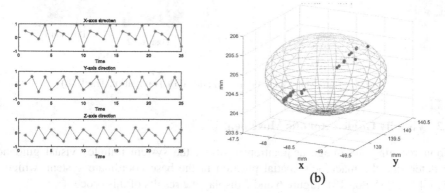

Fig. 8. The Error (a) and Identification Error (b)

In accordance with trajectory planning (Fig. 9), the robot initially navigates from its starting point to the location where the target object becomes visible in the field of view of the camera. This defines the first trajectory. The second trajectory involves movement from the point of target detection in the acquired image to the final position of image capture. Finally, the robot is visually directed to the final destination through the implementation of the third trajectory.

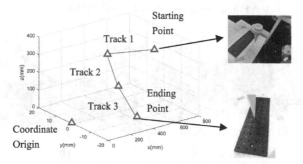

Fig. 9. Robotic Motion Trajectory Map

5   Conclusion

This paper reports on the design of a mobile robot assembly system, integrating a robot, mobile base, lifting tool, end tool, and binocular camera. Communication between the various system components was established using TCP/IP protocols. The control framework was developed, as was the overall control strategy for the entire system. To assess the feasibility of the system design, assembly tasks were set, and shaft-hole assembly experiments conducted. These tests corroborated the design's workability and furnished the foundation for future applications in multiple fields.

Acknowledgement. This work was supported by the National Key Research and Development Program of China under Grant 2022YFB3404102.

References

1. Xu, F., Wang, S., Li, B.: Industrial robot base assembly based on improved Hough transform of circle detection algorithm. In: Proceeding of the 11th World Congress on Intelligent Control and Automation, pp. 2446–2450 (2014). https://doi.org/10.1109/WCICA.2014.7053106
2. Liu, Z., Liu, Q., Xu, W., Wang, L., Zhou, Z.: Robot learning towards smart robotic manufacturing: a review. Robot. Comput.-Integr. Manuf. **77**, 102360 (2022). https://doi.org/10.1016/j.rcim.2022.102360
3. Santos Bottazzi, V., Cruz Fonseca, J.F.: Off-line robot programming framework. In: Joint International Conference on Autonomic and Autonomous Systems and International Conference on Networking and Services - (ICAS-ISNS 2005), p. 71 (2005). https://doi.org/10.1109/ICAS-ICNS.2005.70
4. Chen, Z., Xie, S., Zhang, X.: Position/force visual-sensing-based robotic sheet-like peg-in-hole assembly. IEEE Trans. Instrum. Meas. **71**, 1–11 (2022). https://doi.org/10.1109/TIM.2021.3135552
5. Xu, J., Liu, K., Pei, Y., Yang, C., Cheng, Y., Liu, Z.: A Noncontact control strategy for circular peg-in-hole assembly guided by the 6-DOF robot based on hybrid vision. IEEE Trans. Instrum. Meas. **71**, 1–15 (2022). https://doi.org/10.1109/TIM.2022.3164133
6. Wang, S., Chen, G., Xu, H., Wang, Z.: A robotic peg-in-hole assembly strategy based on variable compliance center. IEEE Access. **7**, 167534–167546 (2019). https://doi.org/10.1109/ACCESS.2019.2954459
7. Jiang, T., Cui, H., Cheng, X., Tian, W.: A measurement method for robot peg-in-hole pre-alignment based on combined two-level visual sensors. IEEE Trans. Instrum. Meas. **70**, 1–12 (2021). https://doi.org/10.1109/TIM.2020.3026802
8. Liu, Z., Liu, X., Cao, Z., Gong, X., Tan, M., Yu, J.: High precision calibration for three-dimensional vision-guided robot system. IEEE Trans. Industr. Electron. **70**, 624–634 (2023). https://doi.org/10.1109/TIE.2022.3152026
9. Yang, Z., Gong, L., Liu, C.: Efficient TCP calibration method for vision guided robots based on inherent constraints of target object. IEEE Access. **9**, 8902–8911 (2021). https://doi.org/10.1109/ACCESS.2021.3049964
10. Fares, F., Souifi, H., Bouslimani, Y., Ghribi, M.: Tool center point calibration method for an industrial robots based on spheres fitting method. In: 2021 IEEE International Symposium on Robotic and Sensors Environments (ROSE), pp. 1–6 (2021). https://doi.org/10.1109/ROSE52750.2021.9611759

11. Krakhmalev, O.N., Petreshin, D.I., Krakhmalev, G.N.: Methods of calibrating the orientation of the industrial robot tool. In: 2018 International Multi-Conference on Industrial Engineering and Modern Technologies (FarEastCon), pp. 1–5 (2018). https://doi.org/10.1109/FarEastCon.2018.8602519

12. Liska, J., Vanicek, O., Chalus, M.: Hand-eye calibration of a laser profile scanner in robotic welding. In: 2018 IEEE/ASME International Conference on Advanced Intelligent Mechatronics (AIM), pp. 316–321 (2018). https://doi.org/10.1109/AIM.2018.8452270

13. Nissler, C., Marton, Z.-C.: Robot-to-camera calibration: a generic approach using 6D detections. In: 2017 First IEEE International Conference on Robotic Computing (IRC), pp. 299–302 (2017). https://doi.org/10.1109/IRC.2017.66

14. Tsai, R.Y., Lenz, R.K.: A new technique for fully autonomous and efficient 3D robotics hand/eye calibration. IEEE Trans. Robot. Autom. **5**, 345–358 (1989). https://doi.org/10.1109/70.34770

15. Liang, R., Mao, J.: Hand-eye calibration with a new linear decomposition algorithm. J. Zhejiang Univ. Sci. A. **9**, 1363–1368 (2008). https://doi.org/10.1631/jzus.A0820318

16. Daniilidis, K.: Hand-eye calibration using dual quaternions. Int. J. Robot. Res. **18**, 286–298 (1999). https://doi.org/10.1177/02783649922066213

Generation of Collision-Free Tool Posture for Robotic Belt Grinding Blisk Using Visualization Toolkit

Anjie Wang, Lai Zou[⊠], and Xinli Wang

The State Key Laboratory of Mechanical Transmissions, Chongqing University, No. 174, Shazhengjie, Shapingba, Chongqing 400044, China
zoulai@cqu.edu.cn

Abstract. In robotic belt grinding of the blisk, the presence of deep and narrow flow channels poses a risk of abrasive belt collisions, potentially causing damage to the tool and blisk. Therefore, a collision-free tool posture generation method is proposed. This method involves discretizing the processing surface into cutter contact (CC) points and establishing local coordinate systems at each CC point. By employing OBB-Tree and leveraging the structural characteristics of the abrasive belt, an efficient collision detection method is developed to establish the relationship between tool posture and the blade. The collision-free posture of the abrasive belt is then determined using a dichotomous method. The feasibility of this approach is verified through a simulation system developed using Visual Studio and VTK (Visualization Toolkit).

Keywords: Blisk · Robotic belt grinding · OBB-Tree · Collision detection

1 Introduction

The blisk, a crucial component of an aircraft engine, plays a vital role in determining the engine's performance due to its impact on surface quality. Therefore, achieving a high-quality surface finish is of utmost importance, necessitating the implementation of grinding techniques. The structure comprises a central hub and a series of blades, resulting in narrow, deep flow channels between them. However, during the grinding process, a potential risk of tool interference with the workpiece exists, which can lead to detrimental effects on both the processing equipment and the workpiece itself. Consequently, it becomes imperative to conduct collision detection prior to commencing the processing operations to effectively prevent such interferences.

In computer simulations, collision detection efficiency can be significantly improved by simplifying the complex models of actual objects by enveloping them with simplified geometries. For instance, Benitez et al. [1] employed spheres as approximations for collision detection, enabling rapid and efficient detection through hierarchical representation and frame-to-frame consistency. In a similar vein, Chang [2] proposed an efficient collision detection method based on Oriented Bounding Boxes (OBB) to enhance the

H. Yang et al. (Eds.): ICIRA 2023, LNAI 14272, pp. 443–455, 2023.
https://doi.org/10.1007/978-981-99-6480-2_37

efficiency of triangle-delta intersection tests. Behzad Danaei [3] et al. used the triangle intersection test method to obtain the collision-free working space of the robot and improved the computational efficiency by the boundary ball method. Prasanth, DR [4] aiming at the collision detection problem in sheet metal bending, the collision detection strategy of sheet metal bending problem considering the boundary volume hierarchy of OBB and AABB methods was studied. To enhance collision detection efficiency in robot processing, Wang et al. [5] transformed interference detection into a distance problem by considering the tool axis and CC points on the workpiece surface, reducing the inspection workload by projecting the tool onto the surface being examined. Similarly, Fan et al. [6] tackled collision problems in robotic motion by introducing the concept of global collision detection feature points, resulting in improved detection efficiency. Based on the above research, it can be found that the elimination of the vast majority of disjoint situations in collision detection is the main means to improve efficiency, but methods used in different situations are not the same, so it is effective to formulate collision detection method according to the actual situation.

In order to address the interference problem in part processing, researchers have developed innovative approaches. Xu et al. [7] introduced the concept of a feasible region, expressing the tool posture of each CC point using inclination and helix angles. By determining the two-dimensional feasible region for each CC point, they effectively avoided overcutting and collisions. Li and Zhang [8–10] divided the surface into collision-free and collision-prone areas, gradually expanding their method to obtain collision-free tool postures. Liang [11] further applied the feasible region concept to blisk machining, planning collision-free tool postures. These studies demonstrate the efficacy of feasible regions in mitigating interference and improving the efficiency of part processing. However, the above tools are all ball-end milling tools, but there is little research on the feasible region of the abrasive belt.

Based on the previous research, this paper introduces the concept of the feasible region in the sanding robotic belt grinding blisk. Initially, a hierarchical bounding box approach is employed to partition the blisk, simplifying the collision detection process by considering the structural characteristics of the abrasive belt. Subsequently, the collision relationship between the tool posture and the blisk is established, and a dichotomy method is utilized to efficiently solve the feasible region, avoiding the time-consuming traversal of tool postures. Finally, a robotic simulation system is developed using Visual Studio and VTK to validate the effectiveness of the proposed method.

2 Preliminary

The blade represents a typical Non-Uniform Rational B-Spline (NURBS) curved surface, and various trajectory planning methods are employed, including the iso-parametric method, iso-chord height method, projection method, and others [12]. It is worth noting that the collision-free tool posture generation algorithm proposed in this paper is not restricted to any particular trajectory planning method. The choice of an appropriate method depends on the specific circumstances and requirements.

After discretizing the surface, the position of each cutter contact (CC) point can be obtained in the workpiece coordinates. However, to determine the tool posture at the robotic end, it is necessary to establish a local coordinate system at the CC point. As illustrated in Fig. 1, the point's normal vector is typically used as the Z-axis, the tangent vector of the curve at the point serves as the X-axis and the Y-axis is derived by applying the right-hand rule to the other two vectors. This information is represented by a 4×4 matrix in formula (1), which describes the local coordinate system {P} of a cutter CC point on a surface.

$$Tp = \left[\begin{array}{ccc|c} X & Y & Z & O \\ \hline & 0 & & 1 \end{array}\right] \tag{1}$$

where O represents the position vector of the CC point in the workpiece coordinate system, and X, Y, and Z represent the three-direction vectors in the workpiece coordinate system.

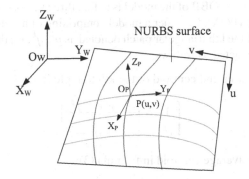

Fig. 1. The local coordinate system of the CC point

Using bounding boxes simplifies testing for complex geometry, but it doesn't reduce the number of tests. However, integrating bounding volumes into a tree structure improves testing efficiency. The Oriented Bounding Box Tree (OBB-Tree) [13] is a hierarchical data structure that uses oriented bounding boxes (OBBs) to represent the model. OBBs are rectangular boxes oriented in 3D space, providing compactness and accurate envelope representation. The collision detection in this study is based on the OBB-Tree. In Sect. 3, the construction of the OBB-Tree for the blade is described (Sect. 3.1). Subsequently, the interference relationship between the tool posture and the blade is established by analyzing the structure of the abrasive belt (Sect. 3.2). Furthermore, a collision detection function is developed (Sect. 3.3) to accurately detect collisions. Finally, this function is applied to determine the feasible domain of the tool (Sect. 3.4).

3 Collision-Free Tool Posture

3.1 Construction of the OBB-Tree of Single Blade

Although the overall structure of the blisk is intricate, the structure of each individual blade remains consistent. Thus, for the purpose of this research, a single blade from the blisk is chosen as the subject of investigation, as illustrated in Fig. 2.

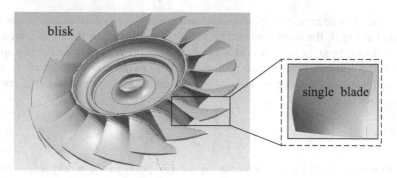

Fig. 2. Structure of the blisk

The key to building an OBB of the model is to find three vectors through the Principal Component Analysis (PCA). Consider a model comprising of n triangles, with the three vertex coordinates of the kth triangular patch denoted as p^k, q^k, r^k, the covariance matrix of the model is constructed as follows:

Step1: Calculate the area and centroid of the kth triangle in formula (2)

$$\begin{cases} A^k = \left| \frac{(q^k - p^k)(r^k - p^k)}{2} \right| \\ c^k = \frac{1}{3}(p^k + q^k + r^k) \end{cases} \qquad (2)$$

Step2: Calculate the average centroid in formula (3):

$$\begin{cases} A^M = \sum_{k=1}^{n} A^k \\ m = \frac{1}{A^M} \sum_{k=1}^{n} A^k c^k \end{cases} \qquad (3)$$

Step3: the covariance matrix is obtained in formula (4):

$$C = [a_{i,j}] = \left(\frac{1}{A^M} \sum_{k=0}^{n} \frac{A^k}{12} (9 c_i^k c_j^k + p_i^k p_j^k + q_i^k q_j^k + r_i^k r_j^k) \right) - m_i m_j \qquad (4)$$

where $i, j = 1, 2, 3$ represent the coordinate components along the coordinate axis X, Y, and Z, respectively, the covariance matrix is constructed. The resulting covariance matrix provides three eigenvectors, which represent the three principal axes of the model's variation. These eigenvectors serve as the axial vectors of OBB). To obtain the bounding box of the model, all the vertices of the model are projected onto these three axes, enabling the determination of the maximum value for each axial projection.

In Fig. 3, the OBB (denote as **A**) of a model is divided along a specific plane, with triangles assigned to the "left" or "right" subgroup based on the centroid's position relative to the dividing plane. This process generates two new OBBs (denote as **A1** and **A2**). **A** represents the parent node, while **A1** and **A2** are its child nodes. The subdivision continues recursively until the number of triangles within a node is below a threshold.

During collision detection, only the parent node is checked for interference with its child nodes, greatly improving efficiency. This hierarchical segmentation approach reduces complexity and ensures accurate collision detection.

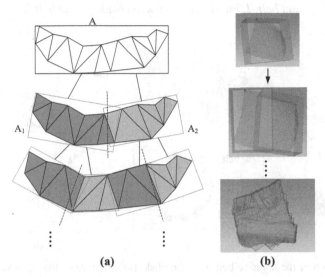

(a)   **(b)**

Fig. 3. The principle of OBB-Tree. (a) The division of OBB. (b) OBB-Tree of the blade

3.2   Structure of the Abrasive Belt

Figure 4(a) depicts a 3D model of the abrasive belt comprising a contact wheel and a grinding belt that wraps around it. The local coordinates for the origin are established at the centre of the contact wheel, with the Z-axis representing the direction of the support axis of the contact wheel and the X-axis representing its axial direction. The relationship between the tool coordinate system {P} and the local coordinate system {M} at the CC point can be defined as follows.

$$T_P trl(0, 0, Z_0) RotY(-90° + \gamma) = T_M \tag{5}$$

where $trl(0, 0, Z_0)$ represents the translation matrix that translates Z_0 along the Z axis, $RotY$ represents the rotation matrix rotating around the Y axis, γ represents the inclination angle of the tool axis vector and the tangent at the machining point. As shown in Fig. 4(b), two interference scenarios can occur during blade grinding: The first is collision with the adjacent blade (*blade_1*), while the second involves interference with the processing blade (*blade_2*).

In the virtual simulation, in order to improve the detection efficiency, a single blade according to Sect. 3.1 to build an OBB-Tree, for the abrasive belt, it can also build the OBB-Tree method of the abrasive belt to improve the detection efficiency, but the intersection test of the two OBB-Trees is very complex. Hense, the structure of the abrasive belt is decomposed as shown in Fig. 5, which is divided into three parts: *belt_1*, *belt_2*, and *belt_3*. Among them, the *belt_3* part is regarded as the part close to the contact wheel, and the processing surface is in contact with the processed surface to achieve polishing, and the two situations of tool interference are subdivided: interference between *blade_1* and *belt_1*, interference between *blade_2* and *belt_2*.

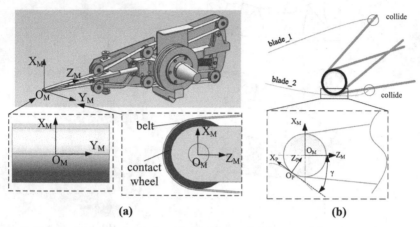

Fig. 4. Collision of the abrasive belt with the blisk. (a) Structure of the abrasive belt. (b) Two positions of collision

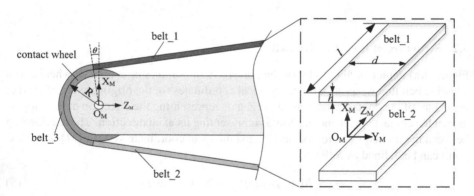

Fig. 5. Decomposition of the abrasive belt

Based on the above analysis, a simple bounding box, denote as $[X_{\min}, X_{\max}, Y_{\min}, Y_{\max}, Z_{\min}, Z_{\max}]$, is employed to describe the geometric information of the abrasive belt. These six quantities represent the maximum and minimum bounds along the three axes of the coordinate system. Taking *belt_1* as an example, bounding box in the local coordinate {*belt_1*} is expressed by formula (6):

$$\begin{cases} T_{belt\_1} = T_M\, RotY(\theta) \\ bounds = [R, R+h, -d/2, d/2, 0, l] \end{cases} \tag{6}$$

where R represents the radius of the contact wheel radius, h represents the thickness of the abrasive belt, d indicates the width of the abrasive belt, l indicates the length of the abrasive belt to be inspected, and θ represents the inclination angle of the abrasive belt.

3.3 Collision Detection Method

The structure of an OBB node is defined as follows:

```
Class OBBNode
{
        double Corner[3];   // center point of OBB
        double Axes[3][3];  // the axes defining OBB
        OBBNode* Parent;  // parent node; nullptr if root
        OBBNode** Kids;  // two children of this node; nullptr if leaf
        IdList* triangles;  // list of triangles in node
}
```

which contains the information of the OBB and the ID of the triangle, and also stores the pointers of the corresponding parent node and child node.

The initial step involves conducting the intersection test between the bounds and the OBB-Tree, the core of which can be seen as a collision check between two bounding boxes (denote as **A** and **B** in Fig. 6). In this implementation, the Separating Axis Theorem (*SAT*) [13] is employed. Illustrated in Fig. 6, each bounding box is characterized by a vertex corner and three axes. When projecting **A** and **B** onto a single axis, if the resulting projections on the axis do not overlap ($A_{max} < B_{min}$ or $B_{max} < A_{min}$), the axis is considered a separating axis. The existence of such a separating axis signifies that **A** and **B** are disjointed. In total, 15 axes need to be examined for searching for the separating axis:

(1) three axes of **A**.
(2) three axes of **B**.
(3) 9 fork-product axes of axis-axis combination between **A** and **B**

Two objects are considered to intersect if none of the above fifteen axes satisfies the condition for separating the axis.

The final accurate detection is a test of the intersection of bounds and triangles (denote as **C**) within leaf nodes, also using *SAT*, except that there are 13 axes that need to be detected [14]:

(1) 9 fork-product axes with edge-to-edge combination between **B** and **C**;
(2) 3 axes of **B**;
(3) the normal vector axis of **C**;

Figure 7 shows the flow chart of the intersection test of the bounding box and OBB-Tree, the input is an OBB-Tree and a bounding box, *col* represents the result of collision detection. A value of 1 denotes a collision occurrence, whereas a value of 0 signifies the absence of collision. *SAT* represents a function that returns 1 when an intersection is detected and 0 otherwise. To perform the intersection test, a stack is employed as a temporary container for storing nodes during the traversal of the tree. When the bounding box intersects with an OBB of a particular node, an exact triangle intersection test is executed for leaf nodes. If the node is not a leaf, the detection process continues for its child nodes. This iterative process is repeated until either an intersection with a triangle is detected ($col = 1$) or traversal is completed ($depth < 0$).

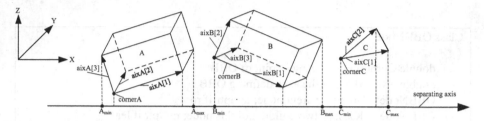

Fig. 6. SAT algorithms between graphs

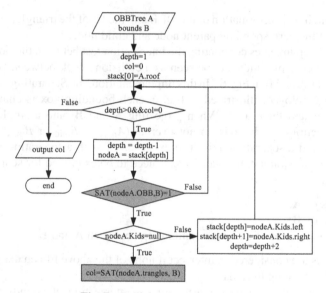

Fig. 7. Collision detection method

3.4 Solution of the Critical Posture

Figure 8(a) illustrates the crucial tool postures that result in collisions between *belt_1* and *blade_1*, denoted as T_{max}, and between *belt_2* and *blade_2*, referred to as T_{min}. These critical tool postures define the boundaries of the feasible region for the tool posture. The tool posture is determined by the variable γ, and the critical tool posture is described by γ_{min} and γ_{max}.

The values of γ_{min} and γ_{max} can be determined by traversing γ directly, but this approach can be time-consuming. To address this, we utilize a dichotomy method to solve the critical tool posture. The flowchart in Fig. 8 outlines the process of solving γ_{min}. Initially, a large step size $\Delta\gamma$ is set, and the search starts from the initial posture. The search continues until γ is found where the collision detection result is 0 (indicating no collision). Subsequently, γ_{min} with an accuracy of *eps* is solved using dichotomy within the interval $[\gamma-\Delta\gamma, \gamma]$. In Fig. 8, the function *Col* represents the collision detection result between the abrasive belt and the blade at a specific posture denoted by γ. The solution for γ_{max} follows a similar approach, except that the initial interval is found in decreasing initial steps starting from the upper limit of the γ (e.g. 90°).

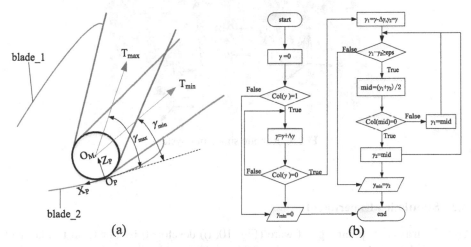

(a)   (b)

Fig. 8. Collision-free tool posture. (a) Critical tool posture. (b) Solution for γ_{min}

4 Simulation Experiment and Result

4.1 Robotic simulation system

A robotic simulation system was developed based on Visual Studio and VTK. The coordinate system of each link in the system is established using the Denavit-Hartenberg (D-H) method. Subsequently, The coordinate system of links is adjusted in UG, and the resulting robotic model is imported into the visualization window of VTK (Fig. 9). During the processing, the robot forms a closed motion chain, and the mathematical relationship of its motor chain can be expressed by the following formula:

$$T_M^B T_P^M = T_W^B T_P^W \tag{7}$$

where the transformation matrix T_W^B describes the relationship between the workpiece coordinate system {W} and the base coordinate system {B}, Similarly, T_P^W represents the relationship between the machining point coordinate system {P} and {W}. These two quantities remain fixed and known throughout the machining process. *TM P* is the transformation matrix of the transformation relationship between {M} and {P}, which determines the interference relationship between the tool and the workpiece. *TB M* represents the transformation matrix of {M} relative to {B}, and the position of each link of the robot can be determined by using the robotic kinematic backsolution through *TB M*, which realizes the simulation of the robotic motion.

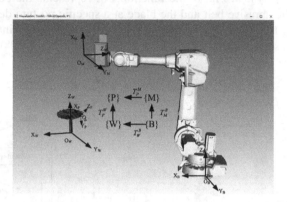

Fig. 9. Robotic simulation system

4.2 Simulation Experiment

Use the trajectory planning software (Fig. 10(a)) developed by our team to plan and generate discrete CC points, and input them into the robotic simulation system. The collision detection algorithm is verified in Fig. 10(b): When a collision between the abrasive belt and the workpiece is detected, the return value of the function is 1 and the abrasive belt is displayed in red. Figure 10(c) shows the collision-free tool posture generation corresponding to this set of CC points.

The set of γ_{min} and γ_{max} obtained in Fig. 10(c) are plotted as two curves, and the area between these two curves is the feasible region of the tool posture, which is shown in Fig. 11, where γ is the angle of the cutter vector to the tangent at a CC point, with an initial range of [0, 90°]. It can be seen that the feasible region is roughly distributed periodically because the part of the tool in the channel gradually increases so that the range of rotation of the tool axis tool becomes a region as the tool is gradually moved by gradually the root of the blade, and the feasible region gradually increases when it is further away from the root. At the same time, the increase in the degree of bending of the blade also leads to the reduction of the feasible region.

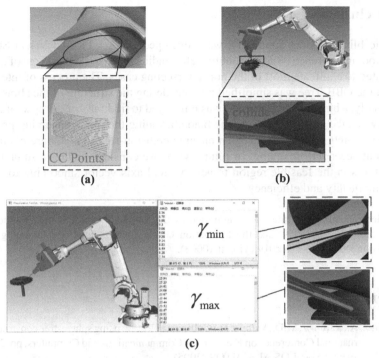

(a)   (b)

(c)

Fig. 10. Simulation experiment. (a) The trajectory planned on the blisk. (b) Implementation of collision detection. (c) Generation of the critical values

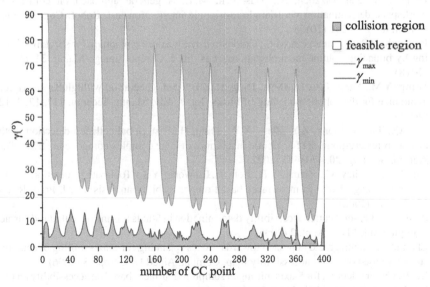

Fig. 11. Feasible region of tool posture

5 Conclusion

A robotic blisk grinding simulation was developed using VTK and Visual Studio to address tool interference issues in robotic belt grinding blisk. The OBB-Tree of the blade was created to eliminate most of the non-intersecting cases. The process of intersecting test with the OBB-Tree was simplified by considering the structure of the abrasive belt. Additionally, a binary search method was employed to find the critical pose of interference between the abrasive belt and the blade, avoiding the time-consuming process of traversing search. The feasible region ensures collision-free tool posture planning for subsequent secondary planning. In future work, we consider finding a suitable set of tool postures in the feasible region to achieve tool axis vector smoothing to improve machining quality and efficiency.

Acknowledgements. This study was supported by the National Natural Science Foundation of China (Grant No. 52075059) and the Innovation Group Science Fund of Chongqing Natural Science Foundation (No. cstc2019jcyj-cxttX0003).

References

1. Benitez, A., Ramirez, M.D., Vallejo, D.: Collision detection using sphere-tree construction. In: 15th International Conference on Electronics, Communications and Computers, pp. 286–291. IEEE Computer Soc, LOS ALAMITOS (2005)
2. Chang, J.W., Kim, M.S.: Efficient triangle-triangle intersection test for OBB-based collision detection. Comput. Graph. **33**, 235–240 (2009)
3. Danaei, B., Karbasizadeh, N., Masouleh, M.T.: A general approach on collision-free workspace determination via triangle-to-triangle intersection test. Robot. Comput. Integr. Manuf. **44**, 230–241 (2017)
4. Prasanth, D.R., Shunmugam, M.S.: Collision detection during planning for sheet metal bending by bounding volume hierarchy approaches. Int. J. Comput. Integr. Manuf. **31**, 893–906 (2018)
5. Wang, Y.M., Yang, J.X., Li, D.W., Ding, H.: Tool path generation with global interference avoidance for the robotic polishing of blisks. Int. J. Adv. Manuf. Technol. **117**, 1223–1232 (2021)
6. Fan, Q., Tao, B., Gong, Z.Y., Zhao, X.W., Ding, H.: Fast global collision detection method based on feature-point-set for robotic machining of large complex components. IEEE Trans. Autom. Sci. Eng. **20**, 470–481 (2022)
7. Xu, X.J., Bradley, C., Zhang, Y.F., Loh, H.T., Wong, Y.S.: Tool-path generation for five-axis machining of free-form surfaces based on accessibility analysis. Int. J. Prod. Res. **40**, 3253–3274 (2002)
8. Zhang, L.: Flat-end cutter accessibility determination in 5-axis milling of sculptured surfaces. Comput. Aided Des. Appl. **2** (2005)
9. Zhang, L.: An integrated approach towards process planning for 5-axis milling of sculptured surfaces based on cutter accessibility map. Comput. Aided Des. Appl. **3** (2006)
10. Li, Z.: Cutter selection for 5-axis milling of sculptured surfaces based on accessibility analysis. Int. J. Prod. Res. **44**, 3303–3323 (2006)
11. Liang, Y.S., Zhang, D.H., Ren, J.X., Chen, Z.Z.C., Xu, Y.Y.: Accessible regions of tool orientations in multi-axis milling of blisks with a ball-end mill. Int. J. Adv. Manuf. Technol. **85**, 1887–1900 (2016)

12. Lv, C., et al.: A trajectory planning method on error compensation of residual height for aero-engine blades of robotic belt grinding. Chin. J. Aeronaut. **35**, 508–520 (2022)
13. Gottschalk, S., Lin, M.C., Manocha, D.: OBBTree: a hierarchical structure for rapid interference detection. In: SIGGRAPH96: Proceedings of the 23rd Annual Conference on Computer Graphics and Interactive Techniques, pp. 171–180 (1996)
14. Akenine-Möllser, T.: Fast 3D triangle-box overlap testing. J. Graph. Tools **6** (2001)

Clinically Oriented Design in Robotic Surgery and Rehabilitation

A Segmented Dynamic Movement Primitives-Based Gait Assistive Strategy for Soft Ankle Exosuit

Fashu Xu[1,2], Wenjun Huang[3], Hao He[4], Nan Li[4], Hongchen He[5(✉)],
and Kang Li[1,2(✉)]

[1] Department of Rehabilitation Medicine and West China Biomedical Big Data
Center, West China Hospital, Sichuan University, Chengdu, China
xufs@wchscu.cn
[2] Med-X Center for Informatics, Sichuan University, Chengdu, China
likang@wchscu.cn
[3] College of Electrical Engineering, Sichuan University, Chengdu, China
[4] Department of Mechanical Engineering, Sichuan University - Pittsburgh Institute,
Sichuan University, Chengdu, China
[5] Department of Rehabilitation Medicine and Institute of Rehabilitation Medicine,
West China Hospital, Sichuan University, Chengdu, China

Abstract. The soft exosuit has been proven to improve the pilot's
walking ability and reduce metabolic consumption, yet, its gait assistance strategy still suffers from the problem of insufficient personalized
adaption. This paper proposes a Segmented Dynamic Movement Primitives (SDMPs) -based gait assistive strategy to address this problem.
This strategy uses a gait detection algorithm to divide a complete gait
cycle into four segments, and establishes independent Dynamic Movement Primitives (DMPs) to learn each segment. Meanwhile, the normal
gait trajectory is referenced and the personalized gait is generated with
the spatial-temporal parameters of each DMPs adjusted automatically
according to the sensor data. Experimental results show that the gait
of SDMPs is superior to those generated by the traditional method and
DMPs. The force feedback indicates that the gait generated using SDMPs
can quickly pull the joint to reach the desired position in the plantar
flexion phase and then quickly complete the tension release, which is
obviously better than other methods. This method can serve as a new
personalized gait assistance strategy for soft ankle exosuits.

Keywords: Soft exosuit · Segmented dynamic movement primitives ·
Gait plan · Assistive strategy

This work was supported by the National Natural Science Foundation of China (Grant
No. 92248304), the 1 3 5 project for disciplines of excellence, West China Hospital,
Sichuan University (ZYYC21004).
F. Xu and W. Huang—Contributed equally to this work and should be considered
co-first authors.

1   Introduction

The design of control algorithms for wearable lower-limb assistive devices has gained significant attention in recent years due to the growing need for efficient and user-friendly tools to facilitate the rehabilitation of patients with lower limb injuries. Exoskeletons are commonly employed devices to assist individuals with walking disabilities or elderly people. However, the rigid framework of exoskeletons introduces substantial inertia to movements, which must be overcome either by motors or the user. Moreover, the static misalignment between the biological joints and the exoskeleton joints can result in dynamic misalignment, leading to user discomfort and potential injury [1,2]. As a potential solution, soft exosuits have been developed to assist users in rehabilitation while minimizing additional mechanical impedance and kinematic restrictions [1,2].

Currently, gait planning algorithms applied to exosuits can be categorized into three main groups: bionics-inspired gait planning, optimization-based gait planning, and machine learning-based gait planning. Bionics-inspired gait planning methods aims to mimic human walking and often rely on accurate sensor data to detect posture and terrain conditions [2,3]. However, these methods may require extensive datasets for sensor accuracy, resulting in a significant computational burden.

Optimization-based gait planning approaches transform the gait planning problem into an optimization problem, aiming to minimize energy cost while satisfying various constraints [4,5]. However, these methods rely on complex mathematical models and algorithms, which can be time-consuming and computationally demanding. Additionally, optimization-based methods may be sensitive to changes in model parameters or environmental conditions, limiting their robustness and adaptability. Machine learning-based gait planning methods utilize artificial intelligence techniques, such as neural networks and reinforcement learning [6–8]. While this approach enables gait planing in diverse walking scenarios and environmental conditions, it often requires a large amount of training data, which can be time-consuming and costly to collect.

To address the aforementioned issues, this paper introduces a soft ankle exosuit design and a new control method based on Segmented Dynamic Movement Primitives (SDMPs) that can generate personalized assistance strategies using a small dataset. The advantages of this approach are as follows:

– it requires a small amount of normal gait sample data and low computational power requirements.
– it has the capability to generate personalized gait trajectories in real-time, by employing feedback from the system.
– it is able to segmentally modulate gait trajectories, with enhancing personalization capabilities and reducing computational burden.

This paper is organized as follows: Sect. 2 introduces the soft exosuit system and describes the Dynamic Movement Primitives (DMPs) and SDMPs algorithms. The design of soft ankle exosuit and SDMPs could be elaborated in details. In Sect. 3, the experiments and results on the soft ankle exosuit would be presented and discussed, especially the effectiveness of the SDMPs. Finally, the conclusion and future work are summarized in Sect. 4.

2   System and Methods

2.1   Soft Exosuit

The soft exosuit discussed in this paper aims to improve walking efficiency and reduce muscular effort by providing tailored assistance to lower extremity joint angles. The ankle joint is a crucial component of human locomotion. Serving as the primary linkage between the foot and lower leg bones, it provides essential mechanical support and regulatory control during movement. While the factors that contribute to effective assistance are not yet fully understood, research has demonstrated the successful implementation of a strategy that capitalizes on the intrinsic dynamics of human walking. Specifically, by adding external torques to complement the normal muscle activity at the lower limb joints, researchers have achieved positive outcomes in previous studies [9,10].

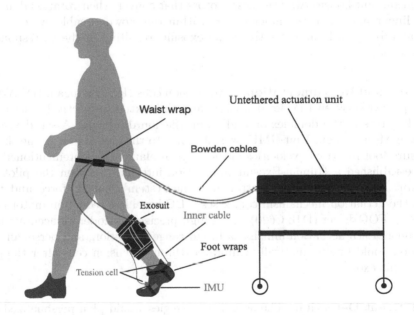

Fig. 1. A soft exosuit schematic diagram including all components of the system. This system is composed of three parts: 1) the untethered actuation unit, including the electronic control and power system; 2) the power transmission line (Bowden cables), delivering the energy from the untethered actuation unit to the exosuit; 3) the soft exosuit, containing the exosuit, foot warps and sensors like tension cells and IMU.

Mechanical Design. The design of this ankle exosuit utilizes flexible materials, such as polyester fabrics, for its primary structure and employs flexible Bowden cables for assisted propulsion. This approach offers several benefits, including a lightweight design, enhanced comfort, and superior adaptability. The ankle exosuit comprises foot straps, lower leg straps, a waist belt, and an untethered actuation unit mounted on a mobile cart. The foot straps are divided into two sections: one section wraps around the dorsum of the forefoot and the medial arch, providing tension during dorsiflexion and housing an inertial sensor; the other section connects to the heel and ankle, offering tension during plantar flexion. Both sections are linked to the inner cables of the Bowden system and pressure sensors, enabling actuation via the Bowden cables and real-time feedback on tension force and motion acceleration. The lower leg straps are constructed from highly elastic polyester fabric, allowing them to adapt to various leg sizes when wrapped around the lower leg. This design ensures both comfort by evenly distributing force across the lower leg and stability by preventing the Bowden cables from shifting on the leg, thus maintaining a consistent direction of applied force. The two Bowden cables pass through the waist belt and are routed to the actuation unit mounted on a mobile cart behind the user. The actuation unit houses two brushless motors that convert their rotational motion into linear motion of the inner cables within the Bowden cable system. This action subsequently actuates the ankle exosuit, resulting in the corresponding movement.

Sensing and Instrumentation. Two tension cells (HY chuangan, HYLY-019) were placed between the Bowden cable and the textile, respectively measuring tensile forces in the dorsiflexion and plantarflexion directions. A self-developed Inertial Measurement Unit (IMU) was attached to the lateral part of the shoe to measure foot rotational velocities in the sagittal plane. The aforementioned sensors established a Human-Exosuit interaction interface between the pilot and exosuit. To achieve precise control over the system's output force and position, the actuation mechanism comprises a DC brushless reduction motor (DJI, M3508), FOC driver (DJI, C620), and a high-precision encoder for accurate measurement. Each actuation unit has a broad range of motion, and personalized 0 position could be automatically calibrated through tension cells after the pilot wears this exosuit.

Gait Event Detection. The assistive strategies would plan personalized gait assistance trajectories during walking, and the effectiveness of the strategies relies on the gait event heavily. According to other studies [11], the gait event detection algorithm would divide each gait cycle into four parts (S1~S4) in real-time, and the initial point and peak value of the specific parts (S2, S3) have a significant impact on gait comfort and efficiency. All parts can be described as fellow:

S1: Stance phase, with foot angular velocity approaching zero. Mean (μ_{50ms}) and variance (σ_{50ms}) of the velocity are calculated over a sliding window of 50 ms. The gait cycle enter S1 only when Eqs. (1) and (2) are met. Otherwise, exit S1.

$$|\mu_{50ms}| < 10 \tag{1}$$

$$\sigma_{50ms}^2 < 100 \tag{2}$$

S2: Pre-swing, starting with the end of S1 and ending with the peak in the negative direction which is relevant to toe off (TO). The time when the peak is detected is marked as t_{TO}.

S3: Early and mid-swing, starting with the end of S2 and lasting for a calculated period length (T_{S3}). T_{S3}, the mean of last five swing period length (T_{swing}), could be described as follows:

$$T_{S3}(k+1) = 0.8 \times \frac{1}{5} \times \sum_{i=k-4}^{k} T_{\text{swing}}(i)$$

$$= 0.8 \times \frac{1}{5} \times \sum_{i=k-4}^{k} [t_{HS}(i) - t_{TO}(i)] \tag{3}$$

in which, $k+1$ and i represent the index of the gait cycle, $T_{S3}(k+1)$ means the predicted period length of S3 in the $(k+1)$th gait cycle, t_{HS} is the time of heel strike (HS).

S4: Late swing and early stance, starting with the end of S3 and ending with when the next S1 starts. t_{HS} would be recorded at the time with a negative peak during S4.

2.2   Dynamic Movement Primitives

As defined in an earlier study [12,13], the DMPs shown as fellows operate by formulating each motion trajectory as a nonlinear dynamical system represented by a set of coupled differential equations. The governing equations are formulated in such a way that the system behavior is controlled by a simple point attractor. This approach allows the system to move toward the desired goal position while also enabling flexible adjustments during the movement execution phase.

$$\tau^2 \dot{v} = K(g - x) - Dv - K(g - x_0)s + Kf(s) \tag{4}$$

$$\tau \dot{x} = v \tag{5}$$

where x and v denote the position and velocity of the system, respectively, while τ is a temporal scaling factor; x_0 and g represent the start and goal positions; K is the elasticity coefficient, and D represents the damping coefficient of the system in a critical state. The function f plays a crucial role in shaping the movement trajectory according to the desired behavior. The differential Eq. (5) indicates a transformation system. Among them, the nonlinear function f can be defined as:

$$f(s) = \frac{\Sigma_i \omega_i \psi_i(s)}{\Sigma_i \psi_i(s)} s \tag{6}$$

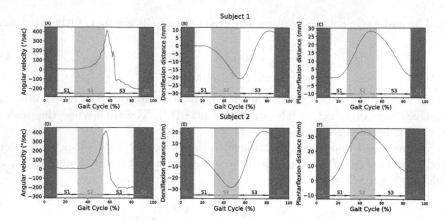

Fig. 2. Angular velocity segmented by gait event detection algorithm for two subjects. This figure contains the angular velocity, dorsiflexion distance, and plantar flexion distance of two subjects during a gait cycle (starting and ending with HS). Through the gait event detection algorithm, the angular velocity curve is divided into four consecutive segments in figure (A) and (D). $S1$ (red regions) indicates the stance phase, the angular velocity is about zero; $S2$ represents the contraction phase of the directions of plantarflexion and dorsiflexion respectively; $S4$ (green regions) means the last swing and early stance of the gait phase. As shown in figure (B), (C), (E) and (F), when the distance value is greater than 0, the ankle joint shrinks in the corresponding direction, other it will loosen. (Color figure online)

where $\psi_i(s)$ is the basic Gaussian function, it can be defined as:

$$\psi_i(s) = \exp\left(-h_i(s - c_i)^2\right) \tag{7}$$

in which, c_i is the center of the function, h_i is the height and w_i is the weight of each Gaussian function.

From Eq. (6), the Gaussian function f is not directly dependent on time parameters, but the phase parameter s, can be expressed as:

$$\tau\dot{s} = -\alpha s \tag{8}$$

where α can be any constant. As can be seen from the Eq. (8), s decreases from 1 to 0 monotonically, that's called the canonical dynamical system. For a given α and τ, the corresponding parameter value s can be calculated, so the f_{target} in the Eq. (4) can be expressed as below:

$$f_{target}(s) = \frac{\tau\dot{v} + Dv}{K} - (g - x) + (g - x_0)s \tag{9}$$

To find the optimal weight value w_i in the Eq. (6), the minimum error criterion expressed in the Eq. (10) will be used. That is, when J is the minimum value, w_i is the optimal weight value. With these parameters above brought into the Eqs. (4) and (5), the position x, speed v and acceleration $\dot{v}$ of the trajectory will be obtained.

$$J = \Sigma_s \left(f_{target}\left(s\right) - f\left(s\right)\right)^2 \tag{10}$$

To tune personalized gait assistance strategies for different objects, the spatial and temporal scaling terms of DMPs would be adjusted based on the feedback sensory data from the system. By changing goal (g) and initial value (y_0) in the $(g - y_0)$ term, the strategies could be spatially scaled, meanwhile, the temporal scaled strategies would appear by adjusting the temporal scaling term (τ). The system would slow down when τ was greater than 1, and when τ was between 0 and 1, the system would accelerate.

2.3   Segmented Dynamic Movement Primitives

Human walking gaits are complex and changeable, and a single DMPs could not represent these curves quickly and directly. When a large number of basis functions were involved, it will cause huge consumption of computation and storage. Although each person's gait has individual differences, the magnitudes of the changes in each gait phase are not the same, because of different factors such as body parameters and health status. Therefore, this paper proposed a Segmented Dynamic Movement Primitives (SDMPs) gait assistive strategy for soft ankle exosuit to generate personalized gait assistive trajectories. Compared with DMPs, SDMPs could divide the gait into four parts with the help of a gait event detection algorithm, and adjust each part of the gait individually according to the system state information. In order to ensure that each part's generated curves could be seamlessly connected, the data from each part was interpolated before generating the final gait.   Each DMPs in the SDMPs is independent, but the starting position of each part is the target position of the previous part. The initial and goal values of all segments Y within the gait trajectory could be expressed as:

$$Y = \begin{bmatrix} \hat{y}_{kS1} \\ \hat{y}_{kS2} \\ \hat{y}_{kS3} \\ \hat{y}_{kS4} \end{bmatrix} = \begin{bmatrix} y^0_{kS1} & y^g_{kS1} \\ y^0_{kS2} & y^g_{kS2} \\ y^0_{kS3} & y^g_{kS3} \\ y^0_{kS4} & y^g_{kS4} \end{bmatrix} = \begin{bmatrix} y^g_{kS4} & y^g_{kS1} \\ y^g_{kS1} & y^g_{kS2} \\ y^g_{kS2} & y^g_{kS3} \\ y^g_{kS3} & y^g_{kS4} \end{bmatrix} \tag{11}$$

in which, $\hat{y}$ represents the adjustment vector for each segment, which includes the initial y^0 and goal y^g values, k is the index of the gait cycle, $S1$, $S2$, $S3$, and $S4$ refer to the four segments obtained by dividing the gait cycle through the gait event detection algorithm. To ensure the continuity of the gait trajectory tuned by SDMPs, the initial value of each segment could be replaced by the goal value of the previous segment.

To achieve better results in gait assistance control, this paper established a control framework of SDMPs as illustrated in Fig. 4. With the help of the system state information, the gait event detection algorithm would determine time

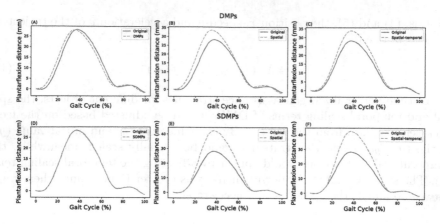

Fig. 3. Comparison of the tuned trajectories of DMPs and SDMPs for plantar flexion distance. The original plantar flexion distance curve (red solid line) was fitted respectively, and then the target planning curve (blue dotted line) was generated by changing on the spatial scale and on the spatial and temporal scales. Since SDMPs can individually tune each part of the gait, this method fits the red curve better than DMPs (figure (A) and (D)). On the basis of maintaining the original curve shape, stretching and adjusting the peak size of the curve on a spatial scale, DMPs modify the entire curve, while SDMPs only modify the peak part of the curve without affecting other gait phase curves (figure (B) and (E)). While changing the spatial scale, the convergence rate of DMPs and SDMPs is modified on the temporal scale (figure (C) and (F)), both of which can better fit the part with smaller amplitudes. (Color figure online)

points for different segments of the gait cycle and pass them into the SDMPs algorithm. Combining with all the inputs including the normal reference gait, system state information, and time points, the SDMPs algorithm could tune a personalized four-segment gait assistive trajectory. Based on the angular velocity data of the IMU in the sagittal plane, the SDMPs algorithm learned the reference gait would act on a temporal and spatial scale to generate a new trajectory. To ensure the smoothness of the generated gait trajectory, a gait interpolation module utilizing cubic spline interpolation functions has been added. Subsequently, the inverse kinematics module would convert this gait trajectory into a cure that is suitable for operation with the actual system, and the motor control system would complete the gait control.

3   Experiments and Results

3.1   Normal Gait Dataset

To establish a normal gait dataset, the range of motion for ankle dorsiflexion and platarflexion of the pilots would be collected at different walking speeds. As shown in Fig. 5, the pilots wearing the ankle exosuit would walk on a treadmill, the exosuit was operating in a force control mode with the target set at 10

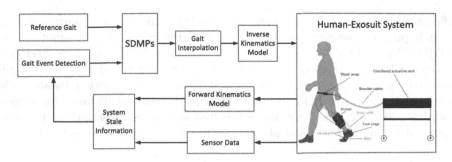

Fig. 4. Control framework of SDMPs.

N, the speed of the treadmill would be set at 3, 4 and 5 km/h according to the experimental requirements. The motion data from two subjects at different speeds would be collected to establish a normal gait dataset in this experiment, and 150 valid gait cycles would be gathered for each speed of each subject. The mean and range of ankle dorsiflexion and plantarflexion motion distances at different speeds for different subjects would be analyzed, which could be used as a reference gait for the SDMPs.

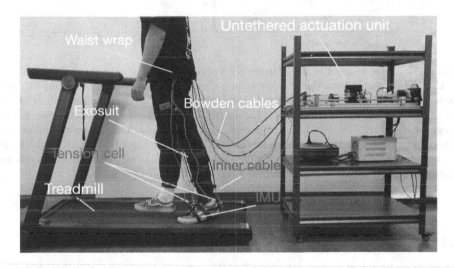

Fig. 5. Untethered soft ankle exosuit. A pilot wearing the exosuit is walking on a treadmill. The exosuit is controlled through an untethered actuation unit that drives Bowden cables. The tension cell and IMU can provide sensory feedback data, and the force control algorithm is completed by using the force and PID algorithm. The IMU data can be used for gait event detection and gait adjustment parameters in SDMPs.

As illustrated in Fig. 6, both subjects exhibit similar trends of ankle dorsiflexion and plantarflexion during walking at 4 km/h, but there are significant differences in the specific range and mean value of motion. The mean gait data of each pilot at the same speed will serve as the reference gait input for the SDMPs. Also, all gait cycles in this figure are normalized to one gait cycle and represented as a percentage from 0 to 100%. The horizontal axis of the figure represents the gait cycle, while the vertical axis represents motion distance. The first and second rows of this figure represent the motion distance for subject 1 and subject 2 respectively, while the first and second columns respectively represent the dorsiflexion and plantarflexion motion data of two subjects.

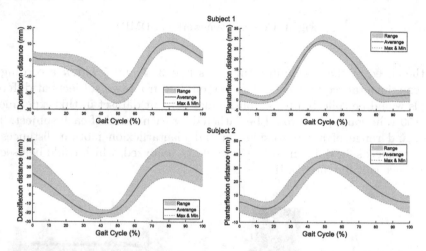

Fig. 6. Example of normal gait dataset for two subjects. The average (solid blue line) in this figure represents the average value after normalization of 150 complete gait cycles, and the blue dashed lines indicate the maximum and minimum values of the range. The range (green region, the blue dashed lines marked) indicates the fluctuation range of the gait. The zero point of dorsiflexion and plantarflexion motion distance is the starting point of the $S1$ phase in the gait detection algorithm, during which the ankle joint angle is approximately 90 °C. The movements in both directions do not yet start at this time. (Color figure online)

3.2   Validation of Segmented Dynamic Movement Primitives

To verify the effectiveness of the SDMPs algorithm, the relationship between the tension force and the gait phase was used for comparative analysis. The gait assistance strategy trajectories of three methods (Traditional, DMPs and SDMPs) for two subjects and their tension force segmented by the gait phase were presented in Fig. 7. The trajectories generated by the traditional method were a predefined gait suitable for the normal waking on flat ground and these tuned by the DMPs were obtained by temporal scaling based on the gait cycle estimated by the IMU. The trajectories tuned by the SDMPs were temporal-spatial scaled based on the gait cycle and amplitude estimated by the IMU.

As shown in the pink region in this figure, the tension transmitted by the traditional method for two pilots in segment $S2$ could not quickly reach the maximum expected value (in (A) and (D)), and there is a problem with a slow release of the tension in segment $S3$ (it is expected that the tension force curve will quickly reach and maintain the peak value in segment $S2$, and become zero in segment $S3$ quickly). The trajectories generated by the DMPs pulled faster in segment $S2$ than the traditional one, but the pull rate in segment $S3$ was still too slow to hinder normal movement (in (B) and (E)), better adaptability to different pilots could be observed when it comes to the strategies tuned by the SDMPs with improved speed and drop rate of the tension force.

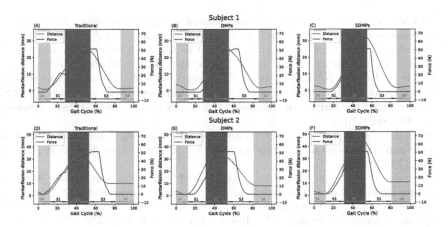

Fig. 7. Comparison of the experimental results of the traditional, DMPs and SDMPs algorithms. The target trajectories (red curves) and corresponding tensions forces (blue curves) generated by different algorithms for two subjects. The differently colored areas of the figure represent individual gait stages as described above. The tension of traditional method can not reach the maximum quickly in $S2$ and release slowly in $S3$(figure (A) and (D)). The trajectories generated by the DMPs can pull up quickly in $S2$ but still not release fast enough in $S3$ (figure (B) and (E)), while tension of the trajectories generated by the SDMPs can raise to the maximum quickly and maintain in $S2$ until it drops to zero at a rapid decline rate in $S3$ (figure (C) and (F)). (Color figure online)

4   Conclusion and Future Work

To generate personalized gaits that suit different pilots with fewer data samples and higher efficiency, this paper proposes a segmented dynamic movement primitives-based gait assistive strategy for soft ankle exosuit. The SDMPs can generate personalized gait assistance strategies in real time based on sensor feedback with normal gaits as references, providing more personalized assistance that fits the pilot's individual movement situation, reducing assistance that does not match the pilot's gait phase, and avoiding impeding the pilot's normal movement. An experimental platform is established to explore the performance of the proposed method.

The method proposed in this paper considers the effectiveness of different personalized gait assistance strategies for pilots in flat walking environments with IMU. However, the actual environment is far more than just flat ground, which is a huge challenge for this algorithm. Future research will focus on improving the algorithm's adaptability to different environments and pilots in order to better adapt to real complex scenarios.

References

1. Wehner, M., et al.: A lightweight soft exosuit for gait assistance. In: 2013 IEEE International Conference on Robotics and Automation, pp. 3362–3369 (2013)
2. Asbeck, A.T., De Rossi, S.M., Holt, K.G., Walsh, C.J.: A biologically inspired soft exosuit for walking assistance. Int. J. Robot. Res. **34**(6), 744–762 (2015)
3. Hu, B.H., Krausz, N.E., Hargrove, L.J.: A novel method for bilateral gait segmentation using a single thigh-mounted depth sensor and IMU. In: 2018 7th IEEE International Conference on Biomedical Robotics and Biomechatronics (Biorob), pp. 807–812 (2018)
4. Park, E.J., et al.: A hinge-free, non-restrictive, lightweight tethered exosuit for knee extension assistance during walking. IEEE Trans. Med. Robot. Bion. **2**(2), 165–175 (2020)
5. Panizzolo, F.A., et al.: A biologically-inspired multi-joint soft exosuit that can reduce the energy cost of loaded walking. J. Neuroeng. Rehabil. **13**(1), 1–14 (2016)
6. Zhang, X., et al.: Enhancing gait assistance control robustness of a hip exosuit by means of machine learning. IEEE Robot. Autom. Lett. **7**(3), 7566–7573 (2022)
7. Chen, L., Chen, C., Fang, T., Zhang, Y., Liu, Y., Wu, X.: A novel gait prediction method for soft exosuit base on limit cycle and neural network. In: 2020 IEEE International Conference on E-health Networking, Application & Services (HEALTHCOM), pp. 1–6 (2021)
8. Wang, Z., Chen, C., Yang, F., Liu, Y., Li, G., Wu, X.: Real-time gait phase estimation based on neural network and assistance strategy based on simulated muscle dynamics for an ankle exosuit. IEEE Trans. Med. Robot. Bion. **5**(1), 100–109 (2023)
9. Shepertycky, M., Burton, S., Dickson, A., Liu, Y.F., Li, Q.: Removing energy with an exoskeleton reduces the metabolic cost of walking. Science **372**(6545), 957–960 (2021)
10. Ding, Y., Kim, M., Kuindersma, S., Walsh, C.J.: Human-in-the-loop optimization of hip assistance with a soft exosuit during walking. Sci. Robot. **3**(15), eaar5438 (2018)
11. Bae, J., et al.: A soft exosuit for patients with stroke: Feasibility study with a mobile off-board actuation unit. In: 2015 IEEE International Conference on Rehabilitation Robotics (ICORR), pp. 131–138 (2015)
12. Pastor, P., Righetti, L., Kalakrishnan, M., Schaal, S.: Online movement adaptation based on previous sensor experiences. In: 2011 IEEE/RSJ International Conference on Intelligent Robots and Systems, pp. 365–371 (2011)
13. Xu, F., Qiu, J., Yuan, W., Cheng, H.: A novel balance control strategy based on enhanced stability pyramid index and dynamic movement primitives for a lower limb human-exoskeleton system. Front. Neurorobot. 15 (2021)

A Magnetically Actuated Diatom-Biohybrid Microrobot as a Drug Delivery Capsule

Mengyue Li[1,2,3], Niandong Jiao[1,2,3(✉)], Xiaodong Wang[1,2,3], and Lianqing Liu[1,2]

[1] State Key Laboratory of Robotics, Shenyang Institute of Automation, Chinese Academy of Sciences, Shenyang 110016, China
ndjiao@sia.cn

[2] Institutes for Robotics and Intelligent Manufacturing, Chinese Academy of Sciences, Shenyang 110016, China

[3] University of Chinese Academy of Sciences, Beijing 100049, China

Abstract. Targeted drug delivery is a strategy to efficiently deliver drugs to a specific target area and has broad application prospects in the treatment of cancer, inflammatory diseases, and neurological diseases. Currently, biohybrid microrobots have been developed as drug-carrying systems and have great potential in the field of drug delivery. However, the efficient carrying and delivery of drugs is still an urgent problem to be solved in the design of drug delivery systems. Here, we fabricated a *Thalassiosira weissflogii*-based biohybrid microrobot as a drug delivery capsule for targeted therapy. Diatom frustules with complete cavities were obtained through a simple and economical preparation method. The drugs were encapsulated into the cavity of the diatom frustules by means of vacuum loading, so that they had good drug-loading properties. The magnetic engine is loaded onto the surface of frustules by electrostatic adsorption, so that they can achieve flexible and controllable movement under the action of an external rotating magnetic field, which is expected to achieve targeted drug delivery. The prepared diatom microrobots have great application potential for drug delivery platforms.

Keywords: Diatom · Biohybrid microrobot · Vacuum loaded drug

1 Introduction

Micro/nanorobots are robots of micron to nanometer size that can convert external energy into their own kinetic energy [1]. Micro/nanorobots have broad application prospects in the medical field [2, 3], and can be used in drug delivery [4–6], disease diagnosis [7], microsurgery [8], cell repair [9], and tissue regeneration [10]. Biohybrid microrobots, a new type of nanodevice, have potential applications for performing various tasks inside the human body [11]. They are a new type of intelligent robotic system that combines biological and microrobot technologies. Using organisms as carriers or components makes them have good biocompatibility. They can interact with living organisms and perform tasks within biological systems, such as drug delivery, tissue repair, and disease diagnosis [12]. Biohybrid microrobots have the ability to move autonomously, respond to environmental stimuli or biological signals, and take corresponding actions [13]. Drug delivery is one of the important applications for biohybrid microrobots. The study of the drug-carrying capacity of biohybrid microrobots is one of the active research areas where material selection as well as the ability of drug encapsulation are to be studied and designed.

Mesoporous silica is a silica material with highly ordered pore structure. Mesoporous silicas have the advantages of tunable pore structure, high specific surface area, chemical stability and biocompatibility [14]. They have a wide range of application potential in the fields of drug delivery [15] and biomedicine [16, 17]. As a drug delivery capsule, mesoporous silica has good biocompatibility, tunable pore structure and surface properties, providing an important tool for customized drug delivery [18, 19]. It has advantages in improving drug stability, controlled release, targeted delivery, and multifunctionality, and promises to be an innovative solution for drug delivery [20, 21]. However, their synthesis requires toxic chemicals and often requires precise process control and high-temperature conditions, which can increase their production costs and limit production at scale. However, diatoms are unicellular photosynthetic microorganisms with porous silica shells that exist in nature [22]. It is a natural alternative to mesoporous silica.

Diatoms are a class of unicellular marine phytoplankton that are widely found in freshwater and marine environments and are one of the most dominant protists in marine and freshwater ecosystems. A distinctive feature of diatoms is their siliceous shell, also known as a frustule. Frustules are composed of silicon dioxide (SiO_2), have complex structures and fine textures, and can assume various shapes and sizes [23]. As a natural biomaterial, diatom frustules have potential applications in medical fields such as tissue engineering and regenerative medicine, drug delivery, diagnosis and imaging, and biosensing detection [24]. The biocompatibility, high pore structure, and surface area of diatom frustules make them an ideal platform for drug delivery [25, 26]. Diatom frustules can be used for drug encapsulation and protection, controlled drug release, and targeted delivery [27]. Diatom frustules have received extensive research and attention as carriers of drug delivery systems in recent years.

Here, we prepared a biohybrid microrobot based on *Thalassiosira weissflogii* with efficient drug loading capability. Figure 1 shows the preparation process of diatom biohybrid microrobots. We obtained a large number of diatom frustules with a complete cavity structure in a simple and economical way. Diatom frustules with a complete cavity structure can be vacuum loaded to allow them to encapsulate larger amounts of drugs and improve their drug delivery performance. This makes diatom frustules have better drug-loading ability as drug delivery capsules, and more advantages in the field of drug delivery. Ferroferric oxide (Fe_3O_4) nanoparticles are modified on the surface of diatom frustules by electrostatic adsorption, and serve as a magnetic drive engine, making them controllable under the action of an external magnetic field, which is expected to achieve targeted drug delivery. The prepared diatom microrobot with a complete cavity structure as a drug delivery capsule provides a new possibility for drug delivery.

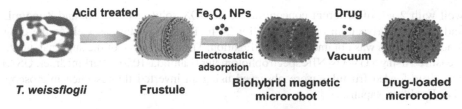

Fig. 1. Preparation process of diatom biohybrid microrobots

2 Materials and Methods

2.1 Materials and Reagents

Fe_3O_4 magnetic nanoparticles (99.5%. 20 nm), doxorubicin hydrochloride (DOX, 98%), anhydrous ethanol (>99.7%), and phosphate-buffered saline (PBS, pH 7.2) were purchased commercially and used as received. All experiments were performed with 18.2 $M\Omega \cdot cm$ ultrapure water (Milli-Q).

2.2 Culture of *T. weissflogii* Cells and Acquisition of Frustules

The purchased *Thalassiosira weissflogii* algae were cultivated in a culture bottle using F/2 medium and placed in a light incubator to provide a suitable culture environment. Twelve hours of white light and 12 h of dark lighting were used with a light intensity of 2000 lx, and the incubation temperature was set at 24 °C.

The concentrated diatom liquid was treated with a mixed solution of hydrogen peroxide (H_2O_2, 30 wt%) and hydrochloric acid (HCl, 2 mol/L) to obtain complete frustules. Concentrated algal solution was obtained by collecting the algal solution using a centrifuge at 3000 r for 5 min. Subsequently, a mixture of HCl and H_2O_2 was added to the concentrated algal solution and left in the dark for 48 h. The complete diatom frustules were collected by centrifugation and washed 5 times with absolute ethanol and ultrapure water.

2.3 Fabrication of Magnetic Diatom Biohybrid Microrobots

The Fe_3O_4 magnetic nanoparticles were formulated into suspensions of different concentrations (0.2, 0.4, 0.5, 0.6, 0.8, 1.0 mg/mL). Subsequently, 1 mg of frustules was added to 1 mL of Fe_3O_4 magnetic particle suspensions of different concentrations. Then, the mixture was shaken on a shaker for 1.5 h to obtain magnetic diatom biohybrid microrobots.

2.4 Drug Load

DOX was used as a simulated drug for electrostatic adsorption drug loading and vacuum drug loading. For electrostatic adsorption loading, 1 mL of DOX solution (2 mg/mL) was mixed with 1 mg of diatom shells, shaken for 24 h at room temperature and centrifuged to obtain the drug-loaded frustules. For vacuum loading, 2 mg of diatom shells were mixed well with 2 mL of different concentrations of DOX solutions (2, 4, 6, and 8 mg/mL) and placed in a vacuum environment for 24 h. The supernatant as well as the drug-loaded frustules was obtained by centrifugation. The absorbance of the supernatant was measured using a UV-vis-NIR spectrophotometer (Lambda-1050+, PerkinElmer, USA). The drug-loaded frustules were observed using an inverted fluorescence microscope (Ti2-E, Nikon, Japan).

3   Results and Discussion

3.1   Fabrication and Characterization of Diatom Biohybrid Microrobots

In the laboratory, diatom cells were cultured in batches in a suitable growth environment, as shown in Fig. 2a. As shown in Fig. 2b, the diatom cells were observed under an inverted fluorescence microscope to appear cylindrical. The absorbance of natural diatom cells was measured with a UV-vis-NIR spectrophotometer, and there was a peak at 677 nm (Fig. 2c). Therefore, under the excitation of the excitation light in the cy5 band of the inverted fluorescence microscope, the natural diatom cells have bright fluorescence (Fig. 2d), because diatoms contain chlorophyll [28].

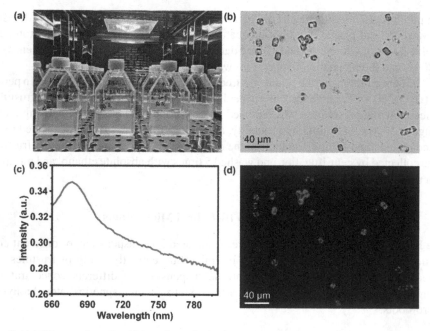

Fig. 2. (a) Diatom algae liquid in culture flask. (b) Light microscopy images of natural diatom cells. (c) Absorption spectra of natural diatom cells. (d) Fluorescence image of natural diatom cells.

Subsequently, the natural diatoms were treated with acid treatment to obtain complete frustules. HCl is mainly used to remove calcareous cemented substances on the surface, and internal organic matter is mainly removed by H_2O_2. Figure 3a shows an optical image of diatom frustules. Compared with natural diatoms, the frustules have the same cylindrical shape, but the middle part is more transparent. The images of the experimental results show that diatom frustules with cavities were obtained by acid treatment, and the internal organic matter was removed at the same time. Figure 3b and 3c are the SEM images of the obtained frustules, which show that there are many porous structures on the surface of the diatom frustules. This provides a larger drug contact area for subsequent electrostatic adsorption drug loading and at the same time provides the possibility of entering the cavity for vacuum drug loading.

Fig. 3. (a) Light microscopy images of frustules. (b-c) SEM images of frustules.

At the same time, we also measured the absorbance of diatom frustules with a UV-vis-NIR spectrophotometer, and found that the peak at 667 nm disappeared (Fig. 4a). Similarly, the fluorescent images of diatom frustules were observed under the excitation light of the cy5 band of the inverted fluorescence microscope, and no bright fluorescence was observed. As shown in Fig. 4b, the mean fluorescence intensity of the fluorescence images of natural diatom cells and diatom frustules after excitation in different wavelength bands was measured. Diatom frustules hardly emit light in the cy5 band, which is due to the removal of chlorophyll in diatoms by acid treatment. At the same time, it was also found that after acid treatment, the fluorescence intensity of diatom frustules became stronger in the DAPI band.

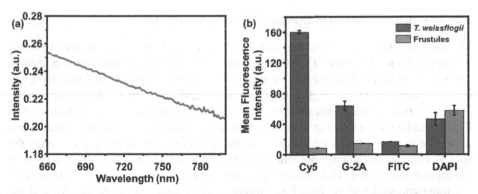

Fig. 4. (a) Absorption spectra of frustules. (b) The mean fluorescence intensity of the fluorescence images of natural diatom cells and frustules.

Diatom frustules and Fe_3O_4 magnetic nanoparticles have different surface zeta potentials, and the nanoparticles adhere to the surface of diatom frustules by electrostatic adsorption. The modification of frustules after treatment with different concentrations of magnetic particle suspensions was tested, as shown in Fig. 5a. When the concentration of magnetic particles was low, the surface of a single diatom frustule was insufficiently modified with magnetic particles. When the concentration of magnetic nanoparticles was high, the diatoms modified with magnetic particles easily agglomerated under the action of the remaining magnetic particles. Based on the situation of exploring the concentration, the magnetic particle concentration of 0.5 mg/mL was finally selected to modify the diatom frustules of 1 mg/mL. Figure 5b-c show SEM images of a diatom frustule after modifying the magnetic particles. It is intuitively indicated that the magnetic particles are successfully modified on the surface of diatom frustules. So far, diatom-based magnetic biohybrid microrobots have been successfully prepared.

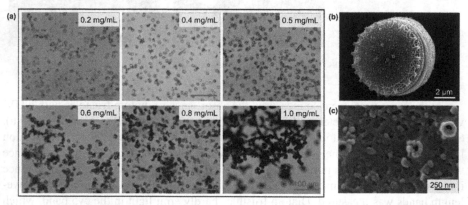

Fig. 5. (a) Optical images of diatom frustules modified with different concentrations of magnetic particles. (b-c) SEM images of a modified magnetic particle diatom frustule

3.2 Magnetic Actuation of Diatom Biohybrid Microrobots

The motion control of biohybrid microrobots determines their basic function in biological applications. Magnetic actuation is particularly useful in biomedical applications due to remote propulsion and precise motion control, biocompatible raw materials, and innocuousness even under high-strength magnetic fields [29]. Here, a five-coil magnetic system is used to control the motion of the prepared diatom microrobot. As shown in Fig. 6a, under the action of an external magnetic field, the diatom microrobot can move under the action of magnetic torque. The change in the pitch angle γ can change the speed of the diatom microrobot, and the direction angle α can control the direction of the diatom microrobot. The motion capability of the diatom microrobots under a rotating magnetic field was studied. First, when the pitch angle was fixed at 120° and the magnetic field strength was 7.5 mT, the moving speed of diatom microrobots at different frequencies of the rotating magnetic field was measured, as shown in Fig. 6b.

The experimental data show that the motion speed of the diatom microrobots increases and then decreases as the frequency of the rotating magnetic field increases. When the rotation frequency is 9 Hz, the speed of the diatom microrobots reaches a maximum of 20.16 μm/s. Then, under the action of a rotating magnetic field of 5 Hz and 7.5 mT, the movement speed of diatom microrobots under different pitch angles was measured. Similarly, the movement speed of diatom microrobots showed a trend of first increasing and then decreasing, as shown in Fig. 6c. These experimental data show that the motion speed of the diatom microrobots can be controlled by controlling the pitch angle γ or frequency of the rotating magnetic field. Subsequently, by changing the direction angle α of the rotating magnetic field, controllable trajectory motion of the diatom microrobot was realized, as shown in Fig. 6d. Therefore, the speed and direction of the diatom microrobot can be controlled by adjusting the frequency, pitch angle γ, and direction angle α of the rotating magnetic field, making the diatom microrobots controllable. This provides the capability of controllable motion for diatom microrobots as drug delivery capsules. The enables the diatom microrobot to be spatiotemporally selective in drug delivery and reach the target location faster.

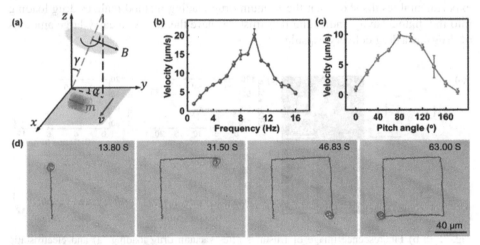

Fig. 6. (a) Schematic diagram of a diatom microrobot actuated by a rotating magnetic field. (b) The relationship between the speed of diatom microrobots and the frequency of the rotating magnetic field (120°, 7.5 mT). (c) The relationship between the speed of diatom microrobots and pitch angle (5 Hz, 7.5 mT). (d) Time-lapse images of diatom microrobots moving according to rectangular trajectories.

3.3   Diatom Vacuum Drug Loading

The complete cavity and surface porous structure of diatom frustules make them capable of carrying large amounts of drugs as a drug delivery capsule. Previous experiments have demonstrated the drug-loading ability of diatom frustules loaded with drugs through electrostatic adsorption [30]. The electrostatic adsorption of diatom frustules for drug loading was mainly based on the large specific surface area of diatoms, so the drug has more attachment points on the diatom frustule. However, the cavity of diatom frustules is underutilized. Here, the drug can enter the cavity of diatom frustules by means of vacuum loading. Similarly, DOX was used as a simulated drug here. The fluorescence properties of DOX can be used to observe the drug distribution on frustules after vacuum or electrostatic adsorption. The fluorescence of frustules after vacuum drug loading (Fig. 7a) and electrostatic adsorption drug loading (Fig. 7b) were observed using an inverted fluorescence microscope. From the fluorescence images, it can be seen intuitively that after vacuum drug loading, the entire diatom frustule has bright fluorescence, which can indicate that DOX enters the cavity. After electrostatic adsorption of drug loading, the fluorescence image showed bright fluorescence on the surface of the frustule, indicating that the drug was more concentrated on the surface of the frustule. At the same time, the fluorescence intensity of the frustules along the long axis (m) and short axis (n) in the fluorescence images were measured. The long axis or short axis of the frustules loaded with DOX in vacuum (Fig. 7c) had higher fluorescence intensity as a whole, while the fluorescence intensity of the frustules loaded with DOX by electrostatic adsorption (Fig. 7d) was lower in the middle area of the long axis or short axis. The experimental results show that the vacuum drug loading method realizes drug loading into the diatom cavity, indicating that frustules have the ability to carry large amounts of drugs as a drug delivery capsule.

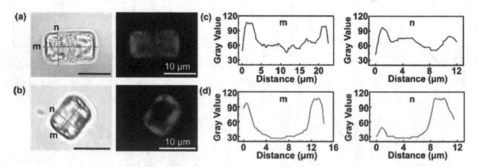

Fig. 7. (a-b) Fluorescence image of frustules after vacuum drug loading (a) and electrostatic adsorption drug loading (b). (c-d) Fluorescence intensity of the frustules along the long (m) and short axes (n) after drug loading in vacuum (c) or electrostatic adsorption (d).

Subsequently, the ability of frustules to load drugs through vacuum was quantified. First, the absorbance (Fig. 8a) of the DOX standard concentration was measured by a UV-vis-NIR spectrophotometer, and the calibration curve (Fig. 8b) of the DOX concentration at 480 nm was obtained by the Beer–Lambert law. The obtained regression equation is:

$$y = 19.39346\,x + 0.04432 \tag{1}$$

where y is the absorbance of the DOX sample and x is the concentration of the DOX drug. The correlation coefficient is 0.99959. The absorbance of the drug in the supernatant after vacuum loading was measured by a spectrophotometer. The concentration of the supernatant was obtained using the calibration curve to calculate the drug load-ing efficiency of the frustules. The drug loading efficiency of frustules is determined as follows:

$$\text{Drug loading efficiency } (\%) = \frac{M_0 - M_s}{M_d} \times 100\% \tag{2}$$

where M_0 is the total mass of DOX, M_s is the mass of DOX drug in the supernatant, and M_d is the mass of frustules. As a drug delivery capsule, the biocompatibility of frustules needs to be considered. 3T3 cells were used to test the biocompatibility of frustules. The cell viability of 3T3 cells was measured after treatment with different concentrations (0.01–2 mg/mL) of frustules for 24 h and 48 h (Fig. 8c). The experimental results show that frustules have good biocompatibility within the determined concentration range. The good biocompatibility makes frustules have great potential as drug delivery capsules. Figure 8d shows the drug loading efficiency of frustules vacuum drug loading under different initial DOX drug concentrations. When the initial drug concentration was 8 mg/mL, the drug loading rate reached 71.31%. The results show that diatom frustules have great potential as drug delivery capsules.

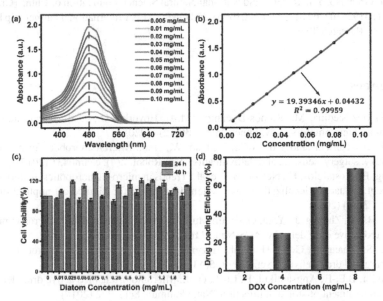

Fig. 8. (a) Absorption spectra of DOX. (b) The calibration curve of DOX absorbance at 480 nm. (c) The biocompatibility testing of diatom frustules with 3T3 cells. (d) Drug loading efficiency of frustules after vacuum loading.

4 Conclusion

Overall, we have prepared a magnetically actuated biohybrid microrobot based on diatom frustules, whose complete cavity and large specific surface area make it a great potential drug delivery capsule. The prepared frustules retain the cylindrical shape of the diatom cells well. The preparation method ensures the integrity of the frustules and the porous structure on the surface. The removal of internal organic matter makes frustules have cavities. This provides favorable conditions for diatom frustules to be used as drug delivery capsules. At the same time, the movement speed of the diatom microrobots can be adjusted by adjusting the frequency and pitch angle of the rotating magnetic field. When the magnetic field strength is 7.5 mT and the pitch angle is 120°, the motion speed of the diatom microrobot can reach 20.16 μm/s. The movement direction of the diatom microrobot can be adjusted by adjusting the direction angle of the rotating magnetic field, thereby realizing the controllable movement of the diatom microrobot. Drugs are loaded into the diatom frustule cavity by vacuum loading. The drug-loading efficiency of the frustules reached 71.31%, and the fluorescence image intuitively showed that the drug entered the cavity. The coculture experiment of different concentrations of frustules and 3T3 cells also showed that they have good biocompatibility. Therefore, diatom microrobots have great potential as drug delivery capsules, providing potential solutions for biomedical applications.

Acknowledgments. This work was supported by the CAS Project for Young Scientists in Basic Research (Grant No. YSBR-036), and National Natural Science Foundation of China (Grant Nos. 62273331, 61925307, 62127811, 61821005), and CAS/SAFEA International Partnership Program for Creative Research Teams.

References

1. Fernandez-Medina, M., Ramos-Docampo, M.A., Hovorka, O., et al.: Recent advances in nano- and micromotors. Adv. Funct. Mater. **30**(12) (2020)
2. Li, J., Esteban-Fernández de Ávila, B., Gao, W., et al.: Micro/nanorobots for biomedicine: delivery, surgery, sensing, and detoxification. Sci. Robot. **2**(4), eaam6431 (2017)
3. Wang, B., Kostarelos, K., Nelson, B.J., et al.: Trends in micro-/nanorobotics: materials development, actuation, localization, and system integration for biomedical applications. Adv. Mater. **33**(4) (2021)
4. Park, B.-W., Zhuang, J., Yasa, O., et al.: Multifunctional bacteria-driven microswimmers for targeted active drug delivery. ACS Nano **11**(9), 8910–8923 (2017)
5. Tang, S., Zhang, F., Gong, H., et al.: Enzyme-powered Janus platelet cell robots for active and targeted drug delivery. Sci. Robot. **5**(43) (2020)
6. de Ávila, B.E.-F., Angsantikul, P., Li, J., et al.: Micromotor-enabled active drug delivery for in vivo treatment of stomach infection. Nat. Commun. **8**(1), 272 (2017)
7. Zhang, Y., Zhang, L., Yang, L., et al.: Real-time tracking of fluorescent magnetic spore–based microrobots for remote detection of C. diff toxins. Sci. Adv. **5**(1), eaau9650
8. Vyskocil, J., Mayorga-Martinez, C.C., Jablonska, E., et al.: Cancer cells microsurgery via asymmetric bent surface Au/Ag/Ni microrobotic scalpels through a transversal rotating magnetic field. ACS Nano **14**(7), 8247–8256 (2020)
9. Chen, X.Z., Liu, J.H., Dong, M., et al.: Magnetically driven piezoelectric soft microswimmers for neuron-like cell delivery and neuronal differentiation. Mater. Horiz. **6**(7), 1512–1516 (2019)
10. Go, G., Jeong, S.-G., Yoo, A., et al.: Human adipose-derived mesenchymal stem cell-based medical microrobot system for knee cartilage regeneration in vivo. Sci. Robot. **5**(38) (2020)

11. Shivalkar, S., Chowdhary, P., Afshan, T., et al.: Nanoengineering of biohybrid micro/nanobots for programmed biomedical applications. Colloids Surfaces B-Biointerfaces **222** (2023)

12. Lin, Z.N., Jiang, T., Shang, J.Z.: The emerging technology of biohybrid micro-robots: a review. Bio-Des. Manuf. **5**(1), 107–132 (2022)

13. Wu, Z., Chen, Y., Mukasa, D., et al.: Medical micro/nanorobots in complex media. Chem. Soc. Rev. **49**(22), 8088–8112 (2020)

14. Kankala, R.K., Han, Y.-H., Na, J., et al.: Nanoarchitectured structure and surface biofunctionality of mesoporous silica nanoparticles. Adv. Mater. **32**(23), 1907035 (2020)

15. Vallet-Regi, M., Colilla, M., Izquierdo-Barba, I., et al.: Mesoporous silica nanoparticles for drug delivery: current insights. Molecules **23**(1) (2018)

16. Xu, C., Lei, C., Yu, C.Z.: Mesoporous silica nanoparticles for protein protection and delivery. Front. Chem. **7** (2019)

17. Li, Z.X., Barnes, J.C., Bosoy, A., et al.: Mesoporous silica nanoparticles in biomedical applications. Chem. Soc. Rev. **41**(7), 2590–2605 (2012)

18. Tang, F., Li, L., Chen, D.: Mesoporous silica nanoparticles: synthesis, biocompatibility and drug delivery. Adv. Mater. **24**(12), 1504–1534 (2012)

19. Li, Y., Deng, G.X., Hu, X.L., et al.: Recent advances in mesoporous silica nanoparticle-based targeted drug-delivery systems for cancer therapy. Nanomedicine **17**(18), 1253–1279 (2022)

20. Diez, P., Lucena-Sanchez, E., Escudero, A., et al.: Ultrafast directional Janus Pt-mesoporous silica nanomotors for smart drug delivery. ACS Nano (2021)

21. Gupta, J., Quadros, M., Momin, M.: Mesoporous silica nanoparticles: synthesis and multifaceted functionalization for controlled drug delivery. J. Drug Deliv. Sci. Technol. **81** (2023)

22. Uthappa, U.T., Brahmkhatri, V., Sriram, G., et al.: Nature engineered diatom biosilica as drug delivery systems. J. Control. Release **281**, 70–83 (2018)

23. Gordon, R., Losic, D., Tiffany, M.A., et al.: The glass menagerie: diatoms for novel applications in nanotechnology. Trends Biotechnol. **27**(2), 116–127 (2009)

24. Maher, S., Kumeria, T., Aw, M.S., et al.: Diatom silica for biomedical applications: recent progress and advances. Adv. Healthc. Mater. **7**(19), 1800552 (2018)

25. Delasoie, J., Zobi, F.: Natural diatom biosilica as microshuttles in drug delivery systems. Pharmaceutics **11**(10), 537 (2019)

26. Terracciano, M., De Stefano, L., Rea, I.: Diatoms green nanotechnology for biosilica-based drug delivery systems. Pharmaceutics **10**(4) (2018)

27. Phogat, S., Saxena, A., Kapoor, N., et al.: Diatom mediated smart drug delivery system. J. Drug Deliv. Sci. Technol. **63**, 102433 (2021)

28. Zhong, D., Du, Z., Zhou, M.: Algae: a natural active material for biomedical applications. View **2**, 20200189 (2021)

29. Choi, J., Hwang, J., Kim, J.Y., et al.: Recent progress in magnetically actuated microrobots for targeted delivery of therapeutic agents. Adv. Healthc. Mater. **10**(6) (2021)

30. Li, M.Y., Wu, J.F., Lin, D.J., et al.: A diatom-based biohybrid microrobot with a high drug-loading capacity and pH-sensitive drug release for target therapy. Acta Biomater. **154**, 443–453 (2022)

Research on Improved Microscope Calibration Method Based on Coplanar Points

Wang Nanfei[1], Cao Haojie[1], and Zhang Xu[1,2(✉)]

[1] School of Mechatronic Engineering and Automation, Shanghai University, Shanghai, China
[2] Huazhong University of Science and Technology Wuxi Research Institute, Wuhan, Jiangsu, China
zhangxu@hust-wuxi.com

Abstract. Camera calibration is the premise and basis for computer vision to obtain three-dimensional space information. Its calibration accuracy directly affects the accuracy of three-dimensional measurement and the results of three-dimensional reconstruction. However, the stereo light microscope has the problems of small depth of field and complex optical path, and the traditional macroscopic calibration method cannot be applied to microscopic calibration. In order to solve this problem, this paper proposes an improved microscope calibration method based on coplanar points. Firstly, the method of varying focal length is used to obtain the camera principal point coordinates. By shooting the same target point at different magnifications, the image coordinates are obtained respectively, then the least square method is used to fit the line, and the intersection of the fitted line is the principal point of the image. Then, based on the coplanar point method, the analytical solution of the camera scale factor is obtained, which improves the robustness of the initial value estimation of the internal parameters. Finally, the initial value estimation of internal parameters is optimized by nonlinear least square method, and the tangential distortion is considered as a factor of nonlinear optimization, so as to obtain accurate microscope calibration parameters. The experimental results show that compared with the traditional Zhang's calibration method, the improved microscope calibration method based on coplanar points has higher calibration accuracy and is suitable for microscope calibration.

Keywords: camera calibration · stereo light microscope · coplanar point · tangential distortion · calibration accuracy

1 Introduction

One of the basic tasks of computer vision is to calculate the three-dimensional spatial information of the actual object from the image information acquired by the camera, and from this three-dimensional measurement and three-dimensional reconstruction can be carried out [1, 2]. The relationship between the three-dimensional geometric position of a point on the surface of a space object and its corresponding point in the image is determined by the geometric model of camera imaging. Furthermore, calibration of a stereo light microscope means acquiring the parameters of the camera's imaging geometry model [3]. The calibration of the camera parameters is crucial and the accuracy of the calibration results directly affects the accuracy of the subsequent 3D reconstruction or 3D measurement.

Because the stereo light microscope has a complex imaging optical path, the macro calibration method cannot be used directly. Schreier et al. [4] proposed a prior distortion estimation combined with traditional bundle adjustment method to estimate imaging system parameters and imaging distortion, but the method is complicated due to the small depth of field of the microscope, which limits its application. Based on Tsai's two-step method, Li et al. [5] proposed an improved method to eliminate lens distortion using orthogonal grids. However, the distortion model only considers first order radial distortions. Kong et al. [6] realized the microscope calibration method based on Tsai's two-step method under various multiples, which is insufficient for the high accuracy requirement of the translational platform. In short, the problem that needs to be solved is to continue to improve the accuracy of the calibration of the stereo light microscope.

In order to further improve the accuracy of microscopic calibration, this paper firstly uses the varying focal length method to obtain the initial values of camera principal point coordinates. Then, based on Zhang's calibration method, an improved camera calibration method based on coplanar points is proposed to obtain the analytical solution of the camera scale factor. Finally, comprehensively considering the distortion model of tangential distortion and radial distortion, the initial value estimation of parameters of camera is optimized by nonlinear least square method. In this paper, the calibration accuracy and calibration errors of this method are experimented and analysed. A comparison test with the Zhang's calibration method shows that this method has a higher calibration accuracy than the Zhang's calibration method.

2 Calibration of Stereomicroscope

Stereomicroscope has two mature types of light path, which are G-type stereomicroscope and CMO-type stereomicroscope. The G-type stereo microscope is low cost, durable and easy to maintain, but it is easy to produce radial image distortion [7, 8], which is slightly insufficient for high-precision precision measurement. The CMO microscope has better optical imaging performance, and has better performance in removing distortion, resolution and zoom ratio, so it is used for scientific research. In this paper, CMO stereomicroscope is used in the experiment. The imaging model of stereomicroscope can be simplified into pinhole imaging model. And the calibration of the microscope is to obtain the camera internal parameters, camera external parameters and distortion parameters of the pinhole imaging model.

In the pinhole imaging model, the commonly used coordinate systems are the world coordinate system $O_W - X_W Y_W Z_W$, the camera coordinate system $O_C - X_C Y_C Z_C$, the image coordinate system $O_s - xy$ and the pixel coordinate system $O - uv$, where the axes of x, y are parallel to the axes of X_c, Y_c. The point P is represented $P_W(X_W, Y_W, Z_W)$ in the world coordinate system, $P_C(X_C, Y_C, Z_C)$ in the camera coordinate system, $P(x, y)$ in the image coordinate system, and $P(u, v)$ in the pixel coordinate system.

According to the pinhole model, the relationship between the feature points on the pixel plane and their corresponding points in the world coordinate system can be expressed as:

$$s \begin{pmatrix} u \\ v \\ 1 \end{pmatrix} = \begin{pmatrix} f_u & 0 & u_0 \\ 0 & f_v & v_0 \\ 0 & 0 & 1 \end{pmatrix} \begin{pmatrix} r_{11} & r_{12} & t_x \\ r_{21} & r_{22} & t_y \\ r_{31} & r_{32} & t_z \end{pmatrix} \begin{pmatrix} X_W \\ Y_W \\ 1 \end{pmatrix}$$

$$= A(RT) \begin{pmatrix} X_W \\ Y_W \\ 1 \end{pmatrix} \tag{1}$$

where, s is the scale factor, f_u, f_v is the camera scale factor, u_0, v_0 is the camera principal point coordinates, A is the internal parameter matrix, and RT is the external parameter matrix.

2.1 The Varying Focal Length Method

In the pinhole imaging model, the straight line perpendicular to the image plane through the focal point of the camera is called the optical axis. The intersection of the optical axis and the image plane is the principal point [9]. Due to the weak perspective of the microscope, the focal point of the microscope is difficult to calculate; the principal point coordinate is the projection of the focal point on the image plane, which is also difficult to calculate. Therefore, it is not feasible to obtain the principal point of the camera through the constraint calculation of the image plane. Because the focal point and the principal point are the origin of the camera coordinate system and the image coordinate system respectively, it greatly affects the projection imaging and distortion correction. Therefore, the accurate calibration of the principal point coordinates is extremely critical. In this paper, the varying focal length method is used to calibrate the principal point of the camera.

The principal point is actually the intersection of the optical axis and the *CCD* imaging plane. When the magnification of the microscope changes, the position of the optical axis is actually unchanged, so the principal point coordinates of the camera remain unchanged. The varying focal length method is based on this characteristics of the microscope. Let the camera coordinate of any point in the space be (X_c, Y_c, Z_c). Ideally, the pixel coordinates of this point is:

$$u' = r \cdot X_c + u_0$$
$$v' = r \cdot Y_c + v_0 \tag{2}$$

where (u', v') is the pixel coordinates of the point, r is any magnification, (u_0, v_0) is the principal point coordinate. Eliminating r in Eq. (2), we can get

$$\frac{u' - u_0}{X_c} = \frac{v' - v_0}{Y_c} \tag{3}$$

It can be seen from Eq. (3) that the pixel coordinates of the point are on the same line at any magnification, and the line must pass through the principal point of the camera. By projecting n non-coincidence spatial points on the image plane at different magnifications (as shown in Fig. 1), n lines intersecting at the same point are formed. This intersection coordinate is the principal point coordinate of the camera (as shown in Fig. 2). There are three magnifications of stereo light microscope: 5 times, 10 times and 20 times.

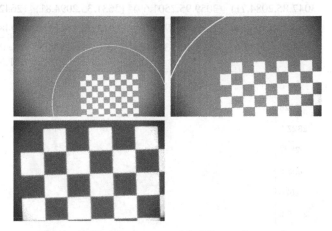

Fig. 1. Calibration images with different times ratios

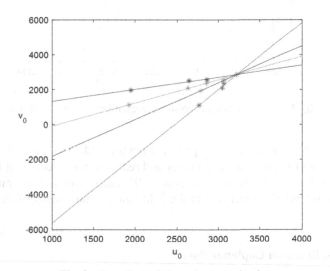

Fig. 2. Coordinate fitting of principal point

Four checkerboard corner points with the upper left corner of the checkerboard as (1,1), (1,2), (2,1) and (2,2) are selected respectively. The corresponding points of the space points at different magnifications are fitted by the least square method (see Table 1), and the accurate linear equation is obtained. Then the intersection of the lines is obtained by the least square method, which is the coordinate of the camera's principal point. The coordinates of the principal point are (3210.7, 2828.0).

Table 1. Straight line fitting table

magnification	Line 1	Line 2	Line 3	Line 4
5	(3064.38,2352.26)	(3069.82,2560.69)	(2854.65,2356.92)	(2860.33,2566.46)
10	(3047.85,2084.71)	(3059.95,2501.69)	(2631.35,2094.81)	(2642.24,2513.51)
20	(2762.29,1105.24)	(2786.40,1944.69)	(1925.38,1127.89)	(1948.27,1965.03)
fitting line	y = 3.81x-9447.6	y = 2.10x-3934.5	y = 1.33x-1435.5	y = 0.69x + 631.68

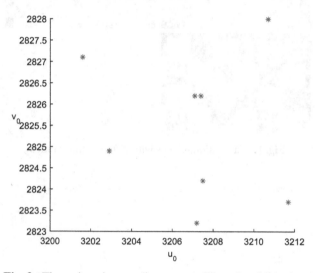

Fig. 3. The main point coordinates are calibrated multiple times

In order to obtain more accurate principal point coordinates, multiple experiments can be performed to eliminate contingency and reduce errors. According to Fig. 3, the mean value of the main point coordinates is (3207, 2825), and the error range is within the range of 3–4 pixels, which meets the calibration requirements of the main point coordinates.

2.2 Method Based on Coplanar Points

The principal point coordinate can be found according to the varying focal length method. If the principal point coordinate is known, the camera parameters can be found without considering distortion by means of ideal perspective projection.

By matrix multiplication, Eq. (1) can be transformed into:

$$s\begin{pmatrix} u - u_0 \\ v - v_0 \\ 1 \end{pmatrix} = \begin{pmatrix} f_u r_{11} & f_u r_{12} & f_u t_x \\ f_v r_{21} & f_v r_{22} & f_v t_y \\ r_{31} & r_{32} & t_z \end{pmatrix} \begin{pmatrix} X_W \\ Y_W \\ 1 \end{pmatrix} \tag{4}$$

$$H = \begin{pmatrix} f_u r_{11} \ f_u r_{12} \ f_u t_x \\ f_v r_{21} \ f_v r_{22} \ f_v t_y \\ r_{31} \quad r_{32} \quad t_z \end{pmatrix} = t_z \begin{pmatrix} h_1 \ h_2 \ h_3 \\ h_4 \ h_5 \ h_6 \\ h_7 \ h_8 \ 1 \end{pmatrix} \tag{5}$$

By eliminating the scaling factors s and t_z, can get

$$\begin{pmatrix} X_W \ Y_W \ 1 \ 0 \quad 0 \ 0 \ -(u-u_0)X_W \ -(u-u_0)Y_W \\ 0 \quad 0 \ 0 \ X_W \ Y_W \ 1 \ -(v-v_0)X_W \ -(v-v_0)Y_W \end{pmatrix} \begin{pmatrix} h_1 \\ h_2 \\ \vdots \\ h_8 \end{pmatrix} = \begin{pmatrix} (u-u_0) \\ (v-v_0) \end{pmatrix} \tag{6}$$

For each corner point on the calibration template, the two equations above correspond. $n(n \geq 4)$ corner points give n sets of the above equations, and the combination of these n sets of equations gives a matrix equation of the form $DX = 0$, D being a $2n \times 8$ matrix. In order to be able to find all the unknown parameters of the matrix equation, it is necessary to ensure that at least 4 points are taken.

Some of the elements of matrix D are world coordinate system coordinates, some are pixel coordinate system coordinates, and some are the multiplication of these two terms, that is, the amount level of each element of matrix D varies greatly. Therefore, $DX = 0$ is a sick system of equations and the direct solution gives a large error in the result, which must be improved. D was improved using Hartley's eight-point algorithm by first normalising the data and then solving for it as follows [10]:

1) Coordinate origin translation: a translation of the coordinates of the world and pixel coordinate systems so that the centre of mass of all point sets is at the origin.
2) Coordinate normalisation: The coordinates of these points are scaled isotropically so that their average distance to the origin is $\sqrt{2}$.

After normalization, the removal of the equations can get better results.

Equation (6) can be solved by using the least squares method to obtain $h_1 \sim h_8$. The rotation matrix R itself is orthogogonal, so there are $r_{11}^2 + r_{21}^2 + r_{31}^2 = 1$, $r_{12}^2 + r_{22}^2 + r_{32}^2 = 1$, $r_{11}r_{12} + r_{21}r_{22} + r_{31}r_{32} = 0$. Combine the above series of formulas to continue separate Eq. (5) and through a series of mathematical transformations to find the value of f_u and f_v:

$$\begin{pmatrix} h_1^2 - h_2^2 \ h_4^2 - h_5^2 \\ h_1 h_2 \quad h_4 h_5 \end{pmatrix} \begin{pmatrix} 1/f_u^2 \\ 1/f_v^2 \end{pmatrix} = \begin{pmatrix} h_8^2 - h_7^2 \\ -h_7 h_8 \end{pmatrix} \tag{7}$$

Since Eq. (7) is a system of homogeneous linear equations, the system of equations has a unique linear solution, which can find out the solution of f_u and f_v directly. However, the f_u and f_v obtained by this direct method are sensitive to noise and are easily affected by error factors such as corner extraction error and camera imaging error. The $h_1 \sim h_8$ obtained from each image is different, corresponding to two equations of Eq. (7). In order to improve the robustness of the solution results, n images can obtain n systems of the above equations, which stand together to form a system of homogeneous linear equations of $2n \times 2$, and solve the solutions of f_u and f_v obtained by linear least squares.

The advantage of this solution is that all the images are taken into account simultaneously, which results in good noise resistance performance and is less affected by the error.

After finding the scale factor of f_u and f_v, the external parameter translation matrix T and the rotation matrix R can also be found. First, from the Equation $r_{11}^2 + r_{21}^2 + r_{31}^2 = 1$, $r_{12}^2 + r_{22}^2 + r_{32}^2 = 1$, we can find t_z.

$$t_z = \sqrt{\frac{1}{\frac{h_1^2}{f_u^2} + \frac{h_4^2}{f_v^2} + h_7^2}} = \sqrt{\frac{1}{\frac{h_2^2}{f_u^2} + \frac{h_5^2}{f_v^2} + h_8^2}} \tag{8}$$

After obtaining t_z, H can also be determined by Eq. (5). When H is known, the values of the elements of the translation matrix T and the first and second columns of the rotation matrix R are solved by Eq. (9).

$$\begin{pmatrix} r_{11} & r_{12} & t_x \\ r_{21} & r_{22} & t_y \\ r_{31} & r_{32} & t_z \end{pmatrix} = \begin{pmatrix} f_u & 0 & 0 \\ 0 & f_v & 0 \\ 0 & 0 & 1 \end{pmatrix}^{-1} H \tag{9}$$

According to the orthogonality of the rotation matrix R, the value of the third column element can be obtained by the cross product of the first column and the second column of the rotation matrix.

$$\begin{pmatrix} r_{13} \\ r_{23} \\ r_{33} \end{pmatrix} = \begin{pmatrix} r_{11} \\ r_{21} \\ r_{31} \end{pmatrix} \times \begin{pmatrix} r_{12} \\ r_{22} \\ r_{32} \end{pmatrix} \tag{10}$$

The initial values of the internal and external parameters of the camera calibration have been obtained, and the initial values are then optimized by the nonlinear least squares method.

2.3 The LM Algorithm Was Used to Optimize the Calibration Initial Values

The ideal lens is free of distortion. However, because of the manufacturing and installation accuracy, the lens always has the distortion, so the nonlinear distortion model needs to be established. The distortion parameters are divided into radial distortion and tangential distortion. There are other types of distortions besides Radial Distortion and Tangential Distortion, but they are not as significant as these two and are therefore ignored.

The radial distortion is caused by the shape defect of the convex lens itself and the light is more curved away from the center of the lens than near the center. The two main types of radial distortion are barrel distortion and pillow distortion. The mathematical model of radial distortion is:

$$x_d = x_u(1 + k_1 r^2 + k_2 r^4 + k_3 r^6)$$
$$y_d = y_u(1 + k_1 r^2 + k_2 r^4 + k_3 r^6) \tag{11}$$

where (x_u, y_u) is the ideal image coordinate, (x_d, y_d) is the distorted image coordinate, r is the radial distance from the image point to the center, $r = \sqrt{x^2 + y^2}$, k_1, k_2, k_3 is the radial distortion coefficient. Usually, the first two terms k_1 and k_2 are used. For lenses with large distortion, k_1, k_2, and k_3 are used.

Tangential distortion is caused by the fact that the lens is not parallel to the imaging plane due to manufacturing defects. The mathematical model of tangential distortion is:

$$x_d = x_u + 2p_1 x_u y_u + p_2(r^2 + 2x_u^2)$$
$$y_d = y_u + 2p_2 x_u y_u + p_1(r^2 + 2y_u^2) \tag{12}$$

where $r = \sqrt{x^2 + y^2}$ represents the distance from the image point to the center point of the image, p_1, p_2 represent the tangential distortion coefficient.

The camera distortion model considering both radial and tangential distortion can be described as:

$$x_d = x_u(1 + k_1 r^2 + k_2 r^4) + 2p_1 x_u y_u + p_2(r^2 + 2x_u^2)$$
$$y_d = y_u(1 + k_1 r^2 + k_2 r^4) + 2p_2 x_u y_u + p_1(r^2 + 2y_u^2) \tag{13}$$

where $r = \sqrt{x^2 + y^2}$ represents the distance from the image point to the center of the image, k_1, k_2 represent the radial distortion coefficient, p_1, p_2 represent the tangential distortion coefficient.

In the previous section to solve the initial value of the camera parameters in the process, do not take into account the impact of any distortion. However, in practice, distortions are always present, so the internal and external camera parameters derived without considering the influence of distortions do not meet the requirements of practical engineering applications. Therefore, the initial values of the camera parameters solved above are optimised non-linearly to estimate the distortion coefficients of the non-linear model of the camera.

In this paper, the effects of both radial and tangential distortion are considered simultaneously. The initial values of the internal and external camera parameters and the initial values of the distortion parameters are obtained previously, and then the spatial points of the world coordinate system are projected onto the image plane according to Eqs. (1) and (13). The square of the difference between the actual image coordinate value and the coordinate value of the corresponding image point after the projection of the spatial point of the world coordinate system is taken as the optimization objective function F. The mathematical model of the optimized objective function F is as follows:

$$F = \sum_{i=1}^{n} \sum_{j=1}^{m} \left\| m_{i,j} - m(A, k_1, k_2, p_1, p_2, R_i, T_i, M_{i,j}) \right\|^2 \tag{14}$$

where m represents the total number of checkerboard corner points of the i-th image, n represents the total number of calibrated images, $M_{i,j}$ represents the spatial points of the world coordinate system, $\tilde{m}(A, k_1, k_2, p_1, p_2, R_i, T_i, M_{i,j})$ represents the projection point of point $M_{i,j}$ in the i-th image according to Eq. (1) and Eq. (13), A is the camera internal parameter matrix, k_1, k_2 are the radial distortion coefficient, p_1, p_2 are the tangential distortion coefficient, R_i and T_i are the external reference matrix of the i-th image.

3   Experimental Results and Analysis

In order to verify the effectiveness and accuracy of the calibration algorithm proposed in this paper, simulation experiments are carried out on MATLAB and compared with the traditional Zhang Zheng you's camera calibration method. The simulation results show that the scale factor calibration results converge quickly when the number of images is at least 18. Considering the radial distortion and tangential distortion, the calibration accuracy of the microscope is improved.

3.1   Correctness Verification of the Calibration Method in This Paper

Figure 4 is the calibration template, with the calibration plate of 1 mm × 1 mm and 0.1 mm × 0.1 mm for each square. Twenty-seven images of the calibration plates were taken from different locations.

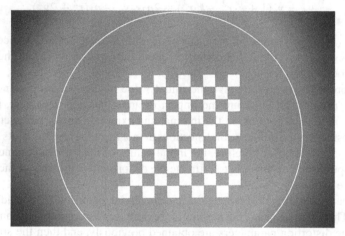

Fig. 4. Calibration plate

The calibration method based on coplanar points in this paper is verified. Scale factor calibration was attempted using 7 to 27 images separately. Then shows the trend of f_u and f_v with the number of images. As can be seen from Fig. 5, when the number of images increases to 18, the scale factor of f_u and f_v begin to remain stable. Therefore, it can be concluded that in this paper, the scale factor calibration based on coplanar points can calibrate the scale factor.

3.2   Comparative Experiment with Zhang Zheng You Calibration Method

The calibration method in this paper is compared with the classical Zhang Zheng you's calibration method. The calibration image used in this paper is consistent with Zhang Zheng you's calibration method. The comparative data of the two methods are shown in Table 2, where RMS is the mean reprojection error and t is the time taken by the algorithm.

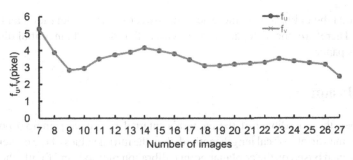

Fig. 5. The variation curves of f_u and f_v

Table 2. Comparison of the camera calibration parameters between the two methods

parameter	using 25 Pictures		using 26 Pictures		using 27 Pictures	
	Zhang's	Ours	Zhang's	Ours	Zhang's	Ours
RMS/pixel	0.72	0.63	0.70	0.60	0.55	0.51
t/s	0.29	0.25	0.31	0.27	0.36	0.27

As can be seen from Table 2, the average reprojection error of the method in this paper is better than that of Zhang Zheng you's calibration method, and the smaller the average reprojection error, the higher the calibration accuracy. In addition, the time t is slightly smaller than that of Zhang Zheng you's calibration method, and the real-time nature of the algorithm has certain advantages.

3.3 Contrasting Experiments Considering Tangential Distortion and not Considering Tangential Distortion

In order to determine the effect of tangential distortion on the non-linear optimization of microscope parameters, two microscope calibrations were carried out for comparison. One parameters of calibration experiment was optimised by considering only radial distortion and the other parameters of calibration experiment was optimised by considering both radial and tangential distortions. A comparison of the two calibrations is shown in Table 3.

Table 3. Comparison of calibration parameters for considering tangential distortion and without considering tangential distortion

parameter	not considering tangential distortion	considering tangential distortion
RMS/pixel	0.52	0.50

As can be seen from Table 3, the reprojection error for considering both radial and tangential distortions is slightly smaller than that for considering only radial distortion, indicating that the calibration is more accurate by considering both radial and tangential distortion. Therefore, the distortion model with both radial and tangential distortions is used in this paper.

4 Conclusion

In this paper, the coordinate of the camera's internal reference principal point is first obtained by the variable focal length method, then the initial values of the camera parameters are obtained based on the coplanar point calibration method, and finally the distortion model is used to optimise parameters by considering the radial and tangential distortions. Through simulation experiments, it can be concluded that the calibration method based on coplanar points in this paper is able to calibrate the scale factor and improve the accuracy compared with the traditional Zhang Zheng you's calibration method. In addition, four distortion factors k_1, k_2, p_1 and p_2 are calibrated in this paper, which makes the calibration results more accurate.

Acknowledgement. This study was supported by the National Natural Science Foundation of China (Grant No. 51975344).

References

1. Xiaowei, T., Yang, Y., et al.: A camera linear calibration method considering distortion. Mach. Des. Manuf. (05), 251–255 (2021)
2. Song, J., Wang, K., et al.: A target recognition and ranging method for eggplant picking robot. Res. Explor. Lab. **34**(09), 54–57 (2015)
3. Longxing, Y., Jiangtao, H., et al.: An analytical improvement of Tsai's camera plane calibration algorithm. Comput. Eng. Sci. **44**(11), 1976–1984 (2022)
4. Schreier, H.W., Garcia, D., Sutton, M.A.: Advances in light microscope stereo vision. Exp. Mech. **44**, 278–288 (2004)
5. Li, K., Wang, Q., Wu, J., et al.: Calibration error for dual-camera digital image correlation at microscale. Opt. Lasers Eng. **50**(7), 971–975 (2012)
6. Kong, C., Zhang, D.: Research on calibration of measurement system based on stereomicroscope. J. Exp. Mech. **32**(01), 9–16 (2017)
7. Wang, Y., Li, D., et al.: Study on the correlation of dual optical paths of stereomicroscope in microscopic stereovision. J. Beijing Univ. Technol. (08), 724–729 (2006)
8. Quinta da Fonseca, J., Mummery, P.M., Withers, P.J.: Full-field strain mapping by optical correlation of micrographs acquired during deformation. J. Microsc. **218**(1), 9–21 (2005)
9. Wu, M., Guo, J., et al.: Calibration method of microscopic Three-dimensional digital image correlation system based on fixed-point rotation. Acta Opt. Sin. **38**(12), 279–287 (2018)
10. Hartley, R.I.: In defense of the eight-point algorithm. IEEE Trans. Pattern Anal. Mach. Intell. **19**(6), 580–593 (1997)

Kinematics Analysis and Control of a Novel Macro-Micro Integrated Hybrid Robot for Medical Surgery

Hao Zheng, Tenghui Wang, Feng Gao[✉], Chenkun Qi, and Renqiang Liu

State Key Laboratory of Mechanical System and Vibration, School of Mechanical Engineering,
Shanghai Jiao Tong University, Shanghai 200240, China
gaofengsjtu@gmail.com

Abstract. An integrated macro-micro medical robot for brain surgery is presented in this paper, aiming to address the challenge of simultaneously achieving high-precision positioning and large-scale motion autonomously. The robot consists of three parallel mechanisms (PMs) connected in series. Among them, two 3PRS mechanisms are connected to form the macro platform, while a 6PSS mechanism independently forms the micro platform. The degree of freedom (DOF) and the forward and inverse kinematics of each individual mechanism and the overall structure have been analyzed. Iterative algorithm system for displacement hierarchy mainly based on damped Newton Method that satisfies the real-time planning and control requirements is established. Additionally, trajectory planning is implemented based on these algorithms, and two modes of a robot force interaction system were developed by combining it with admittance control. Simulation calculations indicate that the solutions meet the accuracy requirements, and planning experiments are conducted to validate the correctness of them. This paper introduces the main components of such a hybrid medical surgical robot system from the perspectives of design, analysis of DOF and kinematics, planning and control.

Keywords: Medical Surgical Robot · Hybrid Mechanism · Kinematics Analysis

1 Introduction

In the past decade, the integration of robotics and the medical field has made significant progress and development [1]. The combination of mechatronics technology and automation has brought new vitality to medical instruments and devices, while the synergy of robotics and computer science has made telesurgery possible [2]. In the field of surgical robotics, the development of miniature medical robotics technology has been relatively more comprehensive. Transoral highly flexible robots [3] have received significant research attention. Single-port laparoscopy bimanual robots [4] and actively stabilized hand-held robots [5, 6] have also provided minimally invasive and more reliable possibilities for many surgical procedures. However, the development of microscopic robots still faces various challenges, such as power supply, positioning, and locomotion

© The Author(s), under exclusive license to Springer Nature Singapore Pte Ltd. 2023
H. Yang et al. (Eds.): ICIRA 2023, LNAI 14272, pp. 493–505, 2023.
https://doi.org/10.1007/978-981-99-6480-2_41

[7]. In addition, many past microdevices still rely heavily on human operation, with their auxiliary capabilities far surpassing their autonomous execution abilities. They are still far from the concept of fully autonomous robots.

In the field of medical surgical robots, in addition to the commonly researched small-sized micro medical robots mentioned above, there are some surgical robots with larger workspaces that have been involved in clinical applications or related medical experiments. For example, the renowned da Vinci surgical system [8] and the RAVEN [9] and Raven-II [10] proposed by Hannaford. Apart from that, many medical experiments have started using robotic arms for medical purposes [11, 12]. The application of serial robotic arms in the medical field primarily faces challenges such as insufficient precision and limited stability. Therefore, parallel mechanisms are used in the design of medical robots due to their high rigidity and high precision [13].Gu proposed a compliant transoral surgical robotic system based on a parallel flexible mechanism [14]. A parallel surgical robot has been developed for precise skull drilling in stereotactic neurosurgical operations [15]. Hybrid mechanisms are also used in the design of medical surgical robots. Pisla proposed a medical robot composed of two subsystems connected in series [16]. Indeed, the application of hybrid mechanisms inherits the advantages of high precision and stability from parallel mechanisms, as well as the large workspace from serial mechanisms. It has gradually become a major structural form in medical robotics.

When multiple parallel mechanisms are connected in series to form a new robotic system, it allows for the simultaneous utilization of both serial and parallel characteristic. Additionally, it enables the separation of large-scale macroscopic movements and small-scale microscopic movements, facilitating the integration of macro and micro motions in a unified medical robot system. However, this hybrid configuration introduces increased complexity of kinematics. Zheng analyzed kinematics of a hybrid serial-parallel manipulator which is consisted with two 3UPU mechanisms [17]. Jaime introduced the kinematics and dynamics of 2(3-RPS) manipulators by means of screw theory and the principle of virtual work [18]. Hu studied the terminal constraint and mobility of serial-parallel manipulators formed by two parallel mechanisms and presented a CGA-based approach to the inverse displacement of them [19–21]. The aforementioned analyses of the kinematics of hybrid parallel-serial mechanisms either remain at the velocity level only or require the use of additional tools, making them challenging to use for real-time trajectory planning in control applications.

This paper proposes a hybrid parallel-serial mechanism consisting of two 3PRS and a 6PSS parallel mechanism in serial term to construct an integrated macro-micro motion medical surgical robot system. Based on related work, kinematic analysis and planning control research were conducted.

2 Systematic Structure

The multi-level macro-micro integrated device for medical surgery, described in this paper, consists of four interconnected stages, as shown in Fig. 1. The first stage is an AGV (Automated Guided Vehicle) with translational and rotational capabilities, which opens four legs around it after reaching the designated position to create a stable support base. The second and the third stage both are 3PRS parallel mechanisms (denoted as

3PRS-I and 3PRS-II), consisting of three chains, capable of providing one translational and two rotational DOFs. All of them have excellent load-bearing capacity and stiffness to ensure minimal deformation when subjected to loads from the upper-level mechanisms and external loads. The two 3PRS parallel mechanisms serve as the macroscopic motion platform of the medical surgical robot, responsible for large-scale positioning. The main purpose of this design is to leverage the high precision, high rigidity, and large payload advantages of parallel mechanisms while expanding the workspace by connecting two parallel mechanisms in series. The fourth stage of this system is a micro-motion platform, namely a 6PSS parallel mechanism.

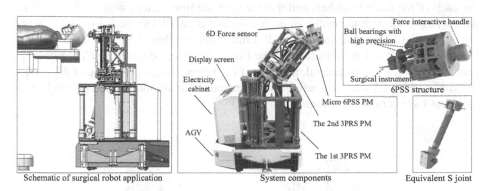

Fig. 1. Systematic structure of the proposed surgical robot

In each branch of the two 3PRS mechanisms as shown in Fig. 1, we use equivalent spherical joint composed of three intersecting rotational axes as a substitute for a ball bearing. The three intersecting rotational axes of the equivalent spherical joint not only offer higher load-bearing capacity and a broader range of rotation but also provide equivalent spherical rotational capability.

To achieve high precision positioning for the micro-motion platform, we use two ball bearings with a tolerance of 1 μm in each branch of the 6DOF PM rather than a typical configuration of 6UPS. Although this introduces local DOFs in the mechanism, it does not have any impact on the end-effector. In addition, we have installed a 6D force/torque sensor on the base of the micro-motion platform to perceive the forces and torques exerted by humans during human-machine interactions.

There are 12 sets of motors and drivers in the system. The communication between the controller and the drivers is based on the EtherCat protocol. The data of force sensor, encoders and other I/O signals will be exchanged with the control system in real-time with a sampling period of 1 ms. The control system's task period is also set to 1 ms.

3 Analysis of DOF and Kinematics

3.1 Analysis of Mechanism DOFs

For the micro-motion platform of the proposed robotic system, its output DOF is undoubtedly 6. However, the DOF of the macro-motion platform may not simply be the sum of the DOF of two 3PRS parallel mechanisms due to the intersection of constrained screw imposed on the mechanisms which leads to the presence of common constraints.

It is known that the constrained screw of a single 3PRS mechanism is generated by each of the three branches, and these screws are line vectors with zero pitch. Each screw passes through the center of the S joint and is parallel to the R axis, while being perpendicular to the direction of the P joint. Based on this, the constrained screw of 3PRS-I and 3PRS-II are illustrated in the Fig. 2, which are denoted as $F_{1,1}^r$, $F_{1,2}^r$, $F_{1,3}^r$ and $F_{2,1}^r$, $F_{2,2}^r$, $F_{2,3}^r$. In general, the rank of the screw system consisting of $F_{1,1}^r$, $F_{1,2}^r$, $F_{1,3}^r$, $F_{2,1}^r$, $F_{2,2}^r$, $F_{2,3}^r$ is 6. Therefore, in the general configuration, this hybrid mechanism does not have common constraints.

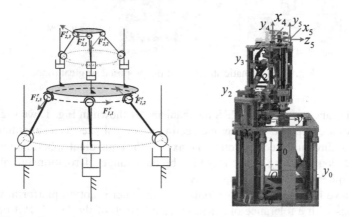

Fig. 2. Constrained screw of hybrid mechanism and definitions of frames

Consequently, according to the modified *Grübler–Kutzzbach* formula, the DOFs at the end-effector of the macro-motion platform are calculated as:

$$M = 6(n - g - 1) + \sum_{i=1}^{g} f_i + \mu = 6(15 - 18 - 1) + 30 = 6 \qquad (1)$$

By analyzing the rank of the six constrained screw, the singularity of the hybrid mechanism can be determined. As a result, the rank of the screw system is less than 6, indicating the presence of common constraints and singularity of such a pose.

The micro-motion platform of the device consists of a 6PSS parallel mechanism, which has 6 DOFs at its end-effector. From a driving perspective, the overall system has 12 driving DOFs.

3.2 Kinematics of the 3PRS PM

Since the 3PRS mechanism embody two translations and one rotation, the free parameters of terminal pose are determined as z, α and β. Therefore, the other three parameters x, y and γ are determined as constrained parameters. Here, we will use 3PRS-I as an example to introduce the kinematics of a single 3PRS.

In the base Frame $O_0 - x_0 y_0 z_0$ (Frame 0), the position of the three U joint is defined as B_i, and the position of the three S joint is defined as A_i. Then we can get:

$$A_i^0 = p_{01} + R_{01}A_i^1, i = 1, 2, 3 \tag{2}$$

where $p_{01} = [x_1, y_1, z_1]^T$. R_{01} is the rotation matrix from the Frame 0 to the Frame 1. A_i^1 represents the position of the S joint in the Frame 1, which is a fixed value as:

$$A_i^1 = [r_{p1} \cos(\frac{2i\pi}{3} - \frac{\pi}{6}), r_{p1} \sin(\frac{2i\pi}{3} - \frac{\pi}{6}), 0]^T, i = 1, 2, 3 \tag{3}$$

where r_{p1} represents the radius of the circular trajectory of the three S joints.

It can be known that the motion of the three PRS chains lies in a plane perpendicular to the axis of R joint. Based on this feature, we can obtain the constrained equations of x_1, y_1, γ_1 by combining Eq. (2) to Eq. (3) as follows:

$$\begin{cases} x_1 = -[R_{01}]_{1,2} r_{p1} \\ y_1 = \frac{1}{2}([R_{01}]_{2,2} - [R_{01}]_{1,1}) r_{p1} \\ [R_{01}]_{1,2} = [R_{01}]_{2,1} \end{cases} \tag{4}$$

where $[R_{01}]_{i,j}$ represents the element in the i th row and j th column of R_{01}.

When the intrinsic constraint equation of the 3PRS mechanism is determined as Eq. (4), the choice of expression for the rotation matrix R_{01} is of significant importance. When using the Euler angles represented by ZXZ convention, it can be obtained that the constrained parameter γ_1 equals negative α_1 from Eq. (4).

Then, the inverse kinematics can be analyzed by establishing a vector equation as:

$$A_i = B_i + q_i e_i + l_i, i = 1, 2, 3 \tag{5}$$

where e_i is the direction vector and q_i is the movement of the i th prismatic joint, and l_i is the vector of the i th link. Since the magnitude of the link vector l_i is the link length L. Therefore, by squaring both sides of Eq. (5) and rearranging it, we can obtain:

$$q_i^2 - 2(A_i - B_i) \cdot e_i q_i + |A_i - B_i|^2 - L^2 = 0 \tag{6}$$

Therefore, the inverse kinematic solution is equivalent to solving a quadratic equation with one variable. Further, it is necessary to analyze the Jacobian matrix for designing an iterative algorithm for the forward kinematics of the 3PRS parallel mechanism. Taking the derivative of Eq. (5), we can get the following expression as:

$$\dot{q}_i e_i = v_1 + \omega_1 \times \left(R_{01}A_i^1\right) - \omega_{li} \times l_i \tag{7}$$

where $\dot{q}_i$ represents the velocity of the i th active joint, v_1 is the terminal velocity, ω_1 is the terminal angular velocity, and ω_{li} is the angular velocity of the i th link. Taking the dot product of both sides of Eq. (7) with l_i, and using the property of $l_i \cdot \omega_{li} \times l_i = 0$ we can transform Eq. (7) to Eq. (8):

$$\dot{q}_i = \frac{l_i}{l_i \cdot e_i} \cdot v_1 + \frac{(R_{01}A_i^1) \times l_i}{l_i \cdot e_i} \cdot \omega_1 = \left[\frac{l_i}{l_i \cdot e_i} \quad \frac{(R_{01}A_i^1) \times l_i}{l_i \cdot e_i} \right] \begin{bmatrix} v_1 \\ \omega_1 \end{bmatrix} \tag{8}$$

By extending Eq. (8) from a single joint to three joints, we can obtain the matrix G in the equation $\dot{q} = G[v_1, w_1]^T$. As the Jacobian matrix J represents the mapping from joint velocities to terminal velocities, it follows that $J = G^{-1}$. However, G is a 3×6 matrix that cannot be directly inverted. Therefore, we use the pseudoinverse to obtain the right pseudoinverse matrix of G and use it as an approximation of J:

$$J = G^T(GG^T)^{-1} \tag{9}$$

It should be noted that in Eq. (7), ω_1 refers to the rigid body angular velocity corresponding to the rotation matrix R_{01}, i.e., $\omega_1 = [\omega_{1x}, \omega_{1y}, \omega_{1z}]^T$. The following transformation relationship exists between the angular velocity vector ω_1 and the Euler angular velocity $\omega_1^{ZXZ} = [\dot{\alpha}, \dot{\beta}, \dot{\gamma}]^T$ in the ZXZ Euler angle system:

$$\omega_1 = R_B^{ZXZ}\omega_1^{ZXZ} = \begin{bmatrix} 0 & \cos\alpha & \sin\alpha\sin\beta \\ 0 & \sin\alpha & -\cos\alpha\sin\beta \\ 1 & 0 & \cos\beta \end{bmatrix} \omega_1^{ZXZ} \tag{10}$$

Clearly, R_B^{ZXZ} is invertible when $\beta = 0$, besides we have $\omega_1^{ZXZ} = \left[R_B^{ZXZ}\right]^{-1}\omega_1$. In addition, we note that when the β expressed in ZXZ Euler angle is 0, we also have $\gamma = -\alpha$. This means that all three Euler angles can be equivalent to 0, indicating no rotation occurs when $\beta = 0$. Based on the mapping relationship $\dot{x} = J\dot{q}$ of the Jacobian matrix, we can further obtain the following equation:

$$\begin{bmatrix} v_1 \\ \omega_1^{ZXZ} \end{bmatrix} = \begin{bmatrix} I_3 & 0 \\ 0 & \left[R_B^{ZXZ}\right]^{-1} \end{bmatrix} \begin{bmatrix} v_1 \\ \omega_1 \end{bmatrix} = \begin{bmatrix} I_3 & 0 \\ 0 & \left[R_B^{ZXZ}\right]^{-1} \end{bmatrix} J \begin{bmatrix} \dot{q}_1 \\ \dot{q}_2 \\ \dot{q}_3 \end{bmatrix} = J^{ZXZ} \begin{bmatrix} \dot{q}_1 \\ \dot{q}_2 \\ \dot{q}_3 \end{bmatrix} \tag{11}$$

where J^{ZXZ} is the Jacobian matrix mapping joint velocity to terminal Euler angular velocity. Then the forward kinematic can be solved through the Newton-Raphson iteration method as:

$$x_{k+1} = x_k - J^{ZXZ}(x_k)(q_k - q) \tag{12}$$

The forward kinematics of the 3PRS mechanism can be continuously calculated using the iterative method based on Eq. (12), where the previous pose is used as the initial value for the next iteration, ensuring a faster convergence rate. It has been demonstrated that this iteration method can generally converge within six steps to enter the accuracy threshold. Therefore, this method for calculating the forward solution can be used for real-time control of a 3PRS mechanism.

3.3   The Overall Kinematics of the Hybrid Macro Mechanism

X_{01} and X_{02} are used to represent the forward kinematics of the 3PRS-I and 3PRS-II mechanism. Correspondingly, they can be transformed into homogeneous transformation matrices $T_{01}(X_{01})$ and $T_{23}(X_{02})$, which represent the pose transformation from Frame 0 to Frame 1 and from Frame 2 to Frame 3.

From the definition of frames in Fig. 2, there should be a total of five homogeneous transformation matrices, denoted as T_{01}, T_{12}, T_{23}, T_{34} and T_{45}. Clearly, among them, matrices T_{12} and T_{34} are constant matrices. Additionally, T_{45} is used to express the forward kinematics of the 6PSS mechanism. Thus, we can derive the forward kinematics of the 3-level macro-micro integrated surgical robot as:

$$T_{05} = T_{01}T_{12}T_{23}T_{34}T_{45} \tag{13}$$

Due to the significant coupling caused by this hybrid mechanism, obtaining an analytical solution for the inverse kinematics becomes challenging. Hence, a numerical iteration method is adopted to solve the inverse kinematics of the macro-motion platform consisting of two 3PRS parallel mechanisms. During the iterative process, determining the iteration step size requires the use of the overall Jacobian matrix of this hybrid mechanism. Therefore, it is necessary to derive the Jacobian matrix J_{04}. Starting from the Frame 0, the vector equation of Frame 4 can be established as:

$$p_4^0 = p_1^0 + R_{01}p_2^1 + R_{01}R_{12}p_3^2 + R_{01}R_{12}R_{23}p_4^3 \tag{14}$$

where p_j^i represents the position of point p_j in Frame i, and R_{ij} is the rotation matrix from Frame i to Frame j. Taking the derivative of Eq. (14), we can get:

$$v_4^0 = v_1^0 + \omega_1^0 \times R_{01}p_2^1 + \omega_1^0 \times R_{01}R_{12}p_3^2 + R_{01}R_{12}v_3^2 + \omega_1^0 \times R_{01}R_{12}R_{23}p_4^3 + R_{01}R_{12}(\omega_3^2 \times R_{23}p_4^3) \tag{15}$$

Using the relationship between cross product and the skew-symmetric matrix, Eq. (15) can be rewritten as follows:

$$v_4^0 = v_1^0 - S(R_{01}p_2^1)\omega_1^0 - S(R_{01}R_{12}p_3^2)\omega_1^0 + R_{01}R_{12}v_3^2 - S(R_{01}R_{12}R_{23}p_4^3)\omega_1^0 - R_{01}R_{12}S(R_{23}p_4^3)\omega_3^2 \tag{16}$$

where $S(a)$ is the skew-symmetric matrix of vector a. Then Eq. (16) can be rearranged as follows:

$$v_4^0 = v_1^0 - A\omega_1^0 - B\omega_3^2 + Cv_3^2 \tag{17}$$

where $A = S(R_{01}p_2^1) + S(R_{01}R_{12}p_3^2) + S(R_{01}R_{12}R_{23}p_4^3)$, $B = R_{01}R_{12}S(R_{23}p_4^3)$, $C = R_{01}R_{12}$

According to Eq. (9) for the Jacobian matrix of a 3PRS mechanism, when the distribution of joints or the terminal pose of the 3PRS is known, we can separately obtain the Jacobian matrices of 3PRS-I and 3PRS-II, which are denoted as J_1 and J_2 respectively. It is evident that J_1 and J_2 are both 6×3 matrices, and we can divide them into upper and lower blocks. Then we denote these divided Jacobian matrices as $J_1 = [J_{1U}, J_{1L}]^T$ and $J_2 = [J_{2U}, J_{2L}]^T$. Therefore, we can obtain:

$$\begin{cases} v_1^0 = J_{1U}[\dot{q}_1, \dot{q}_2, \dot{q}_3]^T, \omega_1^0 = J_{1L}[\dot{q}_1, \dot{q}_2, \dot{q}_3]^T \\ v_3^2 = J_{2U}[\dot{q}_4, \dot{q}_5, \dot{q}_6]^T, \omega_3^2 = J_{2L}[\dot{q}_4, \dot{q}_5, \dot{q}_6]^T \end{cases} \tag{18}$$

Then Eq. (17) can be further expressed as follows:

$$v_4^0 = \left[J_{1U} - AJ_{1L} \ CJ_{2U} - BJ_{2L} \right]_{3\times6} [\dot{q}_1, \dot{q}_2, \dot{q}_3, \dot{q}_4, \dot{q}_5, \dot{q}_6]^T \quad (19)$$

For the angular velocity, we can obtain the following equation:

$$\omega_4^0 = \omega_1^0 + R_{01}R_{12}\omega_3^2 = \left[J_{1L} \ CJ_{2L} \right]_{3\times6} [\dot{q}_1, \dot{q}_2, \dot{q}_3, \dot{q}_4, \dot{q}_5, \dot{q}_6]^T \quad (20)$$

When the terminal orientation is represented with Euler angles, the transformation is performed based on Eq. (10). If we denote the transformation matrix as R_B^E, the rate of change of Euler angles, denoted as ω^E, can be expressed as follows:

$$\omega^E = \left[R_B^E \right]^{-1} \left[J_{1L} \ CJ_{2L} \right] [\dot{q}_1, \dot{q}_2, \dot{q}_3, \dot{q}_4, \dot{q}_5, \dot{q}_6]^T \quad (21)$$

According to Eq. (19) and Eq. (21), the Jacobian matrix corresponding to the terminal pose described in a specific sequence of Euler angles can be obtained as follows:

$$J_{04} = \begin{bmatrix} J_{1U} - AJ_{1L} \ CJ_{2U} - BJ_{2L} \\ \left[R_B^E\right]^{-1} J_{1L} \ \left[R_B^E\right]^{-1} J_{2L} \end{bmatrix}_{6\times6} \quad (22)$$

Furthermore, we can use the Damped Newton iteration method to get the inverse kinematic solution of this mechanism which is shown in Eq. (23).

$$q_{k+1} = q_k - \lambda J_{04}^{-1}(X_{4,k}^0 - X_4^0) \quad (23)$$

where X_4^0 is the given pose and the matrix λ is introduced to incorporate a damping term that helps control the iteration step size effectively, which is represented as $\lambda = diag(\lambda_x, \lambda_y, \lambda_z, \lambda_\alpha, \lambda_\beta, \lambda_\gamma)$. Due to significant differences in the iteration step size among different dimensions in the terminal space, the damping parameters need to be designed separately for each dimension.

Thus, we have successfully completed the forward and inverse kinematics for the macro-motion platform, providing a foundation for the motion planning and control.

3.4 Kinematics of the Micro 6PSS Parallel Mechanism

The micro-motion platform of the robot is composed of a 6PSS parallel mechanism, which is a well-known 6DOFs parallel mechanism with a mature application background. Therefore, this section aims to provide a concise introduction to the kinematics of such a mechanism. The end position is denoted as p_5^4 and its orientation is represented by the rotation matrix R_{45}, the following vector equation can be established:

$$p_5^4 + R_{45}A_i^5 = B_i^4 + q_i^4 e_i^4 + l_i^4, i = 1 \cdots 6 \quad (24)$$

where A_i^5 represents the position of the S joint connected to the moving platform in the Frame 5 for the *ith* branch, B_i^4 represents the position of the S joint connected to the fixed platform in the Frame 4 for the *ith* branch, q_i^4 represents the *ith* active joint, e_i^4

represents the direction vector of the *ith* P joint in the Frame 4, and l_i^4 represents the link vector of the *ith* branch in the Frame 4.

Similar to the 3PRS mechanism, the 6PSS mechanism has a fixed link length L_4 as a parameter. Therefore, by rearranging and squaring Eq. (24), we can obtain:

$$q_i^{4^2} - 2q_i^4 d_i^4 e_i^4 + d_i^4 \cdot d_i^4 - L^{4^2} = 0 \tag{25}$$

where $d_i^4 = p_5^4 + R_{45}A_i^5 - B_i^4$.

Therefore, the inverse kinematic solution can be obtained from Eq. (25). Furthermore, by taking the derivative of Eq. (24) to analyze the Jacobian matrix of this parallel mechanism, the differentiated form of Eq. (24) is obtained as follows:

$$v^4 + \omega^4 \times (R_{45}A_i^5) = \dot{q}_i^4 e_i^4 + \omega_{l_i}^4 \times l_i^4 \tag{26}$$

Considering the orthogonality between l_i^4 and $\omega_{l_i}^4 \times l_i^4$, we can obtain the following equation by left multiplying l_i^4 and rearranging Eq. (26):

$$\dot{q}_i^4 = \frac{l_i^4}{l_i^4 \cdot e_i^4} v^4 + \frac{R_{45}A_i^5 \times l_i^4}{l_i^4 \cdot e_i^4} \omega^4 = \begin{bmatrix} \dfrac{l_i^4}{l_i^4 \cdot e_i^4} & \dfrac{R_{45}A_i^5 \times l_i^4}{l_i^4 \cdot e_i^4} \end{bmatrix} \begin{bmatrix} v^4 \\ \omega^4 \end{bmatrix} \tag{27}$$

Similar to analyze the Jacobian matrix for the 3PRS parallel mechanism, by extending Eq. (27) from a single joint to six joints and then taking its inverse, we can obtain the Jacobian matrix J_{45}. Then we can design the Newton iteration formula for solving the forward kinematics of the 6PSS parallel mechanism as follows:

$$X_{k+1}^4 = X_k^4 - J_{45}(X_k^4)(q_k^4 - q^4) \tag{28}$$

where X^4 represents the terminal pose of the 6PSS mechanism and it is equivalent to T_{45} in Eq. (13), q^4 represents the joint inputs. Obviously, if the orientation of the end effector is represented by a rotation matrix composed of specific Euler angles in a certain sequence, the Jacobian matrix J_{45} needs to be transformed by a matrix.

4 Planning and Control

As a medical surgical robot integrating macro-micro moving platform, a corresponding planning approach needs to be conducted. In practice, it is generally not necessary to define macro or micro space strictly within mathematical constraints. It is sufficient to determine the movement of the macro-motion platform through simple judgment to ensure that the end effector is within the workspace of the micro-motion platform.

When there is no strict requirement for the terminal trajectory and only point-to-point positioning is needed, we recommend planning in the joint space, which offers three main advantages. Firstly, it offers simpler computation and higher precision, as well as better real-time performance. Secondly, it makes it easier to optimize velocity using interpolation methods such as trapezoidal profiles. Lastly, it is beneficial in addressing singularities, such as the infinite height allocation values for a given height in the vertical configuration of two 3PRS mechanisms. In such cases, joint space planning allows us to define a proportional height allocation rule based on stroke.

For the continuous terminal trajectory of the macro-motion platform, we have designed two types of force interaction control modes: force traction mode and force disturbance rejection mode. Both of them are based on the admittance control strategy, which aims to convert the real-time sensed contact force signal into displacement as:

$$\ddot{t}_i = \frac{F_i - F_{id} - B_i\dot{t}_i - k_i(t_i - t_{id})}{M_i}, i = 1\cdots 6 \tag{29}$$

where i represents the dimension of motion or force, t_i represents the position or angle of that dimension, t_{id} represents the desired position, F_i represents the force or torque measured by the force sensor for that dimension, and F_{id} represents the corresponding desired force or torque. B_i, K_i, and M_i are the three corresponding admittance parameters, which generally vary across different dimensions.

Since the frame of the force sensor is aligned with the Frame 4 during installation, the force and torque measured by the sensor can be transformed into position and angular quantities through Eq. (29). These quantities can then be assigned to T_{34} to obtain the new terminal pose. Therefore, the new matrix of T'_{34} can be expressed as:

$$T'_{34} = \begin{bmatrix} R_{34}R(t_4, t_5, t_6) & p_4^3 + [t_4, t_5, t_6]^T \\ 0 \quad 0 \quad 0 & 1 \end{bmatrix} \tag{30}$$

The similarity between the two force interaction modes is that the terminal trajectory will exhibit motion in the direction of the external force when subjected to external forces. The difference between them lies in the k_i in Eq. (29). In the force traction mode, the k_i parameter is set to 0, indicating that the position deviation does not play a role. Therefore, after revoking the force, it will not return to the original position. In the disturbance rejection mode, the k_i parameter is nonzero, the end-effector will go back to the desired position p_{di}.

The planning and control of the micro-motion platform are relatively straightforward. The micro-motion platform performs terminal positioning through inverse kinematics planning. With a movement resolution of 0.1 μ m and angular resolution of $1''$, the micro-motion platform's trajectory is often designed using incremental movements. By leveraging medical amplification equipment, the positioning of the medical instrument at a micron-level precision is achieved by adjusting the pose incrementally.

5 Experiments and Results

In the kinematic analysis of the hybrid mechanism composed of two 3PRS parallel mechanisms, the main challenge lies in the overall inverse kinematics, and the solution heavily relies on the accuracy of the Jacobian matrix. When calculating the Jacobian matrix of the hybrid mechanism, it needs to invert a 3×6 matrix. In such cases, only the right pseudo-inverse matrix can be calculated, leading to precision errors in the calculation of the inverse matrix. A set of predetermined joint trajectories are designed to verify the mapping accuracy of Jacobian matrix at the velocity level, as shown in

Fig. 3(a). Then, the terminal pose trajectory is obtained through forward kinematics, as shown in Fig. 3(b). Finally, by comparing the terminal velocity mapped by the Jacobian matrix with the differentiated velocity of the terminal trajectory, the results are shown in Fig. 3(c). The results indicate that the mapping accuracy of the Jacobian matrix for velocity is within 0.0015 mm/ms, and the mapping accuracy for angular velocity is within 5 μrad/ms. It is evident that the mapping accuracy in the rotational dimension is higher than that in the translational dimension. Additionally, the error levels are not uniformly distributed at different poses, as observed from Fig. 3(c).

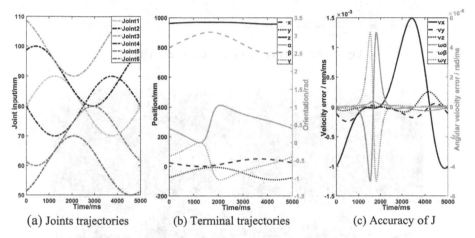

(a) Joints trajectories   (b) Terminal trajectories   (c) Accuracy of J

Fig. 3. Accuracy of the Jacobian matrix J

We designed varied terminal trajectories and get their inverse kinematics solutions to validate the accuracy of the complex overall inverse kinematic. During the solving process, we recorded the pose errors for each output of the inverse solutions, enabling us to evaluate the solving accuracy. Due to the maximum terminal velocities of the macro-motion platform being 50 mm/s and 0.35 rad/s, with a control period of 1 ms, we designed a set of initial poses and they were then incrementally or decrementally varied within the range of [−0.05, 0.05] in the translational directions and [−0.00035, 0.00035] in the rotational directions. The main purpose of designing the terminal trajectory in this way was to ensure that valid inverse kinematic solutions could be obtained for any arbitrary variation in the pose dimensions during the robot's motion planning process.

The results in Fig. 4 indicate that in the translational dimensions, the main errors occur in the x and y directions, and they are kept within 2.5 μm. The error in the z direction remains primarily within 0.1 μm. In the rotational dimensions, the angle errors in α and γ are relatively larger, but they are maintained within 0.5 mrad. The error in β is smaller, remaining within 0.015 mrad, while the angle is in ZXZ Euler angle.

Finally, using the proposed kinematic method and control strategies, the integrated macro-micro medical surgical robot device can be planned correspondingly. Figure 5 shows several different motion poses of this robot.

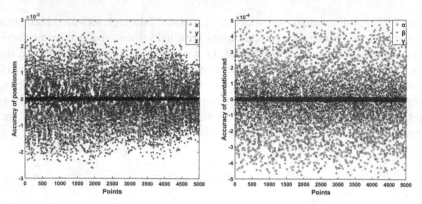

Fig. 4. Accuracy of the inverse kinematic solutions.

Fig. 5. Different poses of the medical surgical robot

6 Conclusion and Discussion

This paper provides a comprehensive analysis of the forward and inverse kinematics of the proposed medical surgical robot system, which consists of a three-level parallel mechanism connected in series. The forward and inverse kinematics of each level and the overall system are thoroughly studied. An iterative solving algorithm is developed to meet the requirements of real-time planning and control. The effectiveness of the proposed method is validated through simulation and experimental results. Based on these methods, further research and development are conducted on related planning and control algorithms. This work serves as a reference for the design, analysis, and planning control of hybrid surgical robots. However, there are still many unfinished tasks in this paper, such as structural optimization, device calibration, and accuracy compensation, which require further research and development.

References

1. Dupont, P.E., et al.: A decade retrospective of medical robotics research from 2010 to 2020. Sci. Robot. **6**(60), 8017 (2021)
2. Marescaux, J., et al.: Transatlantic robot-assisted telesurgery. Nature **413**(6854), 379–380 (2001)
3. Rivera-Serrano, C.M., et al.: A transoral highly flexible robot: novel technology and application. Laryngoscope **122**(5), 1067–1071 (2012)
4. Piccigallo, M., et al.: Design of a novel bimanual robotic system for single-port laparoscopy. IEEE/ASME Trans. Mechatron. **15**(6), 871–878 (2010)
5. Maclachlan, R.A., et al.: Micron: an actively stabilized handheld tool for microsurgery. IEEE Trans. Rob. **28**(1), 195–212 (2012)
6. Payne, C.J., Yang, G.Z.: Hand-held medical robots. Ann. Biomed. Eng. **42**(8), 1594–1605 (2014)
7. Simaan, N., Yasin, R.M., Wang, L.: Medical technologies and challenges of robot-assisted minimally invasive intervention and diagnostics. Ann. Rev. Control Rob. Auton. Syst. **1**(1), 465–490 (2018)
8. Freschi, C., et al.: Technical review of the da Vinci surgical telemanipulator. Int. J. Med. Rob. Comput. Assist. Surg. **9**(4), 396–406 (2013)
9. Lum, M.J.H., et al.: The RAVEN: design and validation of a telesurgery system. Int. J. Rob. Res. **28**(9), 1183–1197 (2009)
10. Hannaford, B., et al.: Raven-II: an open platform for surgical robotics research. IEEE Trans. Biomed. Eng. **60**(4), 954–959 (2012)
11. Ciuti, G., et al.: Robotic magnetic steering and locomotion of capsule endoscope for diagnostic and surgical endoluminal procedures. Robotica **28**(2), 199–207 (2010)
12. Mahoney, A.W., Abbott, J.J.: Five-degree-of-freedom manipulation of an untethered magnetic device in fluid using a single permanent magnet with application in stomach capsule endoscopy. Int. J. Rob. Res. **35**, 129–147 (2016)
13. Afshar, M., et al.: Optimal design of a novel spherical scissor linkage remote center of motion mechanism for medical robotics. In: 2020 IEEE/RSJ International Conference on Intelligent Robots and Systems (IROS), pp. 6459–6465 (2020)
14. Gu, X., et al.: A compliant transoral surgical robotic system based on a parallel flexible mechanism. Ann. Biomed. Eng. **47**(6), 1329–1344 (2019)
15. Tsai, T.C., Hsu, Y.L.: Development of a parallel surgical robot with automatic bone drilling carriage for stereotactic neurosurgery. Biomed. Eng. Appl. Basis Commun. **19**(04), 269–277 (2007)
16. Pisla, D., et al.: An active hybrid parallel robot for minimally invasive surgery. Rob. Comput.-Integr. Manuf. **29**(4), 203–221 (2013)
17. Zheng, X.Z., Bin, H.Z., Luo, Y.G.: Kinematic analysis of a hybrid serial-parallel manipulator. Int. J. Adv. Manuf. Technol. **23**(11), 925–930 (2004)
18. Gallardo-Alvarado, J., et al.: Kinematics and dynamics of 2(3-RPS) manipulators by means of screw theory and the principle of virtual work. Mech. Mach. Theory **43**(10), 1281–1294 (2008)
19. Hu, B., et al.: CGA-based approach for the inverse displacement of serial-parallel manipulators. Mech. Mach. Theory **176**, 105011 (2022)
20. Hu, B., Zhao, J., Cui, H.: Terminal constraint and mobility analysis of serial-parallel manipulators formed by 3-RPS and 3-SPR PMs. Mech. Mach. Theory **134**, 685–703 (2019)
21. Hu, B.: Complete kinematics of a serial–parallel manipulator formed by two Tricept parallel manipulators connected in serials. Nonlinear Dyn. **78**(4), 2685–2698 (2014). https://doi.org/10.1007/s11071-014-1618-4

Comparative Study of Feature-Based Surface Matching Automatic Coarse Registration Algorithms for Neuronavigation

Jiakai Cao⬤, Bai Chen(✉)⬤, and Keming Liu⬤

College of Mechanical and Electrical Engineering, Nanjing University of Aeronautics and Astronautics, Nanjing 210016, Jiangsu, China
chenbye@nuaa.edu.cn

Abstract. Non-invasive surface matching registration is preferred over paired point registration using bone anchor fiducial markers in neurosurgery due to its ability to avoid iatrogenic injuries and eliminate the need for medical image acquisition during navigation. However, the use of the iterative closest point algorithm for surface matching registration requires a manual coarse registration process, leading to a complicated and inconvenient procedure. To automate the coarse registration, this study proposes a method that combines algorithms for automatic surface matching and determination of optimal scale parameters. The method employs feature-based automatic coarse registration using point clouds with unique features at single scale and persistent features at multiple scales. By combining feature detection, description, and matching algorithms, the optimal scale parameters for each algorithm combination are identified. Through a comprehensive evaluation, 19 out of 24 algorithm combinations were found to achieve correct registration at the optimal scale based on considerations of robustness, accuracy, and time efficiency. The most effective combination was the SIFT + FPFH + SAC-IA + ICP algorithm with a scale parameter of $\alpha = 0.09\%$, resulting in a Hausdorff distance of 3.205 mm and a registration time of 5.082 s. This algorithmic combination enables the automatic spatial registration of neuronavigation, providing a convenient and reliable method for establishing accurate pose mapping between the image space and the patient space.

Keywords: Neuronavigation · Surface Matching Registration · Spatial Registration

1 Introduction

Neuronavigation can provide accurate visualization of anatomical structures and location of diseased tissues for surgery, to select optimal surgical path, reduce surgical trauma, and shorten the recovery time of patients [1]. Accuracy is the basis for the effective application of neuronavigation, and spatial registration is a key factor determining the accuracy of neuronavigation, that is: establishing the pose mapping between the coordinate system of the image space (reconstructed anatomical structure model) and the patient space (calibrated digitizer). The robustness, accuracy and time of spatial registration directly affect the surgical process.

© The Author(s), under exclusive license to Springer Nature Singapore Pte Ltd. 2023
H. Yang et al. (Eds.): ICIRA 2023, LNAI 14272, pp. 506–517, 2023.
https://doi.org/10.1007/978-981-99-6480-2_42

The surface matching registration in commercial neuronavigation is based in the iterative closest point (ICP) algorithm [2] and its variants [3], and its registration effect highly dependent on the initial pose between the point clouds to be registered. Therefore, a coarse-to-fine registration strategy is usually adopted, and the two point clouds are roughly matched through a robust but inaccurate coarse registration method before ICP completes the fine registration. Currently, neuronavigation based on surface matching uses manually acquired anatomical landmarks for coarse registration, which increases registration time and suffers from mismatches. Therefore, neuronavigation requires a robust, accurate, and fast automatic spatial registration method. With the continuous development and commercialization of computer imaging technology, various 3D acquisition devices have gradually been introduced into surgical navigation systems, improving the collection efficiency of point cloud data, and promoting the application of point cloud registration algorithms in surface matching registration. Liu et al. [4] proposed a surface matching registration method based on 3D feature matching. This feature-based coarse registration can automatically complete rough registration through keypoints descriptors and is robust. It can provide a reliable initial pose for fine registration but has not explored algorithm combination selection and parameter optimization. However, this coarse-to-fine registration method is greatly influenced by the designer's experience and parameter adjustment ability.

Therefore, this paper conducts a comparative study of different algorithm combinations and scale parameters in each step of feature-based coarse registration based on robustness, accuracy, and time, providing a robust, accurate, and fast automatic coarse-to-fine spatial registration method for neuronavigation.

2 Method

The coarse-to-fine registration method (see Fig. 1). Before registration, the point cloud is preprocessed by filtering, clipping and downsampling. In addition, the part of the point cloud with unique features at a single scale and persistent features at multiple scales is further extracted to ensure the robustness of the algorithm at different scales. Typical feature-based coarse registration consists of feature detection, feature description and feature matching. Feature detection obtains special keypoints within the point cloud, reducing the number of points involved in the registration process. Feature descriptors represent the feature information in the keypoints neighborhood through local feature descriptors that are easy to distinguish and compare and form keypoints descriptors. Feature matching is also a process of transformation estimation. According to the correspondence of keypoints descriptors obtained by matching and error correspondence elimination [5], the least square method or singular value decomposition method is used to obtain the transformation matrix between two points clouds. After the coarse registration, the iterative closest point algorithm is employed to refine the alignment of the two point clouds and improve the accuracy of the pose estimation.

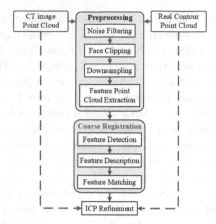

Fig. 1. The overall framework for the coarse-to-fine registration method

3   Data Acquisition and Preprocessing

3.1   Point Cloud Acquisition

Neuronavigation collects cranial CT of patients for diagnosis and preoperative planning. And select the face point cloud with a fixed position relative to the intracranial lesion for registration. The patient's facial skin was segmented and reconstructed from the preoperative CT image by 3D Slicer, and the image point cloud was obtained. The real surface contour point cloud is obtained by scanning the 3D printed patient craniofacial skin model with a line laser 3D scanner (see Fig. 2).

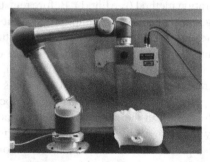

Fig. 2. Acquiring real surface contour point cloud by line laser 3D scanner

3.2   Point Cloud Preprocessing

To begin with, statistical filtering is applied to remove abnormal noise points, ensuring that they do not interfere with subsequent processing steps. Moreover, maintaining consistency in the facial range covered by the skin point clouds of the two craniofacial regions poses a challenge. Applying the feature-based method to two point clouds with different ranges will reduce the efficiency and accuracy of coarse registration, so it is necessary to crop out face regions with similar ranges from the two point clouds. The tip of the nose is in the center of the face, which is the most prominent point on the face and is not affected by the change of expression. Therefore, the nose point is often used as the basis for face clipping. In this paper, the tip of the nose is taken as the center and the Euclidean distance of 85 mm as the radius to crop, and the point cloud of the face regions with a similar range is obtained (see Fig. 3).

Fig. 3. Face regions point cloud clipping. Red: craniofacial skin point cloud, blue: facial regions point cloud, yellow: nasal tip point, green: a clipping sphere centered on the nasal tip point. (Color figure online)

Afterwards, the face regions point cloud is uniformly downsampled. Implementation method: the point cloud is approximated by multiple voxels with a certain resolution, and the point cloud in each voxel is replaced by the point closest to the centroid of voxel. The purpose of downsampling: (1) to reduce the number of points in the two point clouds and improve the processing efficiency of the subsequent steps; (2) the 3D local feature descriptors have better repeatability in two point clouds with similar grid resolution, which can improve the robustness of matching [6].

Finally, a set of continuous and discrete neighborhood radii, determined based on global measurement, is utilized to extract parts from the downsampled point cloud that possess unique features at single scale and persistent features at multiple scales. The optimal neighborhood radius scale is obtained through the registration results of point clouds within this region, allowing for the evaluation of the feature-based coarse registration algorithm's robustness at different scales.

4 Feature-Based Coarse Registration

4.1 Feature Detection

Even after preprocessing, there are still many similar points in the point cloud of the face regions. It is necessary to detect keypoints with special properties through feature detection to reduce the probability of unnecessary calculations and matching errors in feature description and feature matching.

In this paper, three feature detection methods are used: intrinsic shape signatures (ISS) [7], scale invariant feature transform (SIFT) [8], and Harris [9]. ISS applies principal component analysis to local coordinate systems, using points with significant changes in the principal direction as keypoints; SIFT searches for extreme points as keypoints at different scales by constructing a Gaussian pyramid and a Gaussian difference pyramid; Harris uses point cloud normal and local structures to detect corner points as keypoints (see Fig. 4).

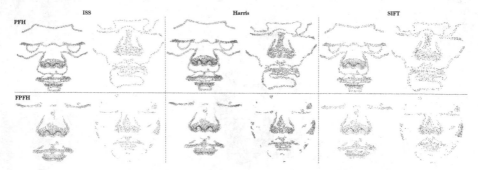

Fig. 4. Unique and persistent point clouds extract based on PFH (top) and FPFH (bottom), respectively. Red: CT image point cloud, Green: real contour point cloud, Blue: key points. (Color figure online)

4.2 Feature Description

The keypoints obtained through feature detection are three-dimensional vectors composed of their coordinates in the corresponding space, which cannot well represent the facial regions feature information they represent. In feature-based coarse registration, it is necessary to explore the geometric attributes or spatial distribution information of keypoints in the point cloud through feature description and express the feature information through feature descriptors that are easy to quantify and compare.

This paper adopts two feature description methods: point feature histograms (PFH) [10] and fast point feature histograms (FPFH) [11]. Both are histogram descriptors based on geometric attributes, which represent the feature information of a query point through a histogram formed by statistical analysis of the distribution of features within its interval in the feature space formed by the geometric structure between the query point and its nearest neighbor within its spherical neighborhood.

The neighborhood radius directly affects the description results of point cloud features by PFH and FPFH. If the neighborhood radius is too small, it cannot accurately represent feature information, and if it is too large, it can cause the loss of small features. Therefore, in addition to finding appropriate feature descriptors for coarse registration of point clouds in the face regions, it is more important to find appropriate neighborhood radius scales. A more robust method is to calculate the same feature descriptor under a set of continuous and discrete neighborhood radius scales and focus on registration at points where the feature descriptor is unique at a single scale and persistent at multiple scales [12]. Rusu et al. [13] proposed a method for extracting points with unique feature histograms at a single scale and persistent feature histograms at multiple scales based on distance metrics: calculate the mean value μ and standard deviation σ of the histograms of all points in the point cloud using distance metrics at a single scale, select points outside the $\mu \pm \alpha \cdot \sigma$ interval of the histogram as feature uniqueness, and select feature uniqueness that exists at multiple scales as feature persistence points.

In this paper, cosine similarity is used as a distance metric for feature histograms, and points outside the $\mu \pm \alpha \cdot \sigma$ interval of the histogram are used as feature uniqueness. Under six different scales, PFH and FPFH are used to extract unique and persistent features from point clouds in two face regions (see Fig. 4). Furthermore, the optimal neighborhood radius for registration can be selected from six different scales by comparing the registration accuracy. In addition, according to the conclusion of Guo et al. [6], the scale of the neighborhood radius will affect the robustness of registration. By comparing registration results at multiple scales, the robustness of feature based coarse registration algorithms can be evaluated to obtain the most robust combination of registration algorithms.

For the selection of these six continuous and discrete neighborhood radii, the global metric-based feature descriptor neighborhood radius calculation method proposed by Zaharescu et al. [15] is used:

$$\rho = \sqrt{\frac{\alpha A_M}{\pi}} \tag{1}$$

where A_M is the total surface area of M, and α is a parameter that controls the size of the neighborhood radius. For a 2.5D model obtained from a single perspective, the total area is estimated to be 4.5 times the area of the 2.5D model. The range of ranges from 0.05% to 0.1%, corresponding to six different neighborhood radii.

4.3 Feature Matching

Feature matching is also a process of transformation estimation, mainly including sample consistency initial alignment (SAC-IA) and feature similarity-based methods. SAC-IA is a method based on the idea of random sample consistency (RANSAC), which involves taking many samples from candidate correspondence relationships and looking at many correspondence relationships to find the correspondence that minimizes the error function and obtain a transformation matrix. The method based on feature similarity determines the corresponding relationship of keypoints by comparing the similarity of feature descriptors of keypoints in the two point cloud and sets constraints to eliminate the incorrect corresponding relationships. Then, the transformation matrix is obtained through singular value decomposition. Among them, there are many common methods for eliminating false correspondence, such as: the median distance (MD) based elimination method does not use a fixed threshold value, but uses the median value of all corresponding point pairs as constraints to adapt to the distance distribution; The elimination method based on the angle between surface normal (SN) constrains the corresponding relationship through the threshold value of the angle between the corresponding point normal; The RANSAC based elimination method extracts correspondence that meets the distance threshold through random sampling and iteration, improving the proportion of correct correspondence in correspondence.

In this paper, SAC-IA and three feature similarity methods based on median distance, normal vector angle, and RANSAC based false correspondence elimination methods are used for feature matching to obtain the transformation matrix between point clouds in two face regions and complete rough registration.

4.4 Evaluation of Registration Results

In point cloud registration problems, similarity metrics are commonly used to evaluate the degree of matching between two clouds. Common similarity measures include mean square error, maximum common point set, chamfer distance, and Hausdorff distance (HD) [15]. In this paper, Hausdorff distance is selected as the evaluation index for registration results. Hausdorff distance can comprehensively consider the similarity between the entire point cloud and is suitable for comparing the differences between different registration algorithms.

Given two point sets A and B, the Hausdorff distance between them is:

$$H(P, Q) = \max(h(P, Q), h(Q, P)) \tag{2}$$

$$\begin{cases} h(P, Q) = \max_{p \in P} \min_{q \in Q} \|p - q\| \\ h(Q, P) = \max_{q \in Q} \min_{p \in P} \|q - p\| \end{cases} \tag{3}$$

where, $h(P, Q)$ is the one-way Hausdorff distance from point set P to point set Q, and $h(Q, P)$ is the one-way Hausdorff distance from point set Q to point set P; $\max_{p \in P} \min_{q \in Q} \|p - q\|$ represents the maximum distance from all points in point set P to the nearest point in point set Q, and $\max_{q \in Q} \min_{p \in P} \|q - p\|$ represents the maximum distance from all points in point set Q to the nearest point in point set P.

5   Registration Experiment and Result Evaluation

The experiment was conducted on a computer configured with a 3.2 GHz Intel Core i7–8700 CPU and 16 GB RAM. The code was implemented in C++ and the Point Cloud Library [16] was used. A total of 24 coarse-to-fine registration combinations are formed by combining algorithms of 3 feature detection, 2 feature descriptions, 4 feature matching and ICP. In addition, each algorithm combination calculates feature descriptors at six neighborhood radius scales to complete the registration of two point clouds. A total of 144 registration results at different algorithm combinations and neighborhood radius scales.

5.1   Registration Results at the Best Neighborhood Radius Scale

The neighborhood radius scale directly affects the accuracy of the feature descriptor's description of keypoints feature information, and an appropriate neighborhood radius scale is a guarantee of good accuracy in registration. Therefore, the optimal neighborhood radius scale for each algorithm combination is selected based on the final accuracy achieved by registration at each scale (see Table 1).

Table 1. Optimal scale parameters and registration accuracy of each algorithm combination

No.	Algorithm combination	Scale (%)	HD (mm)
1	Harris + FPFH + MD + ICP	0.08	3.448
2	Harris + FPFH + RANSAC + ICP	0.09	3.401
3	Harris + FPFH + SAC-IA + ICP	0.09	3.215
4	Harris + FPFH + SN + ICP	×	×
5	Harris + PFH + MD + ICP	×	×
6	Harris + PFH + RANSAC + ICP	0.09	3.303
7	Harris + PFH + SAC-IA + ICP	0.05	3.417
8	Harris + PFH + SN + ICP	×	×
9	ISS + FPFH + MD + ICP	0.08	2.961
10	ISS + FPFH + RANSAC + ICP	0.09	3.259
11	ISS + FPFH + SAC-IA + ICP	0.07	3.212
12	ISS + FPFH + SN + ICP	×	×
13	ISS + PFH + MD + ICP	0.1	3.352
14	ISS + PFH + RANSAC + ICP	0.09	3.431
15	ISS + PFH + SAC-IA + ICP	0.09	3.333
16	ISS + PFH + SN + ICP	×	×
17	SIFT + FPFH + MD + ICP	0.08	3.565
18	SIFT + FPFH + RANSAC + ICP	0.08	3.448
19	SIFT + FPFH + SAC-IA + ICP	0.09	3.205
20	SIFT + FPFH + SN + ICP	0.07	3.621
21	SIFT + PFH + MD + ICP	0.08	3.325
22	SIFT + PFH + RANSAC + ICP	0.09	3.221
23	SIFT + PFH + SAC-IA + ICP	0.08	3.256
24	SIFT + PFH + SN + ICP	0.1	3.656

5.2 Evaluation of Registration Algorithm

Robustness. The robustness of point cloud registration is very important. Point cloud data often contains various types of noise, occlusion, and other abnormal data. If the robustness of the registration algorithm is poor, these abnormal data may cause the algorithm to fail, leading to registration failure. In the preprocessing stage, filtering to remove some abnormal noise can improve the robustness of point cloud registration, and the selection of algorithms and the setting of scale parameters will also directly affect the robustness of registration. This paper evaluates the robustness of each algorithm based on whether it successfully registers under different combinations and scale parameters, using various algorithms used in feature detection, feature description, and feature matching.

The three feature detection algorithms each have 8 algorithm combinations under 6 scales, with a total of 48 registration results (see Fig. 5). The registration algorithms that use SIFT for feature detection under different combinations and scale parameters have the largest number of successful registrations and the best robustness.

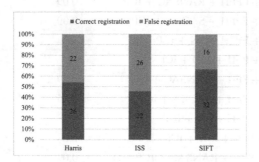

Fig. 5. Correct registration number of feature detection algorithms

The two feature description algorithms each have 12 algorithm combinations under 6 scales, with a total of 72 registration results (see Fig. 6). The registration algorithm that uses FPFH for feature description under different combinations and different scale parameters can achieve the largest number of correct registrations and the best robustness.

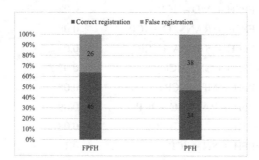

Fig. 6. Correct registration number of feature description algorithms

The four feature matching algorithms each have 6 algorithms combinations under 6 scales, with a total of 36 registration results (see Fig. 7). The registration algorithms that use SAC-IA for feature matching under different combinations and scale parameters have the largest number of correct registrations and the best robustness.

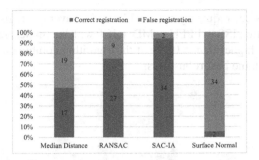

Fig. 7. Correct registration number of feature matching algorithms

Therefore, the combination of SIFT + FPFH + SAC-IA + ICP algorithm has the best robustness, and the registration results for point cloud data under different scale parameters are more stable and reliable, which can better cope with abnormal situation of point cloud registration in the surgical environment.

Accuracy and Time. The accuracy and time of registration are important indicators for measuring point cloud registration algorithms. Accuracy represents the advantages and disadvantages of the registration algorithm, while time represents the practicality and feasibility of the algorithm. There is usually a certain balance between the two, and it is necessary to select an appropriate registration algorithm based on the robustness requirements of point cloud registration in the surgical environment.

The Hausdorff distance is used to evaluate the registration accuracy of each algorithm combination at the optimal scale (see Fig. 8). A total of 19 of the 24 algorithm combinations achieved correct registration. Among them, the Hausdorff distance of the algorithm combination ISS + FPFH + MD + ICP is the smallest, which is 2.961 mm The registration accuracy of the most robust algorithm combination SIFT + FPFH + SAC-IA + ICP is second only to ISS + FPFH + MD + ICP, and the Hausdorff distance is 3.205 mm.

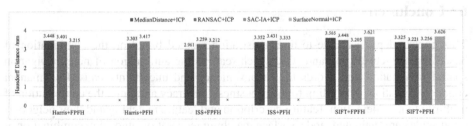

Fig. 8. Combination registration accuracy of various algorithms at optimal scale parameters

Five repeated experiments were conducted on the registration of each algorithm combination at the optimal scale, a total of 120 experiments, and obtain the average registration time (see Fig. 9). All correctly registered algorithm combinations can be registered within 10 s and Harris + FPFH + RANSAC + ICP algorithm combinations have the fastest speed, requiring only 3.779 s. The average registration time of the algorithm combination ISS + FPFH + MD + ICP with the highest registration accuracy is 5.891 s, which is higher than 5.082 s of the algorithm combination SIFT + FPFH + SAC-IA + ICP with the best robustness.

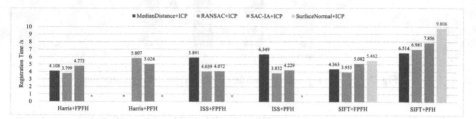

Fig. 9. Combination registration time of various algorithms at optimal scale parameters

Result Analysis. In summary, feature-based coarse registration can provide a reliable initial pose for fine registration of the ICP, enabling registration to be completed correctly in a relatively short time. Different algorithm combinations have different advantages in robustness, accuracy, and time. For surface matching registration in neuronavigation, the complex and variable surgical environment requires high accuracy and reliability of registration results. The feature detection algorithm ISS and feature matching algorithm MD used in the combination of ISS + FPFH + MD + ICP, which has the highest registration accuracy, have poor robustness and are not suitable for neuronavigation. The fastest Harris + FPFH + RANSAC + ICP combination is inferior to SIFT + FPFH + SAC-IA + ICP combination in robustness and registration accuracy. Therefore, the SIFT + FPFH + SAC-IA + ICP combination with a scale parameter of $\alpha = 0.09\%$ can be used as the best algorithm combination for surface matching registration of neuronavigation.

6 Conclusion

This paper adopts a coarse-to-fine registration method based on the combination of based-feature registration and ICP, which realizes the automation of neuronavigation spatial registration and avoids the inconvenience and uncertainty caused by manual coarse registration. According to the robustness, accuracy and time, the combination of multiple feature detection, feature description and feature matching and their neighborhood scales are evaluated, and a surface matching registration algorithm combination at the optimal neighborhood scale is obtained, which can simply the registration process and improve registration reliability. And the follow-up work will focus on integrating the registration algorithm into the neurosurgery robot, and accurately and quickly correspond the preoperative planning path to the patient through feature-based surface matching automatic coarse-to-fine registration.

Acknowledgement. This work was supported by the National Natural Science Foundation of China (U22A20204 and 52205018), the Fundamental Research Funds for the Central Universities, China (NP2022304).

References

1. Thomas, N.W.D., Sinclair, J.: Image-guided neurosurgery: history and current clinical applications. J. Med. Imaging Radiat. Sci. **46**(3), 331–342 (2015)
2. Besl, P.J., McKay, N.D.: A method for registration of 3-D shapes. IEEE Trans. Pattern Anal. Mach. Intell. **14**(2), 239–256 (1992)
3. Elseberg, J., Magnenat, S., Siegwart, R., et al.: Comparison of nearest-neighbor-search strategies and implementations for efficient shape registration. J. Softw. Eng. Rob. **3**, 2–12 (2012)
4. Liu, Y., Song, Z., Wang, M.: A new robust markerless method for automatic image-to-patient registration in image-guided neurosurgery system. Comput. Assist. Surg. **22**(sup1), 319–325 (2017)
5. Buch, A.G., Kraft, D., Kamarainen, J.K., et al.: Pose estimation using local structure-specific shape and appearance context. In: 2013 IEEE International Conference on Robotics and Automation, pp. 2080–2087(2013)
6. Guo, Y., Bennamoun, M., Sohel, F., et al.: A comprehensive performance evaluation of 3D local feature descriptors. Int. J. Comput. Vis **116**(1), 66–89 (2016)
7. Zhong, Y.: Intrinsic shape signatures: a shape descriptor for 3D object recognition. In 2009 IEEE 12th International Conference on Computer Vision Workshops, ICCV Workshops, pp. 689–696(2009)
8. Lowe, D.G.: Distinctive image features from scale-invariant keypoints. Int. J. Comput. Vision **60**(2), 91–110 (2004)
9. Tian, B., Jiang, P., Zhang, X., Zhang, Y., Wang, F.: A novel feature point detection algorithm of unstructured 3D point cloud. In: Huang, D.-S., Han, K., Hussain, A. (eds.) ICIC 2016. LNCS (LNAI), vol. 9773, pp. 736–744. Springer, Cham (2016). https://doi.org/10.1007/978-3-319-42297-8_68
10. Rusu, R.B., Blodow, N., Marton, Z.C., et al.: Aligning point cloud views using persistent feature histograms. In: 2008 IEEE/RSJ International Conference on Intelligent Robots and Systems, pp. 3384–3391 (2008)
11. Rusu, R.B., Blodow, N., Beetz, M.: Fast Point Feature Histograms (FPFH) for 3D registration. In: 2009 IEEE International Conference on Robotics and Automation. Kobe: IEEE, pp. 3212–3217(2009)
12. Holz, D., Ichim, A.E., Tombari, F., et al.: Registration with the point cloud library: a modular framework for aligning in 3-D. IEEE Robot. Autom. Mag. **22**(4), 110–124 (2015)
13. Rusu, R.B., Márton, Z.C., Blodow, N., et al.: Persistent point feature histograms for 3D point clouds. In: Proceedings of the 10th International Conference on Intelligent Autonomous Systems, Baden, Germany, vol. 16(2008)
14. Zaharescu, A., Boyer, E., Horaud, R.: Keypoints and local descriptors of scalar functions on 2D manifolds. Int. J. Comput. Vision **100**(1), 78–98 (2012)
15. Sun, G., Wang, X.: Three-dimensional point cloud reconstruction and morphology measurement method for greenhouse plants based on the kinect sensor self-calibration. Agronomy **9**(10), 596 (2019)
16. Rusu, R.B., Cousins, S.: 3D is here: point cloud library (PCL). In: 2011 IEEE International Conference on Robotics and Automation, pp. 1–4 (2011)

The Effect of Channel Ordering Based on the Entropy Weight Graph on the MI-EEG Classification

Peng Ling[1], Kai Xi[1], Peng Chen[1(✉)], Xi Yu[2,3], and Kang Li[4,5]

[1] School of Mechanical Engineering, Southwest Jiaotong University, Chengdu 610031, China
chenpeng@swjtu.edu.cn

[2] Department of Orthopedic Surgery and Orthopedic Research Institute, West China Hospital, Sichuan University, Chengdu 610041, China

[3] Department of Rehabilitation Medicine, West China Hospital, Sichuan University, Chengdu 610041, China

[4] West China Biomedical Big Data Center, West China Hospital, Sichuan University, Chengdu 610041, China

[5] Med-X Center for Informatics, Sichuan University, Chengdu 610041, China

Abstract. This study investigates the effect of changing channel ordering at the input end of EEGNet on the classification performance of deep learning algorithms, based on the entropy weight graph using phase locking value (PLV). The PLV is computed to reflect the phase synchronization relationship between different EEG channels and an adjacency matrix is constructed to obtain an undirected and non-fully connected graph using an appropriate threshold. The clustering coefficient is then calculated for different channels to determine the central node. Subsequently, the distances from the remaining channels to the central node are calculated using the entropy weight graph based on PLV, which serves as the basis for channel ordering. Additionally, the EEGNet is modified according to the characteristics of the EEG data to make it more suitable for the classification of the recorded motor imagery signals. The classification results demonstrate that channel ordering at the input end of the EEGNet can arrange signals with more synchronized phase information together, thereby enhancing the data separability and improving the classification performance effectively.

Keywords: Phase Locking Value · Entropy Weight · Graph Theory · EEGNet

1 Introduction

Brain-Computer Interface (BCI) technology does not rely on the peripheral neural and muscular outputs. It establishes a communication and control channel between the brain and external devices by analyzing brain neural activity [1]. Based on the placement of sensors used for detecting and acquiring signals from the brain, BCI systems can be categorized into invasive, semi-invasive, and non-invasive types [2]. Non-invasive BCI, in particular, does not require surgical implantation of sensors, which reduces

© The Author(s), under exclusive license to Springer Nature Singapore Pte Ltd. 2023
H. Yang et al. (Eds.): ICIRA 2023, LNAI 14272, pp. 518–526, 2023.
https://doi.org/10.1007/978-981-99-6480-2_43

the associated risks. Utilizing electroencephalogram (EEG) signals, non-invasive BCI systems provide simplicity in operation and real-time capability and have been widely applied in BCI research in recent years [3–6]. Non-invasive BCI technology based on motor imagery EEG (MI-EEG) has the potential to restore motor function by inducing activity-dependent brain plasticity [7–10]. Currently, a number of research focus on the accurate classification of MI-EEG signals.

Several studies have been conducted on classification algorithms for MI-EEG signals. You Y et al. [11] proposed a flexible analytic wavelet transform-based EEG classification method. Yang J et al. [12] introduced an algorithm combining long short-term memory networks with a spatial convolutional network, enabling learning spatial information and temporal correlations from raw MI-EEG signals. Gonuguntla V et al. [13] proposed EEGNet, a convolutional neural network specifically designed for BCI. It performs convolution separately on each channel and time dimension, extracts features then implements classification directly from these two dimensions.

Regarding the input of convolutional neural networks, Zhang H et al. [14] indicated that irrelevant channels could reduce recognition capabilities and influence the control of external devices. Therefore, they developed a sparse squeeze-and-excitation module to extract channel weights based on the contributions of EEG channels to MI classification. This module was used to develop an automatic channel selection strategy. Channel selection is a meaningful approach to improve the separability of EEG signals at the input of convolutional neural networks. However, due to the complexity of the brain, which is regarded as a high-dimensional nonlinear system [15], a strategy considering the phase correlation between channels [16, 17] may be necessary to capture important information that reflects the separability of EEG signals. Samanta et al. [18] investigated the construction of connections between high-dimensional EEG channels from the graph theory perspective of clustering coefficients. Functional connections between channels using graph theory allows for metrics that can serve as features for data classification [19].

It is necessary to study channel ordering based on graph theory for the MI-EEG classification by CNN algorithms. By arranging channels with similar characteristics together and inputting them into modified EEGNet, the separability of the input EEG signals is enhanced while preserving the information of the EEG channels as much as possible. The flowing sections start with the data acquisition and preprocessing of MI-EEG signals, then the determination of central channels based on PLV and channel ordering and MI-EEG classification is presented. The performance comparison of classification is discussed, and the conclusion is drawn.

2 Acquisition and Preprocessing of MI-EEG Signals

The recorded signals in this study come from 9 healthy subjects (S1–S9), all male and right-handed, with an average age of 23 years, without known neurological or psychological disorders, no use of psychotropic drugs, or any effects on the central nervous system Systemic drugs. The data acquisition equipment is the eego system produced by ANT Neuro Company and the supporting software eego™. The sampling channels are 64 channels in the 10–20 international standard, and the sampling frequency is 1024 Hz.

The experimental design for each subject is as follows. Each subject completed 4 sets of experiments, and each experiment performed 40 times motor imagery. In each motor imagery task, the computer screen first displayed a black screen for 5 s, indicating that the experiment was about to be carried out, and then a 3-s motion picture of the fist moving to the left or right appeared on the screen, followed by a picture of moving left or right. Right up arrow for 4 s. There was a 30-s rest between each motor imagery task and a 5-min rest between each group of experiments. The specific experimental process is shown in Fig. 1.

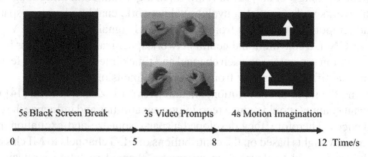

Fig.1. Experiment Process

To obtain relatively clean MI-EEG signals, this study requires preprocessing of the raw EEG signals. Firstly, a 50 Hz notch filter is applied to remove power line interference from the raw EEG signals. Since the rhythmic variations of brainwaves generated during motor imagery primarily concentrate in the mu rhythm (8–12 Hz) and beta rhythm (13–30 Hz) frequency bands [20], a band-pass filter from 1 to 35 Hz is applied in the subsequent steps. To extract the MI-EEG signals during motor imagery tasks, the continuous data is segmented by extracting the MI-EEG data from 0.5 s before the appearance of the cue arrow to 4 s after the appearance of the cue arrow. Lastly, independent component analysis [21] is performed to remove components that are most likely non-brainwave signals from the data.

3   Research on Channel Sorting Algorithm

3.1   Graph Establishment and Channel Ordering

Phase locking value (PLV) can be used to characterize the phase synchronization between EEG signals from two different brain channels [22]. For a pair of real signals $s_1(t)$ and $s_2(t)$, The calculation formula for PLV is shown in Eq. (1).

$$\text{PLV}_{ij} = \left| \frac{1}{N} \sum_{n=1}^{N} e^{j\phi_{ij}^n(t)} \right| \tag{1}$$

where $N = 160$ represents the total number of trials, with each participant requiring 160 times motor imagery, and indicates the relative phase between the two signals in the nth trial, which means when tends to 0, the phase correlation between the two channel signals is worse, and vice versa.

By calculating the phase locking values between all pairs of EEG channels, we can obtain an adjacency matrix P as shown in Eq. (2).

$$P = \begin{pmatrix} \text{PLV}_{11} & \cdots & \text{PLV}_{1m} \\ \vdots & \ddots & \vdots \\ \text{PLV}_{m1} & \cdots & \text{PLV}_{mm} \end{pmatrix} \tag{2}$$

In this equation, PLV_{ij} represents the magnitude of the phase locking value between channel i and channel j, which can also be called an edge. However, some studies indicate that edges with weak correlation between channels can be removed [23, 24]. Kılıç et al. [25] suggest setting a threshold η of 60%. In this study, we adopt this thresholding method to convert the fully connected graph described in Eq. (2) into a partially connected graph $G = (V, E, W)$. Here, V represents the EEG channel set, E represents the edge set, and W represents the weight of E.

$$\text{PLV}_{ij} = \begin{cases} \text{PLV}_{ij}, & \text{if } \text{PLV}_{ij} \geq \eta \\ 0, & \text{else} \end{cases} \tag{3}$$

In this study, the selection of central channels is based on the concept of clustering coefficient, as described by the clustering coefficient of each channel [26].

$$C_i = \frac{E_i}{(k_i(k_i - 1))/2} = \frac{2E_i}{k_i(k_i - 1)} \tag{4}$$

This equation represents the actual number of edges between channel i and its neighboring channels, in which k_i represents the number of possible edges that could exist among the neighbors of channel i. In this study, the channel with the highest clustering coefficient is selected as the central channel, denoted as s.

3.2 Entropy Weight Graph Based on PLV

Based on the previous calculations, in this study, for the ith channel, the defined evaluation indicators for sorting are the magnitude of the phase locking value between that channel and the central channel ($\text{PLV}_{i,s}$) and the clustering coefficient of that channel (C_i). The decision matrix is defined as $X = \{x_{ij}\}_{m \times n}$, where m represents the number of channels and n represents the number of decision criteria. The elements of the decision matrix can be represented in Eq. (5).

$$x_{ij} = \begin{cases} \text{PLV}_{i,s}, & \text{if } i = 1 \\ C_i, & \text{if } i = 2 \end{cases} \tag{5}$$

Next, in this study, the entropy weighting method [27] is used to determine the weights of the two criteria. Ma, Yan, et al. [28] performed a nonlinear dynamic analysis of EEG signals based on entropy, which demonstrated entropy can be a measure of the complex nonlinear system of the brain.

Since this study aims at considering the effect of both the phase-locked value and the clustering coefficient on the sorted results, the Topsis sorting method is useful for decision making and sorting. It considers the shortest distance from the positive ideal solution and the farthest distance from the negative ideal solution [29], and the proximity coefficient is calculated.

This study standardizes the data in the decision matrix by column, and calculates the information entropy of each index, then further obtains the value of information utility. The entropy weight of each indicator can be calculated through the information utility value, and each element is weighted with the help of the entropy weight. Thus, the optimal solution and the worst solution are defined.

For other channels of non-central nodes, the distances from itself to the optimal and worst solution can be obtained respectively through the distance calculation formula [29], and the evaluation value of each channel is calculated accordingly. The channel that is closer to the optimal solution and farthest to the worst solution is the best. The final channel sorting is the result in descending order of evaluation value.

3.3   Modified EEGNet for MI-EEG Classification

Based on the original EEGNet, this study modifies the structure and convolution kernel parameters of EEGNet to avoid overfitting. The CNN structure in this study includes three convolutional layers, two pooling layers, and one fully connected layer. The configuration of the modified EEGNet is shown in Fig. 2.

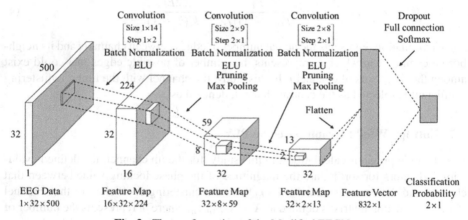

Fig. 2. The configuration of the Modified EEGNet

After preprocessing the experimental data, the individual sample data with dimensions of $1 \times 32 \times 500$ is input into the CNN structure. The first layer mainly performs temporal convolution, its primary purpose is to reduce the length of the signal in the temporal dimension and refine the channel features. The convolutional kernel size is set to 1×14, with a stride of 1×2. After the convolution operation, batch normalization is carried out to accelerate the learning speed and reduce the dependence on the initial weight. Then the exponential linear element (ELU) activation function is used to activate the model to ensure that the average output is close to zero, thus accelerating the convergence of the model.

After convolution, the output consists of 16 channels of feature maps. Moving on to the second convolutional layer, with a kernel size of 2×9 and a stride of 2×1, the neighboring channel's feature information is integrated, assuming that the left and right brain channel signals are not mixed. Batch normalization is applied to the output, followed by activation using the ELU function. Additionally, to avoid overfitting, a pruning operation is performed at a rate of 0.25. Because we add two pooling layers to the new CNN model, the size of the feature map is reduced. Additionally, the new CNN model contains only 3 convolutional layers, so the complexity of the model is reduced. Moreover, after the second and third convolutions, we performed random pruning to inactivate part of the data to further avoid overfitting. Subsequently, a pooling layer with a kernel size of 2×4 is used to extract channel-specific features from the feature maps. The third convolutional layer uses a 2×8 kernel, and the convolutional stride remains at 2×1. Batch normalization is applied again, followed by activation using the ELU function, and pruning is performed at a rate of 0.25. Finally, a 2×4 pooling operation is performed. It is important to note that all convolution operations are conducted in a no-padding mode.

4   Classification Performance Comparison

By utilizing the entropy weight graph using PLV and the initial input described in Sect. 3, this study generates two channel ordering outcomes, denoted as "Original Ordering" and "With the Entropy Weight Graph" (referring to the ordering based on entropy weight graph). After applying these two ordering approaches to the EEG data, they are subsequently fed into EEGNet, resulting in distinct maximum classification accuracies for each channel order, demonstrated in Table 1.

Table 1. Maximum Classification Accuracy After Sorting by Different Channels

Subject	Origin Ordering	With the Entropy Weight Graph
S1	88.6812%	90.6795%
S2	86.6449%	86.9514%
S3	87.4429%	94.6308%
S4	84.6415%	85.5347%
S5	85.5808%	92.8464%
S6	89.3173%	90.1166%
S7	86.6365%	93.1263%
S8	89.3095%	93.9816%
S9	85.6517%	91.3106%

From Table 1, it can be found that the maximum classification accuracy rate after inputting EEGNet after channel sorting will be significantly improved. At the same time,

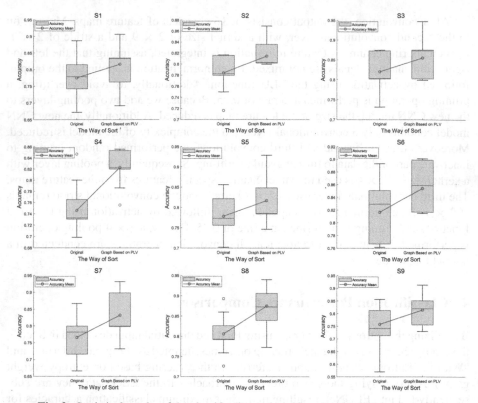

Fig. 3. Statistical results of the classification tasks with and without channel sorting

this study also explored the improvement of classification accuracy by channel sorting by primary statistical analysis, and the results are shown in Fig. 3.

By analyzing Fig. 3, it can be observed that channel reordering through entropy weight graph using PLV can effectively enhance the average classification accuracy. It could be inferred that sorting the EEG channels at the input of EEGNet can group together channels with closer phases, thereby improving the discriminability of the input signals to EEGNet and subsequently enhancing the overall classification accuracy.

5 Conclusion

This study utilizes entropy weight graph using PLV for channel sorting to enhance the classification accuracy. The sorted EEG signals are then input into the modified EEGNet, which preserves the phase correlation information between channels in the input stage of deep learning. In this way, the proposed method enhances the separability of motor imagery EEG signals.

This study also has certain limitations. It did not utilize public datasets to test and compare the performance of the method. In future work, it aims at validating the proposed channel sorting methods by the public datasets for further evaluation. Moreover, this study will explore more about the impact of channel sorting methods on algorithm accuracy. It would attempt to improve channel sorting methods at different scales, and investigate the influence of channel sorting under different metrics on motor imagery EEG signal classification, thereby reveal the underlying patterns of the complex system of the brain.

Acknowledgments. The work has been financially supported by the Sichuan Science and Technology Program (GrantNos. 2022YFH0073, 2022YFS0021, 2023ZHCG0075 and 2023YFH0037), and 1 · 3 · 5 project for disciplines of excellence, West China Hospital, Sichuan University (Grant Nos. ZYYC21004 and ZYJC21081).

References

1. Madiha, T., Trivailo, P.M., Milan, S.: EEG-based BCI control schemes for lower-limb assistive-robots. Front. Human Neurosci. **12**, 312 (2018)
2. Sui, Y., et al.: Deep brain–machine interfaces: sensing and modulating the human deep brain. Natl. Sci. Rev. **9**(10), 212 (2022)
3. Song, Z., et al.: Evaluation and diagnosis of brain diseases based on non-invasive BCI. In: 2021 9th International Winter Conference on Brain-Computer Interface (BCI). IEEE (2021)
4. Zhuang, M., et al.: State-of-the-art non-invasive brain–computer interface for neural rehabilitation: a review. J. Neurorestoratol. **8**(1), 12–25 (2020)
5. Cho, J.-H., et al.: Classification of hand motions within EEG signals for non-invasive BCI-based robot hand control. In: 2018 IEEE International Conference on Systems, Man, and Cybernetics (SMC). IEEE (2018)
6. Dose, H., Møller, J.S., Iversen, H.K., et al.: An end-to-end deep learning approach to MI-EEG signal classification for BCIs. Expert Syst. Appl. **114**, 532–542 (2018)
7. Mane, R., Chouhan, T., Guan, C.: BCI for stroke rehabilitation: motor and beyond. J. Neural Eng. **17**(4), 041001 (2020)
8. Bai, Z., et al.: "Immediate and long-term effects of BCI-based rehabilitation of the upper extremity after stroke: a systematic review and meta-analysis. J. Neuroeng. Rehabil. **17**, 1–20 (2020)
9. Vourvopoulos, A., et al.: Efficacy and brain imaging correlates of an immersive motor imagery BCI-driven VR system for upper limb motor rehabilitation: a clinical case report. Front. Human Neurosci. **13**, 244 (2019)
10. Ang, K.K., et al.: "A randomized controlled trial of EEG-based motor imagery brain-computer interface robotic rehabilitation for stroke. Clin. EEG Neurosci. **46**(4), 310–320 (2015)
11. You, Y., Chen, W., Zhang, T.: Motor imagery EEG classification based on flexible analytic wavelet transform. Biomed. Signal Process. Control **62**, 102069 (2020)
12. Yang, J., Yao, S., Wang, J.: Deep fusion feature learning network for MI-EEG classification. IEEE Access **6**, 79050–79059 (2018)
13. Gonuguntla, V., Wang, Y., Veluvolu, K.C.: Event-related functional network identification: application to EEG classification. IEEE J. Sel. Topics Signal Process. **10**(7), 1284–1294 (2016)
14. Zhang, H., Zhao, X., Wu, Z., et al.: Motor imagery recognition with automatic EEG channel selection and deep learning. J. Neural Eng. **18**(1), 016004 (2021)
15. Li, M., Luo, X.-Y., Yang, J.: Extracting the nonlinear features of motor imagery EEG using parametric t-SNE. Neurocomputing **218**, 371–381 (2016)

16. Yang, F., et al.: "Multi-method fusion of cross-subject emotion recognition based on high-dimensional EEG features. Front. Comput. Neurosci. **13**, 53 (2019)
17. Goshvarpour, A., Goshvarpour, A.: Novel high-dimensional phase space features for EEG emotion recognition. SIViP **17**(2), 417–425 (2023)
18. Samanta, K., Chatterjee, S., Bose, R.: Cross-subject motor imagery tasks EEG signal classification employing multiplex weighted visibility graph and deep feature extraction. IEEE Sensors Lett. **4**(1), 1–4 (2019)
19. Filho, S., Alberto, C., Attux, R., Castellano, G.: Can graph metrics be used for EEG-BCIs based on hand motor imagery? Biomed. Signal Process. Control **40**, 359–365 (2018)
20. Park, Y., Chung, W.: Frequency-optimized local region common spatial pattern approach for motor imagery classification. IEEE Trans. Neural Syst. Rehabil. Eng. **27**(7), 1378–1388 (2019)
21. Radüntz, T., et al.: "Automated EEG artifact elimination by applying machine learning algorithms to ICA-based features. J. Neural Eng. **14**(4), 046004 (2017)
22. Aydore, S., Pantazis, D., Leahy, R.M.: A note on the phase locking value and its properties. Neuroimage **74**, 231–244 (2013)
23. Ismail, L.E., Karwowski, W.: A graph theory-based modeling of functional brain connectivity based on eeg: a systematic review in the context of neuroergonomics. IEEE Access **8**, 155103–155135 (2020)
24. Sun, S., et al.: Graph theory analysis of functional connectivity in major depression disorder with high-density resting state EEG data. IEEE Trans. Neural Syst. Rehabil. Eng. **27**(3), 429–439 (2019)
25. Kılıç, B., Aydın, S.: Classification of contrasting discrete emotional states indicated by EEG based graph theoretical network measures. Neuroinformatics **20**, 1–15 (2022)
26. Demuru, M., et al.: A comparison between power spectral density and network metrics: an EEG study. Biomed. Signal Process. Control **57**, 101760 (2020)
27. Chen, P.: Effects of the entropy weight on TOPSIS. Expert Syst. Appl. **168**(8), 114186 (2020)
28. Ma, Y., et al.: Nonlinear dynamical analysis of sleep electroencephalography using fractal and entropy approaches. Sleep Med. Rev. **37**, 85–93 (2018)
29. Muhammet, G.Ü.L.: A quantitative occupational risk assessment methodology based on TOPSIS-Sort with its application in aluminum extrusion industry. Int. J. Pure Appl. Sci. **7**(1), 163–172 (2021)

Fuzzy Variable Admittance Control-Based End Compliance Control of Puncture Ablation Robot

Yong Tao[1,2](✉), Dongming Han[1], Tianmiao Wang[1], Yufan Zhang[3], He Gao[2], and Jiahao Wan[3]

[1] School of Mechanical Engineering and Automation, Beihang University, Beijing 100191, China
taoy@buaa.edu.cn
[2] Research Institute of Aero-Engine, Beihang University, Beijing 102206, China
[3] School of Large Aircraft Engineering, Beihang University, Beijing 100191, China

Abstract. In the process of remote operation minimally invasive puncture microwave ablation surgery, due to the regular breathing ups and downs of the human chest cavity, it is easy to cause tearing of human tissue near the rigid needle. In order to avoid secondary damage to surrounding living tissues caused by relative movement between the puncture needle and chest skin, we developed a respiratory motion-adaptive robotic end-effector admittance control method for patients undergoing puncture ablation surgery. This method is based on a collaborative robot and incorporates both admittance control and fuzzy control. By continuously monitoring the contact force and velocity at the end-effector, the method dynamically adjusts the admittance parameters through a fuzzy control algorithm. This ensures smoother, more stable and controlled motion of the end-effector, achieving a compliant and force-free motion adaptation. This method can achieve zero-force follow-up of 0.8 N in our physical breathing simulation platform. In addition, on our constructed respiratory simulation platform, we conducted three sets of experiments: rigid stationary end, constant admittance parameters end movement, and variable admittance parameters end movement. These experiments were aimed at validating the superior zero-force tracking characteristics of our designed variable admittance control algorithm. The algorithm demonstrates great clinical applicability as it effectively avoids secondary injuries that patients may encounter during surgery.

Keywords: Puncture ablation surgery · zero-force · variable admittance control

1 Introduction

With the increasing incidence and mortality rates of malignant tumors and cancer in recent years, malignant tumors have become one of the most serious diseases threatening human life and health security. The American Cancer Society's Clinical Oncology Journal predicts that in 2023, the United States will diagnose 1.96 million cases of invasive cancer, an increase from 1.92 million cases in 2022, equivalent to approximately 5,370 new cases per day [1]. The large number of cases has led to a growing demand for minimally invasive percutaneous microwave ablation surgery.

© The Author(s), under exclusive license to Springer Nature Singapore Pte Ltd. 2023
H. Yang et al. (Eds.): ICIRA 2023, LNAI 14272, pp. 527–540, 2023.
https://doi.org/10.1007/978-981-99-6480-2_44

Minimally invasive microwave ablation surgery is a type of minimally invasive procedure that offers advantages such as minimal trauma, minimal bleeding, and fast recovery. In recent years, it has been widely used in the treatment of various solid tumors [2, 3]. However, due to the inevitable respiratory motion of the human body during puncture surgery, especially in the remote puncture scenario in a radiative environment, the lack of an accurate respiratory motion compensation system often requires multiple punctures to reach the lesion site, greatly affecting the surgical incision range and puncture time [4, 5].

In recent years, many research institutions have gradually started using robots to replace physicians in performing remote puncture operations in a radiographic CT environment, and have conducted a series of related studies on the smooth operation of the robotic arm and respiratory compensation during the surgery. For example, Dimeas et al. proposed a human-machine cooperative task admittance control method that combines humanoid decision-making processes with adaptive algorithms in 2014 [6]. Du Zhijiang et al. proposed a hybrid admittance model based on fuzzy Sarsa(a) learning. By changing the virtual damping response to the operator's intention, the robot can follow the operator's intention with zero force, and it was applied to the positioning operation of surgical robots [7]. Grafakos et al. designed a variable admittance controller by monitoring the surface electromechanical signals of the operators [8]. Sharkawy et al. proposed a variable admittance control method in human-machine cooperation based on a multi-layer feedforward neural network and performed online correction of the virtual damping of the admittance controller. [9]. Mohamed Esmail Karar used fuzzy control and variable parameter PID algorithm to design a robot controller for adaptive ultrasound imaging during liver surgery and conducted related simulations, but it lacks practical validation through physical experiments [10]. Gilles P. proposed a practical and cost-effective unidirectional respiratory motion compensation method and conducted tracking experiments using an inline ultrasound imaging probe in ex vivo tissues [11]. Hongbing Li et al. proposed a new position-based force-to-motion controller with amplified force feedback, which can provide enhanced force perception to the operator when inserting a needle into soft tissue [12]. Rongqian Yang et al. designed a respiratory compensation control method based on an optical tracking system and the admittance control of the robot [13, 14], and verified it on their respiratory simulation platform, achieving a certain degree of tracking. However, the overall system is overly complex, and its reliability needs to be further studied.

Based on years of research on admittance control of robotic arms, our team proposes a variable admittance control algorithm based on fuzzy control, which enables the robot to achieve smoother and more stable zero-force motion, thereby better protecting patients. First, we design an actuator for the robot endoscopic needle with a telescopic function, and equip the end of the actuator with a six-axis force sensor to obtain real-time contact force between the puncture needle and the skin. Then, we design a dynamic six-axis force end effector real-time gravity compensation algorithm to accurately obtain the contact force of the robot under different postures. Based on the contact force and the real-time velocity of the robot end, we establish a variable admittance controller based on fuzzy control to generate appropriate admittance control parameters for the robot according to different force and velocity conditions, achieving better zero-force motion tracking. Finally, our robot can achieve zero-force motion below a threshold of 0.8 N, which provides better adaptability and stability compared to traditional fixed admittance zero-force motion.

The organization of this research is as follows: Sect. 2 describes the overall framework of the proposed variable admittance control method, including the real-time gravity compensation algorithm for the six-axis force sensor and the fuzzy control-based variable admittance parameter method. Section 3 introduces the experimental methods and reports the experimental results. Section 4 summarizes this study.

2 Variable Admittance Control Method

2.1 System Composition and Algorithm Framework

The percutaneous ablation surgery platform mainly consists of a puncture robot and a visual navigation system (Fig. 1(a)). The zero-force respiratory motion control algorithm for the robot end of the percutaneous ablation surgery is primarily designed based on the six-axis force sensor and the variable admittance control strategy of the robotic arm (Fig. 1(b)). The puncture surgery robot perceives the respiratory interaction force between the puncture needle at the robot end and the patient through the six-axis force sensor. The force is then compensated for by the sensor's gravity compensation algorithm and coordinate normalization processing, enabling the robot's admittance controller to obtain accurate user contact force. Subsequently, the processed contact force and the robot's velocity information are transmitted to the variable admittance parameter identification algorithm based on fuzzy control algorithm, which determines the appropriate admittance control parameters. Finally, the calculated admittance parameters and interaction force vector information are transmitted to the robot's variable admittance controller, driving the robot to achieve corresponding displacement motion, thereby enabling the robot to achieve smooth zero-force motion.

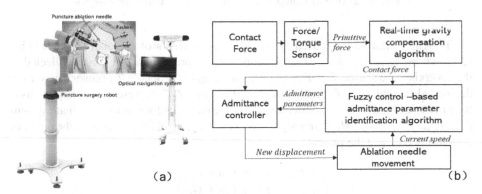

Fig. 1. (a) Puncture Robotic System (b) Variable Admittance Based on Fuzzy Control

The variable admittance control method designed in this research mainly consists of an real-time gravity compensation algorithm for the robot end and a fuzzy control-based admittance parameter identification algorithm. It is also the main innovation of the entire study. We will introduce the specific design and derivation process of these two algorithms in Sects. 2.2 and 2.3, respectively.

2.2 Real-Time Gravity Compensation Algorithm

Due to the presence of a puncture ablation needle gripper at the end of the robot, when the robot end is in different postures, the weight of the gripper and the puncture ablation needle itself will exert a force on the six-axis force sensor. This force causes the six-axis force sensor to collect not only the contact force between the ablation needle and the user but also includes the component of the gripper's gravity and the calibrated zero force during sensor calibration. To eliminate the influence of the gripping force gravity component and the calibrated zero force, we have designed an adaptive real-time dynamic compensation gravity compensation algorithm, as shown in Fig. 2(a) The derivation of the main formulas is as follows.

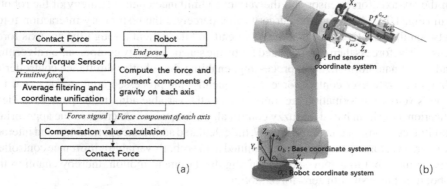

Fig. 2. (a) Gravity Compensation Algorithm (b) End force analysis

The force information sensed by the end-effector sensor of the robot is shown in Eq. (2.1), where F_{x_r}, F_{y_r}, F_{z_r}, M_{x_r}, M_{y_r} and M_{z_r} represent the raw forces collected by the six-axis force sensor. F_{x0}, F_{y0}, F_{z0} M_{x0}, M_{y0}, and M_{z0} denote the sensor's zero force during calibration. G_{x_s}, G_{y_s}, G_{z_s}, M_{gx_s}, M_{gy_s} and M_{gz_s} represent the components of the gravity exerted by the end-effector load in the end-effector sensor coordinate system. f_{x_in}, f_{y_in}, f_{z_in}, M_{x_in}, M_{y_in} and M_{z_in} represent the contact forces between the puncture ablation needle and the patient.

$$\begin{cases} F_{x_r} = f_{x_{in}} + F_{x0} + G_{x_s} \\ F_{y_r} = f_{y_{in}} + F_{y0} + G_{y_s} \\ F_{z_r} = f_{z_{in}} + F_{z0} + G_{z_s} \\ M_{x_r} = M_{x_{in}} + M_{x0} + M_{gx_s} \\ M_{y_r} = M_{y_{in}} + M_{y0} + M_{gy_s} \\ M_{z_r} = M_{z_{in}} + M_{z0} + M_{gz_s} \end{cases} \quad (2.1)$$

The formula that describes the relationship between the torque generated by gravity and the coordinates of the center of gravity, as shown in Eq. (2.2), is as follows:

$$\begin{cases} M_{gx_s} = G_{z_s} \times y - G_{y_s} \times z \\ M_{gy_s} = G_{x_s} \times z - G_{z_s} \times x \\ M_{gz_s} = G_{y_s} \times x - G_{x_s} \times y \end{cases} \tag{2.2}$$

In the equation, x, y and z respectively denote the coordinates of the center of gravity of the end effector in the end effector coordinate system. When the end effector is not in a working state, that is, $f_{x\_in}, f_{y\_in}, f_{z\_in}, M_{x\_in}, M_{y\_in}, M_{z\_in}$ are all equal to 0, the relationship between $M_{x_r}, M_{y_r}, F_{x_r}$ and the center of gravity coordinates $P(x, y, z)$ can be obtained. (where i, j = 1, 2, 3...).

$$\begin{cases} M_{x_r} = F_{z_r} \times y - F_{y_r} \times z + F_{x0} \times z - F_{z0} \times y + M_{x0} \\ M_{y_r} = F_{x_r} \times y - F_{z_r} \times x + F_{z0} \times x - F_{x0} \times z + M_{y0} \\ M_{z_r} = F_{y_r} \times x - F_{x_r} \times y + F_{y0} \times y - F_{y0} \times x + M_{z0} \end{cases} \tag{2.3}$$

In Fig. 2(b), let the world coordinate system be denoted as $O_b - X_b Y_b Z_b$, the robot's base coordinate system as $O_r - X_r Y_r Z_r$, and the coordinate system of the robot's end-effector six-axis force sensor as $O_s - X_s Y_s Z_s$. The coordinate transformation $^r_s R$ between $O_r - X_r Y_r Z_r$ and $O_s - X_s Y_s Z_s$ can be obtained from the robot controller. The origin O_b of the world coordinate system is defined to coincide with the origin O_r of the robot's base coordinate system. Therefore, $O_r - X_r Y_r Z_r$ can be obtained by rotating the $O_b - X_b Y_b Z_b$ coordinate system around the X_b axis by angle U and then around the Y_b axis by angle V. The transformation matrix from $O_b - X_b Y_b Z_b$ to O_r-$O_r - X_r Y_r Z_r$ can be denoted as:

$$^b_r R = \begin{bmatrix} 1 & 0 & 0 \\ 0 & \cos U & -\sin U \\ 0 & \sin U & \cos U \end{bmatrix} \cdot \begin{bmatrix} \cos V & 0 & \sin V \\ 0 & 1 & 0 \\ -\sin V & 0 & \cos V \end{bmatrix} \tag{2.4}$$

Afterwards, by collecting the end effector pose information and the raw readings from the sensor in three different orientations, we can establish a system of equations based on the relationship between torque and the force components along each axis, as well as Eq. (2.3). This will allow us to solve for the coordinates of the center of gravity of the end effector's load. Next, by considering the relationship between the force readings along each axis and the pose of the end effector with respect to the robot's base coordinate system, we can determine the gravitational force components acting on the end effector's load along the X_r, Y_r and Z_r axes in the robot's base coordinate system, as well as the calibrated zero forces on the sensor's axes. At this point, we have the coordinates of F_{x0}, F_{x0}, F_{x0} and the center of gravity (x, y, z), which allows us to calculate M_{x0}, M_{x0} and M_{x0}. Furthermore, the angle between the gravity vector G and the orientation of the robot's base coordinate system with respect to the world coordinate system can be determined using Eqs. (2.5) and (2.6).

$$G = \sqrt[2]{G^2_{x_r} + G^2_{y_r} + G^2_{z_r}} \tag{2.5}$$

$$\begin{cases} U = \arcsin\left(-\dfrac{G_{ry}}{G}\right) \\ V = \arctan\left(-\dfrac{G_{rx}}{G_{rz}}\right) \end{cases} \tag{2.6}$$

Based on Eqs. (2.2) and (2.3), by obtaining the real-time attitude transformation matrix ${}^r_s R$ between the robot coordinate system and the end effector coordinate system, it is possible to calculate the real-time gravitational force components and the torque generated by gravity. By applying Eq. (2.1), the actual interactive forces at the end effector can be calculated. This enables real-time gravity compensation for the end effector load.

2.3 Fuzzy Control-Based Variable Admittance Controller

In the admittance control process of traditional robots, it is usually composed of a constant admittance controller, and it is very easy to produce interactive imbalance, stuttering or even oscillation in the actual interaction process [15, 16]. In order to be able to judge the motion intention in real time according to the force of the robot and the motion of the robot, so as to achieve the corresponding zero-force follow-up effect. According to the force of the puncture ablation needle during the operation, combined with the fuzzy control algorithm, we designed a set of variable admittance controllers with follow-up intention recognition algorithm. The specific establishment process is as follows:

(A) Admittance Controller

The force model during the contact between the puncture needle and the human body is relatively complex. At present, most studies are analyzed based on the three-element muscle structural mechanics model proposed by Hill et al. [17]. The three elements of the muscle mathematical model are contraction element (CE), Series Elastic Elements (SEE) and Parallel Elastic Elements (PEE), however, the specific parameters of these elements are often nonlinear, and the changes are very complicated, so it is difficult to establish an accurate quantitative mathematical model. Here we simplify the force at the needle as an interactive object of complex force, and the robot end as a spring-damper model, as shown in Fig. 3. According to the admittance control model, the force at the end of the robot has the following model:

$$F_p^t = m\ddot{x}_p^t + c\dot{x}_p^t + kx_p^t \tag{2.7}$$

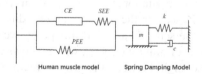

Human muscle model   Spring Damping Model

Fig. 3. Mathematical model of force at the end

In the equation, m, c and k represent virtual mass, virtual damping, and virtual stiffness, respectively. $F_p^t, \ddot{x}_p^t, \dot{x}_p^t$ and x_p^t respectively denote the interaction force, acceleration, velocity, and displacement of the robot's end effector at time t. Similarly, for rotational torque, we have:

$$M_p^t = J\ddot{\theta}_p^t + b\dot{\theta}_p^t + l\theta_p^t \tag{2.8}$$

In the equation, J, b and l represent virtual moment of inertia, rotational damping coefficient, and rotational stiffness, respectively. M_p^t, $\ddot{\theta}_p^t$, $\dot{\theta}_p^t$ and θ_p^t respectively denote the torque, angular acceleration, angular velocity, and angular displacement experienced by the robot's end effector at time t. Due to:

$$\dot{x}_p^t = \frac{x_p^t - x_p^{t-1}}{\Delta t}, \ddot{x}_p^t = \frac{2\left(x_p^{t+1} + x_p^{t-1} - 2x_p^t\right)}{(\Delta t)^2}, \dot{\theta}_p^t = \frac{\theta_p^t - \theta_p^{t-1}}{\Delta t}, \ddot{\theta}_p^t = \frac{2\left(\theta_p^{t+1} + \theta_p^{t-1} - 2\theta_p^t\right)}{(\Delta t)^2}.$$

In the equation, Δt represents the time interval for obtaining the encoder position information. x_p^{t-1} and θ_p^{t-1} represent the displacement and angular displacement of the robot's end effector at time $t-1$, respectively. x_p^{t+1} and θ_p^{t+1} represent the desired displacement of the robot's end effector at time $t+1$.

In practical robot control, the control objective is to determine the new desired displacement increment and angular increment for each control cycle. We can express the velocity and acceleration in the equation in terms of these new values:

$$F_p^t = \frac{2m\left(x_p^{t+1} + x_p^{t-1} - 2x_p^t\right)}{(\Delta t)^2} + \frac{c\left(x_p^t - x_p^{t-1}\right)}{\Delta t} + kx_p^t \tag{2.9}$$

$$M_p^t = \frac{2J\left(\theta_p^{t+1} + \theta_p^{t-1} - 2\theta_p^t\right)}{(\Delta t)^2} + \frac{b\left(\theta_p^t - \theta_p^{t-1}\right)}{\Delta t} + l\theta_p^t \tag{2.10}$$

Since the desired behavior for the robot is to achieve end-effector zero-force tracking, which means the ideal stiffness coefficients k and l are both zero. The desired displacement command for actual robot control x_p^{t+1} and the desired angular displacement command θ_p^{t+1} arc as follows:

$$x_p^{t+1} = 2x_p^t - x_p^{t-1} + \frac{F_p^t(\Delta t)^2 - c\Delta t\left(x_p^t - x_p^{t-1}\right)}{2m} \tag{2.11}$$

$$\theta_p^{t+1} = 2\theta_p^t - \theta_p^{t-1} + \frac{M_p^t(\Delta t)^2 - b\Delta t\left(\theta_p^t - \theta_p^{t-1}\right)}{2J} \tag{2.12}$$

By utilizing the control interface of the robot controller and obtaining real-time end effector displacement x_p^t and angular displacement θ_p^t, you can calculate the corresponding desired displacement and angular displacement using the above formulas. Therefore, the robot can be controlled by providing these desired values to the controller.

(B) Fuzzy Control Based-Admittance Control.

Due to the relatively complex physical model of the interacting object, it is difficult to describe it accurately using a quantified model. In this paper, fuzzy control is employed to address the problem of adjusting the admittance parameters in the absence of a known model. The admittance controllers for each axis of the robot are decoupled, allowing independent adjustment of the admittance parameters along each axis. For fuzzy variable admittance control in any given dimension, the inference process is illustrated in Fig. 4(a).

The inputs to the fuzzy system are the user force F_p^t measured along a single direction and the robot velocity $\dot{x}_p^t$. The output is the virtual damping c of the robot's admittance controller.

First, establish the corresponding membership function for the precise user force F_p^t and robot speed $\dot{x}_p^t$, and fuzzify it to obtain the input variables F_p^t and $\dot{x}_p^t$ of the fuzzy inference engine. In F_p^t, set the F_p^t discrete domain to $\{-50, -20, -10, -3, 3, 10, 20, 50\}$, and the language description is: {NB(Negative big), NM(Negative medium), NS(Negative small), NZ(Negative Zero), PZ(Positive Zero), PS(Positive small), PM(Positive medium), PB(Positive big)}, set the discrete domain of $\dot{x}_p^t$ to $\{-3, -2, -1, 1, 2, 3\}$, the language description is: {NB(Negative big), NM(Negative medium), NS(Negative small), PS(Positive small), PM(Positive medium), PB(Positive big)}. Then define the output variable of the inference engine as c, set its discrete domain as $\{1, 2, 3, 4, 5\}$, and describe the language as: {Min(Minimum), VS(Very small), S(Small), M(Medium), B(Big)}. And design reasoning rules according to common experience, generate fuzzy control table, as shown in Table 1.

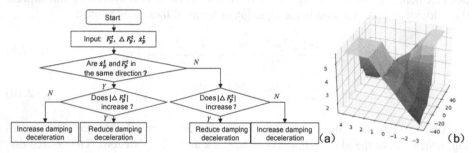

Fig. 4. (a) Fuzzy control inference rules (b) Fuzzy control surface plot

Table 1. Fuzzy Control Table

		F_p^t(N)							
c		NB	NM	NS	NZ	PZ	PS	PM	PB
		[-50,-20]	[-20,-10]	[-10,-3]	[-3,-0]	[0,3]	[3,10]	[10,20]	[20,50]
	NB [-3, -2]	Min	VS	S	S	Max	Max	Max	Max
	NM [-2, -1]	VS	VS	S	M	Max	Max	Max	Max
$\dot{x}_p^t$	NS [-1,0]	S	S	M	B	Max	Max	Max	Max
(mm/s)	PS [0,1]	Max	Max	Max	Max	B	M	S	S
	PM [1,2]	Max	Max	Max	Max	M	S	VS	VS
	PB [2,3]	Max	Max	Max	Max	S	S	VS	Min

The relationship between the input variables F_p^t, $\dot{x}_p^t$, and the output variable c defines the three-dimensional surface distribution of the fuzzy inference rules, as shown in Fig. 4(b). To meet the real-time requirements, the inference engine of the system obtains the fuzzy variable c through table lookup. Finally, the centroid method is used to defuzzify the fuzzy variable c, obtaining the precise value of the virtual damping coefficient c.

To ensure fast system response, the virtual mass m is adjusted in real-time using the same coefficient method to achieve the same mass-damping ratio. The calculation relationship is shown in Eq. (2.13):

$$m(t_i) = \frac{m_0}{c_0} c(t_i) \tag{2.13}$$

In the equation, $m(t_i)$ and $c(t_i)$ represent the virtual mass and virtual damping at time t, where $i = 1, 2, ..., 6$. By passing the precise values of $m(t_i)$ and $c(t_i)$ to the admittance controller, the fuzzy online adjustment of the admittance parameters is achieved in the absence of an exact mathematical model. The same method applies to the adjustment of the virtual moment of inertia and virtual rotational damping coefficient for torque.

3   Experiment and Result

3.1   Experimental Platform and Breathing Simulation Model

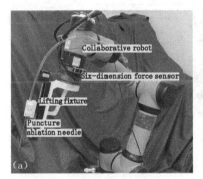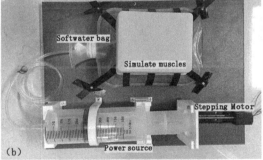

Fig. 5. (a) Composition of the execution end of the puncture robot (b) Composition of a respiratory simulation platform

As shown in Fig. 5(a), the hardware platform for the robot end-effector variable admittance control method developed in this study consists of an AUBO i5 robot and a BlueDot Touch ST-6-200-10 six-axis force sensor. The AUBO i5 robotic arm can achieve a repeatability of 0.0 2mm and a sampling frequency of 250 Hz. The BlueDot Touch ST-6-200-10 six-axis force sensor can achieve a sampling frequency of up to 1000 Hz, with force resolution of 0.2 N and torque resolution of 0.005 Nm, meeting the experimental requirements. The ablation needle is mounted on the ablation needle telescopic frame we designed, and the telescopic frame is driven by a stepper motor, which can achieve a control accuracy of 0.1 m/s. Additionally, we have built a simulation platform that mimics the thoracic breathing of the human body using a hot water bag and biomimetic muscles (Fig. 5(b)). The design of the platform refers to the work of Yang Rongqian et al. [13]. The platform can simulate chest oscillation with a range of 0–2 cm and achieve one complete maximum chest oscillation. The oscillation frequency can range from 0 to 30 cycles per minute. For specific respiratory parameter models, please refer to Section (A) of this chapter.

(A) Construction of the Breathing Model.

The organ movement caused by the human breathing movement is different from the freely designed and determined movement. The complex biomechanical properties of the human body will randomize the process, thereby changing the cycle and amplitude of breathing. In this paper, it is assumed that the period and amplitude of the respiratory model motion are stable, and it can be parameterized, and the mathematical model describing this respiratory motion is obtained as [18, 19].

The image of the mathematical model is shown in Fig. 6(a), which conforms to the characteristics of asymmetric periodic breathing. And it has been reproduced in the simulation model we designed in Fig. 6(b). The frequency and number of pulses sent to the stepper driver are controlled by Arduino, thereby changing the range of motion, speed and acceleration of the stepper motor, and controlling the number of pulses propelled into the hot water bag.

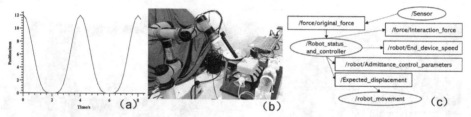

Fig. 6. (a) Position-time diagram of the breathing driver (b) Experimental procedure diagram (c) Robotic nodes diagram

(B) Software Algorithm Framework.

The experimental platform uses ubuntu 20.04 and ROS neotic operating system as the platform to build the algorithm verification platform. Its core Ros node is shown in Fig. 6(c). In the figure, the node "/Sensor" is used to obtain the original force information of the six-dimensional force sensor, and publish the obtained force information through the topic "/force/original_force". The node "/Robot_status_and_controller" is the core of the controller designed by this research institute. It is not only responsible for obtaining the real-time status information of the robot, but also has the function of gravity compensation, and passes the calculated force into the variable admittance controller to obtain the corresponding calculation. Expected displacement. The node "/robot_movement" is responsible for the realization of the robot's motion. By receiving the "/Expected_displacement" topic message, it drives the robot to perform corresponding movements, thereby realizing the corresponding zero-force follow-up. In particular, for this experimental platform, the system sampling period is set to $\Delta t = 1/240$ s in the actual collaborative robot control, that is, the working frequency is 240 Hz.

3.2 Algorithm Verification

(A) Real-Time Gravity Compensation for Six-Axis Force Has the Following Effects
The experiments involved collecting force data from three sets of six-axis force sensors under different orientations. The collected values are shown in Table 2. The corresponding center of gravity coordinates, gravity values, and zero-force values of the sensors were decoupled and are presented in Table 3.

Table 2. The posture of the robot's end effector and the corresponding sensor readings

$\gamma/°$	$\beta/°$	$\alpha/°$	F_x/N	F_y/N	F_z/N	M_x/Nm	M_y/Nm	M_z/Nm
90	0	-180	-0.0077293	0.03326037	0.0147029205	0.001079375	-0.000974825	-0.00022617
90	0	90	-7.13724845	-0.0606918	-6.79612453	-0.3686252	-0.5096709	0.3600089
90	-90	0	0.0902997	-7.1146777	-7.084782296	0.2066474	0.0675725	-0.07679

The variables α, β, and γ represent the angular rotation angles of the end-effector sensor coordinate system with respect to the robot base coordinate system around the x, y, and z axes, respectively. F_x, F_y, F_z, M_x, M_y and M_z represent the raw forces measured by the six-axis force sensor. By inputting the aforementioned data into the gravity compensation algorithm described in Sect. 2.2, the corresponding end-effector gravity compensation data can be obtained.

Table 3. Sensor zero force and end effector load gravity data

	f_{x0}	f_{y0}	f_{z0}	m_{x0}	m_{y0}	m_{z0}
Sensor zero force	0.045 N	−0.55 N	−6.750 N	−0.346 Nm	−0.0101 Nm	0.0093 Nm
	G_{r_x}	G_{r_y}	G_{r_z}	x	y	z
Gravitational force components and center of gravity	0.0499 N	−0.55 N	−6.7501 N	0.0029 mm	5.2419 mm	77.7974 mm

By applying the aforementioned data to the gravity compensation algorithm and placing the sensor end in different postures, the effect of robot gravity compensation can be observed (Fig. 7(a)). The upper part of Fig. 7(b) displays the sensor readings before gravity compensation, indicating significant force components in the Y-axis and Z-axis directions. With the readings after gravity compensation shown in the lower part of Fig. 7(b), the system can accurately capture the user-applied force. To ensure operational stability, based on the compensation effect, we set the activation threshold for interaction to 0.8 N.

(B) Zero Force Follow-Up Experiment and Results.
By applying the same driving force to the simulation platform, with the driving parameters described in section (A) of this chapter, we collected three sets of data with the

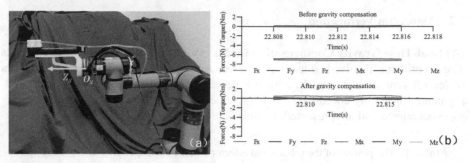

Fig. 7. (a) One posture of robot end effector offset (b) Readings before and after sensor gravity compensation

robot end-effector in a static state. As shown in Fig. 8(a), in the purely static state of the end-effector, the skin experiences a maximum interactive force of 7 N, and it exhibits periodic changes in conjunction with the respiratory fluctuation during exhalation.

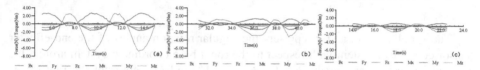

Fig. 8. (a) Force during end stationary state. (b) Constant admittance end movement force (c) Variable admittance end movement force

After enabling conventional fixed-parameter admittance control at the end-effector, the interactive force noticeably decreases (Fig. 8(b)). However, its periodicity becomes inconsistent and disrupted compared to the respiratory cycle. The fluctuation of the interactive force becomes unstable, exhibiting unpredictable variations of magnitude over time.

When our variable admittance controller is enabled (Fig. 8(c)), it is evident that the maximum force decreases to below 1.2 N. Additionally, the fluctuation exhibits a more pronounced periodicity that closely resembles the respiratory cycle imposed by the simulated device.

Based on the three experiments conducted on the respiratory simulation platform, the results clearly indicate that without respiratory motion compensation, the contact force between the chest cavity and the ablation needle can reach up to 7 N, posing a significant risk of secondary injury. When employing zero-force haptic-assisted ablation surgery with fixed admittance control, the contact force noticeably decreases, achieving real-time zero-force tracking below 3.5 N. However, based on the experimental data, it is evident that there are periodic disturbances and abrupt changes in the compensation force during the tracking process, posing considerable risks of instability and potential loss of control.

In comparison to the stationary end effector and the fixed admittance-controlled end effector, our designed variable admittance control algorithm demonstrates excellent performance in achieving zero-force tracking. It effectively tracks the respiratory cycle, exhibiting a smooth tracking effect. Moreover, the peak contact force can be well controlled below 1 N, almost achieving zero-force tracking below 0.8 N. Overall, the algorithm exhibits outstanding performance characteristics.

4 Conclusions

In summary, this study proposes a variable admittance control method based on fuzzy control, which enables the active following of thoracic motion during puncture abla- tion procedures, achieving zero-force tracking of the end-effector needle and effectively avoiding potential secondary injuries such as skin tearing. Additionally, a low-parameter dynamic real-time compensation algorithm for end-effector gravity compensation is designed, simplifying the gravity compensation process and significantly improving the adaptability of the force algorithm. The innovative integration of fuzzy control algorithm into admittance control allows for more sensitive and flexible adaptation to complex contact force variations during surgery, enhancing the robot's stability and flexibility compared to traditional admittance control methods. The research outcomes are partic- ularly clinically significant for puncture surgeries that require remote teleoperation in radiation environments.

Furthermore, the experiments were conducted using our designed thoracic simulation platform. However, further comparative verification is needed to confirm the similarity of the platform's thoracic motion to real human thoracic motion. Overall, this study achieves better zero-force tracking performance and stability compared to traditional end-effector static and fixed-admittance zero-force tracking control methods by proposing a flexible variable admittance control method for robotic puncture ablation procedures. It provides a reference for the development of related robots and inspires research in the field of compliant force control for orthopedic robots, dental robots, neurosurgical robots, and other domains.

References

1. Siegel, R.L., Miller, K.D., Wagle, N.S., Jemal, A.: Cancer statistics, 2023. CA: Cancer J. Clin. **73**(1), 17–48 (2023)
2. Zhao, Z., Wu, F.: Minimally-invasive thermal ablation of early-stage breast cancer: a systemic review. Eur. J. Surg. Oncol. **36**(12), 1149–1155 (2010)
3. Hou, X., Zhuang, X., Zhang, H., Wang, K., Zhang, Y.: Artificial pneumothorax: a safe and simple method to relieve pain during microwave ablation of subpleural lung malignancy. Minim. Invasive Ther. Allied Technol. **26**(4), 220–226 (2017)
4. Musa, M.J., Sharma, K., Cleary, K., Chen, Y.: Respiratory compensated robot for liver cancer treatment: design, fabrication, and benchtop characterization. IEEE/ASME Trans. Mechatron. **27**(1), 268–279 (2021)
5. Ernst, F., Dürichen, R., Schlaefer, A., Schweikard, A.: Evaluating and comparing algorithms for respiratory motion prediction. Phys. Med. Biol. **58**(11), 3911 (2013)
6. Dimeas, F., Aspragathos, N.: Fuzzy learning variable admittance control for human-robot cooperation. In: 2014 IEEE/RSJ International Conference on Intelligent Robots and Systems, pp. 4770–4775. IEEE (2014)

7. Du, Z., Wang, W., Yan, Z., Dong, W., Wang, W.: Variable admittance control based on fuzzy reinforcement learning for minimally invasive surgery manipulator. Sensors **17**(4), 844 (2017)
8. Grafakos, S., Dimeas, F., Aspragathos, N.: Variable admittance control in pHRI using EMG-based arm muscles co-activation. In: 2016 IEEE International Conference on Systems, Man, and Cybernetics (SMC), pp. 001900–001905. IEEE (2016)
9. Sharkawy, A.N., Koustournpardis, P.N., Aspragathos, N.: Variable admittance control for human-robot collaboration based on online neural network training. In: 2018 IEEE/RSJ International Conference on Intelligent Robots and Systems (IROS), pp. 1334–1339. IEEE (2018)
10. Karar, M.E.: A simulation study of adaptive force controller for medical robotic liver ultrasound guidance. Arab. J. Sci. Eng. **43**(8), 4229–4238 (2018)
11. Thomas, G.P., Khokhlova, T.D., Khokhlova, V.A.: Partial respiratory motion compensation for abdominal extracorporeal boiling histotripsy treatments with a robotic arm. IEEE Trans. Ultrason. Ferroelectr. Freq. Control **68**(9), 2861–2870 (2021)
12. Li, H., et al.: An admittance-controlled amplified force tracking scheme for collaborative lumbar puncture surgical robot system. Int. J. Med. Robot. Comput. Assist. Surg. **18**(5), e2428 (2022)
13. Zheng, L., Wu, H., Yang, L., Lao, Y., Lin, Q., Yang, R.: A novel respiratory follow-up robotic system for thoracic-abdominal puncture. IEEE Trans. Ind. Electron. **68**(3), 2368–2378 (2020)
14. Zhang, W., Bao, K., Zheng, L., Cai, L., Yan, B., Yang, R.: A robotic puncture system with optical and mechanical feedback under respiratory motion. Int. J. Med. Robot. Comput. Assist. Surg. **18**(4), e2403 (2022)
15. Ferraguti, F., et al.: An energy tank-based interactive control architecture for autonomous and teleoperated robotic surgery. IEEE Trans. Robot. **31**(5), 1073–1088 (2015)
16. Okunev, V., Nierhoff, T., Hirche, S.: Human-preference-based control design: adaptive robot admittance control for physical human-robot interaction. In: 2012 IEEE RO-MAN: The 21st IEEE International Symposium on Robot and Human Interactive Communication, pp. 443–448. IEEE (2012)
17. Davoodi, R., Brown, I.E., Loeb, G.E.: Advanced modeling environment for developing and testing FES control systems. Med. Eng. Phys. **25**(1), 3–9 (2003)
18. Ritchie, C.J., Hsieh, J., Gard, M.F., Godwin, J.D., Kim, Y., Crawford, C.R.: Predictive respiratory gating: a new method to reduce motion artifacts on CT scans. Radiology **190**(3), 847–852 (1994)
19. Sontag, M.R., Lai, Z.W., McRoy, B.W., Waters, R.D.: Characterization of respiratory motion for pedriatic conformal 3D therapy. Med. Phys. **23**, 1082 (1996)

Deep Forest Model Combined with Neural Networks for Finger Joint Continuous Angle Decoding

Hai Wang(iD) and Qing Tao(✉) (iD)

School of Mechanical Engineering, Xinjiang University, Urumqi 830017, China

Abstract. Many people lose their hand function due to stroke, traffic accidents, and amputation. This paper proposed a new method that can decode hand joint angles from the upper limb's surface electromyography (sEMG). It can be used for the next generation of prosthetic hands, and rehabilitation exoskeletons which will be beneficial for patients and amputees. We simultaneously collect hand joints' angles and sEMG signals by VICON and Noraxon systems. We combine a deep forest algorithm with an artificial neural network to design a comprehensive decoding model. Compared with the Gaussian Process model, its average correlation coefficient has improved by 42%, reaching 0.844. This method shows great potential in prosthetic hand and exoskeleton control. We have also carried out online experiments in which the online experiments achieved a completion rate of more than 90%, as well as a low latency, which is ideal for realistic online prosthetic control scenario applications.

Keywords: sEMG · deep forest · angle decoding · prosthetic hand

1 Introduction

With the rapid development of human-machine interface technology, the prosthetic hand has been more and more used in the amputee's daily life. Limbs, especially the hand burden a lot of daily work in our lives. So how to rebuild the function of the hand is a very hot research point in rehabilitation. High-performance sEMG prosthetic hands have been developed thanks to recent advancements in sEMG signal intention perception technology, which is unquestionably the gospel for amputees and disabled people [1]. The sEMG-controlled prosthesis's prototype system was developed by Reiter with success in 1948. The majority of sEMG prosthetic hand control at this time focuses primarily on the recognition of a few fixed actions. Fang et al. [2] proposed a bio-inspired neural network to recognize six wrist movements. A convolutional neural network was built by Yamanoi et al. [3] to produce an algorithm model with long-term recognition robustness. The current issue is that the sEMG-based prosthetic hand needs to be modified frequently. Through transfer learning, Ulysse et al. [4] realized that the machine learning algorithm training process required fewer data. By developing a novel convolution loop neural network with an attention mechanism, Yong et al. [5] achieved

© The Author(s), under exclusive license to Springer Nature Singapore Pte Ltd. 2023
H. Yang et al. (Eds.): ICIRA 2023, LNAI 14272, pp. 541–557, 2023.
https://doi.org/10.1007/978-981-99-6480-2_45

excellent gesture recognition. Be that as it may, signal acknowledgment by a grouping calculation will experience a quick decrease in acknowledgment exactness when the quantity of activities increments. As a result, we ought to come up with a novel strategy for deciphering the hands' continuous movements.

Many exploration bunches have utilized AI techniques to translate the persistent movements of hands by separating movement information from sEMG. As of now, a few specialists have made a few accomplishments moving congruity unraveling in light of sEMG signals. Xiong's group utilized the sparse Gaussian Process to plan the sEMG signs of 8 lower arm muscles to the points of 5 metacarpophalangeal joints of the fingers, and its online Pearson correlation coefficient can reach 0.91 [6]. By stacking long short-term neural networks, Chen et al. [7] were able to accurately recognize the continuous action angles of the joints in the upper limb. Using high-density sEMG signal acquisition equipment, Zhu's and Dario's teams [8] extracted the corresponding motor neuron action potential to provide a reliable signal source for high-performance intelligent prosthetic limb control. Ali et al. [9] first applied a convolutional neural network to the real-time decoding of wrist motion sEMG signals and reached the coefficient of determination of 0.99. By employing sparse nonnegative matrix decomposition, Lin et al. [10] were able to achieve continuous real-time control of hand motion. Ameri et al. [11] realized continuous online recognition of upper limb motion through a regression convolution neural network. Both Nielsen [12] and Mucelli [13] freely did simultaneous relative control tests given mirror balance preparation, acknowledging coordinated correspond-ing control of wrist joint force and point. Ngeo et al. [14] used the musculoskeletal model, input the eight channels of muscle activation into an artificial neural network, or used Gaussian processes to solve the problem. Their Pearson correlation coefficients can reach 0.71 and 0.84. Celadon and other others use high-density electrodes and the maxi-mum voluntary contraction force (MVC) to establish the mapping relationship between the sEMG signal and the proportional change in the finger joint angle. The linear dis-criminant analysis algorithm and the common space mode algorithm were the specific algorithms used. The two algorithms' combined effect can result in online control with a mean square error of less than 3.6% [15]. To obtain the decoded finger joint angle at this time, Michele et al. [16] used the Gaussian process method to input the last moment's decoded angle as well as this moment's sEMG and Mechanomyogram signal. The Pear-son correlation coefficient is about 0.6. Bao et al. [17] proposed a CNN-lstm model for consistent translating of wrist angle. The regression decoding of hand movements using a recurrent neural network was realized by Koch et al. [18]. The joint's angle and force were simultaneously decoded by Zhang et al. [19] using LSTM and ANN.

Our proposed approach has tested several deep forest models to decode the angle from sEMG in stores the issue of low precision in continuous dethe coding of finger joint angles based on sEMG signals. Additionally, we use an artificial neural network (ANN) to filter the decoding angle to lessen its vibration. Finger joint angles and sEMG signals were synchronously acquired using a customized experimental platform.

2 Methods

In this task, decoding the hand joint angle from the sEMG signal is the main aim. It is vital for high-performance prosthetic limbs. So we design a new experimental scheme to collect sEMG signals and motion data simultaneously. We use the VICON system and Noraxon system to realize this experiment plan. The acquisition frequency of the VICON system is 100 Hz and 2000 Hz for the Noraxon system. This model is verified by offline and online experiments.

2.1 Experimental Protocol

The human hand, including the wrist, has 28 bones, according to physiological research, each with 22 or 23 degrees of freedom. The joint activity produced by the palmar and forearm muscles is what causes the finger activity. The examination of available movement demonstrates that the level of opportunity of the hand is profoundly repetitive, and the movement inside the five fingers and between contiguous fingers has the extent of the second interphalangeal joint and the joint point with the third phalangeal joint which is 3:2. Due to the strong collaborative relationship between the three joint angles in the fingers during flexion and extension, only the metacarpophalangeal joint (MCP) angle is chosen as the regression estimation target for the movement of five fingers. The metacarpophalangeal joint angles of five fingers are depicted schematically in Fig. 1.

1.Thumb finger MCP

2.Index finger MCP

3.Middle finger MCP

4.Ring finger MCP

5.Ring finger MCP

Fig. 1. Schematic diagram of the angle of the metacarpophalangeal joint of the finger to be decoded

Parameter Setting
The experimental muscles (8 muscles in total) were abductor pollicis longus, flexor pollicis longus, flexor carpi radialis, flexor digitorum superficialis, flexor digitorum profundus, extensor digitorum, extensor digitorum and extensor carpi radialis. Figure 2 shows the position of the VICON markers of the finger joints and the sEMG signal acquisition position.

Experimental Procedures
In the experiment, the grasping action of three objects and the independent movement of fingers are included. Each movement is repeated 5 times, and each trial lasts for 2 min. Figure 3 shows the grasping objects in the experiment. Figure 4 shows the whole experimental scene of motion capture and EMG acquisition. We informed each subject

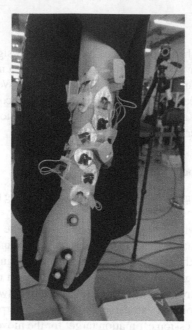

Fig. 2. Schematic diagram of sEMG signal acquisition points and VICON markers

to keep the wrist in the neutral position during the experiment, and use appropriate and stable force during grasping. Subjects were prompted to elicit contractions corresponding to the motions shown in Table 1. A 1 min rest was given between subsequent contractions. Subjects were instructed to perform contractions at a moderate and repeatable force level and given rest periods between trials to avoid fatigue. The average duration of the experiment was approximately 30 min per subject. Some subjects noted minor hand fatigue.

(a) pen   (b) water bottle   (c) Books

Fig. 3. Object for Grasping

Fig. 4. Experiment scene

Table 1. Summary of experimental stages

Stage	Movement	Description	Time of duration
S1	Single finger independent movement	Random free motion	5 * 2 min
S2	Grasping the pen	The natural movement of life	2 min
S3	Raising and lowering the wine glass	The natural movement of life	2 min
S4	Reading books	The natural movement of life	2 min

Model Parameter Acquisition Method

The control of the human hand by the sensory system is exceptionally intricate and complex. The complex coupling of mechanics and neuroscience makes it difficult to solve this problem, and the lack of artificial muscle makes it even more difficult. It is challenging to replicate some fundamental characteristics of human limbs, such as continuity, flexibility, anti-interference, and so on, because the control methods of artificial limbs at the moment are comparable to those of conventional robots. It is necessary to synchronously collect the finger joint angle and sEMG signals of the eight muscles of the forearm to establish a continuous mapping model between two kinds of information. Additionally, it is necessary to seek a regression mapping that can truly obtain the change information of the finger joint angle from the sEMG signal in real-time missions to establish this model.

Five healthy men aged 22 to 30 and five healthy women aged 23 to 26 made up the 10 subjects. The right hand is used by all subjects. The subjects had VICON markers placed on their right hands. And sEMG electrodes adhered to the right forearm by the eight muscles in the abdomen that had been previously selected. The related skin part was cleaned with alcohol ahead of time. An EVA foam support was placed at the volunteer's wrist and elbow, respectively, to prevent the electrode from coming into contact with the tabletop and the unstable extrusion from affecting the collection of sEMG signals. Their forearms were placed on the support platform by volunteers with the arm straight ahead and horizontally. The volunteers can properly move the support so that they can sit in the most comfortable position. The motivation behind this is to forestall the actuation of muscles that support the wrist, for example, the extensor carpi radialis, from influencing the recording of exploratory information. The Vicon motion capture system and the Noraxon sEMG acquisition system are used to collect the 8-channel sEMG signal data as well as the finger joint spatial coordinate data (Fig. 5).

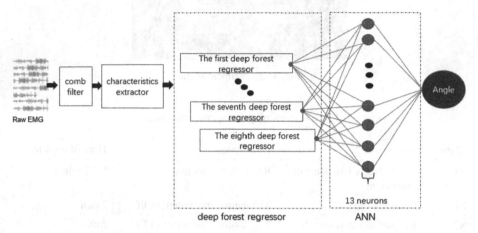

Fig. 5. Schematic diagram of comprehensive regression decoding model

Data Preprocessing

We should choose several features first. Because different features have different performances and different tasks. To realize a good effect on the angle decoding task, we use a random forest model to select the best sEMG feature set for this mission. Random Forest is an ensemble learning method based on a decision tree. It randomly samples multiple subsets on the data set, then constructs a decision tree for each subset, and finally integrates the results of multiple decision trees to get the final prediction result.

The method random forest calculates the importance of features is $n_k = \omega_k * G_k - \omega_{left} * G_{left} - \omega_{right} * G_{right}$, ω_k, ω_{left}, ω_{right} are the ratio of the number of samples in node k and its left and right child nodes to the total number of samples, G_k, G_{left}, G_{right} are the impurity of node k and its surrounding child nodes, it is the mean square error here. After calculating the importance of each node, the importance of each feature can be calculated by the formula (2.1).

$$f_i = \frac{\sum_{j \in nodes\_split\_on\_feature\_i} n_j}{\sum_{k \in all\_nodes} n_k} \tag{2.1}$$

To make the sum of importance e of all features equal to 1, the importance of each feature needs to be normalized, i.e., formula (2.2)

$$f_{i\_norm} = \frac{f_i}{\sum_{j \in all\_features} f_j} \tag{2.2}$$

Through the synchronized and continuous recording data set of finger joint angle and forearm sEMG signals that have been collected mentioned above, the random forest method can be used to further screen the preselected features. Through model training of each group of data, the data of three subjects were used for training. After the training of each set of data, the average value of the feature importance coefficient of five rounds was obtained. After all the data training of the three subjects was completed, the average value of all the feature importance coefficients was calculated to obtain the importance ranking and relevant values of the nine selected time-domain feature values, as shown in Fig. 6.

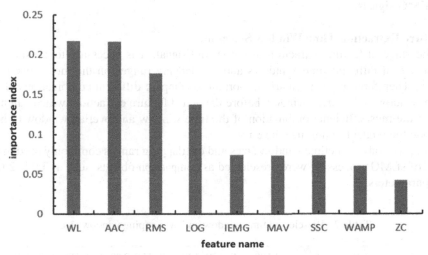

Fig. 6. Time domain features a ranking of nine preselected types and their importance coefficients

The significance of these sEMG features can be obtained by the random forest algorithm after the regression mapping of the hand joints' angle of the electromyographic signals collected in the experiment. To obtain the features hidden in the EMG signal to a large extent and ensure the real-time processing of the signal, the top eight sEMG features were selected as the data sources for subsequent model processing. It can be seen from Fig. 6 that the top eight are waveform length, mean absolute value change, root mean square error, sEMG pair value, integrated EMG value, mean absolute value, and positive and negative slope change of EMG respectively. These features will play a key role in the formal regression model.

The obtained sEMG data need to be filtered to eliminate the power frequency interference. Since China's power system uses a 50 Hz alternating frequency, this study uses a comb filter to filter the integer multiple frequencies of 50 Hz. The specific filtering frequencies are 50 Hz, 100 Hz, 150 Hz, 200 Hz, 250 Hz, 300 Hz, 350 Hz, and 400 Hz.

The change of the three-dimensional coordinates of the finger joint points collected by the VICON optical motion capture device can be transformed to the corresponding angle through the cosine formula in advance.

To extract representative information from the sEMG signals of 8 channels, it is necessary to extract different kinds of features from the sEMG signals after noise reduction. Here, a sliding time window with overlapping parts is used to calculate the features. Figure 6 shows the time window setting during EMG signal processing. The selected characteristics are all time-domain features, which are commonly used in the field of sEMG signals. Which are the mean absolute value, integral sEMG value, root mean square, waveform length, logarithmic characteristics, zero crossing points, slope sign changes, and Willison amplitude of sEMG signals are used to extract the characteristics of sEMG signals.

Feature Extraction Time Window Selection
In the stage of feature extraction of the sEMG signal, it is necessary to consider the influence of different time Windows and overlapping ranges on the model decoding effect. Therefore, it is particularly important to compare different combinations of the time window and overlap window before the actual feature extraction, which can help select the most efficient combination of the time window and overlap window to help decode the model to minimize the error.

In this study, sometime window sizes and overlapping ranges commonly used in the field of sEMG processing were preselected as comparison objects, such as Table 2 lists the parameters.

Table 2. Preselected time window and overlapping window size

Time window (ms)	100, 110, 120, 130, 140, 150, 160, 170, 180, 190, 200
Overlapping percentage (%)	10, 20, 30, 40, 50, 60, 70, 80, 90

Then random forest regression model is used as the basic model for comparative analysis, because the random forest algorithm, as a widely used machine learning algorithm, has the advantages of simple implementation, good effect, and high operating efficiency, which is very suitable for the selection of hyperparameters as a benchmark model.

In the specific training process, such as the screening process of the importance of characteristic values in the previous section, model training is conducted by using the method of 5-fold cross-validation for each group of data, and the data of three subjects are used for training. To improve the operating efficiency of the model, only the most important characteristic value selected in the previous section, namely, the length of the electromyographic waveform, is selected as the data source of the training model. Then, after the training of each set of data, the average value of five rounds of model decoding effect was obtained. The comparison index used here is the Pearson correlation coefficient.

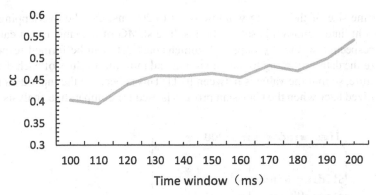

Fig. 7. Actual decoding performance with different time window sizes

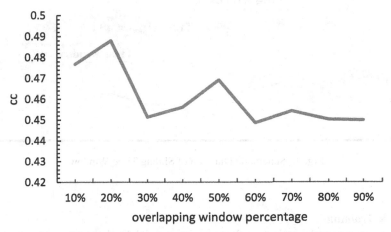

Fig. 8. Actual decoding performance with different overlapped window proportions

Figure 7 shows the actual decoding performance comparison of the selected time window. It can be seen from the figure that the best decoding effect can be achieved when the time window is 200 ms. Figure 8 shows the decoding effect of the model corresponding to different overlap ratios. It can be seen from the figure that the decoding effect is better than that on both sides when the overlap ratio is 50%. Although it can be seen in the figure that the decoding effect is better when the overlap ratio is 10% and 20%, because of the greater data processing demand in real-time control, 50% is chosen as the overlap ratio under the condition of balancing the decoding effect and data processing volume. In subsequent model sliding time window settings, a 200 ms time window size and 50% overlap ratio will be selected to run the decoding model at the optimal level for this task.

The time size of the sliding window is set to 200 ms, and the overlapping part of two adjacent time windows is set to 100 ms. The sEMG of 8 channels can calculate 8 features respectively, and 8 groups of 8-dimensional data can be formed respectively. Normalize the data according to the maximum and minimum values of each dimension of the feature, so that the value is between [0,1]. This is because the input data needs to be normalized later when the Gaussian process is used for comparative analysis (Fig. 9).

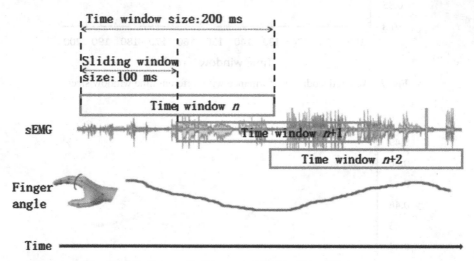

Fig. 9. Schematic Diagram of Sliding Time Window

Network Training

Eight features are used to train a single deep forest model. Each regressor has a three-layer deep forest structure following its adaptive layer construction algorithm. The model's efficiency of operation can be greatly enhanced with fewer layers. After recording the output angles of eight deep forest regressors, an eight-dimensional vector representing the output angles is given to the empirical formula-constructed neural network for further regression training.

The comprehensive regression model optimized with the 8-13-1 structure neural network can increase the correlation coefficient of the single deep forest regressor trained with 8 features by 12% points during the final effect test. Figure 10 shows the general preparation calculation of the whole model. In this study, the Gaussian process is chosen as the comparative model for comparative analysis. The sEMG of 8 channels can calculate 8 features respectively, and 8 groups of 8-dimensional data can be formed respectively. Ten-fold cross-validation is used in this research. After splitting the data into training subsets and test subsets, we normalize the data according to the maximum and minimum values of each dimension of the feature, so that the value is between [0,1]. This is because the input data needs to be normalized to speed up training and get a more accurate model.

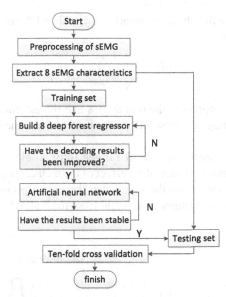

Fig. 10. Training Algorithm for Comprehensive Model Combining Depth Regression Forest and Artificial Neural Network

3 Results

In this paper, we proposed a new decoding model which combines the deep forest model and the ANN model. With the experimental results, we use CC (Pearson correlation coefficient) and RMSE (Root Mean Square Error) to validate the model's offline performance. And we use task completion time and success ratio to verify the model's online performance.

3.1 Offline Test

Performance Metrics
To measure the estimation error and the performance of the angle decoding algorithm, the motion CC and RMSE are used in this study.

$$\rho_{X,Y} = \frac{cov(X, Y)}{\sigma_X \sigma_Y} = \frac{E((X - \mu_X)(Y - \mu_Y))}{\sigma_X \sigma_Y} = \frac{E(XY) - E(X)E(Y)}{\sqrt{E(X^2) - E^2(X)}\sqrt{E(Y^2) - E^2(Y)}} \tag{3.1}$$

where X and Y respectively represent two groups of samples; Cov stands for covariance; E represents expectation; σ represents variance. When the value of ρ is greater than 0.7, the model is considered to have good regression performance. When $\rho = 1$, it means that the model output results are completely linear with the actual results. The reason for using CC is to judge the changing trend of the real and the estimated.

$$RMSE = \sqrt{\frac{1}{m} \sum_{i=1}^{m} (y_i - \hat{y})_i} \qquad (3.2)$$

where and respectively represent the real angles and the estimated angles. The reason for using RMSE is to judge the absolute error of the real and the estimated.

Continuous Estimation and Analysis of Finger Joint Angle

Figure 11 shows the continuous decoding effect of the metacarpophalangeal joint angles of 5 fingers. It can be seen from the figure that the model proposed in this study can accurately decode the actual finger joint angle from the 8 sEMG channel signals of the upper forearm.

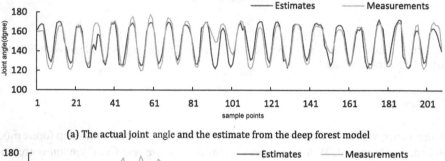

(a) The actual joint angle and the estimate from the deep forest model

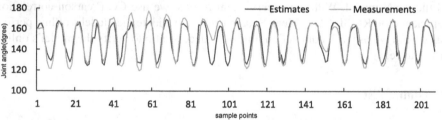

(b) The actual joint angle and the estimate from the comprehensive model combining deep forest and ANN

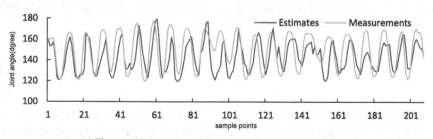

(c) The actual joint angle and the estimate from the GP model

Fig. 11. Comparison between decoding and actual value of metacarpophalangeal joint angles

In the process of analyzing the experimental data of 10 subjects, the analysis method of ten-fold cross-validation was used. Figure 12 shows the comparison of the average motion correlation coefficients of 10 subjects based on DRF, DRF + ANN, and GP methods. Figure 13 shows the comparison of the average correlation coefficients of five fingers based on DRF, DRF + ANN, and GP methods. Figure 14 shows the average coefficients of three grasping tasks based on DRF, DRF + ANN, and GP methods.

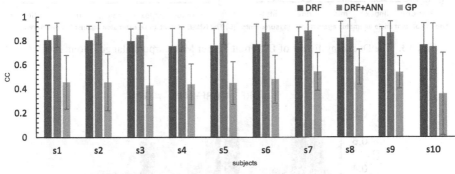

(a) The CC of different subjects' joint angle estimates against the measurements

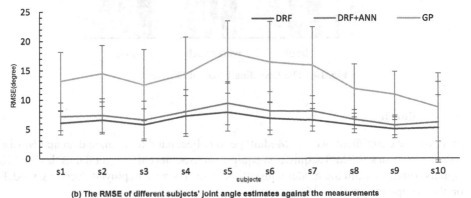

(b) The RMSE of different subjects' joint angle estimates against the measurements

Fig. 12. The Decoding Effect of Different Subjects

As can be seen from Fig. 12, for a group of 10 subjects, the deep regression forest model combined with an artificial neural network has the highest cc, with an average of 0.844, The average RMSE of DRF + ANN is 7.322 and the effect variance among subjects is 0.001378; The second is the single deep regression forest model with eight features, whose Pearson correlation coefficient is also very high, reaching 0.795476. The average RMSE of this model is 6.294277 and the variance is 0.000824. The correlation coefficients of these two models are more than 0.7, which indicates they both have excellent angle decoding performances. Compared with the Gaussian process method commonly used by some research groups in the world in recent years (the average correlation coefficient on this task is 0.473746, the average RMSE is 13.66, and the variance is 0.003845), the proposed method has great progress and strong individual adaptability. It has been verified from the variance that the algorithm model has strong robustness.

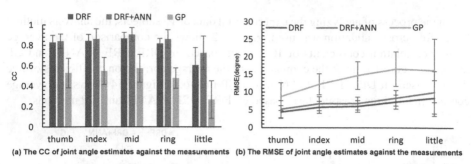

(a) The CC of joint angle estimates against the measurements (b) The RMSE of joint angle estimates against the measurements

Fig. 13. The Decoding Effect of Different Finger Metacarpophalangeal Joint Angles

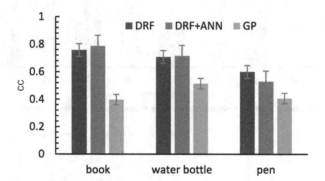

Fig. 14. The Decoding Effect of Different Tasks

3.2 Online Test

In an online experiment, we use MediaPipe to collect hand joint angle data and Biosignalsplux 8 channel sEMG acquisition equipment to achieve the target 8 muscles' sEMG signals. First, we train the model with offline data. Then we deployed decoding models on the computer side (Fig. 15).

Fig. 15. Use MediaPipe to get hand joints' angles

We tested the effectiveness of the online real-time decoding model by testing a single flexion-extension movement of several fingers and an overall coordinated grasping movement. These specific online test scenarios are shown in Fig. 16.

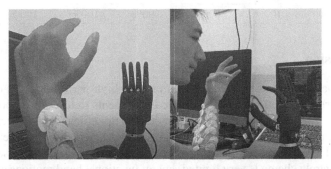

(a) Thumb Angle control   (b) Index finger Angle control

(c) Middle finger Angle control   (d) Ring finger Angle control

(e) Integral grip control

Fig. 16. Experiment scene diagram

In terms of control indicators, the two indicators of completion time and completion rate are mainly investigated, as shown in Table 3.

Time-consuming refers to the time required for each finger to complete one flexion and extension movement, and completion rate refers to the number of successful flexion and extension movements completed in ten tests.

Table 3. Each finger online affect the index

	Thumb	Index	Mid	Ring	Five-finger grip
Time (s)	8	5	7	8	7
Completion rate	100%	90%	90%	100%	100%

4 Discussion

We propose a new decoding model which can get high performance in online tasks. We have carried out both offline and online experiments to test our proposed model's performance. The results have shown the model's high efficiency and accuracy which present great potential for this model used in smart prosthetic hands in the future.

In related research on prosthetic hand control, most focus on hand gesture recognition. This control scheme is very limited., many functional hand motions are combined by different angles of different fingers. So the estimation ability of the fingers' angle is very meaningful for the control of a prosthetic hand.

Besides, the model is very simple, so it is easy to manipulate. We found deep forest model has only three layers in this task. It is very suitable for online usage because of its small size. The online model has a certain system delay of 100 ms because of the overlapping window. But this delay will be compensated due to the existence of electromechanical delay. The research's experimental protocol includes different objects we often use in our daily life. They can verify the proposed model's performance in a more practical mission for future applications in robotic hand control.

5 Conclusion

This work proposes a new comprehensive regression model combining deep regression forest algorithm and artificial neural network. (1) This work uses 8 kinds of sEMG features (the mean absolute value, integral sEMG value, root mean square, waveform length, logarithmic characteristics, zero crossing points, slope sign changes, and Willison amplitude) to form 8 deep forest regressors to get the angles, and then enter the 8 angles into an ANN with the structure of 8-13-1 to filter and optimize the angle curve. Thus, a complete comprehensive regression model was formed to carry out regression mapping of the sEMG signals at the forearm corresponding to the angles of the five metacarpophalangeal joints of the hand. (2) The experimental results show an excellent decoding accuracy, and the Pearson correlation coefficient reaches 0.844, which is 6.16% higher than 0.795 of a single regression integrating multiple features, and significantly higher than the Gaussian process regression that has been studied in sEMG decoding in recent years. And an online experiment has been manipulated in this research. The results have proved that the decoding method is very efficient and robust.

References

1. Beasley, R.W.: General considerations in managing upper limb amputations. Orthop. Clin. North Am. **12**(4), 743–749 (1981)

2. Fang, Y.F., Yang, J.N., Zhou, D.L., et al.: Modeling EMG-driven wrist movements using a bio-inspired neural network. Neurocomputing **470**, 89–98 (2022)
3. Yamanoi, Y., Ogiri, Y., Kato, R.: EMG-based posture classification using a convolutional neural network for a myoelectric hand. Biomed. Signal Process. **55**, 101574 (2020)
4. Cote-Allard, U., Fall, C.L., Drouin, A., et al.: Deep learning for electromyographic hand gesture signal classification using transfer learning. IEEE Trans. Neural Syst. Rehabil. Eng. **27**(4), 760–771 (2019)
5. Hu, Y., Wong, Y., Wei, W., et al.: A novel attention-based hybrid CNN-RNN architecture for sEMG-based gesture recognition. PLoS ONE **13**(10), e0206049 (2018)
6. Zhang, Q., Pi, T., Liu, R.F., et al.: Simultaneous and proportional estimation of multijoint kinematics from EMG signals for myocontrol of robotic hands. IEEE-ASME Trans. Mech. **25**(4), 1953–1960 (2020)
7. Chen, C., Ma, S., Sheng, X., et al.: Adaptive real-time identification of motor unit discharges from non-stationary high-density surface electromyographic signals. IEEE Trans. Biomed. Eng. **67**(12), 3501–3509 (2020)
8. Farina, D., Vujaklija, I., Sartori, M., et al.: Man/machine interface based on the discharge timings of spinal motor neurons after targeted muscle reinnervation. Nat. Biomed. Eng. **1**(2) (2017)
9. Ameri, A., Akhaee, M.A., Scheme, E., et al.: Real-time, simultaneous myoelectric control using a convolutional neural network. PLoS ONE **13**(9), e0203835 (2018)
10. Lin, C., Wang, B., Jiang, N., et al.: Robust extraction of basis functions for simultaneous and proportional myoelectric control via sparse non-negative matrix factorization. J. Neural Eng. **15**(2), 026017 (2018)
11. Ameri, A., Akhaee, M.A, Scheme, E., et al.: Regression convolutional neural network for improved simultaneous EMG control. J. Neural Eng. **16**(3) (2019)
12. Nielsen, J.L.G., Holmgaard, S., Jiang, N., et al.: Simultaneous and proportional force estimation for multifunction myoelectric prostheses using mirrored bilateral training. IEEE Trans. Biomed. Eng. **58**(3), 681–688 (2011)
13. Muceli, S., Farina, D.: Simultaneous and proportional estimation of hand kinematics from EMG during mirrored movements at multiple degrees-of-freedom. IEEE Trans. Neural Syst. Rehabil. Eng. **20**(3), 371–378 (2012)
14. Ngeo, J.G., Tamei, T., Shibata, T.: Continuous and simultaneous estimation of finger kinematics using inputs from an EMG-to-muscle activation model. J. Neuroeng. Rehabil. **11** (2014)
15. Celadon, N., Dosen, S., Binder, I., et al.: Proportional estimation of finger movements from high-density surface electromyography. J. Neuroeng. Rehabil. **13**(1), 73 (2016)
16. Xiloyannis, M., Gavriel, C., Thomik, A.A.C., et al.: Gaussian process autoregression for simultaneous proportional multi-modal prosthetic control with natural hand kinematics. IEEE Trans. Neural Syst. Rehabil. Eng. **25**(10), 1785–1801 (2017)
17. Bao, T.Z., Zaidi, S.A.R., Xie, S.Q., et al.: A CNN-LSTM hybrid model for wrist kinematics estimation using surface electromyography. IEEE Trans. Instrum. Meas. **70**, 1–9 (2021)
18. Koch, P., Dreier, M., Larsen, A., et al.: Regression of hand movements from sEMG data with recurrent neural networks. In: Annual International Conference of the IEEE Engineering in Medicine and Biology Society IEEE Engineering in Medicine and Biology Society Annual International Conference, pp. 3783–3787 (2020)
19. Zhang, Q., Fang, L., Zhang, Q., et al.: Simultaneous estimation of joint angle and interaction force towards sEMG-driven human-robot interaction during constrained tasks. Neurocomputing **484**, 38–45 (2022)

2D/3D Shape Model Registration with X-ray Images for Patient-Specific Spine Geometry Reconstruction

Yanxin Jiang[1], Haoyu Zhai[1], Kang Li[2], Lei Li[3], Hairong Tao[4], Moyu Shao[5], Xiaomin Cheng[5], and Hongkai Wang[1,6(✉)]

[1] School of Biomedical Engineering, Faculty of Medicine, Dalian University of Technology, Dalian 116024, China
18004094066@163.com

[2] West China Biomedical Big Data Center, West China Hospital, Sichuan University, Chengdu 610041, Sichuan, China

[3] Department of Vascular Surgery, The Second Affiliated Hospital of Dalian Medical University, Dalian, Liaoning, China

[4] Shanghai Key Laboratory of Orthopaedic Implants, Department of Orthopaedic Surgery, Shanghai Ninth People's Hospital, Shanghai Jiao Tong University School of Medicine, Shanghai 200011, People's Republic of China

[5] Jiangsu Yunqianbai Digital Technology Co., Ltd., Xuzhou 221000, China

[6] Liaoning Key Laboratory of Integrated Circuit and Biomedical Electronic System, Dalian 116024, China

Abstract. The use of preoperative CT and intraoperative fluoroscopic-guided surgical robotic assistance for spinal disease treatment has gained significant attention among surgeons. However, the intraoperative robotic systems lack guidance based on three-dimensional anatomical structures, rendering them unusable when there is a mismatch between preoperative CT and intraoperative fluoroscopy. Additionally, the continuous X-ray imaging during fluoroscopy exposes the patient to significant radiation risks. This paper proposes a 2D/3D registration method to reconstruct 3D patient spine geometry from frontal-view X-ray images. Our aim is to combine this method with intraoperative robotic assistance for spine procedures, enabling three-dimensional spatial navigation for the robotic system and reducing patient radiation exposure. By utilizing 45 frontal-view X-ray images of patients with scoliosis, we trained a 3D trunk anatomy SSM specific to scoliosis. For the registration, a 2D registration-back projection strategy was employed, which first generates the simulated X-ray projection image of the 3D SSM, then non-rigidly registers the projection image with the patient X-ray image, and finally back-project the 2D registration into 3D to guide the shape deformation of the 3D SSM. This approach was evaluated using X-ray images of 10 scoliosis patients. The results demonstrate the ability to reconstruct the anatomical structure and curvature of the spine in X-ray images. The registration accuracy of the SSM was assessed by visualizing the alignment between the registered model and X-ray images, as well as calculating the average distance between the vertebral disc center points of the model and expert-annotated anatomical landmarks in the patient's

X-rays. The average distance between the registered model's vertebral disc centers and the patient's X-ray anatomical positions was 11.38 mm. The registered model exhibited a high degree of alignment with the curvature of the spine in X-ray images.

Keywords: Scoliosis · Statistical Shape Model · 2D/3D registration · X-ray Images

1 Introduction

Adolescent idiopathic scoliosis is the most common three-dimensional structural deformity of the spine, where the deformed spine compresses the organs within the thoracic and abdominal cavities, posing a significant health risk to patients [1]. In clinical practice, there is growing interest in using image-guided robotic-assisted techniques for the placement of spinal implants in the treatment of spinal deformities and for achieving spinal stability [2]. Robotic-assisted techniques have shown higher accuracy compared to traditional manual surgery [3], reducing surgical time and improving treatment efficiency [4]. One of the current surgical approaches for treating adolescent idiopathic scoliosis involves the use of robot-assisted pedicle screw placement [5]. Robot-assisted spine surgery requires preoperative CT scanning of the patient's spine to create a three-dimensional model of the spine. The region of interest is then uploaded to specific software, which guides the surgeon in placing the pedicle screws using the three-dimensional spine model. Intraoperatively, real-time confirmation of the screw position is achieved using fluoroscopy imaging. Postoperatively, the accuracy of screw placement is evaluated using CT images [6]. However, due to differences between preoperative CT images and intraoperative spinal morphology, a significant mismatch can result in the loss of support from the three-dimensional anatomical structure, rendering the use of robotic-assisted techniques impossible and requiring a switch to manual surgery [2]. Intraoperative fluoroscopy is typically performed using a biplane C-arm fluoroscope, which continuously emits X-rays to obtain images. However, this method exposes the patient to a significant amount of radiation [7].

If an algorithm could be developed to rapidly reconstruct the three-dimensional anatomical structure of a patient's trunk based on intraoperative two-dimensional images, it would not only provide real time three dimensional spatial navigation for surgical robots, enhancing robotic-assisted techniques and facilitating surgeons but also enable the use of intermittent intraoperative X-ray imaging as a substitute for continuous fluoroscopy in robot-assisted spine surgery. This would reduce the dose of X-ray radiation, thereby minimizing the radiation exposure to the patient.

In recent years, there has been significant interest in the three-dimensional reconstruction of patient anatomical structures from 2D X-ray images [8]. The accuracy of patient-specific anatomical models obtained through 2D to 3D reconstruction is lower compared to models derived from CT or MRI imaging. However, 2D X-ray imaging offers lower radiation exposure and cost compared to CT scans, making it more accessible [9]. The reconstruction of 3D models from 2D images is achieved through the optimization of deformable models. A statistical shape model (SSM) is a deformable model that represents the shape of an object using a set of vectors and models the variations in shape using statistical methods [10]. SSMs trained in the field of medical imaging incorporate prior knowledge of three-dimensional anatomy within a specific shape space, allowing for deformations to be constrained within a plausible anatomical shape space. In previous works, SSM-based 2D/3D reconstruction techniques have been applied to various skeletal structures in the human body, such as ribs [11], pelvis [12], femur [13, 14], and extended to atlas-based registration in small animal imaging [15–17]. Regarding the 2D/3D reconstruction of spine models, Novosad et al. [18] proposed a method for three-dimensional reconstruction of the spine from a single X-ray image using explicit rigid 3D/2D registration. This approach introduced prior geometric shape knowledge of individual vertebrae to preserve their shape without significant distortion. However, the rigid registration scheme and the lack of complete prior knowledge of the entire spine may limit the applicability of this method to patients with severe spinal deformities. Zhang et al. [19] utilized the Hough transform technique and deformation matching strategy to reconstruct the spine in three dimensions based on matching vertebral contours from paired-plane X-ray images. This method demonstrated high reconstruction accuracy and reliability. However, this study did not incorporate prior anatomical knowledge, and it required manual identification of the spinal midline in the 3D reconstruction process.

To date, the existing approaches for 3D reconstruction of the human spinal model have not utilized prior anatomical knowledge of spinal curvature deformities. As a result, shape deformations may exceed the boundaries of reasonable anatomical shapes. Furthermore, these methods rely on manual landmark annotations, making them incapable of achieving fully automated reconstruction. Additionally, the reconstruction process typically takes 2 to 3 min, which is impractical for real-time reconstruction during spinal treatment procedures. In this study, we propose a novel approach that addresses these limitations by employing a deformable model known as the SSM to reconstruct a 3D model of the patient's spinal morphology by aligning it with frontal-view X-ray images. The SSM incorporates prior anatomical knowledge derived from a dataset of frontal-view X-rays from multiple scoliosis patients, encompassing a range of spinal curvatures, from mild to severe, within a reasonable shape space. In the following sections, we provide a comprehensive description of our registration method and present the evaluation results of this research.

2 Methods and Materials

2.1 Scoliosis Torso SSM Construction

Construction of the SSM for Scoliosis Torso involved a dataset of X-ray images from 45 cases of adolescent idiopathic scoliosis patients provided by Shanghai Ninth People's Hospital. A 2D/3D registration method was employed to obtain training samples for the SSM. The Chinese torso template mesh [20], which includes the spine, was used for simulating X-ray projections. Each patient's X-ray image was registered with the simulated projection using 2D registration techniques. The deformation field obtained from the registration was applied to the points of the simulated X-ray projection, and the deformed projection points were then back-projected into 3D space. The template mesh was registered with the 45 training samples, yielding a set of deformation coordinates that represented the shape variations across the samples. Generalized Procrustes analysis [21] was employed to normalize the registered torso models, eliminating shape differences among different patients and obtaining shape vectors for the 45 training samples. Principal Component Analysis (PCA) was used to extract shape vectors of the torso and reduce the dimensionality of the shape dataset. PCA identified the main modes of shape variation, generating the average shape and principal components while quantifying the shape changes between different objects. Different shape vectors controlled the deformations of the surface and spinal anatomy in different parts of the torso, combined with the average model's shape, enabling the deformations of the Scoliosis Torso SSM within a fixed shape space. The model expression for the Scoliosis Torso SSM is represented by Eq. (1) [22].

$$X = \overrightarrow{X} + \sum_{m=1}^{45} \alpha_m \beta_m \tag{1}$$

In the Scoliosis Torso SSM, X represents an instance of the shape, $\overline{X}$ denotes the average shape of the SSM. α_m represents the shape coefficients that control the deformation of various anatomical structures, including the body surface and the spine. β_m corresponds to the eigenvectors obtained from the feature decomposition of the shape vectors. By computing different combinations of α values and β, and overlaying them with the average shape of the SSM, one can obtain model shape instances representing different scoliosis morphologies.

2.2 2D/3D Registration

The 2D/3D registration process aims to align the simulated X-ray projections generated by the SSM with the spinal curvature observed in X-ray images of patients with scoliosis. Figure 1 illustrates the algorithmic workflow of the 2D/3D registration.

The first step involves simulating X-ray projections based on the SSM of the scoliosis population. Each simulated projection is then registered to the corresponding patient's X-ray image in 2D. Subsequently, the deformation field obtained from the registration is applied to the points of the simulated X-ray projection. This process ensures that the simulated X-ray projection's spinal curvature matches the spinal curvature observed in the patient's X-ray image. Finally, the deformed projection points are back-projected into the 3D space, resulting in a deformed 3D torso model.

To optimize the registration, the process iteratively repeats the steps of simulating projections, 2D registration, and 3D back-projection. This iterative refinement aims to achieve a 3D human torso model that closely matches the spinal curvature observed in the patient's X-ray images.

Simulated X-ray Projection Algorithm

To achieve better alignment between the spinal morphology of the SSM and the patient's X-ray image, this study utilizes a projection algorithm that simulates the principles of real X-ray imaging. Specifically, the SSM undergoes simulated X-ray projection in the coronal plane.

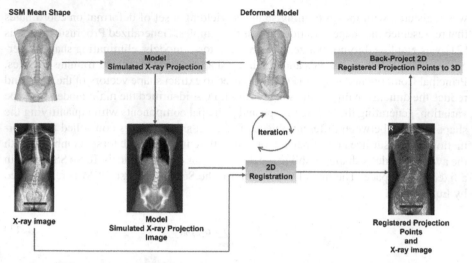

Fig. 1. The 2D/3D SSM registration workflow of the proposed method.

The process of imaging in a normal X-ray involves an X-ray source, the human body, and a detector. The algorithm operates on the following principles:

1) A virtual X-ray source is positioned within the spatial domain of the SSM.
2) A rectangular detection plane is placed in the direction of the model's back.
3) Realistic CT values are assigned to the soft tissues, bones, lungs, and other structures within the model.

For each pixel on the rectangular detection plane, a unique path connecting it to the X-ray source exists within the spatial domain. Along each path, a partial integration is performed based on the corresponding CT values and the path length of the organ tissues represented by the SSM. The integration value is set to zero for the parts of the path that do not intersect with the SSM. Ultimately, the integration values along the entire path are calculated and assigned as the pixel values on the rectangular detection plane. By performing this calculation for each pixel, the resulting array represents the simulated X-ray image of the SSM.

2D Registration of the SSM Projection

The 2D registration process involves two consecutive steps and utilizes specific parameter settings. The first step employs an affine transformation framework with the following settings: transformation method – affine transformation, similarity measure – mutual information, optimization method – adaptive stochastic gradient descent, and interpolation method – B-spline interpolation. The second step utilizes a B-spline transformation framework with the following settings: transformation method – B-spline transformation, similarity measure – mutual information, optimization method – adaptive stochastic gradient descent, and interpolation method – B-spline interpolation.

The primary objective of the first registration step is to achieve a basic alignment between the model's X-ray projection and the patient's X-ray, using an affine transformation. This alignment serves as a foundation for subsequent non-linear transformations. In the second registration step, the goal is to utilize the alignment obtained in the first step and apply the B-spline method to deform the spinal curvature of the SSM in the simulated X-ray projection, aligning it with the actual lateral bending angle observed in the patient's X-ray image.

The 2D registration is conducted using the Elastix software package, which is an open-source software program widely used for solving intensity-based medical image registration problems [23]. Its modular design and command-line interface allow users to quickly configure, test, and compare different registration methods for specific applications, enabling automated processing of large datasets [23]. In this study, Elastix is utilized for 2D registration of the simulated X-ray projection from the SSM with patient X-ray images.

Deformation of Projection Points
Figure 2 shows a comparison between the projection points before deformation and the simulated X-ray image, as well as the validation results of the deformed projection points with the patient X-ray image. For the spine region, which is the focus of this study, the deformed projection points exhibit a deformation that closely matches the contour of the patient's spine in the X-ray image. This indicates that the Transformix deformation vector has been correctly applied to the projection points of the SSM, achieving the desired 2D registration effect between the simulated X-ray projection of the SSM and the patient X-ray image.

The deformation process is conducted using the transformix software, which is a tool that works in conjunction with Elastix to apply transformations to images. It utilizes deformation parameters computed by Elastix to apply the same deformation field to other images or to apply transformations to a single image with different parameter settings [21]. In this study, Transformix was used to apply the deformation field generated from the registration of SSM simulated X-ray projection and patient X-ray images to the SSM 2D projection points.

Deformation Field Back-Projection
Previously, we obtained the simulated X-ray images of the SSM through the process of simulating X-ray imaging. By leveraging the similar triangle relationship between the projection of the SSM and the 3D deformation vector of the model, we can perform a back-projection of the 2D deformation vector. Figure 3 illustrates the principle of the similar triangles between the 2D deformation vector of the model projection and the 3D deformation vector of the SSM.

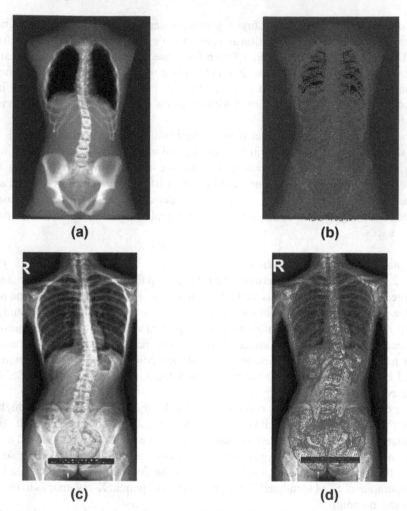

(a)

(b)

(c)

(d)

Fig. 2. Comparison between projection points before deformation and simulated X-ray image, and validation results of deformed projection points with patient X-ray image: (a) Simulated X-ray image of the model, (b) projection of model points before deformation onto the simulated X-ray image, (c) original patient X-ray image, (d) Projection of deformed model points onto the patient X-ray image.

In Fig. 3, plane D represents the rectangular detection plane set in the simulated X-ray projection function, where the model is projected. Model M is the projected SSM. Point O represents the X-ray source set in the projection function. Point N_0 is a point on the SSM, and point P_0 is the two-dimensional projection point of N_0 on plane D. Point P_1 is the transformed two-dimensional projection point obtained by applying Transformix to point P_0. Point N_1 is the point on the deformed SSM corresponding to the transformed projection point P_1. $\overrightarrow{P_0P_1}$ represents the 2D deformation vector, and

$\overrightarrow{N_0N_1}$ represents the 3D deformation vector obtained by back-projecting $\overrightarrow{P_0P_1}$, which represents the deformation of the three-dimensional SSM.

According to the principle of similar triangles, the ratio of the lengths between $\overrightarrow{N_0N_1}$ and $\overrightarrow{P_0P_1}$ is equal to the ratio of the lengths between $\overrightarrow{ON_0}$ and $\overrightarrow{OP_0}$. Therefore, the formula for the length of $\overrightarrow{N_0N_1}$ can be expressed as Eq. (2). By applying the formula (2), we can determine the 3D coordinates of the transformed model point corresponding to the transformed 2D projection point.

$$\left|\overrightarrow{N_0N_1}\right| = \frac{\left|\overrightarrow{ON_0}\right| \times \left|\overrightarrow{P_0P_1}\right|}{\left|\overrightarrow{OP_0}\right|} \tag{2}$$

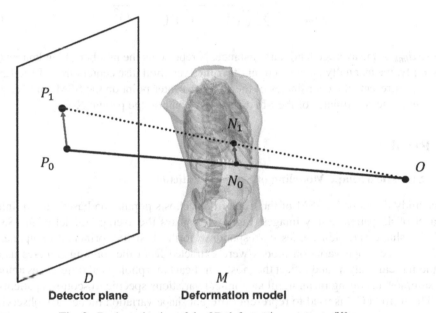

Fig. 3. Back-projection of the 2D deformation vector to 3D space.

The 2D/3D registration strategy applies a deformation to the SSM in 3D space, deformation estimation is based on the transformation achieved through the 2D registration of simulated X-ray projection points with patient X-ray images. The 3D deformation resulting from this transformation applied to skeletal structures such as ribs and spine does not guarantee anatomically plausible shapes. Therefore, it is necessary to adjust this 3D deformation by projecting it onto the shape space of the SSM, obtaining updated shape coefficients (α) for the SSM. These coefficients are then used in Eq. (1) to obtain the updated SSM. Subsequently, this updated SSM serves as the new projection model for the next iteration of the registration process. The iteration stops when the deformation magnitude is below a threshold. At this point, the obtained SSM is considered to represent the three-dimensional anatomical structure of the patient's spinal deformity.

2.3 Registration Accuracy Verification

In this study, the accuracy of the registration results was validated through testing 10 patient X-ray images. The simulated X-ray projection points of the spinal deformity SSM were registered onto the target X-ray images, and the average distance between the registered SSM disc center projection points and the corresponding patient X-ray disc center was calculated as the registration accuracy. This process was repeated for all 10 datasets, resulting in 10 registration accuracies. The coordinates of the disc center points in the patient X-ray images were obtained by manually setting landmarks, while the coordinates of the SSM disc center points were obtained by averaging the coordinates of all vertices of each disc. The formula for calculating the registration error is shown in Eq. (3).

$$d_{lmk} = \frac{1}{N} \sum_{i=1}^{N} \sqrt{\left(x_1^i - x_2^i\right)^2 + \left(y_1^i - y_2^i\right)^2} \tag{3}$$

where d_{lmk} is the average landmark distance, N represents the number of landmarks (In this study, we manually labeled a total of 17 intervertebral disc centers from T1 to L5.), (x_1^i, y_1^i) represents the coordinates of the i-th disc center point on the SSM, and (x_2^i, y_2^i) represents the coordinates of the i-th disc center point on the patient X-ray.

3   Results

3.1 Statistical Shape Modeling of Scoliosis Patients

This study developed a SSM of the trunk in a scoliosis population based on a training dataset of 45 patient X-ray images. Figure 4 displays the average model of the SSM and the shape variation modes corresponding to the first five principal components (PCs). These shape variation modes were extracted from the training samples using mathematical analysis and reflect the most significant morphological differences among the samples, capturing meaningful anatomical variations specific to scoliosis patients.

The term "PC_i" is used to represent different shape variation modes. By observing Fig. 4, it can be noted that different PC_s represent different spinal curvature patterns. PC_1 indicates a significant rightward curvature in the thoracic region and a slight leftward curvature in the lumbar region. PC_2 represents a significant leftward curvature in the lumbar region and a rightward curvature in the lumbar region. PC_3 indicates a significant leftward curvature in the thoracic region and a slight leftward curvature in the lumbar region. PC_4 represents a slight rightward curvature in the thoracic region, while PC_5 represents an S-shaped curvature pattern with rightward curvature in the thoracic region and leftward curvature in the lumbar region. Constructing a shape space that encompasses various spinal curvature patterns in scoliosis patients is crucial for subsequent three-dimensional modeling of individual scoliotic trunks.

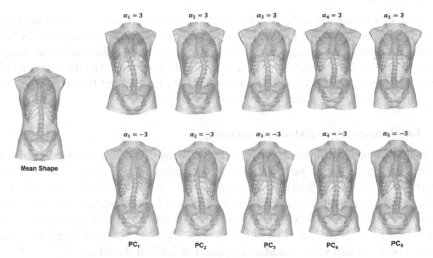

Fig. 4. The SSM of Scoliotic Trunk. The average model is displayed on the far left. Setting the coefficient $\alpha = \pm 3$, each PC is shown overlaid with the average model to visualize the shape instances. The first five PCs capture the most significant shape variations among the training samples. Here, we present the visualization of the first five PCs.

3.2   Registration Results Visualization

This study selected 10 cases with diverse spinal deformities to demonstrate the results. Figure 5 illustrates the 3D registration outcomes using our method overlaid on the frontal

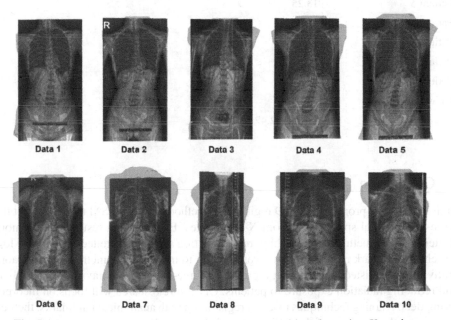

Fig. 5. Visualization of the 3D registration results overlaid on the patient X-ray images.

X-ray images of the 10 patients. The experimental results indicate that our method effectively reconstructs the anatomical structure and curvature of the spine in X-ray images. By observing the alignment between the registration model and X-ray images, it is evident that the restored 3D anatomical model closely matches the corresponding spinal curvature in the X-rays. The curvature of the lumbar and thoracic spine in the X-ray images of all 10 patients can be accurately reconstructed.

3.3 Key Landmark Registration Accuracy

We evaluated the registration accuracy of the SSM by calculating the average distance between the model's intervertebral disc center points and the anatomical landmarks expertly marked on the patient's X-ray images (from T1 to L5, a total of 17 center points). Table 1 presents the test results of 10 patient X-ray images, listing the average distances between the intervertebral disc center points of each X-ray image and the corresponding registered model's center points. The final results showed an average distance of 11.38 mm with a standard deviation of 2.42 for the 10 cases.

Table 1. Average Landmark Distances of the Intervertebral Disc Centers

Patients Data	Average Distance of Intervertebral Disc Centers (mm)
Patient 1	6.36
Patient 2	10.35
Patient 3	10.02
Patient 4	14.15
Patient 5	13.25
Patient 6	9.15
Patient 7	12.42
Patient 8	10.58
Patient 9	13.01
Patient 10	14.53
mean ± std.	11.38 ± 2.42

4 Conclusion

In this paper, we propose a 2D/3D registration method based on SSM to reconstruct the three-dimensional spine shape from X-ray images. Experimental results have demonstrated that this method achieves high reconstruction accuracy as reflected from the low vertebrae landmark reconstruction error. We aim to integrate this method with intraoperative robot-assisted spinal surgery, providing three-dimensional navigation for robots and reducing radiation exposure to patients. Our future research will focus on incorporating deep learning techniques to assist registration with anatomical landmarks, thereby improving the accuracy of three-dimensional anatomical structure reconstruction.

Acknowledgements. This work was supported in part by the National Key Research and Development Program No. 2020YFB1711500, 2020YFB1711501, 2020YFB1711503, the general program of the National Natural Science Fund of China (No. 81971693, 61971445), the funding of Dalian Engineering Research Center for Artificial Intelligence in Medical Imaging, Hainan Province Key Research and Development Plan ZDYF2021SHFZ244, the Fundamental Research Funds for the Central Universities Fundamental Research Funds for the Central Universities (No. DUT22YG229 and DUT22YG205), the funding of Liaoning Key Lab of IC & BME System and the 1-3-5 project for disciplines of excellence, West China Hospital, Sichuan University (ZYYC21004).

References

1. Cheng, J., Castelein, R., Chu, W., Danielsson, A.: Adolescent idiopathic scoliosis. Nat. Rev. Dis. Primers **1**(1), 15030 (2015)
2. Hu, X., Ohnmeiss, D.D., Lieberman, I.H.: Robotic-assisted pedicle screw placement: lessons learned from the first 102 patients. Eur. Spine J. **22**(3), 661–666 (2013)
3. Fan, Y., et al.: Accuracy of pedicle screw placement comparing robot-assisted technology and the free-hand with fluoroscopy-guided method in spine surgery: an updated meta-analysis. Medicine (Baltimore) **97**(22), e10970 (2018)
4. Ueno, J., et al.: Robotics is useful for less-experienced surgeons in spinal deformity surgery. Eur. J. Orthop. Surg. Traumatol. 1–6 (2022)
5. Macke, J.J., Woo, R., Varich, L.: Accuracy of robot-assisted pedicle screw placement for adolescent idiopathic scoliosis in the pediatric population. J. Robot. Surg. **10**(2), 145–150 (2016)
6. Akazawa, T., et al.: Accuracy of computer-assisted pedicle screw placement for adolescent idiopathic scoliosis: a comparison between robotics and navigation. Eur. Spine J. **32**(2), 651–658 (2023)
7. Hyun, S.J., Kim, K.J., Jahng, T.A., Kim, H.J.: Minimally invasive robotic versus open fluoroscopic-guided spinal instrumented fusions: a randomized controlled trial. Spine **42**(6), 353–358 (2017)
8. Goswami, B., Misra, S.K.: 3D modeling of X-ray images: a review. Int. J. Comput. Appl. **132**, 40–46 (2015)
9. Reyneke, C.J.F., Luthi, M., Burdin, V., Douglas, T.S., Vetter, T., Mutsvangwa, T.E.M.: Review of 2-D/3-D reconstruction using statistical shape and intensity models and X-ray image synthesis: toward a unified framework. IEEE Rev. Biomed. Eng. **12**, 269–286 (2019)
10. Heimann, T., Meinzer, H.P.: Statistical shape models for 3D medical image segmentation: a review. Med. Image Anal. **13**(4), 543–563 (2009)
11. Dworzak, J., et al.: 3D reconstruction of the human rib cage from 2D projection images using a statistical shape model. Int. J. Comput. Assist. Radiol. Surg. **5**(2), 111–124 (2010)
12. Sadowsky, O., Lee, J., Sutter, E.G., Wall, S.J., Prince, J.L., Taylor, R.H.: Hybrid cone-beam tomographic reconstruction: incorporation of prior anatomical models to compensate for missing data. IEEE Trans. Med. Imaging **30**(1), 69–83 (2011)
13. Zheng, G., Gollmer, S., Schumann, S., Dong, X., Feilkas, T., González Ballester, M.A.: A 2D/3D correspondence building method for reconstruction of a patient-specific 3D bone surface model using point distribution models and calibrated X-ray images. Med. Image Anal. **13**(6), 883–899 (2009)
14. Baka, N., et al.: 2D–3D shape reconstruction of the distal femur from stereo X-ray imaging using statistical shape models. Med. Image Anal. **15**(6), 840–850 (2011)

15. Wang, H., Stout, D.B., Chatziioannou, A.F.: Mouse atlas registration with non-tomographic imaging modalities – a pilot study based on simulation. Mol. Imag. Biol. **14**(4), 408–419 (2012)

16. Wang, H., et al.: MARS: a mouse atlas registration system based on a planar x-ray projector and an optical camera. Phys. Med. Biol. **57**(19), 6063–6077 (2012)

17. Wang, H., Stout, D.B., Chatziioannou, A.F.: A method of 2D/3D registration of a statistical mouse atlas with a planar X-ray projection and an optical photo. Med. Image Anal. **17**(4), 401–416 (2013)

18. Novosad, J., Cheriet, F., Petit, Y., Labelle, H.: Three-dimensional (3-D) reconstruction of the spine from a single X-ray image and prior vertebra models. IEEE Trans. Biomed. Eng. **51**(9), 1628–1639 (2004)

19. Zhang, J., et al.: 3-D reconstruction of the spine from biplanar radiographs based on contour matching using the Hough transform. IEEE Trans. Biomed. Eng. **60**(7), 1954–1964 (2013)

20. Sun, X., et al.: A statistical model of spine shape and material for population-oriented biomechanical simulation. IEEE Access **9**, 155805–155814 (2021)

21. Bookstein, F.L.: Landmark methods for forms without landmarks: morphometrics of group differences in outline shape. Med. Image Anal. **1**(3), 225–243 (1997)

22. Wang, H., Yu, D., Tan, Z., Hu, R., Zhang, B., Yu, J.: Estimation of thyroid volume from scintigraphy through 2D/3D registration of a statistical shape model. Phys. Med. Biol. **64**(9), 095015 (2019)

23. Klein, S., Staring, M., Murphy, K., Viergever, M.A., Pluim, J.P.: Elastix: a toolbox for intensity-based medical image registration. IEEE Trans. Med. Imaging **29**, 196–205 (2010)

Visual and Visual-Tactile Perception for Robotics

Real-Time Detection of Surface Floating Garbage Based on Improved YOLOv7

Liang Li[1,2,3,4(✉)], Yiping Li[1,2,3], Zhibin Jiang[1,2], and Hailin Wang[1,2,3,4]

[1] State Key Laboratory of Robotics, Shenyang Institute of Automation, Chinese Academy of Sciences, Shenyang 110016, China
liliang@sia.cn
[2] Institutes for Robotics and Intelligent Manufacturing, Chinese Academy of Sciences, Shenyang 110169, China
[3] Key Laboratory of Marine Robotics, Shenyang 110169, Liaoning, China
[4] University of Chinese Academy of Sciences, Beijing 100049, China

Abstract. Cleaning up surface floating garbage is of great significance to improve the ecological environment of the waters, of which the detection of surface floating garbage is a crucial step. It is difficult to distinguish the background and garbage and solve the problem of small targets of the existing target detection methods. Therefore, an improved YOLOv7 network is proposed to achieve efficient and high-precision detection of surface floating garbage. The newly proposed DS method is applied to original YOLOv7 network for multi-scale feature fusion. Meanwhile, CBAM attention mechanism module is applied to network backbone to improve detection precision. The public data set FLOW is used to validate the method in this paper. The simulation test results show that the proposed method significantly improves the detection precision without reducing too much detection speed, which proves the effectiveness of the proposed method. Finally, the proposed method is deployed to an NVIDIA Jetson device and applied to real-time surface floating garbage detection, which proves its practicability.

Keywords: Surface Floating Garbage · Target Detection · Deep Learning · YOLOv7

1 Introduction

At present, many rivers, lakes, and oceans float a large amount of surface garbage due to the increasing scope of human activities [1]. This surface garbage not only destroys the beauty of the natural environment but also has a serious impact on the survival of underwater plants and animals. If the garbage can be recovered and reused, it will improve the ecological environment and bring economic benefits [2]. Currently, most of the surface garbage is removed by manually driving a surface ship, which wastes a lot of humans, material, and financial resources. Therefore, the research on the automatic cleaning of surface garbage is receiving more and more attention from researchers. The automatic garbage cleaning task is mainly divided into three parts, namely garbage

H. Yang et al. (Eds.): ICIRA 2023, LNAI 14272, pp. 573–582, 2023.
https://doi.org/10.1007/978-981-99-6480-2_47

detection, garbage capture, and garbage recovery. Among them, garbage detection is the key step of the task, and it is responsible for providing the location and type information of the garbage. In general, there are three ways to detect surface garbage, including infrared imaging sensors, lidar-based images, and optical images. Among them, the object information obtained by optical images has significant differences in color, texture, corner, and other features, to facilitate more accurate identification of the type and amount of surface garbage. Therefore, this paper intends to study the surface garbage detection method based on optical images.

Surface garbage target detection methods are classified as traditional [3–6] and deep learning based methods [7–10]. Traditional methods mainly extract the color, texture, and edge information on targets in the image to establish the template, and then use the corresponding classifier, such as the SVM, for category recognition. This method achieves a degree of intelligence, but it also has some limitations. For example, feature extraction is difficult and requires expert supervision. Feature extraction and target classification are carried out separately, so the speed and accuracy of the detection cannot reach optimal. Overall, traditional surface garbage detection methods generally suffer from slow detection speed, low detection accuracy as well as poor robustness. As computer science develops, deep learning techniques have achieved good results in the field of surface garbage detection, which includes two-stage and one-stage detection methods. Two-stage methods mainly include R-CNN [11] and its variants, which have relatively high detection accuracy and slow detection speed; one-stage detection methods mainly include YOLO [12] and its variants, SSD [13], etc., which are more balanced with respect to detection accuracy and efficiency. In [7], the author improved the YOLOv3 network by reducing the number of detection heads from 3 to 2, which improved the target detection speed. In [8], the author proposed a PC-Net network on the basis of the Faster R-CNN to improve the detection accuracy of surface floating garbage. In [9], the author presented a real-time detection method for surface garbage based on the improved RefineDet network, which includes three modules: anchor refinement module, transmission connection block, and target detection module. In [10], the author put forward a garbage detection method based on improved YOLOv4, which can realize fast and high-precision detection.

Based on the above research results, we propose an improved YOLOv7 target detection method for surface floating garbage detection. Specifically, the DS, a new downsampling module, is proposed for information fusion between different layers of the network. Then the CBAM method is embedded into the YOLOv7 network to improve target detection accuracy. Finally, the proposed method is verified on a public data set and deployed to the edge computing device to prove its effectiveness and practicability.

2 Methodology

YOLOv7 network is an advanced target detection algorithm at present. Based on this network, this paper makes improvements by adding the newly proposed downsampling module DS and the attention mechanism module CBAM to solve the problems that the surface garbage is difficult to detect from background and garbage size is small.

2.1   Original YOLOv7 Network

The YOLOv7 network consists of the input, backbone, and detection head.

The input part mainly reuses preprocessing method of the YOLOv5 network, using mosaic data enhancement, adaptive anchor frame calculation, adaptive picture scaling, and other tricks. Mosaic data enhancement technology adopts four images to splice using random scaling, clipping, and arrangement, which is mainly used to solve the problem of small target detection and can enrich the data set. Adaptive anchor frame computation refers to the adaptive computation of the optimal anchor frame in different training data sets, which can improve the convergence speed of the network. Adaptive picture scaling adaptively adds minimal black borders to the original image, scaling the original image uniformly to a size that can be used as the input.

The backbone network mainly uses ELAN and MP structures with the Silu activation function. ELAN allows deeper networks to learn and converge effectively by controlling the shortest longest gradient paths. E-ELAN designed based on ELAN adopts expand, shuffle, and merge cardinality to achieve continuously enhancing network learning capabilities without destroying the original gradient path. In the process of downsampling, the MP structure adopts max pooling and convolution layers to replace the original structure using only max pooling. Meanwhile, the number of channels before and after the MP structure remains unchanged.

The overall structure of the detection head is similar to that of the YOLOv5 network. It is still an anchor-based structure, including the SPPCSPC module, ELAN-W module, MP module, and currently popular reparametrized Rep structure.

2.2   DS Module

The methods of downsampling in convolutional neural networks are mainly pooling and convolution operation. The feature map will lose some underlying information after the downsampling. The Focus module in YOLOv5 divides the input feature map into several small blocks and then rearranges these blocks into the output feature map according to certain rules. The main function of this module is to convert large feature maps into smaller ones to improve computational efficiency while maintaining the size of the perceptual field. In addition, it can also help the network learn more underlying features and improve detection accuracy.

Therefore, this paper proposes a new downsampling module (DS module), as shown in Fig. 1, which combines pooling, convolution, and Focus to better preserve the underlying features of targets to improve detection accuracy of small targets. After DS module, width and height of feature maps become half of input size, and the number of channels becomes twice input size.

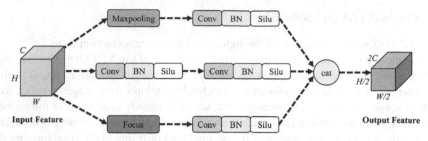

Fig. 1. Structure of the DS module

2.3 CBAM Module

CBAM [14] is a lightweight convolutional channel space hybrid attention module, which combines the channel attention mechanism (CAM) and the spatial attention mechanism (SAM), as shown in Fig. 2. The two modules use the attention mechanism in channel and space respectively. This structure can not only reduce the number of parameters but also ensure that it can be integrated into the existing network architecture as a plug-and-play module.

The CAM module focuses on the meaningful information in the input. The channel dimension does not change and the dimension of the space is compressed. The input feature map goes through the maximum pooling layer and average pooling layer, and the size changes from C * H * W to C * 1 * 1. The two outputs are then obtained by the shared multilayer perceptron module. The two results are added, and output of the CAM module is finally obtained through a sigmoid activation function.

The SAM module focuses on the location information of the target, with the same spatial dimension and the compressed channel dimension. The output of CAM is pooled and averaged to obtain two feature maps of 1 * H * W size, and then the two feature maps are stitched together by the concat operation and turned into a 1-channel feature map by a 7 * 7 convolution. Finally, the output of the SAM module is obtained through a sigmoid activation function.

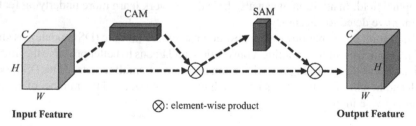

Fig. 2. Structure of the CBAM module

2.4 Improved YOLOv7 Network

The MP module in the original YOLOv7 network is replaced with the DS module, and the CBAM attention mechanism module is added to the backbone of the original YOLOv7 network. The improved YOLOv7 network is shown in Fig. 3. The improved network can theoretically obtain better target detection performance than the original YOLOv7 network, especially for the detection of small targets in the complex background, due to the addition of attention mechanism and improved multi-scale information fusion.

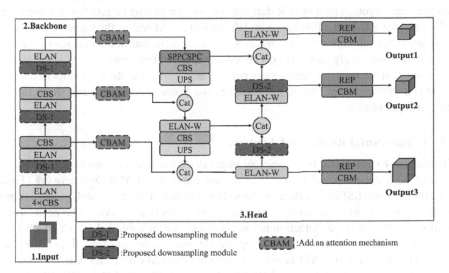

Fig. 3. Structure of the improved YOLOv7 network

3 Results

This section first introduces the data set and its division as well as the hardware configuration used for network training, and then proposes the evaluation metrics. Finally, the network is trained and deployed on an NVIDIA Jetson, and the results are summarized and analyzed.

3.1 Data Set and Hardware Configuration

In this paper, we adopt the Flow data set, which is the world's first floating garbage data set from the viewpoint of an unmanned surface vessel (USV). It contains only one class, containing 2000 pictures and 5271 labeled targets. The proportion of small targets in the data set is the largest. 1200 pictures are randomly selected as the training set, 400 pictures as the validation set, and another 400 pictures as the test set.

The hardware configuration for network training is as follows: The Central Processing Unit (CPU) is Intel (R) Core (TM) I9-10940X @ 3.30 GHz, and the memory is

128G. The Graphics Processing Unit (GPU) is 4 GeForce RTX2080TI. The experimental environment is Ubuntu 18.04.6, and the Python language is used as a programming language. The architecture used in deep learning networks is PyTorch v.1.10.1.

3.2 Evaluation Metrics

To verify the performance of the method in this paper, some common evaluation metrics are used, including Precision (P), Recall (R), Average Precision (AP), F1-score, and Frames Per Second (FPS). The metric P denotes the number of predicted positive samples that are true targets. The metric R denotes the number of true targets that are predicted. AP is calculated from the P-R curve, and the higher the AP value, the higher the detection accuracy of the network on a certain class. F1-score is the harmonic average of P and R. It can comprehensively reflect the precision and recall of the network. FPS is the number of frames that the network can process per second. It is one of the indicators to measure the speed performance. The higher the FPS, the faster the network and the better the real-time performance.

3.3 Experimental Results and Analysis

Simulation Experiment. Four classical target detection networks are selected for comparison with the proposed method, including the original YOLOv7 network, Faster R-CNN network, SSD network, and CenterNet network. The grid search method is used to obtain the best hyperparameters for each target detection network. The performance results of different target detection networks are shown in Table 1. In the YOLOv7+DS network, the MP module is replaced by the DS module in the original YOLOv7 network. The YOLOv7+CBAM network represents the addition of the CBAM attention mechanism module to the original YOLOv7 network. The YOLOv7+DS+CBAM network indicates that both the MP module in the YOLOv7 network is replaced by the DS module and the CBAM attention mechanism module is added, which is the proposed method in this paper.

Table 1. Performance of different target detection networks.

Networks	P	R	AP	F1-score	FPS
YOLOv7 (base)	**0.761**	**0.689**	**0.742**	**0.723**	**116**
Faster R-CNN	0.742	0.658	0.704	0.707	87
SSD	0.644	0.527	0.598	0.58	105
CenterNet	0.728	0.674	0.692	0.7	111
YOLOv7+DS	0.821	0.75	0.808	0.784	110
YOLOv7+CBAM	0.786	0.736	0.771	0.847	108
YOLOv7+DS+CBAM (ours)	**0.881**	**0.846**	**0.897**	**0.863**	**106**

From Table 1, it can be seen that the original YOLOv7 network is better than the Faster R-CNN network, SSD network, and CenterNet network in each evaluation metric, indicating that the original YOLOv7 network is more applicable to surface floating garbage detection. The network that adds the DS module has better retained the low-level information of the target, so it has improved the detection accuracy; however, the detection efficiency is somewhat reduced. The network with added CBAM attention mechanism can reduce the effect of complex backgrounds on target detection and also improve detection accuracy. However, because the added CBAM module increases the network size, the detection speed decreases. The network with both DS and CBAM modules added, which is the proposed network in this paper, improves 15.8%, 22.8%, 20.9%, and 19.4% in P, R, AP, and F1-score metrics, respectively. Compared with the original YOLOv7 network, the proposed method effectively improves detection accuracy. At the same time, the detection speed metric FPS decreases a little for the addition of MP and DS module. The results indicate that the improved YOLOv7 method greatly improves the detection accuracy while sacrificing little detection speed. The validity of the proposed method is demonstrated.

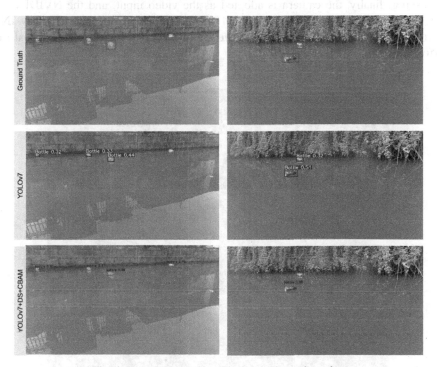

Fig. 4. Results of surface floating garbage detection

To better display the experimental results, two pictures are randomly selected to test the well-trained original YOLOv7 network and the YOLOv7+DS+CBAM network. The predicted results are presented in Fig. 4. Original YOLOv7 network has low confidence in the prediction of the surface garbage targets, and there are missed detections. While the YOLOv7+DS+CBAM network can accurately detect each target with higher prediction accuracy and has a better detection effect.

Field Test. To realize the real-time detection of surface garbage, the improved target detection network in this paper is deployed to edge computing equipment. NVIDIA Jetson Xavier NX is a small, high-performance embedded computer, which is suitable for smart edge devices and embedded systems. It has six Carmel ARM V8.2 64-bit CPUs and an NVIDIA Volta GPU, which can provide AI performance up to 21 TOPS. Therefore, this paper proposes to install an NVIDIA Jetson Xavier NX device on the USV to detect surface floating garbage.

The following describes how to deploy the well-trained improved YOLOv7 network on the NVIDIA Jetson Xavier NX and accelerate the inference process to improve the real-time performance of garbage detection. Firstly, Jetpack SDK is installed on the Jetson Xavier NX, which can provide the basic development environment and software libraries; secondly, necessary dependencies such as OpenCV and Python are installed; then the well-trained network model is transformed into ONNX files for subsequent processing; finally, the camera is adopted as the video input, and the NVIDIA TensorRT library is used to optimize the model to improve performance and accuracy. INT8 precision quantization is used to accelerate the inference process to improve real-time performance.

Fig. 5. Real-time detection results in the local river

Jetson Xavier NX, deployed with the improved YOLOv7 model, is used to detect surface floating garbage in the local river. Some test results are illustrated in Fig. 5. The proposed method performs the task of surface garbage detection excellently. In terms of detection accuracy, the proposed method can meet the requirements. All objects in the video can be detected in real time with high confidence. In terms of detection speed, the average FPS is as high as 32.58, which also meets the real-time requirement of the task.

4 Conclusion

To improve the accuracy and speed of surface floating garbage detection, this paper proposes an improved YOLOv7 target detection method and successfully deploys the method into NVIDIA Jetson Xavier NX embedded computer. The newly added DS module and CBAM attention mechanism module in the YOLOv7 network improve the detection accuracy of surface garbage targets. To improve the detection speed, this paper also uses the NVIDIA TensorRT library to accelerate the inference of the improved YOLOv7 model. Finally, the effectiveness and practicality of the proposed method are verified by field tests. The results show that the proposed method can detect surface garbage with high precision based on the FPS up to 32.58. The method presented in this paper can provide the location and type information of surface garbage, which can be used for the actual surface garbage cleaning task. However, due to the limitation of the types of garbage in the data set, the proposed method can only identify bottle garbage. It is proposed to collect more types of surface floating garbage data to train the network in the future to expand its practical application.

Acknowledgments. This work was supported by the Liaoning Province Science and technology Fund Project (Grant No. 2021-MS-035) and the Research Fund of State Key Laboratory of Robotics (Grant No. 2020-Z04, No. 2021-Z11L02).

References

1. Themistocleous, K., Papoutsa, C., Michaelides, S., Hadjimitsis, D.: Investigating detection of floating plastic litter from space using sentinel-2 imagery. Remote Sens. **12**(16) (2020)
2. Dickens, C., McCartney, M., Tickner, D., Harrison, I.J., Pacheco, P., Ndhlovu, B.: Evaluating the global state of ecosystems and natural resources: within and beyond the SDGs. Sustainability **12**(18) (2020)
3. Ma, Z., Wen, J., Liang, X., Chen, H., Zhao, X.: Extraction and recognition of features from multi-types of surface targets for visual systems in unmanned surface vehicle. J. Xi'an Jiaotong Univ. **48**(8), 60–66 (2014)
4. Fefilatyev, S., Goldgof, D.: Detection and tracking of maritime vehicles in video. In: 19th International Conference on Pattern Recognition, USA, pp. 1–4 (2008)
5. Chen, J., Zhao, G., Pietikainen, M.: Unsupervised dynamic texture segmentation using local spatiotemporal descriptors. In: 19th International Conference on Pattern Recognition, USA, pp. 2937–2940 (2008)
6. Socek, D., Culibrk, D., Marques, O., Kalva, H., Furht, B.: A hybrid color-based foreground object detection method for automated marine surveillance. In: Blanc-Talon, J., Philips, W., Popescu, D., Scheunders, P. (eds.) ACIVS 2005. LNCS, vol. 3708, pp. 340–347. Springer, Heidelberg (2005). https://doi.org/10.1007/11558484_43
7. Li, X., Tian, M., Kong, S., Wu, L., Yu, J.: A modified YOLOv3 detection method for vision-based water surface garbage capture robot. Int. J. Adv. Robot. Syst. **17**(3), (2020)

8. Li, N., Huang, H., Wang, X., Yuan, B., Liu, Y., Xu, S.: Detection of floating garbage on water surface based on PC-Net. Sustainability **14**(18) (2022)
9. Zhang, L., Wei, Y., Wang, H., Shao, Y., Shen, J.: Real-time detection of river surface floating object based on improved RefineDet. IEEE Access **9**, 81147–81160 (2021)
10. Tian, M.,. Li, X, Kong, S., Wu, L., Yu, J.: A modified YOLOv4 detection method for a vision-based underwater garbage cleaning robot. Front. Inf. Technol. Electron. Eng. **23**(8), 1217–1228 (2022)
11. Girshick, R., Donahue, J., Darrell, T., Malik, J.: Rich feature hierarchies for accurate object detection and semantic segmentation. In: 27th IEEE Conference on Computer Vision and Pattern Recognition, Columbus, OH, pp. 580–587 (2014)
12. Redmon, J., Divvala, S., Girshick, R., Farhadi, A.: You only look once: unified, real-time object detection. In: IEEE Conference on Computer Vision and Pattern Recognition, Seattle, WA , pp. 779–788 (2016)
13. Liu, W., et al.: SSD: single shot MultiBox detector. In: 14th European Conference on Computer Vision, Amsterdam, Netherlands, pp. 21–37 (2016)
14. Woo, S., Park, J., Lee, J.-Y., Kweon, I.S.: CBAM: convolutional block attention module. In: 15th European Conference on Computer Vision, Munich, Germany, vol. 11211, pp. 3–19 (2018)

Real-Time Map Compression Method Based on Boolean Operation and Moore-Neighborhood Search

Chengcheng Niu[1,2], Hongyao Shen[1,2(✉)], Zhiwei Lin[1,2], and Jianzhong Fu[1,2]

[1] The State Key Laboratory of Fluid Power and Mechatronic Systems, College of Mechanical Engineering, Zhejiang University, Hangzhou 310027, China
shenhongyao@zju.edu.cn

[2] Key Laboratory of 3D Printing Process and Equipment of Zhejiang Province, College of Mechanical Engineering, Zhejiang University, Hangzhou 310027, China

Abstract. Presently, the topics of sensor network information sharing and multi-robot mapping in robotics have gained considerable research interest. This paper introduces a real-time map compression methodology developed to address the time-intensive problem associated with large-scale map cross-system transmission. This method employs neighborhood filtering, a modified Moore-Neighborhood tracking algorithm, and polygonal Boolean operation technology to extract the inner and outer boundaries of a 2D raster map, thereby enabling map reconstruction. The proposed methodology specifically focuses on the removal of burrs from the outer boundary and reoptimization of the inner boundary search process. This is done to enhance the efficacy of the map reconstruction. Additionally, the extracted inner and outer boundaries are utilized for the reconstruction of the map. The performance of the proposed algorithm was evaluated using several types of maps. The results indicate a relatively low execution time of 300 ms for a map comprising 2 million pixels, which essentially fulfills the real-time requirements for large-scale map transmission and reconstruction. Furthermore, the quality of the map reconstruction was assessed using the Universal Image Quality Index (UIQI), Multi-Scale Structural Similarity (MS-SSIM), and Peak signal-to-noise ratio (PSNR) image evaluation metrics. The reconstruction results reveal that the map effectively satisfies the requirements with a UIQI exceeding 0.9984, an MS-SSIM surpassing 0.9282, and a PSNR above 27.7089. Simultaneously, the map's compression rate exceeded 99.0%, thereby demonstrating that the algorithm can accomplish a significantly high compression rate. This evidence suggests the algorithm's potential for effective deployment in real-world applications requiring large-scale map transmission and reconstruction.

Keywords: Boolean operation · Moore-Neighborhood search · Lightweight map · Boundary extraction · Map reconstruction · Map compression

© The Author(s), under exclusive license to Springer Nature Singapore Pte Ltd. 2023
H. Yang et al. (Eds.): ICIRA 2023, LNAI 14272, pp. 583–596, 2023.
https://doi.org/10.1007/978-981-99-6480-2_48

1 Introduction

As Simultaneous Localization and Mapping (SLAM) technology continues to evolve [1–3], the efficient utilization of large-scale maps constructed by mobile robots presents a significant challenge in the field. Currently, the sharing of information through robot sensor networks and multi-robot mapping has become an area of active research [4, 5]. The demand for effective map compression techniques that facilitate real-time map transmission, including the transfer of maps between different operating systems, is becoming increasingly apparent.

Notably, there is a scarcity of research on real-time compression and transmission of 2D maps. Map compression methods are typically employed in scenarios involving high-precision, large-scale mapping. In contrast, a significant body of research has been devoted to the compression and transmission of 3D point clouds. Current 3D point cloud compression methods primarily focus on the compression of data received by 3D point cloud sensors, whereas 2D map compression methods concentrate on real-time map establishment. Despite the differences in data sources and types between the two, they share a commonality in point cloud data compression.

Point cloud compression is generally categorized into real-time and non-real-time types. Few algorithms exist for real-time 3D point cloud transmission due to the complexity of the algorithms leading to extended compression times. Compression methods based on height maps and octrees can fulfill the implementation requirements. An octree is a tree-like data structure in which each node has eight child nodes. This structure is frequently employed for three-dimensional space division and for accelerating spatial queries. However, many tree-based methods fail to extract random data features, and their compression rates cannot compete with height maps.

Prominent methods include octree-based point cloud coding by Huang et al. [6], and octree-based progressive point cloud compression by Ruwen Schnabel et al. [7]. Armin Hornung et al. [8] proposed a real-time 3D mapping framework based on octrees in 2013, designed for 3D environment modeling and potential compression applications. This has been successfully implemented in numerous real-world robotic projects.

In 2015, Tim Golla et al. [9] introduced a method based on local 2D parameterization of surface point clouds to compress 3D point clouds. This method maintains an advanced compression ratio while ensuring method speed. Erik et al. [10] utilized the self-similarity of the point cloud to complete the 3D point cloud compression and is suitable for datasets of millions of points. Julius Kammerl et al. [11] proposed a real-time point cloud stream compression method based on octree in 2012. This method eliminates redundancy in the point cloud stream but is only suitable for a fixed point cloud stream output by a single sensor. Pauly and Gross et al. [12] pioneered the description of point clouds based on height maps, using these to perform spectral analysis of point clouds.

Opdenbosch et al. [13] proposed a method based on feature coding and a minimum spanning tree for compressing the environment map obtained by 3D vision SLAM. This method retains effective compression characteristics and high observability, but is mainly applicable to sparse maps of 3D vision and not to dense maps. Chenxi et al. [14] employed a recursive neural network and residual block method to compress the point cloud of a 3D LiDAR sensor. Compared with the commonly used octree point cloud compression method, this method requires less volume for the same accuracy. Nagasaka et al. [15–17] proposed a dictionary-based point cloud compression method that yields superior results in compression speed and data compactness. This method is primarily used in point cloud compression during the SLAM mapping process, but it does not delve into grayscale map compression. In this research, we introduce a technique for real-time map compression, specifically developed to mitigate the complexities and time-intensity related to the cross-system transmission of large-scale maps.

2   Map Compression and Reconstruction Approach

The process of map compression and reconstruction primarily encompasses four significant stages: preprocessing and outline acquisition of the map, removal of burrs from $Boundary_{outer}$, acquisition of internal boundaries within the map, and re-optimized search for the internal boundary within the map. Each of these stages will be elaborated upon in the following sections.

2.1   Map Preprocessing and Outline Acquisition

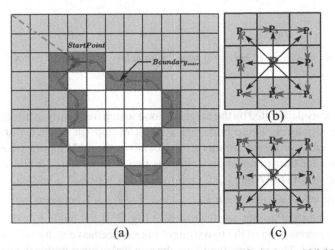

Fig. 1. Modified Moore-Neighborhood algorithm: (a) the Modified Moore-Neighborhood algorithm and its tracking direction (b) clockwise, and (c) counterclockwise.

Map preprocessing, a fundamental step in our proposed method, consists of map cropping and black pixel neighborhood filtering. The preprocessing phase establishes the foundation for subsequent operations. In this study, we employ a modified version of the Moore-Neighborhood algorithm [18], also referred to as the 8-Neighborhood algorithm. This algorithm offers two search directions: clockwise and counterclockwise. For the purposes of our research, we opted for the clockwise search direction. In a bid to accelerate the initial point search within the Modified Moore-Neighborhood algorithm, we applied Bresenham's line interpolation [20] to the starting point and the center point of the map. The initial point is then sought along the interpolated line, as depicted in Fig. 1. To extract the boundary of the map, we applied the modified Moore-Neighborhood algorithm, utilizing Jacob's stopping criterion [19]. For the sake of brevity, we denote the boundary of the map as $Boundary_{outer}$.

2.2 Removal of Burrs from $Boundary_{outer}$

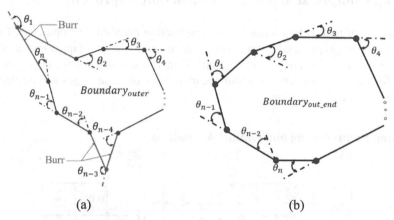

Fig. 2. Schematic diagram of burrs: (a) burrs in $Boundary_{outer}$, and (b) removal of burrs from $Boundary_{out\_end}$.

The boundary delineated by the neighborhood search frequently exhibits burrs, which are long, slender lines. These burrs are a result of gaps in obstacles or uneven surfaces encountered during the Simultaneous Localization and Mapping (SLAM) process. The procedure for burr removal encompasses two primary steps. Initially, we traverse the positions within $Boundary_{outer}$, eliminating any repeated coordinate points. Subsequently, we calculate the angle $\theta_n = \cos^{-1}\left(\frac{BA \cdot BC}{|BA| \cdot |BC|}\right)$ between two straight lines composed of adjacent points, as illustrated in Fig. 2. If the angle θ_n exceeds a certain threshold, the intersection of the two straight lines is deemed a sharp point and is consequently eliminated. This method facilitates the removal of burrs within the $Boundary_{outer}$. Following this operation, the final outline of the map is denoted as $Boundary_{out\_end}$.

2.3 Map Internal Boundaries Acquisition

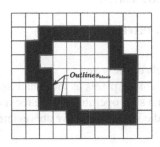

Fig. 3. Rectangles Boolean operation effect chart.

The black pixel is expanded into rectangle with the pixel as the center and side length of one. And the Boolean sum operation is performed on the rectangles to obtain $Outlines_{black}$ as shown in Figs. 3 and 4.

Each black pixel is expanded into a rectangle with the pixel at its center and a side length of one. We subsequently perform a Boolean sum operation on these rectangles to acquire $Outlines_{black}$, as demonstrated in Figs. 3 and 4. In Fig. 4, the set within $Boundary_{ounter}$ represents a set that requires evaluation for internal boundary determination; all other sets can be disregarded. When all points of $Boundary_{inner\_n}$ are situated within $Boundary_n$, $Boundary_{inner\_n}$ is deemed the internal boundary.

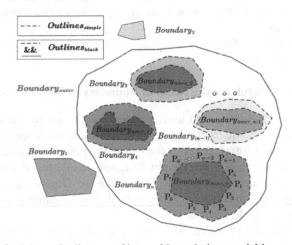

Fig. 4. Schematic diagram of internal boundaries acquisition method.

The algorithm discussed in this section primarily encompasses three steps: obtaining the outline of black pixels, reducing the number of black pixel outlines, and conducting an initial search for internal boundaries.

Obtain the Outline of Black Pixels:

Step 1. Extract the black pixels of the map.
Step 2. Create rectangles with black pixels as the center and side length one.
Step 3. The offset and Boolean sum operation of the rectangle.
Step 4. Obtain the outline of the black pixels, we abbreviate it as $Outlines_{black}$ as shown in Fig. 4.

Reduce the Number of the Outline of Black Pixels:

Step 1. Offset $Boundary_{out\_end}$ inward by a certain threshold.
Step 2. Boolean intersection operation between $Boundary_{out_{end}}$ and $Outlines_{black}$.
Step 3. If the two intersect, the black pixel outline is retained; otherwise, the black pixel outline is deleted, we abbreviate it as $Outlines_{simple}$ as shown in Fig. 4.

Initial Search of Internal Boundaries:

Step 1. In Fig. 4, if all vertices of $Boundary_{inner\_n}$ are within $Boundary_n$, $Boundary_{inner\_n}$ is the internal boundary and add it to $Boundary_{inner1}$, otherwise $Boundary_{inner\_n}$ isn't the internal boundary.
Step 2. Traverse every outline in $Outlines_{simple}$, if the outline is the internal boundary, add it to $Boundary_{inner1}$.

2.4 Re-optimized Search for the Internal Boundary Within the Map

We deploy a purposefully designed neighborhood search operator, as demonstrated in Fig. 5(a), to ascertain the quantity of gray pixels surrounding a specific pixel along a boundary. If the count of gray pixels exceeds one, the pixel is designated as the initial search point for the boundary. Utilizing this designed neighborhood search operator, we proceed to search for the initial search point within the $Outlines_{simple}$. Based on this search point, we employ an enhanced Moore neighborhood search algorithm to identify the internal boundary, as depicted in Fig. 5(b).

The re-optimization of the internal boundary search within the map is crucial. It is worth noting that only two-layer nested closed outlines can be acknowledged as internal boundaries, while certain individual smaller outlines might not qualify for recognition. Thus, the re-optimization of the internal boundary search is necessitated to augment the quality of map boundary extraction.

This algorithm is primarily composed of three procedural steps: determining boundaries that satisfy the predetermined conditions, acquiring the initial search position, and

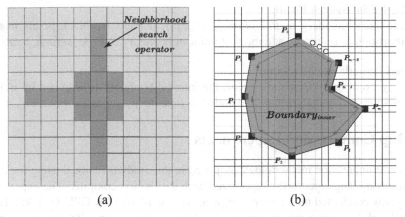

Fig. 5. Re-optimized search for the internal boundary: (a) neighbor search operator, and (b) internal boundaries search.

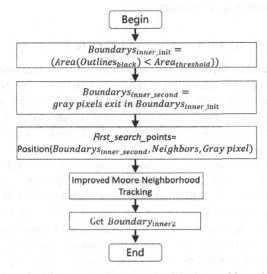

Fig. 6. Flow chart for re-optimized search of the internal boundary in the map.

subsequently tracking the internal boundaries. These steps are visually represented in Fig. 6.

Determine Boundaries That Meets the Requirements:

Step 1. Delete outlines smaller than the area threshold in $Outlines_{black}$, we will get $Boundarys_{inner\_init}$.

Step 2. Traverse each boundary in $Boundarys_{inner\_init}$, if there are black pixels in the neighbor search operator as shown in Fig. 4 of boundary add boundary to $Boundarys_{inner\_second}$.

Get the Initial Search Position:

Traverse each boundary in $Boundarys_{inner\_second}$, if there are black pixels in the 8-Neighborhood of boundary add the first point of boundary to $First\_serach\_point$.

Internal Boundaries Tracking:

For every point in $First\_serach\_point$, the internal boundary is searched by modified Moore-Neighborhood algorithm and added to $Boundary_{inner2}$ as shown in Fig. 4.

3　Map Compression Experiments

The map compression methodology proposed in this study is realized using the Python programming language, further optimized with the Cython compiler. The experimental testing was conducted on a laptop equipped with an i7-10700K CPU @ 3.80 GHz and 32GB RAM. In our experiments, we assessed map compression and reconstruction, program execution time, and the compression rate of the map. We provide a comprehensive display of the map compression and decompression processes, in addition to comparing three maps both pre and post-reconstruction.

3.1　Map Compression and Reconstruction Effect Test

In an effort to evaluate the efficacy of our map compression and reconstruction method, we employed three different maps varying in size and structure for testing. The results of these tests are visualized in Fig. 7. Overall, the original and reconstructed maps are congruent, without any significant compromise to the visualization effect. Compared to the direct transmission of the original map, our method drastically reduces the network resources needed for map transmission.

To quantitatively assess the quality of map reconstruction, we utilized three image quality evaluation metrics: Peak Signal-to-Noise Ratio (PSNR), Universal Image Quality Index (UIQI), and Multi-Scale Structural Similarity (MS-SSIM). PSNR, a commonly used quality evaluation method, calculates the difference between the gray values of corresponding pixels in the distorted and original images, offering a statistical view of the quality of the distorted image. However, it does not account for local visual factors of the human eye, and thus, performs poorly in evaluating the local quality of an image [21].

On the other hand, UIQI, a simple measure reliant solely on the first and second order statistics of the original and distorted images, serves as a measure of instability and often exhibits inconsistency with subjective evaluations [22]. MS-SSIM, a more advanced form of SSIM, operates on multiple scales through a multi-stage process of sub-sampling. It demonstrates equivalent or superior performance to SSIM across various image and video databases [23–25].

The reconstruction effects on three maps of varying sizes and structures were tested. The test maps consisted of cropped maps and their reconstructed counterparts, with both maps sharing the same dimensions. The results revealed that all UIQI indicators exceeded 0.9984, all MSSSIM indicators surpassed 0.9282, and all PSNR indicators exceeded 27.7089. These results suggest that the map reconstruction using our proposed method satisfactorily meets the requirements.

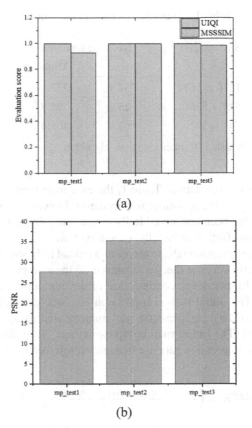

Fig. 7. Evaluation of map reconstruction effect: (a) UIQI, MSSSIM, and (b) PSNR.

3.2 Map Executing Time Comparison

This algorithm, developed in Python and optimized with Cython, was evaluated using three maps of varying sizes and structures to measure its efficiency. The associated statistics, including the size of each map and the execution time of our program, are presented in Table 1. It is evident that the program execution time increases proportionally with the size of the map. As displayed in Table 1, for a test map consisting of approximately 2,000,000 pixels, the duration from outlines extraction to map reconstruction was 274.4 ms. Conversely, for a smaller test map, containing about 300,000 pixels, the process required only 20.4 ms.

Notably, the execution time of the algorithm is influenced not only by the size of the map but also by the structure of the map. This is exemplified in Table 1, where a test map with approximately 300,000 pixels required 20.4 ms for outlines extraction to map reconstruction, while another map with fewer pixels (200,000) required a longer time of 73.0 ms.

The time complexity of the algorithm is suitable for real-time applications. For larger scale maps, it is desirable to have an algorithm with a shorter execution time, hence lower

Table 1. Algorithm executing time statistics

	Size (pixels)	Executing time (ms)		
		Mean	Minimum	Maximum
Test map one	1216 × 1632	337.4	332.1	333.8
Test map two	512 × 576	25.8	25.7	26.1
Test map three	541 × 309	103.6	101.4	107.2

Note: Each map above is tested 10 times using our algorithm

time complexity. As per the data in Table 1, the execution time for each test map was below 300 ms, satisfying the real-time requirements. However, it should be noted that while the algorithm has been optimized in Python, a transition to C++ could potentially improve efficiency and further reduce the execution time.

As for the map compression rate, it serves as a crucial indicator for map compression methods, as it directly reflects the performance of the compression method. In this study, we performed a two-stage compression of the contour data to achieve a higher compression ratio. The initial map compression rate was calculated using the IMCR method, and the secondary compression was implemented using the Google Encoded Polyline Format [26]. The initial map compression rate, secondary map compression rate, and final map compression rate are henceforth referred to as IMCR, SMCR, and FMCR, respectively.

$$IMCR = \left(1 - \frac{Pixels_{BL} + Pixels_{IN} + Pixels_{OT}}{Pixels_{OM}}\right) \times 100\% \tag{1}$$

in which MCR is map compression rate, $Pixels_{BL}$ are black pixels, $Pixels_{IN}$ are pixels of $Bounday_{inner1}$ and $Bounday_{inner2}$, $Pixels_{OT}$ are pixels of $Boundary_{out\_end}$, $Pixels_{OM}$ are original map pixels.

$$FMCR = (1 - IMCR) \times (1 - SMCR) \times 100 \tag{2}$$

The statistics regarding the number of original map pixels, the number of compressed map pixels, and the map compression rate for our test maps are detailed in Table 2. The compression rate of the map is contingent on both the sizes and structures of the map. Upon testing three different maps, it was observed that the final compression rate exceeded 99.0% for each one. This finding validates the capability of our proposed algorithm to achieve high compression rates.

3.3 Map Compression and Reconstruction Comparison

Figure 8 delineates the entire process of map compression and reconstruction. Additionally, Fig. 9 provides a comparative illustration of the compression and reconstruction of three maps, each with distinct sizes and structures.

Table 2. Map compression rate statistics

	Size (pixels)	Initial map compression rate	Secondary map compression rate	Final map compression rate
Test map I	$1,216 \times 1,632$	99.03%	93.80%	99.93%
Test map II	512×576	98.08%	93.21%	99.87%
Test map III	541×309	95.30%	93.54%	99.70%

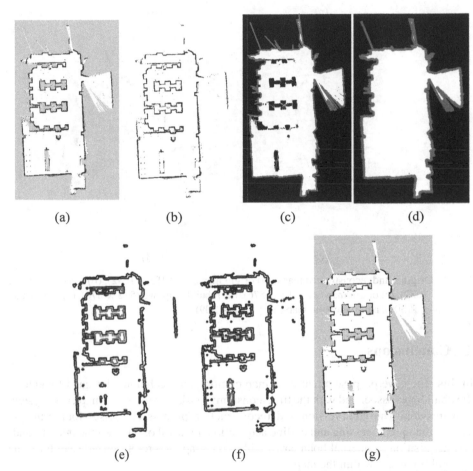

Fig. 8. The entire process of map compression and reconstruction: (a) map cropping: (b) the results of filtering black pixels, (c) obtaining the effect of map outline, (d) the effect of removing burr of $Boundary_{out\_end}$, (e) obtain $Boundary_{inner1}$ in the map, (f) re-optimized search result of $Boundary_{inner2}$ in the map, and (g) map reconstruction rendering.

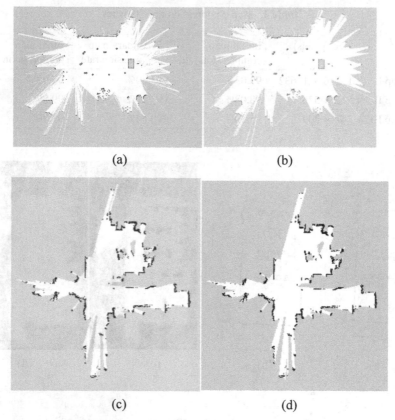

Fig. 9. Original and reconstructed maps: (a) origin map one (1216 × 1632), (b) rebuild map one (1216 × 1632), (c) origin map two (512 × 576), (d) rebuild map two (512 × 576), (e) origin map three (541 × 309), and (f) rebuild map three (541 × 309).

4   Conclusions

In this study, we propose a real-time map compression technique designed to address the challenges associated with the time-consuming task of large-scale map cross-system transmission. The compression and reconstruction process comprises four principal stages: map preprocessing and outline acquisition, removal of burrs on the outer boundary, acquisition of internal boundaries within the map, and re-optimized search for the internal boundary within the map.

During the initial stage, map cropping and black pixel neighborhood filtering are utilized to simplify subsequent operations. A modified Moore-Neighborhood algorithm is employed to acquire the outer boundary, denoted as $Boundary_{outer}$. Notably, Bresenham's line interpolation is utilized to expedite the search for the initial point. In the second stage, we focus on the elimination of long and narrow protruding lines, often referred to as burrs, on the outer boundary. These lines are usually artifacts resulting from small holes and uneven surfaces on the object rather than being inherent features of the object. To further optimize the outer boundary, we set an angle threshold between adjacent straight lines to eliminate these burrs, resulting in the optimized outer boundary, $Boundary_{out\_end}$. The third stage involves the use of Boolean operations to extract and reduce the number of black pixel outlines. The initial internal boundaries, $Boundary_{inner1}$, are then generated using the modified Moore-Neighborhood algorithm. In the final stage, we enhance the efficacy of the internal boundaries search. A novel neighbor search operator, in conjunction with the modified Moore-Neighborhood algorithm, is used to derive the re-optimized internal boundaries, $Boundary_{inner2}$.

We conducted an experimental evaluation involving map compression reconstruction, program execution time, and map compression rate tests. A variety of maps were used to assess algorithm performance. The results revealed that the algorithm execution time was relatively low at 300 ms for a map consisting of 2 million pixels. This essentially meets the real-time requirements for large-scale map transmission and reconstruction. The quality of the map reconstruction was evaluated using the Universal Image Quality Index (UIQI), Multi-Scale Structural Similarity (MS-SSIM), and Peak Signal-to-Noise Ratio (PSNR) image evaluation indicators. The reconstruction results demonstrate that the map effectively meets the requirements with a UIQI exceeding 0.9984, an MS-SSIM surpassing 0.9282, and a PSNR above 27.7089. Simultaneously, the compression rate of the map exceeded 99.0%, thereby providing evidence that the algorithm can achieve a significantly high compression rate. Furthermore, given that the algorithm is written in Python, although it has been optimized, substituting Python with C++ could potentially enhance efficiency and reduce algorithm execution time further.

Acknowledgements. This work was financially supported by the National Nature Science Foundation of China (51975518) and Natural Science Foundation of Zhejiang Province for Distinguished Young Scholars (LR22E050002).

References

1. Grisetti, G., Stachniss, C., Burgard, W.: Improved techniques for grid mapping with Rao-blackwellized particle filters. IEEE Trans. Rob. **23**, 34–46 (2007)
2. Kohlbrecher, S., von Stryk, O., Meyer, J., Klingauf, U.: A flexible and scalable SLAM system with full 3D motion estimation. In: 2011 IEEE International Symposium on Safety, Security, and Rescue Robotics, pp. 155–160 (2011)
3. Hess, W., Kohler, D., Rapp, H.H., Andor, D.: Real-time loop closure in 2D LIDAR SLAM. In: 2016 IEEE International Conference on Robotics and Automation (ICRA), pp. 1271–1278 (2016)
4. Andersson, L.A.A., Nygårds, J.: C-SAM: multi-robot SLAM using square root information smoothing. In: 2008 IEEE International Conference on Robotics and Automation, pp. 2798–2805 (2008)
5. Menegatti, E., Zanella, A., Zilli, S., Zorzi, F., Pagello, E.: Range-only SLAM with a mobile robot and a Wireless Sensor Networks. In: 2009 IEEE International Conference on Robotics and Automation, pp. 8–14 (2009)
6. Huang, Y., Peng, J., Kuo, C.-C.J., Gopi, M.: Octree-based progressive geometry coding of point clouds. In: PBG@SIGGRAPH (2006)
7. Schnabel, R., Klein, R.: Octree-based point-cloud compression. In: PBG@SIGGRAPH (2006)

8. Hornung, A., Wurm, K.M., Bennewitz, M., Stachniss, C., Burgard, W.: OctoMap: an efficient probabilistic 3D mapping framework based on octrees. Auton. Robot. **34**, 189–206 (2013)
9. Golla, T., Klein, R.: Real-time point cloud compression. In: 2015 IEEE/RSJ International Conference on Intelligent Robots and Systems (IROS), pp. 5087–5092 (2015)
10. Hubo, E., Mertens, T., Haber, T., Bekaert, P.: Self-similarity-based compression of point clouds, with application to ray tracing. In: PBG@Eurographics (2007)
11. Kammerl, J., Blodow, N., Rusu, R.B., Gedikli, S., Beetz, M., Steinbach, E.G.: Real-time compression of point cloud streams. In: 2012 IEEE International Conference on Robotics and Automation, pp. 778–785 (2012)
12. Pauly, M., Gross, M.H.: Spectral processing of point-sampled geometry. In: Proceedings of the 28th Annual Conference on Computer Graphics and Interactive Techniques (2001)
13. Opdenbosch, D.V., Aykut, T., Alt, N., Steinbach, E.G.: Efficient map compression for collaborative visual SLAM. In: 2018 IEEE Winter Conference on Applications of Computer Vision (WACV), pp. 992–1000 (2018)
14. Tu, C., Takeuchi, E., Carballo, A., Takeda, K.: Point cloud compression for 3d lidar sensor using recurrent neural network with residual blocks. In: 2019 International Conference on Robotics and Automation (ICRA), pp. 3274–3280 (2019)
15. Tomomi, N., Kanji, T.: An incremental scheme for dictionary-based compressive SLAM. In: 2011 IEEE/RSJ International Conference on Intelligent Robots and Systems, pp. 872–879 (2011)
16. Tomomi, N., Kanji, T.: Dictionary-based map compression using modified RANSAC map-matching. In: 2010 IEEE International Conference on Robotics and Biomimetics, pp. 980–985 (2010)
17. Tomomi, N., Kanji, T.: Dictionary-based map compression for sparse feature maps. In: 2011 IEEE International Conference on Robotics and Automation, pp. 2329–2336 (2011)
18. Sharma, P., Diwakar, M., Lal, N.: Edge detection using Moore neighborhood. Int. J. Comput. Appl. **61**, 26–30 (2013)
19. Reddy, P.R., Amarnadh, V., Bhaskar, M.: Evaluation of Stopping Criterion in Contour Tracing Algorithms (2012)
20. Bresenham, J.: Algorithm for computer control of a digital plotter. Semin. Graph. (1965)
21. Huynh-Thu, Q., Ghanbari, M.: Scope of validity of PSNR in image/video quality assessment. Electron. Lett **44**, 800–801 (2008)
22. Al-Najjar, Y., Soong, C.: Comparison of Image Quality Assessment: PSNR, HVS, SSIM, UIQI (2012)
23. Wang, Z., Simoncelli, E.P., Bovik, A.C.: Multiscale structural similarity for image quality assessment. In: The Thirty-Seventh Asilomar Conference on Signals, Systems and Computers, vol. 1392, pp. 1398–1402 (2003)
24. Søgaard, J., Krasula, L., Shahid, M., Temel, D., Brunnström, K., Razaak, M.: Applicability of existing objective metrics of perceptual quality for adaptive video streaming. In: Image Quality and System Performance (2016)
25. Dosselmann, R., Yang, X.D.: A comprehensive assessment of the structural similarity index. SIViP **5**, 81–91 (2011)
26. Google Encoded Polyline Format. https://developers.google.com/maps/documentation/utilities/polylinealgorithm

Research on Location Algorithm of 5G Ceramic Filter Based on Machine Vision

Zuhao Zhu[1], Yi Long[2,3]([✉]), Long He[3], Yaoan Lu[4], Jian Li[5], and Liangsheng Guo[5]

[1] College of Information Science and Engineering, Northeastern University, Shenyang, Liaoning, China

[2] Faculty of Robot Science and Engineering, Northeastern University, Shenyang, Liaoning, China
longyi@mail.neu.edu.cn

[3] Zhiyuan Research Institute, Hangzhou, Zhejiang, China

[4] Guangdong Provincial Key Laboratory of Minimally Invasive Surgical Instruments and Manufacturing Technology, Guangdong University of Technology, Guangzhou, China

[5] Department of Orthopaedics, The Second Affiliated Hospital of Soochow University, Suzhou, China

Abstract. In order to solve the problem of insufficient positioning accuracy in the detection process of ceramic filters, a high-precision positioning algorithm based on edge detection fitting is proposed. The algorithm combines hierarchical pyramid model to locate ceramic filter step by step and obtain ROI region. Secondly, according to the rough location results of the target area, combined with the improved Canny detection algorithm, the ceramic filter is sub-pixel extracted, and a hierarchical screening method is proposed to obtain the contour information of the circular hole, which improves the stability of the algorithm. The minimum circumscribed circle algorithm based on Tukey is used to fit the extracted sub-pixel contour by weight, and the center position of the circular hole is obtained. Finally, according to the geometric relationship between the center of the circular hole and the ceramic filter, the center coordinates and offset angle of the ceramic filter are solved. The results of the experiment demonstrate that the ceramic filter positioning algorithm described in this paper can accomplish accurate and precise positioning of ceramic filters, in which the center repeated positioning error is 1.86 pixels and the angle error is 0.1137°, which meets the requirements for the positioning accuracy of ceramic filters.

Keywords: Machine Vision · Subpixel Extraction · Graded Screening · High Precision Positioning

Fund project: Supported by Guangdong Basic and Applied Basic Research Foundation(2020A1515110121), State Key Laboratory of Robotics and System (HIT) (SKLRS-2022-KF-05).

H. Yang et al. (Eds.): ICIRA 2023, LNAI 14272, pp. 597–607, 2023.
https://doi.org/10.1007/978-981-99-6480-2_49

1 Introduction

With the advent of the information age, the construction of 5G base stations is in full swing, and the demand for corresponding RF components has also increased greatly. As an important component of RF components, 5G ceramic filter plays an important role in signal processing of 5G signals. Compared with traditional metal ceramic filters, ceramic filters have the advantages of high dielectric constant, low loss and small size, and gradually replace traditional metal ceramic filters and become the mainstream of the market [1, 2]. However, due to the brittleness and low impact resistance of ceramic materials, in order to avoid the damage to the ceramic filters caused by secondary loading, we consider using robots to suck the 31 mm * 17.5 mm ceramic filter in the material tray and put it in the detection position of 32 mm * 18 mm. Because the rotation and translation of the ceramic filters are involved in the process of placing materials, and the camera field of view of the detection platform is relatively small, it puts forward higher requirements for the positioning accuracy of the ceramic filters.

Usually, locating and identifying the workpiece visually is a very important link in the industrial manufacturing process in recent years. At present, template matching method [3, 4], region growing method [5, 6], minimum circumscribed rectangle method [7, 8] and other methods are commonly used in workpiece positioning, identification and detection. Template matching method is universal, but it takes a long time to calculate and needs a lot of storage space, which greatly affects the efficiency of workpiece positioning and the accuracy of template matching is also lacking. Region growing method has a large amount of calculation and is greatly influenced by factors such as illumination, which often leads to over-segmentation or under-segmentation of images. The minimum circumscribed rectangle method is simple in calculation, but the stability of the algorithm is not good if the background of the workpiece is complex. Yu [9] according to the imaging characteristics of SOP package patch components, median ceramic filtering is used to detect the edge of the image, and the outline of the pin foot is selected according to the area and outline perimeter, and then the offset angle of the component is calculated by the adjacent rectangle and the improved least square method, so as to realize the high-precision positioning of the component. Wang [10] and others proposed a tag location algorithm to improve the accuracy and stability of tag location, and adopted a composite template to improve the location quality of template matching. Baygin [11] and others proposed Otsu thresholding and Hough transform to extract features from reference images, and finally matched the models to detect the size of holes.

In view of the above research on workpiece positioning algorithm and the structural characteristics of the ceramic filter, this paper proposes a fast and accurate ceramic filter positioning algorithm. By utilizing template matching, this approach is capable of identifying the general location of the targeted area and deriving an estimated position for the circular hole located on the ceramic filter. In order to improve the positioning accuracy and stability, the algorithm combining hierarchical screening and minimum circumscribed circle fitting based on turkey is use to find the edge of the template imaged accurately locate the center of the circular hole. Finally, the center position and offset angle of the ceramic filter are calculated according to the geometric relationship.

2   ROI Region Extraction

2.1   Material Tray Positioning Algorithm

In the search stage, the ceramic filters are randomly placed in the material tray, so it is necessary to make a preliminary positioning of the material tray. Through the preliminary positioning of the material tray, it can not only avoid the collision between the manipulator and the edge of the material tray because the ceramic filter is close to the material tray, but also reduce the template matching area and improve the template matching speed. The specific steps are shown in the following figure (Fig. 1):

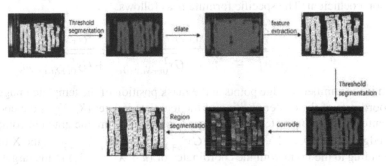

Fig. 1. Material tray positioning algorithm

Through the above steps, we can initially locate the location of the ceramic filters. Because the ceramic filters are too dense, it is difficult to ensure that all ceramic filters are separated by Blob analysis, so it is necessary to use template matching to roughly locate the ceramic filters and obtain the approximate location of each ceramic filter.

2.2   Template Matching Based on Image Pyramid

Template Matching. By template matching of ceramic filter, we can roughly obtain the ROI region of ceramic filter, which lays the foundation for subsequent accurate positioning. The specific process is as follows:

(1) The Sobel operator is used to obtain the output G_x and G_y in the X and Y directions in the template image, and then the gradient intensity and gradient angle are obtained.

$$\text{Magnitude} = \sqrt{Gx^2 + Gy^2}. \tag{1}$$

$$\text{Direction} = \text{invtan}\left(\frac{Gy}{Gx}\right). \tag{2}$$

(2) For the pixel in the template image, its gradient amplitude is compared with that of two adjacent pixels along its gradient direction. If the gradient value of the current pixel is the largest, the current pixel is retained; Otherwise, its value is set to zero.

(3) The gradient amplitudes of edge pixels and non-edge pixels are compared with a set of thresholds. The pixels with gradient amplitudes higher than the high threshold are regarded as edge pixels, and the pixels below the low threshold are excluded, while the pixels in between are regarded as edge pixels only when they are connected to the high threshold pixels.

(4) After extracting the edge, we save the x and y derivatives of the selected edge as a template model together with the coordinate information.

By performing NCC operation on the template image on the image to be matched, the correlation coefficient between the template image and the template image is calculated, and the similarity between the two regions is expressed by the magnitude of the correlation coefficient. The specific formula is as follows.

$$S_{u,v} = \frac{1}{n}\sum_{i=1}^{n} \frac{\left(Gx_i^T \cdot Gx_{(u+Xi,v+Yi)}^S\right) + \left(Gy_i^T \cdot Gy_{(u+Xi,v+Yi)}^S\right)}{\sqrt{Gx_i^{T^2} + Gy_i^{T^2}} \cdot \sqrt{Gx_{(u+Xi,v+Yi)}^T{}^2 + Gy_{(u+Xi,v+YV_Y)}^T}}. \tag{3}$$

where: n is the number of edge points at the mask position of the template image; (u, v) is the coordinate of the center position of the template image; (X_i, Y_i) is the coordinate of the center position of the template image; Gx_i^T and Gy_i^T are the gradient components of each edge point in X and Y directions; $Gx_{(u+Xi,v+Yi)}^S$, $Gy_{(u+Xi,v+Yi)}^S$ is the X direction corresponding to the point with the coordinates of $(u + X_i, v + Y_i)$ in the target image.

Image Pyramid. Template matching based on edge gradient NCC can avoid mutual interference between ceramic filters and locate the ROI area. However, searching the 212 pixel * 375 pixel area directly in the 5672 pixel * 3628 pixel area takes too long to meet the real-time requirements. Consider using hierarchical pyramid to improve the matching speed. The image pyramid is constructed by continuously downsampling the template map and the search map. When matching, only the top layer of the pyramid is traversed, and the subsequent matching areas are obtained according to the candidate points obtained at the top layer. The specific steps are as follows:

1. The matched images and templates are preprocessed and processed into a series of image sequences from high to low resolution and from large to small size.
2. The first round of correlation search is carried out from the layer with low resolution and small size, and the similarity S of each position is calculated, and the possible central point position (x, y) and offset angle θ are obtained. Judge whether the lowest resolution layer has been reached, and if not, repeat step 2.
3. The high-scoring image is turned into a low-resolution image through the image pyramid, and then the pyramid of the template image is matched with the pyramid of the matching image by using the NCC template matching algorithm, and the image is matched only at the lowest resolution layer at the top, so as to realize fast image matching.

3   Center Location Algorithm Based on Plane Three Points

Because of the low positioning accuracy of template matching and the great influence of template selection, the precise positioning of the ceramic filter can't be realized. In order to improve the positioning accuracy, we combine the characteristics of the ceramic filter, extract and fit the sub-pixel contour of the ceramic filter, obtain the center coordinates of the circular hole, and calculate the center coordinates and offset angle of the ceramic filter according to the coordinates of the circular hole.

3.1 Sub-Pixel Edge Detection

Image Preprocessing. Because the surface gray level of ceramic filter is not very drastic, it puts forward higher requirements for sub-pixel contour extraction. Firstly, we need to preprocess the image to eliminate the influence of some noise signals on ceramic filter contour extraction.

In the process of camera image acquisition and transmission, noise may be introduced due to signal interference, which seriously affects the image processing effect, among which salt and pepper noise is the most typical. Because salt and pepper noise belong to high frequency noise, linear ceramic filters are mostly low-pass ceramic filters. The median ceramic filter is a typical nonlinear ceramic filter operator, which has a good denoising effect on isolated noise and can also preserve the edge features of the image. The principle is to sort the gray values of the images in the neighborhood, and then use the middle gray value as the output pixel value. Median ceramic filtering of two-dimensional images is defined as:

$$y_i = \text{Med}\{f_{i-v}, \cdots\cdots, f_i, \cdots\cdots f_{i+v}\} i \in N, v = \frac{m-1}{2}. \tag{4}$$

where y_i is the ceramic filtered pixel gray value; $f_{i-v}, \cdots\cdots, f_i, \cdots\cdots f_{i+v}$ are the pixel values before ceramic filtering; Med is median operation (Figs. 2 and 3).

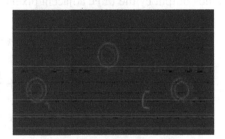

Fig. 2. Profile before pretreatment   **Fig. 3.** Pre-processed contour

By gray stretching, linear transformation and median ceramic filtering, the contrast of image edges can be effectively enhanced, the influence of noise on edge extraction can be reduced, and the contour information of the target object can be retained to the greatest extent.

Sub-pixel Contour Extraction. At present, the mainstream sub-pixel extraction methods can mainly include three kinds of methods, namely moment method [12], interpolation method [13] and curve fitting method [14]. Moment method is to determine the position of the actual edge by assuming the consistency of gray moment between the actual image and the theoretical edge image. However, the moment method is very sensitive to noise, and it is easy to make the edge solution offset. Interpolation method needs to interpolate the image and calculate the gray transformation rate of each pixel. For large-size images, the amount of calculation will be large, which can not meet the real-time requirements. Curve fitting method solves the edge model first, and then solves the sub-pixel edge according to the existing edge model. This method is accurate and not easily affected by edge noise.

In order to extract the sub-pixel contour of the ceramic filter circular hole, we use Canny edge detection algorithm to extract the pixel-level edge, and then get the sub-pixel edge position by quadratic curve fitting. Because Canny algorithm is relatively mature, we mainly introduce the process of fitting sub-pixel edge with quadratic curve.

According to the sampling theorem of square aperture, the output value of a pixel is that the photosensitive surface of the pixel can be expressed as:

$$f(i,j) = \int_{j-\frac{1}{2}}^{j+\frac{1}{2}} \int_{i-\frac{1}{2}}^{i+\frac{1}{2}} g(x,y)dxdy. \tag{5}$$

where $f(i,j)$ is the pixel output value; $g(x,y)$ is the light intensity distribution of continuous images.

Let the quadratic curve equation be in the form:

$$y = ax^2 + bx + c. \tag{6}$$

First, find the point with the most intense gray level in the image and make its serial number 1, and its gray value represents f_0 The serial numbers of the two adjacent points are -1 and 1, respectively, and the corresponding gray values are f_{-1}, f_1 so that the gray values output by the three adjacent pixels can be obtained:

$$\begin{aligned} f_1 &= \int_{\frac{1}{2}}^{\frac{3}{2}}(ax^2 + bx + c)dx \\ &= \left[\frac{1}{3}ax^3 + \frac{1}{2}bx^2 + cx\right]_{\frac{1}{2}}^{\frac{3}{2}} \cdot \\ &= \frac{13}{12}a + b + c \end{aligned} \tag{7}$$

In the same way, we can ask in turn:

$$f_0 = \frac{1}{12}a + c. \tag{8}$$

$$f_{-1} = \frac{13}{12}a - b + c. \tag{9}$$

Combining Eqs. (7), (8) and (9), the expressions of a, b and c can be obtained as follows:

$$a = \frac{1}{2}(f_1 + f_{-1} + 2f_0). \tag{10}$$

$$b = \frac{1}{2}(f_1 - f_{-1}).\tag{11}$$

$$c = \frac{13}{12}f_0 - \frac{1}{24}f_{-1} - \frac{1}{24}f_1.\tag{12}$$

When the abscissa value of the vertex of the conic is $x = -\frac{b}{2a}$, and the values of a and b are brought in respectively, the edge position with sub-pixel accuracy can be obtained.

$$x = \frac{f_1 - f_{-1}}{2(2f_0 - f_{-1} - f_1)}.\tag{13}$$

Because the ceramic filter boundary is not obvious, if the ceramic filter is smoothed excessively, the edge of the circular hole will be blurred, and if the smoothing degree is not enough, new sub-pixel errors will be introduced, which greatly affects the sub-pixel extraction of the circular hole. In view of the above situation, we adopt a multi-level screening processing mode, that is, first, the interference of some sub-pixel edges is eliminated by the limitation of length and roundness, then the similar edges are connected by edge connection, and finally the sub-pixel contour of the circular hole is extracted according to the contour characteristics. The results show that, as shown in Fig. 5, the sub-pixel contour of the circular hole can be extracted stably by this method (Fig. 4).

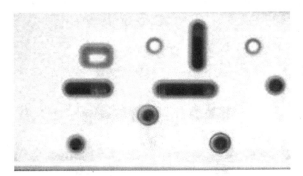

Fig. 4. Sub-pixel contour extraction

Sub-pixel Contour Fitting. After extracting the sub-pixel edge of the ceramic filter circular hole, we need to fit the sub-pixel feature information of the arc. The least square method is a general method to approximate the circular boundary contour to be detected, which finds a set of functions that are closest to the sub-pixel contour to match it by minimizing the error. Even if the edge of the circular object in the image is missing due to uneven illumination and other factors, it will not affect the positioning of the center of the circle and the detection of the radius.

First, suppose that the center coordinates and radius of the circle to be fitted are (x_0, y_0) and r, respectively, then the curve of the fitted circle can be expressed as:

$$f(x, y) = (x - x_0)^2 + (y - y_0)^2 - r^2).\tag{14}$$

If the coordinates of the contour point set extracted from the edge are marked as (x_i, y_i), the distance from the contour point set to the center of the circle is:

$$d_i = \sqrt{(x_i - x_0)^2 + (y_i - y_0)^2}. \tag{15}$$

Considering the influence of outliers on the fitting effect, we introduce weights to reduce the influence of outliers. The weight function can be expressed according to the point to the center of the circle:

$$\delta = \sqrt{(x_i - x_0)^2 + (y_i - y_0)^2}. \tag{16}$$

$$\omega(\delta) = \begin{cases} [1 - (\delta/\tau)^2]^2 & |\delta| \leq \tau \\ 0 & |\delta| > \tau \end{cases}. \tag{17}$$

For all edge points in the image, the optimization residual can be expressed as:

$$Q_\omega = \sum_{i=0}^{n} \omega_i (d_i - r)^2. \tag{18}$$

According to the principle of least squares, when Q_ω is the minimum, the parameters (x_0, y_0) obtained are the parameters of the best fitting element. The fitting result is as shown in the Fig. 6:

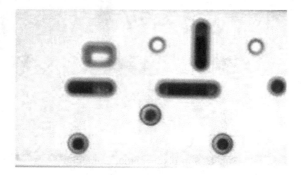

Fig. 5. Sub-pixel contour fitting

3.2   Calculation of the Center Coordinates and Offset Angle of the Ceramic Filter

The position of the cavity on the ceramic filter is always constant. After obtaining the coordinates of the three circular cavities of the ceramic filter, we can calculate the center point (x_0, y_0) and the offset angle θ of the ceramic filter according to the geometric relationship of the model. The specific formula is as follows:

$$\theta = \frac{y_3 - y_1}{y_3 - y_1}. \tag{19}$$

$$x_0 = x_2 + d * sin\theta. \tag{20}$$

$$y_0 = y_2 + d * cos\theta. \tag{21}$$

From the above formula, we can get the center point (x_0, y_0) and offset angle θ of the ceramic filter, and analyze the error to get the actual accuracy of the above algorithm.

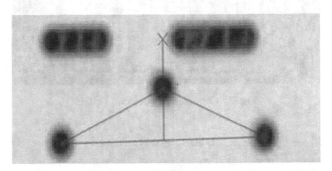

Fig. 6. Central point positioning

4   Parameter Analysis and Experimental Results

4.1   Coordinate Extraction Results

In this paper, 125 ceramic filters with different fouling conditions are detected, as shown in Fig. 7, in which 12 ceramic filters of other types are mixed. Finally, 108 ceramic filters of target type are detected, with a recognition rate of 95.57% and a false positive rate of 0. By analyzing the unidentified ceramic filters, it is found that the edge of the circular cavity of most ceramic filters is damaged and the surface is seriously dirty, so this detection method can also ceramic filter the defective ceramic filters in advance and improve the operating efficiency of the equipment.

4.2   Parameter Analysis

By manually marking coordinate points in Photoshop software and solving the angle between the ceramic filter and the Z axis, the algorithm used in this paper is compared. As shown in Table 1, the average error in the image is 1.83 pixels.

As shown in Table 2, the average error of the angle between the ceramic filter and the Z axis is 0.1137° by comparing the results obtained by the algorithm in this paper with those obtained by manual marking, and the angle deviation is small, which has little influence on the manipulator to take and put materials.

Fig. 7. Ceramic filter detection effect

Table 1. Pixel Error.

Picture	Output coordinates (pixel)	Calibration coordinates (pixel)	Absolute error (pixel)
Image 1	(607.03, 2291.58)	(606, 2290)	1.89
Image 2	(799.61, 2814.72)	(800, 2813)	1.76
Image 3	(615.62, 3897.06)	(617, 3897)	1.38
Image 4	(826.02, 3407.09)	(825, 3409)	2.17
Image 5	(1046.56, 3908.08)	(1047, 1910)	1.97
Image 6	(576.90, 2820.21)	(577, 2822)	1.79
average error	~	~	1.83

Table 2. Angle error

Picture	Output angle (°)	Calibration angle (°)	Absolute error (°)
Image 1	−0.1373	−0.3	0.1627
Image 2	−0.5648	−0.7	0.1352
Image 3	1.0823	1.2	0.1177
Image 4	−1.6584	−1.5	0.1584
Image 5	−0.8986	−0.8	0.0986
Image 6	−2.4904	−2.5	0.0096
average error	~	~	0.1137

5 Conclusion

In this paper, the method of locating the ceramic filter by machine vision technology is proposed, and the image recognition and location algorithm is given. Firstly, Blob analysis is used to locate the material tray and determine the ROI area, and then template matching is used to roughly locate the ceramic filter. Finally, a plane three-point center positioning method is proposed to obtain the center coordinates and offset angle of the ceramic filter. Experiments show that this method can accurately locate the chaotic ceramic filters and meet the needs of industrial production in which the center repeated positioning error is 1.83 pixels and the angle error is 0.1137°.

References

1. Liu, Y.: Research on key technologies of automatic production of ceramic filters. Electron. Qual. (08), 1–5 (2020)
2. Yi, G.: New infrastructure drives the development of key materials in the 5G industrial chain. New Mater. Ind. **05**, 2–5 (2020)
3. Guo, X., Liu, X., Gupta, M.K., Hou, S., Królczyk, G., Li, Z.: Machine vision-based intelligent manufacturing using a novel dual-template matching: a case study for lithium battery positioning. Int. J. Adv. Manuf. Technol. (2021, prepublish)
4. Cai, J., Lei, T.: An autonomous positioning method of tube-to-tubesheet welding robot based on coordinate transformation and template matching. IEEE Robot. Autom. Lett. **6**(2) (2021)
5. Liu, Y., Wang, Y., Zuo, S.: Confocal probe positioning algorithm based on region growth and prior endoscope size. J. Biomed. Eng. **39**(05), 945–957 (2022)
6. Zhang, X., He, J., Niu, Y., Zhang, Y.: Application of improved Canny operator in part size measurement. Mech. Sci. Technol., 1–7 (2023)
7. Wu, Z.: Design and Research of Meat Sorting System Based on Machine Vision. Jiangnan University (2022)
8. Song, C., Jiao, L., Wang, X., Liu, Z., Chen, H.: Improved minimum zone circle method for roundness error evaluation of shaft and hole parts. China Mech. Eng. **33**(09), 1090–1097+1114 (2022)
9. Yu, S., Xiao, S.: Research on positioning detection method of SOP patch components based on machine vision. Mach. Tool Hydraul. **48**(07), 29–33+46 (2020)
10. Wang, R., Yang, K., Zhu, Y.: A high-precision Mark positioning algorithm based on sub-pixel shape template matching in wafer bonding alignment. Precis. Eng. **80,** 104–114 (2023)
11. Qin, Y., Na, Q., Liu, F., Wu, H., Sun, K.: Strain gauges position based on machine vision positioning. Integr. Ferroelectr. **200**(1) (2019)
12. Research on Sub-Pixel Edge Detection Technology of Small Module Gear Image Based on Moment Method. China Metrology University (2019)
13. Xuan, Y., Silong, Z., Long, C., Hui, Z.: Improved interpolation with sub-pixel relocation method for strong barrel distortion. Signal Process. **203** (2023)
14. Yu, M., Wang, G., Yang, L., et al.: Sub-pixel edge location of gray code based on complementary curve fitting. Sci. Technol. Eng. **21**(21), 8999–9004 (2021)

MLP Neural Network-Based Precise Localization of Robot Assembly Parts

Bin Cheng, Zonggang Li[✉], Jianjun Jiao, and Guanglin An

School of Mechanical and Electrical Engineering, Robotics Institute, Lanzhou Jiaotong University, Lanzhou, Gansu, China

lizongg@126.com

Abstract. Traditional visual servoing encounters challenges in achieving target localization during the assembly process of riveted components when target features out of the field of view or when image feature motion extends beyond the image boundaries, resulting in feature loss and inability to accomplish visual servoing positioning. To address these issues, this paper first proposes a target localization method based on the ORB feature matching algorithm to solve the problem of the target features out of the field of view. A multi-layer perceptron neural network is applied to estimate the relative error between the current camera attitude and the desired attitude through the target image features obtained by the camera at the initial pose and the preset reference image features. The robot reaches the intermediate posture according to the predicted motion vector, Then the adaptive visual control method is used for fine-tuning, which can realize the accurate positioning and grasping tasks of the assembly with fewer iterations than the traditional visual servo.

Keywords: Visual servoing · Multilayer perceptron · Feature matching Predictive control

1 Introduction

The assembly process is a crucial stage in industrial production, and the use of robots for automation not only saves labor costs but also improves production efficiency. Offline program based robot operations have drawbacks such as low compatibility and poor autonomy, as well as absolute positioning and repeated positioning errors. By integrating visual sensors, robots can achieve higher adaptability and can be applied to robot positioning, path planning, and posture correction [1–3].

The robot visual control system can be classified into two types based on the feedback information: image-based visual servoing (IBVS) and position-based visual servoing [4, 5]. In IBVS control laws are established based on the difference between the current image features and the desired image features to control robot motion. This method is widely adopted due to its ease of implementation and robustness to camera calibration errors [6]. However, when the camera undergoes large-angle rotations around its optical axis, it may exhibit redundant motions such as forward or backward movements, and

H. Yang et al. (Eds.): ICIRA 2023, LNAI 14272, pp. 608–618, 2023.
https://doi.org/10.1007/978-981-99-6480-2_50

there is a possibility of image features extending beyond the camera's field of view or being occluded by obstacles [7, 8]. These issues can lead to the failure of visual servoing due to the inability to extract sufficient feature information. In PBVS, the relative pose of the robot with respect to the target object is calculated using image feature informations, followed by Cartesian space motion control commands [4, 9]. The advantage of this method is the decoupling of visual information processing and robot control. However, it is sensitive to image noise, requires high computational precision, is sensitive to calibration errors of the camera and robot, and requires additional image analysis and inverse kinematic calculations. These factors directly affect the accuracy of robot visual control. Arif et al. [10] proposed an IBVS scheme based on the partial manipulator Jacobian matrix, established a mixed switching partition task Jacobian matrix without the need to define the Jacobian matrix, and constructed an adaptive switching controller based on efficient second-order minimization (ESM) to solve the camera's backward motion problem. However, it lack of robustness when the target move out of the field of view.

In recent years, the application of neural networks in robot visual control systems has been widely researched. Bateux et al. [11] proposes using a Convolutional Neural Network (CNN) to estimate the relative pose between two images for eye-in-hand visual servoing control tasks. This method exhibits robustness against local lighting variations and occlusions. Xuejian Zhang et al. [12] presents a groove cutting speed inference and planning system based on machine vision and a two-stage fuzzy neural hybrid network to ensure the cutting quality and efficiency of sheet metal grooves. The model combines the advantages of fuzzy reasoning and neural networks. It accurately captures the contour information of the workpiece through machine vision and derives the optimal cutting speed for trajectory segments based on relevant processing parameters using the two-stage fuzzy neural hybrid network, enabling autonomous design and planning of cutting speeds. Yan et al. [13] proposes a robot assembly method for high-precision alignment of aviation circular connectors based on a Convolutional Neural Network (CNN). By constructing a CNN, the point and line features of the gripper are obtained, and a visual servoing system is established based on the acquired geometric features. The control law for aligning the gripper's orientation and posture is designed, achieving high-precision alignment of the 6-DOF connector.

Multilayer perceptron is a kind of artificial neural network, based on back-propagation learning, is a typical feedforward network, in addition to the input and output layer, it can have multiple hidden layers in the middle, the simplest MLP contains only one hidden layer, that is, a three-layer structure [14]. The direction of information processing is carried out layer by layer from the input layer to each hidden layer and then to the output layer. The hidden layer realizes the nonlinear mapping of the input space, and the output layer realizes the linear classification. The nonlinear mapping mode and the linear discriminant function can be learned simultaneously. MLP has the advantages of high nonlinear global action and strong adaptive learning function, and can be used in image recognition, classification and other fields [15–17].

In this paper, the problem of target feature moving out of the field of view in visual servo is discussed. Firstly, the ORB feature matching algorithm is employed to locate the target based on the images obtained by the camera in the initial position, determining the pixel coordinates of the target feature points. Then MLP neural network is utilized to estimate the relative pose of the two optic angle according to the initial image feature information. Finally, parameter adaptive visual servoing control is employed to fine-tune the camera or end-effector pose, ultimately achieving precise localization of the assembly parts for subsequent grasping and assembly tasks.

2 Target Localization

Feature matching as an important component of computer vision and digital image processing, plays a crucial role in various applications such as target recognition and 3D reconstruction. Rublee proposed a fast matching algorithm called ORB (Oriented FAST and Rotated BRIEF), which combines the real-time advantages of FAST (Features from Accelerated Segment Test) and BRIEF (Binary Robust Independent Elementary Features) algorithms [18].

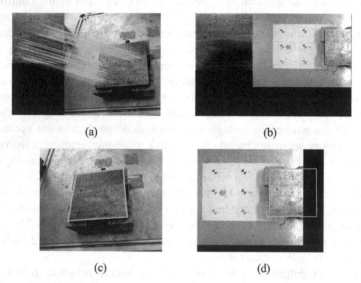

(a)   (b)

(c)   (d)

Fig. 1. Matching results of features(a)-(b), Location of object(c) and object partially outside the field of view(d)

The ORB algorithm takes advantage of FAST and BRIEF for efficient computation. It first applies the FAST algorithm for corner detection and then utilizes the BRIEF algorithm for feature description. Both algorithms exhibit excellent performance with low computational cost and memory overhead [19]. ORB can also employ a pyramid strategy to achieve scale invariance. As a result, ORB features exhibit good translation, rotation, and scale invariance.

After identifying the feature points in the images, the next step is to establish correspondences between these points. The simplest and most intuitive approach is to use the brute-force matching method, which calculates the distances between the descriptor of a particular feature point and all other feature point descriptors. The closest distance is considered as the matching point. The cross-check matching method is used to solve the possible incorrect matching in brute-force matching.

When there are at least 8 correct matching point pairs, the homography matrix, which represents the mapping relationship between points in two images, can be computed as shown in Eq. (1). The RANSAC algorithm is used to find the best homography matrix H, where the goal is to find the optimal parameter matrix that maximizes the number of data points satisfying this matrix.

$$H = \begin{bmatrix} h_{11} & h_{12} & h_{13} \\ h_{21} & h_{22} & h_{23} \\ h_{31} & h_{32} & h_{33} \end{bmatrix} \tag{1}$$

$$\begin{bmatrix} x \\ y \\ 1 \end{bmatrix} = \begin{bmatrix} h_{11} & h_{12} & h_{13} \\ h_{21} & h_{22} & h_{23} \\ h_{31} & h_{32} & h_{33} \end{bmatrix} \begin{bmatrix} x_1 \\ y_1 \\ 1 \end{bmatrix} \tag{2}$$

The target image needs to be resampled after obtaining the homography matrix. ORB feature extraction and description were carried out on the resampled image and the benchmark image to complete the fine matching, and then the target positioning in the image was realized, and the pixel coordinates of the feature points corresponding to the template in the current image were obtained. Figure 1(a)–(b) shows the result of feature matching and Fig. 1(c)–(d) shows the result of target positioning.

3 Robot Hand-Eye Visual Localization System

3.1 Assembly Task

To achieve high-precision autonomous alignment in the assembly process of multi-axis riveted components, as shown in Fig. 2(Left), a robot vision system is constructed. It consists of a 6-DOF robot, a camera mounted on the end of the robot, and an end effector used for gripping the riveted components. The riveted component P1 is fixed on the workbench, and the end effector of the robot grips the riveted component P2 to achieve alignment and assembly with the riveted component P1 through pose control. Since P1 is preinstalled with multiple rivets and there is a small gap between the rivets and the rivet holes, precise alignment of each rivet with its corresponding hole is required to complete the assembly of the riveted component P2 into the riveted component P1. In the system, {B} represents the robot base coordinate system, {E} represents the end effector coordinate system, {C} represents the camera coordinate system, and {O} represents the target coordinate system.

3.2 Vision Control Method

Motion Prediction Based on Neural Networks. The artificial neural network can be used as the fitting method of any function to learn the complex nonlinear relationship between input and output through the data set [20]. In this paper, a neural network based on a multilayer perceptron is employed to estimate the motion vector from

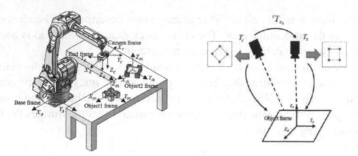

Fig. 2. Left: Vision based robot assembly scheme diagram. **Right:** Initial pose of the camera and riveted part.

the current camera pose T_c to the reference pose T_0. $s = [u_1, v_1, u_2, v_2, \cdots u_n, v_n]$ represents the current image features. The image features obtained by the camera under the reference attitude are regarded as the desired features and represented by $s* = [u_1*, v*_1, u*_2, v*_2, \cdots u*_n, v*_n]$. The output of the neural network is given by:

$$D = net(s, s*) \tag{3}$$

Vector $D = [\Delta V, \Delta W]^T = [\Delta x, \Delta y, \Delta z, \Delta\alpha, \Delta\beta, \Delta\gamma]^T$ represents the error between the current camera pose and the desired pose, where $\Delta V = [\Delta x, \Delta y, \Delta z]^T$ represents the positional error of the camera, and $\Delta W = [\Delta\alpha, \Delta\beta, \Delta\gamma]^T$ represents the orientation error. The reference pose that corresponding to the desired image feature where the camera needs to reach is represented by $T_0 = T_c {}^cT_{c_0}$, as shown in Fig. 2(Right), ${}^cT_{c_0}$ represents the transformation matrix from the current pose to the reference pose, where $P = \Delta V$ represents the translation vector, and R represents the rotation matrix obtained by sequentially rotating around the three axes of a fixed coordinate system. In this case, it represents the rotation around the three axes of the initial camera coordinate system.

$$^cT_{c0} = \begin{bmatrix} R & P \\ O & 1 \end{bmatrix} \tag{4}$$

$$P = \begin{bmatrix} \Delta x & \Delta y & \Delta z \end{bmatrix}^T \tag{5}$$

$$R = R(Z, \Delta\alpha)R(Y, \Delta\beta)R(X, \Delta\gamma) \tag{6}$$

$$R(X, \Delta\alpha) = \begin{bmatrix} 1 & 0 & 0 \\ 0 & \cos\Delta\alpha & \sin\Delta\alpha \\ 0 & -\sin\Delta\alpha & \cos\Delta\alpha \end{bmatrix}, \quad R(Y, \Delta\beta) = \begin{bmatrix} \cos\Delta\beta & 0 & -\sin\Delta\beta \\ 0 & 1 & 0 \\ \sin\Delta\beta & 0 & \cos\Delta\beta \end{bmatrix},$$

$$R(Z, \Delta\gamma) = \begin{bmatrix} \cos\Delta\gamma & \sin\Delta\gamma & 0 \\ -\sin\Delta\gamma & \cos\Delta\gamma & 0 \\ 0 & 0 & 1 \end{bmatrix} \tag{7}$$

The positional relationship between the camera frame, target frame, and robot base frame is illustrated in Fig. 2(Left). The feature points obtained by the camera from the target object serve as input to the neural network, which then predicts the transformation matrix of the camera's current pose relative to the reference pose. The pose of the robot end in robot base frame can be obtained from the robot controller, then get ${}^bT_c = {}^bT_e\,{}^eT_c$, ${}^bT_c$ represents the pose of the camera in the robot base frame, after predicting the camera transformation matrix using the neural network, we have:

$$ {}^bT_{c0} = {}^bT_e\,{}^eT_c\,{}^cT_{c0} \tag{8} $$

where ${}^bT_{c0}$ represents the desired pose of the camera in the robot base frame. Therefore, the desired pose of the robot end effector is determined.

$$ {}^bT_e = {}^bT_{c0}\,{}^eT_c^{-1} \tag{9} $$

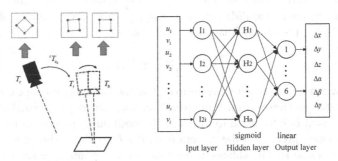

Fig. 3. Left: Camera at three different positions, **Right:** Multilayer perceptron neural network

Adaptive Visual Servo Controller. Due to the existence of certain errors in the predicted values of the neural network, there may still be a discrepancy between the camera pose and the desired pose after the robot moves according to the predicted values. In this case, the adaptive Visual Servoing (IBVS) method is employed to fine-tune the position of the end effector.

The current image feature is denoted by $s = [u_1, v_1, u_2, v_2, \cdots u_n, v_n]$, the desired image feature is denoted by $s* = [u_1*, v_1*, u_2*, v_2*, \cdots u_n*, v_n*]$. The goal of the IBVS controller is to reduce the error between the current image feature and the desired image feature, which is defined as e and represented by $e = s - s*$. The relationship between the camera velocity and the derivative of e in visual control is expressed by Eq. (10), where V_c represents the spatial velocity of the camera.

$$ \dot{e} = LV_c \tag{10} $$

$$ V_c = [v_e, \omega_e]^T = [v_x, v_y, v_z, \omega_x, \omega_y, \omega_z]^T \tag{11} $$

$$ L = \begin{bmatrix} \frac{f}{\alpha_u Z} & 0 & \frac{\bar{u}}{Z} & \frac{\alpha_u \bar{u}\bar{v}}{f} & -\frac{f^2+\alpha_v^2\bar{u}^2}{f} & \bar{v} \\ 0 & \frac{f}{\alpha_v Z} & \frac{\bar{v}}{Z} & \frac{f^2+\alpha_v\bar{v}^2}{f} & -\frac{\alpha_v \bar{u}\bar{v}}{f} & -\bar{u} \end{bmatrix} \tag{12} $$

$L_s = [L_1; L_2; ...; L_n]$ represents the image Jacobian matrix or interaction matrix, where $\bar{u} = u - u_0, \bar{v} = v - v_0$, and (u_0, v_0) are the pixel coordinates of the center of the image plane. In order to achieve exponential decay of the error, proportional control is applied to the objective function. By substitute $\dot{e} = -\lambda e$ into Eq. (10), the control law for IBVS can be obtained:

$$V_c = -\lambda L_s^+ e \qquad (13)$$

L_s^+ is the pseudo-inverse of the interaction matrix L_s. Tahri [21] proposes the use of Second-Order Minimization (ESM) technique for quadratic convergence in IBVS to address the camera zoom-out problem. This technique approximates the feature Jacobian matrix using the average of the current and desired image Jacobian matrices. Under the ESM scheme, two methods have been developed, namely the pseudoinverse of the mean of the feature Jacobian matrix (PMJ) and the mean of the pseudoinverse of the feature Jacobian matrix (MJP), where the PMJ method is superior to the MJP method [10, 21]. Therefore, in this paper, the PMJ method is employed to calculate the Jacobian matrix, represented by Eq. (14) as the image Jacobian matrix.

$$\hat{L}_s = -\frac{1}{2}[L_s^+ + L_{s*}^+] \qquad (14)$$

When the camera approaches the desired pose, the variation of image error becomes smaller, resulting in slower camera motion, Therefore, an adaptive visual servo control (A-IBVS) method is introduced to fine-tune the positioning process at the final stage, that is, the motion process of the camera from the T_i to T_0, as shown in Fig. 3(Left), this method is introduced to address the issues of slow response speed and local minima near the camera's arrival at the desired pose domain. It allows the controller to maintain a responsive behavior near the convergence region while achieving faster convergence. A proportional gain λ_a is designed to adaptively adjust based on the error, as shown in Eq. (15)

$$\lambda_a = (\lambda_0 - \lambda_m)e^{-\frac{\lambda'_0}{\lambda_0 - \lambda_m}\|e\|_\infty} + \lambda_m \qquad (15)$$

λ_a is the adaptive gain, λ_0 is the lower limit of the gain, λ_m is the upper of the gain, and λ'_0 is the slope of λ_a at $\lambda_a = \lambda_0$. Then, we obtain the relationship between the rate of change of image feature error and the camera's spatial velocity as shown in Eq. (16). The relationship between the robot end-effector Cartesian velocity and the joint space velocity is represented by Eq. (17).

$$V_c = -\lambda_a \hat{L}_s e \qquad (16)$$

$$\dot{q} = J^+ T V_c \qquad (17)$$

where, J^+ is the inverse of the Jacobian matrix for robotics. The rotation angle of the robot joint, denoted as q_d, can be obtained by integrating the velocity of joint, and the value is sent to the robot controller to drive the robot joint rotation.

$$q_d(t) = q(t_0) + \int_{t_0}^{t} \dot{q}(t)dt \qquad (18)$$

4 Neural Network Training

In this paper, a multilayer perceptron (MLP) network with a feedforward topology is employed, as shown in Fig. 3(Right). The network is trained using the Bayesian regularization algorithm, which provides strong generalization capability. The hidden layers use the sigmoid function as the activation function, while the output layer uses a linear activation function. The input of the neural network is the current image feature information represented by $s = (p_1, p_2, \cdots, p_n), p_i = (u_i, v_i)$ are the pixel coordinates of the feature points. In this paper, the feature information of the four corner points of the target object is used as the input of the neural network. $s* = (p_1*, p_2*, \cdots, p_n*)$ represents the desired image feature coordinates, and the output is the attitude error vector, representing by $D = [\Delta x, \Delta y, \Delta z, \Delta\alpha, \Delta\beta, \Delta\gamma]$. Based on the QJR20 industrial robot model, a simulation model is established in Simulink for data acquisition to train the neural network. This approach is more efficient and convenient compared to directly using the real robot hand-eye system to record image feature and pose data. The dataset consists of 2000 randomly generated camera poses and the pixel coordinates of the target's corner points projected onto the image plane for training. Validation was performed using separate validation data on the neural network trained with the Levenberg-Marquardt(L-M) algorithm and the neural network trained with the Bayesian regularization algorithm. Figure 4(Left) shows the estimation error distribution based on the Bayesian regularization algorithm, while Fig. 4(Right) shows the estimation error distribution based on the L-M algorithm. It can be observed that the neural network trained with the Bayesian regularization algorithm achieves higher prediction accuracy compared to the neural network trained with the L-M algorithm.

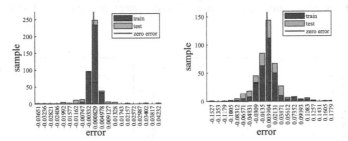

Fig. 4. Left: Estimation error distribution based on Bayesian algorithm **Right:** Estimation error distribution based on L-M algorithm

5 Simulation Experiment

The camera model used in this study has a focal length is $16mm$, resolution is 2592×1944, image center pixel coordinates is $u_0 = 1296$ and $v_0 = 972$, and pixel size is $a_x = 1 \times 10^{-5}$, $a_y = 1 \times 10^{-5}$.

In the test, the initial joint angles of the robot are set to $[-0.45, 0.15, -0.16, 0, 0, 0.1, 0.45]$rad, Fig. 5(Left) shows the image feature trajectory when the robot performs localization using the traditional IBVS method. The image feature trajectory when the robot moves based on the neural network prediction and the Adaptive Visual Servoing Control (P+AIBVS) method is shown in Fig. 5(Right), it includes the intermediate image features obtained by the camera after the robot moved according to the predicted motion vector, and the image features after fine tuning, and the feature motion trajectory of the whole process. In the predictive control phase, the motion vector of the robot end effector has been given. Although the image features may go beyond the field of view, it does not affect the robot end effector reaching the intermediate pose. Figure 6 (Left) shows the image feature error variation based on IBVS, where the convergence speed decreases as the feature error decreases, resulting in a longer convergence time. Figure 6 (Right) shows the feature error variation based on predictive control and adaptive visual servoing control, after the predictive control motion ends, the gain-adaptive visual servoing control is applied, which maintains the convergence speed. Compared to the fixed-gain IBVS method, the convergence speed is faster, reducing the time required for visual positioning.

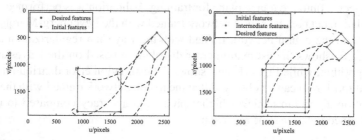

Fig. 5. Left: Image feature trajectory. **Right**: Image feature trajectory based on IBVS based on P+AIBVS

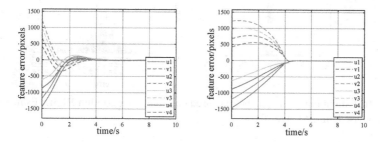

Fig. 6. Left: Feature error based on IBVS. **Right**: Feature error based on P+AIBVS

By comparing the two feature trajectories in Fig. 7(Right), it is evident that the use of predictive control can significantly reduce redundant camera movements. Compared to the traditional IBVS method, the visual control approach based on MLP prediction combined with AIBVS demonstrates faster convergence speed. This leads to a significant reduction in the overall execution time of the task, thereby enhancing the efficiency of industrial robot operations.

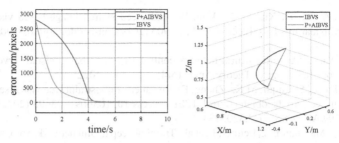

Fig. 7. Left: Image feature error norm. **Right:** End effector trajectory in space on IBVS and P+AIBVS

6 Conclusion

This paper first adopted the target localization method based on the ORB feature matching algorithm to address the issue of locating partially out-of-field features. It further utilizes a multilayer perceptron neural network to estimate the relative pose between the current camera posture and the desired posture based on the target image features acquired at the initial camera pose and the predefined reference image features. This approach reduces the reliance of the visual control system on camera calibration, system modeling, and Jacobian matrix calculations. Instead, it leverages the approximation capability of neural networks to map the complex nonlinear relationship between feature pixel positions and camera poses. The proposed method exhibits robustness when the object partially exits the camera's field of view. Moreover, due to the larger initial camera movements, the overall convergence time of the task is noticeably accelerated. Therefore, this method enables faster and more accurate task execution, leading to improved productivity in industrial settings.

References

1. Pagano, S., Russo, R., Savino, S.: A vision guided robotic system for flexible gluing process in the footwear industry. Robot. Comput. Integr. Manuf. **65**, 101965 (2020)
2. Zhuang, S., Dai, C., Shan, G., et al.: Robotic rotational positioning of end effectors for micromanipulation. IEEE Trans. Robot. **38**(4), 2251–2261 (2022)
3. Gilmour, A., Jackson, W., Zhang, D., et al.: Robotic positioning for quality assurance of feature sparse components using a depth-sensing camera. IEEE Sens. J. **23**(9), 10032–10040 (2023)
4. Cong, V.D.: Visual servoing control of 4-DOF palletizing robotic arm for vision based sorting robot system. Int. J. Interact. Des. Manuf. **17**(2), 717–728 (2023)
5. Xu, X., Tang, R., Gong, L., Chen, B., Zuo, S.: Two dimensional position-based visual servoing for soft tissue endomicroscopy. IEEE Robot. Autom. Lett. **6**(3), 5728–5735 (2021). https://doi.org/10.1109/LRA.2021.3084885
6. Rotithor, G., Salehi, I., Tunstel, E., et al.: Stitching dynamic movement primitives and image-based visual servo control. IEEE Trans. Syst. **53**(5), 2583–2593 (2023)
7. Dong, J.X., Zhang, J.: A new image-based visual servoing method with velocity direction control. J. Franklin Inst. **357**(7), 3993–4007 (2020). https://doi.org/10.1016/j.jfranklin.2020.01.012

8. Ghasemi, A., Li, P., Xie, W.-F., Tian, W.: Enhanced switch image-based visual servoing dealing with features loss. Electronics **8**(8), 903 (2019). https://doi.org/10.3390/electronics8 080903

9. Qiu, Z., Wu, Z.: Adaptive neural network control for image-based visual servoing of robot manipulators. IET Control Theory Appl. **16**(4), 443–453 (2022)

10. Arif, Z., Fu, Y., Siddiqui, M.K., Zhang, F.: Visual error constraint free visual servoing using novel switched part Jacobian control. IEEE Access **10**, 103669–103693 (2022). https://doi. org/10.1109/ACCESS.2022.3203734

11. Bateux, Q., Marchand, E., Leitner, J., et al.: Training deep neural networks for visual servoing. In: IEEE International Conference on Robotics and Automation (ICRA), Brisbane, QLD, Australia, pp. 3307–3314 (2018)

12. Xuejian, Z., Xiaobing, H., Hang, L.: A speed inference planning of groove cutting robot based on machine vision and improved fuzzy neural network. J. Intell. Fuzzy Syst. **42**(4), 3251–3264 (2022)

13. Yan, S., Tao, X., Xu, D.: Image-based visual servoing system for components alignment using point and line features. IEEE Trans. Instrum. Meas. **71**, 1–11 (2022)

14. Popescu, M.C., Balas, V., Perescu-Popescu, L.: Multilayer perceptron and neural net-works. WSEAS Transactions on Circuits and Systems **8** (2009)

15. Tolstikhin, I., Houlsby, N., Kolesnikov, A., et al.: MLP-Mixer: an all-MLP architecture for vision. In: Neural Information Processing Systems (2021)

16. Yang, L.F., Li, X., Song, R.J., et al.: Dynamic MLP for fine-grained image classification by leveraging geographical and temporal information. In: IEEE/CVF Conference on Computer Vision and Pattern Recognition (CVPR), New Orleans, LA, USA, pp. 10935–10944 (2022)

17. Lv, T.X., Bai, C.Y., Wang, C.J.: MDMLP: Image Classification from Scratch on Small Datasets with MLP. *AtXir* abs/2205.14477 (2022)

18. Rublee, E., Rabaud, V., Konolige, K., et al.: ORB: an efficient alternative to SIFT or SURF. In: 2011 International Conference on Computer Vision, Barcelona, Spain, pp. 2564–2571 (2011)

19. Sun, C., Wu, X., Sun, J., et al.: Multi-stage refinement feature matching using adaptive ORB features for robotic vision navigation. IEEE Sens. J. **22**(3), 2603–2617 (2022)

20. Chen, Q., Zhang, W., Lou, Y.: Forecasting stock prices using a hybrid deep learning model integrating attention mechanism, multi-layer perceptron, and bidirectional long-short term memory neural network. IEEE Access **8**, 117365–117376 (2020). https://doi.org/10.1109/ ACCESS.2020.3004284

21. Tahri, O., Mezouar, Y.: On visual servoing based on efficient second order minimization. Robot. Auton. Syst. **58**(5), 712–719 (2010). https://doi.org/10.1016/j.robot.2009.11.003

Author Index

Printed in the United States
by Baker & Taylor Publisher Services